CENGAGE**brain**.com

Cases from prior editions of Michael C. Knapp's **Contemporary Auditing** are available exclusively online via **www.CengageBrain.com**. In addition to the option to purchase the current edition in multiple formats, CengageBrain.com offers the following cases from prior editions for purchase as an eBook or as individual eChapters. This range of options allows you the flexibility to choose the content that best fits your needs!

COMPREHENSIVE CASES

1A Jamaica Water Properties
1B AMRE, Inc.
1C United States Surgical Corporation

AUDITS OF HIGH-RISK ACCOUNTS

2A CapitalBanc Corporation
2B Dollar General Stores, Inc.
2C General Technologies Group Ltd.
2D SmarTalk Teleservices, Inc.
2E Campbell Soup Company
2F Perry Drug Stores, Inc.
2G Rocky Mount Undergarment Company, Inc.

INTERNAL CONTROL ISSUES

3A Saks Fifth Avenue
3B Triton Energy Ltd.
3C Troberg Stores

ETHICAL RESPONSIBILITIES OF ACCOUNTANTS

4A Oak Industries, Inc.
4B Thomas Forehand, CPA
4C Laurel Valley Estates
4D Jack Bass, Accounting Professor

ETHICAL RESPONSIBILITIES OF INDEPENDENT AUDITORS

5A Mallon Resources Corporation
5B The PTL Club
5C Zaveral Boosalis Raisch
5D Koger Properties, Inc.

PROFESSIONAL ROLES

6A David Myers, WorldCom Controller

PROFESSIONAL ISSUES

7A HealthSouth Corporation
7B PricewaterhouseCoopers Securities, LLC
7C Stephen Gray, CPA
7D Scott Fane, CPA
7E National Medical Transportation Network

INTERNATIONAL CASES

8A Royal Ahold, N.V.
8B Australian Wheat Board
8C Tata Finance Limited
8D Baan Company, N.V.

CLASSIC LITIGATION CASES

9A National Student Marketing Corporation
9B Equity Funding Corporation of America

Discover why CengageBrain.com is your one-stop solution!

CengageBrain.com offers students a wealth of options in both price and format of their course materials. To access additional course materials, visit www.cengagebrain.com. At the CengageBrain.com home page, fill in the author or ISBN of your textbook. This will take you to the product page where you will find various purchasing options and access to free companion study resources.

CONTEMPORARY AUDITING
REAL ISSUES AND CASES

Ninth Edition

CONTEMPORARY AUDITING
REAL ISSUES AND CASES

Ninth Edition

Michael C. Knapp
University of Oklahoma

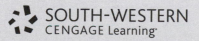
SOUTH-WESTERN
CENGAGE Learning

Australia • Brazil • Japan • Korea • Mexico • Singapore • Spain • United Kingdom • United States

SOUTH-WESTERN
CENGAGE Learning·

Contemporary Auditing: Real Issues and Cases, Ninth Edition
Michael C. Knapp

Vice President of Editorial, Business:
Jack W. Calhoun

Editor-in-Chief: Rob Dewey

Acquisitions Editor: Matt Filimonov

Developmental Editor: Ann Loch

Editorial Assistant: Ann Loch

Marketing Manager: Heather Mooney

Content Project Management:
PreMediaGlobal

Media Editor: Bryan England

Manufacturing Planner: Doug Wilke

Marketing Communications Manager:
Libby Shipp

Production Service: PreMediaGlobal

Art Director: Kristina Mose-Libon

Internal Designer: PreMediaGlobal

Cover Designer: PreMediaGlobal

Cover Image: ©Sailorr/Shutterstock; Bottom
photo (background graph): ©Photoredaktor/
Dreamstime.com; Small photos: Left small
photo (gold map and pen): ©ronfromyork/
Shutterstock; 2nd photo from left (man
at computers): ©Steve Cole Images/
iStockphoto.com; 3rd photo from left (gavel
and paper): ©Chris Reed/ iStockphoto;
4th photo from left: (blue money and men
in circle): ©Photos.com/Getty Images/
Thinkstock

Rights Acquisitions Specialist: Sam Marshall

For product information and technology assistance, contact us at
Cengage Learning Customer & Sales Support, 1-800-354-9706

For permission to use material from this text or product,
submit all requests online at **www.cengage.com/permissions**
Further permissions questions can be emailed to
permissionrequest@cengage.com

Library of Congress Control Number: 2011941655

ISBN-13: 978-1-133-18789-9

ISBN-10: 1-133-18789-7

South-Western
5191 Natorp Boulevard
Mason, OH 45040
USA

Cengage Learning is a leading provider of customized learning solutions
with office locations around the globe, including Singapore, the United
Kingdom, Australia, Mexico, Brazil, and Japan. Locate your local office at:
international.cengage.com/region

Cengage Learning products are represented in Canada by
Nelson Education, Ltd.

For your course and learning solutions, visit **www.cengage.com**.

Purchase any of our products at your local college store or at our
preferred online store **www.cengagebrain.com**.

Printed in the United States of America
1 2 3 4 5 6 7 15 14 13 12 11

DEDICATION

To Paula, Suzie, and Becky

BRIEF CONTENTS

CONTENTS

Arthur Edward Andersen established a simple motto that he required his subordinates and clients to invoke: "Think straight, talk straight." For decades, that motto served Arthur Andersen & Co. well. Unfortunately, the firm's association with one client, Enron Corporation, abruptly ended Andersen's long and proud history in the public accounting profession.

KEY TOPICS: history of the public accounting profession in the United States, scope of professional services provided to audit clients, auditor independence, and retention of audit workpapers.

Wall Street was stunned in September 2008 when this iconic investment banking firm filed for bankruptcy. Lehman's bankruptcy examiner charged that the company had engaged in tens of billions of dollars of "accounting-motivated" transactions to enhance its apparent financial condition.

KEY TOPICS: "accounting-motivated" transactions, materiality decisions by auditors, responsibility of auditors to investigate whistleblower allegations, auditors' legal exposure, communications with audit committee.

In the fall of 1999, just a few months after reporting a record profit for fiscal 1998, Just for FEET collapsed and filed for bankruptcy. Subsequent investigations by law enforcement authorities revealed a massive accounting fraud that had grossly misrepresented the company's reported operating results. Key features of the fraud were improper accounting for "vendor allowances" and intentional understatements of the company's inventory valuation allowance.

KEY TOPICS: applying analytical procedures, identifying inherent risk and control risk factors, need for auditors to monitor key developments within the client's industry, assessing the health of a client's industry, and receivables confirmation procedures.

The Private Securities Litigation Reform Act (PSLRA) of 1995 amended the Securities Exchange Act of 1934. This new federal statute was projected to have a major impact on auditors' legal liability under the 1934 Act. The first major test of the PSLRA was triggered by a class-action lawsuit filed against BDO Seidman for its 1995 audit of Health Management, Inc., a New York–based pharmaceuticals distributor.

KEY TOPICS: inventory audit procedures, auditor independence, content of audit workpapers, inherent risk factors, and auditors' civil liability under the federal securities laws.

Paul Polishan, the former chief financial officer of The Leslie Fay Companies, received a nine-year prison sentence for fraudulently misrepresenting Leslie Fay's financial

controls by stealing a large amount of inventory, which he then sold to other parties.

The general manager of Buranello's set up a "sting" operation–with the owner's approval–to test the honesty of the employee who he believed was stealing from the business. But the plan backfired, and Buranello's eventually found itself on the wrong end of a "malicious prosecution" lawsuit.

Foamex's auditors repeatedly reported internal control problems to the company's management and audit committee. Because the company's management refused to adopt effective and timely measures to remediate those problems, Foamex became the first public company sanctioned by the SEC solely for having inadequate internal controls.

Intrigue and espionage seem far removed from accounting . . . but not in this case. Creve Couer's CPA was actually a double agent. While providing accounting services to his client, the CPA also supplied incriminating evidence regarding the client to the IRS.

A financial fraud spelled the end of a company with a proud history and tested the ethics of several of its key management and accounting personnel.

Suzette Washington was a college senior majoring in accounting when she came face-to-face with an important ethical decision. Since accounting majors are entering a profession with a rigorous code of ethics, do they have a greater responsibility than other students to behave ethically?

Partners and employees of accounting firms often have access to confidential client information that they could use to gain an unfair advantage over other investors. In recent years, law enforcement authorities have filed insider trading charges against several public accountants, including a partner assigned to a professional services engagement for Freescale.

"To tell or not to tell" was the gist of an ethical dilemma faced by Wiley Jackson while completing a pre-employment document for his future employer, a major accounting firm.

The South African economy was rocked in recent years by a series of financial reporting scandals. To restore the credibility of the nation's capital markets, the South African Parliament passed a controversial new law, the Auditing Profession Act (APA). The APA established a new auditing regulatory agency and a new professional credential for independent auditors. The APA also mandated that independent auditors immediately disclose to the new auditing agency any "reportable irregularities" committed by an audit client.

The Big Four accounting firms view China as one of the most lucrative markets for accounting and auditing services worldwide. However, those firms face major challenges in that market. Among these challenges are an increasing litigation risk and the difficulty of coping with the often heavy-handed tactics of China's authoritarian central government.

This case focuses on the 1999 murder of Michael Wansley, a partner with Deloitte Touche Tohmatsu. Wansley was supervising a debt-restructuring engagement in a remote region of Thailand when he was gunned down by a professional assassin.

PricewaterhouseCoopers (PwC) accepted a lucrative, unusual, and very controversial engagement for the transitional government established for Somalia by the United Nations. The case questions require students to consider the significant risks and thorny ethical issues that engagement poses for PwC.

Business Week referred to the huge Gazprom debacle as "Russia's Enron." For the first time in the history of the new Russian republic, a Big Four accounting firm was sued for allegedly issuing improper audit opinions on a Russian company's financial statements.

This case addresses the surprising decision made by Societe Generale, *France's second largest bank, to backdate a 6.4 billion euro loss that resulted from unauthorized securities trades made by one of its employees. Although that huge loss occurred in 2008, the bank included the loss in its audited financial statements for 2007. To justify that decision, the bank's management invoked a controversial provision of International Financial Reporting Standards (IFRS).*

The Institute of Chartered Accountants of India (ICAI) is the federal agency that oversees India's accounting profession. In 2002, the ICAI commissioned a study of the alleged takeover of that profession by the major international accounting firms.

The resulting 900-page report charged that those firms had used a variety of illicit and even illegal methods to "colonize" India's market for accounting, auditing, and related services to the detriment of the nation's domestic accounting firms.

In 2004, the SEC began requiring domestic and foreign registrants to disclose any business operations within, or other relationships with, Sudan and other countries identified as state sponsors of terrorism. Three years later, the SEC included a Web page on its EDGAR website that listed all such companies. This SEC "blacklist" proved to be extremely controversial and triggered a contentious debate over the federal agency's regulatory mandate and its definition of "materiality."

Islamic companies are prohibited from engaging in transactions that violate Shari'a, *that is, Islamic religious law. To ensure that they have complied with* Shari'a, *Islamic companies have their operations subjected to a* Shari'a *compliance audit each year. Recently, Big Four firms have begun offering* Shari'a *audit services.*

Accountants sometimes find themselves in situations in which they must report unethical or even illegal conduct by other members of their organization. This case examines the trials and tribulations of an internal auditor who "blew the whistle" on his immediate superior for embezzling large sums of cash from their employer, the Washington, D.C., embassy of the United Arab Emirates.

"Environmental and labor practices" audits are one of many nontraditional services that major accounting firms have begun offering in recent years to generate new revenue streams. Ernst & Young provided such an audit for Nike, which had been accused of operating foreign "sweatshops" to produce its footwear products. This case documents the unexpected challenges and problems that accounting firms may face when they provide services outside their traditional areas of professional expertise.

PREFACE

The past decade has arguably been the most turbulent and traumatic in the history of the accounting profession and the independent audit function. Shortly after the turn of the century, the Enron and WorldCom fiascoes focused the attention of the investing public, the press, Wall Street, and, eventually, Congress on our profession. Those scandals resulted in the passage of the Sarbanes-Oxley Act of 2002 (SOX) and the creation of the Public Company Accounting Oversight Board (PCAOB).

Next came the campaign to replace U.S. generally accepted accounting principles (GAAP) with International Financial Reporting Standards (IFRS). That campaign stalled when the subprime mortgage crisis in the United States caused global stock markets to implode and global credit markets to "freeze" during the fall of 2008. Many parties insisted that inadequate audits were a major factor that led to the onset of the most severe global economic downturn since the Great Depression. That economic downturn claimed many companies that had been stalwarts of the U.S. economy, most notably Lehman Brothers. The huge investment banking firm filed for bankruptcy in September 2008 just a few months after having had its annual financial statements "blessed" by its audit firm.

As Congress and regulatory authorities struggled to revive the U.S. economy, news of the largest Ponzi scheme in world history grabbed the headlines in early 2009. Investors worldwide were shocked to learn that Bernie Madoff, an alleged "wizard of Wall Street," was a fraud. Law enforcement authorities determined that billions of dollars of client investments supposedly being held by Madoff's company, Madoff Securities, did not exist. The business press was quick to report that for decades Madoff Securities' financial statements had been audited by a New York accounting firm and had received unqualified audit opinions each year from that firm. The auditing discipline absorbed another body blow in 2010 when a court-appointed bankruptcy examiner publicly singled out Lehman Brothers' audit firm as one of the parties most responsible for the Lehman Brothers debacle.

As academics, we have a responsibility to help shepherd our profession through these turbulent times. Auditing instructors, in particular, have an obligation to help restore the credibility of the independent audit function that has been adversely impacted by the events of the past decade. To accomplish this latter goal, one strategy we can use is to embrace the litany of reforms recommended several years ago by the Accounting Education Change Commission (AECC). Among the AECC's recommendations was that accounting educators employ a broader array of instructional resources, particularly experiential resources, designed to stimulate active learning by students. In fact, the intent of my casebook is to provide auditing instructors with a source of such materials that can be used in both undergraduate and graduate auditing courses.

This casebook stresses the "people" aspect of independent audits. If you review a sample of recent "audit failures," you will find that problem audits seldom result from inadequate audit technology. Instead, deficient audits typically result from the presence of one, or both, of the following two conditions: client personnel who intentionally subvert an audit and auditors who fail to carry out the responsibilities assigned to them. Exposing students to problem audits will help them recognize the red flags that often accompany audit failures. An ability to recognize these red flags and the insight gained by discussing and dissecting problem audits will allow students to cope more effectively with the problematic situations they are certain to encounter in their own careers. In addition, this experiential approach provides students with context-specific situations that make it much easier for them to grasp the relevance of important auditing topics, concepts, and procedures.

The cases in this text also acquaint students with the work environment of auditors. After studying these cases, students will better appreciate how client pressure, peer pressure, time budgets, and related factors complicate the work roles of independent auditors. Also embedded in these cases are the ambiguity and lack of structure that auditors face each day. Missing documents, conflicting audit evidence, auditors' dual obligations to the client and to financial statement users, and the lack of definitive professional standards for many situations are additional aspects of the audit environment woven into these cases.

The ninth edition of my casebook contains the following eight sections of cases: Comprehensive Cases, Audits of High-Risk Accounts, Internal Control Issues, Ethical Responsibilities of Accountants, Ethical Responsibilities of Independent Auditors, Professional Roles, Professional Issues, and International Cases. This organizational structure is intended to help adopters readily identify cases best suited for their particular needs.

In preparing this edition, I retained those cases that have been among the most widely used by adopters. These cases include, among many others, Crazy Eddie, Enron Corporation, Golden Bear Golf, Leigh Ann Walker, Lincoln Savings and Loan Association, Livent, The Trolley Dodgers, and ZZZZ Best Company. You will find that many of the "returning" cases have been updated for relevant circumstances and events that have occurred since the publication of the previous edition.

New To This Edition This edition features 13 new cases. Two of these cases are included in the international section. Easily the most dramatic trend in the business world over the past few decades has been the "globalization" of markets, including the market for professional accounting services. Business schools have responded to this dramatic trend by establishing new international majors, study-abroad programs, and a slew of international courses across all business disciplines. Accounting may very well be the business discipline that has been the slowest to "internationalize" its curriculum. The 14 international cases in this edition provide auditing instructors with an efficient and cost-effective way to introduce their students to a wide range of important issues within the global accounting profession that will have far-reaching implications for their careers.

The new Parmalat Finanziaria case provides an opportunity for students to compare and contrast the independent audit functions of Italy and the United States. This case demonstrates the significant impact that cultural norms and influences can have on the nature and effectiveness of a nation's independent audit function. Another important focus of the Parmalat case is a legal issue that has become very troublesome for the major international accounting firms in recent years. This issue is whether those firms' global organizations should face joint and several liability for the malfeasance of any one national practice unit.

The other international case new to this edition is The Republic of Somalia, which transports students to one of the most troubled "hotspots" in the world. For more than 20 years, anarchy has reigned in Somalia, a country that sits astride one of the world's most important oceanic trade routes. In 2009, the world's largest accounting firm, PricewaterhouseCoopers (PwC), accepted a controversial professional services engagement in Somalia. Under the terms of that engagement, PwC serves as an overseer of the financial affairs for the provisional government that the United Nations established for the war-torn country. The Somalia case requires students to consider the significant risks and thorny ethical issues that engagement poses for PwC.

Eight of the new cases in this edition are included in two sections of my casebook that historically have been among the most popular: Audits of High-Risk Accounts and Internal Control Issues. New cases in the Audits of High-Risk Accounts section include General Motors Company, Lipper Holdings, Geo Securities, Belot Enterprises, and Regina Company. The General Motors case examines the controversy surrounding GM's pension-related accounting decisions and the role of the company's longtime audit firm, Deloitte, in those decisions. Hedge funds have been among the most controversial and mysterious investment vehicles on Wall Street over the past decade and have presented major challenges for the firms that audit them. In the Lipper Holdings case, the organization's audit firm was criticized for failing to uncover a fraudulent scheme that materially inflated the market values of investments held by three Lipper hedge funds.

In the present business environment, many, if not most, companies routinely deal with the worrisome problems posed by material loss contingencies. Loss contingencies also pose major challenges for independent auditors. Geo Securities' audit engagement partner faced SEC sanctions for the decisions he made regarding a pending loss contingency for that company. Client executives who face pressure to meet unrealistic earnings goals are often tempted to understate period-ending expense accruals. A senior auditor assigned to the audit engagement team for Belot Enterprises faced the unpleasant task of challenging the client's decision to implement a new approach for estimating its period-ending discretionary expense accruals. That decision by client management coincided with the end of a promotional campaign intended to boost Belot's sagging operating results. The final new "High-Risk" case, Regina Company, is actually a refurbished version of a case that appeared in earlier editions of my casebook. This case, which focuses on a high-profile financial fraud involving revenue recognition issues, was not previously available in the custom publishing database for my casebook.

First Keystone Bank, Buranello's Ristorante, and Foamex International are the three new cases in the Internal Controls Issues section. The First Keystone case revolves around a collusive fraud involving three employees of a small branch of a Pennsylvania-based bank. The case questions require students to examine internal control and audit issues linked to a device that plays an important role in many, if not most, of their everyday lives, namely, the local ATM. In the Buranello's case, the central focus is internal controls for cash receipts. A frustrated manager of a popular restaurant organized a "sting" operation to snag red-handed a subordinate who he believed was stealing from the business. Unfortunately, the sting went awry leaving the manager red-faced and his employer on the wrong end of a malicious prosecution lawsuit. Finally, Foamex International became the first company in the post-SOX era to be sanctioned by the SEC for the sole reason that it had inadequate internal controls.

Lehman Brothers Holdings is a new comprehensive case in the ninth edition of my casebook. The principal source for this case is the massive 2,200-page report prepared by the bankruptcy examiner for this former iconic investment banking firm. Lehman played a leading and notorious role in the global economic crisis of 2008–2009. To enhance their company's apparent financial condition, Lehman's executives engaged in tens of billions of dollars of "accounting-motivated" financing transactions referred to as Repo 105s. Lehman's controversial actions prompted a debate within the profession regarding whether "intent matters" in accounting and financial reporting decisions.

The final two new cases in this edition are the Freescale Semiconductor and Phillips Petroleum Company cases. Freescale Semiconductor appears in Section 4, Ethical Responsibilities of Accountants, while Phillips Petroleum is included in Section 5, Ethical Responsibilities of Independent Auditors. The Freescale case provides an overview of a series of recent insider trading incidents involving partners or employees of the major international accounting firms, including the former vice chairman of one of those firms. In the Phillips Petroleum case, the partner in charge of the company's annual audit was found in contempt of court by a federal judge and jailed when he refused to compromise the confidentiality of his client's accounting records.

My casebook can be used in several different ways. Professors can use the casebook as a supplemental text for an undergraduate auditing course or as a primary text for a graduate-level seminar in auditing. The instructor's manual contains a syllabus for a graduate auditing course organized around this text. This casebook can also be used in the capstone professional practice course incorporated in many five-year accounting programs. Customized versions of this casebook are suitable for a wide range of accounting courses as explained later.

Organization of Casebook Listed next are brief descriptions of the eight groups of cases included in this text. The casebook's Table of Contents presents an annotated description of each case.

Comprehensive Cases Most of these cases deal with highly publicized problem audits performed by the major international accounting firms. Among the clients involved in these audits are Enron Corporation, The Leslie Fay Companies, Lincoln Savings and Loan Association, Madoff Securities, and ZZZZ Best Company. Each of these cases addresses a wide range of auditing, accounting, and ethical issues.

Audits of High-Risk Accounts In contrast to the cases in the prior section, these cases highlight contentious accounting and auditing issues posed by a single account or group of accounts. For example, the Jack Greenberg case focuses primarily on inventory audit procedures. The Happiness Express case raises audit issues relevant to accounts receivable, while the Golden Bear case examines a series of revenue recognition issues.

Internal Control Issues In recent years, leading authorities in the public accounting profession have emphasized the need for auditors to thoroughly understand their clients' internal control policies and procedures. The cases in this section introduce students to control issues in a variety of contexts. For example, the Goodner Brothers case examines control issues for a wholesaler, while the Howard Street Jewelers case raises important control issues relevant to retail businesses.

Ethical Responsibilities of Accountants Integrating ethics into an auditing course requires much more than simply discussing the AICPA's *Code of Professional Conduct*. This section presents specific scenarios in which accountants have been forced to deal with perplexing ethical dilemmas. By requiring students to study actual situations in which important ethical issues have arisen, they will be better prepared to resolve similar situations in their own professional careers. Three of the cases in this section will "strike close to home" for your students since they involve accounting majors. For example, in the Wiley Jackson case, a soon-to-graduate accounting major must decide whether to disclose in a pre-employment document a minor-in-possession charge that is pending against him. Another case in this section, F&C International, profiles three corporate executives who had to decide whether to compromise their personal code of ethics in the face of a large-scale fraud masterminded by their company's chief executive.

Ethical Responsibilities of Independent Auditors The cases in this section highlight ethical dilemmas encountered by independent auditors. In the Cardillo Travel Systems case, two audit partners face an ethical dilemma that most audit practitioners will experience at some point during their careers. The two partners are forced to decide whether to accept implausible explanations for a suspicious client transaction given to them by client executives or, alternatively, whether to "complicate" the given engagement by insisting on fully investigating the transaction.

Professional Roles Cases in this section examine specific work roles in the accounting profession. These cases explore the responsibilities associated with those roles and related challenges that professionals occupying them commonly encounter. The Tommy O'Connell case involves a young auditor recently promoted to audit senior. Shortly following his promotion, Tommy finds himself assigned to supervise a small but challenging audit. Tommy's sole subordinate on that engagement happens to be a young man whose integrity and work ethic have been questioned by seniors he has worked for previously. Two cases in this section spotlight the staff accountant work role, which many of your students will experience first-hand following graduation.

Professional Issues The dynamic nature of the public accounting profession continually impacts the work environment of public accountants and the nature of the services they provide. The cases in this section highlight important issues presently facing accounting firms. For example, the *Hopkins v. Price Waterhouse* case explores the unique problems that women face in pursuing careers in public accounting, while the Ligand Pharmaceuticals case addresses the responsibility accounting firms have to ensure that their audit partners are qualified to supervise audit engagements. Finally, the Fred Stern and First Securities cases examine the most important legal liability issues within the public accounting profession.

International Cases The purpose of these cases is to provide your students with an introduction to important issues facing the global accounting profession and auditing discipline. After studying these cases, students will discover that most of the technical, professional, and ethical challenges facing U.S. practitioners are shared by auditors and accountants across the globe. Then again, some of these cases document unique challenges that must be dealt with by auditors and accountants in certain countries or regions of the world. For example, the Chinese case (*Zuan Yan*) demonstrates the problems that an authoritarian central government can present for independent auditors and accounting practitioners. Likewise, the Kaset Thai Sugar Company case vividly demonstrates that auditors and accountants may be forced to cope with hostile and sometimes dangerous working conditions in developing countries where their professional roles and responsibilities are not well understood or appreciated.

Customize Your Own Casebook To maximize your flexibility in using these cases, South-Western/Cengage Learning has included *Contemporary Auditing: Real Issues and Cases* in its customized publishing program, Make It Yours. Adopters have the option of creating a customized version of this casebook ideally suited for their specific needs. At the University of Oklahoma, a customized selection of my cases is used to add an ethics component to the undergraduate managerial accounting course. In fact, since the cases in this text examine ethical issues across a wide swath of different contexts, adopters can develop a customized ethics casebook to supplement almost any accounting course.

This casebook is ideally suited to be customized for the undergraduate auditing course. For example, auditing instructors who want to add a strong international component to their courses can develop a customized edition of this text that includes

a series of the international cases. Likewise, to enhance the coverage of ethical issues in the undergraduate auditing course, instructors could choose a series of cases
from this text that highlight important ethical issues. Following are several examples
of customized versions of this casebook that could be easily integrated into the undergraduate auditing course.

International Focus: Parmalat Finanziaria (8.2), *Kansayaku* (8.3), Registered
Auditors, South Africa (8.4), *Zuan Yan* (8.5), OAO Gazprom (8.8), Institute of
Chartered Accountants of India (8.10). This custom casebook would provide
your students with an in-depth understanding of the current state of the auditing
discipline in several of the world's most important countries.

Ethics Focus (I): Suzette Washington, Accounting Major (4.3), Wiley Jackson,
Accounting Major (4.5), Arvel Smart, Accounting Major (4.6), Leigh Ann Walker,
Staff Accountant (6.1), Hamilton Wong, In-Charge Accountant (6.3), Avis Love,
Staff Accountant (6.5). The first three of these cases give your students an
opportunity to discuss and debate ethical issues directly pertinent to them as
accounting majors. The final three cases expose students to important ethical
issues they may encounter shortly after graduation if they choose to enter public
accounting.

Ethics Focus (II): Creve Couer Pizza, Inc. (4.1), F&C International, Inc. (4.2),
Freescale Semiconductor (4.4), David Quinn, Tax Accountant (4.7), American
International Group (5.2), Waverly Holland, Audit Senior (5.4). This selection of
cases is suitable for auditing instructors who have a particular interest in covering
a variety of ethical topics relevant to the AICPA's *Code of Professional Conduct,*
several of which are not directly or exclusively related to auditing.

Applied Focus: Enron Corporation (1.1), NextCard, Inc. (1.6), ZZZZ Best
Company, Inc. (1.9), Belot Enterprises (2.8), American Fuel & Supply Company,
Inc. (5.6), Livent, Inc. (8.1). This series of cases will provide students with a
broad-brush introduction to the *real world* of independent auditing. These cases
raise a wide range of technical, professional, and ethical issues in a variety of
client contexts.

Professional Roles Focus: Leigh Ann Walker, Staff Accountant (6.1), Bill DeBurger,
In-Charge Accountant (6.2), Tommy O'Connell, Audit Senior (6.4), Avis Love,
Staff Accountant (6.5), Charles Tollison, Audit Manager (6.6), Bud Carriker, Audit
Senior (7.3). This custom casebook would be useful for auditing instructors
who choose to rely on a standard textbook to cover key technical topics in
auditing—but who also want to expose their students to the everyday ethical and
professional challenges faced by individuals occupying various levels of the
employment hierarchy within auditing firms.

High-Risk Accounts Focus: Each of the cases in Section 2, Audits of High-Risk
Accounts. This series of cases will provide your students with relatively intense
homework assignments that focus almost exclusively on the financial statement
line items that pose the greatest challenges for auditors.

Of course, realize that you are free to choose any "mix" of my cases to include in a
customized casebook for an undergraduate auditing course or another accounting

course that you teach. For more information on how to design your customized case-book, please contact your South-Western/Cengage Learning sales representative or visit the textbook website: www.cengage.com/custom/makeityours/knapp.

Acknowledgements I greatly appreciate the insight and suggestions provided by the following reviewers of earlier editions of this text: Alex Ampadu, University at Buffalo; Barbara Apostolou, Louisiana State University; Sandra A. Augustine, Hilbert College; Jane Baird, Mankato State University; Jason Bergner, University of Kentucky; James Bierstaker, Villanova University; Ed Blocher, University of North Carolina; Susan Cain, Southern Oregon University; Kurt Chaloupecky, Missouri State University; Ray Clay, University of North Texas; Jeffrey Cohen, Boston College; Mary Doucet, University of Georgia; Rafik Elias, California State University, Los Angeles; Ruth Engle, Lafayette College; Diana Franz, University of Toledo; Chrislynn Freed, University of Southern California; Carolyn Galantine, Pepperdine University; Soha Ghallab, Brooklyn College; Russell Hardin, University of South Alabama; Michele C. Henney, University of Oregon; Laurence Johnson, Colorado State University; Donald McConnell, University of Texas at Arlington; Heidi Meier, Cleveland State University; Don Nichols, Texas Christian University; Marcia Niles, University of Idaho; Thomas Noland, University of South Alabama; Les Nunn, University of Southern Indiana; Robert J. Ramsay, Ph.D., CPA, University of Kentucky; John Rigsby, Mississippi State University; Mike Shapeero, Bloomsburg University of Pennsylvania; Edward F. Smith, Boston College; Dr. Gene Smith, Eastern New Mexico University; Rajendra Srivastava, University of Kansas; Richard Allen Turpen, University of Alabama at Birmingham; T. Sterling Wetzel, Oklahoma State University; and Jim Yardley, Virginia Polytechnic University. This project also benefitted greatly from the editorial assistance of my sister, Paula Kay Conatser, my wife, Carol Ann Knapp, and my son, John William Knapp. I would also like to thank Glen McLaughlin for his continuing generosity in funding the development of instructional materials that highlight important ethical issues. Finally, I would like to acknowledge the contributions of my students, who have provided invaluable comments and suggestions on the content and use of these cases.

Michael C. Knapp
McLaughlin Chair in Business
Ethics, David Ross Boyd Professor,
and Professor of Accounting
University of Oklahoma

SECTION 1

COMPREHENSIVE CASES

1

Enron Corporation

John and Mary Andersen immigrated to the United States from their native Norway in 1881. The young couple made their way to the small farming community of Plano, Illinois, some 40 miles southwest of downtown Chicago. Over the previous few decades, hundreds of Norwegian families had settled in Plano and surrounding communities. In fact, the aptly named Norway, Illinois, was located just a few miles away from the couple's new hometown. In 1885, Arthur Edward Andersen was born. From an early age, the Andersens' son had a fascination with numbers. Little did his parents realize that Arthur's interest in numbers would become the driving force in his life. Less than one century after he was born, an accounting firm bearing Arthur Andersen's name would become the world's largest professional services organization with more than 1,000 partners and operations in dozens of countries scattered across the globe.

Think Straight, Talk Straight

Discipline, honesty, and a strong work ethic were three key traits that John and Mary Andersen instilled in their son. The Andersens also constantly impressed upon him the importance of obtaining an education. Unfortunately, Arthur's parents did not survive to help him achieve that goal. Orphaned by the time he was a young teenager, Andersen was forced to take a fulltime job as a mail clerk and attend night classes to work his way through high school. After graduating from high school, Andersen attended the University of Illinois while working as an accountant for Allis-Chalmers, a Chicago-based company that manufactured tractors and other farming equipment. In 1908, Andersen accepted a position with the Chicago office of Price Waterhouse. At the time, Price Waterhouse, which was organized in Great Britain during the early nineteenth century, easily qualified as the United States' most prominent public accounting firm.

At age 23, Andersen became the youngest CPA in the state of Illinois. A few years later, Andersen and a friend, Clarence Delany, established a partnership to provide accounting, auditing, and related services. The two young accountants named their firm Andersen, Delany & Company. When Delany decided to go his own way, Andersen renamed the firm Arthur Andersen & Company.

In 1915, Arthur Andersen faced a dilemma that would help shape the remainder of his professional life. One of his audit clients was a freight company that owned and operated several steam freighters that delivered various commodities to ports located on Lake Michigan. Following the close of the company's fiscal year but before Andersen had issued his audit report on its financial statements, one of the client's ships sank in Lake Michigan. At the time, there were few formal rules for companies to follow in preparing their annual financial statements and certainly no rule that required the company to report a material "subsequent event" occurring after the close of its fiscal year-such as the loss of a major asset. Nevertheless, Andersen insisted that his client disclose the loss of the ship. Andersen reasoned that third parties who would use the company's financial statements, among them the company's banker, would want to be informed of the loss. Although unhappy with Andersen's position, the client eventually acquiesced and reported the loss in the footnotes to its financial statements.

Two decades after the steamship dilemma, Arthur Andersen faced a similar situation with an audit client that was much larger, much more prominent, and much more profitable for his firm. Arthur Andersen & Co. served as the independent auditor for the giant chemical company, du Pont. As the company's audit neared completion one year, members of the audit engagement team and executives of du Pont quarreled over how to define the company's operating income. Du Pont's management insisted on a liberal definition of operating income that included income earned on certain investments. Arthur Andersen was brought in to arbitrate the dispute. When he sided with his subordinates, du Pont's management team dismissed the firm and hired another auditor.

Throughout his professional career, Arthur E. Andersen relied on a simple, four-word motto to serve as a guiding principle in making important personal and professional decisions: "Think straight, talk straight." Andersen insisted that his partners and other personnel in his firm invoke that simple rule when dealing with clients, potential clients, bankers, regulatory authorities, and any other parties they interacted with while representing Arthur Andersen & Co. He also insisted that audit clients "talk straight" in their financial statements. Former colleagues and associates often described Andersen as opinionated, stubborn and, in some cases, "difficult." But even his critics readily admitted that Andersen was point-blank honest. "Arthur Andersen wouldn't put up with anything that wasn't complete, 100% integrity. If anybody did anything otherwise, he'd fire them. And if clients wanted to do something he didn't agree with, he'd either try to change them or quit."[1]

As a young professional attempting to grow his firm, Arthur Andersen quickly recognized the importance of carving out a niche in the rapidly developing accounting services industry. Andersen realized that the nation's bustling economy of the 1920s depended heavily on companies involved in the production and distribution of energy. As the economy grew, Andersen knew there would be a steadily increasing need for electricity, oil and gas, and other energy resources. So he focused his practice development efforts on obtaining clients involved in the various energy industries. Andersen was particularly successful in recruiting electric utilities as clients. By the early 1930s, Arthur Andersen & Co. had a thriving practice in the upper Midwest and was among the leading regional accounting firms in the nation.

The U.S. economy's precipitous downturn during the Great Depression of the 1930s posed huge financial problems for many of Arthur Andersen & Co.'s audit clients in the electric utilities industry. As the Depression wore on, Arthur Andersen personally worked with several of the nation's largest metropolitan banks to help his clients obtain the financing they desperately needed to continue operating. The bankers and other leading financiers who dealt with Arthur Andersen quickly learned of his commitment to honesty and proper, forthright accounting and financial reporting practices. Andersen's reputation for honesty and integrity allowed lenders to use with confidence financial data stamped with his approval. The end result was that many troubled firms received the financing they needed to survive the harrowing days of the 1930s. In turn, the respect that Arthur Andersen earned among leading financial executives nationwide resulted in Arthur Andersen & Co. receiving a growing number of referrals for potential clients located outside of the Midwest.

During the later years of his career, Arthur Andersen became a spokesperson for his discipline. He authored numerous books and presented speeches throughout the nation regarding the need for rigorous accounting, auditing, and ethical standards for the emerging public accounting profession. Andersen continually urged his fellow

---

1. R. Frammolino and J. Leeds, "Andersen's Reputation in Shreds," *Los Angeles Times* (online), 30 January 2002.

accountants to adopt the public service ideal that had long served as the underlying premise of the more mature professions such as law and medicine. He also lobbied for the adoption of a mandatory continuing professional education (CPE) requirement. Andersen realized that CPAs needed CPE to stay abreast of developments in the business world that had significant implications for accounting and financial reporting practices. In fact, Arthur Andersen & Co. made CPE mandatory for its employees long before state boards of accountancy adopted such a requirement.

By the mid-1940s, Arthur Andersen & Co. had offices scattered across the eastern one-half of the United States and employed more than 1,000 accountants. When Arthur Andersen died in 1947, many business leaders expected that the firm would disband without its founder, who had single-handedly managed its operations over the previous four decades. But, after several months of internal turmoil and dissension, the firm's remaining partners chose Andersen's most trusted associate and protégé to replace him.

Like his predecessor and close friend who had personally hired him in 1928, Leonard Spacek soon earned a reputation as a no-nonsense professional—an auditor's auditor. He passionately believed that the primary role of independent auditors was to ensure that their clients reported fully and honestly regarding their financial affairs to the investing and lending public. Spacek continued Arthur Andersen's campaign to improve accounting and auditing practices in the United States during his long tenure as his firm's chief executive. "Spacek openly criticized the profession for tolerating what he considered a sloppy patchwork of accounting standards that left the investing public no way to compare the financial performance of different companies."[2] Such criticism compelled the accounting profession to develop a more formal and rigorous rule-making process. In the late 1950s, the profession created the Accounting Principles Board (APB) to study contentious accounting issues and develop appropriate new standards. The APB was replaced in 1973 by the Financial Accounting Standards Board (FASB). Another legacy of Arthur Andersen that Leonard Spacek sustained was requiring the firm's professional employees to continue their education throughout their careers. During Spacek's tenure, Arthur Andersen & Co. established the world's largest private university, the Arthur Andersen & Co. Center for Professional Education, located in St. Charles, Illinois, not far from Arthur Andersen's birthplace.

Leonard Spacek's strong leadership and business skills transformed Arthur Andersen & Co. into a major international accounting firm. When Spacek retired in 1973, Arthur Andersen & Co. was arguably the most respected accounting firm not only in the United States, but worldwide as well. Three decades later, shortly after the dawn of the new millennium, Arthur Andersen & Co. employed more than 80,000 professionals, had practice offices in more than 80 countries, and had annual revenues approaching $10 billion. However, in late 2001, the firm, which by that time had adopted the one-word name "Andersen," faced the most significant crisis in its history since the death of its founder. Ironically, that crisis stemmed from Andersen's audits of an energy company, a company founded in 1930 that, like many of Arthur Andersen's clients, had struggled to survive the Depression.

The World's Greatest Company

Northern Natural Gas Company was founded in Omaha, Nebraska, in 1930. The principal investors in the new venture included a Texas-based company, Lone Star Gas Corporation. During its first few years of existence, Northern wrestled with the problem

---

2. *Ibid.*

of persuading consumers to use natural gas to heat their homes. Concern produced by several unfortunate and widely publicized home "explosions" caused by natural gas leaks drove away many of Northern's potential customers. But, as the Depression wore on, the relatively cheap cost of natural gas convinced increasing numbers of cold-stricken and shallow-pocketed consumers to become Northern customers.

The availability of a virtually unlimited source of cheap manual labor during the 1930s allowed Northern to develop an extensive pipeline network to deliver natural gas to the residential and industrial markets that it served in the Great Plains states. As the company's revenues and profits grew, Northern's management launched a campaign to acquire dozens of its smaller competitors. This campaign was prompted by management's goal of making Northern the largest natural gas supplier in the United States. In 1947, the company, which was still relatively unknown outside of its geographical market, reached a major milestone when its stock was listed on the New York Stock Exchange. That listing provided the company with greater access to the nation's capital markets and the financing needed to continue its growth-through-acquisition strategy over the following two decades.

During the 1970s, Northern became a principal investor in the development of the Alaskan pipeline. When completed, that pipeline allowed Northern to tap vast natural gas reserves it had acquired in Canada. In 1980, Northern changed its name to InterNorth, Inc. Over the next few years, company management extended the scope of the company's operations by investing in ventures outside of the natural gas industry, including oil exploration, chemicals, coal mining, and fuel-trading operations. But the company's principal focus remained the natural gas industry. In 1985, InterNorth purchased Houston Natural Gas Company for $2.3 billion. That acquisition resulted in InterNorth controlling a 40,000-mile network of natural gas pipelines and allowed it to achieve its long-sought goal of becoming the largest natural gas company in the United States.

In 1986, InterNorth changed its name to Enron. Kenneth Lay, the former chairman of Houston Natural Gas, emerged as the top executive of the newly created firm that chose Houston, Texas, as its corporate headquarters. Lay quickly adopted the aggressive growth strategy that had long dominated the management policies of InterNorth and its predecessor. Lay hired Jeffrey Skilling to serve as one of his top subordinates. During the 1990s, Skilling developed and implemented a plan to transform Enron from a conventional natural gas supplier into an energy-trading company that served as an intermediary between producers of energy products, principally natural gas and electricity, and end users of those commodities. In early 2001, Skilling assumed Lay's position as Enron's chief executive officer (CEO), although Lay retained the title of chairman of the board. In the management letter to shareholders included in Enron's 2000 annual report, Lay and Skilling explained the metamorphosis that Enron had undergone over the previous 15 years:

> Enron hardly resembles the company we were in the early days. During our 15-year history, we have stretched ourselves beyond our own expectations. We have metamorphosed from an asset-based pipeline and power generating company to a marketing and logistics company whose biggest assets are its well-established business approach and its innovative people.

Enron's 2000 annual report discussed the company's four principal lines of business. Energy Wholesale Services ranked as the company's largest revenue producer. That division's 60 percent increase in transaction volume during 2000 was fueled by the rapid development of EnronOnline, a B2B (business-to-business) electronic marketplace for the energy industries created in late 1999 by Enron. During fiscal 2000

EXHIBIT 1

ENRON
CORPORATION
2000 ANNUAL
REPORT FINANCIAL
HIGHLIGHTS TABLE
(IN MILLIONS EXCEPT
FOR PER SHARE
AMOUNTS)

	2000	1999	1998	1997	1996
Revenues	$100,789	$40,112	$31,260	$20,273	$13,289
Net Income:					
Operating Results	1,266	957	698	515	493
Items Impacting Comparability	(287)	(64)	5	(410)	91
Total	979	893	703	105	584
Earnings Per Share:					
Operating Results	1.47	1.18	1.00	.87	.91
Items Impacting Comparability	(.35)	(.08)	.01	(.71)	.17
Total	1.12	1.10	1.01	.16	1.08
Dividends Per Share:	.50	.50	.48	.46	.43
Total Assets:	65,503	33,381	29,350	22,552	16,137
Cash from Operating Activities:	3,010	2,228	1,873	276	742
Capital Expenditures and Equity Investments:	3,314	3,085	3,564	2,092	1,483
NYSE Price Range:					
High	90.56	44.88	29.38	22.56	23.75
Low	41.38	28.75	19.06	17.50	17.31
Close, December 31	83.12	44.38	28.53	20.78	21.56

alone, EnronOnline processed more than $335 billion of transactions, easily making Enron the largest e-commerce company in the world. Enron's three other principal lines of business included Enron Energy Services, the company's retail operating unit; Enron Transportation Services, which was responsible for the company's pipeline operations; and Enron Broadband Services, a new operating unit intended to be an intermediary between users and suppliers of broadband (Internet access) services. Exhibit 1 presents the five-year financial highlights table included in Enron's 2000 annual report.

The New Economy business model that Enron pioneered for the previously staid energy industries caused Kenneth Lay, Jeffrey Skilling, and their top subordinates to be recognized as skillful entrepreneurs and to gain superstar status in the business world. Lay's position as the chief executive of the nation's seventh-largest firm gave him direct access to key political and governmental officials. In 2001, Lay served on the "transition team" responsible for helping usher in the administration of President-elect George W. Bush. In June 2001, Skilling was singled out as "the No. 1 CEO in the entire country," while Enron was hailed as "America's most innovative company."[3]

---

3. K. Eichenwald and D. B. Henriques, "Web of Details Did Enron In as Warnings Went Unheeded," *The New York Times* (online), 10 February 2002.

Enron's chief financial officer (CFO) Andrew Fastow was recognized for creating the financial infrastructure for one of the nation's largest and most complex companies. In 1999, *CFO Magazine* presented Fastow the Excellence Award for Capital Structure Management for his "pioneering work on unique financing techniques."[4]

Throughout their tenure with Enron, Kenneth Lay and Jeffrey Skilling continually focused on enhancing their company's operating results. In the letter to shareholders in Enron's 2000 annual report, Lay and Skilling noted that "Enron is laser-focused on earnings per share, and we expect to continue strong earnings performance." Another important goal of Enron's top executives was to increase their company's stature in the business world. During a speech in January 2001, Lay revealed that his ultimate goal was for Enron to become "the world's greatest company."[5]

As Enron's revenues and profits swelled, its top executives were often guilty of a certain degree of chutzpah. In particular, Skilling became known for making brassy, if not tacky, comments concerning his firm's competitors and critics. During the crisis that gripped California's electric utility industry during 2001, numerous elected officials and corporate executives criticized Enron for allegedly profiteering by selling electricity at inflated prices to the Golden State. Skilling brushed aside such criticism. During a speech at a major business convention, Skilling asked the crowd if they knew the difference between the state of California and the Titanic. After an appropriate pause, Skilling provided the punch line: "At least when the Titanic went down, the lights were on."[6]

Unfortunately for Lay, Skilling, Fastow, and thousands of Enron employees and stockholders, Lay failed to achieve his goal of creating the world's greatest company. In a matter of months during 2001, Enron quickly unraveled. Enron's sudden collapse panicked investors nationwide, leading to what one *Newsweek* columnist described as the "the biggest crisis investors have had since 1929."[7] Enron's dire financial problems were triggered by public revelations of questionable accounting and financial reporting decisions made by the company's accountants. Those decisions had been reviewed, analyzed, and apparently approved by Andersen, the company's independent audit firm.

Debits, Credits, and Enron

Throughout 2001, Enron's stock price drifted lower. Publicly, Enron executives blamed the company's slumping stock price on falling natural gas prices, concerns regarding the long-range potential of electronic marketplaces such as EnronOnline, and overall weakness in the national economy. By mid-October, the stock price had fallen into the mid-$30s from a high in the lower $80s earlier in the year. On October 16, 2001, Enron issued its quarterly earnings report for the third quarter of 2001. That report revealed that the firm had suffered a huge loss during the quarter. Even more problematic to many financial analysts was a mysterious $1.2 billion reduction in Enron's owners' equity and assets that was disclosed seemingly as an afterthought in the earnings press release. This write-down resulted from the reversal of previously recorded transactions involving the swap of Enron stock for notes receivable. Enron had acquired the notes receivable from related third parties who had invested in limited partnerships organized and sponsored by the company. After studying those transactions in more depth, Enron's accounting staff and its Andersen auditors concluded

4. E. Thomas, "Every Man for Himself," *Newsweek*, 18 February 2002, 25.

5. Eichenwald and Henriques, "Web of Details."

6. *Ibid.*

7. N. Byrnes, "Paying for the Sins of Enron," *Newsweek*, 11 February 2002, 35.

that the notes receivable should not have been reported in the assets section of the company's balance sheet but rather as a reduction to owners' equity.

The October 16, 2001, press release sent Enron's stock price into a free fall. Three weeks later on November 8, Enron restated its reported earnings for the previous five years, wiping out approximately $600 million of profits the company had reported over that time frame. That restatement proved to be the death knell for Enron. On December 2, 2001, intense pressure from creditors, pending and threatened litigation against the company and its officers, and investigations initiated by law enforcement authorities forced Enron to file for bankruptcy. Instead of becoming the nation's greatest company, Enron laid claim to being the largest corporate bankruptcy in U.S. history, imposing more than $60 billion of losses on its stockholders alone. Enron's "claim to fame" would be eclipsed the following year by the more than $100 billion of losses produced when another Andersen client, WorldCom, filed for bankruptcy.

The massive and understandable public outcry over Enron's implosion during the fall of 2001 spawned a mad frenzy on the part of the print and electronic media to determine how the nation's seventh-largest public company, a company that had posted impressive and steadily rising profits over the previous few years, could crumple into insolvency in a matter of months. From the early days of this public drama, skeptics in the financial community charged that Enron's balance sheet and earnings restatements in the fall of 2001 demonstrated that the company's exceptional financial performance during the late 1990s and 2000 had been a charade, a hoax orchestrated by the company's management with the help of a squad of creative accountants. Any doubt regarding the validity of that theory was wiped away—at least in the minds of most members of the press and the general public—when a letter that an Enron accountant had sent to Kenneth Lay in August 2001 was discovered. The contents of that letter were posted on numerous websites and lengthy quotes taken from it appeared in virtually every major newspaper in the nation.

Exhibit 2 contains key excerpts from the letter that Sherron Watkins wrote to Kenneth Lay in August 2001. Watkins' job title was vice president of corporate development, but she was an accountant by training, having worked previously with Andersen, Enron's audit firm. The sudden and unexpected resignation of Jeffrey Skilling as Enron's CEO after serving in that capacity for only six months had prompted Watkins to write the letter to Lay. Before communicating her concerns to Lay, Watkins had attempted to discuss those issues with one of Lay's senior subordinates. When Watkins offered to show that individual a document that identified significant problems in accounting decisions made previously by Enron, Watkins reported that he rebuffed her. "He said he'd rather not see it."[8]

Watkins was intimately familiar with aggressive accounting decisions made for a series of large and complex transactions involving Enron and dozens of limited partnerships created by the company. These partnerships were so-called SPEs or special purpose entities that Enron executives had tagged with a variety of creative names, including Braveheart, Rawhide, Raptor, Condor, and Talon. Andrew Fastow, Enron's CFO who was involved in the creation and operation of several of the SPEs, named a series of them after his three children.

SPEs—sometimes referred to as SPVs (special purpose vehicles)—can take several legal forms but are commonly organized as limited partnerships. During the 1990s, hundreds of large corporations began establishing SPEs. In most cases, SPEs

---

8. T. Hamburger, "Watkins Tells of 'Arrogant' Culture; Enron Stifled Staff Whistle-Blowing," *The Wall Street Journal* (online), 14 February 2002.

EXHIBIT 2

SELECTED EXCERPTS
FROM SHERRON
WATKINS' AUGUST
2001 LETTER TO
KENNETH LAY

Dear Mr. Lay,

Has Enron become a risky place to work? For those of us who didn't get rich over the last few years, can we afford to stay?

Skilling's abrupt departure will raise suspicions of accounting improprieties and valuation issues. Enron has been very aggressive in its accounting—most notably the Raptor transactions and the Condor vehicle. . . .

We have recognized over $550 million of fair value gains on stocks via our swaps with Raptor, much of that stock has declined significantly. . . . The value in the swaps won't be there for Raptor, so once again Enron will issue stock to offset these losses. Raptor is an LJM entity. It sure looks to the layman on the street that we are hiding losses in a related company and will compensate that company with Enron stock in the future.

I am incredibly nervous that we will implode in a wave of scandals. My 8 years of Enron work history will be worth nothing on my resume, the business world will consider the past successes as nothing but an elaborate accounting hoax. Skilling is resigning now for "personal reasons" but I think he wasn't having fun, looked down the road and knew this stuff was unfixable and would rather abandon ship now than resign in shame in 2 years.

Is there a way our accounting gurus can unwind these deals now? I have thought and thought about how to do this, but I keep bumping into one big problem—we booked the Condor and Raptor deals in 1999 and 2000, we enjoyed a wonderfully high stock price, many executives sold stock, we then try and reverse or fix the deals in 2001 and it's a bit like robbing the bank in 1 year and trying to pay it back 2 years later. . . .

I realize that we have had a lot of smart people looking at this and a lot of accountants including AA & Co. have blessed the accounting treatment. None of this will protect Enron if these transactions are ever disclosed in the bright light of day. . . .

The overriding basic principle of accounting is that if you explain the "accounting treatment" to a man on the street, would you influence his investing decisions? Would he sell or buy the stock based on a thorough understanding of the facts?

My concern is that the footnotes don't adequately explain the transactions. If adequately explained, the investor would know that the "Entities" described in our related party footnote are thinly capitalized, the equity holders have no skin in the game, and all the value in the entities comes from the underlying value of the derivatives (unfortunately in this case, a big loss) AND Enron stock and N/P. . . .

The related party footnote tries to explain these transactions. Don't you think that several interested companies, be they stock analysts, journalists, hedge fund managers, etc., are busy trying to discover the reason Skilling left? Don't you think their smartest people are pouring [sic] over that footnote disclosure right now? I can just hear the discussions—"It looks like they booked a $500 million gain from this related party company and I think, from all the undecipherable 1/2 page on Enron's contingent contributions to this related party entity, I think the related party entity is capitalized with Enron stock." . . . "No, no, no, you must have it all wrong, it can't be that, that's just too bad, too fraudulent, surely AA & Co. wouldn't let them get away with that?"

were used to finance the acquisition of an asset or fund a construction project or related activity. Regardless, the underlying motivation for creating an SPE was nearly always "debt avoidance." That is, SPEs provided large companies with a mechanism to raise needed financing for various purposes without being required to report the debt in their balance sheets. *Fortune* magazine charged that corporate CFOs were using SPEs as scalpels "to perform cosmetic surgery on their balance sheets."[9] During the early 1990s, the Securities and Exchange Commission (SEC) and the FASB had wrestled with the contentious accounting and financial reporting issues posed by SPEs. Despite intense debate and discussions, the SEC and the FASB provided little in the way of formal guidance for companies to follow in accounting and reporting for SPEs.

The most important guideline that the authoritative bodies implemented for SPEs, the so-called 3 percent rule, proved to be extremely controversial. This rule allowed a company to omit an SPE's assets and liabilities from its consolidated financial statements as long as parties independent of the company provided a minimum of 3 percent of the SPE's capital. Almost immediately, the 3 percent threshold became both a technical minimum and a practical maximum. That is, large companies using the SPE structure arranged for external parties to provide exactly 3 percent of an SPE's total capital. The remaining 97 percent of an SPE's capital was typically contributed by loans from external lenders, loans arranged and generally collateralized by the company that created the SPE.

Many critics charged that the 3 percent rule undercut the fundamental principle within the accounting profession that consolidated financial statements should be prepared for entities controlled by a common ownership group. "There is a presumption that consolidated financial statements are more meaningful than separate statements and that they are usually necessary for a fair presentation when one of the companies in the group directly or indirectly has a controlling financial interest in the other companies."[10] *Business Week* chided the SEC and FASB for effectively endorsing the 3 percent rule.

> *Because of a gaping loophole in accounting practice, companies can create arcane legal structures, often called special-purpose entities (SPEs). Then, the parent can bankroll up to 97 percent of the initial investment in an SPE without having to consolidate it. . . . The controversial exception that outsiders need invest only 3 percent of an SPE's capital for it to be independent and off the balance sheet came about through fumbles by the Securities and Exchange Commission and the Financial Accounting Standards Board.*[11]

Throughout the 1990s, many companies took advantage of the minimal legal and accounting guidelines for SPEs to divert huge amounts of their liabilities to off-balance sheet entities. Among the most aggressive and innovative users of the SPE structure was Enron, which created hundreds of SPEs. Unlike most companies, Enron did not limit its SPEs to financing activities. In many cases, Enron used SPEs for the sole purpose of downloading underperforming assets from its financial statements to the financial statements of related but unconsolidated entities. For example, Enron would arrange for a third party to invest the minimum 3 percent capital required in an SPE and then sell assets to that SPE. The SPE would finance the purchase of those assets by loans collateralized by Enron common stock. In some cases, undisclosed side

9. J. Kahn, "Off Balance Sheet—And Out of Control," *Fortune,* 18 February 2002, 84.

10. *Accounting Research Bulletin No. 51*, "Consolidated Financial Statements" (New York: AICPA, 1959).

11. D. Henry, H. Timmons, S. Rosenbush, and M. Arndt, "Who Else Is Hiding Debt?" *Business Week,* 28 January 2002, 36–37.

agreements made by Enron with an SPE's nominal owners insulated those individuals from any losses on their investments and, in fact, guaranteed them a windfall profit. Even more troubling, Enron often sold assets at grossly inflated prices to their SPEs, allowing the company to manufacture large "paper" gains on those transactions.

Enron made only nominal financial statement disclosures for its SPE transactions and those disclosures were typically presented in confusing, if not cryptic, language. One accounting professor observed that the inadequate disclosures that companies such as Enron provided for their SPE transactions meant that, "the nonprofessional [investor] has no idea of the extent of the [given firm's] real liabilities."[12] *The Wall Street Journal* added to that sentiment when it suggested that Enron's brief and obscure disclosures for its off-balance sheet liabilities and related-party transactions "were so complicated as to be practically indecipherable."[13]

Just as difficult to analyze for most investors was the integrity of the hefty profits reported each successive period by Enron. As Sherron Watkins revealed in the letter she sent to Kenneth Lay in August 2001, many of Enron's SPE transactions resulted in the company's profits being inflated by unrealized gains on increases in the market value of its own common stock. In the fall of 2001, Enron's board of directors appointed a Special Investigative Committee chaired by William C. Powers, dean of the University of Texas Law School, to study the company's large SPE transactions. In February 2002, that committee issued a lengthy report of its findings, a document commonly referred to as the Powers Report by the press. This report discussed at length the "Byzantine" nature of Enron's SPE transactions and the enormous and improper gains those transactions produced for the company.

> *Accounting principles generally forbid a company from recognizing an increase in the value of its capital stock in its income statement. . . . The substance of the Raptors [SPE transactions] effectively allowed Enron to report gains on its income statement that were . . . [attributable to] Enron stock, and contracts to receive Enron stock, held by the Raptors.*[14]

The primary motivation for Enron's extensive use of SPEs and the related accounting machinations was the company's growing need for capital during the 1990s. As Kenneth Lay and Jeffrey Skilling transformed Enron from a fairly standard natural gas supplier into a New Economy intermediary for the energy industries, the company had a constant need for additional capital to finance that transformation. Like most new business endeavors, Enron's Internet-based operations did not produce positive cash flows immediately. To convince lenders to continue pumping cash into Enron, the company's management team realized that their firm would have to maintain a high credit rating, which, in turn, required the company to release impressive financial statements each succeeding period.

A related factor that motivated Enron's executives to window dress their company's financial statements was the need to sustain Enron's stock price at a high level. Many of the SPE loan agreements negotiated by Enron included so-called price "triggers." If the market price of Enron's stock dropped below a designated level (trigger), Enron was required to provide additional stock to collateralize the given loan, to make significant cash payments to the SPE, or to restructure prior transactions with the SPE.

---

12. *Ibid.*

13. J. Emshwiller and R. Smith, "Murky Waters: A Primer on the Enron Partnerships," *The Wall Street Journal* (online), 21 January 2002.

14. W. C. Powers, R. S. Troubh, and H. S. Winokur, "Report of Investigation by the Special Investigative Committee of the Board of Directors of Enron Corporation," 1 February 2002, 129–130.

In a worst-case scenario, Enron might be forced to dissolve an SPE and merge its assets and liabilities into the company's consolidated financial statements.

> *What made Enron's stock price so important was the fact that some of the company's most important deals with the partnerships [SPEs] run by Mr. Fastow—deals that had allowed Enron to keep hundreds of millions of dollars of potential losses off its books—were financed, in effect, with Enron stock. Those transactions could fall apart if the stock price fell too far.*[15]

As Enron's stock price drifted lower throughout 2001, the complex labyrinth of legal and accounting gimmicks underlying the company's finances became a shaky house of cards. Making matters worse were large losses suffered by many of Enron's SPEs on the assets they had purchased from Enron. Enron executives were forced to pour additional resources into many of those SPEs to keep them solvent. Contributing to the financial problems of Enron's major SPEs was alleged self-dealing by Enron officials involved in operating those SPEs. Andrew Fastow realized $30 million in profits on his investments in Enron SPEs that he oversaw at the same time he was serving as the company's CFO. Several of his friends also reaped windfall profits on investments in those same SPEs. Some of these individuals "earned" a profit of as much as $1 million on an initial investment of $5,800. Even more startling was the fact that Fastow's friends realized these gains in as little as 60 days.

By October 2001, the falling price of Enron's stock, the weight of the losses suffered by the company's large SPEs, and concerns being raised by Andersen auditors forced company executives to act. Enron's management assumed control and ownership of several of the company's troubled SPEs and incorporated their dismal financial statement data into Enron's consolidated financial statements. This decision led to the large loss reported by Enron in the fall of 2001 and the related restatement of the company's earnings for the previous five years. On December 2, 2001, the transformed New Age company filed its bankruptcy petition in New Age fashion—via the Internet. Only six months earlier, Jeffrey Skilling had been buoyant when commenting on Enron's first quarter results for 2001. "So in conclusion, first-quarter results were great. We are very optimistic about our new businesses and are confident that our record of growth is sustainable for many years to come."[16]

As law enforcement authorities, Congressional investigative committees, and business journalists rifled through the mass of Enron documents that became publicly available during early 2002, the abusive accounting and financial reporting practices that had been used by the company surfaced. Enron's creative use of SPEs became the primary target of critics; however, the company also made extensive use of other accounting gimmicks. For example, Enron had abused the mark-to-market accounting method for its long-term contracts involving various energy commodities, primarily natural gas and electricity. Given the nature of their business, energy-trading firms regularly enter into long-term contracts to deliver energy commodities. Some of Enron's commodity contracts extended over periods of more than 20 years and involved massive quantities of the given commodity. When Enron finalized these deals, company officials often made tenuous assumptions that inflated the profits booked on the contracts.

> *Energy traders must book all the projected profits from a supply contract in the quarter in which the deal is made, even if the contract spans many years. That means companies can inflate profits by using unrealistic price forecasts, as Enron has been accused of doing. If a company contracted to buy natural gas through 2010 for $3 per thousand*

---

15. Eichenwald and Henriques, "Web of Details."

16. *Ibid.*

cubic feet, an energy-trading desk could aggressively assume it would be able to sup-ply gas in each year at a cost of just $2, for a $1 profit margin.[17]

The avalanche of startling revelations regarding Enron's aggressive business, ac-counting, and financial reporting decisions reported by the business press during the early weeks of 2002 created a firestorm of anger and criticism directed at Enron's key executives, principally Kenneth Lay, Jeffrey Skilling, and Andrew Fastow. A common theme of the allegations leveled at the three executives was that they had created a corporate culture that fostered, if not encouraged, "rule breaking." *Fortune* magazine observed that, "If nothing else, Lay allowed a culture of rule breaking to flourish,"[18] while Sherron Watkins testified that Enron's corporate culture was "arrogant" and "intimidating" and discouraged employees from reporting and investigating ethical lapses and questionable business dealings.[19] Finally, a top executive of Dynegy, a company that briefly considered merging with Enron during late 2001, reported that "the lack of internal controls [within Enron] was mindboggling."[20]

Both Kenneth Lay and Andrew Fastow invoked their Fifth Amendment rights against self-incrimination when asked to testify before Congress in early 2002. Jeffrey Skilling did not. While being peppered by Congressional investigators regarding Enron's ques-tionable accounting and financial reporting decisions, Skilling replied calmly and re-peatedly: "I am not an accountant." A well-accepted premise in the financial reporting domain is that corporate executives and their accountants are ultimately responsible for the integrity of their company's financial statements. Nevertheless, frustration stemming from the lack of answers provided by Enron insiders to key accounting and financial reporting-related questions eventually caused Congressional investigators, the business press, and the public to focus their attention, their questions, and their scorn on Enron's independent audit firm, Andersen. These parties insisted that Andersen representatives explain why their audits of Enron had failed to result in more transparent, if not reli-able, financial statements for the company. More pointedly, those critics demanded that Andersen explain how it was able to issue unqualified audit opinions on Enron's finan-cial statements throughout its 15-year tenure as the company's independent audit firm.

Say It Ain't So Joe

Joseph Berardino became Andersen's chief executive shortly before the firm was swamped by the storm of criticism surrounding the collapse of its second-largest cli-ent, Enron Corporation. Berardino launched his business career with Andersen in 1972 immediately after graduating from college and just a few months before Leonard Spacek ended his long and illustrious career with the firm. Throughout its history, the Andersen firm had a policy of speaking with one voice, the voice of its chief ex-ecutive. So, the unpleasant task of responding to the angry and often self-righteous accusations hurled at Andersen following Enron's demise fell to Berardino, although he had not been a party to the key decisions made during the Enron audits.

A common question directed at Berardino was whether his firm had been aware of the allegations Sherron Watkins made during August 2001 and, if so, how had Andersen responded to those allegations. Watkins testified before Congress that shortly after she communicated her concerns regarding Enron's questionable ac-counting and financial reporting decisions to Kenneth Lay, she had met with a

---

17. P. Coy, S. A. Forest, and D. Foust, "Enron: How Good an Energy Trader?" *Business Week*, 11 February 2002, 42–43.

18. B. McLean, "Monster Mess," *Fortune*, 4 February 2002, 94.

19. Hamburger, "Watkins Tells of 'Arrogant' Culture."

20. N. Banjeree, D. Barboza, and A. Warren, "At Enron, Lavish Excess Often Came before Success," *The New York Times* (online), 26 February 2002.

member of the Andersen firm with whom she had worked several years earlier. In an internal Andersen memorandum, that individual relayed Watkins' concerns to several colleagues, including the Enron audit engagement partner, David Duncan. At that point, Andersen officials in the firm's Chicago headquarters began systematically reviewing previous decisions made by the Enron's audit engagement team.

In fact, several months earlier, Andersen representatives had become aware of Enron's rapidly deteriorating financial condition and become deeply involved in helping the company's executives cope with that crisis. Andersen's efforts included assisting Enron officials in restructuring certain of the company's SPEs so that they could continue to qualify as unconsolidated entities. Subsequent press reports revealed that in February 2001, frustration over the aggressive nature of Enron's accounting and financial reporting decisions caused some Andersen officials to suggest dropping the company as an audit client.[21]

On December 12, 2001, Joseph Berardino testified before the Committee on Financial Services of the U.S. House of Representatives. Early in that testimony, Berardino freely admitted that members of the Enron audit engagement team had made one major error while analyzing a large SPE transaction that occurred in 1999. "We made a professional judgment about the appropriate accounting treatment that turned out to be wrong."[22] According to Berardino, when Andersen officials discovered this error in the fall of 2001, they promptly notified Enron's executives and told them to "correct it." Approximately 20 percent of the $600 million restatement of prior earnings announced by Enron on November 8, 2001, was due to this item.

The remaining 80 percent of the earnings restatement involved another SPE that Enron created in 1997. Unknown to Andersen auditors, one-half of that SPE's minimum 3 percent "external" equity had been effectively contributed by Enron. As a result, that entity did not qualify for SPE treatment, meaning that its financial data should have been included in Enron's consolidated financial statements from its inception. When Andersen auditors discovered this violation of the 3 percent rule in the fall of 2001, they immediately informed Enron's accounting staff. Andersen also informed the company's audit committee that the failure of Enron officials to reveal the source of the SPE's initial funding could possibly be construed as an illegal act under the Securities Exchange Act of 1934. Berardino implied that the client's lack of candor regarding this SPE exempted Andersen of responsibility for the resulting accounting and financial reporting errors linked to that entity.

Berardino also explained to Congress that Andersen auditors had been only minimally involved in the transactions that eventually resulted in the $1.2 billion reduction of owners' equity reported by Enron on October 16, 2001. The bulk of those transactions had occurred in early 2001. Andersen had not audited the 2001 quarterly financial statements that had been prepared following the initial recording of those transactions—public companies are not required to have their quarterly financial statements audited.

Berardino's testimony before Congress in December 2001 failed to appease Andersen's critics. Over the next several months, Berardino continually found himself defending Andersen against a growing torrent of accusations. Most of these accusations centered on three key issues. First, many critics raised the controversial and longstanding "scope of services" issue when criticizing Andersen's role in the Enron debacle. Over the final few decades of the twentieth century,

---

21. S. Labaton, "S.E.C. Leader Sees Outside Monitors for Auditing Firms," *The New York Times* (online), 18 January 2002.

22. J. Kahn and J. D. Glater, "Enron Auditor Raises Specter of Crime," *The New York Times* (online), 13 December 2001.

the major accounting firms had gradually extended the product line of professional services they offered to their major audit clients. A research study focusing on nearly 600 large companies that released financial statements in early 1999 revealed that for every $1 of audit fees those companies had paid their independent auditors, they had paid those firms $2.69 for nonaudit consulting services.[23] These services included a wide range of activities such as feasibility studies of various types, internal auditing, design of accounting systems, development of e-commerce initiatives, and a varied assortment of other information technology (IT) services.

In an interview with *The New York Times* in March 2002, Leonard Spacek's daughter revealed that her father had adamantly opposed accounting firms providing consulting services to their audit clients. "I remember him ranting and raving, saying Andersen couldn't consult and audit the same firms because it was a conflict of interest. Well, now I'm sure he's twirling in his grave saying, 'I told you so.'"[24] In the late 1990s, Arthur Levitt, the chairman of the SEC, had led a vigorous, one-man campaign to limit the scope of consulting services that accounting firms could provide to their audit clients. In particular, Levitt wanted to restrict the ability of accounting firms to provide IT and internal audit services to their audit clients. An extensive and costly lobbying campaign that the Big Five firms carried out in the press and among elected officials allowed those firms to defeat the bulk of Levitt's proposals.

Public reports that Andersen earned approximately $52 million in fees from Enron during 2000, only $25 million of which was directly linked to the 2000 audit, caused the scope of services issue to resurface. Critics charged that the enormous consulting fees accounting firms earned from their audit clients jeopardized those firms' independence. "It's obvious that Andersen helped Enron cook the books. Andersen's Houston office was pulling in $1 million a week from Enron—their objectivity went out the window."[25] These same critics reiterated an allegation that had widely circulated a few years earlier, namely, that the large accounting firms had resorted to using the independent audit function as "a loss leader, a way of getting in the door at a company to sell more profitable consulting contracts."[26] One former partner of a Big Five accounting firm provided anecdotal evidence corroborating that allegation. This individual revealed that he had been under constant pressure from his former firm to market various professional services to his audit clients. So relentless were his efforts that at one point a frustrated client executive asked him, "Are you my auditor or a salesperson?"[27]

A second source of criticism directed at Andersen stemmed from the firm's alleged central role in Enron's aggressive accounting and financial reporting treatments for its SPE-related transactions. The Powers Report released to the public in February 2002 spawned much of this criticism. That lengthy report examined in detail several of Enron's largest and most questionable SPE transactions. The Powers Report pointedly and repeatedly documented that Andersen personnel had been deeply involved in those transactions. Exhibit 3 contains a sample of selected excerpts from the Powers Report that refers to Andersen's role in "analyzing" and "reviewing" Enron's SPE transactions.

---

23. N. Byrnes, "Accounting in Crisis," *Business Week,* 28 January 2002, 46.

24. D. Barboza, "Where Pain of Arthur Andersen Is Personal," *The New York Times* (online), 13 March 2002.

25. *SmartPros.com*, "Lawsuit Seeks to Hold Andersen Accountable for Defrauding Enron Investors, Employees," 4 December 2001.

26. J. Kahn, "One Plus One Makes *What*?" *Fortune*, 7 January 2002, 89.

27. I. J. Dugan, "Before Enron, Greed Helped Sink the Respectability of Accounting," *The Wall Street Journal* (online), 14 March 2002.

Page 5: In virtually all of the [SPE] transactions Enron's accounting treatment was determined with the extensive participation and structuring advice from Andersen, which reported to the Board.

Page 17: Various disclosures [regarding Enron's SPE transactions] were approved by one or more of Enron's outside [Andersen] auditors and its inside and outside counsel. However, these disclosures were obtuse, did not communicate the essence of the transactions completely or clearly, and failed to convey the substance of what was going on between Enron and the partnerships.

Page 24: The evidence available to us suggests that Andersen did not fulfill its professional responsibilities in connection with its audits of Enron's financial statements, or its obligation to bring to the attention of Enron's Board (or the Audit and Compliance Committee) concerns about Enron's internal controls over the related-party [SPE] transactions.

Page 24: Andersen participated in the structuring and accounting treatment of the Raptor transactions, and charged over $1 million for its services, yet it apparently failed to provide the objective accounting judgment that should have prevented these transactions from going forward.

Page 25: According to recent public disclosures, Andersen also failed to bring to the attention of Enron's Audit and Compliance Committee serious reservations Andersen partners voiced internally about the related-party transactions.

Page 25: The Board appears to have reasonably relied upon the professional judgment of Andersen concerning Enron's financial statements and the adequacy of controls for the related-party transactions. Our review indicates that Andersen failed to meet its responsibilities in both respects.

Page 100: Accountants from Andersen were closely involved in structuring the Raptors [SPE transactions]. . . . Enron's records show that Andersen billed Enron approximately $335,000 in connection with its work on the creation of the Raptors in the first several months of 2000.

Page 107: Causey [Enron's chief accounting officer] informed the Finance Committee that Andersen "had spent considerable time analyzing the Talon structure and the governance structure of LJM2 and was comfortable with the proposed [SPE] transaction."

Page 126: At the time [September 2001], Enron accounting personnel and Andersen concluded (using qualitative analysis) that the error [in a prior SPE transaction] was not material and a restatement was not necessary.

Page 129: Proper financial accounting does not permit this result [questionable accounting treatment for certain of Enron's SPE transactions]. To reach it, the accountants at Enron and Andersen—including the local engagement team and, apparently, Andersen's national office experts in Chicago—had to surmount numerous obstacles presented by pertinent accounting rules.

Page 132: It is particularly surprising that the accountants at Andersen, who should have brought a measure of objectivity and perspective to these transactions, did not do so. Based on the recollections of those involved in the transactions and a large collection of documentary evidence, there is no question that Andersen accountants were in a position to understand all the critical features of the Raptors and offer advice on the appropriate accounting treatment. Andersen's total bill for Raptor-related work came to approximately $1.3 million. Indeed, there is abundant evidence that Andersen in fact offered Enron advice

EXHIBIT 3

SELECTED EXCERPTS FROM THE POWERS REPORT REGARDING ANDERSEN'S INVOLVEMENT IN KEY ACCOUNTING AND FINANCIAL REPORTING DECISIONS FOR ENRON'S SPE TRANSACTIONS

(continued)

EXHIBIT 3—
continued

SELECTED EXCERPTS
FROM THE POWERS
REPORT REGARDING
ANDERSEN'S
INVOLVEMENT IN
KEY ACCOUNTING
AND FINANCIAL
REPORTING
DECISIONS FOR
ENRON'S SPE
TRANSACTIONS

at every step, from inception through restructuring and ultimately to terminating the Raptors. Enron followed that advice.

Page 202: While we have not had the benefit of Andersen's position on a number of these issues, the evidence we have seen suggests Andersen accountants did not function as an effective check on the disclosure approach taken by the company. Andersen was copied on drafts of the financial statement footnotes and the proxy statements, and we were told that it routinely provided comments on the related-party transaction disclosures in response. We also understand that the Andersen auditors closest to Enron Global Finance were involved in drafting of at least some of the disclosures. An internal Andersen e-mail from February 2001 released in connection with recent Congressional hearings suggests that Andersen may have had concerns about the disclosures of the related-party transactions in the financial statement footnotes. Andersen did not express such concerns to the Board. On the contrary, Andersen's engagement partner told the Audit and Compliance Committee just a week after the internal e-mail that, with respect to related-party transactions, "'[r]equired disclosure [had been] reviewed for adequacy,' and that Andersen would issue an unqualified audit opinion on the financial statements."

Source: W. C. Powers, R. S. Troubh, and H. S. Winokur, "Report of Investigation by the Special Investigative Committee of the Board of Directors of Enron Corporation," 1 February 2002.

Among the parties most critical of Andersen's extensive involvement in Enron's accounting and financial reporting decisions for SPE transactions was former SEC Chief Accountant Lynn Turner. During his tenure with the SEC in the 1990s, Turner had participated in the federal agency's investigation of Andersen's audits of Waste Management Inc. That investigation culminated in sanctions against several Andersen auditors and in a $1.4 billion restatement of Waste Management's financial statements, the largest accounting restatement in U.S. history at that time. Andersen eventually paid a reported $75 million in settlements to resolve various civil lawsuits linked to those audits and a $7 million fine to settle charges filed against the firm by the SEC.

In an interview with *The New York Times*, Turner suggested that the charges of shoddy audit work that had plagued Andersen in connection with its audits of Waste Management, Sunbeam, Enron, and other high-profile public clients was well-deserved.

Turner compared Andersen's problems with those experienced several years earlier by Coopers & Lybrand, a firm for which he had been an audit partner. According to Turner, a series of "blown audits" was the source of Coopers' problems. "We got bludgeoned to death in the press. People did not even want to see us at their doorsteps. It was brutal, but we deserved it. We had gotten into this mentality in the firm of making business judgment calls."[28] Clearly, the role of independent auditors does not include "making business judgments" for their clients. Instead, auditors have a responsibility to provide an objective point of view regarding the proper accounting and financial reporting decisions for those judgments.

Easily the source of the most embarrassment for Berardino and his Andersen colleagues was the widely publicized effort of the firm's Houston office to shred a large quantity of documents pertaining to various Enron audits. In early January 2002, Andersen officials informed federal investigators that personnel in the Houston office had "destroyed a significant but undetermined number of documents relating

---

28. F. Norris, "From Sunbeam to Enron, Andersen's Reputation Suffers," *The New York Times* (online), 23 November 2001.

to the company [Enron] and its finances."[29] That large-scale effort began in September 2001 and apparently continued into November after the SEC revealed it was conducting a formal investigation of Enron's financial affairs. The report of the shredding effort immediately caused many critics to suggest that Andersen's Houston office was attempting to prevent law enforcement authorities from obtaining potentially incriminating evidence regarding Andersen's role in Enron's demise. Senator Joseph Lieberman, chairman of the U.S. Senate Governmental Affairs Committee that would be investigating the Enron debacle, warned that the effort to dispose of the Enron-related documents might be particularly problematic for Andersen.

> It [the document-shredding] came at a time when people inside, including the executives of Arthur Andersen and Enron, knew that Enron was in real trouble and that the roof was about to collapse on them, and there was about to be a corporate scandal. . . . [This] raises very serious questions about whether obstruction of justice occurred here. The folks at Arthur Andersen could be on the other end of an indictment before this is over. This Enron episode may end this company's history.[30]

The barrage of criticism directed at Andersen continued unabated during the early months of 2002. Ironically, some of that criticism was directed at Andersen by Enron's top management. On January 17, 2002, Kenneth Lay issued a press release reporting that his company had decided to discharge Andersen as its independent audit firm.[31]

> As announced on Oct. 31, the Enron Board of Directors convened a Special Committee to look into accounting and other issues relating to certain transactions. While we had been willing to give Andersen the benefit of the doubt until the completion of that investigation, we can't afford to wait any longer in light of recent events, including the reported destruction of documents by Andersen personnel and the disciplinary actions against several of Andersen's partners in its Houston office.[32]

Throughout the public relations nightmare that besieged Andersen following Enron's bankruptcy filing, a primary tactic employed by Joseph Berardino was to insist repeatedly that poor business decisions, not errors on the part of Andersen, were responsible for Enron's downfall and the massive losses that ensued for investors, creditors, and other parties. "At the end of the day, we do not cause companies to fail."[33] Such statements failed to generate sympathy for Andersen. Even the editor-in-chief of *Accounting Today*, one of the accounting profession's leading publications, was unmoved by Berardino's continual assertions that his firm was not responsible for the Enron fiasco. "If you accept the audit and collect the fee, then be prepared to accept the blame. Otherwise you're not part of the solution but rather part of the problem."[34]

---

29. K. Eichenwald and F. Norris, "Enron Auditor Admits It Destroyed Documents," *The New York Times* (online), 11 January 2002.

30. R. A. Oppel, "Andersen Says Lawyer Let Its Staff Destroy Files," *The New York Times* (online), 14 January 2002.

31. Kenneth Lay resigned as Enron's chairman of the board and CEO on January 23, 2002, one day after a court-appointed "creditors committee" had requested him to step down.

32. M. Palmer, "Enron Board Discharges Arthur Andersen in All Capacities," *Enron.com*, 17 January 2002.

33. M. Gordon, "Labor Secretary to Address Enron Hearings," *Associated Press* (online), 6 February 2002.

34. B. Carlino, "Enron Simply Newest Player in National Auditing Crisis," *The Electronic Accountant* (online), 17 December 2001.

Ridicule and Retrospection

As 2001 came to a close, *The New York Times* reported that the year had easily been the worst ever for Andersen, "the accounting firm that once deserved the title of the conscience of the industry."[35] The following year would prove to be an even darker time for the firm. During the early months of 2002, Andersen faced scathing criticism from Congressional investigators, enormous class-action lawsuits filed by angry Enron stockholders and creditors, and a federal criminal indictment stemming from the shredding of Enron-related documents.

In late March 2002, Joseph Berardino unexpectedly resigned as Andersen's CEO after failing to negotiate a merger of Andersen with one of the other Big Five firms. During the following few weeks, dozens of Andersen clients dropped the firm as their independent auditor out of concern that the firm might not survive if it was found guilty of the pending criminal indictment. The staggering loss of clients forced Andersen to lay off more than 25 percent of its workforce in mid-April. Shortly after that layoff was announced, U.S. Justice Department officials revealed that David Duncan, the former Enron audit engagement partner, had pleaded guilty to obstruction of justice and agreed to testify against his former firm. Duncan's plea proved to be the death knell for Andersen. In June 2002, a federal jury found the firm guilty of obstruction of justice. That conviction forced the firm to terminate its relationship with its remaining public clients, effectively ending Andersen's long and proud history within the U.S. accounting profession.

Three years later, the U.S. Supreme Court unanimously overturned the felony conviction handed down against Andersen. In an opinion written by Chief Justice William Rehnquist, the High court ruled that federal prosecutors did not prove that Andersen had *intended* to interfere with a federal investigation when the firm shredded the Enron audit workpapers. The Supreme Court's decision was little consolation to the more than 20,000 Andersen partners and employees who had lost their jobs when the accounting firm was forced out of business by the felony conviction.

Numerous Enron officials faced criminal indictments for their roles in the Enron fraud, among them Andrew Fastow, Jeffrey Skilling, and Kenneth Lay. Fastow pleaded guilty to conspiracy to commit securities fraud as well as to other charges. The former CFO received a 10-year prison term, which was reduced to six years after he testified against Skilling and Lay. Fastow was also required to forfeit nearly $25 million of personal assets that he had accumulated during his tenure at Enron. Largely as a result of Fastow's testimony against them, Skilling and Lay were convicted on multiple counts of fraud and conspiracy in May 2006. In September 2006, Skilling was sentenced to 24 years in prison. Kenneth Lay, who was to be sentenced at the same time, died of a massive heart attack in July 2006. Three months later, a federal judge overturned Lay's conviction since Lay was no longer able to pursue his appeal of that conviction.

The toll taken on the public accounting profession by the Enron debacle was not limited to Andersen, its partners, or its employees. An unending flood of jokes and ridicule directed at Andersen tainted and embarrassed practically every accountant in the nation, including both accountants in public practice and those working in the private sector. The Enron nightmare also prompted widespread soul-searching within the profession and a public outcry to strengthen the independent audit function and improve accounting and financial reporting practices. Legislative and regulatory authorities quickly responded to the public's demand for reforms.

The FASB imposed stricter accounting and financial reporting guidelines on SPEs as a direct result of the Enron case. Those new rules require most companies to include

---

35. Norris, "From Sunbeam to Enron."

the financial data for SPEs in their consolidated financial statements. In 2002, Congress passed the Sarbanes-Oxley Act to strengthen financial reporting for public companies, principally by improving the rigor and quality of independent audits. Among other requirements, the Sarbanes-Oxley Act limits the types of consulting services that independent auditors can provide to their clients and requires public companies to prepare annual reports on the quality of their internal controls. The most sweeping change in the profession resulting from the Enron fiasco was the creation of a new federal agency, the Public Company Accounting Oversight Board, to oversee the rule-making process for the independent audit function.

Among the prominent individuals who commented on the challenges and problems facing the accounting profession was former SEC Chairman Richard Breeden when he testified before Congress in early 2002. Chairman Breeden observed that there was a simple solution to the quagmire facing the profession. He called on accountants and auditors to adopt a simple rule of thumb when analyzing, recording, and reporting on business transactions, regardless of whether those transactions involved "New Economy" or "Old Economy" business ventures. "When you're all done, the result had better fairly reflect what you see in reality."[36]

In retrospect, Commissioner Breeden's recommendation seems to be a restatement of the "Think straight, talk straight" motto of Arthur E. Andersen. Andersen and his colleagues insisted that their audit clients adhere to a high standard of integrity when preparing their financial statements. An interview with Joseph Berardino by *The New York Times* in December 2001 suggests that Mr. Berardino and his contemporaries may have had a different attitude when it came to dealing with cantankerous clients such as Enron: "In an interview yesterday, Mr. Berardino said Andersen had no power to force a company to disclose that it had hidden risks and losses in special-purpose entities. 'A client says: 'There is no requirement to disclose this. You can't hold me to a higher standard.'"[37]

Berardino is certainly correct in his assertion. An audit firm cannot force a client to adhere to a higher standard. In fact, even Arthur Edward Andersen did not have that power. But Mr. Andersen did have the resolve to tell such clients to immediately begin searching for another audit firm.

Questions

1. The Enron debacle created what one public official reported was a "crisis of confidence" on the part of the public in the accounting profession. List the parties who you believe were most responsible for that crisis. Briefly justify each of your choices.

2. List three types of consulting services that audit firms are now prohibited from providing to clients that are public companies. For each item, indicate the specific threats, if any, that the provision of the given service could pose for an audit firm's independence.

3. For purposes of this question, assume that the excerpts from the Powers Report shown in Exhibit 3 provide accurate descriptions of Andersen's involvement in Enron's accounting and financial reporting decisions. Given this assumption, do you believe that Andersen's involvement in those decisions violated any professional auditing standards? If so, list those standards and briefly explain your rationale.

---

36. R. Schlank, "Former SEC Chairmen Urge Congress to Free FASB," *AccountingWeb* (online), 15 February 2002.

37. F. Norris, "The Distorted Numbers at Enron," *The New York Times* (online), 14 December 2001.

4. Briefly describe the key requirements included in professional auditing standards regarding the preparation and retention of audit workpapers. Which party "owns" audit workpapers: the client or the audit firm?

5. Identify five recommendations made to strengthen the independent audit function following the Enron scandal. For each of these recommendations, indicate why you support or do not support the given measure. Also indicate which of these recommendations were eventually implemented.

6. Do you believe that there has been a significant shift or evolution over the past several decades in the concept of "professionalism" as it relates to the public accounting discipline? If so, explain how you believe that concept has changed or evolved over that time frame, and identify the key factors responsible for any apparent changes.

7. As pointed out in this case, the SEC does not require public companies to have their quarterly financial statements audited. What responsibilities, if any, do audit firms have with regard to the quarterly financial statements of their clients? In your opinion, should quarterly financial statements be audited? Defend your answer.

Lehman Brothers Holdings, Inc.

Debt is a prolific mother of folly and crime.

Benjamin Disraeli

Thursday, October 24, 1929, easily ranks as the most dramatic day that Wall Street has ever seen.[1] That day witnessed the beginning of the Great Stock Market Crash that over the following few years would result in an almost ninety percent decline in the Dow Jones Industrial Average (DJIA). Although not nearly as dramatic as "Black Thursday," September 15, 2008, is a date that modern day Wall Street insiders will not soon forget. On that day, one of Wall Street's iconic investment banking firms, Lehman Brothers, filed for bankruptcy. That bankruptcy filing ended the proud history of a firm that had played a major role in shaping the nation's securities markets and economy for more than a century.

Lehman Brothers had approximately $700 billion in assets when it failed, which makes it the largest corporate bankruptcy in U.S. history, easily surpassing the previous headline-grabbing bankruptcies of Enron, General Motors, and WorldCom. By comparison, the telecommunications giant WorldCom, which temporarily held the title of the nation's largest business failure after collapsing in 2002, had less than one-sixth the total assets claimed by Lehman Brothers.

The shocking announcement that Lehman had filed for bankruptcy caused the DJIA to plunge more than 500 points within a few hours. That large loss was only a harbinger of things to come. Within six months, the DJIA had declined by more than 50 percent from its all-time high of 14,164.53 that it had reached on October 9, 2007. That market decline wiped out nearly ten *trillion* dollars of "paper" wealth for stock market investors and plunged the U.S. and world economies into what became known as the Great Recession.

In the spring of 2010, the Lehman bankruptcy once again captured the nation's attention when the company's court-appointed bankruptcy examiner released his 2200-page report. In preparing the highly anticipated report, the bankruptcy examiner and his staff reviewed 20 million documents and 10 million e-mails and spent $38 million. The massive report documented the circumstances and events that had contributed to Lehman's collapse and the parties that the bankruptcy examiner believed could be held civilly liable for it.

The release of the bankruptcy report prompted a public outcry because it revealed that Lehman's executives had routinely used multi-billion dollar "accounting-motivated" transactions to embellish their company's financial data. Allegedly, those transactions had been executed for the express purpose of enhancing a financial ratio that regulatory authorities, stock market analysts, and investors considered to be a key indicator of the company's overall financial condition.

As the company's financial health was rapidly deteriorating in 2007 and 2008, Lehman's executives had ramped up their use of the controversial transactions, resulting in the company's liabilities being understated by as much as $50 billion. Arguably most shocking was that Lehman never disclosed or referred to those transactions in the 10-K and 10-Q registration statements it filed periodically with the Securities and Exchange Commission (SEC).

---

1. I would like to thank Glen McLaughlin for his generous and continuing support of efforts to integrate ethics into business curricula. I would also like to thank T.J. Gillette for his excellent research that was instrumental in the development of this case.

Another revelation in the bankruptcy report that stunned the public was the fact that Lehman's audit firm had been aware of the billion-dollar transactions the company had used to window-dress its financial statements. According to the bankruptcy examiner, the Big Four audit firm had discussed those transactions on many occasions with company officials but had not insisted or, apparently, even suggested that the company disclose them in their financial statements or the accompanying notes.

The bankruptcy examiner also maintained that the audit firm had not properly informed Lehman's management and audit committee of an internal whistleblower's allegations that management was intentionally misrepresenting the company's financial statements. Because of alleged professional malpractice, Lehman's audit firm was among the parties the bankruptcy examiner suggested could be held civilly liable for the enormous losses suffered by the company's stockholders and creditors.

The Cotton Kings

Political unrest and poor economic conditions in their homeland prompted six million Germans to immigrate to the United States during the nineteenth century. Those immigrants included three brothers from Bavaria, the beautiful mountainous region of southeastern Germany. In 1844, 23-year-old Henry Lehman arrived in Montgomery, Alabama, a small city with fewer than 5,000 inhabitants in south central Alabama. Over the next few years, Henry's two brothers, Emanuel and Mayer, joined him in Montgomery.

The three brothers established a small retail store that stocked a wide range of merchandise including groceries, clothing, and hardware. Among the brothers' principal customers were cotton farmers from nearby rural areas who often paid for the merchandise they purchased with cotton bales. The brothers soon realized that there were more profits to be made in buying and selling cotton than operating a retail store, so they became cotton merchants.

By 1860, "King Cotton" ruled the South. The southern states accounted for three-fourths of the cotton produced worldwide. Cotton was also the nation's largest export, accounting for 60 percent of the U.S.'s total annual exports. In 1858, the huge demand for cotton in New England's booming textiles industry had convinced the Lehman brothers to establish an office in lower Manhattan, just a few blocks from the Wall Street financial district. But the outbreak of the Civil War in 1861 forced the Lehmans, who supported the Confederacy, to close that office.

The economic embargo imposed by President Lincoln on the South during the Civil War meant that cotton merchants such as the Lehman brothers lost their biggest market. Because the Lehmans realized that the demand for cotton would spike dramatically following the war, they bought large quantities of cotton produced during the war years and stored it in well-hidden warehouses scattered across the South. The post-war profits the brothers realized from selling that cotton helped them reestablish their firm as one of the South's largest cotton merchants following the war. By 1870, the Lehman brothers had reopened their New York City office; a short time later, they made that office the headquarters of their business.

In the latter decades of the nineteenth century, the Lehman brothers gradually expanded their business to include the trading of other commodities, such as coffee, sugar, wheat, and petroleum products. The three brothers also decided to purchase a seat on the New York Stock Exchange. They realized that there was a need for financial intermediaries to funnel private investment capital to the large companies that were fueling the nation's rapid economic growth. Because of the nature of their business, the three brothers were well acquainted with the banking and credit industries and believed they could use that experience to easily segue into the emerging and very lucrative investment banking industry.

By the early years of the twentieth century, the Lehman firm, which by then was being managed by the second generation of the Lehman family, had cut its ties to the cotton industry and focused its attention almost exclusively on investment banking. During that time frame, the firm served as the underwriter for several companies that would become stalwarts of the U.S. economy. These companies included B.F. Goodrich, Campbell Soup, F.W. Woolworth, R.H. Macy & Co., and Sears, Roebuck & Co.

Investment banks facilitate the flow of investment capital in a free market economy by effectively "pricing risk." That is, investment bankers help buyers and sellers determine the appropriate relationship between the risk posed by given securities and the price at which those securities should be initially sold. This pricing process helps ensure that scarce investment capital is allocated in an efficient manner to corporations, other business organizations, and governmental agencies that need external funds to finance their operations.

Investment banking firms face a wide range of business risks. For example, investment banks sometimes absorb large losses on new client securities that they acquire during the underwriting process and are unable to sell to third parties. The most important factor contributing to the risk profile of investment banks is the degree of financial leverage they utilize. Similar to commercial banks, investment banks rely heavily on debt capital rather than invested capital. This high degree of financial leverage typically results in significant profits accruing to the firms' stockholders in a strong economic environment when the investment banking industry prospers. On the other hand, during economic downturns, investment banks often incur large losses that wipe out much of their stockholders' equity.

Throughout its history, Lehman Brothers experienced the highs and lows of the volatile business cycle common to the investment banking industry. The intensity of that cycle was magnified by a new line of investment products that Lehman and its competitors made popular on Wall Street during the 1990s.

Playing with Fire

Lehman Brothers and the other large investment banks became major players in the financial derivatives markets that emerged in the final decade of the twentieth century. Investopedia (www.investopedia.com) defines a financial "derivative" as follows:

> A security whose price is dependent upon or derived from one or more underlying assets. The derivative itself is merely a contract between two or more parties. Its value is determined by fluctuations in the underlying asset. The most common underlying assets include stocks, bonds, commodities, currencies, interest rates and market indexes. Most derivatives are characterized by high leverage.

Many types of financial derivatives have existed for decades, including the most generic, namely, put and call options on common stocks. In the mid-1990s, however, a new genre of exotic financial derivatives became increasingly prevalent. These new derivatives included collateralized debt obligations, credit default swaps, and interest rate swaps, among many others. Institutional investors accounted for the bulk of the trading volume in these new securities because they were poorly understood and thus shunned by most individual investors.

The new breed of derivatives produced large and profitable revenue streams for the investment banking industry. On the downside, the risks posed by these new securities were often difficult to assess, which, in turn, made those risks difficult, if not impossible, to manage. Some economists and Wall Street experts suggested that the risks posed by many of these derivatives were, in fact, disproportionately high compared to the rates of return they generated. Further enhancing the risk profile of these investments was the fact that they were subject to only minimal regulatory oversight.

In a 2009 retrospective overview of the securities markets, President Obama observed that over the prior two decades those markets had been characterized by "wild risk-taking."[2] The president added that many of the new securities that became popular during that time frame were so complex and multifaceted that the "old regulatory schemes" developed for the securities markets in the 1930s did not provide adequate oversight for them.

Lehman flourished financially as the derivatives markets mushroomed in size and prominence during the 1990s and beyond. The firm was particularly active in the market for residential mortgage-backed securities (RMBS). By the turn of the century, government agencies, brokerage firms, and investment banks were producing a huge volume of RMBS each year. This "securitization" process involved purchasing residential mortgages from the banks, mortgage companies and other entities that originated them, bundling or "pooling" these mortgages together, and then selling ownership interests (securities) in these pools. The purchasers of RMBS were actually purchasing a claim on the cash flows generated by the mortgages that "backed" those securities. By 2004, Lehman produced more RMBS annually than any other entity.[3]

The high yields on RMBS created a surging demand for these new hybrid securities. In turn, the increasing demand for RMBS caused mortgage originators to become increasingly aggressive in extending loans to individuals who in years past had not been able to qualify for a home mortgage because of an insufficient income, a poor credit history, or other issues. These mostly first-time home buyers were referred to as "subprime" borrowers. Mortgage originators were not concerned by the sizable default risk posed by subprime borrowers since they intended to sell their loans "downstream" and thereby transfer that risk to the purchasers of RMBS.

The critical factor that influenced the riskiness of RMBS was the underlying health of the housing market in the United States. Steadily rising housing prices during the decade from 1995 through 2005 made the default risk on residential mortgages minimal. Wall Street analysts warned, however, that a downturn in housing prices would trigger a rise in mortgage defaults that would be problematic for parties having significant investments in RMBS. On the other hand, a sudden and sharp downturn in housing prices could prove to be catastrophic for those investors. Sadly, the latter doomsday scenario took place.

Housing prices peaked in the United States in 2006. By late 2007, housing prices had begun to tumble, declining in many residential markets by 20 percent or more by mid-2008. In some of the residential markets that had seen the sharpest increases over the previous several years, such as Las Vegas and south Florida, housing prices plunged by 50 percent.

---

2. S. Labaton, "Obama Sought a Range of Views on Finance Rules," *The New York Times* (online), 17 June 2009.

3. Lehman purchased a large portion of the residential mortgages that it securitized from New Century Financial Corporation, one of the nation's major subprime mortgage companies. Case 1.11 documents New Century's brief and turbulent history.

Falling housing prices caused a growing number of U.S. homeowners to be "upside down," meaning that the market values of their homes were lower than the unpaid balances of their mortgages. By early 2008, an estimated 9 million Americans had a negative equity in their homes, which caused a rapid rise in mortgage defaults and foreclosures. It was only a matter of time before the sharp decline in housing prices undercut the market for RMBS.

Government agencies, large institutional investors, and investment banks having an ownership interest in RMBS suddenly found the value of those securities spiraling downward when it became obvious that housing prices would continue their freefall. In some cases, the markets for mortgage-backed securities simply "froze," meaning that the securities could not be sold at any price. Lehman was among those entities that held a large inventory of mortgage-backed securities when the housing market crumbled. At the end of 2007, the company owned nearly $90 billion of those "toxic" assets. By comparison, Lehman's total stockholders' equity at the time was only $22.5 billion.

Prior to the collapse of the housing market, Lehman's high-risk business model had produced a string of record-breaking years. Exhibit 1 presents a financial highlights table for Lehman for the five-year period 2003 through 2007, which is a condensed version of a similar table included in the company's 2007 annual report. Notice that during that time period the company reported record revenues and net income each successive year. Lehman's string of impressive reported operating results continued in early 2008. When the company posted stronger than expected results for the first quarter of 2008, the price of its common stock soared by nearly 50 percent in one day.

Lehman's top executives profited enormously from the consistently strong reported financial performance of their company. Richard Fuld served as Lehman's chief executive officer (CEO) from 1994 through 2008. Over that time, Fuld earned nearly $500 million in compensation. In addition to monetary rewards, Lehman's executives were lavished with praise and accolades. Just as Lehman's financial empire was beginning to buckle in 2008, *Barron's* included Fuld in its list of the top 30 CEOs nationwide and tagged him with the title of "Mr. Wall Street."

	2007	2006	2005	2004	2003
Revenues	$ 19.3	$ 17.6	$ 14.6	$ 11.6	$ 8.7
Net Income	4.2	4.0	3.3	2.4	1.7
Total Assets	691.1	503.6	410.1	357.2	312.1
Total Stockholders' Equity	22.5	19.2	16.8	14.9	13.2
Earnings per Share	7.26	6.81	5.43	3.95	3.17
Dividends per Share	.60	.48	.40	.32	.24
Year-end Stock Price	62.63	73.67	63.00	41.89	36.11
Return on Equity	20.8%	23.4%	21.6%	17.9%	18.2%
Leverage Ratio	30.7	26.2	24.4	23.9	23.7
Net Leverage Ratio	16.1	14.5	13.6	13.9	15.3

*In billions of dollars except for per share amounts.

EXHIBIT 1

LEHMAN BROTHERS FINANCIAL HIGHLIGHTS, 2003–2007*

Despite the glowing operating results reported for fiscal 2007 and the first quarter of 2008, Lehman's management recognized that the company faced daunting challenges. "Lehman was publicly presenting a rosy outlook about its future while it was privately scrambling for a solution to its deepening problems."[4] Complicating matters for Lehman's management was the fact that financial analysts and other parties closely monitoring the investment banking industry had begun raising serious questions regarding the company's financial health. Those questions stemmed primarily from two issues facing Lehman, one of which was the mayhem taking place within the housing market. The second and more important issue facing the large investment banking firm was the fact that it was "wildly overleveraged."[5] This issue was critical because by this time there was a general consensus on Wall Street that an investment bank's degree of financial leverage was the most important metric to use in evaluating its financial health.

Lehman's financial highlights table in Exhibit 1 presents two measures of financial leverage. The company's conventional leverage ratio was computed by dividing total assets by total stockholders' equity. At fiscal year-end 2007, this ratio was 30.7 for Lehman, meaning that the company had only $1 of stockholders' equity for every $30.70 of assets that it held. In the company's 2007 annual report, Lehman's management suggested that the "net leverage ratio" was a much better measure of the company's financial leverage than the conventional leverage ratio. In computing the net leverage ratio, the company excluded from total assets a large volume of "low-risk" assets. Notice that Lehman's 2007 net leverage ratio was nearly fifty percent lower than its conventional leverage ratio.

The importance being ascribed to Lehman's leverage ratios, in particular, its net leverage ratio, by financial analysts in late 2007 prompted Dick Fuld to order a company-wide "deleveraging strategy." In an intercompany communication during this time frame, one of Fuld's subordinates noted that "reducing leverage is necessary to . . . win back the confidence of the market, lenders, and investors."[6] Another of Fuld's subordinates subsequently testified that beginning in late 2007 "Lehman set balance sheet targets with an eye to reaching [reducing] certain leverage ratios that rating agencies used to measure and gauge Lehman's performance."

Lehman's management chose an unconventional method to reduce the company's net leverage ratio. This improvised tactic involved engaging in a large volume of "accounting-motivated" transactions, known internally as Repo 105 transactions, near the end of each quarterly reporting period. Because the Repo 105 transactions were not disclosed in Lehman's SEC filings, third-party financial statement users were unaware that the company's net leverage ratio was being intentionally "sculpted" by management. "Lehman never disclosed that its net leverage ratio—which Lehman publicly touted as evidence of its discipline and financial health—depended upon the Repo 105 practice."

---

4. L. Story and B. White, "The Road to Lehman's Failure Was Littered With Lost Chances," *The New York Times* (online), 6 October 2008.

5. D. Leonard, "How Lehman Brothers Got Its Real Estate Fix," *The New York Times* (online), 3 May 2009.

6. This and all subsequent quotes, unless indicated otherwise, were taken from the following source: *In re*: *Lehman Brothers Holdings Inc., et al., Debtors*, "Report of Anton R. Valukas, Examiner," U.S. Bankruptcy Court for the Southern District of New York, Chapter 11 Case No. 08-13555, 11 March 2010.

Repo Central

In a repurchase or "repo" agreement, one party sells securities to another party while making a contractual commitment to repurchase those securities at a later date. The agreed-upon repurchase price for the given securities is nominally greater than the original selling price. In substance, the original "seller" of the securities is actually borrowing money from the original "purchaser" and using the securities transferred to the purchaser as collateral for the loan. The difference between the original selling price and the repurchase price is the interest earned on the loan by the original purchaser.

Another feature of repo transactions is what is known as the "haircut." The borrowing party (seller) transfers more than the face value of the securities involved in the transaction as collateral to the lender (purchaser). For example, if Lehman borrowed $100 million from another party under a conventional repo agreement, it would transfer more than $100 million of securities to the lender to serve as collateral for the loan. The haircut for Lehman's normal repos was typically two percent. So, in the example just provided, Lehman would have transferred $102 million of securities to the lender even though the actual amount of the loan was only $100 million.

Repos are a common financing tool used by large companies that need to raise a significant amount of funds for a short period of time. Repo lenders, on the other hand, view these transactions as a relatively safe way to invest excess cash at a modest rate of return without "tying up" those funds for an extended period of time. Similar to other investment banks, Lehman used repos as a major source of short-term financing.

For accounting purposes, repo agreements are nearly always treated as financing (borrowing) transactions by the borrower rather than as true sales of securities—Lehman recorded all of its normal repos as financing transactions. This accounting treatment is dictated by *Statement of Financial Accounting Standards (SFAS) No. 140*, "Accounting for Transfers and Servicing of Financial Assets and Extinguishment of Liabilities." When certain unusual conditions are met, however, *SFAS No. 140* provides for an exception to this general rule, meaning that repo borrowers can record the transactions as sales of securities.[7]

Lehman's executives realized that the *SFAS No. 140* exception could be used to their advantage, namely, to reduce their company's net leverage ratio. The lynchpin of this strategy was engaging in a large volume of "Repo 105s" that were repurchase agreements that the company recorded as sales rather than as financing transactions. The company's justification for treating a Repo 105 as a sale was the size of the "haircut" involved in the transaction. For Repo 105s, the amount of the haircut was 5 percent—which explained the label applied to them by the company. Lehman's accounting staff maintained that the larger haircut for the Repo 105s allowed them to be treated as sales under the exception included in *SFAS No. 140*.[8,9] Because this interpretation of *SFAS No. 140* was controversial, prior to engaging in any Repo 105s, company management decided to obtain a legal opinion confirming that the transactions could be considered "true sales" of securities.

---

7. *SFAS No. 140* has been revised in recent years, principally by *SFAS No. 166*, "Accounting for Transfers of Financial Assets."

8. Lehman Brothers' detailed justification for this accounting treatment is documented in several sources, including a lengthy explanation in the bankruptcy examiner's report. For a more concise discussion of Lehman Brothers' defense of this accounting treatment, see the following source: S.K. Dutta, D. Caplan, and R. Lawson, "Poor Risk Management," *Strategic Finance*, August 2010, 23–29. Essentially, Lehman maintained that the larger haircut involved in a Repo 105 was evidence that it had surrendered control over the securities transferred to the other party, a condition required for a repo to be treated as a sale under *SFAS No. 140*.

9. Recognize that the "haircut" is not equal to the amount of interest paid by the borrower to the lender in a repo transaction. Since repos tend to be for a short period of time, the amount of interest paid by the borrower is typically a fraction of 1 percent, although the annualized interest rate might be, for example, 8 percent.

Lehman's management could not find a law firm in the United States willing to issue a legal opinion that Repo 105s were true sales. Undeterred, the company's executives began searching for a foreign law firm that would issue such an opinion. The law firm that the company eventually retained for that purpose was Linklaters, a large British firm.

> *Unable to find a United States law firm that would provide it with an opinion letter permitting the true sale accounting treatment under United States law, Lehman conducted its Repo 105 program under the aegis of an opinion letter the Linklaters law firm in London wrote for LBIE, Lehman's European broker-dealer in London, under English law.*

Because the Repo 105s had to be consummated in Great Britain, Lehman transferred securities that would be involved in those transactions from a U.S. division of the firm to a British-based division, namely, Lehman Brothers International Europe (LBIE), its London-based brokerage. Although these transactions were consummated in Great Britain, they were ultimately included in Lehman's consolidated financial statements issued in the United States.

There were actually two "legs" to each Repo 105 transaction. The first leg involved the "sale" of the securities to a third party; in the second leg of these transactions, Lehman used the proceeds from the sale to pay off a portion of its outstanding liabilities. When taken together, the two legs of Repo 105 transactions allowed Lehman to reduce its net leverage ratio and thereby strengthen its apparent financial condition.

Recognize that the impact of the first leg of a Repo 105 on net assets was zero. When securities were sold in a Repo 105, the journal entry to record the transaction included a "debit" to a cash account that was offset by an equal "credit" to the appropriate investments account.[10] However, the second leg of the transaction, that is, the use of Repo 105 cash proceeds to pay down liabilities, resulted in Lehman's total assets being reduced, which, in turn, reduced Lehman's net leverage ratio. The accounting treatment applied to conventional repos, which were simply recorded as short-term loans, did not yield this "leverage-reduction" benefit.[11]

Lehman's bankruptcy examiner documented the fact that the volume of Lehman's Repo 105s spiked dramatically at the end of each quarterly reporting period. This opportunistic timing of the transactions allowed the company to significantly reduce its net leverage ratio just days or even hours before its accounting staff "closed" the accounting records to prepare the company's quarterly or annual financial statements. A few days later, Lehman would reverse or unwind the Repo 105s by re-acquiring the given securities with newly-borrowed funds. At the end of fiscal 2007, Lehman had $39 billion of "open" Repo 105 transactions; three months later, that figure had risen to $50 billion.

Lehman's use of Repo 105s to strengthen its reported financial condition in 2007 and 2008 was the major focus of the 2200-page report that was filed by the company's bankruptcy examiner with a federal court. Particularly appalling to the bankruptcy examiner was the efforts of Lehman's management to draw attention to the company's declining leverage while concealing the fact that Repo 105s were responsible for much of that improvement. In "earnings calls" with financial

---

10. This is a brief and simplified summary of the accounting treatment applied to Repo 105s by Lehman. Examples of hypothetical accounting entries used by Lehman to record its Repo 105 transactions are presented in the following article: S.K. Dutta, D. Caplan, and R. Lawson, "Poor Risk Management," *Strategic Finance*, August 2010, 23–29.

11. The conventional strategy for reducing the net leverage ratio would have been to simply sell assets and then use the proceeds to pay down liabilities. Lehman could not avail itself of that strategy since the markets for the assets (investments) that it had available for sale were highly illiquid. To sell those assets, Lehman would have been forced to absorb large losses, losses that would have reduced its stockholders' equity and thus largely negated the intended reduction of its net leverage ratio.

analysts tracking Lehman's stock, for example, the company's chief financial officer (CFO) stressed the fact that the company's financial leverage was being reduced; however, she "said nothing about the firm's use of Repo 105 transactions." At the same time, the CFO told those analysts that her company was committed to providing them "a great amount of transparency" regarding the company's balance sheet.

The bankruptcy examiner maintained that even if the accounting treatment applied to the Repo 105s technically complied with *SFAS No. 140*, that accounting treatment violated Generally Accepted Accounting Principles (GAAP) by causing Lehman's financial statements to be misleading. To support his position, the bankruptcy examiner referred to a ruling handed down by a federal district court in a case involving an accounting matter. "GAAP itself recognizes that technical compliance with particular GAAP rules may lead to misleading financial statements, and imposes an overall requirement that the statements taken as a whole accurately reflect the financial status of the company."

According to the bankruptcy examiner, there had been no underlying business purpose for the Repo 105s. Instead, the sole purpose of the transactions had been to make Lehman's "balance sheet appear stronger than it actually was." In sum, the transactions had been "accounting-motivated." The bankruptcy examiner referred to a prior SEC release to define that term.

> *"Accounting-motivated structured transactions"* are *"transactions that are structured in an attempt to achieve reporting results that are not consistent with the economics of the transaction, and thereby impair the transparency of financial reports."* [Attempts] *to portray the transactions differently from their substance do not operate in the interests of investors, and may be in violation of the securities laws.*

The bankruptcy examiner uncovered numerous instances of intercompany communications that suggested the Repo 105s had been accounting-driven. In responding to an inquiry regarding why Lehman was engaging in a large volume of Repo 105s at the end of each quarter, one company executive had told another, "It's basically window-dressing. We are calling repos true sales based on legal technicalities." Another company executive testified that "It was universally accepted throughout the entire institution [company] that Repo 105 was used for balance sheet relief at quarter end." A lower-level Lehman employee had referred to Repo 105s as an "accounting gimmick" and a "lazy way of managing the balance sheet." Finally, a high-ranking accounting officer admitted to the bankruptcy examiner that "there was no substance to these transactions" and that their only "purpose or motive was reduction [of assets] in the balance sheet."

Further validating the bankruptcy examiner's argument that the Repo 105s had been purely accounting-driven was the fact that they had been more expensive than Lehman's normal repo transactions. That is, the company could have secured the short-term financing provided by the several hundred billions of dollars of its Repo 105s at a lower cost by using conventional repo agreements. "Lehman could have obtained the same financing at a lower cost by engaging in ordinary repo transactions with substantially the same counterparties using the same assets involved in the Repo 105 transactions."

When considering the issue of whether the accounting treatment applied to the Repo 105s made Lehman's financial statements *materially* misleading, the bankruptcy examiner effectively invoked the definition of that construct found in *Statement of Financial Accounting Concepts No. 2*, "Qualitative Characteristics of Accounting Information."

The magnitude of an omission or misstatement of accounting information that, in light of the surrounding circumstances, makes it probable that the judgment of a reasonable person relying on the information would have been changed or influenced by the omission or misstatement.

The bankruptcy examiner surveyed a wide range of "reasonable" parties that had relied on Lehman's financial statements. Nearly all of these parties insisted that they would have wanted to know that the company was using the Repo 105 transactions to distort its balance sheet and key financial ratios. "Lehman's directors, the rating agencies, and government regulators—all of whom were unaware of Lehman's use of Repo 105 transactions—have advised the examiner that Lehman's Repo 105 usage was material or significant information that they would have wanted to know." In fact, in 2008, the controller of Lehman's European operations had e-mailed a Lehman colleague in the United States and warned him that the Repo 105s "are understating what we have at risk by a material amount especially around quarter ends." The bankruptcy examiner relied on such statements in arriving at his decision that a "trier of fact," that is, a court, would likely find that the Repo 105s had resulted in Lehman's financial statements being materially misleading.

To bolster this conclusion, the bankruptcy examiner referred to a discussion of materiality included in the 2007 workpapers of Lehman's independent audit firm, Ernst & Young. "Indeed, audit walk-through papers prepared by Lehman's outside auditor, Ernst & Young, regarding the process for reopening or adjusting a closed balance sheet stated: 'Materially is usually defined as any item individually, or in the aggregate, that moves net leverage by 0.1 or more (typically $1.8 billion). Repo 105 moved net leverage not by tenths, but by whole points." As shown in Exhibit 1, Lehman's reported net leverage ratio as of the end of fiscal 2007 was 16.1. According to the bankruptcy examiner, the actual ratio would have been 17.8 if the company had accounted for the Repo 105s as financing transactions.

During his investigation, the bankruptcy examiner spent considerable time reviewing the Ernst & Young (E&Y) audit workpapers. The prominent accounting firm ultimately became a major focus of that investigation and the target of scathing criticism by the bankruptcy examiner.

Auditors on the Firing Line

E&Y served as Lehman's independent audit firm from 1994 through 2008. For the 2007 audit, the final audit of the company prior to its collapse, Lehman paid E&Y approximately $29.5 million. That figure included the fee for the 2007 audit, fees for tax services provided to the company, and miscellaneous fees. William Schlich served as the engagement audit partner for the 2007 audit of Lehman. In July 2008, Schlich, a longtime E&Y partner, was named the head of E&Y's "Global Banking & Capital Markets" practice, the firm's largest individual industry practice.

Lehman's bankruptcy examiner interviewed Schlich extensively during his investigation. Schlich told the bankruptcy examiner that E&Y had been aware of the Repo 105 transactions and was also aware that Lehman had not disclosed the transactions in financial statements filed with the SEC. Schlich also revealed that Lehman officials had consulted with E&Y while they were developing the company's Repo 105 accounting policy, although he reported that his firm had not been directly involved in that process and had not formally approved the accounting policy.

Martin Kelly, Lehman's former Financial Controller, testified that he discussed the Repo 105 transactions with Schlich in late 2007. Kelly told the bankruptcy examiner that he had a certain degree of "discomfort" with the Repo 105s, ostensibly because

Lehman had been unable to obtain a legal opinion from a U.S. law firm that supported the company's decision to record those transactions as sales of securities. Kelly recalled that he had discussed Lehman's inability to obtain such a legal opinion with the E&Y auditors.

Surprisingly, Schlich told the examiner that he did not know whether anyone on the E&Y engagement team had actually reviewed the legal opinion on the Repo 105 transactions issued by Linklaters, the British law firm. Schlich suggested that the responsibility for reviewing that letter would have rested with his firm's British affiliate, E&Y United Kingdom, which had audited the accounting records of LBIE, the British arm of Lehman Brothers that had executed the Repo 105 transactions.

Throughout his investigation and in his report, the bankruptcy examiner repeatedly characterized the Repo 105s as "accounting-motivated" transactions without an underlying business purpose that had been intended to embellish Lehman's financial statements and its net leverage ratio. While being interviewed by the examiner, however, Schlich staunchly defended the accounting treatment that had been applied to those transactions. The E&Y partner insisted that the "off-balance sheet treatment" of the Repo 105s was purely a "consequence of the accounting rules" rather than the underlying "motive for the transactions." When the examiner asked Schlich whether "technical adherence" to *SFAS No. 140* or any other specific accounting rule could have resulted in Lehman's financial statements being misstated, "Schlich refrained from comment." On two occasions, the examiner "offered Ernst & Young the opportunity" to explain or identify the "business purpose of Lehman's Repo 105 transactions." On each occasion, the E&Y representative (apparently Schlich) "declined that invitation."

The bankruptcy examiner subsequently criticized E&Y for not addressing the possibility that Lehman's "Repo 105 transactions were accounting-motivated transactions that lacked a business purpose." According to the examiner, E&Y should have recognized, or at least considered the possibility, that the Repo 105s were simply intended to improve Lehman's apparent financial condition, in particular, its net leverage ratio. The examiner stated that there was "no question that Ernst & Young had a full understanding of the net leverage ratio" and that the auditors understood the importance of that ratio to third-party financial statement users.

The bankruptcy examiner focused considerable attention on the materiality of the Repo 105 transactions while he was interviewing Schlich. At one point, the examiner asked Schlich what volume of Repo 105 transactions would have been considered "material" by E&Y. "Schlich replied that Ernst & Young did not have a hard and fast rule defining materiality in the balance sheet context, and that, with respect to balance sheet issues, 'materiality' depends upon the facts and circumstances." In his report, the bankruptcy examiner juxtaposed this statement of Schlich with the fact that E&Y's 2007 Lehman workpapers had identified the following precise materiality threshold for the company's net leverage ratio: "Materiality is usually defined as any item individually, or in the aggregate, that moves net leverage by 0.1 or more (typically $1.8 billion)."

When questioned further regarding the materiality of the Repo 105s, Schlich told the bankruptcy examiner that E&Y's audit plan had not required the Lehman engagement team to "review the volume or timing of Repo 105 transactions." Consequently, "as part of its year-end 2007 audit, E&Y did not ask Lehman about any directional trends, such as whether its Repo 105 activity was increasing during fiscal year 2007." The bankruptcy examiner reported that Schlich was unable to "confirm or deny that Lehman's use of Repo 105 transactions was increasing in late 2007 and into mid-2008."

A final major issue raised with William Schlich by the bankruptcy examiner was E&Y's response to the whistleblower letter sent to company management in May 2008 by a senior member of Lehman's accounting staff. Lehman's management had asked E&Y to be involved in investigating the allegations in that letter.[12] Among other allegations, the whistleblower suggested that Lehman's assets and liabilities were routinely misstated by "tens of billions of dollars" in the company's periodic balance sheets. To remind his superiors of their responsibilities related to financial reporting, the whistleblower had included in his letter the following excerpt from Lehman's Code of Ethics.[13]

> All employees . . . must endeavor to ensure that information in documents that Lehman Brothers files with or submits to the SEC, or otherwise discloses to the public, is presented in a full, fair, accurate, timely and understandable manner. Additionally, each individual involved in the preparation of the Firm's financial statements must prepare those statements in accordance with Generally Accepted Accounting Principles, consistently applied, and any other applicable accounting standards and rules so that the financial statements present fairly, in all material respects, the financial position, results of operations and cash flows of the Firm.

Approximately four weeks passed before E&Y interviewed the author of the whistleblower letter. Schlich and Hillary Hansen, another E&Y partner, conducted that interview. Hansen's handwritten notes compiled during the interview indicated that the whistleblower alleged that Lehman had used tens of billions of dollars of Repo 105 transactions to strengthen its quarter-ending balance sheets. According to the examiner, E&Y never interviewed the whistleblower a second time and never "followed up" on his allegation regarding Lehman's improper use of Repo 105s.

The day after interviewing the whistleblower, E&Y auditors met with Lehman's audit committee but, according to the bankruptcy examiner, did not inform the committee members of the whistleblower's Repo 105 allegation. Three weeks later, E&Y auditors met once more with Lehman's audit committee and again reportedly failed to mention that allegation. The bankruptcy examiner subsequently reviewed E&Y's work papers for the 2007 audit and the 2008 quarterly reviews and "found no reference to any communication with the audit committee about Repo 105."

During his interview with the bankruptcy examiner, Schlich indicated that he did not recall the whistleblower mentioning the Repo 105 transactions when he and Hansen met with him. When informed that Hansen's handwritten notes of that meeting indicated that the whistleblower had referred to those transactions, Schlich "did not dispute the authenticity" of those notes.

In summarizing his investigation of E&Y's role as Lehman's auditor, the bankruptcy examiner reported that there was "sufficient evidence to support at least three colorable claims that could be asserted against Ernst & Young relating to Lehman's Repo 105 activities and reporting."[14] The first colorable claim involved E&Y's alleged failure to "conduct an adequate inquiry" into the whistleblower's allegations and failing "to properly inform management and the audit committee" of those allegations. Second, the bankruptcy examiner charged that E&Y had failed to "take proper action" to investigate whether Lehman's financial statements for the first two quarters of 2008 were materially misleading due to the company's failure to disclose its Repo 105 transactions. The final colorable claim involved

---

12. After reading the whistleblower letter, Schlich confided to two colleagues in an e-mail that the letter was "pretty ugly" and that it "will take us a significant amount of time to get through."

13. The whistleblower was dismissed approximately one month after sending his letter to Lehman's top management. He was reportedly dismissed as a result of a corporate-wide "downsizing" campaign.

14. "Colorable claim" is a legal term. A colorable claim is generally a "plausible legal claim," that is, a claim "strong enough to have a reasonable chance of being valid if the legal basis is generally correct and the facts can be proven in court" (http://topics.law.cornell.edu).

E&Y's alleged failure to "take proper action" to investigate whether Lehman's financial statements for fiscal 2007 were materially misleading due to the Repo 105s.[15]

The allegations that the bankruptcy examiner filed against E&Y spawned widespread discussion and debate within the accounting profession. One accounting professor defended the accounting treatment that Lehman applied to its Repo 105s and, by implication, E&Y's tacit approval of that treatment. In responding to the question of whether Lehman was entitled to account for those transactions as sales of securities, the professor responded, "Absolutely. Even if intended to influence (or deceitfully change) the numbers reported? Yes, intent doesn't matter. It [Lehman] found a rule it could utilize to its advantage and followed it."[16] The professor went on to explain that the given "rule" was a bad one that should be amended.

Three other accounting professors expressed a very different point of view. These professors noted that "a fundamental financial reporting objective that overrides the application of any specific rule is that the accounting of a transaction should not obfuscate its economic substance."[17] The professors then noted that "parties with meaningful roles in the financial reporting process" shouldn't be involved in applying "accounting rules with the intent to obfuscate the economic substance"[18] of given transactions. Finally, the professors made the following observation regarding the professional responsibilities of the accountants and auditors involved in the Lehman debacle.

> *External auditors, internal auditors, and management accountants all have professional standards that are aspirational in nature, and, regardless of whether Lehman's auditors and accountants met the minimum standards that might shield them from legal liability and formal professional sanction, it seems clear that they fell short of the higher standards to which all management accountants and auditors should aspire.*[19]

EPILOGUE

The revelations and allegations included in the report issued by Lehman's bankruptcy examiner evoked an immediate response from the SEC. In March 2010, an SEC spokesperson reported that the federal agency had been unaware that Wall Street firms were using Repo 105-type transactions to enhance their apparent financial condition. The SEC revealed that it was contacting twenty major financial institutions to determine if they had used similar tactics to "manage" their balance sheets. To date, the SEC has not commented on the results of that survey or identified the specific firms that were contacted.

Lehman's bankruptcy report served as an "open invitation"[20] to file civil lawsuits against E&Y. And that is exactly what happened. Throughout 2010, numerous lawsuits that named E&Y as a defendant or co-defendant were filed on behalf of parties that suffered losses due to Lehman's collapse. Among these lawsuits, the one with arguably the highest profile was a civil fraud lawsuit filed against E&Y in late December 2010 by Andrew Cuomo, New York's

---

15. The bankruptcy examiner noted that E&Y "may have valid defenses" to the colorable claims that he asserted against the firm. The examiner discussed some of these defenses including the fact that many auditing standards do not impose "bright line rules" but instead provide only "general guidance" to auditors.

16. D. Albrecht, "Repo 105 Explained with Numbers and Detail," 24 April 2010, http://profalbrecht.wordpress.com/2010/04/24.

17. S.K. Dutta, D. Caplan, and R. Lawson, "Poor Risk Management," *Strategic Finance*, August 2010, 29.

18. *Ibid.*

19. *Ibid.*

20. Texas Society of Certified Public Accountants, "Accounting Web—April 2, 2010," http://www.tscpa.org.

Attorney General and Governor-elect. In commenting on the lawsuit, Cuomo noted that Lehman had been a "house-of-cards" and that E&Y had "helped hide" this fact "from the investing public."[21]

Shortly after the release of the Lehman bankruptcy report, E&Y issued the following statement defending its unqualified opinion on Lehman's 2007 financial statements: "Our opinion stated that Lehman's financial statements for 2007 were fairly presented in accordance with U.S. GAAP, and we remain of that view."[22] E&Y's statement went on to observe that "Lehman's bankruptcy was the result of a series of unprecedented adverse events in the financial markets . . . It was not caused by accounting issues or disclosures issues."[23]

E&Y's responses to Lehman-related lawsuits have typically included rebuttals of allegations initially made by the company's bankruptcy examiner. For example, E&Y has repeatedly insisted that the accounting treatment applied by Lehman to its Repo 105 transactions was GAAP-compliant. In a legal document filed with a federal court, E&Y's defense counsel maintained that Lehman's Repo 105s were properly recorded as true sales of securities under *SFAS No. 140.*[24] Likewise, E&Y has maintained that at the time Lehman was not required to disclose the Repo 105 transactions in its financial statements. E&Y's attorneys have pointed out that *SFAS No. 166*, "Accounting for Transfers of Financial Assets," which was issued in June 2009, now mandates such disclosure, which, from the attorneys' perspective, reinforces their argument that such disclosure was *not* required in 2007.[25]

Considerable attention was focused by the bankruptcy examiner on the impact that Lehman's Repo 105 transactions had on the company's reported net leverage ratio. E&Y, however, has pointed out that the ratio was not included in the company's audited financial statements and thus was not a "GAAP financial measure" subject to being audited.[26] E&Y has also strongly contested the assertion that the Lehman auditors failed to properly inform the company's audit committee of the allegations included in the infamous whistleblower letter received by Lehman's management in May 2008.

The media has inaccurately reported that E&Y concealed a May 2008 whistleblower letter from Lehman's Audit Committee. The whistleblower letter, which raised significant potential concerns about Lehman's financial controls and reporting but did not mention Repo 105, was directed to Lehman's management. When we learned of the letter, our lead partner promptly called the Audit Committee Chair; we also insisted that Lehman's management inform the Securities & Exchange Commission and the Federal Reserve Bank of the letter. E&Y's lead partner discussed the whistleblower letter with the Lehman Audit Committee on at least three occasions during June and July 2008.[27,28]

---

21. P. Lattman, "Cuomo Sues Ernst & Young Over Lehman," *The New York Times* (online), 21 December 2010.

22. M. Cohn, "Ernst & Young Defends Lehman Audits," *WebCPA*, 25 March 2010. (http://www.accounting today.com)

23. *Ibid.*

24. *In Re Lehman Brothers Equity/Debt Securities Litigation*, No. 08 Civ. 5523 (LAK), "Civil Action No. 09 MD 2017 (LAK), U.S. District Court for the Southern District of New York. E&Y's legal counsel contended that Lehman had relinquished "effective control" of the securities involved in the Repo 105 transactions and, as a result, was permitted to record those transactions as sales of securities under *SFAS No. 140*. Not surprisingly, the plaintiff attorneys disagreed with that interpretation of *SFAS No. 140*.

25. *Ibid.*

26. Texas Society of Certified Public Accountants, "Accounting Web—April 2, 2010." Recall that Lehman's net leverage ratio was included in a financial highlights table in its 2007 annual report. That ratio was also referred to in the Management's Discussion & Analysis (MD&A) section of that report.

27. Texas Society of Certified Public Accountants, "Accounting Web—April 2, 2010."

28. Notice that E&Y asserts that it discussed the whistleblower letter with Lehman's audit committee. The bankruptcy examiner, however, alleges that E&Y did not bring the Repo 105s to the attention of the audit committee members. E&Y is correct that the Repo 105s were not specifically identified in the whistleblower letter, although they were apparently alluded to in the letter and were referred to by the whistleblower during his subsequent interview with Schlich and Hansen.

Over the years to come, the gaggle of Lehman-related lawsuits that have been filed will work their way through the courts. No doubt, over that time frame a clearer picture will emerge regarding the veracity of the claims and counterclaims in those lawsuits as well as the veracity of the allegations made by Lehman's bankruptcy examiner.

Similar to the Enron and WorldCom fiascoes in the past, the Lehman debacle has prompted widespread calls for accounting, auditing, and financial reporting reforms. In particular, many parties critical of Lehman's accountants and auditors have urged rule-making bodies to clarify the accounting and financial reporting rules for complex transactions, such as Repo 105-type transactions. In fact, the Financial Accounting Standards Board attempted to do just that by issuing multiple amendments to *SFAS No. 140* in the aftermath of Lehman's collapse.

The authors of an article in a practice-oriented accounting periodical, however, suggest that promulgating new, more precise accounting rules is unlikely to prevent Lehman-type accounting scandals in the future. In their view, the most effective way to prevent the recurrence of such scandals is to develop a more robust "ethical culture" within the accounting profession, a culture that encourages accountants and auditors to embrace the profession's core values such as integrity, objectivity, and commitment to public service.

Ethical behavior is not about abiding by the law. Individuals and organizations can act legally and still be acting unethically. Ethical behavior is driven by compliance with a set of values that act as the touchstone for situational decisions where rules may not exist to cover every alternative.[29]

Questions

1. When Lehman was developing its Repo 105 accounting policy, did E&Y have a responsibility to be involved in that process? In general, what role should an audit firm have when a client develops an important new accounting policy? Comment on an audit firm's responsibilities during and following that process.

2. Do you agree with the assertion that "intent doesn't matter" when applying accounting rules? That is, should reporting entities be allowed to apply accounting rules or approved exceptions to accounting rules for the express purpose of intentionally embellishing their financial statements or related financial data? Defend your answer.

3. Do auditors have a responsibility to determine whether important transactions of a client are "accounting-motivated"? Defend your answer.

4. William Schlich implied that E&Y's British affiliate had the responsibility for reviewing the legal opinion issued by a British law firm regarding the treatment of Repo 105s as sales of securities. Do you believe that Schlich or one of his subordinates should have reviewed that letter? Why or why not? In general, how should the responsibility for different facets of a multinational audit be allocated between or among the individual practice offices involved in the engagement?

5. Lehman's net leverage ratio was not reported within the company's audited financial statements but rather in the company's financial highlights table and MD&A section of its annual report. What responsibility, if any, do auditors have to assess the material accuracy of financial data included in those two sections of a client's annual report?

---

29. Dutta *et al.*, "Poor Risk Management."

6. The Repo 105 transactions reduced Lehman's net leverage ratio from 17.8 to 16.1 at the end of fiscal 2007. Do you believe that was a "material difference"? Why or why not?

7. In general, what responsibility do auditors have to investigate whistleblower allegations that relate to the material accuracy of an audit client's financial statements?

8. E&Y is a defendant in Lehman-related lawsuits filed in both state and federal courts. Identify the factors that influence E&Y's legal exposure between lawsuits filed in state courts versus those filed in federal courts.

Just For FEET, Inc.

Life is so fragile. A single bad choice in a single moment can cause a life to turn irrevocably 180 degrees.

U.S. District Judge C. Lynwood Smith, Jr.

In 1971, 25-year-old Thomas Shine founded a small sporting goods company, Logo 7, that would eventually become known as Logo Athletic. Shine's company manufactured and marketed a wide range of shirts, hats, jackets, and other apparel items that boldly displayed the logos of the Denver Broncos, Detroit Red Wings, San Diego Padres, and dozens of other professional sports teams. In 2001, Shine sold Logo to Reebok and became that company's senior vice president of sports and entertainment marketing. In that position, Shine wined and dined major sports stars with the intent of persuading them to sign exclusive endorsement contracts with Reebok.

During his long career, Thomas Shine became one of the most well-known and respected leaders of the sporting goods industry. Shine's prominence and credibility in that industry took a severe blow in February 2004 when he pleaded guilty to a criminal indictment filed against him by the U.S. Department of Justice. The Justice Department charged that Shine had signed a false audit confirmation sent to him in early 1999 by one of Logo's largest customers. The confirmation indicated that Logo owed that customer approximately $700,000. Although Shine knew that no such debt existed, he signed the confirmation and returned it to the customer's independent audit firm, Deloitte & Touche, after being pressured to do so by an executive of the customer. As a result of his guilty plea, Shine faced a possible sentence of five years in federal prison and a fine of up to $250,000.

Out of South Africa

At approximately the same time that Thomas Shine was launching his business career in the retail industry in the United States, Harold Ruttenberg was doing the same in South Africa. Ruttenberg, a native of Johannesburg, paid for his college education by working nights and weekends as a sales clerk in an upscale men's clothing store. After graduation, he began importing Levi's jeans from the United States and selling them from his car, his eventual goal being to accumulate sufficient capital to open a retail store. Ruttenberg quickly accomplished that goal. In fact, by the time he was 30, he owned a small chain of men's apparel stores.

Mounting political and economic troubles in his home country during the early and mid-1970s eventually convinced Ruttenberg to move his family to the United States. South Africa's strict emigration laws forced Ruttenberg to leave practically all of his net worth behind. When he arrived in California in 1976 with his spouse and three small children, Ruttenberg had less than $30,000. Despite his limited financial resources and unfamiliarity with U.S. business practices, the strong-willed South African was committed to once again establishing himself as a successful entrepreneur in the retailing industry.

Ruttenberg soon realized that the exorbitant rents for commercial retail properties in the major metropolitan areas of California were far beyond his reach. So, he moved his family once more, this time to the more affordable business environment of Birmingham, Alabama. Ruttenberg leased a vacant storefront in a Birmingham mall and a few months later opened Hang Ten Sports World, a retail store that marketed children's sportswear products. Thanks largely to his work ethic and intense desire to succeed, Ruttenberg's business prospered over the next decade.

In 1988, Ruttenberg decided to take a gamble on a new business venture. Ruttenberg had come to believe that there was an opportunity to make large profits in the retail shoe business. At the time, the market for high-priced athletic shoes—basketball shoes, in particular—was growing dramatically and becoming an ever-larger segment of the retail shoe industry. The principal retail outlets for the shoes produced by Adidas, Nike, Reebok, and other major athletic shoe manufacturers were relatively small stores located in thousands of suburban malls scattered across the country, meaning that the retail athletic shoe "subindustry" was highly fragmented. The five largest retailers in this market niche accounted for less than 10 percent of the annual sales of athletic shoes.

Ruttenberg realized that the relatively small floor space of retail shoe stores in suburban malls limited a retailer's ability to display the wide and growing array of products being produced by the major shoe manufacturers. Likewise, the high cost of floor space in malls with heavy traffic served to limit the profitability of shoe retailers. To overcome these problems, Ruttenberg decided that he would build freestanding "Just for FEET" superstores located near malls. To lure consumers away from mall-based shoe stores, Ruttenberg developed a three-pronged business strategy focusing on "selection," "service," and "entertainment."

The business plan that Ruttenberg developed for his superstores involved a stores-within-a-store concept; that is, he intended to create several mini-stores within his large retail outlets, each of which would be devoted exclusively to the products of individual shoe manufacturers. He believed this store design would appeal to both consumers and vendors. Consumers who were committed to one particular brand would not have to search through store displays that included a wide assortment of branded products. Likewise, his proposed floor design would provide major vendors an opportunity to participate in marketing their products. Ruttenberg hoped that his planned floor design would spur the major vendors to compete with each other in providing so-called vendor allowances to his superstores to make their individual displays more attractive than those of competitors.

Customer service was the second major element of Ruttenberg's business plan for his shoe superstores. Ruttenberg planned to staff his stores so that there would be an unusually large ratio of sales associates to customers. Sales associates would be required to complete an extensive training course in "footwear technology" so that they would be well equipped to answer any questions posed by customers. When a customer chose to try on a particular shoe product, he or she would have to ask a sales associate to retrieve that item from the "back shop." Sales associates were trained to interact with customers in such a way that they would earn their trust and thus create a stronger bond with them.

Just for Feet's 1998 Form 10-K described the third feature of Harold Ruttenberg's business plan as creating an "Entertainment Shopping Experience." Rock and roll music and brightly colored displays greeted customers when they entered the superstores. When they tired of shopping, customers could play a game of "horse" on an enclosed basketball half-court located near the store's entrance or sit back and enjoy a multiscreen video bank in the store's customer lounge. Frequent promotional events included autograph sessions with major sports celebrities such as Bart Starr, the former Green Bay Packers quarterback who was also on the company's board of directors.

Ruttenberg would eventually include two other key features in the floor plans of his superstores. Although Just for Feet did not target price-conscious customers, Ruttenberg added a "Combat Zone" to each superstore where such customers could rummage through piles of discontinued shoe lines, "seconds," and other discounted items. For those customers who simply wanted a pair of shoes and did not have a strong preference for a given brand, Ruttenberg developed a "Great Wall" that contained a wide array of shoes sorted not by brand but rather by function. In this large display, customers could quickly compare and contrast the key features of dozens of different types of running shoes, walking shoes, basketball shoes, and cross-trainers.

Quite a FEET

Just for Feet's initial superstore in Birmingham proved to be a huge financial success. That success convinced Harold Ruttenberg to open similar retail outlets in several major metropolitan areas in the southern United States and to develop a showcase superstore within the glitzy Caesar's Forum shopping mall on the Las Vegas Strip. By 1992, Just for Feet owned and operated five superstores and had sold franchise rights for several additional stores. The company's annual sales were approaching $20 million, but that total accounted for a nominal proportion of the retail shoe industry's estimated $15 billion of annual sales.

To become a major force in the shoe industry, Ruttenberg knew that he would have to expand his retail chain nationwide, which would require large amounts of additional capital. To acquire that capital, Ruttenberg decided to take his company public. On March 9, 1994, Just for Feet's common stock began trading on the NASDAQ exchange under the ticker symbol FEET. The stock, which sold initially for $6.22 per share, would quickly rise over the next two years to more than $37 per share.

Ruttenberg used the funds produced by Just for Feet's initial public offering (IPO) to pursue an aggressive expansion program. The company opened dozens of new superstores during the mid-1990s and acquired several smaller competitors, including Athletic Attic in March 1997 and Sneaker Stadium in July 1998. For fiscal 1996, which ended January 31, 1997, the company reported a profit of $13.9 million on sales of $250 million. Two years later, the company earned a profit of $26.7 million on sales of nearly $775 million. By the end of 1998, Just for Feet was the second largest athletic shoe retailer in the United States with 300 retail outlets.

During the mid-1990s, Just for Feet's common stock was among the most closely monitored and hyped securities on Wall Street. Analysts and investors tracking the stock marveled at the company's ability to consistently outperform its major competitors. By the late 1990s, market saturation and declining profit margins were becoming major concerns within the athletic shoe segment of the shoe industry. Despite the lackluster profits and faltering revenues of other athletic shoe retailers, Harold Ruttenberg continued to issue press releases touting his company's record profits and steadily growing sales. Most impressive was the company's 21 straight quarterly increases in same-store sales through the fourth quarter of fiscal 1998.

In November 1997, Delphi Investments released a lengthy analytical report focusing on Just for Feet's future prospects. In that report, which included a strong "buy" recommendation for the company's common stock, Delphi commented on the "Harold Ruttenberg factor." The report largely attributed the company's financial success and rosy future to "the larger-than-life founder and inventor of the Just for Feet concept."

In frequent interviews with business journalists, Harold Ruttenberg was not modest in discussing the huge challenges that he had personally overcome to establish himself as one of the leading corporate executives in the retail apparel industry. Nor was

Ruttenberg reluctant to point out that he had sketched out the general framework of Just for Feet's successful business plan over a three-day vacation in the late 1980s. After being named one of 1996's Retail Entrepreneurs of the Year, Ruttenberg noted that Just for Feet had succeeded principally because of the unique marketing strategies he had developed for the company. "Customers love our stores because they are so unique. We are not a copycat retailer. Nobody does what we do, the way we do it. The proof is in our performance."[1] In this same interview, Ruttenberg reported that he had never been tempted to check out a competitor's stores. "I have nothing to learn from them. I'm certainly not going to copy anything they are doing."[2] Finally, Ruttenberg did not dispute, or apologize for, his reputation as a domineering, if not imposing, superior. "I can be a very demanding, difficult boss. But I know how to build teams. And I have made a lot of people very rich."[3]

Ruttenberg realized that one of his primary responsibilities was training a new management team to assume the leadership of the company following his retirement. "As the founder, my job is to put the right people in place for the future. I'm preparing this company for 25 years down the road when I won't be here."[4] One of the individuals who Ruttenberg handpicked to lead the company into its future was his son, Don-Allen Ruttenberg, who shared his father's single-minded determination and tenacious business temperament. In 1997, at the age of 29, Don-Allen Ruttenberg was named Just for Feet's Vice President of New Store Development. Two years later, the younger Ruttenberg was promoted to the position of Executive Vice President.

Similar to most successful companies, Just for Feet's path to success was not without occasional pitfalls. In 1995, Wall Street's zeal for Just for Feet's common stock was tempered somewhat by an accounting controversy involving "store opening" costs. Throughout its existence, Just for Feet had accumulated such costs for each new store in an asset account and then amortized the costs over the 12-month period following the store's grand opening. A more common practice within the retail industry was to expense such costs in the month that a new store opened. Criticism of Just for Feet's accounting for store opening costs goaded company management to adopt the industry convention, which resulted in the company recording a $2.1 million cumulative effect of a change in accounting principle during fiscal 1996.

In the summer of 1996, Wall Street took notice when Harold Ruttenberg, his wife, Pamela, and their son, Don-Allen, sold large blocks of their Just for Feet common stock in a secondary offering to the general public. Collectively, the three members of the Ruttenberg family received nearly $49.5 million from the sale of those securities. Major investors and financial analysts questioned why the Ruttenbergs would dispose of much of their Just for Feet stock while, at the same time, the senior Ruttenberg was issuing glowing projections of the company's future prospects.

Clay Feet

No one could deny the impressive revenue and profit trends that Just for Feet established during the mid- and late 1990s. Exhibit 1 and Exhibit 2, which present the company's primary financial statements for the three-year period fiscal 1996 through fiscal 1998, document those trends. However, hidden within the company's financial data for that three-year period was a red flag. Notice in the statements of cash flows

---

1. *Chain Store Age*, "Retail Entrepreneurs of the Year: Harold Ruttenberg," December 1996, 68.

2. *Ibid.*

3. *Ibid.*

4. *Ibid.*

shown in Exhibit 2 that despite the rising profits Just for Feet reported in the late 1990s, the company's operating cash flows during that period were negative. By early 1999, these negative operating cash flows posed a huge liquidity problem for the company. To address this problem, Just for Feet sold $200 million of high-yield "junk" bonds in April 1999.

A few weeks after selling the junk bonds, Just for Feet issued an earnings warning. This press release alerted investors that the company would likely post its first-ever quarterly loss during the second quarter of fiscal 1999. One month later, Just for Feet shocked its investors and creditors when it announced that it might default on its first interest payment on the $200 million of junk bonds. Investors received more disturbing news in July 1999 when Harold Ruttenberg unexpectedly resigned as Just for Feet's CEO. The company replaced Ruttenberg with a corporate turnaround

JUST FOR FEET, INC.
BALANCE SHEETS (000s omitted)

EXHIBIT 1

JUST FOR FEET, INC., 1996–1998 BALANCE SHEETS

	1999	January 31, 1998	1997
Current assets:			
Cash and cash equivalents	$ 12,412	$ 82,490	$138,785
Marketable securities available for sale	—	—	33,961
Accounts receivable	18,875	15,840	6,553
Inventory	399,901	206,128	133,323
Other current assets	18,302	6,709	2,121
Total current assets	449,490	311,167	314,743
Property and equipment, net	160,592	94,529	54,922
Goodwill, net	71,084	36,106	—
Other	8,230	6,550	6,169
Total assets	$689,396	$448,352	$375,834
Current liabilities:			
Short-term borrowings	$ —	$ 90,667	$100,000
Accounts payable	100,322	51,162	38,897
Accrued expenses	24,829	9,292	5,487
Income taxes payable	902	1,363	425
Current maturities of long-term debt	6,639	3,222	2,105
Total current liabilities	132,692	155,706	146,914
Long-term debt and obligations	230,998	24,562	10,364
Total liabilities	$363,690	$180,268	$157,278
Shareholders' equity:			
Common stock	3	3	3
Paid-in capital	249,590	218,616	190,492
Retained earnings	76,113	49,465	28,061
Total shareholders' equity	325,706	268,084	218,556
Total liabilities and shareholders' equity	$689,396	$448,352	$375,834

specialist, Helen Rockey. Upon resigning, Ruttenberg insisted that Just for Feet's financial problems were only temporary and that the company would likely post a profit during the third quarter of fiscal 1999.

Harold Ruttenberg's statement did not reassure investors. The company's stock price went into a freefall during the spring and summer of 1999, slipping to near $4 per share by the end of July. In September, the company announced that it had lost $25.9 million during the second quarter of fiscal 1999, a much larger loss than had been expected by Wall Street. Less than two months later, on November 2, 1999, the company shocked its investors and creditors once more when it filed for Chapter 11 bankruptcy protection in the federal courts.

Just for Feet's startling collapse over a period of a few months sparked a flurry of lawsuits against the company and its executives. Allegations of financial mismanagement and accounting irregularities triggered investigations of the company's financial affairs by state and federal law enforcement authorities, including the Alabama Securities Commission, the FBI, the Securities and Exchange Commission (SEC), and the U.S. Department of Justice. In May 2003, the Justice Department announced that a former Just for Feet executive, Adam Gilburne, had pleaded guilty to conspiracy to

EXHIBIT 2

JUST FOR FEET, INC., 1996–1998 INCOME STATEMENTS AND STATEMENTS OF CASH FLOWS

JUST FOR FEET, INC.
CONSOLIDATED STATEMENTS OF EARNINGS (000s omitted)

	Year Ended January 31,		
	1999	1998	1997
Net sales	$774,863	$478,638	$256,397
Cost of sales	452,330	279,816	147,526
Gross profit	322,533	198,822	108,871
Other revenues	1,299	1,101	581
Operating expenses:			
Store operating	232,505	139,659	69,329
Store opening costs	13,669	6,728	11,240
Amortization of intangibles	2,072	1,200	180
General and administrative	24,341	18,040	7,878
Total operating expenses	272,587	165,627	88,627
Operating income	51,245	34,296	20,825
Interest expense	(8,059)	(1,446)	(832)
Interest income	143	1,370	4,750
Earnings before income taxes and cumulative effect of change in accounting principle	43,329	34,220	24,743
Provision for income taxes	16,681	12,817	8,783
Earnings before cumulative effect of a change in accounting principle	26,648	21,403	15,960
Cumulative effect on prior years of change in accounting principle	—	—	(2,041)
Net earnings	$ 26,648	$ 21,403	$ 13,919

EXHIBIT 2—
continued

JUST FOR FEET,
INC., 1996–1998
INCOME
STATEMENTS AND
STATEMENTS OF
CASH FLOWS

JUST FOR FEET, INC.
CONSOLIDATED STATEMENTS OF CASH FLOWS (000s omitted)

| | Year Ended January 31, | | |
	1999	1998	1997
Operating activities:			
Net earnings	$ 26,648	$ 21,403	$ 13,919
Adjustments to reconcile net earnings to net cash used by operating activities:			
Cumulative effect of a change in accounting principle	—	—	2,041
Depreciation and amortization	16,129	8,783	3,971
Deferred income taxes	12,100	2,194	(744)
Deferred lease rentals	2,655	2,111	1,456
Changes in assets and liabilities providing (using) cash, net of effects of acquisitions:			
(Increase) decrease in accounts receivable	(2,795)	(8,918)	(3,143)
(Increase) decrease in inventory	(170,169)	(56,616)	(76,685)
(Increase) decrease in other assets	(8,228)	(5,643)	271
Increase (decrease) in accounts payable	34,638	7,495	16,628
Increase (decrease) in accrued expenses	7,133	2,264	2,709
Increase (decrease) in income taxes payable	(181)	543	(2,506)
Net cash used by operating activities	(82,070)	(26,384)	(42,083)
Investing activities:			
Purchases of property and equipment, net of disposals	(78,984)	(43,446)	(33,206)
Acquisitions, net of cash acquired	(199)	(25,548)	—
Purchases of marketable securities	—	(14,726)	(44,778)
Maturities and sales of marketable securities	—	51,653	63,132
Net cash used for investing activities	(79,183)	(32,067)	(14,852)
Financing activities:			
Borrowings (repayments) under credit facilities, net	(90,667)	(9,333)	45,000
Borrowings of long-term obligations	291,076	12,739	479
Principal payments on long-term obligations	(132,290)	(2,054)	(1,335)
Proceeds from issuance of common stock, net	20,000	—	52,900
Proceeds from exercise of options	3,056	804	1,822
Net cash provided by financing activities	91,175	2,156	98,866
Net increase (decrease) in cash and equivalents	(70,078)	(56,295)	41,931
Cash and equivalents, beginning of year	82,490	138,785	96,854
Cash and equivalents, end of year	$ 12,412	$ 82,490	$138,785

commit wire and securities fraud. Gilburne, who had served in various executive positions with Just for Feet, revealed that he and other members of the company's top management had conspired to inflate the company's reported earnings from 1996 through 1999.

> *The information [testimony provided by Gilburne] alleges that beginning in about 1996, Just for Feet's CEO [Harold Ruttenberg] would conduct meetings at the end of every quarter in which he would lay out analysts' expectations of the company's earnings, and then draw up a list of "goods"—items which produced or added income— and "bads"—those which reduced income. The information alleges that the CEO*

directed Just for Feet's employees to increase the "goods" and decrease the "bads" in order to meet his own earnings expectations and those of Wall Street analysts.[5]

Approximately two years following Gilburne's guilty plea, the SEC issued a series of enforcement releases that documented the three key facets of the fraudulent scheme perpetrated by Just for Feet's management team. "Just for Feet falsified its financial statements by (1) improperly recognizing unearned and fictitious receivables from its vendors, (2) failing to properly account for excess inventory, and (3) improperly recording as income the value of display booths provided by its vendors."[6]

As noted earlier, the stores-within-a-store floor plan developed by Harold Ruttenberg provided an opportunity for Just for Feet's vendors to become directly involved in the marketing of their products within the company's superstores. Each year, Just for Feet received millions of dollars of "vendor allowances" or "advertising co-op" from its major suppliers. These allowances were intended to subsidize Just for Feet's advertising expenditures for its superstores.

Despite the large size of the vendor allowances, there was typically not a written agreement that documented the conditions under which Just for Feet was entitled to an allowance. Instead, an account manager of each vendor generally had considerable discretion in determining the size and timing of the allowances to be granted to Just for Feet. After Just for Feet had run a series of advertisements or other promotional announcements for a vendor's product, copies of the advertising materials would be submitted to the vendor. The vendor would then pay Just for Feet an allowance based largely upon the amount of the advertised products that the company had purchased.

Generally accepted accounting principles (GAAP) dictate that vendor allowances not be offset against advertising expense until the given advertisements have been run or other promotional efforts have been completed. However, Just for Feet began routinely recording *anticipated* vendor allowances as receivables and advertising expense offsets well before the related advertising or promotional programs had been completed. Just for Feet's management team was particularly aggressive in "front-loading" vendor allowances during fiscal 1998. At the end of fiscal 1997, Just for Feet had slightly more than $400,000 of outstanding vendor allowance receivables; twelve months later, at the end of fiscal 1998, that total had soared to almost $29 million.[7]

During fiscal 1998, Just for Feet's merchandise inventory nearly doubled, rising from $206 million on January 31, 1998, to almost $400 million on January 31, 1999. Although Just for Feet had a large amount of slow-moving inventory, the company's management team refused to properly apply the lower of cost or market rule in arriving at a year-end valuation reserve for that important asset. As a result, at the end of both fiscal 1997 and fiscal 1998, the company's allowance for inventory obsolescence stood at a nominal $150,000.

The major athletic shoe vendors frequently erected promotional displays or booths in the Just for Feet superstores. These booths were maintained by sales representatives of the vendors and were the property of those vendors. In early 1998, Don-Allen Ruttenberg concocted a fraudulent scheme to produce millions of dollars of

---

5. U.S. Department of Justice, "Former 'Just for Feet, Inc.' Executive Pleads Guilty to Conspiracy to Commit Wire, Securities Fraud," www.usdoj.gov, 12 May 2003.

6. U.S. Securities and Exchange Commission, "SEC Charges Deloitte & Touche and Two of Its Personnel for Failures in Their Audits of Just for Feet," www.sec.gov, 26 April 2005.

7. Although technically receivables, the vendor allowances purportedly due to Just for Feet were netted against the given vendor's accounts payable balance, which explains why these receivables do not appear explicitly in the company's balance sheets shown in Exhibit 1.

"booth income" for Just for Feet. Without the knowledge of its vendors, Just for Feet began recording in its accounting records monthly booth income amounts allegedly earned from those vendors. The offsets to these revenue amounts for accounting purposes were booked (debited) to a booth assets account.[8] By the end of fiscal 1998, Just for Feet had recorded $9 million of bogus assets and related revenues as a result of this scheme. More than 80 percent of these bogus transactions were recorded during the final two quarters of fiscal 1998, ostensibly to allow Just for Feet to reach its previously announced earnings targets for those two periods.

An important feature of the Just for Feet accounting fraud was Don-Allen Ruttenberg's close relationship with key executives of the major athletic shoe vendors. Since Just for Feet was among the largest customers of each of those vendors, the company had a significant amount of economic leverage on their executives. The younger Ruttenberg used this leverage to persuade those executives to return false confirmations to Just for Feet's independent audit firm, Deloitte & Touche. Those confirmations were sent to Just for Feet's vendors to confirm bogus receivables that were a product of the company's fraudulent accounting scheme. In most cases, the bogus receivables resulted from inflated or otherwise improper vendor allowances booked by Just for Feet. One of the five vendor executives who capitulated to Don-Allen Ruttenberg's demands was Thomas Shine, the senior executive of Logo Athletic. Executives of four Just for Feet vendors steadfastly refused to provide false confirmations to Deloitte. Those executives were employed by Asics-Tiger, New Balance, Reebok, and Timberland. Ironically, in 2001, Thomas Shine became an executive of Reebok when that company purchased Logo Athletic.

Footing & Cross-Footing

Deloitte & Touche served as Just for Feet's independent audit firm from 1992 through early December 1999, one month after the company filed for Chapter 11 bankruptcy. Deloitte issued unqualified audit opinions each year on Just for Feet's financial statements, including the financial statements in the S-1 registration statement the company filed with the SEC when it went public in 1994.

Steven Barry served as Just for Feet's engagement partner for the fiscal 1998 audit. Barry was initially an employee of Touche Ross & Co. and was promoted to partner with that firm in 1988. The next year, Barry became a Deloitte & Touche partner following the merger of Touche Ross with Deloitte, Haskins, & Sells. In 1996, Barry was promoted to managing partner of Deloitte's Birmingham, Alabama, office. Barry's principal subordinate on the 1998 Just for Feet audit was Karen Baker, who had been assigned to the company's audit engagement team since 1993. Initially the audit senior on that engagement team, she became the engagement audit manager after being promoted to that rank in 1995.

Deloitte assigned a "greater than normal" level of audit risk to the fiscal 1998 Just for Feet audit during the planning phase of that engagement. To help monitor high-risk audit engagements, Deloitte had established a "National Risk Management Program." In both 1997 and 1998, Just for Feet was included in that program. Each client involved in this program was assigned a "National Review Partner." This partner's duties included "discussing specific risk areas and plans to respond to them . . . reviewing the audit workpapers concerning risk areas of the engagement, and reviewing the financial statements and Deloitte's audit reports with an emphasis on the

---

8. This fraudulent scheme actually replaced a similar but smaller-scale scam that the younger Ruttenberg had used since December 1996 to inflate Just for Feet's operating results.

identification of specific risk areas as well as the adequacy of the audit report and disclosures regarding these risk areas."[9]

The audit workpapers for the fiscal 1997 audit identified several specific audit risk factors. These factors included "management accepts high levels of risk," "places significant emphasis on earnings," and "has historically interpreted accounting standards aggressively." Another 1997 workpaper noted that the company's management team placed a heavy emphasis on achieving previously released earnings targets, expressed an "excessive" interest in maintaining the company's stock price at a high level, and engaged in "unique and highly complex" transactions near fiscal year-end. A summary 1997 workpaper entitled "Risk Factors Worksheet" also noted that Harold Ruttenberg exercised "one-man rule (autocrat)" rule over Just for Feet and that the company practiced "creative accounting."

For both the 1997 and 1998 audit engagements, Deloitte personnel prepared a "Client Risk Profile." This workpaper for those two audits identified vendor allowances and inventory valuation as key audit risk areas. In 1996, Deloitte's headquarters office had issued a firm-wide "Risk Alert" informing practice offices that vendor allowances should be considered a "high-risk area" for retail clients.

During the 1998 audit, the Deloitte engagement team identified several factors that, according to the SEC, should have caused both Barry and Baker to have "heightened professional skepticism" regarding Just for Feet's vendor allowances. The most important of these factors was the huge increase in the vendor allowance receivables between the end of fiscal 1997 and fiscal 1998. In the final few weeks of fiscal 1998, Just for Feet recorded $14.4 million of vendor allowances, accounting for almost one-half of the year-end balance of that account. Deloitte was never provided with supporting documentation for $11.3 million of those vendor allowances, although a Just for Feet executive had promised to provide that documentation. Deloitte completed its fieldwork for the fiscal 1998 audit on April 23, 1999, almost three months following the fiscal year-end. As of that date, Just for Feet had not received any payments from its suppliers for the $11.3 million of undocumented vendor allowances.

In March 1999, Deloitte mailed receivables confirmations to 13 of Just for Feet's suppliers. Collectively, those vendors accounted for $22 million of the $28.9 million of year-end vendor allowances. Again, Don-Allen Ruttenberg persuaded executives of five Just for Feet vendors to sign and return confirmations to Deloitte even though the vendor allowance receivables listed on those confirmations did not exist or were grossly inflated. The confirmations returned by the other eight vendors were generally "nonstandard," according to the SEC. That is, these confirmations included caveats, disclaimers, or other statements that should have alerted Deloitte to the possibility that the given receivable balances were unreliable. "Five vendors returned non-standard letters that, instead of unambiguously confirming amounts owed to Just for Feet at the end of the fiscal 1998 year, as requested by the auditors, provided ambiguous information on amounts of co-op [vendor allowances] that the Company had earned, accrued, or had available during the year" [emphasis added by SEC]. Another of the returned confirmations explicitly noted that "no additional funds" were due to Just for Feet.

The eight nonstandard confirmations accounted for approximately $16 million of the $22 million of vendor allowance receivables that Deloitte attempted to confirm at year-end. "Despite these and other flaws, the Respondents [Deloitte, Barry and

---

9. Securities and Exchange Commission, *Accounting and Auditing Enforcement Release No. 2238*, 26 May 2005. Unless noted otherwise, the remaining quotations in this case were taken from this source.

Baker] nonetheless accepted these letters as confirming approximately $16 million in receivables claimed by Just for Feet." The SEC's investigation of Deloitte's Just for Feet audits revealed that although Barry and Baker accepted these flawed confirmations, two subordinates assigned to the 1998 engagement team continued to investigate the obvious discrepancies in those confirmations well after the completion of that audit. These two individuals, who were audit seniors, twice contacted a Just for Feet executive in the months following the completion of the 1998 audit in an attempt to obtain plausible explanations for the eight nonstandard and suspicious confirmations. That executive did not respond to the audit seniors and neither Barry, nor Baker, apparently, insisted that he provide appropriate documentation and/or explanations regarding the amounts in question.

Just for Feet's large increase in inventory during fiscal 1998 raised several important issues that the Deloitte auditors had to address during the 1998 audit, the most important being whether the client's reserve for inventory obsolescence was sufficient. The primary audit procedure used by Deloitte during the 1998 audit to assess the reasonableness of the client's inventory valuation reserve was to obtain and test an inventory "reserve analysis" prepared by a company vice president. This latter document was supposed to include the following three classes of inventory items for which company policy required application of the lower of cost or market rule: (1) shoe styles for which the company had four or fewer pairs, (2) shoes and other apparel that were selling for less than cost, and (3) any inventory styles for which no items had been sold during the previous 12 months. The reserve analysis for 1998, however, excluded those inventory styles for which no sales had been made during the previous 12 months, an oversight that the Deloitte auditors never questioned or investigated. The Deloitte auditors also discovered that a large amount of inventory included in a Just for Feet warehouse had been excluded from the reserve analysis prepared by the company vice president. Again, the auditors chose not to question client personnel regarding this oversight.

After completing their inventory audit procedures, the Deloitte auditors concluded that Just for Feet's year-end reserve for inventory obsolescence was significantly understated. The SEC noted that this conclusion was reached by the Deloitte auditors despite the obvious deficiencies in audit procedures applied to Just for Feet's reserve for inventory obsolescence:

> *Even using the flawed inventory analysis provided by the Vice President and the deficient inventory information that excluded the goods from the New Jersey warehouse, the Respondents concluded that Just for Feet's obsolescence reserve should have been in the range of $441,000 to over $1 million.*

The Deloitte audit team proposed an audit adjustment to increase the reserve for inventory obsolescence by more than $400,000; however, the client rejected that audit adjustment, meaning that the year-end balance of that account remained at a meager $150,000.

Although not specifically identified as a "key audit risk area" during the 1998 audit, the Deloitte auditors focused considerable attention on Just for Feet's accounting decisions for the approximately $9 million of "booth income" the company recorded during that year. The Deloitte auditors discovered the monthly booth income journal entries recorded by Just for Feet during fiscal 1998 and prepared a workpaper documenting those entries. "An analysis at the end of the workpaper, which Baker reviewed, showed that the net effect of Just for Feet's booth-related journal entries was to increase assets with a corresponding increase in income. The respondents [Deloitte, Barry, and Baker] performed no further analysis to determine the basis and propriety of these journal entries." Instead of independently investigating these entries, the Deloitte auditors accepted the representation of a Just for Feet executive that the entries had no effect on the company's net income. According to this executive, the monthly booth income amounts were offset by preexisting "co-op" or advertising credits that had been granted to Just for Feet by its major vendors. In other words, instead of using those advertising credits to reduce reported advertising expenses, Just for Feet was allegedly converting those credits into booth income or revenue amounts.

By the end of 1998, the bogus booth income journal entries had produced $9 million of nonexistent "booth assets" in Just for Feet's accounting records. Since "neither the Company nor the auditors had internal evidence supporting the recording of $9 million of booth assets," the Deloitte engagement team decided to corroborate the existence and ownership assertions for those assets by obtaining confirmations from the relevant Just for Feet vendors. These confirmations were prepared with the assistance of certain Just for Feet executives who were aware of the fraudulent nature of the booth income/booth assets amounts. Apparently, these executives contacted the vendor representatives to whom the confirmations were mailed and told them how to respond to the confirmations. The booth assets confirmations returned by the vendors to Deloitte were replete with errors and ambiguous statements. A frustrated audit senior who reviewed the confirmations brought this matter to the attention of both Barry and Baker.

> An audit senior reviewed these confirmations and informed Barry and Baker that she was in some cases sending multiple confirmation requests to the vendors because many of their initial requests came back in forms different from that requested. The Respondents failed to discover from these indications that Just for Feet might not actually . . . [own] . . . the booths as claimed.

EPILOGUE

In February 2000, after realizing that Just for Feet was no longer salvageable, Helen Rockey began the process of liquidating the company under Chapter 7 of the federal bankruptcy code. Over the next few years, settlements were announced to a number of large lawsuits linked to the Just for Feet accounting fraud and the company's subsequent bankruptcy. Just for Feet's former executives and Deloitte were among the principal defendants in those lawsuits. One of those cases, a class-action lawsuit filed by Just for Feet's former stockholders, was settled for a reported $32.4 million in 2002.

Several of Just for Feet's former executives pleaded guilty to criminal charges for their roles in the company's massive accounting fraud. Among these individuals was Don-Allen Ruttenberg. In April 2005, a federal judge sentenced Ruttenberg to 20 months in federal prison and fined him $50,000. At the same time that the younger Ruttenberg's sentence was announced, a Department of Justice official reported that Harold Ruttenberg, who was gravely ill with brain cancer, would not be charged in the case. In January 2006, Harold Ruttenberg died at the age of 63.

Five executives of Just for Feet's former vendors also pleaded guilty to various criminal charges for providing false confirmations to the company's auditors. Most of these individuals, including Thomas Shine, received probationary sentences. An exception was Timothy McCool, the former director of apparel sales for Adidas, who received a four-month "noncustodial" sentence. While sentencing McCool, U.S. District Judge C. Lynwood Smith, Jr., noted, " Life is so fragile. A single bad choice in a single moment can cause a life to turn irrevocably 180 degrees. I think that is where you find yourself."[10]

Arguably, the party to the Just for Feet scandal that received the most condemnation from the courts and the business press was Deloitte. In April 2005, the SEC berated the prominent accounting firm for the poor quality of its Just for Feet audits in *Accounting and Auditing Enforcement Release No. 2238*. In that same enforcement release, the SEC fined Deloitte $375,000 and suspended Steven Barry from serving on audit engagements involving SEC registrants for two years; Karen Baker received a one-year suspension.

On the same date that the SEC announced the sanctions that it had imposed on Deloitte for its Just for Feet audits, the federal agency also revealed the sanctions that Deloitte received for its allegedly deficient audits of a large telecommunications company, Adelphia Communications. Similar to Just for Feet, the once high-flying Adelphia had suddenly collapsed in 2002 following revelations that its previously issued financial statements that had been audited by Deloitte were riddled with errors. The SEC stunned the public accounting profession by fining Deloitte $50 million for its role in the huge Adelphia scandal, which was easily the largest fine ever imposed on an accounting firm by the federal agency.

Shortly after the SEC announced the sanctions that it had levied on Deloitte for its Just for Feet and Adelphia Communications audits, James Quigley, Deloitte's CEO, issued a press release responding to those sanctions. Quigley noted in his press release that, "Among our most significant challenges is the early detection of fraud, particularly when the client, its management and others collude specifically to deceive a company's auditors."[11] This statement infuriated SEC officials. An SEC spokesperson responded to Quigley's press release by stating that, "Deloitte was not deceived in this case. The findings in the order show that the relevant information was right in front of their eyes. Deloitte just didn't do its job, plain and simple. They didn't miss red flags. They pulled the flag over their head and claimed they couldn't see."[12]

The SEC also suggested that Quigley's press release violated the terms of the agreement that the agency had reached with Deloitte in settling the Just for Feet and Adelphia cases. Under the terms of that agreement, Deloitte was not required to "admit" to the SEC's findings, nor was it allowed to "deny" those findings. Deloitte subsequently rescinded Quigley's press release and issued another that eliminated some, but not all, of the statements that had offended the SEC.

Questions

1. Prepare common-sized balance sheets and income statements for Just for Feet for the period 1996–1998. Also compute key liquidity, solvency, activity, and profitability ratios for 1997 and 1998. Given these data, comment on what you believe were the high-risk financial statement items for the 1998 Just for Feet audit.

2. Just for Feet operated large, high-volume retail stores. Identify internal control risks common to such businesses. How should these risks affect the audit planning decisions for such a client?

---

10. *The Associated Press State & Local Wire*, "Adidas America Executive Sentenced in Just for Feet Case," 22 March 2004.

11. S. Laub, "Deloitte Statement Irks SEC," *CFO.com*, 28 April 2005.

12. S. Hughes, "SEC Rebukes Deloitte over Spin of Adelphia Audit," *The Associated Press State & Local Wire*, 27 April 2005.

3. Just for Feet operated in an extremely competitive industry, or sub-industry. Identify inherent risk factors common to businesses facing such competitive conditions. How should these risks affect the audit planning decisions for such a client?

4. Prepare a comprehensive list, in a bullet format, of the audit risk factors present for the 1998 Just for Feet audit. Identify the five audit risk factors that you believe were most critical to the successful completion of that audit. Rank these risk factors from the least to most important, and be prepared to defend your rankings. Briefly explain whether or not you believe that the Deloitte auditors responded appropriately to the five critical audit risk factors that you identified.

5. Put yourself in the position of Thomas Shine in this case. How would you have responded when Don-Allen Ruttenberg asked you to send a false confirmation to Deloitte & Touche? Before responding, identify the parties who will be affected by your decision.

Health Management, Inc.

Clifford Hotte had a problem. His company had come up short of its earnings target. For the fiscal year ended April 30, 1995, financial analysts had projected that Health Management, Inc. (HMI), a New York—based pharmaceuticals distributor, would post earnings per share of $0.74. Following the close of fiscal 1995, Drew Bergman, HMI's chief financial officer (CFO), informed Hotte, the company's founder and chief executive officer (CEO), that the actual earnings figure for fiscal 1995 would be approximately $0.54 per share. According to Bergman, Hotte refused to "take the hit," that is, the almost certain drop in HMI's stock price that would follow the announcement of the disappointing earnings.[1] Instead, Hotte wanted HMI to report 1995 earnings in line with analysts' predictions.[2]

Bergman altered HMI's accounting records to allow the company to reach its 1995 earnings target. To lower cost of sales and increase HMI's gross profit and net income, Bergman inflated the company's year-end inventory by approximately $1.8 million. Bergman also posted a few other smaller "adjustments" to HMI's accounting records. Both Bergman and Hotte realized that the company would have to take elaborate measures to conceal the accounting fraud from its audit firm. Bergman was very familiar with BDO Seidman and its audit procedures since he had been employed by that accounting firm several years earlier. In fact, Bergman had supervised BDO Seidman's 1989 and 1990 audits of HMI.

HMI's inventory fraud was not particularly innovative. Corporate executives who want to embellish their company's operating results are aware that among the easiest methods of achieving that goal is overstating year-end inventory. What was unique about HMI's inventory hoax was that it triggered one of the first major tests of an important and controversial new federal law, the 1995 Private Securities Litigation Reform Act (PSLRA). The PSLRA was the only law passed by Congress during President Clinton's first administration that overcame a presidential veto.

Among the parties most pleased by the passage of the PSLRA were the large, international accounting firms. These firms' mounting litigation losses in the latter decades of the twentieth century had prompted them to lobby Congress to reform the nation's civil litigation system. In particular, the firms argued that they were being unfairly victimized by the growing number of class-action lawsuits. The bulk of these lawsuits were being filed under the Securities Exchange Act of 1934, one of the federal statutes that created the regulatory infrastructure for the nation's securities markets in the early 1930s. Top officials of the major accounting firms believed that the PSLRA, which amended key provisions of the 1934 Act, would make it much more difficult for plaintiff attorneys to extract large legal judgments or settlements from their firms. The jury's verdict in favor of BDO Seidman in the HMI lawsuit seemed to support that conclusion. HMI's stockholders filed suit against BDO Seidman for failing to detect

---

1. Unless indicated otherwise, the quotations in this case were drawn from court transcripts obtained for the *In Re Health Management, Inc. Securities Litigation* case that was tried in U.S. District Court (Eastern District of New York) in October 1999.

2. I would like to acknowledge a former student of mine, Amy Hollis, for her excellent research that contributed to this case. I would also like to acknowledge the kind assistance of Michael Young.

the inventory fraud masterminded by Drew Bergman and Clifford Hotte. Michael Young, a prominent New York attorney who headed BDO Seidman's legal defense team, predicted that the case would become a "watershed event" in the accounting profession's struggle to curb its litigation losses.[3]

Thinly Veiled Extortion

The federal securities laws passed by Congress in the early 1930s not only established a formal regulatory structure for the securities markets, they also strengthened an informal control mechanism that had long served to promote and preserve the integrity of the capital markets. That control mechanism was private securities litigation. The federal securities laws make it unlawful for companies registered with the SEC to issue financial statements that misrepresent their financial condition and operating results. However, the courts have also permitted those statutes to be used as the basis for civil actions. Investors and creditors can file tort actions to recover damages they suffer at the hands of parties who prepare or are otherwise associated with misrepresented financial statements of SEC registrants.

Prior to the passage of the federal securities laws and for several decades thereafter, major institutional investors and large creditors, such as metropolitan banks, filed most private securities lawsuits. Individual investors and creditors who suffered damages as a result of relying on misrepresented financial statements generally found that it was not economically feasible to use the courts to recover their losses. During the 1970s, resourceful attorneys cured this "problem" by employing the concept of a "class-action" lawsuit. In such lawsuits, the legal claims of a large number of individual plaintiffs are consolidated into one joint claim. In exchange for representing these joint plaintiffs, attorneys receive a contingent fee equal to a percentage of any collective judgment or settlement awarded to the plaintiffs.

Thanks to their newfound ability to file class-action lawsuits, attorneys specializing in private securities litigation began vigorously suing parties directly or indirectly linked to allegedly false or misleading financial statements filed with the SEC. Most of these lawsuits claimed one or more violations of Rule 10b-5 of the Securities Exchange Act of 1934. That section of the 1934 Act prohibits the "employment of manipulative and deceptive devices" in connection with the preparation and distribution of the financial statements of SEC-registered companies.[4]

By the late 1970s, class-action lawsuits predicated on Rule 10b-5 violations were commonplace. One legal scholar observed that the "low transaction cost" of filing a class-action lawsuit under the federal securities laws invited abuse of that tactic by plaintiff attorneys.[5] Former SEC Chairman Richard Breeden frequently spoke out against the epidemic of class-action securities lawsuits plaguing corporations, their executives, and related parties. Breeden characterized the securities class-action system "as a legal regime disconnected from principles of right and wrong that is riddled with abuse and that involves nothing less than thinly veiled extortion."[6]

---

3. G. Cheney, "BDO Wins Landmark Case under New Tort Reform Law," *Accounting Today*, November 22–December 12, 1999, 3.

4. Case 7.6, "*First Securities Company of Chicago*," presents the complete text of Rule 10b-5.

5. H. E. Milstein, "Recent Developments in the Private Securities Litigation Reform Act," *Securities Litigation & Regulation Reporter*, 12 January 2000, 12.

6. R. M. Phillips and G. C. Miller, "The Private Securities Litigation Reform Act of 1995: Rebalancing Litigation Risks and Rewards for Class Action Plaintiffs, Defendants, and Lawyers," *The Business Lawyer*, August 1996, 51 Bus. Law. 1009.

Class-action securities lawsuits proved to be particularly problematic for the large accounting firms that audit the financial statements of most major public companies. An unavoidable facet of these firms' primary line of business is being burdened occasionally with a client whose executives choose to use "creative" or even blatantly fraudulent accounting methods. An audit firm that fails to detect irregularities in a public client's financial statements faces a considerable risk of being named a defendant in a class-action lawsuit if those irregularities eventually surface. An accounting firm that issues an unqualified opinion on financial statements later proven to contain material errors may only be guilty of accepting a client whose management is inept and/or unethical. Nevertheless, the financial resources of the large accounting firms make them inviting targets for investors and creditors who have relied, to their detriment, on misleading financial statements.

The executives of many large accounting firms decided that the most rational approach to dealing with class-action lawsuits filed against them was to settle those lawsuits out of court as quickly and quietly as possible. Michael Cook, former CEO of Deloitte & Touche, testified before Congress that his firm often used that strategy because of the leverage plaintiff attorneys had on his firm. That leverage stemmed from the enormous judgments Deloitte & Touche potentially faced if it allowed class-action lawsuits in which it was named as a defendant to go to trial. Most frustrating to Cook and his colleagues at other accounting firms was the need to pay large sums to settle cases in which they were convinced their firms were not at fault. According to Cook, "I am forced to settle cases in which I believe our firm did nothing wrong."[7]

Skeptics questioned the veracity of such statements by Cook and other top executives of major accounting firms. However, empirical research by Professor Zoe-Vonna Palmrose, an authority on audit-related litigation, suggested that the large accounting firms were often named as defendants in class-action lawsuits because of their "deep pockets" rather than because they were at fault.[8] The ability of plaintiff attorneys to goad defendants into settling was borne out by a study of class-action securities lawsuits filed prior to the mid-1990s. Only 2 percent of those lawsuits went to trial, while 20 percent were dismissed. In the remaining 78 percent of those cases, the plaintiffs received out-of-court settlements, often multimillion-dollar settlements, from the defendants.[9]

"Relief" Is Spelled . . . PSLRA

In 1991, the Big Six accounting firms launched a costly and coordinated campaign to persuade Congress to reform the nation's private securities litigation system. Congress finally took up that cause during the mid-1990s. The resulting congressional debate was heated, far-reaching, and drew extensive coverage by the media. The most contentious issue addressed in this debate was what "pleading standard" federal judges should invoke when deciding whether a given lawsuit should be allowed to proceed to trial. The Big Six firms wanted Congress to raise the pleading standard, making it more likely that class-action securities lawsuits would be dismissed shortly after being filed.

Congress sided with the Big Six firms when it enacted the PSLRA in December 1995 after overriding President Clinton's veto of the bill. President Clinton vetoed the

---

7. *Ibid.*

8. Z-V. Palmrose, "The Joint and Several vs. Proportionate Liability Debate: An Empirical Investigation of Audit-Related Litigation," *Stanford Journal of Law, Business and Finance*, 1994 (Vol.1), 53–72.

9. W. Hamilton, "Stock-Fraud Suits Increase Despite '95 Law," *Los Angeles Times*, 1 July 1998, D1.

bill because he believed the PSLRA's tough pleading standard would make it too difficult for plaintiffs with legitimate claims to have their day in court. Generally, the federal courts have interpreted the PSLRA to require plaintiffs to allege that a defendant was at least "reckless" for a case to proceed to trial. Among other requirements, the law mandates that plaintiffs identify or plead specific facts to support their allegations against defendants. No longer do the federal courts allow "fishing expeditions" by plaintiff attorneys. For example, plaintiff attorneys are now barred from making general, broad-brush allegations of professional misconduct when filing class-action lawsuits against accounting firms, a tactic they commonly used prior to the PSLRA.[10]

Congress's inclusion of a proportionate liability rule in the PSLRA was also a major victory for accounting firms. Previously, the federal courts had imposed joint and several liability on defendants proven to have violated federal securities laws in a civil case. Under this standard, each such defendant was responsible for the entire judgment awarded the plaintiff. If one or more defendants could not pay their share of a judgment, their portion had to be paid by any remaining defendants that were solvent. The joint and several liability rule served to punish accounting firms since they were often the only solvent defendant in a class-action lawsuit. The PSLRA imposes joint and several liability only on defendants that knowingly participated in a fraud. A defendant guilty of no more than "recklessness" is generally responsible for only a percentage of the plaintiffs' losses. This percentage is equal to the defendant's percentage of responsibility or fault for the given series of events that produced those losses.

Another important feature of the PSLRA for the accounting profession is a clause permitting federal judges to fine plaintiff attorneys who file frivolous securities lawsuits. The PSLRA also contains several clauses that relate directly to the independent audit function, some of which were adapted from the profession's own technical standards. The statute requires audit firms to design audits to provide reasonable assurance of detecting illegal acts that have a material and direct effect on a client's financial statements. Likewise, the law mandates that auditors use appropriate procedures to identify a client's related-party transactions and to assess the client's ability to remain a going concern over the following 12 months. A new requirement that the PSLRA imposed on auditors was reporting to the SEC any illegal acts by a client that had a material effect on the client's financial statements—assuming the client refused to report such items to the SEC.

Following the passage of the PSLRA, members of the accounting profession, trial attorneys, and other interested parties waited anxiously for a major litigation case to test the new statute's key features. That test would ultimately be provided by the class-action lawsuit filed by HMI's stockholders against BDO Seidman.

Hotte Inventory

Clifford Hotte, a licensed pharmacist with a Ph.D in nuclear pharmacology and a former president of the New York State Board of Pharmacy, founded Homecare Management in 1986. This small company sold medical supplies and equipment to the public and to individuals and firms that provided in-home medical services. Hotte's company grew rapidly and expanded into other lines of business. By the mid-1990s, Hotte had taken his company public and renamed it Health Management, Inc. (HMI). At this point, the company's principal line of business was "chronic disease

---

10. Recognize that since the PSLRA served as an amendment to the Securities Exchange Act of 1934, this statute applies only to lawsuits involving the financial statements of public companies, that is, companies that file periodic financial statements with the SEC.

management." The company specialized in marketing expensive drugs needed by individuals suffering from a wide range of chronic illnesses including AIDS, Alzheimer's, Parkinson's, and schizophrenia.

Hotte retained BDO Seidman as his company's audit firm in 1989. According to subsequent court testimony, the company's prior audit firm resigned because of concerns it had regarding HMI's inventory accounting procedures. One of the auditors assigned to the 1989 and 1990 HMI audit engagement teams was Drew Bergman. Bergman graduated from Queens College in 1979 and accepted an entry-level position with a small accounting firm that later merged with BDO Seidman's predecessor. In 1987, Bergman transferred to BDO Seidman's Long Island office. Bergman served as the senior audit manager on the 1989 and 1990 HMI audits. In court testimony, Bergman provided the following description of his responsibilities as a senior audit manager:

> In that position, I was responsible for running the engagement from the time that we started working on a particular job, making sure that the staffing was accurate [sic], that we had the appropriate levels of people to do the work that was necessary, and accumulate the work product necessary to support the conclusions that we needed to reach before reaching an opinion on the financial statements.

One of Bergman's subordinates on the 1989 and 1990 HMI audits was Mei-ya Tsai. During the three years Bergman worked for BDO Seidman's Long Island office, Tsai was assigned to approximately 20 engagements he supervised. On the 1989 and 1990 HMI audits, Tsai served as the audit senior. When Drew Bergman resigned from BDO Seidman, Tsai was promoted to audit manager and assumed Bergman's responsibilities on subsequent HMI audits. After Bergman left BDO Seidman, he and Tsai maintained the friendship they had developed while working together at the audit firm. That friendship was strengthened by a relationship between Tsai and Bergman's wife, Nancy. From 1986 through the mid-1990s, Nancy Bergman was the marketing director and administrative office manager for BDO Seidman's Long Island office. Nancy Bergman and Mei-ya Tsai became close friends during that time. The two women, their spouses, and their children frequently visited each other and occasionally spent holidays together.

Clifford Hotte hired Drew Bergman away from BDO Seidman in 1990 and appointed him HMI's CFO. Bergman testified that he was "ultimately responsible" for HMI's accounting records and for "generating financial statements which then were sent to various governmental agencies." In his role as CFO, Bergman met frequently with Hotte to discuss important accounting and financial matters for HMI. During the first week of June 1995, Bergman delivered the unpleasant news to Hotte that HMI's net income for the fiscal year ended April 30, 1995, had fallen short of the company's forecasted profit for that period. After scouring HMI's accounting records with Bergman and confirming the earnings shortfall, Hotte told his CFO that HMI would not report an earnings figure significantly lower than the $0.74 per share financial analysts had predicted the company would earn during fiscal 1995. A flabbergasted Bergman responded, "We are already at the end of the year . . . we're in June. April ended already, sales are done. Inventories have been taken." Following an awkward period of silence, Hotte made himself even more clear to Bergman when he stated that reporting disappointing earnings was "not an option." At this point, Bergman finally realized what Hotte was implying.

After "stewing over" the predicament he found himself in, Bergman went to Hotte's office later that same day with a proposition. "I went back into Dr. Hotte, and I said, 'Dr. Hotte, I said, listen, recruiting people for this, I don't want anything to do with it . . . [but] if you can go out and get them [other subordinates] to go along with this, then I'd be willing to make the [accounting] adjustments.'" Over the next two weeks, Bergman and Hotte worked on their plan. Eventually, Bergman decided to increase the company's April 30, 1995, inventory by approximately $1.8 million. His justification for this increase? He had overlooked $1.8 million of inventory in transit on April 30 when compiling the results of the company's year-end physical inventory. Bergman and Hotte invented a series of bogus events and fabricated several documents to support the in-transit inventory tale. Bergman later admitted in court that these efforts were intended to "fool BDO Seidman," in other words, to conceal the inventory fraud from the auditors.

The centerpiece of the in-transit inventory hoax was a $1.3 million inventory transfer that had supposedly taken place between HMI's Pittsburgh warehouse and another HMI warehouse in New York City. An HMI truck driver had allegedly left the company's Pittsburgh facility on Friday, April 28, 1995, in a company van that contained nearly $1.3 million of drugs. (These drugs were among the most expensive marketed by HMI, which explained why such a sizable dollar value of inventory could plausibly be transported in a relatively small vehicle.) Since the driver left the Pittsburgh warehouse before the inventory counting procedures were begun at that location, the drugs in the van were not included in that site's year-end physical inventory. When the truck driver arrived at the New York warehouse on the afternoon of Monday, May 1, 1995, the inventory counting had been completed at that facility.[11] So the $1.3 million of drugs were also excluded from the year-end physical inventory of the New York warehouse.

Another bogus inventory transfer of more than $500,000 accounted for the remaining portion of the year-end in-transit inventory conjured up by Bergman. These drugs had allegedly been segregated from the other pharmaceuticals in the New York warehouse and intentionally excluded from that site's year-end physical inventory. On his return trip to Pittsburgh, the truck driver had supposedly transported this $500,000 of inventory to HMI's Pittsburgh warehouse. According to Bergman's yarn, this inventory had arrived at the Pittsburgh site too late to be included in its physical inventory.

The seven HMI employees who served as accomplices in the inventory hoax included the truck driver, pharmacists who worked at the HMI warehouses, and the company controller who reported directly to Bergman. These employees were given specific instructions on what they should tell the BDO Seidman auditors regarding the year-end inventory transfers, the objective being to ensure that each conspirator's "story" was consistent with the scam as laid out by Bergman. HMI's controller subsequently testified that Tom Boyle, the audit senior who supervised the fieldwork on the 1995 HMI audit, asked him why the $1.3 million year-end inventory transfer had been necessary. "Drew Bergman basically told me what I had to tell the auditors, and I just reiterated [to Boyle] what he [Bergman] had told me."

Bergman realized that HMI's lack of a perpetual inventory system would make it difficult for BDO Seidman's auditors to uncover the inventory scam that he and Hotte had masterminded. Nevertheless, he was very concerned that BDO Seidman would perform an "inventory rollback" to substantiate the existence assertion for the in-transit inventory. In responding to a question posed by the federal judge who presided over the HMI lawsuit, Bergman explained why he was so concerned by this possibility.

> Your Honor, assuming again that I had all the information, all of the units that were sold and all of the units that were purchased for that period of time, I—you would know conclusively what the ending inventory would have been and whether this inventory in transit would have existed or did not exist.

---

11. The truck driver, who was a relative of Hotte, spent the weekend (supposedly) visiting his aunt in New Jersey, meaning that the $1.3 million of inventory was (supposedly) left unguarded in a residential driveway for more than two days.

"Oh, by the way . . ."

Mei-ya Tsai planned to begin the 1995 audit of HMI in mid-June 1995. But Drew Bergman insisted that the auditors arrive one week later than originally planned. Bergman and his confederates needed the extra week to finalize and shore up the details of the in-transit inventory ruse. The BDO Seidman audit team finally arrived at HMI's headquarters during the latter part of June. On that first day at the client's office, Tsai received a rude shock from her old friend. During a meeting with Tsai, Bergman informed her of the $1.8 million of in-transit inventory at year-end. According to Bergman, Tsai responded to that revelation with a rhetorical question: "Inventory in transit of $1,800,000?"[12] Tsai, no doubt, was alarmed by that figure since it represented nearly 20 percent of HMI's year-end inventory of $9.8 million and approximately one-half of the year-end inventory of HMI's New York warehouse. The company typically had no, or only negligible amounts of, inventory in transit at year-end. Another unusual feature of the year-end inventory transfers was that they had been transported in an HMI vehicle. The company typically used common carriers, such as United Parcel Service (UPS), to transfer significant amounts of inventory from one location to another.

Bergman testified that he only discussed the in-transit inventory on one other occasion with members of the audit engagement team. This second discussion involved Tsai and two BDO Seidman audit partners. One of those partners was Fred Bornstein, the HMI audit engagement partner, while the other partner was Warren Fisk, who served as the concurring review partner on the engagement. During this second meeting, which took place on approximately July 15, 10 days or so before the completion of the audit, Fred Bornstein chastised his former subordinate. "I [Bornstein] said how could you ever have let this happen? I said, you are an accountant, and you have been an accountant for 20 years, and you know that something like this never should have happened." Warren Fisk, who was scheduled to replace Bornstein as the HMI audit partner in 1996, told Bergman that the in-transit inventory made him "uncomfortable." Fisk informed Bergman that he and his colleagues were considering various additional tests to verify the in-transit inventory and would likely require HMI officials to sign a separate management representation letter confirming that item. Bergman recalled telling Fisk that "you have to do what you have to do."

The in-transit inventory was a key focus of the month-long 1995 audit of HMI. During the engagement, several BDO Seidman auditors questioned, investigated, and fretted over that item. Those individuals included Warren Fisk, Fred Bornstein, Mei-ya Tsai, Tom Boyle, and Jill Karnick, the semi-senior who had been assigned the primary responsibility for auditing inventory. Exhibit 1 lists the principal audit procedures BDO Seidman applied to the in-transit inventory.

Despite the inordinate time and effort BDO Seidman focused on HMI's inventory account, the audit team also wrestled with several other contentious issues during the 1995 audit. Near the end of the audit, a dispute arose between HMI management and the auditors regarding the adequacy of the allowance for doubtful accounts for the company's more than $30 million of accounts receivable. The auditors proposed an adjusting entry to increase the year-end balance of the allowance account by $1.2 million. Management insisted that an increase of only one-half of that amount was necessary. Complicating BDO Seidman's decision regarding whether to accept

---

12. The trial in the HMI case took place in October 1999, more than four years after the 1995 audit was completed. Not surprisingly, the witnesses in the case often had differing recollections of key events that occurred during that audit. Mei-ya Tsai testified that she first learned of the in-transit inventory from Tom Boyle, the audit senior assigned to the 1995 HMI audit. According to Tsai's testimony, early in the audit Boyle called her at BDO Seidman's Long Island office and informed her of the in-transit inventory.

EXHIBIT 1

AUDIT PROCEDURES
APPLIED BY BDO
SEIDMAN TO
HMI'S IN-TRANSIT
INVENTORY

1. Requested the usual documentation that HMI prepared for all inventory transfers.

2. Verified that the inventory transfer documents were signed by both the shipping and receiving pharmacists, identified on the documents the pharmaceuticals reportedly included in the transfers, confirmed that the quantities and per unit prices of those pharmaceuticals agreed with the information previously provided to the auditors by HMI management.

3. Interviewed the truck driver who allegedly transported the year-end inventory transfers. Compared his chronology of the relevant events with the inventory transfer documents and found no inconsistencies.

4. Examined the expense report filed by the truck driver and found it consistent with his chronology of the relevant events and the chronology of those events provided by other HMI personnel.

5. Discussed the inventory transfers with HMI's controller who provided a credible explanation for why the transfers were necessary.

6. Discussed the inventory transfers with HMI's CFO (Bergman) who indicated that he had not been able to prevent the transfers because he had not learned of them until after the fact.

7. Used various mathematical tests, including a gross profit percentage test, to challenge the reasonableness of the company's total year-end inventory; these tests suggested that the year-end inventory was reasonable.

8. Obtained a standard management representations letter and a separate representation letter from company officials focusing exclusively on the in-transit inventory; each of these letters confirmed the existence of the in-transit inventory.

Source: Trial brief prepared for BDO Seidman *In Re Health Management, Inc. Securities Litigation*, U.S. District Court, Eastern District of New York, Civil Action No. 96-CV-889 (ADS) (ARL).

the client's proposed adjustment was a letter of inquiry the audit firm had received from the SEC several months earlier. In that letter, the SEC had expressed concern and requested information concerning the method HMI was using to arrive at its allowance for doubtful accounts. Despite the unusual nature of that inquiry, an expert witness for the plaintiffs testified that he found no reference to it in BDO Seidman's 1995 workpapers, nor any evidence that the auditors had modified their audit procedures for the allowance account as a result of the inquiry.

After considerable discussion with HMI's officers, Fred Bornstein decided to accept the client's proposed adjustment of $600,000 for the allowance account. Bornstein provided the following justification for that decision during testimony in the HMI lawsuit: "First of all, it is the client's financial statements. It is not our financial statements. Secondly, we may not be right all the time. The client looks at them [proposed audit adjustments] and decides which ones he agrees with and which ones he doesn't agree with. It is a give and take. And as long as we are satisfied with the client's explanation . . . [we accept the client's decisions regarding those adjustments]."

Another problem the HMI audit team faced during the 1995 engagement was an earnings release issued by the company approximately one week prior to the date that the fieldwork was begun. That press release reported HMI's anticipated, post-audit net income, a figure that had been materially inflated by the fraudulent inventory scheme. This earnings release distressed Mei-ya Tsai and her superiors.

Although not required to do so, client executives customarily delay such press releases until their auditors are fairly certain that the anticipated earnings figure is a "firm" number. A company that reports its earnings before the completion of the annual audit exerts subtle but significant pressure on the auditors to "pass" on proposed adjustments that would materially reduce the prematurely released earnings figure. If the auditors insist that a lower earnings figure be included in the audited financial statements, the resulting "earnings surprise" may cause a sharp drop in the client's stock price.

Apparently even more distressing to BDO Seidman than the SEC's inquiry regarding HMI's allowance for doubtful accounts and the client's premature earnings release was an anonymous letter the audit firm received in May 1995. That letter criticized certain HMI accounting procedures and suggested the company was misleading financial analysts tracking the company's stock. The letter also charged that BDO Seidman's independence was being undermined by a close friendship involving Drew Bergman and an undisclosed member of the audit engagement team. (As discussed during the trial, Mei-ya Tsai was the auditor alluded to by the letter.) During subsequent court testimony, Fred Bornstein revealed that in his 30 years of professional audit experience he had never received such a letter. Bornstein reported that he discussed the letter's contents during a meeting with the individuals assigned to the 1995 HMI audit. But neither during that meeting nor afterwards did Bornstein directly ask individual members of the audit team whether they had a relationship with Bergman that would impair their independence.

BDO Seidman completed the 1995 HMI audit in late July. Similar to the audit opinions issued by the firm in previous years on HMI's financial statements, the 1995 audit opinion was unqualified. In December 1995, Drew Bergman was given a new title at HMI, Corporate Development Officer.[13] Paul Jurewicz, an individual with considerable accounting experience in the healthcare industry, was hired to replace Bergman as HMI's CFO. Shortly after he joined HMI, Jurewicz was having a casual conversation with the company's controller, one of Bergman and Hotte's co-conspirators. During that conversation, the controller matter-of-factly referred to the inventory fraud, believing that Jurewicz was aware of it. According to the controller, Jurewicz "turned white as a ghost" and abruptly ended the conversation. Immediately, the controller knew the "gig was up."

Jurewicz informed Clifford Hotte of the information he had accidentally obtained from the controller. Hotte denied any knowledge of the inventory fraud and refused to refer the matter to other members of HMI's board or the company's legal counsel. Jurewicz then took matters into his own hands and informed the company's legal counsel. In short order, the company's board retained the services of a former federal prosecutor to investigate the alleged inventory fraud. In February 1996, HMI issued a press release indicating that irregularities had been discovered in the company's accounting records. That press release sent HMI's stock price spiraling downward and prompted BDO Seidman to withdraw its audit opinion on the company's 1995 financial statements. Next, a flurry of lawsuits and criminal indictments swamped HMI, its corporate officers, and other parties associated with the 1995 financial statements.

Federal prosecutors filed a litany of fraud charges against Clifford Hotte and his co-conspirators. In exchange for agreeing to testify against Hotte and the other

---

13. Effective May 1, 1995, HMI's board of directors had more than doubled Bergman's annual salary to $200,000.

conspirators, Drew Bergman was granted immunity from prosecution.[14] Hotte's initial trial ended in a hung jury. Throughout that first trial, Hotte insisted that Bergman had been responsible for the fraudulent inventory scheme. But, in a second trial, a jury convicted Hotte of 14 counts of conspiracy and securities fraud. The former CEO was sentenced to nine years in federal prison, ordered to pay a $250,000 fine, and to make $9.6 million of restitution to the victims of the inventory hoax. HMI never recovered from the trauma inflicted on it by Bergman and Hotte. In October 1997, another healthcare firm acquired HMI for a nominal amount.

The class-action securities lawsuit filed against BDO Seidman by more than 4,000 HMI stockholders initially included several defendants, most of whom were Hotte and Bergman's co-conspirators. Those co-conspirators reached out-of-court settlements and were dismissed from the lawsuit. Bergman was also dismissed from the lawsuit after agreeing to testify truthfully regarding the HMI inventory fraud and other relevant events and circumstances during his tenure at HMI. The two remaining defendants were Hotte and BDO Seidman. Judge Arthur Spatt, who presided over the HMI case, ordered a "directed verdict" against Hotte, who refused to participate in the trial after invoking his Fifth Amendment rights against self-incrimination. As a result, BDO Seidman took center stage as the sole defendant in the class-action lawsuit. The attorneys for HMI's stockholders claimed that the inventory fraud had cost their clients approximately $37 million and that BDO Seidman was responsible for 75 percent of those damages.

As suggested earlier, prior to the passage of the PSLRA, large accounting firms were reluctant to "gamble" that a jury would resolve a class-action lawsuit in their favor. But the team of attorneys retained by BDO Seidman believed the PSLRA gave their client a very reasonable chance of prevailing in court. BDO Seidman followed those attorneys' advice and "rolled the dice." The large accounting firm lost its first gamble when Judge Spatt ruled that the plaintiffs had made sufficiently credible and specific allegations to allow the case to proceed to trial.

Red Flags & Crooks

The skilled teams of attorneys retained by the plaintiffs and defendants in the HMI lawsuit faced many challenges in representing their clients. One of those challenges was shared by both teams of attorneys. The jury that would decide the outcome of the case was composed principally of individuals from blue-collar backgrounds, that is, individuals who had little familiarity with the complex accounting issues, financial reporting matters, and capital market phenomena that would be discussed during the trial. To clarify and strengthen their arguments, each team of attorneys retained prominent expert witnesses to testify during the trial. Plaintiff counsel hired a CPA specializing in forensic services to identify and explain alleged deficiencies in BDO Seidman's audit procedures. To refute much of that individual's testimony, the defense attorneys relied on a former member of the Auditing Standards Board. Each team of attorneys also hired a damages expert to estimate the losses suffered by the HMI stockholders who had filed the lawsuit. According to the trial transcripts, the two teams paid these expert witnesses approximately $600,000 in total. That amount was four times larger than the approximately $140,000 BDO Seidman received for performing the 1995 HMI audit.

Each team of attorneys went into the trial with a well-rehearsed "game plan." The principal objective of the plaintiff attorneys was to convince the jury that the

---

14. Drew Bergman was sanctioned by the SEC. The federal agency barred him from serving as an officer or director of a public company and fined him approximately $75,000.

auditors, at a minimum, had recklessly ignored the auditing profession's technical standards during the 1995 audit and that this reckless conduct had prevented them from uncovering the inventory fraud. To paint a "reckless" image of the auditors in the minds of the jurors, the plaintiff attorneys repeatedly drew attention to the red flags the auditors had allegedly overlooked or, at least, slighted during the 1995 HMI audit. These red flags included, among other items, the SEC's inquiry regarding HMI's allowance for doubtful accounts, the premature press release reporting the company's 1995 earnings, the allegations included in the anonymous letter that BDO Seidman received before the beginning of the 1995 audit, and the suspicious circumstances surrounding the in-transit inventory at year-end.

The plaintiff attorneys faced two major problems in presenting their case to the jury. First, they were forced to use Drew Bergman as their principal witness to attack the credibility and professionalism of the BDO Seidman auditors. Since Bergman admitted on the stand that he had been a primary architect of HMI's inventory fraud, the jury had an obvious reason to question his credibility.

A second and related challenge facing plaintiff counsel was to divert the jury's attention away from the flagrantly criminal conduct of Bergman, Hotte, and the other conspirators who had carried out the inventory fraud. Because of the PSLRA's proportionate liability rule, the plaintiff attorneys had to convince the jury that the BDO Seidman auditors had been reckless during the 1995 HMI audit *and* that they were responsible for a large proportion of the losses suffered by HMI's stockholders. A possible outcome of the trial would be the jury finding the auditors reckless but then concluding that they were responsible for only a negligible percentage of the stockholder losses. Throughout the trial, the plaintiff attorneys struggled with the awkward task of having Bergman describe the fraud that he had designed, while attempting to convince the jury that BDO Seidman was responsible for the bulk of the stockholder losses resulting from that fraud.

The team of defense attorneys led by Michael Young used a three-prong strategy during the trial to help their client prevail. First, at every opportunity, Young and his colleagues attempted to portray the auditors as victims of the inventory fraud rather than as "reckless" accomplices of Bergman and Hotte. Young and the other defense attorneys drew repeated and stark contrasts between the BDO Seidman auditors and the HMI conspirators. In his opening statement, Michael Young introduced the jury one by one to the four BDO Seidman auditors seated in the courtroom who had been deeply involved in the 1995 audit. "Next, I would like to introduce Mei-ya Tsai . . . [She] lives in Bellmore with her husband and two children." This tactic was apparently meant to convey to the jury members that the auditors were similar to themselves: hard working, family-oriented individuals who lived in local communities. In contrast, when referring to the participants in the HMI fraud, the defense counsel often invoked derisive epithets such as "those crooks" or "those liars." Near the end of the trial, one of the defense attorneys told the jury members that they had to "distinguish between the liars, and those who were lied to."

A second strategy of the defense counsel was to repeatedly "thump the bible" of the auditing profession, that is, the professional auditing standards. Young and his cohorts constantly challenged the plaintiff attorneys and their witnesses to identify specific requirements in the professional standards that the auditors had violated. The defense attorneys charged that the allegations filed against the auditors were based upon abstract and largely indefensible interpretations of those standards.

The final feature of the defense counsel's trial strategy was intended to blunt the repeated allegations of the plaintiff attorneys that BDO Seidman had failed to properly investigate the $1.8 million of in-transit inventory. Throughout the trial, the defense attorneys used a phrase to characterize the auditors' consideration of that item: "But they didn't stop there." On several occasions when the plaintiff attorneys focused the jurors' attention on the bogus in-transit inventory, the defense attorneys responded by using a flip chart to sequentially and forcefully list the series of audit tests and other procedures shown in Exhibit 1 that the auditors had used to corroborate the year-end inventory transfers. After each audit test or procedure was explained, the defense attorneys would typically turn to the jury and remark, "But they didn't stop there"—before proceeding to a discussion of the next item.

The Trial: Rollbacks and Relationships

The two most contentious issues that arose during the trial centered on whether the auditors should have completed an inventory rollback during the 1995 HMI audit and whether the relationship between Drew Bergman and Mei-ya Tsai impaired BDO Seidman's independence. As noted earlier, Bergman feared that the auditors would perform an inventory rollback to test the reasonableness of the $1.8 million of in-transit inventory. The CPA who testified as an expert witness for the plaintiff attorneys insisted that had the auditors completed an inventory rollback, they would have determined that the in-transit inventory had never existed.

> Mr. Fox (plaintiff attorney): *Have you seen any evidence that BDO Seidman even attempted to do any tests which resemble an inventory rollback?*
>
> Mr. Moore (plaintiff expert witness): *Not that was included in the workpapers, no.*
>
> Mr. Fox: *And do you have an opinion about whether BDO Seidman could have done an inventory roll back in this case?*
>
> Mr. Moore: *Yes, I do.*
>
> Mr. Fox: *And what is that opinion?*
>
> Mr. Moore: *I think it would have been very easy to do. They could have done a rollback. And it was the only test that would have substantiated without a doubt whether or not the in-transit inventory existed.*
>
> Mr. Fox: *If an inventory rollback was performed by BDO Seidman, what would it have shown?*
>
> Mr. Moore: *It would have shown that the in-transit inventory didn't exist and couldn't have existed.*

The expert witness then used a flip chart presentation to walk the jury through an example of how an inventory rollback is performed. Instead of completing an inventory rollback, the expert witness charged BDO Seidman with applying an "audit by conversation" approach to the in-transit inventory. That is, the expert charged that the auditors relied heavily on client representations to support the existence of that inventory.

Michael Young bluntly contested the expert witness's assertion that BDO Seidman should have performed an inventory rollback. Young began by getting the witness to agree that generally accepted auditing standards (GAAS) are the accepted benchmark for assessing the work of independent auditors. Young then produced a bound copy of those standards.

> Mr. Young: *This is the bible?*
>
> Mr. Moore: *Basically for auditors, yes.*
>
> Mr. Young: *Okay. There is no section of this book—there is no section of generally accepted auditing standards—entitled "in-transit inventory," is there?*
>
> Mr. Moore: *No. There is only a section entitled inventory that we have already discussed.*
>
> Mr. Young: *Right. It doesn't tell you exactly how to go about testing in-transit inventory, does it?*

Following these exchanges, Young quoted the following section of the auditing standards: "The independent auditor must exercise his judgment in determining which auditing procedures to apply." Young maintained that this statement demonstrated that the members of the HMI engagement team were well within their rights as professional auditors to decide whether or not to perform an inventory rollback during the 1995 audit. Young was still not satisfied the jury recognized that the expert witness's opinion regarding the need for an inventory rollback during the 1995 audit was just that—one man's opinion. So, in a subsequent exchange, Young pointedly asked the witness: "Now, is it fair to say that this notion that generally accepted auditing standards required an inventory rollback is just something you made up?" The witness responded with a firm "No." Young then handed the witness a copy of the bound auditing standards and asked him to identify the phrase "inventory roll back" in the alphabetical index of those standards. Of course, Young realized that phrase was not included in the index.

Mr. Young: *Is it fair to say that the reference to rollback appears nowhere in the "bible"?*

Mr. Moore: *Yes.*

Mr. Young: *So, basically, it all boils down to your opinion that the auditors should have done more [that is, an inventory rollback]; is that correct?*

Mr. Moore: *Yes.*

Later in the trial, Jill Karnick, the BDO Seidman semi-senior who had been assigned the primary responsibility for auditing HMI's inventory account, took the witness stand. Karnick surprised the jury when she revealed that, in fact, she had attempted during the audit to perform an "inventory rollforward," which is essentially equivalent to an inventory rollback.[15] After spending three days on this task, Karnick became frustrated and decided not to continue. She testified that the volume of inventory purchases and sales was simply too large to allow her to complete the rollforward. Karnick was then asked why there was no indication in the audit workpapers that an inventory rollforward had been attempted. She replied that it was "normal practice" to discard the results of "inconclusive" audit tests.

Another surprising revelation made by Karnick during her testimony was that she never spoke directly to either Mei-ya Tsai, the audit manager on the 1995 HMI audit, or Fred Bornstein, the audit engagement partner, regarding the in-transit inventory.

Mr. Strauss   (plaintiff attorney): *Ms. Karnick, isn't it true you never spoke to your superior, Mei-ya Tsai, about the in-transit inventory?*

Ms. Karnick: *Face to face verbally, no, that's true.*

Mr. Strauss: *In fact, isn't it true that Mei-ya Tsai never even asked you to do anything concerning inventory in-transit?*

Ms. Karnick: *Not directly, no.*

Mr. Strauss: *And Mr. Bornstein never instructed you to do anything relating to inventory in-transit either, did he?*

Ms. Karnick: *Not directly, no.*

Mr. Strauss: *So, the two most senior people on the audit, the partner and the senior manager never spoke to you about, or instructed you to do anything concerning inventory in-transit. Correct?*

Ms. Karnick: *Yes.*

---

15. Ms. Karnick attempted to roll the April 30, 1994, inventory forward to April 30, 1995, by using inventory purchases and sales data for that 12-month period.

On cross-examination, Michael Young had Karnick clarify that it was BDO Seidman's policy for semi-seniors to receive their work instructions and be supervised by their immediate superior on an audit engagement. During the 1995 HMI audit, Tom Boyle, the audit senior assigned to that engagement, had supervised Karnick. In his brief time on the witness stand, Boyle reported that he had only a "limited role" in auditing inventory during the HMI audit. "Jill [Karnick] dealt mostly directly with Mei-ya Tsai on that, as I was out in the field being Jill's supervisor. . . . I would provide guidance basically as to the questions she had." (The fact that this testimony seemed at odds with Karnick's assertion that she never spoke directly to Tsai regarding the in-transit inventory was apparently not addressed by either the plaintiff or defendant attorneys.)

Of all the issues raised during the trial, the one that had the most pervasive implications was the question of whether the close friendship between Drew Bergman and Mei-ya Tsai had impaired BDO Seidman's independence during the 1995 HMI audit. The auditing profession has long maintained that independence is the cornerstone of the independent audit function. If a key member of an audit team loses his or her independence, then all other issues or questions regarding the quality or integrity of the given audit become moot.

The CPA who served as an expert witness for the plaintiffs testified that he believed the social relationship between Bergman and Tsai violated the independence standard included in GAAS: "In all matters relating to the assignment, an independence of mental attitude is to be maintained by the auditor or auditors." According to the expert witness, the Bergman-Tsai friendship "made it extremely difficult to maintain a real level of professional skepticism on the part of the auditor [Ms. Tsai] in looking at the financial statements of HMI." More to the point, the expert witness believed the friendship of the two individuals would have prevented Tsai from going to Bergman after uncovering the inventory scam and telling him, "I think you are a thief, I think you are a fraud."

During her testimony, Mei-ya Tsai acknowledged that BDO Seidman's policy and procedures manual commented on independence concerns posed by social or personal relationships between auditors and officers of a client. A related issue arising during her testimony was that at some point during 1995 she had been offered the position of chief accounting officer (CAO) at HMI, an offer she eventually turned down. Tsai testified that she was unclear regarding the timing of the offer.

Mr. Strauss (plaintiff attorney): *Isn't it true, Ms. Tsai, that during the 1995 audit, you were being considered for the chief accounting officer position at Health Management?*

Ms. Tsai: *At one time. I don't remember exactly when the job offer was made to me.*

Mr. Strauss: *And you were being considered for that job during the 1995 audit; isn't that correct?*

Ms. Tsai: *I don't know the timing.*

Mr. Strauss: *Isn't it—*

Ms. Tsai: *Definitely not during the audit, no.*

Mr. Strauss: *Isn't it true that your friend, Drew Bergman, recommended you for that job during the 1995 audit?*

Ms. Tsai: *As I said, I don't know the timing. But it can't be during the audit.*

Mr. Strauss: *You are sure of that?*

Ms. Tsai: *I don't believe it's during the audit.*

Later in the trial, the plaintiff attorneys introduced evidence indicating that Drew Bergman apparently recommended that Tsai be offered the CAO position during an HMI board meeting that took place on July 20, 1995. That was one week prior to the date of the audit report issued by BDO Seidman on HMI's 1995 financial statements.

Michael Young resorted to one of his key defense strategies when tackling the contentious question of whether the Bergman–Tsai friendship impaired BDO Seidman's independence. While cross-examining Mr. Moore, the plaintiff's expert witness, Young once more handed him a bound copy of the profession's auditing standards and a copy of the *AICPA Code of Professional Conduct* and asked: "Would you please read to the jury the part where it says that an auditor may not be friends with an audit client?" Moore replied that those "specific words" were not included in either item. Young then asked Moore another question: "Isn't it possible for a representative of an audit firm to be social friends with a representative of a client company and for the audit firm to still be independent? Is that possible, Mr. Moore?" Moore grudgingly replied, "It's possible."

Once the testimony in a jury trial is complete, the presiding judge must give the jury detailed instructions for them to follow during their deliberations. Near the completion of the HMI trial, the two teams of attorneys spent three days debating before Judge Spatt—in the absence of the jury—the information that should be included in the jury instructions. The key issue facing Judge Spatt was how to define "recklessness" in the jury instructions. Both sets of attorneys realized that the outcome of the trial might hinge on Judge Spatt's definition of that critical term. Judge Spatt eventually settled on the following description of recklessness: "The plaintiff must prove that there was an egregious refusal to see the obvious or to investigate the doubtful, or that the auditing judgments made were such that no reasonable auditor would have made the same decision if confronted with the same facts."

The Verdict

During the jury's deliberations, the jury foreman sent a note to Judge Spatt asking for further clarification of the term "recklessness." Judge Spatt then brought the jury members back into the courtroom and gave them additional instructions. Judge Spatt reiterated the important distinction between negligence and recklessness: "I want to make clear that an auditor is not liable under Section 10(b) and Rule 10b-5 [of the Securities Exchange Act of 1934] merely because he or she made a mistake or was merely negligent. I repeat, recklessness is more than mere negligence. Reckless conduct represents grossly unreasonable or rash behavior."

Shortly after being sequestered once more, the jury arrived at its verdict in favor of BDO Seidman. In celebrating the victory, Michael Young commented on the PSLRA's impact on the case: "It is questionable whether an accounting firm could muster the courage to take a case like this to trial absent the innovations under the Reform Act."[16] Young went on to explain that the PSLRA's elimination of joint and several liability for auditors guilty of no more than recklessness was the principal source of BDO Seidman's "courage" to defend itself in court.

Jeffrey Zwerling, one of the plaintiff attorneys, spoke with several of the jurors following the trial.[17] Zwerling reported that the jurors had difficulty grasping the legal

---

16. M. Riccardi, "Accounting Fraud Trial Breaks New Ground," *New York Law Journal*, 29 October 1999, 1.

17. E. L. Rosen, "Defendants Heartened by the First Trial of PSLRA Case," *The National Law Journal*, 15 November 1999, B5.

definition of recklessness even after asking Judge Spatt to clarify that term. Zwerling implied that confusion might have predisposed the jury to rule in favor of the auditors. BDO Seidman's general legal counsel put a different "spin" on the outcome of the trial. He maintained that the plaintiff attorneys' strategy of relying on Drew Bergman's testimony "blew up in their faces" since Bergman admitted during the trial that he had specifically designed the fraud to deceive the auditors.[18]

Despite the favorable outcome of the HMI lawsuit for BDO Seidman, the post-PSLRA litigation trends have been mixed for the public accounting profession. Since 1995, class-action securities lawsuits have trended downward on an annual basis when expressed as a percentage of the total number of public companies.[19] However, the percentage of such lawsuits predicated on accounting irregularities has generally risen since 1995. This is bad news for auditors since they are more likely to be named as defendants in a class-action securities lawsuit when a client is charged with manipulating its accounting records. More bad news for audit firms: The average settlement paid to resolve class-action lawsuits involving charges of accounting irregularities has also been rising.

Questions

1. BDO Seidman's attorneys pointed out correctly that professional standards do not prohibit auditors and client personnel from being "friends." At what point do such relationships result in violations of the auditor independence rules and guidelines? Provide hypothetical examples to strengthen your answer.

2. According to court testimony, on July 20, 1995, Drew Bergman recommended to HMI's board of directors that Mei-ya Tsai be hired as the company's chief accounting officer (CAO). One week later, BDO Seidman issued its audit report on HMI's 1995 financial statements. Under presently existing professional standards, would this situation have presented an independence "problem" for BDO Seidman? Defend your answer.

3. Under what circumstances is an inventory rollback or rollfoward typically performed? How valid is the evidence yielded by this audit procedure? Explain.

4. Jill Karnick abandoned her attempt to complete an inventory rollforward because of the considerable amount of work the procedure involved. Do you believe she made an appropriate decision given the circumstances she faced? How should auditors weigh the cost of an audit procedure, in terms of time and other resources, against the quantity and quality of evidence that it yields?

5. Should the results of inconclusive audit tests be included in audit workpapers? Defend your answer.

6. A major focus of the trial in this case was BDO Seidman's consideration of, and response to, the "red flags" apparent during the 1995 HMI audit. Define or describe the phrase "red flags." Explain the impact of red flags identified by auditors on each major phase of an audit.

---

18. E. MacDonald, "Federal Jury Exonerates BDO Seidman in Accounting Suit over Audit of Firm," *The Wall Street Journal*, 28 October 1999, B2.

19. An exception to this trend was 2001. The bursting of the "dot-com" bubble in the stock market triggered an unusually large number of class-action securities lawsuits in that year. Likewise, there was a modest spike in such lawsuits in 2009 and 2010 as a consequence of the worldwide economic crisis linked to the subprime mortgage industry in the United States.

7. The PSLRA requires auditors to report to the SEC illegal acts "that would have a material effect" on a client's financial statements, assuming client management refuses to do so. Briefly describe three hypothetical situations involving potential illegal acts discovered by auditors. Indicate whether the auditors involved in these situations should insist that client management report the given item to the SEC. Defend your decision for each item.

The Leslie Fay Companies

Paul Polishan graduated with an accounting degree in 1969 and immediately accepted an entry-level position in the accounting department of The Leslie Fay Companies, a women's apparel manufacturer based in New York City. Fred Pomerantz, Leslie Fay's founder, personally hired Polishan. Company insiders recall that Pomerantz saw in the young accounting graduate many of the same traits that he possessed. Both men were ambitious, hard driving, and impetuous by nature.

After joining Leslie Fay, Polishan quickly struck up a relationship with John Pomerantz, the son of the company's founder. John had joined the company in 1960 after earning an economics degree from the Wharton School at the University of Pennsylvania. In 1972, the younger Pomerantz became Leslie Fay's president and assumed responsibility for the company's day-to-day operations. Over the next few years, Polishan would become one of John Pomerantz's most trusted allies within the company. Polishan quickly rose through the ranks of Leslie Fay, eventually becoming the company's chief financial officer (CFO) and senior vice president of finance.

Leslie Fay's corporate headquarters were located in the heart of Manhattan's bustling garment district. The company's accounting offices, however, were 100 miles to the northwest in Wilkes-Barre, Pennsylvania. During Polishan's tenure as Leslie Fay's top accounting and finance officer, the Wilkes-Barre location was tagged with the nickname "Poliworld."

The strict and autocratic Polishan ruled the Wilkes-Barre site with an iron fist. When closing the books at the end of an accounting period, Polishan often required his subordinates to put in 16-hour shifts and to work through the weekend. Arriving two minutes late for work exposed Poliworld inhabitants to a scathing reprimand from the CFO. To make certain that his employees understood what he expected of them, Polishan posted a list of rules within the Wilkes-Barre offices that documented their rights and privileges in minute detail. For example, they had the right to place one, and only one, family photo on their desks. Even Leslie Fay personnel in the company's Manhattan headquarters had to cope with Polishan's domineering manner. When senior managers in the headquarters office requested financial information from Wilkes-Barre, Polishan often sent them a note demanding to know why they needed the information.

Polishan's top lieutenant at the Wilkes-Barre site was the company controller, Donald Kenia. On Polishan's frequent trips to Manhattan, Kenia assumed control of the accounting offices. Unlike his boss, Kenia was a soft-spoken individual who apparently enjoyed following orders much more than giving them. Because of Kenia's meek personality, friends and coworkers were stunned in early February 1993 when he took full responsibility for a large accounting fraud revealed to the press by John Pomerantz. Investigators subsequently determined that Leslie Fay's earnings had been overstated by approximately $80 million from 1990 through 1992.

Following the public disclosure of the large fraud, John Pomerantz repeatedly and adamantly insisted that he and the other top executives of Leslie Fay, including Paul Polishan, had been unaware of the massive accounting irregularities perpetrated by Kenia. Nevertheless, many parties inside and outside the company expressed doubts regarding Pomerantz's indignant denials. Kenia was not a major stockholder and did not have an incentive-based compensation contract tied to the company's earnings, meaning that he had not benefited directly from the grossly inflated earnings figures he had manufactured. On the other hand, Pomerantz, Polishan, and several other Leslie Fay executives held large blocks of the company's stock and had received substantial year-end bonuses, in some cases bonuses larger than their annual salaries, as a result of Kenia's alleged scam.

Even after Kenia pleaded guilty to fraud charges, many third parties remained unconvinced that he had directed the fraud. When asked by a reporter to comment on Kenia's confession, a Leslie Fay employee and close friend of Kenia indicated that he was a "straight arrow, a real decent guy" and then went on to observe that, "something doesn't add up here."[1]

Lipstick-Red Rolls Royces and the Orient Express

Similar to many of his peers, Fred Pomerantz served his country during World War II. But instead of storming the beaches of Normandy or pursuing Rommel across North Africa, Pomerantz had served his country by making uniforms—uniforms for the Women's Army Corps. Following the war, Pomerantz decided to make use of the skills he had acquired in the military by creating a company to manufacture women's dresses. He named the company after his daughter, Leslie Fay.

Pomerantz's former subordinates and colleagues in the industry recall that he was a "character." Over the years, he reportedly developed a strong interest in gambling, enjoyed throwing extravagant parties, and reveled in shocking new friends and business associates by pulling up his shirt to reveal knife scars he had collected in encounters with ruffians in some of New York's tougher neighborhoods. Adding to Pomerantz's legend within the top rung of New York's high society was his lipstick-red Rolls Royce that he used to cruise up and down Manhattan's crowded streets.

Pomerantz's penchant for adventure and revelry did not prevent him from quickly establishing his company as a key player in the volatile and intensely competitive women's apparel industry. From the beginning, Pomerantz focused Leslie Fay on one key segment of that industry. He and his designers developed moderately priced and stylishly conservative dresses for women aged 30 through 55.

Leslie Fay's principal customers were the large department store chains that flourished in major metropolitan areas in the decades following World War II. By the late 1980s, Leslie Fay was the largest supplier of women's dresses to department stores. At the time, Leslie Fay's principal competitors included Donna Karan, Oscar de la Renta, Nichole Miller, Jones New York, and Albert Nipon. But, in the minds of most industry observers, Liz Claiborne, an upstart company that had been founded in 1976 by an unknown designer and her husband, easily ranked as Leslie Fay's closest and fiercest rival. Liz Claiborne was the only publicly owned women's apparel manufacturer in the late 1980s that had larger annual sales than Leslie Fay.

Fred Pomerantz took his company public in 1952. In the early 1980s, the company went private for a period of several years via a leveraged buyout orchestrated by John Pomerantz, who became the company's CEO and chairman of the board following his father's death in 1982. The younger Pomerantz pocketed $40 million and a large bundle of Leslie Fay stock when the firm re-emerged as a public company in 1986.

Like his father before him, John Pomerantz believed that the top executive of a company involved in the world of fashion should exhibit a certain amount of panache. As a result, the popular and outgoing businessman invested in several Broadway shows

---

1. S. Strom, "Accounting Scandal at Leslie Fay," *The New York Times*, 2 February 1993, D1.

and became a mainstay on Manhattan's celebrity circuit. The windfall that Pomerantz realized in the early 1980s allowed him to buy an elegant, Mediterranean-style estate in Palm Beach, Florida, where he often consorted during the winter months with New York City's rich and famous. To reward his company's best clients, he once rented the legendary Orient Express for a festive railway jaunt from Paris to Istanbul.

Despite Leslie Fay's size and prominence in the apparel industry, John Pomerantz continued operating the company much like his father had for decades. Unlike his competitors, Pomerantz shunned extensive market testing to gauge women's changing tastes in clothes. Instead, he relied on his and his designers' intuition in developing each season's new offerings. Pomerantz was also slow to integrate computers into his company's key internal functions. Long after most women apparel manufacturers had developed computer networks to monitor daily sales of their products at major customer outlets, Leslie Fay officials continued to track the progress of their sales by telephoning large customers on a weekly basis. Pomerantz's insistence on doing business the "old-fashioned way" also meant that the company's Wilkes-Barre location was slow to take advantage of the speed and efficiency of computerized data processing.

Management's aversion to modern business practices and the intense competition within the women's apparel industry did not prevent Leslie Fay from prospering after John Pomerantz succeeded his father. Thanks to the younger Pomerantz's business skills, Leslie Fay's annual revenues and earnings grew robustly under his leadership.

Fashion Becomes Unfashionable

By the late 1980s, a trend that had been developing within the women's apparel industry for several years became even more evident. During that decade, fashion gradually became unfashionable. The so-called "casualization" of America meant that millions of consumers began balking at the new designs marketed by apparel manufacturers, opting instead for denims, t-shirts, and other more comfortable attire, including well-worn, if not tattered, garments that they had purchased years earlier. Initially, this trend had a much more pronounced impact on the buying habits of younger women. But, gradually, even women in the 30 to 55-year-old age bracket, the consumers targeted by Leslie Fay, decided that casual was the way to go.

The trend toward casual clothing had the most dramatic impact on women's dress sales. Since Leslie Fay's inception, the company had concentrated its product offerings on dresses, even after pantsuits became widely recognized as suitable and stylish for women of all ages during the 1970s. In the early 1970s, annual dress sales began gradually declining. Most corporate executives in the women's apparel industry believed this trend would eventually reverse. The preference for more casual apparel that developed during the 1980s, however, resulted in declining dress sales throughout the end of the century.

The recession of the late 1980s and early 1990s compounded the problems facing the women's apparel industry. That recession caused many consumers to curtail their discretionary expenditures, including purchases of new clothes. The economy-wide decline in retail spending had particularly far-reaching implications for the nation's major department store chains, Leslie Fay's principal customers.

Even as other segments of the economy improved, continued weakness in the retail sector cut deeply into the sales and earnings of department stores. Eventually, several large chains were forced to merge with competitors or to liquidate. In late 1989, Leslie Fay incurred a substantial loss when it wrote off a receivable from Allied/Federated Department Stores after the large retailer filed for bankruptcy. Many of the department store chains that survived wrangled financial concessions from their suppliers. These concessions included longer payment terms, more lenient return policies, and increased financial assistance to develop and maintain in-store displays, kiosks, and apparel boutiques.

The structural and economic changes affecting the women's apparel industry during the late 1980s and early 1990s had a major impact on most of its leading companies. Even Liz Claiborne, whose revenues had zoomed from $47 million in 1979 to more than $1 billion by 1987, faced slowing sales from its major product lines and was eventually forced to take large inventory write-downs. Occasionally, industry publications reported modest quarterly sales increases. But the companies that benefited the most from those increases were not the leading apparel manufacturers but rather firms such as Clothestime that marketed their wares to discount merchandisers.

Despite the trauma being experienced by its key competitors, Leslie Fay reported impressive sales and earnings throughout the late 1980s and early 1990s. Leslie Fay's typical quarterly earnings release during that timeframe indicated that the company had posted record earnings and sales for the just completed period. For example, in October 1991, John Pomerantz announced that Leslie Fay had achieved record earnings for the third quarter of the year despite the "continued sluggishness in retail sales and consumer spending."[2]

Exhibit 1 presents Leslie Fay's consolidated balance sheets and income statements for 1987 through 1991. For comparison purposes, Exhibit 2 presents norms for key financial ratios within the women's apparel industry in 1991. These benchmark ratios are composite amounts derived from data reported by the investment services that publish financial ratios and other financial measures for major industries.

The gregarious John Pomerantz remained upbeat with the business press regarding his company's future prospects even as Leslie Fay's competitors questioned how the company was able to sustain strong sales and earnings in the face of the stubborn recession gripping the retail sector. Privately, though, Pomerantz was worried. Pomerantz realized that retailers were increasingly critical of Leslie Fay's product line. "Old-fashioned," "matronly," "drab," and "overpriced" were adjectives that the company's sales reps routinely heard as they made their sales calls.

To keep his major customers happy, Pomerantz had to approve significant markdowns in Leslie Fay's wholesale prices and grant those customers large rebates when they found themselves "stuck" with excess quantities of the company's products. To keep investors happy, Pomerantz lobbied financial analysts tracking Leslie Fay's stock. One analyst reported that an "irate" Pomerantz called her in 1992 and chastised her for issuing an earnings forecast for Leslie Fay that was too "pessimistic."[3]

"Houston, We Have a Problem"

On Friday morning, January 29, 1993, Paul Polishan called John Pomerantz who was on a business trip in Canada. Polishan told Pomerantz, "We got a problem . . . maybe a little more than just a problem."[4] Polishan then informed his boss of the enormous accounting hoax that Donald Kenia had secretively carried out over the past several years. According to Polishan, Kenia had admitted to masterminding the fraud, although some of his subordinates had helped him implement and conceal the various scams. Pomerantz's first reaction to the startling news? Disbelief. "I thought it was a joke."[5]

When revealing the fraud to the press the following Monday, Pomerantz denied having any clue as to what might have motivated Kenia to misrepresent Leslie Fay's

2. *Business Wire*, "Leslie Fay Announces Record Earnings," 17 October 1991.

3. T. Agins, "Dressmaker Leslie Fay Is an Old-Style Firm That's in a Modern Fix," *The Wall Street Journal*, 23 February 1993, A8.

4. Strom, "Accounting Scandal at Leslie Fay."

5. T. Agins, "Leslie Fay Says Irregularities in Books Could Wipe Out '92 Profit; Stock Skids," *The Wall Street Journal*, 2 February 1993, A5.

EXHIBIT 1

THE LESLIE FAY
COMPANIES
1987–1991
BALANCE SHEETS

The Leslie Fay Companies
Consolidated Balance Sheets 1987–1991
(in millions)

ASSETS	1991	1990	1989	1988	1987
Current Assets:					
Cash	$ 4.7	$ 4.7	$ 5.5	$ 5.5	$ 4.1
Receivables (net)	118.9	139.5	117.3	109.9	82.9
Inventories	126.8	147.9	121.1	107.0	83.0
Prepaid Expenses & Other Current					
Assets	19.7	22.5	19.5	16.4	15.9
Total Current Assets	270.1	314.6	263.4	238.8	185.9
Property, Plant, and Equipment	39.2	30.0	27.2	25.9	24.1
Goodwill	81.3	88.1	91.2	94.1	90.3
Deferred Charges and Other Assets	5.2	6.2	5.5	4.2	5.1
Total Assets	$395.8	$438.9	$387.3	$363.0	$305.4
LIABILITIES AND STOCKHOLDERS' EQUITY					
Current Liabilities:					
Notes Payable	35.0	48.0	23.0	29.0	15.5
Current Maturities of Long-term Debt	.3	.3	.3	.3	1.4
Accounts Payable	31.9	43.3	38.6	45.6	31.6
Accrued Interest Payable	3.0	3.8	4.1	3.9	3.7
Accrued Compensation	16.9	14.9	19.5	16.6	10.6
Accrued Expenses & Other	4.3	6.4	5.8	7.2	7.4
Income Taxes Payable	1.4	2.3	4.6	6.1	1.8
Total Current Liabilities	92.8	119.0	95.9	108.7	72.0
Long-term Debt	84.4	129.7	129.0	116.3	116.6
Deferred Credits & Other Noncurrent					
Liabilities	2.8	2.6	2.7	4.2	4.9
Stockholders' Equity:					
Common Stock	20.0	20.0	20.0	20.0	20.0
Capital in Excess of Par Value	82.2	82.2	82.1	82.2	82.2
Retained Earnings	156.9	127.6	98.5	72.8	50.5
Other	(34.3)	(31.5)	(31.9)	(32.0)	(31.7)
Treasury Stock	(9.0)	(10.7)	(9.0)	(9.1)	(9.1)
Total Stockholders' Equity	215.8	187.6	159.7	133.8	111.9
Total Liabilities and					
Stockholders' Equity	$395.8	$438.9	$387.3	$363.0	$305.4

(continued)

financial data. Pomerantz also denied that he and the other top executives of Leslie Fay had suspected Kenia of any wrongdoing. He was particularly strident in defending his close friend Paul Polishan who had supervised Kenia and who was directly responsible for the integrity of Leslie Fay's accounting records. Pomerantz firmly told a reporter that Polishan "didn't know anything about this."[6]

---

6. *Ibid.*

EXHIBIT 1—
continued

THE LESLIE FAY
COMPANIES
1987–1991
INCOME
STATEMENTS

The Leslie Fay Companies
Consolidated Income Statements 1987–1991
(in millions)

	1991	1990	1989	1988	1987
Net Sales	$836.6	$858.8	$786.3	$682.7	$582.0
Cost of Sales	585.1	589.4	536.8	466.3	403.1
Gross Profit	251.5	269.4	249.5	216.4	178.9
Operating Expenses:					
Selling, Warehouse, General and Administrative	186.3	199.0	183.8	156.2	132.5
Amortization of Intangibles	2.7	2.9	2.6	3.3	3.8
Total Operating Expenses	189.0	201.9	186.4	159.5	136.3
Operating Income	62.5	67.5	63.1	56.9	42.6
Interest Expense	18.3	18.7	19.3	18.2	16.4
Income Before Non-recurring Charges (Credits)	44.2	48.8	43.8	38.7	26.2
Non-recurring Charges (Credits)	—	—	—	—	(5.0)
Income Before Taxes on Income	44.2	48.8	43.8	38.7	31.2
Income Taxes	14.8	19.7	18.0	16.4	11.5
Net Income	$ 29.4	$ 29.1	$ 25.8	$ 22.3	$ 19.7
Net Income per Share	$ 1.55	$ 1.53	$ 1.35	$ 1.17	$ 1.03

EXHIBIT 2

THE LESLIE FAY
COMPANIES 1991
INDUSTRY NORMS
FOR KEY FINANCIAL
RATIOS

Liquidity:
Current Ratio	1.8
Quick Ratio	.9

Solvency:
Debt to Assets	.53
Times Interest Earned	4.2
Long-term Debt to Equity	.14

Activity:
Inventory Turnover	6.7
Age of Inventory	53.7 days
Accounts Receivable Turnover	8.0
Age of Accounts Receivable	45.5 days
Total Asset Turnover	3.1

Profitability:
Gross Margin	31.5%
Profit Margin on Sales	2.2%
Return on Total Assets	6.0%
Return on Equity	14.0%

During the following weeks and months, an increasingly hostile business press hounded Pomerantz for more details of the fraud, while critics openly questioned whether he was being totally forthcoming regarding his lack of knowledge of Kenia's accounting scams. Responding to those critics, the beleaguered CEO maintained that rather than being involved in the fraud, he was its principal victim. "Do I hold myself personally responsible? No. In my heart of hearts, I feel that I'm a victim.

I know there are other victims. But I'm the biggest victim."[7] Such protestations did not prevent critics from questioning why Pomerantz had blithely accepted Leslie Fay's impressive operating results while many of the company's competitors were struggling financially.

Shortly after Pomerantz publicly disclosed Kenia's fraud, Leslie Fay's audit committee launched an intensive investigation of its impact on the company's financial statements for the previous several years. The audit committee retained Arthur Andersen & Co. to help complete that study. Pending the outcome of the investigation, Pomerantz reluctantly placed Polishan on temporary paid leave.

BDO Seidman had served as Leslie Fay's audit firm since the mid-1970s and issued unqualified opinions each year on the company's financial statements. Following Pomerantz's disclosure of the fraud, BDO Seidman withdrew its audit opinions on the company's 1990 and 1991 financial statements. In the ensuing weeks, Leslie Fay stockholders filed several large lawsuits naming the company's management team and BDO Seidman as defendants.

In April 1993, BDO Seidman officials contacted the Securities and Exchange Commission (SEC) and inquired regarding the status of their firm's independence from Leslie Fay given the pending lawsuits. The SEC informed BDO Seidman that its independence was jeopardized by those lawsuits, which forced the firm to resign as Leslie Fay's auditor in early May 1993. Company management immediately appointed Arthur Andersen as Leslie's Fay new auditor.

In September 1993, Leslie Fay's audit committee completed its eight-month investigation of the accounting fraud. The resulting 600-page report was reviewed by members of Leslie Fay's board and then submitted to the SEC and federal prosecutors. Although the report was not released publicly, several of its key findings were leaked to the press. The most startling feature of the fraud was its pervasive nature. According to a company insider who read the report, "There wasn't an entry on the cost side of the company's ledgers for those years that wasn't subject to some type of rejiggering."[8]

The key focus of the fraudulent activity was Leslie Fay's inventory. Kenia and his subordinates had inflated the number of dresses manufactured each quarterly period to reduce the per-unit cost of finished goods and increase the company's gross profit margin on sales. During period-ending physical inventories, the conspirators "manufactured" the phantom inventory they had previously entered in the company's accounting records. Forging inventory tags for nonexistent products, inflating the number of dresses of a specific style on hand, and fabricating large amounts of bogus in-transit inventory were common ruses used to overstate inventory during the period-ending counts.

Other accounting gimmicks used by Kenia included failing to accrue period-ending expenses and liabilities, "pre-recording" orders received from customers as consummated sales to boost Leslie Fay's revenues near the end of an accounting period, failing to write off uncollectible receivables, and ignoring discounts on outstanding receivables granted to large customers experiencing slow sales of the company's products. Allegedly, Kenia decided each period what amount of profit Leslie Fay should report. He and his subordinates then adjusted Leslie Fay's key financial numbers until that profit figure was achieved. From 1990 through the end of 1992, approximately $130 million of bogus entries were made in Leslie Fay's accounting records. These fraudulent entries overstated the company's profits by approximately $80 million.

---

7. E. Lesly, "Who Played Dress-up with the Books?" *Business Week*, 15 March 1993, 34.

8. T. Agins, "Report Is Said to Show Pervasive Fraud at Leslie Fay," *The Wall Street Journal*, 27 September 1993, B3.

Kenia and his co-conspirators molded Leslie Fay's financial statements so that key financial ratios would be consistent with historical trends. The financial ratio that the fraudsters paid particular attention to was Leslie Fay's gross profit percentage. For several years, the company's gross profit percentage had hovered near 30 percent. Leslie Fay's actual gross profit percentage was approximately 20 percent by the early 1990s, but Kenia relied on his assorted bag of accounting tricks to inflate that financial ratio to near its historical norm.

Excerpts released to the press from the audit committee's report largely exonerated John Pomerantz of responsibility for Leslie Fay's accounting irregularities. The report indicated that there was no evidence that he and other members of Leslie Fay's headquarters management team had been aware of those irregularities, but the report did criticize those executives for failing to aggressively pursue unusual and suspicious circumstances they had encountered during the course of Kenia's fraud. If those circumstances had been vigorously investigated, the audit committee concluded that the fraud might have been uncovered much earlier than January 1993.

In particular, the audit committee questioned why Pomerantz had not investigated Leslie Fay's remarkably stable gross profit percentage in the early 1990s, given the significant problems facing other women's dress manufacturers and the apparently poor response to many of the company's new product offerings during that period.

Following the completion of the audit committee's investigation in September 1993, Leslie Fay's board of directors allowed John Pomerantz to remain as the CEO but relieved him of all financial responsibilities related to the company's operations. The board created a committee of outside directors to oversee the company's operations while Leslie Fay dealt with the aftermath of the large-scale fraud. The board also dismissed Paul Polishan as Leslie Fay's CFO and senior vice president of finance and replaced him with an Arthur Andersen partner who had been involved in the audit committee investigation.

BDO Seidman: Odd Man Out

In April 1993, Leslie Fay filed for protection from its creditors under Chapter 11 of the federal bankruptcy code. Press reports of Kenia's fraudulent scheme had cut off the company's access to the additional debt and equity capital that it needed to continue normal operations. By early April 1993, the price of Leslie Fay's stock had dropped by nearly 85 percent since the first details of the fraud had become public two months earlier. The company's plummeting stock price and the mounting criticism of its officers in the business press triggered additional lawsuits by angry stockholders against Pomerantz, other Leslie Fay executives, and the company's longtime auditor, BDO Seidman.

The lawsuits that named BDO Seidman as a defendant charged that the firm had been at least reckless in auditing Leslie Fay's periodic financial statements during the early 1990s. Howard Schilit, an accounting professor and forensic accounting specialist, suggested in the business press that Leslie Fay's financial data had been replete with red flags. These red flags included implausible trend lines in the company's financial data, implausible relationships between key financial statement items, and unreasonably generous bonuses paid to top executives, bonuses linked directly to the record earnings Leslie Fay reported each successive period. For 1991, John Pomerantz had received total salary and bonuses of $3.6 million, three times more than the 1991 compensation of Liz Claiborne's CEO, whose company reported sales more than double those of Leslie Fay's.

BDO Seidman officials chafed at published reports criticizing their firm's Leslie Fay audits. Those officials insisted that BDO Seidman was being indicted in the press on the basis of innuendo and incomplete information. These same individuals also maintained that Leslie Fay's top management, principally John Pomerantz, should shoulder the bulk of the responsibility for the massive fraud.

During various court proceedings following the disclosure of the Leslie Fay fraud, many parties questioned the objectivity of the forensic investigation supervised by Leslie Fay's audit committee that had effectively vindicated Pomerantz. These skeptics suggested that the members of the audit committee had been reluctant to criticize Pomerantz. To squelch such criticism, the federal judge presiding over Leslie Fay's bankruptcy filing appointed an independent examiner, Charles Stillman, to prepare another report on the details of the fraud. Stillman was also charged with identifying the individuals responsible for the fraud and those responsible for failing to discover it.

In August 1994, the U.S. Bankruptcy Court released the so-called Stillman Report. This document corroborated the key findings of the audit committee investigation. Similar to the audit committee report, the Stillman Report largely exonerated Pomerantz: "The examiner's report concludes there is no evidence to suggest that viable claims exist against any members of Leslie Fay's current management or its board of directors."[9]

The Stillman Report went on to suggest that although there were likely "viable claims" against former company executives Kenia and Polishan based upon "presently available information,"[10] the limited assets of those individuals made it economically infeasible for the bankruptcy court to pursue those claims. Finally, the Stillman Report indicted the quality of BDO Seidman's audits of Leslie Fay by asserting that there may be "claims worth pursuing against . . . BDO Seidman,"[11] and that "it is likely BDO Seidman acted negligently in performing accounting services for Leslie Fay."[12]

Following the release of the Stillman Report, Leslie Fay's stockholders filed a large civil lawsuit against BDO Seidman in the federal bankruptcy courts. At approximately the same time, BDO Seidman filed a lawsuit against Leslie Fay's principal officers, including John Pomerantz. In commenting on this latter lawsuit, BDO Seidman officials reported that "Leslie Fay's upper management not only tolerated fraud to bolster reported financial results but they benefited directly from its execution. As BDO Seidman has said from the beginning, we are victims of this fraud. As Leslie Fay's outside auditors, we were deceived by the company. Our reputation has suffered needlessly as a result of Leslie Fay's deliberate deception."[13]

Leslie Fay's management responded immediately to the news that BDO Seidman had named John Pomerantz and his fellow officers as defendants in a large civil lawsuit. "The unsubstantiated and unfounded allegations made today by BDO Seidman are a classic example of 'revisionist history' and are clearly an attempt by the accounting firm to divert attention from its own apparent negligence by blaming others."[14]

---

9. *Business Wire*, "Independent Examiner Confirms Findings of Leslie Fay's Audit Committee Investigation," 16 August 1994.

10. *Ibid.*

11. *Ibid.*

12. *Business Wire*, "Leslie Fay Responds to Unfounded Allegations by BDO Seidman," 29 March 1995.

13. *PR Newswire*, "BDO Seidman Announces Cross-Claims and Third Party Complaints Against Key Leslie Fay Figures," 29 March 1995.

14. *Business Wire*, "Leslie Fay Responds to Unfounded Allegations."

EPILOGUE

In July 1997, a federal judge approved a $34 million settlement to the large number of lawsuits filed by Leslie Fay's stockholders and creditors against the company, its executives, and BDO Seidman. BDO Seidman contributed $8 million to the settlement pool, although the firm reported that it was agreeing to the settlement only because it was the most economical and expeditious way to "put this matter behind us."[15] In June 1997, Leslie Fay emerged from federal bankruptcy court. Over the next several years, the much smaller company returned to a profitable condition before being purchased in late 2001 by a large investment fund. A few months later, in April 2002, John Pomerantz received a lifetime achievement award at the annual American Image Awards, a glitzy event sponsored by the major companies and organizations in the fashion industries.

On October 31, 1996, federal prosecutors filed a 21-count fraud indictment against Paul Polishan. The specific charges included conspiracy, making false statements to the SEC, bank fraud, and wire fraud. Unknown to the public, three years earlier, Donald Kenia had broken down under relentless questioning by federal investigators and admitted that Polishan, his former boss, had been the architect of the Leslie Fay fraud. According to Kenia's testimony, Polishan had overseen and directed every major facet of the fraud. Because of Polishan's intimidating personality, Kenia and several of his subordinates had agreed to make the enormous number of fraudulent entries in Leslie Fay's accounting records that he had demanded. Polishan had also compelled Kenia to accept full responsibility for the accounting irregularities when it became apparent in late January 1993 that the fraud would soon be exposed.

Following a series of lengthy and fiercely contested pre-trial hearings, Polishan's criminal case was finally heard in federal court in the summer of 2000. Polishan was convicted on 18 of the 21 fraud counts filed against him. His attorneys immediately appealed the guilty verdict. The attorneys' principal contention during the appeal was that there was almost no physical evidence to link their client to the fraud. Instead, they maintained that Polishan's conviction had hinged almost entirely upon the veracity of Kenia's testimony.

The federal judge who presided over Polishan's appeal did not dispute his attorneys' principal contention. Throughout the fraud, the former CFO had painstakingly avoided leaving incriminating physical evidence that linked him directly to the accounting irregularities. Despite that fact, the judge denied Polishan's appeal. The judge observed that a substantial amount of circumstantial evidence had been presented during the trial. After studying the evidence in painstaking detail, the judge ruled that it was much more consistent with Kenia's testimony than that of Polishan.

A key factor contributing to the judge's decision was the unusual relationship that had existed between Polishan and Kenia during their long tenure with Leslie Fay, a relationship that had been documented and discussed at length during the trial. The judge noted that Polishan had "dominated" Kenia through intimidation and fear. In the opinion he issued in the case, the judge referred on multiple occasions to an episode during 1992 to demonstrate how completely Polishan had controlled Kenia. In forcing Kenia to take responsibility for an accounting error that had been discovered in Leslie Fay's accounting records, Polishan had insisted Kenia to tell another company executive, "I am a _____ idiot."[16]

On January 21, 2002, almost exactly nine years after the news of the Leslie Fay fraud

---

15. *The Electronic Accountant* (online), "BDO to Pay $8 Million to Settle Leslie Fay Lawsuit," 10 March 1997. As a point of information, there is no public report of any resolution to the lawsuit filed against John Pomerantz *et al.* by BDO Seidman. Most likely, that lawsuit was dropped by BDO Seidman following the settlement approved by the federal judge.

16. *United States of America v. Paul Polishan*, 2001 U.S. Dist. LEXIS 10662.

surfaced in the press, Paul Polishan was sentenced to serve nine years in federal prison for his role in plotting and overseeing that fraud.[17] Polishan, who filed for personal bankruptcy in 1999 claiming assets of only $17,000, was also fined $900. After losing an appeal to overturn his conviction, Polishan reported to the federal correctional facility in Schuylkill County, Pennsylvania, in early September 2003 to begin serving his nine-year sentence. In exchange for his testimony against Polishan, Donald Kenia was allowed to plead guilty to two counts of making false statements to the SEC. In 2001, Kenia was sentenced to two years in the Allenwood Federal Prison Camp in Montgomery, Pennsylvania.

Questions

1. Prepare common-sized financial statements for Leslie Fay for the period 1987–1991. For that same period, compute for Leslie Fay the ratios shown in Exhibit 2. Given these data, which financial statement items do you believe should have been of particular interest to BDO Seidman during that firm's 1991 audit of Leslie Fay? Explain.

2. In addition to the data shown in Exhibit 1 and Exhibit 2, what other financial information would you have obtained if you had been responsible for planning the 1991 Leslie Fay audit?

3. List nonfinancial variables or factors regarding a client's industry that auditors should consider when planning an audit. For each of these items, briefly describe their audit implications.

4. Paul Polishan apparently dominated Leslie Fay's accounting and financial reporting functions and the individuals who were his subordinates. What implications do such circumstances pose for a company's independent auditors? How should auditors take such circumstances into consideration when planning an audit?

5. Explain why the SEC ruled that BDO Seidman's independence was jeopardized by the lawsuits that named the accounting firm, Leslie Fay, and top executives of Leslie Fay as co-defendants.

---

17. Polishan's attorneys asked the presiding judge to reduce their client's sentence because Polishan allegedly suffered from a narcissistic personality disorder. The judge denied that request.

Nextcard, Inc.

In the late 1990s, the investing public's fascination with Internet-based companies prompted the cyberspace equivalent of the Oklahoma Land Rush, according to one prominent Wall Street analyst. "In a land rush, you suspend rules because your perception is that time is of the essence."[1] That perception caused many anxious investors who feared missing out on a once-in-a-lifetime investment opportunity to bid the prices of Internet stocks to ever-higher levels. Those investors readily discounted the fact that most Internet companies were reporting minimal revenues and sizable, if not staggering, operating losses. Over a 15-month stretch between late 1998 and March 2000, the dot-com-laced NASDAQ stock exchange rose by more than 150 percent. By comparison, over the same time frame, the largely "Old Economy" Dow Jones Industrial Average managed a much less impressive 15 percent gain.

Dot-com fever caused many investment services and publications to create new stock indices dedicated strictly to Internet companies. On June 30, 1999, *USA Today* launched the *Internet 100* to track the stock prices of 100 high-profile companies whose primary lines of business were directly or exclusively related to the Internet. Within a few months, the collective value of that index had risen by more than 60 percent. Other Internet stock indices realized similar increases. By early March 2000, the 300 companies included in the *Forbes Internet Index* had a collective market value of $1.2 trillion, which was approximately equal to the total value of all publicly traded U.S. stocks a little more than one decade earlier.

The public's feeding frenzy on Internet stocks produced numerous paper billionaires among dot-com bigwigs. Dot-com billionaires making appearances in the *Forbes 400*, a list of the 400 "richest people in America," included, among several others, Jeff Bezos (Amazon), Stephen Case (AOL), Mark Cuban (Broadcast.com), Andrew McKelvey (Monster.com), Pierre Omidyar (eBay), Jay Walker (Priceline), David Wetherell (CMGI), and Jerry Yang and David Filo (Yahoo!). As you might expect, the surging prices of Internet stocks added an even larger number of new members to the millionaires' club. By early 2000, one publication reported that in northern California's Silicon Valley alone, the Internet revolution was creating 64 new millionaires each day.[2] Among these millionaires were Jeremy and Molly Lent, a husband-and-wife team that founded the Internet-based NextCard, Inc., in 1997.

Credit on the Fly

Jeremy Lent served as the chief financial officer (CFO) of Providian Financial Corporation during the early 1990s. At the time, Providian ranked among the largest financial services companies in the United States. Experts in the financial services industry attributed Providian's success to the direct-mail marketing methods the company used to identify and then recruit as customers, individuals who made extensive use of credit cards. In the late 1990s, Lent decided that the marketing tactics used by

---

1. G. Ip, S. Pulliam, S. Thurm, and R. Simon, "How the Internet Bubble Broke Records, Rules, Bank Accounts," *The Wall Street Journal* (online), 14 July 2000.

2. *The Economist* (online), "The Country-Club Vote," 20 May 2000.

Providian could be easily adapted to the Internet, which prompted him and his wife to create NextCard, an online company that would offer Internet users the opportunity to obtain a credit card in a matter of moments.

Because of his tenure at Providian, Lent realized that a key metric in the credit card industry is the acquisition cost of a new customer. Lent was convinced that he could use the Internet to undercut the average acquisition cost of a new customer incurred by brick-and-mortar credit card companies, such as Providian. Likewise, Lent believed that his company would have significantly lower bad debt losses than conventional credit card issuers. Marketing research had found that Internet users were generally more affluent, and thus better credit risks, than individuals drawn from the general population of consumers.

One of Lent's first major strategic initiatives was hiring dozens of marketing researchers to analyze a large database of "clickstream data" that documented the "surfing" habits of Internet users. After analyzing these data, the company's marketing team developed Internet-based advertising campaigns targeting Internet users who made frequent use of, and maintained large balances on, their credit cards. NextCard's online ads encouraged such individuals to apply for a credit card with NextBank, a virtual bank that was NextCard's largest operating unit, and to transfer their existing credit card balances to this new card. The key inducement used by Lent to convince potential customers to apply for a NextBank credit card was a lower interest rate than that charged by conventional credit card issuers. Lent also promised those potential customers that a decision regarding their online credit card application would be made within 30 seconds of their submitting that application.

Initially, Lent's business model for NextCard appeared to be a huge success as the company quickly became recognized as one of the leaders of the Internet Revolution that made the term *e-commerce* the hottest buzzword among Wall Street analysts and individual investors. The company's website was regularly named one of the top 50 financial websites by *Money* magazine and by 2000 had more daily "hits" or visits than any other website in the financial services industry. More importantly, for several consecutive years, NextCard issued more credit cards online than any other credit card issuer, including such large and well-established firms as American Express, Bank of America, Citibank, and MBNA. Lent used NextCard's prominent position in the Internet industry to create a network of 60,000 online "affiliates" that referred potential credit card customers to NextCard. Several of these affiliates, including Amazon.com, purchased significant ownership interests in NextCard.

By early 2000, NextCard was well on its way to achieving one of Lent's primary goals for the company: obtaining one million credit card customers. During that year, NextCard extended more than $1 billion of credit to its customers. Those impressive operating statistics did not translate into immediate profits for NextCard, a fact that Lent and other company executives frequently downplayed or simply ignored in press releases and other public disclosures. In February 2000, a NextCard executive boasted that "we continue to beat our aggressive growth targets while maintaining very strong parameters in the other core elements of our business model. Our average balance per account, which is one of the major drivers of success in the credit card business, remains approximately $2,000. Our acquisition cost, credit quality, and yield—all major drivers of profitability—continue to be strong and stable, leading to continued very strong revenue results."[3] This statement conveniently overlooked the

---

3. *Business Wire* (online), "NextCard Announces Significant Growth Milestones Ahead of Plan," 22 February 2000.

fact that NextCard's New Age business model had produced a large loss during the company's just completed 1999 fiscal year, $77.2 million to be exact.

Despite the fact that NextCard was posting large losses each reporting period, Lent had taken the company public in 1999. On the first day NextCard's stock was traded, the stock's price rose from an initial selling price of $20 per share to more than $40, making Lent and several other NextCard executives instant multimillionaires. A few months later, the stock surged past $50 per share. When the "lock-up" period mandated by the Securities and Exchange Commission (SEC) following an initial public offering expired, Lent and his colleagues sold large chunks of their ownership interests in the company.

When NextCard reported an unexpectedly large loss of $81.9 million for fiscal 2000, company executives could no longer sidestep the recurring question posed by persistent Wall Street analysts, namely, "When would NextCard earn its first quarterly profit?" NextCard's management team insisted that the company had "turned the corner" and pledged that NextCard would report its first-ever quarterly profit by the fourth-quarter of fiscal 2001. At the same time, company officials predicted that NextCard would report a net income of $150 million by fiscal 2003.

In March 2000, the NASDAQ stock index crested at an all-time high of more than 5,000. Over the following 18 months, the Internet "bubble" in the stock market burst, causing the stock prices of most Internet companies, including NextCard, to spiral downward. Many of these New Age companies survived, including such firms as Amazon.com, eBay, Monster.com, and Yahoo!. NextCard would not be among those survivors.

Loose Credit = Bad Debts

The bursting of the Internet bubble in the stock market quickly cut off NextCard's access to the debt and equity markets. Without the ability to raise additional debt or equity capital, NextCard suddenly faced the need to raise capital the "old-fashioned way," namely, via profitable operations.

Despite the promises and predictions of NextCard's executives, the company never reported a profit, principally because two of the key premises on which Jeremy Lent had predicated NextCard's business model proved to be invalid. First, the average acquisition cost NextCard incurred to obtain new customers proved to be much higher than the figure Lent had originally projected. NextCard spent huge amounts on Internet advertising campaigns to recruit customers only to find that Internet users routinely ignored, if not treated with contempt, most efforts of online advertisers to attract their attention. In fact, the "click-through" rate for most Internet advertisements hovered at a fraction of 1 percent, considerably lower than the response rate to direct or "junk" mail advertisements used by conventional credit card issuers.

Lent's other major miscalculation had even more serious consequences for NextCard. Internet users, at least the subpopulation of Internet users who signed up for a NextBank credit card, proved to be much higher credit risks than Lent had expected. A large proportion of the Internet users who took advantage of NextCard's liberal credit policies were individuals who could not obtain credit from any other source. For these desperate and shallow-pocketed consumers, NextCard effectively served as the "lender of last resort." These individuals eventually produced the large balances that Lent had expected Internet users to carry on their credit cards but they often allowed those balances to go unpaid, resulting in large credit losses for NextCard.

In sum, instead of incurring minimal marketing expenditures to acquire "good" credit card customers, NextCard spent large amounts to acquire "bad" credit card customers. Making matters worse, many of NextCard's competitors, including American Express, "went to school" on NextCard's mistakes. These competitors learned from those mistakes and developed more cost-effective—and ultimately profitable—Internet marketing strategies to expand their market shares in the intensely competitive credit card industry.

Early in NextCard's history, the company's executives apparently realized that their business model contained serious flaws. Despite that realization, those executives continued to pursue Jeremy Lent's dream of creating one of the dominant companies in the credit card industry. To shore up the company's stock price and to maintain credibility on Wall Street and among private investors, NextCard's executives chose to conceal the extent and source of the company's financial problems. The principal means used to accomplish this goal was understating NextCard's massive credit losses by refusing to provide sufficient allowances each period for expected bad debts.

Because NextBank was subject to federal banking regulations, the Office of the Comptroller of the Currency (OCC) regularly reviewed the company's accounting records and operating policies and procedures. During 2001, OCC auditors forced NextCard to significantly increase its allowance for bad debts. When NextCard publicly reported the OCC's decision, company management denied that the larger allowance for bad debts was due to unexpectedly high credit losses. Instead, NextCard officials insisted that the increase in the allowance for bad debts was necessary because the company had suffered large losses as a result of fraudulent schemes perpetrated by hackers and other Internet miscreants. In November 2001, a skeptical Wall Street analyst questioned how such a massive problem could "pop up" so unexpectedly and without any previous warning from company officials.[4] In fact, subsequent investigations would reveal that NextCard officials had routinely and materially understated the company's allowance for credit losses.

In late 2001, angry NextCard investors filed a large class-action lawsuit against the company and its executives. Among other charges, that lawsuit alleged that NextCard's management team had intentionally concealed the extent and nature of the company's financial problems. In addition, the plaintiffs charged that the NextCard executives had engaged in insider trading by selling off large portions of their ownership interests in the company before NextCard's true financial condition became apparent. This large class-action lawsuit and widespread concerns regarding the integrity of NextCard's publicly reported financial data caused federal regulatory authorities, including the SEC, to launch investigations of the company's financial affairs.

Suspicious Audit Trails

Discovering that your largest client is the subject of a series of federal investigations for tampering with its accounting records and issuing materially misleading financial statements is, no doubt, among the life events feared most by audit partners of major accounting firms. Thirty-six-year-old Thomas Trauger found himself facing that disturbing scenario in the fall of 2001. Trauger, a partner in the San Francisco office of Ernst & Young (E&Y), had served for several years as the audit engagement partner for NextCard. In March 2001, Trauger had authorized the unqualified opinion issued on NextCard's 2000 financial statements.

After considering his options, including doing nothing and simply awaiting the outcome of the federal investigations of NextCard, Trauger decided to take matters

---

4. J. Graham, "What's the Next Move for Troubled NextCard?" *Investor's Business Daily*, 1 November 2001, 6.

into his own hands. His first decision was to contact his top subordinate on the 2000 NextCard audit, Oliver Flanagan.

Like most accounting professionals, Oliver Flanagan enjoyed challenging assignments. A native of Ireland, Flanagan accepted an entry-level position on the auditing staff of the London, England, office of E&Y in the mid-1990s. Flanagan left E&Y in late 1999 to accept a position in the banking industry but quickly discovered that he missed working as an independent auditor. So, Flanagan asked E&Y for his job back. In the late 1990s, the Internet bubble had created a huge demand for the services of public accounting firms, which caused E&Y to be more than happy to rehire Flanagan. Among the locations having the greatest need for auditors at the time was the booming Silicon Valley region near San Francisco. Given his interest in the banking industry and the "adventure" of going stateside, Flanagan quickly accepted the opportunity to move to San Francisco and become a member of the NextCard audit engagement team.

Despite the fact that he had only a few years of auditing experience, Flanagan was assigned to serve as the senior audit manager on the NextCard engagement, a position in which he would report directly to Thomas Trauger. Flanagan realized that Trauger was a "fast track" partner in the San Francisco office of E&Y since he was in charge of the prestigious NextCard engagement. The young Irishman hoped that Trauger would serve as his mentor and help him advance quickly within E&Y.

In early November 2001, more than six months after the 2000 NextCard audit was completed, Thomas Trauger left a message instructing Oliver Flanagan to meet him in the E&Y office the following Saturday morning. Flanagan was probably not surprised by the request since weekend work was nothing unusual with a major accounting firm. Plus, the planning phase for the 2001 audit of the financially troubled NextCard was nearing completion. If Flanagan expected Trauger to discuss the 2001 audit during the weekend meeting, he was wrong. Instead, when Flanagan contacted Trauger, the audit partner told him to gather all of the workpapers for the 2000 NextCard audit and "have them ready for revisions"[5] during that meeting. Flanagan knew that it was not common to revise prior-year audit workpapers once they had been archived. Almost certainly, NextCard's well-documented financial problems and the insinuations of an accounting scandal within the company caused Flanagan to wonder what types of "revisions" Trauger intended to make to the NextCard workpapers.

Before meeting with Flanagan, Trauger contacted the other audit manager on the NextCard engagement team, Michael Mullen—Mullen had not been involved in the 2000 NextCard audit as he had only been assigned to the engagement team since June 2001. Trauger instructed Mullen to determine whether it was possible to "manipulate E&Y's computer system so that he [Trauger] could alter electronically archived working papers without being discovered."[6] Trauger wanted to revise the original NextCard workpapers without leaving any evidence that they had been altered. For the conventional "hard copy" workpapers, this goal did not pose any particular challenge. But accomplishing that same goal for the electronic workpapers meant that Trauger had to change the electronic "time stamps" on those files.

Mullen complied with Trauger's request and eventually learned from another E&Y employee that it was possible to "de-archive" previously completed electronic audit workpapers and thereby change the time stamps posted on those workpapers.

---

5. Securities and Exchange Commission, *Accounting and Auditing Enforcement Release No. 1871,* 25 September 2003.

6. *Ibid.*

Mullen sent this information to both Trauger and Flanagan. During their weekend meeting, Trauger and Flanagan reviewed the 2000 NextCard audit workpapers and made numerous additions and deletions to those workpaper files. The principal items changed were the "Summary Review Memorandum" and the receivables work-papers. In a subsequent enforcement release that focused on the conduct of Oliver Flanagan, the SEC described the process used by Trauger and Flanagan to alter the NextCard workpapers. (Note: In this enforcement release, the SEC referred to Trauger as simply the "audit partner.")

> The audit partner marked up printed versions of the documents and gave them to Flanagan for Flanagan to input using Flanagan's laptop computer. In order to ensure that the revised documents appeared to have been created as part of the original working papers, the audit partner instructed Flanagan to reset the date on his com-puter so that any documents bearing computer-generated dates would reflect a date in early 2001. Some documents went through more than one edit, as Flanagan input the audit partner's changes and then printed out the revised version for the audit partner's further review."[7]

NextCard's deteriorating financial condition in late 2001 and the increasing scru-tiny of the company by federal regulatory authorities apparently prompted Trauger to ask Flanagan to meet with him once more to make additional alterations to the 2000 NextCard workpapers. Trauger also asked Michael Mullen to attend this second meeting, which took place in late November 2001. The SEC provided the following overview of what transpired during this second meeting.

> The audit partner marked up printed versions of the memoranda he was revising and then the other audit manager [Mullen] input the changes. At the audit partner's direction, the other audit manager deleted charts, portions of tables, and discussion sections that indicated problems with NextCard's charge-off numbers and trends. The audit partner also added information and altered the tone of certain sections. One of the documents altered during this meeting was a memorandum entitled "Analysis for Loan Losses." Flanagan remained involved in the process by proofreading the other audit manager's work to ensure that all of the audit partner's changes were made.[8]

The SEC issued multiple enforcement releases that documented the improper professional conduct of Thomas Trauger, Oliver Flanagan, and Michael Mullen. In those enforcement releases, the SEC noted on several occasions that Trauger's intent in revising the 2000 NextCard audit workpapers was to "make it appear that there was a more satisfactory basis" for the key E&Y conclusions reached during that en-gagement. The *New York Times* reported that "Mr. Trauger told Mr. Flanagan that he wanted to 'beef up' the workpapers to make it appear as if the auditing team had been 'right on the mark' all along."[9] During the course of the federal investigations of NextCard, the FBI retrieved e-mails that Trauger had sent to his subordinates. One of those e-mails provided a more pointed statement of Trauger's intent in modifying the NextCard workpapers. According to an FBI affidavit, in one of those e-mails Trauger stated that he did not want "some smart-ass lawyer"[10] second-guessing the decisions that he had made during the 2000 NextCard audit.

---

7. *Ibid.*

8. *Ibid.*

9. K. Eichenwald, "U.S. Charges Ernst & Young Ex-Partner in Audit Case," *The New York Times*, 26 September 2003, 1.

10. J. Hoppin, "Snared by SOX," *Corporate Counsel*, December 2003, 24.

Following the two meetings in which the E&Y auditors had altered the NextCard workpapers, Trauger had instructed Flanagan "to scour his hard drive and delete documents or e-mails inconsistent with the altered versions of the working papers."[11] Once more, Flanagan followed his mentor's instructions. Approximately three months later, E&Y received a subpoena from the OCC that instructed the firm to give the federal agency certain NextCard workpapers. At that time, Trauger discovered that Michael Mullen had kept a computer diskette containing some of the original NextCard workpapers that had been altered in November 2001. Trauger ordered Flanagan to obtain that diskette and destroy it. Flanagan obtained the diskette and told Trauger that he had destroyed it. In fact, Flanagan kept the diskette and subsequently gave it to federal authorities.

EPILOGUE

The computer diskette that Oliver Flanagan turned over to federal authorities investigating NextCard ultimately resulted in the FBI arresting Thomas Trauger in September 2003. The U.S. Department of Justice filed criminal charges against Trauger for obstructing the federal investigations of NextCard. Trauger was the first partner of a major accounting firm to be prosecuted for destroying audit-related documents under the criminal provisions of the Sarbanes-Oxley Act of 2002. Those provisions were included in the Sarbanes-Oxley Act as a direct consequence of the widely publicized scandal involving Enron Corporation. During an SEC investigation of Enron, Andersen, the company's audit firm, had shredded certain Enron workpapers. The subsequent felony conviction handed down against Andersen by a federal court effectively put the prominent accounting firm out of business.[12] Ironically, Trauger and his subordinates were altering the NextCard workpapers in November 2001, the same time frame during which Andersen personnel were shredding the Enron work papers.

Shortly after being arrested in September 2003, Thomas Trauger insisted that he was innocent of the charges filed against him. When Trauger was released after posting a $1 million bail, his attorney issued the following public statement defending his client: "He's a good man, a well-respected accountant, and I'm confident he will be exonerated."[13] Despite those assertions, a little more than one year later on October 28, 2004, Thomas Trauger pled guilty to one count of impeding a federal investigation. As a result of that plea, Trauger faced a prison sentence of up to 25 years and a fine of $500,000. On January 27, 2005, a federal judge sentenced Trauger to one year in prison and two years of "supervised release." The judge also ordered Trauger to pay a $5,000 fine. In his plea agreement, Trauger admitted he had failed to inform federal authorities that he and his subordinates had altered certain of the NextCard audit workpapers subpoenaed by those authorities.

Ernst & Young disavowed responsibility for the actions of Trauger, Flanagan, and Mullen. In a press release, an E&Y spokesperson pointed out that the actions of the three individuals were in clear violation of the firm's professional standards and internal policies. That spokesperson also noted that when E&Y discovered the nature of the individuals' conduct, firm officials cooperated fully with federal law enforcement authorities.

Not surprisingly, federal authorities were elated with the outcome of the Trauger case. In commenting on the case, a spokesperson for the U.S. Department of Justice observed that the proper functioning of the nation's capital

11. Securities and Exchange Commission, *Accounting and Auditing Enforcement Release No. 1871.*

12. The U.S. Supreme Court overturned Andersen's felony conviction in May 2005; however, by that time, the firm was in the process of being disbanded.

13. E. Iwata, "Accountant Arrested under Sarbanes-Oxley," *USA Today*, 26 September 2003, 2B.

markets depends, in large part, on the integrity of auditors and other professionals involved in the financial reporting process:

> This is one of the first cases in the country in which an auditor has been accused of destroying key documents in an effort to obstruct an investigation. Our financial markets depend on the integrity of auditors, lawyers and other professionals to do their jobs ethically and fairly. Where they fail to do so because of negligence, markets are compromised. Where they fail to do so because of criminal intent, all of us are at risk. The U.S. Attorney's Office will bring those professionals to justice who join in criminal acts they are supposed to uncover and expose.[14]

Stephen Cutler, the SEC's Director of Enforcement, echoed these sentiments and stressed the importance of auditors' maintaining the integrity of the audit process:

> Complete and accurate workpapers are critical to the integrity of the audit process and the efficacy of our investigative work. We will aggressively pursue auditors who alter or destroy workpapers or otherwise undermine the financial reporting process, and will work closely with criminal authorities to ensure that those who engage in such conduct are held accountable.[15]

Finally, an FBI spokesperson observed: "We look to certified public accountants to maintain the integrity of publicly traded companies. The criminal acts of auditors who abuse their authority, act in their own self-interest, and violate the sacred trust of shareholders will not be tolerated."[16]

In October 2004, Michael Mullen pled guilty to lying to an FBI agent involved in the NextCard investigation. Mullen was sentenced to one year of probation and ordered to pay a $100 fine. As a result of his guilty plea, Mullen's right to practice before the SEC was suspended. In August 2003, Oliver Flanagan pled guilty to one count of criminal obstruction of justice. After cooperating with federal authorities in the prosecution of Thomas Trauger, Flanagan was allowed to return to his native Ireland. Flanagan's attorney noted that "Oliver has made peace with our [U.S.] government."[17] The attorney then added that Flanagan's only wish is that Thomas Trauger had been a "better mentor."[18]

NextCard's financial problems steadily worsened following the announcement in late 2001 that federal law enforcement authorities were investigating the company's financial affairs. In February 2002, the OCC ruled that NextBank was operating in an "unsafe and unsound" manner and placed the bank under the control of the Federal Deposit Insurance Corporation (FDIC). At the time, NextCard's stock was trading for $0.14 per share, down from its all-time high of $53.12. In the summer of 2003, a federal bankruptcy court liquidated the company. NextCard had total liabilities of nearly $470 million, which far exceeded its realizable assets of approximately $20 million.

In November 2006, the SEC announced that it had reached an agreement to settle fraud charges filed in 2004 against five former NextCard executives, including Jeremy Lent. In total, the SEC required the executives to pay $1.4 million of fines and other monetary damages. Approximately $900,000 of that amount was paid by Lent. The SEC allowed the five executives to consent to the settlement "without admitting or denying" the charges that had been filed against them.[19] One year earlier, in December 2005, the class-action lawsuit filed against NextCard and its former executives had been settled out of court. Ernst & Young contributed $23.5 million to the settlement pool, while Jeremy Lent contributed $635,000.

---

14. Securities and Exchange Commission, "Former Ernst & Young Audit Partner Arrested for Obstruction Charges and Criminal Violations of the Sarbanes-Oxley Act," *Release No. 2003-123*, 25 September 2003.

15. *Ibid.*

16. *Ibid.*

17. V. Colliver, "FBI Arrests Suspect in Fraud," *San Francisco Chronicle*, 26 September 2003, B1.

18. *Ibid.*

19. Securities and Exchange Commission, *Litigation Release No. 19903*, November 2006.

Questions

1. Should auditors evaluate the soundness of a client's business model? Defend your answer.

2. Identify and briefly describe the specific fraud risk factors present during the 2000 NextCard audit. How should these factors have affected the planning and execution of that engagement?

3. What are the primary objectives an audit team hopes to accomplish by preparing a proper set of audit workpapers?

4. Identify the generally accepted auditing standards violated by the E&Y auditors in this case. Briefly explain how each standard was violated.

5. When he became a member of the NextCard audit engagement team, Oliver Flanagan hoped that Thomas Trauger would serve as his mentor. What responsibility, if any, do senior audit personnel have to serve as mentors for their subordinates?

6. Assume the role of Oliver Flanagan in this case. What would you have done when Thomas Trauger asked you to help him alter the 2000 NextCard audit workpapers? In answering this question, identify the alternative courses of action available to you. Also identify the individuals who may be affected by your decision, and briefly describe how they may be affected.

Lincoln Savings and Loan Association

Charles Keating, Jr., was a scholar-athlete at the University of Cincinnati during the mid-1940s. In 1946, Keating won an NCAA individual championship in the 200-yard butterfly, a swimming event, and two years later graduated from the University of Cincinnati Law School. Over the next 30 years, Keating established himself as the nation's leading critic of the pornography industry. In 1960, he founded the Citizens for Decency through Law, an organization dedicated to "stamping out smut." A decade later, Keating was appointed to President Nixon's Commission on Pornography. Keating became best known nationally for his successful effort to help law enforcement authorities prosecute magazine publisher Larry Flynt, another native of Cincinnati, on obscenity charges.

In 1978, Keating began focusing his time and energy on his business endeavors when he founded the real estate firm, American Continental Corporation (ACC). Six years later, ACC acquired Lincoln Savings and Loan Association, which was headquartered in Phoenix, although its principal operations were in California. In his application to purchase Lincoln, Keating pledged to regulatory authorities that he would retain the Lincoln management team, that he would not use brokered deposits to expand the size of the savings and loan, and that residential home loans would remain Lincoln's principal line of business. After gaining control of Lincoln, Keating replaced the management team; began accepting large deposits from money brokers, which allowed him to nearly triple the size of the savings and loan in two years; and shifted the focus of Lincoln's lending activity from residential mortgage loans to land development projects.

On April 14, 1989, the Federal Home Loan Bank Board (FHLBB) seized control of Lincoln Savings and Loan, alleging that Lincoln was dissipating its assets by operating in an unsafe and unsound manner. On that date, Lincoln's balance sheet reported total assets of $5.3 billion, only 2.3 percent of which were investments in residential mortgage loans. Nearly two-thirds of Lincoln's asset portfolio was invested directly or indirectly in high-risk land ventures and other commercial development projects. At the time, federal authorities estimated that the closure of Lincoln Savings and Loan would cost U.S. taxpayers at least $2.5 billion.

Congressional hearings into the collapse of Lincoln Savings and Loan initially focused on the methods Keating used to circumvent banking laws and on disclosures that five U.S. senators intervened on Keating's behalf with federal banking regulators. Eventually, the hearings centered on the failure of Lincoln's independent auditors to expose fraudulent real estate transactions that allowed the savings and loan to report millions of dollars of nonexistent profits. In summarizing the Lincoln debacle, U.S. Representative Jim Leach laid the blame for the costly savings and loan failure on a number of parties, including Lincoln's auditors and the accounting profession as a whole:

I am stunned. As I look at these transactions, I am stunned at the conclusions of an independent auditing firm. I am stunned at the result. And let me just tell you, I think that this whole circumstance of a potential $2.5 billion cost to the United States taxpayers is a scandal for the United States Congress. It is a scandal for the Texas and California *legislatures. It is a scandal for the Reagan administration regulators. And it is a scandal for the accounting profession.*[1]

Creative Accounting, Influence Peddling, and Other Abuses at Lincoln Savings and Loan

Representative Henry Gonzalez, chairman of the U.S. House Committee on Banking, Finance and Urban Affairs, charged that over the five years Charles Keating owned Lincoln, he employed accounting schemes to divert the savings and loan's federally insured deposits into ACC's treasury. Keating was aware that he would be permitted to withdraw funds from Lincoln and invest them in ACC or use them for other purposes only to the extent that Lincoln reported after-tax profits. Consequently, he and his associates wove together complex real estate transactions involving Lincoln, ACC, and related third parties to manufacture paper profits for Lincoln. Kenneth Leventhal & Company, an accounting firm retained by regulatory authorities to analyze and report on Lincoln's accounting practices, used a few simple examples to explain the saving and loan's fraudulent schemes. Exhibit 1 contains a portion of the

EXHIBIT 1

CONGRESSIONAL TESTIMONY OF KENNETH LEVENTHAL & COMPANY REGARDING LINCOLN'S REAL ESTATE TRANSACTIONS

To illustrate the accounting concepts Lincoln used, let me give you a few simple, hypothetical examples. Suppose you own a house that you paid $100,000 for, and against which you still owe $60,000. Now, suppose you could not find a buyer for your house. Therefore, you go out and find an individual who agrees to pay you the $200,000 you want for your house, but is only willing to give you one dollar in cash and a nonrecourse note for the balance of $199,999. A nonrecourse note means that you cannot get at him personally. If he defaults on the note, your only recourse is to take the house back.

So now you have one dollar in your pocket, and a note for the rest. You very likely have not parted company with your house in this situation, because your so-called buyer may be unable to pay you, or he may simply decide that he does not want to pay you. Economically, he has an option to stick to the deal if the price of the house appreciates, or he can walk away from it if it does not. That is not a sale.

Now, suppose you have the same house again. Your next-door neighbor has a different house, but it is worth the same as yours, and has the same outstanding mortgage balance. You then swap houses and mortgages with your neighbor.

You now have a house which is different, but very similar to the one that you did have. I think that you will agree, there is no profit realized on this exchange. By the accounting theory that Lincoln appears to have followed, you would be able to record a $100,000 profit: the difference between what you originally paid for your house and what you think your neighbor's house is worth.

Really, it could have been more, if you could have found an appraiser to tell you that your neighbor's house was worth $300,000. And it could have been still more if you and your neighbor had simply chosen to agree upon a stated price which was even in excess of these amounts.

As you can see, all sales of real estate are not created equal. Over the years, accountants have had to wrestle with what is economically a sale and what is not. The economic substance of a transaction should of course be the controlling consideration.

---

1. This and all subsequent quotations, unless indicated otherwise, were taken from the following source: U.S. Congress, House, Committee on Banking, Finance and Urban Affairs; *Investigation of Lincoln Savings and Loan Association, Part 4* (Washington, DC: U.S. Government Printing Office, 1990).

Leventhal firm's testimony before Representative Gonzalez's committee, which sponsored the lengthy Congressional investigation of Lincoln Savings and Loan.

One of the most scrutinized of Lincoln's multimillion-dollar real estate deals was the large Hidden Valley transaction that took place in the spring of 1987. On March 30, 1987, Lincoln loaned $19.6 million to E. C. Garcia & Company. On that same day, Ernie Garcia, a close friend of Keating and the owner of the land development company bearing his name, extended a $3.5 million loan to Wescon, a mortgage real estate concern owned by Garcia's friend, Fernando Acosta. The following day, Wescon purchased 1,000 acres of unimproved desert land in central Arizona from Lincoln for $14 million, nearly twice the value established for the land by an independent appraiser one week earlier. Acosta used the loan from Garcia as the down payment on the tract of land and signed a nonrecourse note for the balance. Lincoln recorded a profit of $11.1 million on the transaction—profit that was never realized, since the savings and loan never received payment on the nonrecourse note.

In fact, Lincoln never expected to be paid the balance of the nonrecourse note. Lincoln executives arranged the loan simply to allow the savings and loan to book a large paper gain. Garcia later testified that he agreed to become involved in the deceptive Hidden Valley transaction only because he wanted the $19.6 million loan from Lincoln.[2] Recognizing a profit on the Hidden Valley transaction would have openly violated financial accounting standards if Garcia had acquired the property directly from Lincoln and used for his down payment funds loaned to him by the savings and loan.

Fernando Acosta eventually admitted that his company, Wescon, which prior to the Hidden Valley transaction had total assets of $87,000 and a net worth of $30,000, was only a "straw buyer" of the Hidden Valley property. In a *Los Angeles Times* article, Acosta reported that Wescon "was too small to buy the property and that he signed the documents without reading them to help his friend, Ernie Garcia."[3] Exhibit 2 contains a letter that a worried Acosta wrote to Garcia in 1988 regarding the Hidden Valley transaction. In that letter, Acosta encouraged Garcia to assume title to the property so that he could take it off Wescon's books.

Keating and his associates repeatedly used bogus real estate transactions, such as the Hidden Valley charade, to produce enormous gains for Lincoln. In 1986 and 1987 alone, Lincoln recognized more than $135 million of profits on such transactions. That amount represented more than one-half of the savings and loan's total reported profits for the two-year period.

The gains recorded by Lincoln on its real estate transactions allowed ACC to withdraw huge sums of cash from the savings and loan in the form of intercompany dividend payments, funds that were actually federally insured deposits. When the "purchasers" of these tracts of land defaulted on their nonrecourse notes, Lincoln was forced to recognize losses--losses that the savings and loan offset with additional "profitable" real estate transactions. This recurring cycle of events ensured that Lincoln would eventually fail. However, since the Federal Savings and Loan Insurance Corporation (FSLIC) guaranteed Lincoln's liabilities (that is, its deposits), and since ACC had little equity capital invested in Lincoln, Keating was not overly concerned by the inevitable demise of his company's savings and loan subsidiary.

Lincoln's convoluted and contrived real estate transactions appalled members of Representative Gonzalez's Congressional committee. One of the Leventhal partners

---

2. K. Kerwin and C. Yang, "Everything Was Fine Until I Met Charlie: The Rise and Stumble of Whiz Kid and Keating Crony Ernie Garcia," *Business Week*, 12 March 1990, 44, 46.

3. J. Granelli, "Firm Says It Was a 'Straw Man' in Lincoln Deal," *Los Angeles Times*, 3 January 1990, D1, D13.

EXHIBIT 2

LETTER FROM
WESCON TO
ERNIE GARCIA
REGARDING HIDDEN
VALLEY PROPERTY

[This letter was addressed to Mr. E.C. Garcia, E.C. Garcia and Company, Inc., and appeared on Wescon letterhead.]

Re: Hidden Valley Project/Property

Dear Ernie:

The time when we should have been out of this project is well past.

For various reasons, our discomfort with continuation in the project is growing. Particularly of late, we have been concerned with how to report this to the IRS. We are convinced that all we can do is report as if the corporation were not the true/beneficial owner, but merely the nominal title holder, which is consistent with the facts and the reality of the situation. Correspondingly, it seems you should have, and report, the real tax burdens and benefits arising from this property.

Also, we are increasingly uncomfortable with showing this property on our company's financial statements (and explaining why it is there). We absolutely need to extract this item.

In order to expedite relief for us on this matter, in line with your repeated assurances, please arrange for the transfer of this property to its rightful owner as soon as possible.

Sincerely,

FRA/Wescon

Fernando R. Acosta

who testified before the Congressional committee provided the following overview of his firm's report on Lincoln's accounting schemes:

> Seldom in our experience have we encountered a more egregious example of misapplication of generally accepted accounting principles. This association [Lincoln] was made to function as an engine, designed to funnel insured deposits to its parent in tax allocation payments and dividends. To do this, it had to generate reportable earnings. It created profits by making loans. Many of these loans were bad. Lincoln was manufacturing profits by giving money away.

Critics chastised Charles Keating not only for employing creative accounting methods but for several other abusive practices as well. In 1979, Keating signed a consent decree with the Securities and Exchange Commission (SEC) to settle conflict of interest charges the agency had filed against him. In 1985, Keating handpicked his 24-year-old son, Charles Keating III, to serve as Lincoln's president. Along with the impressive job title came an annual salary of $1 million. At the time, the young man's only prior work experience was as a busperson in a country club restaurant. Years later, the younger Keating testified that he did not understand many of the transactions he signed off on as Lincoln's president.

The elder Keating's gaudy lifestyle and ostentatious spending habits were legendary. U.S. taxpayers absorbed many of the excessive expenses rung up by Keating since he pawned them off as business expenses of Lincoln. The bill for a 1987 dinner Keating hosted at an upscale Washington, D.C., restaurant came to just slightly less than $2,500. One of the guests at that dinner was a former SEC commissioner. In another incident, after inadvertently scuffing a secretary's $30 shoes, Keating wrote her a check for $5,000 to replace them—and the rest of her wardrobe as well, apparently. Other Keating excesses documented by federal and state investigators included safaris, vacations in European castles, numerous trips to the south of France, and lavish parties for relatives and government officials.

The most serious charges leveled at Keating involved allegations of influence peddling. Keating contributed heavily to the election campaigns of five prominent senators, including John Glenn of Ohio and John McCain of Arizona. These five senators, who became known as the Keating Five, met with federal banking regulators and lobbied for favorable treatment of Lincoln Savings and Loan. The key issue in these lobbying efforts was the so-called direct investment rule adopted by the FHLBB in 1985. This rule limited the amount that savings and loans could invest directly in subsidiaries, development projects, and other commercial ventures to 10 percent of their total assets. Because such investments were central to Lincoln's operations, the direct investment rule imposed severe restrictions on Keating—restrictions that he repeatedly ignored.

In 1986, a close associate of Keating's was appointed to fill an unexpired term on the FHLBB. Following his appointment, this individual proposed an amendment to the direct investment rule that would have exempted Lincoln from its requirements. The amendment failed to be seconded and thus was never adopted. Shortly before Alan Greenspan was appointed to the powerful position of chairman of the Federal Reserve Board, Keating retained him to represent Lincoln before the FHLBB. In a legal brief submitted to the FHLBB, Greenspan reported that Lincoln's management team was "seasoned and expert" and that the savings and loan was a "financially strong" institution. Congressional testimony also disclosed that Keating loaned $250,000, with very favorable payback terms, to a former SEC commissioner, who then lobbied the SEC on Lincoln's behalf.

The charges of influence peddling failed to concern or distract Keating. In responding to these charges, Keating made the following remarks during a press conference: "One question, among the many raised in recent weeks, has to do with whether my financial support in any way influenced several political figures to take up my cause. I want to say in the most forceful way I can: I certainly hope so."[4]

Federal authorities eventually indicted Keating on various racketeering and securities fraud charges. He was also sued by the Resolution Trust Corporation, the federal agency created to manage the massive savings and loan crisis that threatened the integrity of the nation's banking system during the 1980s. That agency charged Keating with insider dealing, illegal loans, sham real estate and tax transactions, and the fraudulent sale of Lincoln securities.

Audit History of Lincoln Savings and Loan

Arthur Andersen served as Lincoln's independent auditor until 1985 when it resigned "to lessen its exposure to liability from savings and loan audits," according to a *New York Times* article.[5] That same article described the very competitive nature of the Phoenix audit market during the mid-1980s when Lincoln was seeking a replacement auditor. Because of the large size of the Lincoln audit, several audit firms pursued the engagement, including Arthur Young & Company.[6] From 1978 through 1984, Arthur

---

4. D.J. Jefferson, "Keating of American Continental Corp. Comes Out Fighting," *The Wall Street Journal,* 18 April 1989, B2.

5. E.N. Berg, "The Lapses by Lincoln's Auditors," *The New York Times,* 28 December 1989, D1, D6.

6. Arthur Andersen and, subsequently, Arthur Young audited both ACC and Lincoln, a wholly owned subsidiary of ACC. However, the Lincoln audit was much more complex and required much more time to complete than the ACC audit. Reportedly, the ACC/Lincoln audit accounted for one-fifth of the annual audit revenues of Arthur Young's Phoenix office during 1986 and 1987.

Young suffered a net loss of 63 clients nationwide.[7] Over the next five years, an intense marketing effort produced a net increase of more than 100 audit clients for the firm. During the 1980s, critics of the accounting profession suggested that the extremely competitive audit market induced many audit firms to accept high-risk clients, such as Lincoln, in exchange for large audit fees.

> The savings industry crisis has revived questions repeatedly raised in the past about the profession's independence in auditing big corporate clients: whether the accounts need more controls and whether some firms are willing to sanction questionable financial statements in exchange for high fees, a practice called "bottom fishing."[8]

Before pursuing Lincoln as an audit client, Jack Atchison, an Arthur Young partner in Phoenix, contacted the former Lincoln engagement partner at Arthur Andersen. The Arthur Andersen partner told Atchison that he had no reason to question the integrity of Lincoln's management and that no major disagreements preceded the resignation of his firm as Lincoln's auditor. At the time of Arthur Andersen's resignation, Lincoln was undergoing an intensive examination by FHLBB auditors, who were raising serious questions regarding Lincoln's financial records. Arthur Young was not informed of this investigation by Arthur Andersen. Years later, Arthur Andersen partners denied that they were aware of the examination when they resigned from the audit.

Shortly after accepting Lincoln as an audit client, Arthur Young learned of the FHLBB audit. Among the most serious charges of the FHLBB auditors was that Lincoln had provided interest-free loans to ACC—a violation of federal banking laws—and had falsified loan documents. Three years later, officials from the Office of Thrift Supervision testified before Congress that Arthur Andersen and Lincoln employees had engaged in so-called file-stuffing. These charges resulted in formal inquiries by the Federal Bureau of Investigation and the U.S. Department of Justice.[9] Arthur Andersen officials denied involvement in any illegal activities but did acknowledge that employees of their firm had worked "under the direction of client [Lincoln] personnel to assist them in organizing certain [loan] files."[10] Later, a representative of Lincoln admitted that "memorialization" had been used for certain loan files.

Congressional testimony of several Arthur Young representatives revealed that the 1986 and 1987 Lincoln audits were very complex engagements. William Gladstone, the co-managing partner of Ernst & Young (the firm formed by the 1989 merger of Ernst & Whinney and Arthur Young), testified that the 1987 audit required 30,000 hours to complete. Despite concerns being raised by regulatory authorities, Arthur Young issued an unqualified opinion on Lincoln's financial statements in both 1986 and 1987. Critics contend that these clean opinions allowed Lincoln to continue engaging in illicit activities. Of particular concern to Congressional investigators was that during this time Keating and his associates sold ACC's high-yield "junk" bonds in the lobbies of Lincoln's numerous branches. The sale of these bonds, which were destined to become totally worthless, raised more than $250 million for ACC. The marketing campaign for the bonds targeted retired individuals, many of whom believed that the bonds were federally insured since they were being sold on the premises of a savings and loan.

---

7. L. Berton, "Spotlight on Arthur Young Is Likely to Intensify as Lincoln Hearings Resume," *The Wall Street Journal*, 21 November 1989, A20.

8. N.C. Nash, "Auditors of Lincoln On the Spot," *The New York Times*, 14 November 1989, D1, D19.

9. P. Thomas and B. Jackson, "Regulators Cite Delays and Phone Bugs in Examination, Seizure of Lincoln S&L," *The Wall Street Journal*, 27 October 1989, A4; Berg, "The Lapses by Lincoln's Auditors."

10. Thomas and Jackson, "Regulators Cite Delays and Phone Bugs."

When called to testify before the U.S. House committee, SEC Commissioner Richard Breeden was asked to explain why his agency did not force ACC to stop selling the junk bonds in Lincoln's branches.

Congressman Hubbard: *Didn't the SEC have not one, not two, but actually three or more opportunities to stop the sale of the ACC subordinated debt?*

Commissioner Breeden: *We did not have any opportunity—the only way in which the SEC can stop the sale of securities is if we are able to prove those securities are being distributed based on false and misleading information. And we have to prove that in court. We cannot have reasons to be concerned about it, we cannot have suspicions, we cannot just have cause to be concerned; we have to be able to prove that in court.*

And remember that this is a situation in which one of the Big Eight accounting firms is certifying that these accounts comply fully with generally accepted accounting principles, without caveat or limitation in any way. That is an important factor in that kind of decision [Emphasis added.].

Following the completion of the 1987 Lincoln audit, the engagement audit partner, Jack Atchison, resigned from Arthur Young and accepted a position with ACC. Exhibit 3 contains the memorandum Atchison wrote to William Gladstone, who at the time was Arthur Young's managing partner, to inform Gladstone of his resignation. Gladstone later testified that Atchison earned approximately $225,000 annually as an Arthur Young partner before his resignation. ACC records revealed that Atchison's new position came with an annual salary of approximately $930,000.

The close relationship that Atchison developed with Keating before resigning from Arthur Young alarmed Congressional investigators. Testimony before the Congressional committee disclosed that Atchison, while he was serving as the engagement partner on the Lincoln audit, wrote several letters to banking regulators and U.S. senators vigorously supporting the activities of Keating and Lincoln: "Atchison seemed to drop the auditor's traditional stance of independence by repeatedly defending the practices of Lincoln and its corporate parent to Congress and federal regulators. . . . Since when does the outside accountant—the public watchdog—become a proponent of the client's affairs?"[11]

Congressman Gonzalez's committee also questioned Arthur Young representatives regarding Atchison's relationship with the Arthur Young audit team after he joined ACC. The committee was concerned that Atchison may have been in a position to improperly influence the auditors he had supervised just weeks earlier.

Congressman Lehman: *Did anyone at AY have any contact with Mr. Atchison after he left and went to work for Lincoln?*

Mr. Gladstone: *Yes, sir.*

Congressman Lehman: *In the course of the audit?*

Mr. Gladstone: *Yes.*

Congressman Lehman: *So he went from one side of the table to the other for $700,000 more?*

Mr. Gladstone: *That is what happened.*

Congressman Lehman: *And he—just tell me what his role was in the audits . . . when he was on the other side of the table.*

---

11. Berg, "The Lapses by Lincoln's Auditors."

EXHIBIT 3

MEMORANDUM
FROM JACK
ATCHISON
TO WILLIAM
GLADSTONE

[This memorandum appeared on Arthur Young letterhead.]

TO: Office of Chairman   FROM: Phoenix Office
    William L. Gladstone   Jack D. Atchison
    Hugh Grant, West Regional Office
    Al Boos, Phoenix Office

SUBJECT:

Several weeks ago, Charles H. Keating, Jr., Chairman of American Continental Corporation, asked me to consider joining his company at a senior executive level. Because we were in the process of conducting an audit, I informed Mr. Keating that any discussions regarding future employment would have to await the conclusion of the audit. I also informed Hugh Grant of Mr. Keating's overtures to me.

Knowing Mr. Keating would raise the subject again at the conclusion of the audit, I began to seriously consider the possibility of leaving Arthur Young to join American Continental. Arthur Young has been my professional home for over 24 years, providing a comfortable source of income and rewarding professional environment. My closest personal friends are also my partners. To even consider no longer being a part of Arthur Young was difficult and traumatic, since serving as a partner in Arthur Young has been my single professional goal since 1962.

On April 8 and 11, 1988, I had discussions with Mr. Keating wherein he presented an employment offer which was very rewarding economically and very challenging professionally. His offer addressed all of my economic, job security and position description requirements and concerns. American Continental offers some unique challenges and potential rewards not presently available in Arthur Young. It also presents some risks not present in the Arthur Young environment.

Based on American Continental's offer and my perception of the future there, I have decided to accept their offer and seek to withdraw from the Arthur Young partnership at the earliest possible date. Since American Continental is an SEC client and active issuer of securities requiring registration, and Arthur Young's consent to the use of its report is needed in such filings, an expedited withdrawal arrangement would protect against any real or apparent conflicts of interest between Arthur Young and American Continental.

Mr. Gladstone: *He was a senior vice president for American Continental when he joined them in May 1988.*

Congressman Lehman: *Did the job he had there have anything to do with interfacing with the auditors?*

Mr. Gladstone: *To some extent, yes.*

Congressman Lehman: *What does "to some extent" mean?*

Mr. Gladstone: *On major accounting issues that were discussed in the Form 8-K, we did have conversations with Jack Atchison.*

Congressman Lehman: *So he was the person Mr. Keating had to interface with you in major decisions?*

Mr. Gladstone: *Him, and other officers of American Continental.*

During the summer of 1988, the relationship between Lincoln's executives and the Arthur Young's audit team gradually soured. Janice Vincent, who became the Lincoln engagement partner following Atchison's resignation, testified that disagreements arose with client management that summer over the accounting treatment applied to several large real estate transactions. The most serious disagreement involved a proposed exchange of assets between Lincoln and another corporation—a transaction for which Lincoln intended to record a $50 million profit. Lincoln management insisted that the exchange involved dissimilar assets. Vincent, on the other hand, stubbornly maintained that the transaction involved the exchange of similar assets and, consequently, that the gain on the transaction could not be recognized. During the Congressional hearings, Vincent described how this dispute and related disputes eventually led to the resignation of Arthur Young as Lincoln's auditor.

> *These disagreements created an adversarial relationship between members of Arthur Young's audit team and American Continental officials, which resulted in Mr. Keating requesting a meeting with Bill Gladstone. . . . While in New York at that meeting, Mr. Keating turned to me at one point and said, "Lady, you have just lost a job." That did not happen. Rather, he had lost an accounting firm.*

Following Arthur Young's resignation in October 1988, Keating retained Touche Ross to audit Lincoln's 1988 financial statements. Touche Ross became ensnared, along with Arthur Andersen and Arthur Young, in the web of litigation following Lincoln's collapse. Purchasers of the ACC bonds sold in Lincoln's branches named Touche Ross as a defendant in a large class-action lawsuit. The suit alleged that had Touche Ross not accepted Lincoln as an audit client, ACC's ability to sell the bonds would have been diminished significantly.

Criticism of Arthur Young Following Lincoln's Collapse

Both Arthur Young and its successor, Ernst & Young, were criticized for the former's role in the Lincoln Savings and Loan debacle. One of the most common criticisms was that Arthur Young readily accepted questionable documentary evidence provided by Lincoln employees to corroborate the savings and loan's real estate transactions. During the Congressional hearings into the collapse of Lincoln, William Gladstone commented on the appraisals that Arthur Young obtained to support those transactions: "All appraisals of land [owned by Lincoln] were done by appraisers hired by the company, and we had to rely on them." Certainly, these appraisals were relevant evidence to be used in auditing Lincoln's real estate transactions. However, appraisals obtained by Arthur Young from independent third parties would have been just as relevant and less subject to bias.[12]

Among Arthur Young's most vocal critics during the Congressional hearings was the newly appointed SEC commissioner, Richard Breeden. Commissioner Breeden berated Arthur Young for failing to cooperate with an SEC investigation into Lincoln's financial affairs.

Commissioner Breeden: *We subpoenaed the accountants [Arthur Young] to provide all of their workpapers and their back-up.*

Congressman Hubbard: *Do you know if they were forthcoming and helpful in helping you resolve some of these questions, or helping the SEC resolve some of these questions?*

Commissioner Breeden: *No. I would characterize them as very unhelpful, very unforthcoming, and very resistant to cooperate in any way, shape or form.*

Earlier, Commissioner Breeden had testified that many of the subpoenaed documents that Arthur Young eventually produced were illegible or obscured: "The firm [Arthur Young] ultimately, after much discussion, produced legible copies of the documents, but not before the Commission [SEC] was forced to prepare court

---

12. Quite possibly, Arthur Young did obtain independent appraisals in certain cases, although Gladstone's testimony suggests otherwise.

enforcement requests to overcome Arthur Young's uncooperative stance. Unfortunately, a substantial amount of staff time and resources was devoted unnecessarily to overcoming this resistance to the Commission's subpoenas."

When given an opportunity to respond to Commissioner Breeden's charges, William Gladstone maintained that the delays in providing the SEC with the requested documents were not intentional: "We did not stonewall the SEC. There are Arizona state privilege statutes and ethics rules which prohibit our producing our work papers without a client consent. . . . I also take issue with the allegation that we obliterated some papers. . . . The SEC itself requires a confidentiality stamp on all papers on which confidentiality was requested."

The most stinging criticism of Arthur Young during the Congressional hearings was triggered by the report prepared by Kenneth Leventhal & Company on Lincoln's accounting decisions for its major real estate transactions. Although the Leventhal report served as the basis for much of the criticism directed at Arthur Young, the report did not mention Arthur Young or, in any way, explicitly criticize its Lincoln audits. Nevertheless, since Arthur Young had issued unqualified opinions on Lincoln's financial statements, many parties, including Ernst & Young officials, regarded the Leventhal report as an indictment of the quality of Arthur Young's audits.

The key finding of the Leventhal report was that Lincoln had repeatedly violated the substance-over-form concept by engaging in "accounting-driven" deals among related parties to manufacture illusory profits. Ernst & Young representatives contested this conclusion by pointing out that Leventhal reviewed only 15 of the hundreds of real estate transactions that Lincoln engaged in during Arthur Young's tenure. The Ernst & Young representatives were particularly upset that, based upon a review of those 15 transactions, Leventhal implied that none of Lincoln's major real estate transactions were accounted for properly. In Leventhal's defense, a Congressman noted that the 15 transactions in question were all very large and, collectively, accounted for one-half of Lincoln's pretax profits during 1986 and 1987.

At times, the debate over the Leventhal report became very heated. William Gladstone maligned the report, stating that it was gratuitous; contained broad, sweeping generalizations; in certain cases was "flatly wrong"; and, in his opinion, was unprofessional. In responding to these charges, Congressman Leach questioned the professionalism of Gladstone's firm.

Congressman Leach: *[addressing William Gladstone] I am going to be very frank with you, that I am not impressed with the professional ethics of your firm vis-a-vis the United States Congress. Several days ago, my office was contacted by your firm and asked if we would be interested in questions to ask of Leventhal. We said, "Surely." The questions you provided were of an offensive nature. They were to request of Leventhal how much they were paid, implying that perhaps based upon their payment from the U.S. Government that their decisions as CPAs would be biased. I consider that to be very offensive.*

Now, in addition, one of the questions that was suggested I might ask of the Leventhal firm was: Could it be that their firm is biased because a partner in their firm did not make partner in your firm? I consider that exceedingly unprofessional. Would you care to respond to that?

Mr. Gladstone: *I do not know who contacted you, and I certainly do not know how the questions were raised.*

Later in the hearings, the individual who had submitted the questions to Congressman Leach's office was identified as an Ernst & Young employee.

Congressman Leach also took issue with the contention of Ernst & Young representatives that Leventhal's report contained angry and vengeful comments regarding their firm.

Congressman Leach: *I read that report very carefully, and I found no angry, vengeful sweeping statements. But I did find a conclusion that Arthur Young had erred rather grievously.*

In any regard, what we are looking at is an issue that is anything but an accounting kind of debate. One of the techniques of Lincoln vis-a-vis the U.S. government was to attack the opposition. You are employing the same tactics toward Leventhal. . . . I think that is unprofessional, unethical, and, based upon a very careful reading of their statement, irresponsible.

Now, I would like to ask you if you would care to apologize to the Leventhal firm.

Mr. Gladstone: *First, Mr. Leach, I stated in my opening remarks that I believed that their report was general and sweeping and unprofessional, because what I would call unprofessional about it is the statement that looking at 15 transactions, that therefore they would conclude that nothing Lincoln did had the substance——*

Congressman Leach: *I have carefully read their report, and they note that they have just been allowed to look at 15 transactions. They could not go into more detail, but they were saying that ACC batted 15 for 15, that all 15 transactions were unusual, perplexing, and in their judgment in each case breached ethical standards in terms of generally accepted accounting principles.*

Your firm in effect is saying, "We think that there may be some legal liabilities. Therefore, we are going to stonewall, and we are going to defend each and every one of these transactions."

I believe that you are one of the great firms in the history of accounting. But I also believe that big and great people and institutions can sometimes err. And it is better to acknowledge error than to put one's head in the sand.

I think before our committee you have rather righteously done that.

EPILOGUE

Anthony Elliot, a widower and retired accountant in his 80s, was one of thousands of elderly Californians who invested heavily in the junk bonds of Lincoln Savings and Loan's parent company, ACC. In fact, Elliot invested practically all of his life savings, approximately $200,000, in the ACC bonds. Like many of his friends who had also purchased the bonds—which they, along with Elliot, believed were federally insured—Elliot was forced to scrape by each month on his small Social Security check after ACC defaulted on the bonds. On Thanksgiving Day in 1990, Elliot slashed his wrists and bled to death in his bathtub. In a suicide note, he remarked that there was "nothing left for me."[13] Elliot's story is just one of many personal tragedies resulting from the Lincoln Savings and Loan scandal.

The estimated losses linked to the demise of Lincoln Savings and Loan eventually rose to $3.4 billion, making it the most costly savings and loan failure in U.S. history at the time. In March 1991, after posting huge losses—approximately

---

13. M. Connelly, "Victim of S&L Loss Kills Self," *Los Angeles Times*, 29 November 1990, B1.

$1 billion in 1989 alone--most of Lincoln's remaining assets were sold to another financial institution by the Resolution Trust Corporation, which had been operating the savings and loan for more than one year. One month later, Lincoln's parent company, ACC, filed for protection from its creditors under the federal bankruptcy laws.

In late 1992, Ernst & Young paid $400 million to settle four lawsuits filed against it by the federal government. These lawsuits charged Ernst & Young with substandard audits of four savings and loans, including Lincoln Savings and Loan. In a similar settlement reported in 1993, Arthur Andersen paid $85 million to the federal government to settle lawsuits that charged the firm with shoddy audits of five savings and loans, including Lincoln. Finally, although Touche Ross served as Lincoln's auditor for only five months, that firm's successor, Deloitte & Touche, paid nearly $8 million to the federal government to settle charges filed against it for its role in the Lincoln debacle.

In April 1991, Ernst & Young agreed to pay the California State Board of Accountancy $1.5 million to settle negligence complaints that the state agency filed against the firm for Arthur Young's audits of Lincoln. An Ernst & Young spokesman noted that the accounting firm agreed to the settlement to "avoid protracted and costly litigation" and insisted that the settlement did not involve the "admission of any fault by the firm or any partner."[14] In August 1994, Arthur Andersen agreed to pay $1.7 million to the California State Board of Accountancy for its alleged negligence in auditing Lincoln. Andersen personnel were also required to perform 10,000 hours of community service. Like Ernst & Young, Andersen denied any wrongdoing when its settlement with the California State Board was announced.

In October 1990, Ernie Garcia pleaded guilty to fraud for his involvement in the Hidden Valley real estate transaction. His plea bargain agreement with federal prosecutors required him to assist them in their investigation of Charles Keating, Jr. In March 1991, the Lincoln executive who oversaw the sale of ACC's junk bonds through Lincoln's branches pleaded guilty to eight state and federal fraud charges that he had misled the investors who purchased those bonds. Two years later, Charles Keating III was sentenced to eight years in prison after being convicted of fraud and conspiracy charges.

In a California jury trial presided over by Judge Lance Ito, Charles Keating, Jr., was convicted in 1991 on 17 counts of securities fraud for his role in marketing ACC's junk bonds. While serving a 10-year prison term for that conviction, Keating was convicted of similar fraud charges in a federal court and sentenced to an additional 12 years in prison.

In April 1996, a federal appeals court overturned Keating's 1991 conviction. The appellate court ruled that Judge Lance Ito had given improper instructions to the jurors who found Keating guilty of securities fraud. Several months later, a U.S. District judge overturned Keating's federal conviction on fraud charges. The judge ruled that several jurors in the federal trial had been aware of Keating's 1991 conviction. According to the judge, that knowledge had likely prejudiced the federal jury in favor of convicting Keating. For the same reason, the judge overturned the 1993 conviction of Charles Keating III.

With both of his convictions overturned, Charles Keating was released from federal prison in December 1996 after serving four-and-a-half years. In January 1999, federal prosecutors announced that they would retry the 75-year-old Keating on various fraud charges. Three months later, the federal prosecutors and Keating reached an agreement, an agreement that gave both parties what they wanted most. In federal court, Keating admitted for the first time that he had committed various fraudulent acts while serving as ACC's chief executive. In return, Keating was sentenced to the time he had already served in prison. Even more important to Keating, his plea bargain arrangement required federal prosecutors to drop all charges still outstanding against his son, Charles Keating III.[15]

---

14. "E&Y Pays $1.5M in Lincoln Failure," *Accounting Today*, 13 May 1991, 1, 25.

15. In November 2000, California state prosecutors announced that they would not retry Charles Keating for his role in marketing ACC's junk bonds. This announcement effectively ended Keating's legal problems linked to the collapse of Lincoln Savings and Loan.

Questions

1. Arthur Young was criticized for not encouraging Lincoln to invoke the substance-over-form principle when accounting for its large real estate transactions. Briefly describe the substance-over-form concept and exactly what it requires. What responsibilities, if any, do auditors have when a client violates this principle?

2. Explain how the acceptance of large, high-risk audit clients for relatively high audit fees may threaten an audit firm's *de facto* and perceived independence. Under what circumstances should such prospective clients be avoided?

3. How is an auditor's examination affected when a client has engaged in significant related party transactions? What measures should an auditor take to determine that such transactions have been properly recorded by a client?

4. Professional standards require auditors to consider a client's "control environment." Define *control environment*. What weaknesses, if any, were evident in Lincoln's control environment?

5. What was the significance of Lincoln receiving nonrecourse notes rather than recourse notes as payment or partial payment on many of the properties it sold?

6. Professional auditing standards identify the principal "management assertions" that underlie a set of financial statements. What are the key assertions that Arthur Young should have attempted to substantiate for the Hidden Valley transaction? What procedures should Arthur Young have used for this purpose, and what types of evidence should have been collected?

7. Do you believe that Jack Atchison's close relationship with Lincoln and Charles Keating prior to his leaving Arthur Young was proper? Why or why not? After joining Lincoln's parent company, ACC, should Atchison have "interfaced" with Arthur Young's auditors assigned to the Lincoln and ACC engagements? Again, support your answer.

8. Does the *AICPA Code of Professional Conduct* discuss the collegial responsibilities of CPA firms? In your opinion, were representatives of either Ernst & Young or Kenneth Leventhal & Company unprofessional in this regard during their Congressional testimony?

9. What responsibilities does an auditor have to uncover fraud perpetrated by client management? Discuss factors that mitigate this responsibility and factors that compound it. Relate this discussion to Arthur Young's audits of Lincoln.

CASE 1.8

Crazy Eddie, Inc.

In 1969, Eddie Antar, a 21-year-old high school dropout from Brooklyn, opened a consumer electronics store with 150 square feet of floor space in New York City.[1] Despite this modest beginning, Antar would eventually dominate the retail consumer electronics market in the New York City metropolitan area. By 1987, Antar's firm, Crazy Eddie, Inc., had 43 retail outlets, sales exceeding $350 million, and outstanding stock with a collective market value of $600 million. Antar personally realized more than $70 million from the sale of Crazy Eddie stock during his tenure as the company's chief executive.

A classic rags-to-riches story became a spectacular business failure in the late 1980s when Crazy Eddie collapsed following allegations of extensive financial wrongdoing by Antar and his associates. Shortly after a hostile takeover of the company in November 1987, the firm's new owners discovered that Crazy Eddie's inventory was overstated by more than $65 million. This inventory shortage had been concealed from the public in registration statements filed with the Securities and Exchange Commission (SEC). Subsequent investigations by regulatory authorities revealed that Eddie Antar and his subordinates had grossly overstated Crazy Eddie's reported profits throughout its existence.[2]

Eddie Antar: The Man Behind the Legend

Eddie Antar was born into a large, closely knit Syrian family in 1947. After dropping out of high school at the age of 16, Antar began peddling television sets in his Brooklyn neighborhood. Within a few years, Antar and one of his cousins scraped together enough cash to open an electronics store near Coney Island. It was at this tiny store that Antar acquired the nickname "Crazy Eddie." When a customer attempted to leave the store empty-handed, Antar would block the store's exit, sometimes locking the door until the individual agreed to buy something—anything. To entice a reluctant customer to make a purchase, Antar first determined which product the customer was considering and then lowered the price until the customer finally capitulated.

Antar became well known in his neighborhood not only for his unusual sales tactics but also for his unconventional, if not asocial, behavior. A bodybuilder and fitness fanatic, he typically came to work in his exercise togs, accompanied by a menacing German shepherd. His quick temper caused repeated problems with vendors, competitors, and subordinates. Antar's most distinctive trait was his inability to trust anyone outside of his large extended family. In later years, when he needed someone to serve in an executive capacity in his company, Antar nearly always tapped a family member, although the individual seldom had the appropriate training or experience

---

1. This case was coauthored by Carol Knapp, Assistant Professor at the University of Oklahoma.

2. The facts of this case were drawn from numerous articles and SEC enforcement releases published over a period of several years. *The New York Times* and *The Wall Street Journal*, in particular, closely followed the colorful saga of Crazy Eddie and its founder, Eddie Antar. One of the more comprehensive investigative reports that documented the history of Crazy Eddie, Inc., is the following article: G. Belsky and P. Furman, "Calculated Madness: The Rise and Fall of Crazy Eddie Antar," *Crain's New York Business*, 5 June 1989, 21–33. That article provided much of the background information regarding Eddie Antar included in this case.

for the position. Eventually, Antar's father, sister, two brothers, uncle, brother-in-law, and several cousins would assume leadership positions with Crazy Eddie, while more than one dozen other relatives would hold minor positions with the firm.

Crazy Eddie's Formula for Success

In the early 1980s, sales in the consumer electronics industry exploded, doubling in the four-year period from 1981 to 1984 alone. As the public's demand for electronic products grew at an ever-increasing pace, Antar converted his Crazy Eddie stores into consumer electronics supermarkets. Antar stocked the shelves of Crazy Eddie's retail outlets with every electronic gadget he could find and with as many different brands of those products as possible. By 1987, the company featured seven product lines. Following are those product lines and their percentage contributions to Crazy Eddie's 1987 sales.

Televisions	53%
Audio products and systems	15
Portable and personal electronics	10
Car stereos	5
Accessories and tapes	4
Computers and games	3
Miscellaneous items—including microwaves, air conditioners, and small appliances	10
Total	100%

Antar encouraged his salespeople to supplement each store's profits by pressuring customers to buy extended product warranties. Many, if not most, of the repair costs that Crazy Eddie paid under these warranties were recovered by the company from manufacturers that had issued factory warranties on the products. As a result, the company realized a 100 percent profit margin on much of its warranty revenue.

As his firm grew rapidly during the late 1970s and early 1980s, Antar began extracting large price concessions from his suppliers. His ability to purchase electronic products in large quantities and at cut-rate prices enabled him to become a "transhipper," or secondary supplier, of these goods to smaller consumer electronics retailers in the New York City area. Although manufacturers frowned on this practice and often threatened to stop selling to him, Antar continually increased the scale of his transhipping operation.

The most important ingredient in Antar's marketing strategy was large-scale advertising. Antar created an advertising "umbrella" over his company's principal retail market that included the densely populated area within a 150-mile radius of New York City. Antar blanketed this region with raucous, sometimes annoying but always memorable, radio and television commercials.

In 1972, Antar hired a local radio personality and part-time actor known as Doctor Jerry to serve as Crazy Eddie's advertising spokesperson. Over the 15 years that the bug-eyed Doctor Jerry hawked products for Crazy Eddie, he achieved a higher "recognition quotient" among the public than Ed Koch, the longtime mayor of New York City. Doctor Jerry's series of ear-piercing television commercials that featured him screaming "Crazy Eddie—His prices are insane!" brought the company national notoriety when they were parodied by Dan Akroyd on *Saturday Night Live*.

Crazy Eddie's discounting policy served as the focal theme of the company's advertising campaigns. The company promised to refund the difference between the selling price of a product and any lower price for that same item that a customer found within 30 days of the purchase date. Despite the advertising barrage intended to convince the public that Crazy Eddie was a deep-discounter, the company's prices on most products were in line with those of its major competitors. Customers drawn to Crazy Eddie outlets by "advertised specials" were routinely diverted by sales staff to higher-priced merchandise.

Crazy Eddie Goes Public

In 1983, Antar decided to sell stock in Crazy Eddie to raise capital to finance his aggressive expansion program. The underwriting firm retained by Antar delayed Crazy Eddie's initial public offering (IPO) for more than one year after discovering that the company's financial records were in disarray. Among other problems uncovered by the underwriter were extensive related-party transactions, interest-free loans to employees, and speculative investments unrelated to the company's principal line of business. The underwriting firm was also disturbed to find that nearly all of the company's key executives were members of the Antar family. Certain of these individuals, including Antar's wife and mother, were receiving salaries approaching $100,000 for little or no work.

To prepare for the IPO, the underwriter encouraged Antar, Crazy Eddie's chairman of the board and president, to clean up the company's accounting records and financial affairs. The underwriter also urged Antar to hire a chief financial officer (CFO) who had experience with a public company and who was not a member of the Antar family. The underwriter warned Antar that investors would question the competence of Crazy Eddie's executives who were his relatives. Despite the underwriter's concern, Antar hired his first cousin, Sam E. Antar, to serve as Crazy Eddie's CFO.

The sale of Crazy Eddie's stock to the public was a tremendous success. Because the IPO was oversubscribed, the company's underwriter obtained permission from the SEC to sell 200,000 more shares than originally planned. Following the public offering, Antar worked hard to convince the investment community, particularly financial analysts, that his firm was financially strong and well managed. At every opportunity, Antar painted a picture of continued growth and increased market share for Crazy Eddie.

One tactic Antar used to convince financial analysts that the company had a rosy future was to invite them to a store and demonstrate in person his uncanny ability to "close" sales. Such tactics worked to perfection as analysts from prominent investment firms released glowing reports regarding Crazy Eddie's management team and the company's bright prospects. One analyst wrote, "Crazy Eddie is a disciplined, competently organized firm with a sophisticated management and a well-trained, dedicated staff."[3] Another analyst wrote that Antar is a "brilliant merchant surrounded by a deeply dedicated organization eager to create an important retail business."[4] Because of such reports and continued strong operating results (as reflected by the company's 1984—1987 financial statements shown in Exhibit 1 and Exhibit 2), the price of Crazy Eddie's stock skyrocketed. Many investors who purchased the company's stock in the IPO realized a 1,000 percent increase in the value of their investments.

Crazy Eddie Goes . . . Bust

Despite Crazy Eddie's impressive operating results during the mid-1980s and the fact that the company's stock was one of the hottest investments on Wall Street, all was not well within the firm. By 1986, the company was in deep trouble. By the latter

---

3. J. E. Tannenbaum, "How Mounting Woes at Crazy Eddie Sank Turnaround Effort," *The Wall Street Journal*, 10 July 1989, A1, A4.

4. G. Belsky and P. Furman, "Calculated Madness: The Rise and Fall of Crazy Eddie Antar," *Crain's New York Business*, 5 June 1989, 26.

EXHIBIT 1

1984–1987
BALANCE SHEETS
OF CRAZY EDDIE

CRAZY EDDIE, INC.
BALANCE SHEETS (000s omitted)

	March 1, 1987	March 2, 1986	March 3, 1985	May 31, 1984
Current assets:				
Cash	$ 9,347	$ 13,296	$22,273	$ 1,375
Short-term investments	121,957	26,840	—	—
Receivables	10,846	2,246	2,740	2,604
Merchandise inventories	109,072	59,864	26,543	23,343
Prepaid expenses	10,639	2,363	645	514
Total current assets	261,861	104,609	52,201	27,836
Restricted cash	—	3,356	7,058	—
Due from affiliates	—	—	—	5,739
Property, plant and equipment	26,401	7,172	3,696	1,845
Construction in process	—	6,253	1,154	—
Other assets	6,596	5,560	1,419	1,149
Total assets	$294,858	$126,950	$65,528	$36,569
Current liabilities:				
Accounts payable	$ 50,022	$ 51,723	$23,078	$20,106
Notes payable	—	—	—	2,900
Short-term debt	49,571	2,254	423	124
Unearned revenue	3,641	3,696	1,173	764
Accrued expenses	5,593	17,126	8,733	6,078
Total current liabilities	108,827	74,799	33,407	29,972
Long-term debt	8,459	7,701	7,625	46
Convertible subordinated debentures	80,975	—	—	—
Unearned revenue	3,337	1,829	635	327
Stockholders' equity:				
Common stock	313	280	134	50
Additional paid-in capital	57,678	17,668	12,298	574
Retained earnings	35,269	24,673	11,429	5,600
Total stockholders' equity	93,260	42,621	23,861	6,224
Total liabilities and stockholders' equity	$294,858	$126,950	$65,528	$36,569

part of that year, the boom days had ended for the consumer electronics industry. Although sales of consumer electronics were still increasing, the rate of growth had tapered off considerably as compared with the dramatic growth rates realized by the industry during the early 1980s. Additionally, the industry had become saturated with retailers, particularly in major metropolitan areas such as New York City, Crazy Eddie's home base. Increased competition meant smaller profit margins for Crazy Eddie and diminished Antar's ability to extract sweetheart deals from his suppliers.

Besides the problems posed by the increasingly competitive consumer electronics industry, Crazy Eddie faced a corporate meltdown in the late 1980s. The tripling of the company's annual sales volume between 1984 and 1987 and the more complex

EXHIBIT 2

1984–1987 INCOME
STATEMENTS OF
CRAZY EDDIE

	Year Ended March 1, 1987	Year Ended March 2, 1986	Nine Months Ended March 3, 1985	Year Ended May 31, 1984
CRAZY EDDIE, INC. INCOME STATEMENTS (000s omitted)				
Net sales	$352,523	$262,268	$136,319	$137,285
Cost of goods sold	(272,255)	(194,371)	(103,421)	(106,934)
Gross profit	80,268	67,897	32,898	30,351
Selling, general and administrative expense	(61,341)	(42,975)	(20,508)	(22,560)
Interest and other income	7,403	3,210	1,211	706
Interest expense	(5,233)	(820)	(438)	(522)
Income before taxes	21,097	27,312	13,163	7,975
Pension contribution	(500)	(800)	(600)	—
Income taxes	(10,001)	(13,268)	(6,734)	(4,202)
Net income	$ 10,596	$ 13,244	$ 5,829	$ 3,773
Net income per share	$.34	$.48	$.24	$.18

responsibilities associated with managing a public company imposed an enormous administrative burden on Crazy Eddie's executives. Complicating matters was the disintegration of Antar's inner circle of relatives, who had served as his principal advisers during the first 15 years of his company's existence. Antar forced many of his relatives to leave the firm after they sided with his former wife in a bitter divorce. Even as Crazy Eddie's internal affairs spiraled into chaos and the firm lurched toward financial disaster, Wall Street continued to tout the company's stock as a "can't miss" investment.

In late 1986, Eddie Antar resigned as company president, although he retained the title of chairman of the board. A few weeks later, he simply dropped out of sight. In the absence of Antar, Crazy Eddie's financial condition worsened rapidly. Poor operating results that the company reported for the fourth quarter of fiscal 1987—which ended March 1, 1987—sent Crazy Eddie's stock price into a tailspin from which it never recovered. In November 1987, a takeover group headed by two well-known financiers gained control of the company. A company-wide physical inventory taken by the new owners uncovered the $65 million shortage of inventory alluded to earlier. That inventory shortage, which was larger than the cumulative profits the company had reported since it went public in 1984, would eventually plunge Crazy Eddie into bankruptcy and send regulatory authorities in pursuit of Eddie Antar for an explanation.

Charges of Accounting Irregularities

Extensive investigations of Crazy Eddie's financial records by the new owners and regulatory authorities culminated in fraud charges being filed against Eddie Antar and his former associates. The SEC alleged that after Crazy Eddie went public in 1984,

Antar became preoccupied with the price of his company's stock. Antar realized that Crazy Eddie had to keep posting impressive operating results to maintain the upward trend in the stock's price. An SEC investigation revealed that within the first six months after the company went public, Antar ordered a subordinate to overstate inventory by $2 million, resulting in the firm's gross profit being overstated by the same amount. The following year Antar ordered year-end inventory to be overstated by $9 million and accounts payable to be understated by $3 million. Court records documented that Crazy Eddie employees overstated year-end inventory by preparing inventory count sheets for items that did not exist. To understate accounts payable, employees prepared bogus debit memos from vendors and entered them in the company's accounting records.

As the economic fortunes of Crazy Eddie began to fade in the late 1980s, Antar became more desperate in his efforts to enhance the company's reported revenues and profits. He ordered company employees to include in inventory consigned merchandise and goods being returned to suppliers. Another fraudulent tactic Antar used to overstate inventory involved transhipping transactions, the large-volume transactions between Crazy Eddie and many of its smaller competitors.

Antar knew that financial analysts closely monitor the annual percentage change in "same-store" sales for retailers. A decline in this percentage is seen as a negative indicator of a retailer's future financial performance. As the consumer electronics industry became increasingly crowded, the revenues of Crazy Eddie's individual stores began to fall, although the firm's total revenues continued to climb due to new stores being opened each year. To remedy the drop in same-store sales, Antar instructed his employees to record selected transhipping transactions as retail sales of individual stores. For instance, suppose that Crazy Eddie sold 100 microwaves costing $180 each to another retailer at a per unit price of $200. The $20,000 in sales would be recorded as retail sales with a normal gross profit margin of 30 to 50 percent—meaning that inventory would not be credited for the total number of microwaves actually sold. This practice killed two birds with the proverbial stone. Same-store sales were inflated for selected operating units, and inventory was overstated with a corresponding increase in gross profit from sales.

Where Were the Auditors?

"Where were the auditors?" was a question posed repeatedly by investors, creditors, and other interested parties when the public learned of the Crazy Eddie fraud. Four different accounting firms audited Crazy Eddie's financial statements over its turbulent history. Antar dismissed Crazy Eddie's first accounting firm, a local firm, before he took the company public. The underwriter that managed Crazy Eddie's IPO urged Antar to retain a more prestigious accounting firm to increase the public's confidence in the company's financial statements. As a result, Antar retained Main Hurdman to serve as Crazy Eddie's audit firm. Main Hurdman had a nationwide accounting practice with several prominent clients in the consumer electronics industry. In the mid-1980s, Peat Marwick became Crazy Eddie's audit firm when it merged with Main Hurdman. Following the corporate takeover of Crazy Eddie in 1987, the new owners replaced Peat Marwick with Touche Ross.

Much of the criticism triggered by the Crazy Eddie scandal centered on Main Hurdman and its successor, Peat Marwick. Main Hurdman charged Crazy Eddie comparatively modest fees for the company's annual audits. A leading critic of major accounting firms alleged that Main Hurdman had "lowballed" to obtain Crazy Eddie as an audit client, realizing that it could make up for any lost audit revenue by selling the company consulting services.

> In one year, Main Hurdman charged only $85,000 to do a complete audit of Crazy Eddie—a business with hundreds of millions of dollars in reported revenues, dozens of retail stores, and two large warehouses. At the very same time that Main Hurdman was charging the bargain basement price of $85,000 for supposedly conducting an audit, its consulting division was charging Crazy Eddie millions of dollars to computerize Crazy Eddie's inventory system.[5]

This same individual challenged Main Hurdman's ability to objectively audit an inventory system that it had effectively developed. Main Hurdman's independence was also questioned because many of Crazy Eddie's accountants were former members of that accounting firm. Critics charge that a company that hires one or more of its former auditors can more easily conceal fraudulent activities during the course of subsequent audits. That is, a former auditor may help his or her new employer undermine subsequent audits. In fact, Crazy Eddie's practice of hiring its former auditors is not unusual. Many accounting firms actually arrange such "placements" with audit clients.

> You would think that if an auditor wanted to leave a public accounting firm, he or she would be discouraged from going to work for clients they had audited. Instead, just the opposite is true with big accounting firms encouraging their personnel to work for clients in the apparent belief that it helps cement the accountant—client relationship.[6]

Most of the criticism directed at Crazy Eddie's auditors stemmed from their failure to uncover the huge overstatement of the company's inventory and the material understatement of accounts payable. Third parties who filed suit against the auditors accused them of "aiding and abetting" the fraud by failing to thoroughly investigate numerous suspicious circumstances they discovered. Of particular concern were several reported instances in which the auditors requested client documents, only to be told that those documents had been lost or inadvertently destroyed.

In Peat Marwick and Main Hurdman's defense, Antar and his associates engaged in a large-scale plan to deceive the auditors. For example, after determining which inventory sites the auditors would be visiting at year-end, Antar shipped sufficient inventory to those stores or warehouses to conceal any shortages. Likewise, Crazy Eddie personnel systematically destroyed incriminating documents to conceal inventory shortages from the auditors. Antar also ordered his employees to "junk" the sophisticated, computer-based inventory system designed by Main Hurdman and to return to the outdated manual inventory system previously used by the company. The absence of a computer-based inventory system made it much more difficult for the auditors to determine exactly how much inventory the firm had at any point in time.

A particularly disturbing aspect of the Crazy Eddie scandal was the involvement of several key accounting employees in the various fraudulent schemes. These parties included the director of the internal audit staff, the acting controller, and the director of accounts payable. Past audit failures demonstrate that a fraud involving the collusion of key accounting personnel is difficult for auditors to uncover.

5. M. I. Weiss, "Auditors: Be Watchdogs, Not Just Bean Counters," *Accounting Today*, 15 November 1993, 41.
6. *Ibid.*, 42.

EPILOGUE

In June 1989, Crazy Eddie filed a Chapter 11 bankruptcy petition after losing its line of credit. Later that year, the company closed its remaining stores and liquidated its assets. Meanwhile, Eddie Antar was named as a defendant in several lawsuits, including a large civil suit filed by the SEC and a criminal indictment filed by a U.S. district attorney. In January 1990, a federal judge ordered Antar to repatriate $52 million that he had transferred to foreign bank accounts in 1987.

The following month, federal marshals began searching for Antar after he failed to appear in the federal court. A judge had scheduled a hearing to force Antar to account for the funds he had transferred to overseas bank accounts. After Antar surrendered to federal marshals, the judge found him in contempt and released him on his own recognizance. Following this court appearance, Antar became a fugitive. For the next two years, Antar eluded federal authorities despite reported sightings of him in Brooklyn, Jerusalem, and South America.

On June 25, 1992, Israeli police arrested Eddie Antar. At the time, he was living in a small town outside Tel Aviv and posing as an Israeli citizen, David Jacob Levi Cohen. On December 31, 1992, Antar's attorney announced that an extradition agreement had been reached with the U.S. Department of Justice and Israeli authorities. After being extradited, Antar was convicted in July 1993 on 17 counts of financial fraud including racketeering, conspiracy, and mail fraud. In May 1994, a federal judge sentenced Antar to 12-1/2 years in federal prison and ordered him to pay restitution of $121 million to former stockholders and creditors.

A federal appeals court overturned Antar's fraud conviction in April 1995. The appeals court ruled that the judge who had presided over Antar's trial had been biased against him and ordered that a new trial be held under a different judge. In May 1996, Antar's attorneys

and federal prosecutors arranged a plea bargain agreement to settle the charges outstanding against him. Under the terms of this agreement, Antar pleaded guilty to one federal charge of racketeering and publicly admitted, for the first time, that he had defrauded investors by manipulating his company's accounting records. Following his admission of guilt, one of the prosecuting attorneys commented: "Crazy Eddie wasn't crazy, he was crooked."[7]

In early 1997, Eddie Antar was sentenced to seven years in federal prison. Antar, who had remained in custody since being extradited to the United States in 1993, received credit for the time he had already spent in prison. As a result, he was required to serve only two years of his seven-year sentence.

Several of Antar's former cohorts have also been convicted or have pleaded guilty to fraud charges, including Sam E. Antar, Crazy Eddie's former CFO. After being released from prison, Sam E. Antar openly described and discussed his role in the fraud masterminded by his cousin. He revealed that Eddie had financed his college degree in accounting because the family needed an expert accountant to help design, manage, and conceal the company's fraudulent schemes. Sam graduated *magna cum laude* in accounting and passed the CPA exam on his first attempt. Upon joining Crazy Eddie, Sam confessed that he became a "thug" and a willing participant in the massive fraud:

> Crazy Eddie was an empire built on deceit. The company was rotten to its core. Eddie Antar, his father, brothers, brother-in-law, me and others formed the nucleus of this massive criminal enterprise. In our day, we considered the humanity of others as weaknesses to be exploited in our efforts to commit our crimes. We simply gave investors, creditors, and many customers a raw deal. . . . We were nothing but cold-hearted and soulless criminals. We were two-bit thugs.[8]

---

7. F. A. McMorris, "Crazy Eddie Inc.,'s Antar Admits Guilt in Racketeering Conspiracy," *The Wall Street Journal*, 9 May 1996, B7.

8. Sam E. Antar, "Crazy Eddie Speaks, Cousin Sam E. Antar Responds," *White Collar Fraud* (http://whitecollarfraud.blogspot.com), 25 June 2007.

In March 1993, an agreement was reached to settle dozens of pending civil lawsuits spawned by the Crazy Eddie fraud. The contributions of the various defendants to the $42 million settlement pool were not disclosed; however, the defendants contributing to that pool included Peat Marwick and the local accounting firm used by Crazy Eddie before the company went public. Law enforcement authorities recovered more than $150 million from the parties that profited from the fraud. Those funds included more than $40 million that a federal judge ordered Sam Antar, Eddie Antar's father, to surrender in August 2002.

In the late 1990s, Eddie Antar's mother purchased the Crazy Eddie logo and the company's former advertising catch phrase, "Crazy Eddie—His prices are insane!" which had been sold in bankruptcy proceedings years earlier. In 1998, two nephews of Eddie Antar revived their uncle's business. The "new" Crazy Eddie operated principally as a mail-order and Internet-based retailer of consumer electronics. In June 2001, a New York business publication reported that the company had hired a former executive in the consumer electronics industry to serve as the "creative force" behind its marketing efforts.[9] That individual was none other than Crazy Eddie Antar.[10]

Questions

1. Compute key ratios and other financial measures for Crazy Eddie during the period 1984–1987. Identify and briefly explain the red flags in Crazy Eddie's financial statements that suggested the firm posed a higher-than-normal level of audit risk.

2. Identify specific audit procedures that might have led to the detection of the following accounting irregularities perpetrated by Crazy Eddie personnel: (a) the falsification of inventory count sheets, (b) the bogus debit memos for accounts payable, (c) the recording of transhipping transactions as retail sales, and (d) the inclusion of consigned merchandise in year-end inventory.

3. The retail consumer electronics industry was undergoing rapid and dramatic changes during the 1980s. Discuss how changes in an audit client's industry should affect audit planning decisions. Relate this discussion to Crazy Eddie.

4. Explain what is implied by the term *lowballing* in an audit context. How can this practice potentially affect the quality of independent audit services?

5. Assume that you were a member of the Crazy Eddie audit team in 1986. You were assigned to test the client's year-end inventory cutoff procedures. You selected 30 invoices entered in the accounting records near year-end, 15 in the few days prior to the client's fiscal year-end, and 15 in the first few days of the new year. Assume that client personnel were unable to locate 10 of these invoices. How should you and your superiors have responded to this situation? Explain.

6. Should companies be allowed to hire individuals who formerly served as their independent auditors? Discuss the pros and cons of this practice.

9. "Week in Review," *Crain's New York Business*, 11 June 2001, 34.

10. In 2004, the "new" Crazy Eddie failed. The company's trademarks were purchased by a Texas-based firm.

ZZZZ Best Company, Inc.

On May 19, 1987, a short article in *The Wall Street Journal* reported that ZZZZ Best Company, Inc., of Reseda, California, had signed a contract for a $13.8 million insurance restoration project. This project was just the most recent of a series of large restoration jobs obtained by ZZZZ Best (pronounced "zee best"). Located in the San Fernando Valley of southern California, ZZZZ Best had begun operations in the fall of 1982 as a small, door-to-door carpet cleaning business. Under the direction of Barry Minkow, the extroverted 16-year-old who founded the company and initially operated it out of his parents' garage, ZZZZ Best experienced explosive growth in both revenues and profits during the first several years of its existence. In the three-year period from 1984 to 1987, the company's net income surged from less than $200,000 to more than $5 million on revenues of $50 million.

When ZZZZ Best went public in 1986, Minkow and several of his close associates became multimillionaires overnight. By the late spring of 1987, the market value of Minkow's stock in the company exceeded $100 million, while the total market value of ZZZZ Best surpassed $200 million. The youngest chief executive officer in the nation enjoyed the "good life," which included an elegant home in an exclusive suburb of Los Angeles and a fire-engine–red Ferrari. Minkow's charm and entrepreneurial genius made him a sought-after commodity on the television talk show circuit and caused the print and visual media to tout him as an example of what America's youth could attain if they would only apply themselves. During an appearance on *The Oprah Winfrey Show* in April 1987, Minkow exhorted his peers with evangelistic zeal to "Think big, be big" and encouraged them to adopt his personal motto, "The sky is the limit."

Less than two years after appearing on *Oprah*, Barry Minkow began serving a 25-year prison sentence. Tried and convicted on 57 counts of securities fraud, Minkow had been exposed as a fast-talking con artist who swindled his closest friends and Wall Street out of millions of dollars. Federal prosecutors estimate that, at a minimum, Minkow cost investors and creditors $100 million. The company that Minkow founded was, in fact, an elaborate Ponzi scheme. The reported profits of the firm were nonexistent and the large restoration contracts, imaginary. As one journalist reported, rather than building a corporation, Minkow created a hologram of a corporation. In July 1987, just three months after the company's stock reached a market value of $220 million, an auction of its assets netted only $62,000.

Unlike most financial frauds, the ZZZZ Best scam was perpetrated under the watchful eye of the Securities and Exchange Commission (SEC). The SEC, a large and reputable West Coast law firm that served as the company's general counsel, a prominent Wall Street brokerage firm, and an international public accounting firm all failed to uncover Minkow's daring scheme. Ultimately, the persistence of an indignant homemaker who had been bilked out of a few hundred dollars by ZZZZ Best resulted in Minkow being exposed as a fraud.

How a teenage flimflam artist could make a mockery of the complex regulatory structure that oversees the U.S. securities markets was the central question posed by a Congressional subcommittee that investigated the ZZZZ Best debacle. That subcommittee was headed by Representative John D. Dingell, chairman of the U.S. House Committee on Energy and Commerce. Throughout the investigation, Representative

Dingell and his colleagues focused on the role the company's independent auditors played in the ZZZZ Best scandal.

> *The ZZZZ Best prospectus told the public that revenues and earnings from insurance restoration contracts were skyrocketing but did not reveal that the contracts were completely fictitious. Where were the independent auditors and the others that are paid to alert the public to fraud and deceit?*[1]

Like many other daring financial frauds, the ZZZZ Best scandal caused Congress to reexamine the maze of rules that regulate financial reporting and serve as the foundation of the U.S. system of corporate oversight. However, Daniel Akst, a reporter for *The Wall Street Journal* who documented the rise and fall of Barry Minkow, suggested that another ZZZZ Best was inevitable. "Changing the accounting rules and securities laws will help, but every now and then a Barry Minkow will come along, and ZZZZ Best will happen again. Such frauds are in the natural order of things, I suspect, as old and enduring as human needs."[2]

The Early History of ZZZZ Best Company

Barry Minkow was introduced to the carpet cleaning industry at the age of 12 by his mother, who helped make ends meet by working as a telephone solicitor for a small carpet cleaning firm. Although the great majority of companies in the carpet cleaning industry are legitimate, the nature of the business attracts a disproportionate number of shady characters. There are essentially no barriers to entry: no licensing requirements, no apprenticeships to be served, and only a minimal amount of start-up capital is needed. A 16-year-old youth with a driver's license can easily become what industry insiders refer to as a "rug sucker," which is exactly what Minkow did when he founded ZZZZ Best Company.

Minkow quickly learned that carpet cleaning was a difficult way to earn a livelihood. Customer complaints, ruthless competition, bad checks, and nagging vendors demanding payment complicated the young entrepreneur's life. Within months of striking out on his own, Minkow faced the ultimate nemesis of the small businessperson: a shortage of working capital. Because of his age and the fact that ZZZZ Best was only marginally profitable, local banks refused to loan him money. Ever resourceful, the brassy teenager came up with his own innovative ways to finance his business: check kiting, credit card forgeries, and the staging of thefts to fleece his insurance company. Minkow's age and personal charm allowed him to escape unscathed from his early brushes with the law that resulted from his creative financing methods. The ease with which the "system" could be beaten encouraged him to exploit it on a broader scale.

Throughout his tenure with ZZZZ Best, Minkow recognized the benefits of having an extensive social network of friends and acquaintances. Many of these relationships he developed and cultivated at a Los Angeles health club. After becoming a friend of Tom Padgett, an insurance claims adjuster, Minkow devised a scheme to exploit that friendship. Minkow promised to pay Padgett $100 per week if he would simply confirm over the telephone to banks and any other interested third parties that ZZZZ Best was the recipient of occasional insurance restoration contracts. Ostensibly, Minkow had

---

1. This and all subsequent quotations, unless indicated otherwise, were taken from the following source: U.S. Congress, House, Subcommittee on Oversight and Investigations of the Committee on Energy and Commerce, *Failure of ZZZZ Best Co.* (Washington, DC: U.S. Government Printing Office, 1988). Each of the exhibits in this case was also taken from this source.

2. D. Akst, *Wonder Boy, Barry Minkow—The Kid Who Swindled Wall Street* (New York: Scribner, 1990), 271.

obtained these contracts to clean and do minor remodeling work on properties damaged by fire, storms, or other catastrophes. Minkow convinced the gullible Padgett that the sole purpose of the confirmations was to allow ZZZZ Best to circumvent much of the bureaucratic red tape in the insurance industry.

From this modest beginning, the ZZZZ Best fraud blossomed. Initially, Minkow used the phony insurance restoration contracts to generate the paper profits and revenues he needed to convince bankers to loan him money. Minkow's phony financial statements served their purpose, and he expanded his operations by opening several carpet cleaning outlets across the San Fernando Valley. Minkow soon realized that there was no need to tie his future to the cutthroat carpet cleaning industry when he could literally dictate the size and profitability of his insurance restoration "business." Within a short period of time, insurance restoration, rather than carpet cleaning, became the major source of revenue appearing on ZZZZ Best's income statements.

Minkow's "the sky is the limit" philosophy drove him to be even more innovative. The charming young entrepreneur began using his bogus financial statements to entice wealthy individuals in his ever-expanding social network to invest in ZZZZ Best. Eventually, Minkow recognized that the ultimate scam would be to take his company public, a move that would allow him to tap the bank accounts of unsuspecting investors nationwide.

Going Public with ZZZZ Best

Minkow's decision to take ZZZZ Best public meant that he could no longer completely control his firm's financial disclosures. Registering with the SEC required auditors, investment bankers, and outside attorneys to peruse ZZZZ Best's periodic financial statements.

ZZZZ Best was first subjected to a full-scope independent audit for the 12 months ended April 30, 1986. George Greenspan, the sole practitioner who performed that audit, confirmed the existence of ZZZZ Best's major insurance restoration contracts by contacting Tom Padgett. Padgett served as the principal officer of Interstate Appraisal Services, which reportedly contracted the jobs out to ZZZZ Best. By this time, Padgett was an active and willing participant in Minkow's fraudulent schemes. Minkow established Interstate Appraisal Services and Assured Property Management for the sole purpose of generating fake insurance restoration contracts for ZZZZ Best.

In testimony before the Congressional subcommittee that investigated the ZZZZ Best scandal, Greenspan insisted that he had properly audited Minkow's company. Greenspan testified that while planning the 1986 audit he had performed various analytical procedures to identify unusual relationships in ZZZZ Best's financial data. These procedures allegedly included comparing ZZZZ Best's key financial ratios with industry norms. Regarding the insurance contracts, Greenspan testified that he had obtained and reviewed copies of all key documents pertaining to those jobs. However, Greenspan admitted that he had not inspected any of the insurance restoration sites.

Congressman Lent: *Mr. Greenspan, I am interested in the SEC Form S-1 that ZZZZ Best Company filed with the SEC. . . . You say in that report that you made your examination in accordance with generally accepted auditing standards and accordingly included such tests of the accounting records and other auditing procedures as we consider necessary in the circumstances. . . . You don't say in that statement that you made any personal on-site inspections.*

Mr. Greenspan:	*It's not required. Sometimes you do; sometimes you don't. I was satisfied that these jobs existed and I was satisfied from at least six different sources, including payment for the job. What could you want better than that?*
Congressman Lent:	*Your position is that you are an honest and reputable accountant.*
Mr. Greenspan:	*Yes, sir.*
Congressman Lent:	*You were as much a victim as some of the investors in this company?*
Mr. Greenspan:	*I was a victim all right. . . . I am as much aghast as anyone. And every night I sit down and say, why didn't I detect this damned fraud.*

Retention of Ernst & Whinney by ZZZZ Best

Shortly after Greenspan completed his audit of ZZZZ Best's financial statements for fiscal 1986, which ended April 30, 1986, Minkow dismissed him and retained Ernst & Whinney to perform the following year's audit. Apparently, ZZZZ Best's investment banker insisted that Minkow obtain a Big Eight accounting firm to enhance the credibility of the company's financial statements. At approximately the same time, and for the same reason, Minkow retained a high-profile Los Angeles law firm to represent ZZZZ Best as its legal counsel.

The Congressional subcommittee asked Greenspan what information he provided to Ernst & Whinney regarding his former client. In particular, the subcommittee wanted to know whether Greenspan discussed the insurance restoration contracts with the new auditors.

Congressman Wyden:	*Mr. Greenspan, in September 1986, Ernst & Whinney came on as the new independent accountant for ZZZZ Best. What did you communicate to Ernst & Whinney with respect to the restoration contracts?*
Mr. Greenspan:	*Nothing. I did--there was nothing because they never got in touch with me. It's protocol for the new accountant to get in touch with the old accountant. They never got in touch with me, and it's still a mystery to me.*

Representatives of Ernst & Whinney later testified that they did, in fact, communicate with Greenspan prior to accepting ZZZZ Best as an audit client. However, Ernst & Whinney did not comment on the nature or content of that communication. (Greenspan was not recalled to rebut Ernst & Whinney's testimony on this issue.)[3]

Exhibit 1 contains the engagement letter signed by Ernst & Whinney and Barry Minkow in September 1986. The engagement letter outlined four services that the audit firm intended to provide ZZZZ Best: a review of the company's financial statements for the three-month period ending July 31, 1986; assistance in the preparation of a registration statement to be filed with the SEC; a comfort letter to be submitted to ZZZZ Best's underwriters; and a full-scope audit for the fiscal year ending April 30, 1987. Ernst & Whinney completed the review, provided the comfort letter to ZZZZ Best's underwriters, and apparently assisted the company in preparing the registration statement for the SEC; however, Ernst & Whinney never completed the 1987 audit.

---

3. After a lengthy investigation, the American Institute of Certified Public Accountants ruled in 1998 that there was no "prima facie evidence" that Greenspan had violated the organization's *Code of Professional Conduct* during the time that ZZZZ Best was his client. A similar conclusion was reached by two state boards of accountancy with which Greenspan was registered to practice public accounting.

EXHIBIT 1

ERNST &
WHINNEY'S ZZZZ
BEST ENGAGEMENT
LETTER

September 12, 1986

Mr. Barry Minkow
Chairman of the Board
ZZZZ Best Co., Inc.
7040 Darby Avenue
Reseda, California

Dear Mr. Minkow:

This letter is to confirm our understanding regarding our engagement as independent accountants of ZZZZ BEST CO., INC. (the Company) and the nature and limitations of the services we will provide.

We will perform the following services:

1. We will review the balance sheet of the Company as of July 31, 1986, and the related statements of income, retained earnings, and changes in financial position for the three months then ended, in accordance with standards established by the American Institute of Certified Public Accountants. We will not perform an audit of such financial statements, the objective of which is the expressing of an opinion regarding the financial statements taken as a whole, and, accordingly, we will not express an opinion on them. Our report on the financial statements is presently expected to read as follows:

> "We have made a review of the condensed consolidated balance sheet of ZZZZ BEST CO., INC. and subsidiaries as of July 31, 1986, and the related condensed consolidated statements of income and changes in financial position for the three-month period ended July 31, 1986, in accordance with standards established by the American Institute of Certified Public Accountants. A review of the condensed consolidated financial statements for the comparative period of the prior year was not made.
>
> A review of financial information consists principally of obtaining an understanding of the system for the preparation of interim financial information, applying analytical review procedures to financial data, and making inquiries of persons responsible for financial and accounting matters. It is substantially less in scope than an examination in accordance with generally accepted auditing standards, which will be performed for the full year with the objective of expressing an opinion regarding the financial statements taken as a whole. Accordingly, we do not express such an opinion. Based on our review, we are not aware of any material modifications that should be made to the condensed consolidated interim financial statements referred to above for them to be in conformity with generally accepted accounting principles."

Our engagement cannot be relied upon to disclose errors, irregularities, or illegal acts, including fraud or defalcations, that may exist. However, we will inform you of any such matters that come to our attention.

2. We will assist in the preparation of a Registration Statement (Form S-1) under the Securities Act of 1933 including advice and counsel in conforming the financial statements and related information to Regulation S-X.

3. We will assist in resolving the accounting and financial reporting questions which will arise as a part of the preparation of the Registration Statement referred to above.

4. We will prepare a letter for the underwriters, if required (i.e., a Comfort Letter), bearing in mind the limited nature of the work we have done with respect to the financial data.

(continued)

EXHIBIT 1—
continued

ERNST &
WHINNEY'S ZZZZ
BEST ENGAGEMENT
LETTER

5. We will examine the consolidated financial statements of the Company as of April 30, 1987, and for the year then ended and issue our report in accordance with generally accepted auditing standards approved by the American Institute of Certified Public Accountants. These standards contemplate, among other things, that (1) we will study and evaluate the Company's internal control system as a basis for reliance on the accounting records and for determining the extent of our audit tests; and (2) that we will be able to obtain sufficient evidential matter to afford a reasonable basis for our opinion on the financial statements. However, it should be understood that our reports will necessarily be governed by the findings developed in the course of our examination and that we could be required, depending upon the circumstances, to modify our reporting from the typical unqualified opinion. We will advise you, as our examination progresses, if any developments indicate that we will be unable to express an unqualified opinion. Because our examination will be performed generally on a test basis, it will not necessarily disclose irregularities, if any, that may exist. However, we will promptly report to you any irregularities which our examination does disclose.

Our fees will be derived from our customary rates for the various personnel involved plus out-of-pocket expenses. Certain factors can have an effect on the time incurred in the conduct of our work. Among these are the general condition of the accounting records, the amount of assistance received from your personnel in the accumulation of data, the size and transaction volume of business, any significant financial reporting issues that arise in connection with the SEC's review of the S-1, as well as unforeseen circumstances. Based upon our current understanding of the situation, the amount of our proposed billing for the various services which we will be providing are estimated to be:

Review of the July 31, 1986, financial statements	$ 5,000–$ 7,500
Assistance in the preparation of the Registration Statement	8,000–30,000
Comfort Letter	4,000–6,000
Audit of financial statements as of April 30, 1987	24,000–29,000

We will invoice you each month for the time charges and expenses incurred in the previous month and such invoices are due and payable upon presentation.

Larry D. Gray, Partner, is the Client Service Executive assigned to the engagement. Peter Griffith, Audit Manager, and Michael McCormick, Tax Manager, have also been assigned.

We greatly appreciate your engagement of our firm; if you have any questions, we shall be pleased to discuss them with you. Please indicate your acceptance of the above arrangements by signing and returning the enclosed copy. This letter constitutes the full understanding of the terms of our engagement.

Very truly yours,
Ernst & Whinney
By Larry D. Gray, Partner
ACCEPTED:
ZZZZ BEST CO., INC.
Barry J. Minkow, Chairman of the Board (signed)
9/16/86

The audit firm resigned on June 2, 1987, amid growing concerns that ZZZZ Best's financial statements were grossly misstated.

The Congressional subcommittee investigating the ZZZZ Best fraud questioned Ernst & Whinney representatives at length regarding the bogus insurance restoration contracts—contracts that accounted for 90 percent of ZZZZ Best's reported profits.

Congressional testimony disclosed that Ernst & Whinney repeatedly insisted on visiting several of the largest of these contract sites and that Minkow and his associates attempted to discourage such visits. Eventually, Minkow realized that the auditors would not relent and agreed to allow them to visit certain of the restoration sites, knowing fully well that none of the sites actually existed.

To convince Ernst & Whinney that the insurance restoration contracts were authentic, Minkow plotted and carried out a series of sting operations that collectively cost millions of dollars. In the late fall of 1986, Larry Gray, the engagement audit partner for ZZZZ Best, told client personnel that he wanted to inspect a restoration site in Sacramento on which ZZZZ Best had reported obtaining a multimillion-dollar contract. Minkow sent two of his subordinates to Sacramento to find a large building under construction or renovation that would provide a plausible site for a restoration contract. Gray had visited Sacramento a few weeks earlier to search for the site that Minkow had refused to divulge. As chance would have it, the building chosen by the ZZZZ Best conspirators was the same one Gray had identified as the most likely site of the insurance restoration job.

Minkow's two confederates posed as leasing agents of a property management firm and convinced the supervisor of the construction site to provide the keys to the building one weekend on the pretext that a large, prospective tenant wished to tour the facility. Prior to the arrival of Larry Gray and an attorney representing ZZZZ Best's law firm, Minkow's subordinates visited the site and placed placards on the walls at conspicuous locations indicating that ZZZZ Best was the contractor for the building renovation. No details were overlooked by the two co-conspirators. They even paid the building's security officer to greet the visitors and demonstrate that he was aware in advance of their tour of the site and its purpose. Although the building had not been damaged and instead was simply in the process of being completed, the sting operation went off as planned. Exhibit 2 presents the memorandum Gray wrote describing his tour of the building—a memorandum included in Ernst & Whinney's ZZZZ Best workpapers.

Congressional investigators quizzed Gray regarding the measures he took to confirm that ZZZZ Best actually had a restoration contract on the Sacramento building. They were particularly concerned that he never discovered the building had not suffered several million dollars in damages a few months earlier, as claimed by ZZZZ Best personnel.

Congressman Lent: . . . *Did you check the building permit or construction permit?*

Mr. Gray: *No, sir. That wouldn't be necessary to accomplish what I was setting out to accomplish.*

Congressman Lent: *And you did not check with the building's owners to see if an insurance claim had been filed?*

Mr. Gray: *Same answer. It wasn't necessary. I had seen the paperwork internally of our client, the support for a great amount of detail. So, I had no need to ask—to pursue that.*

Congressman Lent: *You understand that what you saw was not anything that was real in any sense of the word? . . . You are saying you were duped, are you not?*

Mr. Gray: *Absolutely.*

Before allowing Ernst & Whinney auditors to visit a bogus restoration project, Minkow insisted that the firm sign a standard confidentiality agreement. Exhibit 3 presents a copy of that agreement. Members of the Congressional subcommittee were troubled by the following stipulation of the confidentiality agreement: "We will

EXHIBIT 2

Ernst & Whinney
Internal Memo
Regarding Visit
to ZZZZ Best
Restoration
Project

TO: ZZZZ Best Co., Inc. File

FROM: Larry D. Gray

RE: Visit to Sacramento Job

At our request, the Company arranged for a tour of the job site in Sacramento on November 23rd [1986]. The site (not previously identified for us because of the confidentiality agreement with their customer) had been informally visited by me on October 27. I knew approximately where the job was, and was able to identify it through the construction activity going on.

On November 23, Mark Morse accompanied Mark Moskowitz of Hughes Hubbard & Reed and myself to Sacramento. We visited first the offices of the Building Manager, Mark Roddy of Assured Property Management, Inc. Roddy was hired by the insurance company (at Tom Padgett's suggestion according to Morse) to oversee the renovation activities and the leasing of the space. Roddy accompanied us to the building site.

We were informed that the damage occurred from the water storage on the roof of the building. The storage was for the sprinkler systems, but the water was somehow released in total, causing construction damage to floors 17 and 18, primarily in bathrooms which were directly under the water holding tower, then the water spread out and flooded floors 16 down through about 5 or 6, where it started to spread out even further and be held in pools.

We toured floor 17 briefly (it is currently occupied by a law firm) then visited floor 12 (which had a considerable amount of unoccupied space) and floor 7. Morse pointed out to us the carpet, painting and clean up work which had been ZZZZ Best's responsibility. We noted some work not done in some other areas (and in unoccupied tenant space). But per Mark, this was not ZZZZ Best's responsibility, rather was work being undertaken by tenants for their own purposes.

Per Morse (and Roddy) ZZZZ Best's work is substantially complete and has passed final inspection. Final sign-off is expected shortly, with final payment due to ZZZZ Best in early December.

Morse was well versed in the building history and in the work scope for ZZZZ Best. The tour was beneficial in gaining insight as to the scope of the damage that had occurred and the type of work that the Company can do.

not make any follow-up telephone calls to any contractors, insurance companies, the building owner, or other individuals involved in the restoration contract." This restriction effectively precluded the auditors from corroborating the insurance restoration contracts with independent third parties.

Resignation of Ernst & Whinney

Ernst & Whinney resigned as ZZZZ Best's auditor on June 2, 1987, following a series of disturbing events that caused the firm to question Barry Minkow's integrity. First, Ernst & Whinney was alarmed by a *Los Angeles Times* article in mid-May 1987 that revealed Minkow had been involved in a string of credit card forgeries as a teenager. Second, on May 28, 1987, ZZZZ Best issued a press release, without consulting or notifying Ernst & Whinney, that reported record profits and revenues. Minkow intended

EXHIBIT 3

ERNST &
WHINNEY'S
CONFIDENTIALITY
AGREEMENT
WITH ZZZZ BEST
REGARDING VISITS
TO RESTORATION
PROJECTS

Mr. Barry Minkow, President
ZZZZ Best Co., Inc.
7040 Darby Avenue
Reseda, California

Dear Barry,

In connection with the proposed public offering (the Offering) of units consisting of common stock and warrants of ZZZZ Best Co., Inc. (the Company), we have requested a tour of the site of the Company's insurance restoration project in Sacramento, California, Contract No. 18886. Subject to the representations and warranties below, the Company has agreed to arrange such a tour, which will be conducted by a representative of Assured Property Management Inc. (the Representative), which company is unaffiliated with Interstate Appraisal Services. The undersigned, personally and on behalf of Ernst & Whinney, hereby represents and warrants that:

1. We will not disclose the location of such building, or any other information with respect to the project or the building, to any third parties or to any other members or employees of our firm;

2. We will not make any follow-up telephone calls to any contractors, insurance companies, the building owner, or other individuals involved in the restoration project;

3. We will obey all on-site safety and other rules and regulations established by the Company, Interstate Appraisal Services, and the Representative;

4. The undersigned will be the only representative of this Firm present on the tour.

This Confidentiality Letter is also being furnished for the benefit of Interstate Appraisal Services, to the same extent as if it were furnished directly to such company.

this press release to restore investors' confidence in the company—confidence that had been shaken by the damaging *Los Angeles Times* story. Third, and most important, on May 29, Ernst & Whinney auditors discovered evidence supporting allegations made several weeks earlier by a third-party informant that ZZZZ Best's insurance restoration business was fictitious.

The informant had contacted Ernst & Whinney in April 1987 and asked for $25,000 in exchange for information proving that one of the firm's clients was engaging in a massive fraud. Ernst & Whinney refused to pay the sum, and the individual recanted shortly thereafter, but not until the firm determined that the allegation involved ZZZZ Best. (Congressional testimony disclosed that the individual recanted because of a bribe paid to him by Minkow.) Despite the retraction, Ernst & Whinney questioned Minkow and ZZZZ Best's board of directors regarding the matter. Minkow insisted that he did not know the individual who had made the allegation. On May 29, 1987, however, Ernst & Whinney auditors discovered several cancelled checks that Minkow had personally written to the informant several months earlier.

Because ZZZZ Best was a public company, the resignation of its independent auditor had to be reported to the SEC in an 8-K filing. This requirement alerts investors and creditors of circumstances that may have led to the change in auditors. At the time, SEC registrants were allowed 15 days to file an 8-K auditor change announcement. After waiting the maximum permissible time, ZZZZ Best reported the change in auditors but, despite Ernst & Whinney's insistence, made no mention in the 8-K of the fraud allegation that had been subsequently recanted.

The SEC requires a former audit firm to prepare a letter to be filed as an exhibit to its former client's 8-K auditor change announcement. That exhibit letter must comment on the 8-K's accuracy and completeness. In 1987, former audit firms had 30 days to file an exhibit letter, which was the length of time Ernst & Whinney waited before submitting its exhibit letter to the SEC. In that letter, Ernst & Whinney revealed that ZZZZ Best's insurance contracts might be fraudulent.

The Congressional subcommittee was alarmed that 45 days passed before the charges of fraudulent misrepresentations in ZZZZ Best's financial statements were disclosed to the public. By the time the SEC released Ernst & Whinney's exhibit letter to the public, ZZZZ Best had filed for protection from its creditors under Chapter 11 of the federal bankruptcy code. During the period that elapsed between Ernst & Whinney's resignation and the public release of its 8-K exhibit letter, ZZZZ Best obtained significant financing from several parties, including $1 million from one of Minkow's close friends. These parties never recovered the funds invested in, or loaned to, ZZZZ Best. As a direct result of the ZZZZ Best debacle, the SEC shortened the length of time that registrants and their former auditors may wait before filing auditor change documents.

The Congressional subcommittee also quizzed Ernst & Whinney representatives regarding the information they disclosed to Price Waterhouse, the audit firm Minkow retained to replace Ernst & Whinney.[4] Congressman Wyden wanted to know whether Ernst & Whinney had candidly discussed its concerns regarding Minkow's integrity with Price Waterhouse.

> **Congressman Wyden:** *I am going to insert into the record at this point a memo entitled "Discussion with successor auditor," written by Mr. Gray and dated June 9, 1987. Regarding a June 4 meeting, Mr. Gray, with Dan Lyle of Price Waterhouse concerning the integrity of ZZZZ Best's management, you stated that you had no reportable disagreements and no reservations about management integrity pending the results of a board of directors' investigation. Then you went on to say that you resigned because, and I quote here: "We came to a conclusion that we didn't want to become associated with the financial statements." Is that correct?*
>
> **Mr. Gray:** *That is correct.*
>
> **Mr. Wyden:** *. . . Mr. Gray, you told the committee staff on May 29, 1987, that when you uncovered evidence to support allegations of fraud that you decided to pack up your workpapers and leave the ZZZZ Best audit site. How did your leaving without telling anybody except the ZZZZ Best management and board of directors the reasons for leaving help the public and investors?*

A final twist to the ZZZZ Best scandal was an anonymous letter Ernst & Whinney received one week after the firm resigned as ZZZZ Best's auditor. At that time, no one other than Ernst & Whinney and ZZZZ Best's officers was aware of the firm's resignation. The letter, shown in Exhibit 4, contained several allegations suggesting that ZZZZ Best's financial statements were fraudulent. According to the Congressional testimony, Ernst & Whinney forwarded this letter to the SEC on June 17, 1987.

---

4. Price Waterhouse never issued an audit report on ZZZZ Best's financial statements. ZZZZ Best was liquidated less than two months after Price Waterhouse was retained.

EXHIBIT 4

Anonymous Letter Received by Ernst & Whinney Regarding ZZZZ Best

June 9, 1987

Mr. Guy Wilson
Ernst & Whinney
515 South Flower
Los Angeles, California 90021

Dear Mr. Wilson,

I am an individual having certain confidential information regarding the financial condition of ZZZZ Best Co., Inc. I have read the prospectus and your Review Report dated October 3, 1986 and recognize you have not done an examination in accordance with generally accepted auditing standards, but that such audit will be forthcoming by you.

I wish to make you aware of the following material facts which require you to confirm or disaffirm:

1. The electric generators which appear on the balance sheet under Note 6 as being purchased for $1,970,000 were purchased for scrap for less than $100,000 thru intermediaries of ZZZZ Best and resold to ZZZZ Best at the inflated value. The sole purpose was to boost the assets on the balance sheet. These generators have never been used and have no utility to the company.

2. Note 5 of the balance sheet discusses joint ventures and two restoration contracts. These contracts are fictitious as are the bookkeeping entries to support their validity. Interstate Appraisal Service [sic] did not let such contracts although they confirm their existence. The same is true for the alleged $7,000,000 Sacramento contract and the $40–100 million contracts with Interstate.

3. Further, checks made and passed between ZZZZ Best, its joint venturers and some of its vendors are no more than transactions among conspirators to support the validity of these restoration contracts.

4. Earnings reported by ZZZZ Best are being reported as billings in excess of costs and estimated earnings on restoration contracts. These contracts do not exist nor do the earnings. This can be confirmed directly by contacting the alleged insurance carriers as well as physical inspections as to the existence and extent of the contracts.

5. Billings and earnings for 1985 and 1986 were fabricated by the company before being presented to other accountants for certification.

Confirmation of these allegations can be accomplished by a careful due diligence. Such due diligence on your behalf is imperative for your protection.

Very truly yours,

B. Cautious
(Signed)

Collapse of ZZZZ Best

The *Los Angeles Times* article published in mid-May 1987 that disparaged Barry Minkow ultimately doomed the young entrepreneur and his company. Several years earlier, a homemaker had fallen victim to Minkow's credit card forgeries. Minkow had added a fraudulent charge to a credit charge slip the woman had used to make a payment on her account. Despite her persistence, Minkow avoided repaying the small amount. The woman never forgot the insult and tracked down, and kept a record of, individuals who had been similarly harmed by Minkow. At the urging of this woman, a reporter for the *Los Angeles Times* investigated her allegations. The woman's diary eventually became the basis for the *Los Angeles Times* article that, for the first time, cast doubt on the integrity of the "boy wonder" who was the talk of Wall Street.

The newspaper article triggered a chain of events that caused ZZZZ Best to collapse and disappear less than three months later. First, a small brokerage firm specializing in newly registered companies with suspicious earnings histories began short-selling ZZZZ Best stock, forcing the stock's price into a tailspin. Second, Ernst & Whinney, ZZZZ Best's law firm, and ZZZZ Best's investment banker began giving more credence to the allegations and rumors of financial wrongdoing by Minkow and his associates. Third, and most important, the article panicked Minkow and compelled him to make several daring moves that cost him even more credibility. The most critical mistake was his issuance of the May 28, 1987, press release that boldly reported record profits and revenues for his firm.

EPILOGUE

Among the parties most vilified for their role in the ZZZZ Best scandal was Ernst & Whinney. The transcripts of the Congressional testimony focusing on the ZZZZ Best fraud included a list of 10 "red flags" that the audit firm had allegedly overlooked while examining ZZZZ Best's financial statements (see Exhibit 5). Ernst & Whinney officials flatly rejected assertions that their firm was even partially to blame for the ZZZZ Best fiasco. In his Congressional testimony, Leroy Gardner, the West Coast director of accounting and auditing for Ernst & Whinney, maintained that when all the facts were revealed, his firm would be totally vindicated:

> The ZZZZ Best situation proves at least one thing: a well-orchestrated fraud will often succeed even against careful, honest, hardworking people.... The facts that have begun to emerge establish that Minkow along with confederates both inside and outside ZZZZ Best went to extraordinary lengths to deceive Ernst & Whinney. For example, Thomas Padgett, an alleged conspirator, revealed in a recent televised interview that Minkow spent $4 million to deceive Ernst & Whinney during a visit to one of ZZZZ Best's job sites. . . . Ernst & Whinney never misled investors about the reliability of ZZZZ

> Best's financial statements. Ernst & Whinney never even issued an audit opinion for ZZZZ Best. . . . We are not part of the problem in this case. We were part of the solution.

In one of the largest civil suits stemming from the ZZZZ Best fraud, a court ruled that Ernst & Whinney was not liable to a large California bank that had extended ZZZZ Best a multimillion-dollar loan in 1986. The bank alleged that in granting the loan, it had relied upon the review report issued by Ernst & Whinney on ZZZZ Best's financial statements for the three-month period ending July 31, 1986. However, an appellate judge ruled that the bank was not justified in relying on the review report since Ernst & Whinney had expressly stated in the report that it was not issuing an opinion on the ZZZZ Best financial statements: "Ernst, because it issued only a review report, specifically declined to express an opinion on ZZZZ Best's financial statements. The report expressly disclaimed any right to rely on its content."[5]

In the late 1980s, ZZZZ Best's former stockholders filed a class-action lawsuit against Ernst & Whinney, ZZZZ Best's former law firm, and ZZZZ Best's former investment banker. An Internet publication reported in March 1996 that

---

5. "Ernst & Young Not Liable in ZZZZ Best Case," *Journal of Accountancy*, July 1991, 22.

EXHIBIT 5

TEN RED FLAGS
THAT ZZZZ
BEST'S AUDITORS
ALLEGEDLY
OVERLOOKED

1. The amounts called for by the insurance restoration contracts were unrealistically large.

2. The number of multimillion-dollar insurance restoration contracts reportedly obtained by ZZZZ Best exceeded the total number available nationwide during the relevant time period.

3. The purported contracts failed to identify the insured parties, the insurance companies, or the locations of the jobs.

4. The contracts consisted of a single page which failed to contain details and specifications of the work to be done, such as the square yardage of carpet to be replaced, which were usual and customary in the restoration business.

5. Virtually all of the insurance restoration contracts were with the same party.

6. A large proportion of the ZZZZ Best insurance restoration contracts occurred immediately, and opportunistically, prior to a planned offering of stock.

7. The purported contracts provided for payments to ZZZZ Best or Minkow alone rather than to the insured or jointly with ZZZZ Best and the insured, contrary to the practice of the industry.

8. The purported contracts provided for payments by the insurance adjustor contrary to normal practice in the industry, under which payments are customarily made by the insurance company directly to its insured or jointly to its insured and the restorer.

9. ZZZZ Best's purported gross profit margins for its restoration business were greatly in excess of the normal profit margins for the restoration industry.

10. The internal controls at ZZZZ Best were grossly inadequate.

---

this lawsuit had been settled privately. The defendants reportedly paid the former ZZZZ Best stockholders $35 million. However, the contribution of each defendant to the settlement pool was not disclosed.[6]

Barry Minkow was released from prison in late 1994. Minkow secured the reduction in his 25-year prison sentence for "good behavior and efforts to improve himself."[7] These efforts included earning by correspondence bachelor's and master's degrees in religion from Liberty University. Shortly after being paroled, Minkow married a young woman introduced to him by a fellow inmate. That inmate was a former subordinate of Charles Keating, the principal architect of the massive Lincoln Savings and Loan fraud.

In early 1995, Minkow began serving as the associate pastor of an evangelical church in a community near his hometown of Reseda. Two years later, Minkow was appointed the senior pastor of a large nondenominational church in San Diego. Besides his pastoral duties, Minkow served as the spokesperson for an Internet company, the Fraud Discovery Institute, which markets various fraud prevention and detection services.

For more than a decade, Minkow regularly presented lectures and seminars across the United States that focused on his "experience" with corporate fraud. He spoke to groups of CPAs, educational institutions, and, most notably, the FBI Academy at Quantico, Virginia. Minkow often chastised the accountants and auditors in his audience. During one presentation, Minkow noted that, "CPAs are creatures of habit. You're interested in making tick marks and footnotes, not in thinking

---

6. C. Byron, "$26 Million in the Hole," *Worth Online*, March 1996.

7. M. Matzer, "Barry Minkow," *Forbes*, 15 August 1994, 134.

outside of the box."[8] Minkow also chided auditors for being overly willing to accept weak forms of audit evidence, such as client representations. He warned auditors, "Don't give up objectivity for convenience."[9]

Unfortunately, the redemptive phase of Barry Minkow's life ended abruptly in 2011. In May of that year, Minkow pleaded guilty to conspiracy to commit securities fraud. Law enforcement authorities established that Minkow had participated in a scheme during January 2009 to drive down the stock price of Lennar Corporation and to extort money from the company's executives. At the time, Minkow wrongfully accused Lennar of fraudulently misrepresenting its publicly released financial statements.

On July 21, 2011, Barry Minkow appeared before Judge Patricia Seitz in a federal courtroom in Miami, Florida. Judge Seitz denied Minkow's request for leniency and sentenced him to five years in federal prison, the maximum sentence requested by federal prosecutors.

Questions

1. Ernst & Whinney never issued an audit opinion on financial statements of ZZZZ Best but did issue a review report on the company's quarterly statements for the three months ended July 31, 1986. How does a review differ from an audit, particularly in terms of the level of assurance implied by the auditor's report?

2. Professional auditing standards identify the principal "management assertions" that underlie a set of financial statements. The occurrence assertion was particularly critical for ZZZZ Best's insurance restoration contracts. ZZZZ Best's auditors obtained third-party confirmations to support the contracts, reviewed available documentation, performed analytical procedures to evaluate the reasonableness of the revenues recorded on the contracts, and visited selected restoration sites. Comment on the limitations of the evidence that these procedures provide with regard to the management assertion of occurrence.

3. In testimony before Congress, George Greenspan reported that one means he used to audit the insurance restoration contracts was to verify that his client actually received payment on those jobs. How can such apparently reliable evidence lead an auditor to an improper conclusion?

4. What is the purpose of predecessor–successor auditor communications? Which party, the predecessor or successor auditor, has the responsibility for initiating these communications? Briefly summarize the information that a successor auditor should obtain from the predecessor auditor.

5. Did the confidentiality agreement that Minkow required Ernst & Whinney to sign improperly limit the scope of the ZZZZ Best audit? Why or why not? Discuss general circumstances under which confidentiality concerns on the part of a client may properly affect audit planning decisions. At what point do client-imposed audit scope limitations affect the type of audit opinion issued?

6. What procedures, if any, do professional standards require auditors to perform when reviewing a client's pre-audit report but post-year-end earnings press release?

8. T. Sickinger, "Ex-Con Artist Helps Find Fraud," *The Kansas City Star*, 18 October 1995, B1.

9. *Ibid.*

Gemstar-TV Guide International, Inc.

The United States prides itself in being first in a wide range of socioeconomic, scientific, and cultural "top ten" lists. One ranking that does nothing to bolster national pride among United States citizens, however, is the nation's claim to watching more television programs than any other country across the globe. In 2007, the *Economist*, an international business periodical, reported that the average U.S. household spends 8 hours and 11 minutes each day viewing television programming, far surpassing the runner-up, the typical Turkish household, which spends exactly five hours watching the boob tube. Rounding out the top five in this inauspicious list were the sedentary citizens of Italy, Belgium, and Japan, respectively.

Over the past two decades, surfing the World Wide Web has become an important pastime for many former couch potatoes. The increasing popularity of the Internet during the 1990s convinced several e-commerce companies, principal among them AOL and Yahoo!, to establish massive websites intended to serve as "portals" to the Internet. These Internet portals were designed to "capture" Internet users when they went online and then direct them to the specific entertainment, business, sports, or other sites that they wanted to visit. AOL, Yahoo!, and their competitors expected to produce huge revenue streams by selling advertising on their portal websites to the large number of companies that wanted to market their products and services to Internet users who typically have deeper pockets than the average consumer.

Several insightful business executives recognized that the portal concept could be even more lucrative if applied to the "old school" but still dominant electronic information and entertainment medium, namely, the television. Despite the far-reaching impact that the Internet has had on U.S. culture over the past two decades, television viewing remains much more prevalent in the United States than surfing the World Wide Web. The Nielsen Company reported recently that the typical Internet user in the United States spends only 20 minutes online each day, a small fraction of the time that individual spends glued to his or her television screen.

The most successful television "portal" to date has been the ubiquitous scrolling programming guide that millions of bleary-eyed television addicts scan each day to find an upcoming episode of *NYPD Blue*, *Seinfeld*, or *The Beverly Hillbillies*. During the 1990s, several companies struggled to gain control over that very low-tech but also very important television portal. That struggle eventually culminated in a large-scale financial fraud that imposed billions of dollars of losses on investors worldwide.

From Shanghai to Fenway Park

Che-Chuen Yuen was born in 1948 in Shanghai during the bloody civil war that rocked China following the conclusion of World War II. After the Chinese civil war ended in 1949, Mao Zedung, the leader of the Communist forces that gained control of the country, established an authoritarian central government and renamed the nation the People's Republic of China. The new Communist government forced business owners, professionals, and other Chinese citizens who were perceived to be counter-revolutionaries to leave the country. Che-Chuen's father, a businessman, was among those banished. The elder Yuen moved his family, including his infant son, to Hong Kong, which had been a British colony since the mid-1800s. Fifteen years later, Che-Chuen immigrated to the United States where he assumed the name Henry.

After finishing his undergraduate degree in mathematics at the University of Wisconsin, the quiet and studious Yuen decided to pursue a doctorate in applied mathematics at the prestigious California Institute of Technology in Pasadena, California. Upon completing his doctorate, Yuen remained in southern California, working for 14 years as a research scientist for TRW, a large conglomerate. Because he had always been fascinated by the U.S. legal system, Yuen spent several years attending law school on a part-time basis while employed by TRW. He eventually earned a law degree from Loyola Law School near downtown Los Angeles.

While working toward his doctorate at CalTech, Henry Yuen became close friends with Daniel Kwoh, a doctoral student in the university's physics department. Like Yuen, Kwoh accepted a research position with TRW after completing his doctorate. In addition to having the same employer, the two friends had a mutual interest in sports, an interest that would eventually prove to be extremely lucrative for both of them.

As a young man, Yuen had aspired to becoming a world class soccer player. When he failed to achieve that goal, he became a martial arts expert, specializing in Wing Chun, a form of martial arts that involves aggressive, close range combat. After coming to the United States, Yuen became a hardcore baseball fan—his favorite team was the Boston Red Sox. Yuen's full-time job at TRW and his evening law school classes typically prevented him from watching Red Sox games that were televised on the West Coast. So, he would program his VCR to record those games. Unfortunately, Yuen often came home to find that his VCR had failed to record a game, leaving him frustrated and angry. In his mind, if a research scientist with a doctorate from CalTech could not successfully use a VCR's recording technology, then there was something wrong with that technology.

In 1988, Yuen and Kwoh teamed together to develop a simplified method for programming VCRs that they referred to as VCR Plus. This technology became the flagship product of a small company they co-founded, Gemstar Development Corporation. Although Gemstar produced only modest revenues during its first few years of operation, the company's impressive technology and seemingly bright future persuaded *Business Week* to name Yuen and Kwoh as the nation's "best entrepreneurs" in 1990. Five years later, Yuen and Kwoh took their company public, listing its stock on the NASDAQ stock exchange. That exchange would eventually include Gemstar in the NASDAQ 100, the stock index used to track the performance of companies listed on the world's largest electronic securities exchange. In 1997, a reported "falling out" between the two men resulted in Kwoh leaving the company to become an independent venture capitalist.

During the first five years that Gemstar was a public company, its revenues steadily increased, rising from $42 million in 1995 to $167 million in 1999. After incurring operating losses from 1995 through 1997, the company posted its first profit of $39 million in 1998. The following year, the company's net income increased to $74 million.

Gemstar generated revenues by licensing the various generations of its VCR Plus product and related technologies that it developed to companies in the broadcasting and electronic communications industries. A major feature of Gemstar's business model was acquiring a wide range of patents that allowed the company to gain effective control of programming and search technologies vital to companies in those industries. Gemstar eventually acquired nearly 100 such patents. Another feature of Gemstar's business model was closely monitoring the efforts of other companies to develop technologies similar to those that it had patented. When a potential infringement of a Gemstar patent was discovered, Yuen would immediately file a lawsuit or multiple lawsuits against the offending company. Yuen's legal background was a key factor that helped Gemstar prevail in most of these lawsuits.

"Patent Terrorist"

Henry Yuen quickly earned a reputation as a ruthless competitor because of his litigious business strategy. So ruthless, in fact, that certain of his rivals referred to him as a "patent terrorist." During an interview with *Business Week*, an executive in the cable TV industry, who asked to remain anonymous, candidly admitted that "he scares the hell out of us."[1] Yuen defended his aggressive legal tactics and insisted that they were not improper or unethical. "I am no terrorist. A terrorist is someone who breaks the law. I am only doing what the U.S. Congress and patent law allow."[2]

A few of Yuen's competitors begrudgingly complimented the tactics he used to establish Gemstar as a significant player in the fiercely competitive and rapidly evolving broadcasting and electronic communications industries. Rupert Murdoch, the chairman and CEO of the Australia-based News Corporation, easily the largest media company worldwide, fought repeated legal battles with Yuen. Nevertheless, Murdoch often referred to Yuen as a brilliant strategist and "genius." Another competitor noted that Yuen was "the smartest guy in television."[3] *U.S. News and World Report* referred to Yuen, who was effectively unknown outside the inner circle of top executives in the broadcasting and electronic communications industries, as "the Bill Gates of television."[4]

Yuen was among the first corporate executives to envision the revenue streams that a television portal could produce. As the turn of the century approached, he believed that the television medium would change dramatically over the following decade. Yuen expected television to become a highly interactive medium, similar to the Internet, in which the viewing public would have hundreds of television channels, movies, games, and other entertainment options to choose from. When that happened, he was convinced that a company that controlled television information and navigation services would be a formidable force within the broadcasting and electronic communications industries.

Among the first companies to provide on-screen navigation guides was United Video, a small technology company based in Tulsa, Oklahoma. That company marketed the Prevue Network, a scrolling on-screen programming guide, to cable TV networks during the mid-1980s. United Video's executives surprised their much larger competitors in 1999 when they launched a successful takeover of TV Guide International, a company they purchased from Rupert Murdoch's News Corporation. Following the takeover, Murdoch was one of the largest shareholders of the new company, which assumed the name TV Guide, Inc. The company planned to use its prominent brand name to market the on-screen programming guide that it renamed the TV Guide Network.

Following the merger of United Video and TV Guide International, the new company's management team began butting heads with Henry Yuen. By this time, Gemstar controlled most patents related to the use of what had become known as EPG—electronic programming guide—technology. Yuen blocked every effort by TV Guide to

---

1. R. Grover, T. Lowry, and L. Armstrong, "Henry Yuen: TV Guy," *Business Week* (online), 12 March 2001.
2. *Ibid.*
2. *Ibid.*
4. F. Vogelstein, "Meet the Bill Gates of TV," *U.S. News and World Report*, 7 August 2000, 50.

upgrade its onscreen navigation guide. To solve this problem, Rupert Murdoch goaded TV Guide to launch a hostile takeover bid for Gemstar. But Murdoch and the TV Guide management team were no match for the crafty and hardnosed Yuen who turned the tables on them by forcing them to sell their company to him in 2000.

Financial analysts and other members of the investment community had high expectations for the new company. Those expectations caused the company's stock price to surge. Thanks to that surging stock price, Henry Yuen became the third wealthiest Asian-American in the United States, according to *Forbes* magazine. Yuen's net worth of $1.3 billion easily secured him a spot in the Forbes 400, the publication's annual compilation of the 400 richest U.S. citizens. At the age of 51, the Chinese immigrant whose family had been forced to leave its homeland following the Communist takeover of that nation was among the most successful capitalists in the world and was proudly living the "American dream." But he wasn't satisfied. According to *The New York Times*, Yuen believed that his company's "on-screen guide would be the ultimate toll-keeper for the media [television] and told colleagues that Gemstar would someday be bigger than Microsoft."[5]

A Rocky Start for GTGI

Following the $15 billion purchase of TV Guide by Gemstar, Henry Yuen and Rupert Murdoch, who had been fierce rivals, were the new company's largest and most influential stockholders. Yuen was also the company's chief executive officer (CEO) and chairman of the board of directors. Gemstar's former stockholders, led by Yuen, controlled 55 percent of the company's common stock, while TV Guide's former stockholders, led by Murdoch, controlled the remainder. To take advantage of TV Guide's brand name, Yuen decided that the newly formed company would be named Gemstar-TV Guide International, Inc. (GTGI).

Yuen organized GTGI into three business segments. Easily the largest of these segments was the Media and Services Sector, which accounted for approximately 70 percent of GTGI's consolidated revenues. This sector produced the bulk of its revenues from the *TV Guide*, the largest weekly publication in the world at the time in terms of circulation and readership. The second business segment was the technology and licensing sector that included the former operations of Gemstar International.

Following the acquisition of TV Guide, Yuen's principal strategic initiative was to use Gemstar's EPG patents and TV Guide's brand name to establish a product line of interactive information and navigation services for use by cable TV networks. This product line of services was included in GTGI's third and smallest business segment, the Interactive Platform Sector. Advertising was the principal revenue producer for this sector, which accounted for less than two percent of GTGI's total revenues for fiscal 2000. Yuen was convinced that over the years to come major retailers and service companies would allocate a large portion of their advertising budgets to ads placed on GTGI's electronic navigation guides, most notably the TV Guide Network. By 2000, the profit potential of the TV Guide Network seemed enormous since it reached more than 50 million U.S. households.

Despite Yuen's glowing forecasts for GTGI's business model, the company's financial performance worsened dramatically during 2001, its second year of operation. In 2001, GTGI reported a net loss of $600 million, three times greater than the net loss it reported the previous year. Yuen downplayed this disappointing news in earnings releases and

---

5. R. Siklos, "The Math Whiz vs. the Media Moguls in a Battle for Millions," *The New York Times*, 3 April 2006, 1.

conference calls by focusing the attention of analysts and investors on the rapidly growing revenues of the interactive platform sector. In fiscal 2001, that sector's revenues
increased by more than 400 percent. He attributed this large increase to "advertisers'
growing acceptance" of the new advertising medium offered by that sector.[6]

Explaining GTGI's large loss during fiscal 2001 wasn't the only challenge that Yuen
faced in early 2002. During the merger deliberations with TV Guide, Yuen had negotiated an incentive-laden compensation contract for himself. During 2001, that contract
resulted in Yuen earning nearly $20 million, which was three times his compensa-
tion the previous year. Financial analysts, investors, and other parties berated Yuen
for that huge pay increase in the face of GTGI's $600 million loss for the year. That
criticism was met with indifference and silence by Yuen. Two years earlier, several
Gemstar shareholders had also suggested that Yuen was being overpaid. Yuen had
responded to that criticism by brusquely noting that "I deserve every bit of it."[7]

An Unhappy Marriage

When Yuen orchestrated the takeover of TV Guide, he realized that the newly created
company would pose a wide range of challenging problems due to its size, the highly
competitive nature of its principal lines of business, and the strong personalities—
including his own—that would play key roles in overseeing its operations. The most
intractable of the company's problems proved to be its schizoid personality. Yuen
and his associates from Gemstar were intent on creating a New Age, high-technology
company that would serve as a traffic cop for literally billions of television viewers
around the world. The former executives and major stockholders of TV Guide, Inc.,
wanted to maintain and increase the revenues from the "old school" media empire
that had revolved for decades around the *TV Guide*. Rupert Murdoch served as the
principal spokesperson for the latter individuals.

Enhancing GTGI's "split" personality was the composition of the company's
12-member board of directors. Six of those directors were former Gemstar executives, while the remaining six directors were former TV Guide executives or major
stockholders. Most prominent among the latter individuals was Rupert Murdoch. The
Gemstar–TV Guide merger agreement gave Yuen the right to cast the tie-breaking
vote to resolve deadlocks between the two factions of the GTGI board. To counter-
balance Yuen's powerful position on the GTGI board, Murdoch had a stipulation
included in the merger agreement that allowed the former TV Guide directors to dismiss Yuen as GTGI's chairman of the board and CEO after five years. Yuen accepted
that unusual stipulation of the merger agreement only after Murdoch and the remaining GTGI board members agreed that Yuen would receive a huge severance payment
if he was dismissed.

The troubled relationship between Henry Yuen and Rupert Murdoch became even
more problematic in the months following the merger of Gemstar and TV Guide. Yuen
focused most of his attention on GTGI's interactive platform sector since he was convinced that the electronic programming services it marketed would eventually become
the company's principal revenue stream. The inordinate attention placed by Yuen on
that sector angered and frustrated Murdoch. Particularly upsetting to Murdoch was
Yuen's continual hyping of the interactive platform sector to the business press each

---

6. *Securities and Exchange Commission v. Henry C. Yuen and Elsie M. Leung*, Case No. CV 03-4376 NM,
U.S. District Court for the Central District of California, Western Division, 29 June 2003.

7. L. Armstrong, "What's on TV? Ask Henry Yuen," *Business Week*, 14 September 1998, 164.

quarterly reporting period since that sector, despite its impressive revenue growth, still accounted for just a small fraction of GTGI's total revenues each quarter.

Murdoch believed that the principal focus of GTGI's operations should be the company's media and services sector that had been consistently profitable for decades because of *TV Guide's* popularity. During the first two years that Yuen oversaw GTGI's operations, *TV Guide's* circulation dropped dramatically, falling by approximately one million subscribers. *TV Guide's* declining circulation and advertising revenues was the principal factor responsible for the large loss that GTGI reported for fiscal 2001.

By early 2002, Murdoch was pressuring Yuen to resign as GTGI's CEO. Yuen resisted that pressure. When Murdoch initiated weekly management meetings to address GTGI's declining health, Yuen often skipped those meetings. When he did attend, Yuen reportedly refused to participate, choosing instead to carry on conversations in Cantonese with his longtime confidant, Elsie Leung, GTGI's chief financial officer (CFO). As Gemstar's financial condition continued to deteriorate, Yuen became increasingly "abrupt" and "secretive,"[8] further undercutting his ability to work with Murdoch and key GTGI executives. Years later, his personal attorney would defend Yuen's management style, while admitting that his interpersonal skills, a skill set so critical to top corporate executives, were sub-par: "I would not say of Henry that sweetness and diplomacy were his strong suit."[9]

Re-Re-Restatements

In April 2002, Henry Yuen and GTGI faced a major crisis when certain financial analysts began questioning the company's revenue recognition policies. Those analysts pointed out two questionable accounting decisions documented in the company's 2001 Form 10-K. The two decisions involved $100 million of disputed licensing fees that GTGI had booked as revenue and $20 million of revenue from an unusual barter transaction. Another third party pointed out that these items had significantly enhanced the reported operating results of the company's interactive platform sector, the business segment that Henry Yuen had been regularly touting. These news reports caused several investment rating services to downgrade GTGI's stock, which, in turn, caused the stock's price to decline more than 40 percent in one day.

In an interview a few days later with a *USA Today* reporter, Yuen dismissed the concerns raised regarding Gemstar's revenue recognition policies by pointing out that Gemstar's auditor, KPMG, "had no problem with the accounting."[10] Another source reinforced Yuen's position by noting that the accounting decisions in question had been "blessed" by KPMG.[11] Two months later, in June 2002, *Business Week* revealed that Rupert Murdoch had been responsible for forcing Yuen to highlight the two questionable accounting decisions in GTGI's 2001 Form 10-K despite the fact that KPMG had "approved" them.[12]

The public controversy over GTGI's revenue recognition decisions prompted the company's audit committee to investigate the matter. In October 2002, GTGI released the results of that investigation. The audit committee's report revealed additional problems with the company's accounting and financial disclosure decisions over the previous two years, which resulted in the SEC launching its own investigation of GTGI.

---

8. Siklos, "The Math Whiz vs. The Media Moguls."

9. *Ibid.*

10. D. Lieberman, "Accounting Issue Dulls Gemstar Stock," *USA Today*, 3 April 2002, 1B.

11. M. Scanlon, "Gemstar Bitten by Accounting Bug," *BNET.com*, 8 April 2002.

12. R. Grover, " Gemstar Wars: Murdoch Strikes Back," *Business Week*, 3 June 2002, 42.

Shortly after the release of the audit committee's report, Henry Yuen was replaced as GTGI's CEO by one of Murdoch's top subordinates. GTGI also disclosed that Ernst & Young had been retained to replace KPMG as its independent audit firm. At the same time that it announced the change in auditors, GTGI disclosed that it would likely be required to restate its financial statements for the past several years. In fact, GTGI would subsequently issue multiple restatements of those financial statements. These restatements resulted in a more than $250 million reduction of the revenues that the company had previously reported for the period 1999 through 2001 and increased the company's previously reported losses for that period by nearly $200 million.

In June 2003, the SEC announced that it was filing securities fraud charges against Henry Yuen and Elsie Leung for their role in misrepresenting GTGI's financial statements. The federal agency subsequently filed similar charges against several other GTGI executives who were allegedly involved in the scheme and/or were aware of it. The SEC also charged the company, as a separate entity, with releasing materially misrepresented financial statements.

In June 2004, the SEC disclosed that it had settled the charges pending against GTGI. This settlement did not include Yuen, Leung, and the other GTGI executives allegedly involved in the fraudulent accounting scheme. The federal agency would deal with those officers on an individual basis in subsequent litigation or out-of-court settlements. The SEC's settlement with GTGI required the company to pay a $10 million fine and permanently enjoined it from future violations of federal securities laws. In the settlement agreement, the SEC disclosed a litany of accounting gimmicks that GTGI had used to misrepresent its financial statements, each of which involved intentional misapplications of the revenue recognition rule.

The methods used by GTGI to inflate its operating results included recognizing revenue under "expired, disputed, or non-existent" contracts. A significant portion of this revenue was recorded by the company's "highly touted" interactive platform sector, according to the SEC.[13] GTGI also accelerated revenue recognized under certain long-term contracts and improperly recorded revenue for large non-monetary and barter transactions. The SEC also reported that certain revenues earned by GTGI's media and services sector had been diverted for accounting purposes to the interactive platform sector. Finally, GTGI used a series of "multiple-element" transactions to inflate the reported revenue of the interactive platform sector.

"Repeated Audit Failures"

The SEC issued multiple enforcement and litigation releases that documented the GTGI accounting fraud. One of these releases analyzed the "repeated audit failures"[14] of KPMG, GTGI's independent audit firm during the course of that fraud. The SEC's criticism of KPMG focused on three facets of the firm's GTGI audits.

According to the SEC, the GTGI audit engagement team should have contacted KPMG's technical staff in the firm's headquarters office when the auditors uncovered suspicious and unusual transactions recorded by the client. The federal agency believed that such consultation would almost certainly have resulted in more thorough investigations of those transactions and ultimately led to KPMG discovering their fraudulent nature. Although KPMG had a "consultation policy" at the time, the SEC suggested that the policy was not sufficiently comprehensive or rigorous, which

---

13. Securities and Exchange Commission, *Litigation Release No. 18760*, 23 June 2004.

14. Securities and Exchange Commission, "KPMG LLP and Four Auditors Sanctioned for Improper Professional Conduct in Connection with Gemstar-TV Guide International, Inc. Audits," www.sec.gov, 20 October 2004.

explained why the GTGI engagement team had failed to ask for the assistance of the firm's technical staff.

The SEC also faulted the "materiality determinations" of the GTGI audit engagement team. A key feature of the GTGI fraud was Henry Yuen's effort to inflate the operating results of the new interactive platform sector. According to the SEC, the GTGI auditors should have been aware of that sector's disproportionate importance to not only Yuen but also to financial analysts and other parties tracking the company's financial performance. Because the KPMG auditors relied on quantitative measures of materiality, they failed to adequately investigate the relatively nominal operating results of the interactive platform sector.

> . . . the KPMG auditors . . . unreasonably determined that the [Interactive Platform Sector] revenues were immaterial to Gemstar's financial statements. The KPMG auditors' materiality determinations were unreasonable in that they only considered quantitative materiality (i.e., that the amount of revenue was not a large percentage of Gemstar's consolidated financial results) and failed to also consider qualitative materiality (i.e., that the revenue related to business lines that were closely watched by securities analysts and had a material effect on the valuation of Gemstar stock).[15]

The bulk of the lengthy SEC enforcement release that examined the role of KPMG in the GTGI debacle focused on the audit firm's consideration of several large revenue transactions that the company used to inflate and distort its operating results. Listed next are the most important of these transactions and the SEC's related criticism of the GTGI audit engagement team.

Licensing Agreement with AOL

In early April 2000, AOL, the large Internet service provider, paid GTGI a nonrefundable fee of $23.5 million in exchange for an eight-year license on a patented technology controlled by GTGI. The agreement between the two companies required GTGI to provide AOL with technical assistance and support over the entire eight-year term of the contract. Despite these contractual terms, GTGI management convinced the KPMG auditors that the $23.5 million fee was "for transfer of the license and for 12 months of technical assistance and engineering support." Because the auditors did not challenge that assertion, they allowed GTGI to recognize the entire fee as revenue over a 12-month period from April 2000 through March 2001.

The SEC maintained that the KPMG auditors "unreasonably failed to exercise professional care and skepticism in reviewing the [AOL-GTGI] contract and in testing Gemstar's representations regarding the purpose of the upfront nonrefundable fee." If the auditors had properly investigated that contract and management's related representations, they would have determined that the $23.5 million fee paid to GTGI by AOL should have been prorated for revenue recognition purposes over the eight-year term of the contract.

Disputed Scientific-Atlanta Revenue

Scientific-Atlanta manufactures equipment used by cable TV networks, Internet service suppliers, and various other companies involved in the broadcasting and electronic communications industries. Gemstar Development Corporation, the predecessor of GTGI, had a three-year licensing agreement with Scientific-Atlanta.

---

15. Unless noted otherwise, the remaining citations in this text were drawn from the following source: Securities and Exchange Commission, *Accounting and Auditing Enforcement Release No. 2125*, 20 October 2004.

This agreement allowed Scientific-Atlanta to use certain patented technologies controlled by Gemstar. The agreement expired in 1999 and was not renewed. Following the expiration of that agreement, Gemstar sued Scientific-Atlanta, alleging that the company was infringing on patented technologies that were Gemstar's exclusive intellectual property.

During this ongoing litigation, Gemstar continued to record licensing revenue from Scientific-Atlanta as if it still had a contractual relationship with that company. Following the 2000 merger with TV Guide, GTGI's accounting staff did the same. From early 2000 through the first quarter of fiscal 2002, GTGI recorded more than $100 million of disputed licensing revenue from Scientific-Atlanta.

According to the SEC, there was no defensible basis for Gemstar and later GTGI to record revenue from Scientific-Atlanta after the contract with that company expired in 1999. The federal agency identified the following four conditions that precluded the recording of that revenue.

1) GTGI did not have a current contract with Scientific-Atlanta;
2) GTGI did not receive any payments of the disputed revenues;
3) Scientific-Atlanta was insisting that it did not owe the revenues to GTGI;
4) any subsequent receipt of the disputed revenues by GTGI was contingent on a favorable outcome to the litigation between it and Scientific-Atlanta.

Because KPMG "knew or reasonably should have known" of each of these conditions, the auditors should have refused to endorse their client's decision to record that revenue.

Improper Recording of Revenue from Multiple-Element Transactions

During 2001, GTGI engaged in large "multiple-element" revenue transactions with Motorola, Inc., which manufactures various electronic products, and the Tribune Company, a broadcasting company whose flagship television station is Chicago-based WGN. In each of these transactions, Motorola and the Tribune Company purchased certain assets from GTGI's media and services sector. GTGI executives negotiated payment terms for the two transactions that required Motorola and the Tribune Company to purchase large amounts of advertising revenue from the interactive platform sector. Collectively, those payment terms produced more than $100 million of revenue for that sector. GTGI's segment disclosures in the notes to its audited financial statements did not disclose that a material portion of the interactive platform sector's revenues resulted from the two multiple-element transactions.

The SEC ruled that GTGI did not have a sufficient basis for ascertaining the fair value of the advertising revenues that were a major component of the Motorola and Tribune Company transactions.

> Gemstar did not have sufficient stand-alone IPG [Interactive Platform Sector] advertising revenue (i.e., revenue from advertising that was not part of a related-party, nonmonetary, or multi-element transaction) to provide a basis on which to fair value the Motorola and Tribune IPG [Interactive Platform Sector] advertising components of the multi-element transactions.

In fact, GTGI had structured the Motorola and Tribune Company transactions to divert disproportionate amounts of the revenues from those transactions to the interactive platform sector. GTGI executives also took explicit steps to conceal this fact from the public and other parties. For example, in the case of the Tribune Company transaction, a GTGI executive threatened to cancel the transaction if Tribune's management insisted on complete disclosure of its terms.

The SEC concluded that KPMG failed to adequately audit these multiple-element transactions. In particular, the SEC found that KPMG did not collect "sufficient competent evidence" to substantiate the fair value of the advertising revenues that were components of those two transactions. Instead, the KPMG auditors accepted management's representations that the advertising revenue component of each transaction was determined on an arm's length or fair value basis. The SEC also criticized KPMG for failing to insist that GTGI disclose that a major portion of the revenues reported by the interactive platform sector was attributable to multiple-element transactions.

Improper Recording of Revenue from Barter Transactions

In fiscal 2001, GTGI acquired certain intellectual property from another company, Fantasy Sports. In exchange for that property that was supposedly worth $20.75 million, GTGI gave Fantasy Sports $750,000 cash and $20 million of future advertising credits. Fantasy Sports used these advertising credits during fiscal 2001, which produced $20 million of advertising revenue for the interactive platform sector that period. The SEC once again faulted KPMG for not recognizing that GTGI had insufficient "stand-alone IPG [interactive platform sector] advertising revenue to provide a basis on which to fair value" the $20 million of advertising credits. Likewise, the SEC pointed out that GTGI's financial statements on which KPMG had issued an unqualified opinion did not provide adequate disclosure of this barter transaction.

After reviewing these and similar GTGI revenue transactions audited by KPMG, the SEC ruled that the accounting firm had failed to comply with generally accepted auditing standards. This lack of compliance had been manifested in the following ways, according to the federal agency:

1) Failure to exercise professional care and skepticism, failure to obtain sufficient competent evidential matter, and over-reliance on management representations;

2) Failure to take appropriate action to correct disclosure that did not comply with GAAP and/or was not consistent with Gemstar's financial statements;

3) Failure to render accurate reports.

EPILOGUE

In June 2004, the SEC and KPMG reached an agreement to resolve the allegations that the firm's GTGI audits had been deficient. KPMG agreed to pay a $10 million fine, which at the time was the largest fine ever imposed on an independent audit firm by the SEC.[16] The SEC also censured KPMG and sanction four of the firm's auditors involved in the relevant GTGI audit engagements. The latter individuals included the engagement audit partner, co-engagement audit partner, review partner, and senior audit manager who had been assigned to one or more of those engagements. Each of these individuals was suspended from practicing before the SEC for one or more years.

In February 2006, Elsie Leung, GTGI's former CFO, agreed to pay $1.3 million to resolve pending SEC charges that she had participated in the fraudulent scheme to misrepresent GTGI's financial statements. Leung was also permanently barred from serving as an officer or director of a public company.

---

16. In 2005, the SEC would levy a $22.5 million fine on KPMG for allegedly deficient audits of Xerox Corporation.

After a three-year court battle in a civil case, a federal judge ruled in March 2006 that Henry Yuen was guilty of securities fraud, falsifying GTGI's accounting records, and lying to his former company's independent auditors. The judge ruled that Yuen had to pay the victims of the GTGI accounting fraud $22.3 million. To date, the only criminal complaint filed against Yuen has been for obstruction of justice. Yuen allegedly destroyed documents during the course of the federal investigation into the GTGI accounting fraud. Yuen resolved the obstruction charge by agreeing to a plea bargain deal offered by the U.S. Department of Justice. This deal required Yuen to pay approximately $1 million in fines and to serve six months of home detention.

In December 2007, GTGI was purchased by another company for $2.8 billion, an amount that was a small fraction of the company's total market value shortly after the merger with TV Guide International. To date, Yuen's much-hyped EPG technology has not lived up to its great expectations. According to a *New York Times* reporter, "Mr. Yuen's vision for the electronic programming guide as a major money maker has yet to materialize."[17]

Questions

1. What fundamental principles dictate when a company should recognize or record revenue in its accounting records? Revenue recognition issues can be particularly complex for companies that sell software and/or license technology. Identify specific rules or concepts in the professional standards that accountants and auditors can rely on to make proper revenue recognition decisions for such companies.

2. The SEC charged KPMG with "repeated audit failures" in this case. Identify general conditions, specific circumstances, and other factors that are common causes of, or, at a minimum, commonly associated with, "audit failures." What quality control mechanisms can audit firms implement to minimize the likelihood of audit failures?

3. The SEC criticized KPMG for relying on "quantitative" measures in arriving at materiality judgments while ignoring important "qualitative" issues relevant to those judgments. Under what circumstances should auditors rely more heavily on quantitative measures rather than qualitative issues in making materiality judgments? Under what circumstances should auditors rely more heavily on qualitative issues rather than quantitative measures in making materiality judgments? Explain.

4. Do you agree with Henry Yuen's assertion that a businessperson who is complying with all applicable laws and regulations is, by definition, behaving "ethically"? Defend your answer.

---

17. Siklos, "The Math Whiz vs. the Medial Moguls."

New Century Financial Corporation

*It is well enough that people of the nation do not understand
our banking and monetary system, for if they did, I believe there
would be a revolution before tomorrow morning.*

Henry Ford

From 1962 to 1992, Ed McMahon served as the quintessential sidekick and straight man to Johnny Carson on the long-running and popular television program *The Tonight Show*. After leaving that program, McMahon stayed in the television spotlight for 12 years by serving as the host of *Star Search*, a syndicated talent show. McMahon's resume also included long stints as cohost of *TV Bloopers and Practical Jokes*, the annual Macy's Thanksgiving Day Parade, and the Jerry Lewis Labor Day Telethon, and as commercial spokesperson for such companies as Budweiser and American Family Publishing.

McMahon's 50-year-plus career in television made him one of the most recognized celebrities in that medium. Understandably then, the American public was shocked when press reports in June 2007 revealed that McMahon was more than $600,000 past due on his home mortgage payments. The $5 million mortgage on McMahon's Beverly Hills mansion was held by Countrywide Financial Corporation.

Unfortunately, millions of everyday Americans with mortgage balances only a fraction of Ed McMahon's have recently faced the unhappy prospect of losing their homes due to the worst financial crisis to strike the United States economy since the Great Depression. As that crisis quickly worsened and spread to the global economy, the search began for the parties responsible for it. Among the potential culprits identified by the press was the accounting profession, in particular, independent auditors.

Mortgage Mess

Nearly one-half of recent mortgage foreclosure victims in the United States obtained their loans from so-called subprime lenders that became dominant forces in the mortgage industry over the past two decades. The largest of those lenders were Countrywide, HSBC, New Century Financial Corporation (New Century), and Wells Fargo, but more than a dozen other large companies provided loans to borrowers with suspect credit histories. The implosion of the lucrative but high-risk subprime sector of the mortgage industry in 2007 and 2008 ignited a financial crisis in the United States that would quickly engulf the global economy.

The origins of the subprime mortgage debacle in the United States can be traced to the collapse of New Century, the nation's second largest subprime lender. New Century was founded in 1995 by three friends who had previously worked together at a mortgage banking company. New Century, which was based in Irvine, California, grew dramatically over its brief existence. In 1996, New Century reported total revenues of $14.5 million and total assets of $4.4 million. Nine years later, the company reported total revenues of $2.4 billion and total assets of $26 billion.

During the heyday of subprime mortgage lending in 2005 and 2006, New Century funded $200 million of new mortgage loans on a typical business day. In early February 2007, just a few months after company executives insisted that New Century was financially strong, those same executives unsettled Wall Street when they revealed that the company would be restating previously released financial statements as a result of the misapplication of generally accepted accounting principles (GAAP).

Two months later, New Century declared bankruptcy. A court-appointed bankruptcy examiner summarized the far-reaching implications that New Century's downfall had for the global economy.

> *The increasingly risky nature of New Century's loan originations created a ticking time bomb that detonated in 2007. . . The demise of New Century was an early contributor to the subprime market meltdown. The fallout from this market catastrophe has been massive and unprecedented. Global equity markets were rocked, credit markets tightened, recession fears spread, and losses are in the hundreds of billions of dollars and growing.*[1]

In fact, New Century would be just the first of many high-profile companies brought down by the turmoil in the mortgage industry. Other longtime stalwarts of the nation's financial services industries that fell victim to that turmoil included Bear Stearns, Lehman Brothers, and Merrill Lynch.

In September 2008, the federal government assumed control of the Federal National Mortgage Association and the Federal Home Loan Mortgage Company, two "government-sponsored" but publicly owned companies better known as Fannie Mae and Freddie Mac, respectively. At the time, the two organizations owned or guaranteed nearly one-half of the approximately $12 trillion of home mortgages in the United States. For decades, the federal government had used Fannie Mae and Freddie Mac to create an orderly and liquid market for homeowner mortgages, but the enormous losses each suffered in 2007 and 2008 undercut that role and forced the U.S. Department of the Treasury to take over their operations.

Angry investors lashed out at a wide range of parties who they believed bore some measure of responsibility for the massive financial crisis. Those parties included the major subprime mortgage lenders in the United States, such as New Century, and the politicians, regulatory authorities, ratings agencies, and independent auditors who had failed to prevent or rein in the imprudent business practices of those lending institutions.

Only a few years removed from the sweeping reforms prompted by the Enron and WorldCom scandals, the accounting profession was once again forced to defend itself from a wide range of angry and often self-righteous critics. Among these critics was *The New York Times*. The prominent newspaper castigated the auditors of subprime lenders for stamping those institutions' financial statements with the accounting profession's equivalent of the Good Housekeeping Seal of Approval. "While accounting firms don't exert legal or regulatory authority over their clients, they do bestow seals of approval, the way rating agencies do. People in the financial industry, as well as investors, have reason to believe that a green light from an auditor means that a company's accounting practices have passed muster."[2]

---

1. "Final Report of Michael J. Missal, Bankruptcy Court Examiner," In re: New Century TRS Holdings, Inc., a Delaware corporation, *et al.*, U.S. Bankruptcy Court for the District Delaware, Case No. 07-10416 (KJC), 29 February 2008. Unless indicated otherwise, the quotations appearing in this case were taken from this source.

2. V. Bajaj and J. Creswell, "A Lender Failed. Did Its Auditor?" *The New York Times* (online), 13 April 2008.

The following section of this case provides a historical overview of subprime mortgage lending in the United States. Next, the history and operations of New Century Financial Corporation are reviewed with a particular focus on the company's major role in the subprime mortgage fiasco. The case then examines the criticism of KPMG, New Century's longtime independent audit firm, by the federal bankruptcy examiner appointed to investigate the company's sudden collapse in early 2007.

Subprime Lending: A Historical Perspective

Like all businesses, mortgage companies struggle to achieve a proper balance between "risk" and "return" in their operations. The principal risk historically faced by mortgage lenders is the possibility that their clients will be unable or unwilling to pay the principal and interest on their mortgage loans.

Prior to the 1980s, individuals who were poor credit risks effectively had only two choices for obtaining a mortgage to purchase a home. Those alternatives were obtaining a home loan insured by either the Federal Housing Administration (FHA) or the Department of Veteran Affairs (VA). Borrowers with good credit histories, so-called prime borrowers, would typically seek financing for a new loan directly from a bank, savings and loan, or other financial institutions.

The deregulation of the lending industry, beginning in the 1980s, made it much easier for subprime borrowers to obtain mortgage loans to finance the purchase of a new home. The Depository Institutions Deregulation and Monetary Control Act of 1980 did away with restrictions that imposed a ceiling on the interest rates lending institutions could charge on new mortgage loans. Subsequent legislation allowed mortgage lenders to create a wide array of financing alternatives to compete with the standard 30-year, fixed-interest rate mortgage loan that had long been the industry's principal product. Most notably, these non-traditional mortgage loans included ARMs, or adjustable rate mortgages, that would become particularly popular with mortgage borrowers who had impaired or "subprime" credit histories or profiles.

Despite the deregulatory legislation of the 1980s, the subprime sector of the mortgage industry did not experience explosive growth until the "securitization" of mortgage loans became increasingly common following the turn of the century. Wikipedia defines securitization as "a structured finance process in which assets, receivables, or financial instruments [such as mortgage loans] are acquired, classified into pools, and offered as collateral for third-party investment."

The securitization option caused many mortgage lenders to adopt an "originate to distribute" business model. This new business model meant that the credit risk posed by new mortgages was no longer exclusively absorbed by lending institutions but rather was shared with investors worldwide who purchased so-called mortgage-backed securities or MBS. By 2006, nearly one-fourth of all new residential mortgage loans in the United States were made to subprime borrowers; three-fourths of those mortgages were securitized and sold to investors in the United States and around the world.

The insatiable demand for high-yield MBS among investors, particularly institutional investors such as large banks and hedge funds, caused subprime lenders to ratchet up their marketing efforts. To persuade individuals who were high credit risks to obtain mortgage loans, the subprime lenders developed new products designed specifically for that sector of the mortgage market.

Among the most popular mortgage products developed for the subprime lending market were "stated-income" and "interest-only" mortgages. An applicant for a stated-income loan was simply asked to report his or her annual income during the application process for the loan. The applicant's self-reported income was used by the lender to determine the size of the loan that the individual could afford. Not surprisingly, many applicants for stated-income loans, commonly known as "liars' loans" in the mortgage industry, grossly overstated their annual incomes so that they could purchase a larger home than was economically feasible given their actual annual incomes.

A borrower who obtained an interest-only or IO mortgage loan was required to pay only interest on his or her loan balance for a fixed period of the mortgage term. The IO feature of these loans typically extended over either the first 5 or the first 10 years of the mortgage term. Similar to other mortgage loans, the most common term of an IO loan was 30 years.

Housing prices in those regions of the country where subprime lending was particularly prevalent—such as Arizona; California; south Florida; and Las Vegas, Nevada—rose steeply during the late 1990s and into the early years of the new century. Many subprime borrowers in those housing markets purchased a home with the express intention of reaping a short-term windfall profit. An individual who obtained a 100 per cent loan to acquire a $2 million home could realize a more than $400,000 "profit" on that home in two years if housing prices rose 10 percent each year. After two years, the borrower could extract that profit by refinancing his or her mortgage. That profit could then be used to make the monthly payments on the new mortgage. Or, that individual could sell the home and use the resulting profit to purchase a much larger home—with a much larger mortgage—that he or she could also "flip" in a few years.

Housing prices generally reached their peak in the United States in mid-2006, although they had been declining in some regions of the country over the previous twelve months. By late 2007, prices in several major regional housing markets had declined by 10 percent from their peak levels. By mid-2008, housing prices in those same markets had declined by 20 percent, or more, from their high water marks.

As housing prices steadily fell, a growing number of subprime borrowers began defaulting on their monthly mortgage payments. In fact, many of those individuals quickly became "upside down in their homes," that is, the unpaid balances of their mortgages exceeded the market values of their homes. By early 2008, an estimated 9 million U.S. homeowners had a negative equity in their homes.

The sharp downturn in the housing market had an immediate and drastic impact on mortgage lenders, particularly subprime mortgage lenders such as New Century. Many of the subprime loans originated and packaged for sale by New Century included repurchase clauses. If the default rate on those packages of loans exceeded a certain rate, New Century could be forced to repurchase those loans. As the housing market weakened, New Century and other subprime lenders were flooded with loan repurchase requests.

The financial problems facing the mortgage industry soon spread to other sectors of the economy because of the securitization of subprime mortgage loans. Many high-profile companies in the financial services industry, such as Merrill Lynch, that had no direct connection to the large subprime lenders suffered huge losses as the market value of MBS plunged. Making matters worse, a large proportion of MBS that originated in the United States was sold worldwide. As one observer of the mortgage market noted, the securitization process effectively "spread the cancer of subprime mortgages to investors throughout the U.S. and the rest of the world."[3]

---

3. K. Amadeo, "Understanding the Subprime Mortgage Crisis," *About.com* (online), 9 October 2008.

New Century: Poster Child for Subprime Mortgage Lending

Bob Cole, Ed Gotschall, and Brad Morrice found themselves without jobs in 1995 when the company for which they had worked for several years, Plaza Home Mortgage, was purchased by a much larger competitor. The three friends decided to pool their resources and establish their own mortgage company, a company that would focus on the "low-end" or subprime sector of the mortgage market. Cole served as New Century Financial Corporation's chief executive officer (CEO), Gotschall was the company's chief financial officer, and Morrice oversaw New Century's lending operations as the company's chief operating officer (COO). Morrice would eventually replace Cole as New Century's CEO In June 1997, the company went public by listing its stock on the NASDAQ—New Century's stock would be switched to the New York Stock Exchange in late 2004.

Cole, Gotschall, and Morrice earned relatively modest annual salaries throughout their tenure with the company. For example, in 2005, each of them received a salary of $569,250. However, New Century's incentive compensation plan rewarded the three co-founders handsomely with significant bonuses and stock option grants when the company met or exceeded its financial goals. During 2005, the three executives received total compensation of approximately $15 million each. In addition, *The New York Times* reported that, collectively, they realized more than $40 million in trading profits on the sale of New Century stock between 2004 and 2006.[4]

New Century thrived from its inception, thanks largely to three key factors. First, mortgage interest rates, which had spiked during the mid-1990s, stabilized and then generally trended downward for more than a decade—lower mortgage rates serve to fuel the housing and mortgage industries. Second, the economic and regulatory environment at the time made subprime lending the most lucrative sector of the mortgage industry. Finally, the booming housing market in Orange County, California, where the company was located, provided New Century a large and easily accessible market to tap.

Once New Century was well established in Orange County, the company's ruling troika of Cole, Gotschall, and Morrice began pursuing expansion opportunities for their company in other "hot" real estate markets in the United States. At its zenith, New Century operated more than 200 retail mortgage offices in the United States from which company employees originated new mortgage loans. The company's wholesale division, which produced the bulk of its loan originations, operated through a far-flung network of more than 35,000 independent mortgage brokers.

New Century's 2003 Form 10-K filed with the Securities Exchange Commission (SEC) provided a concise summary of the company's business model.

> We offer mortgage products designed for borrowers who generally do not satisfy the credit, documentation or other underwriting standards prescribed by conventional mortgage lenders and loan buyers, such as Fannie Mae and Freddie Mac. We originate and purchase loans on the basis of the borrower's ability to repay the mortgage loan, the borrower's historical pattern of debt repayment and the amount of equity in the borrower's property (as measured by the borrower's loan-to-value ratio, or LTV). We have been originating and purchasing these types of loans since 1996 and believe we have developed a comprehensive and sophisticated process of credit evaluation and risk-based pricing that allows us to effectively manage the potentially higher risks associated with this segment of the mortgage industry.

In 2004, New Century's management reorganized the company as a real estate investment trust (REIT) so that it would qualify for favorable tax treatment under

---

4. V. Bajaj, "Report Assails Auditor for Work at Failed Home Lender," *The New York Times* (online), 26 March 2008.

the Internal Revenue Code. This organizational change had little impact on the company's operations or the underlying nature of its principal line of business, that is, originating subprime mortgage loans.

New Century experienced impressive growth from its founding in 1996 through 2001; however, a significant increase in subprime lending activity quadrupled New Century's revenues from fiscal 2002 to fiscal 2005. In the latter fiscal year, New Century originated or purchased more than $56 billion of mortgage loans and securitized $17 billion of those loans, resulting in net earnings of $411 million for the company.

The decision by New Century's management to focus the company's marketing efforts principally on stated-income and IO loans contributed significantly to its remarkable growth in revenues beginning in 2002. By 2005, approximately three-fourths of the company's loan originations involved one of those two products.

Throughout the period that New Century's revenues were increasing dramatically, company spokespeople repeatedly insisted in press releases and public filings with the SEC that the company had a strong and sophisticated system of internal controls. That contention was subsequently questioned by the bankruptcy examiner appointed to investigate the collapse of New Century.

> *Several interviewees told the Examiner that they thought New Century's information technology and data entry and processing systems were not "state of the art" and were not sufficient for a business of the size and nature of New Century's. In particular, New Century's loan production processes were apparently manual and people-intensive through the fall of 2005. Up until that time, New Century apparently used an outdated DOS-based loan underwriting and appraising operating system, which according to one Management interviewee, allowed users to "finagle anything."*

The bankruptcy examiner's report went on to note that the company's accounting system was particularly lax with regard to tracking "loan repurchase claims." According to the examiner, New Century did not develop an "automated system or protocol" for tracking such claims until late 2006. By that time, the company was being swamped by loan repurchase requests due to the weakening housing markets in the principal geographical areas that it served. Besides failing to properly track loan repurchase requests throughout most of its history, New Century "did not have a formal policy spelling out exactly how to calculate reserves"[5] for loans that it would be required to repurchase.

By late 2005, several members of New Century's board of directors were openly challenging top management's high-risk business strategies as well as questionable accounting and financial reporting decisions made by the company. The most vocal of these critics was Richard Zona, an outside director who also served on the company's audit committee.

Earlier in his long and distinguished career, Zona had been a senior partner with Ernst & Young (E&Y) and had served for a time as E&Y's National Director of Financial Services, a position in which he oversaw the firm's audit, tax, and management consulting services. In the late 1990s, Zona had also served on an advisory council to the Federal Reserve Board.

In late 2005, Zona drafted a resignation letter, which he addressed to New Century's board of directors. In that letter, Zona suggested that company management was manipulating reported earnings, employing "aggressive" revenue recognition methods, and failing to provide an adequate allowance for loan losses.[6] Excerpts from Zona's letter are included in Exhibit 1.

---

5. Bajaj and Creswell, "A Lender Failed."

6. Zona eventually rescinded the 2005 resignation letter and remained on the company's board until September 2007.

EXHIBIT 1

Excerpts from
Draft of 2005
Resignation
Letter
Submitted by
Richard Zona to
New Century's
Board

At the October 25th and 26th [2005] Board meeting, Management informed the Board that its current forecast and analyst consensus for third quarter EPS of $2.24 per share could not be achieved unless Management reversed $.26 per share of loan loss reserves . . . Obviously, Management's desire to reverse reserves in the third quarter smacked of earnings manipulation.

Management use of off balance sheet gain on sale accounting substantially overstates earnings when compared to cash flows, thus generating extremely aggressive income recognition.

Our largest shareholder has questioned the appropriateness of our accounting for loan losses.

As to accounting for loan losses, it is a long standing accounting maxim that accounting should be designed and applied to match revenues with expenses. Management's methodology to provide for loan losses based upon their estimate of charge offs over the next 18 months does not accomplish that objective . . . Management's methodology does not result in a proper matching of revenues with costs, (loan loss provisions), because charge offs are back ended.

Source: "Final Report of Michael J. Missal, Bankruptcy Court Examiner," In re: New Century TRS Holdings, Inc., a Delaware corporation, *et al.*, U.S. Bankruptcy Court for the District Delaware, Case No. 07-10416 (KJC), 29 February 2008.

Throughout 2006, New Century's financial condition and operating results deteriorated rapidly. To quell concerns regarding the company's health, New Century management repeatedly assured Wall Street that the company was financially sound. In August 2006, New Century reported a significant increase in its earnings for the second quarter of the year compared with that for the same period of the prior year. A company spokesperson noted that those operating results were "evidence of the strength and stability of our franchise." New Century's third quarter earnings press release for 2006 admitted that subprime lenders faced "challenging" market conditions because of increasing loan delinquencies. Nevertheless, the press release assured the investing public that New Century was "adequately reserved for the expected higher level of loan losses."

On January 31, 2007, New Century's management team met with the company's board of directors and audit committee. At that meeting, management told the board and audit committee that New Century had understated its reserve for loan repurchase losses for each of the first three quarterly reporting periods of 2006. New Century's controller, David Kenneally, attributed those understatements to an "inadvertent oversight" in the method used to compute the reserve. Members of New Century's board and audit committee testified that they were "shocked" by this revelation and described the January 31 meeting as "ugly" and "very emotional."

On February 7, 2007, New Century filed a Form 8-K with the SEC, which publicly disclosed the prior understatements of the loan repurchase loss reserve. The 8-K indicated that the understatements were due to the company failing "to account for expected discounts upon the disposition of repurchased loans" and due to its failure to "properly consider the growing volume of repurchase claims outstanding that resulted from the increasing pace of repurchase requests." The 8-K filing did not disclose to what extent the loan repurchase loss reserve had been understated but instead simply indicated that the previously reported earnings for the first three quarters of 2006 "should no longer be relied upon."

EXHIBIT 2

FICTITIOUS LETTER
SUPPOSEDLY
WRITTEN BY
FORMER NEW
CENTURY CEO
FOLLOWING
THE COMPANY'S
BANKRUPTCY FILING

Dear BankNet360 Readers:

Hi, my name is Brad Morrice and I've just bailed out of my sinking ship, the SS New Century Financial.

But don't feel bad for me; I'll be doing just fine. I may have bankrupt the company, treated mortgage underwriting like a bad cold, and helped cause more layoffs than a recession, but I should still bank about $25 million. To the creditors I say, "nanee-nanee billy goat."

Regrets? Sure, I've got some. I should have cashed in more of my options when the NEW stock was on a rocket ship fueled by option ARMs and I.O. loans from heaven. Ah, those were the days, when loans fell from the sky—and into the laps of subprime borrowers who can more easily discern Britney from J-Lo than understand all the conditions of their upcoming loan repricings.

You know, I wonder also how I can walk away from New Century with so much dough. This Chief Restructuring Officer, Holly Etlin, I don't know what planet she is from, but she can come over to my palace, er, place, anytime.

Oh, look at the time. That money's going to hit my account any moment now, and I've got shopping to do. Well, my regards to the subprime mortgage industry. All you Wall Street guys—hope you can handle the risk.

Sincerely yours,

Brad A. Morrice
Founder (ret.)
New Century Financial Corp. (bankrupt)

Source: BankNet360.com (www.banknet360.com/viewpoints/Discussion.do?discussion_id=191), 13 June 2007.

On March 2, 2007, New Century informed the SEC that its 2006 Form 10-K would be delayed and that it would eventually report a loss for the entire year. At the same time, New Century disclosed that KPMG was considering issuing a going-concern opinion on the company's 2006 financial statements—KPMG resigned as New Century's auditor a few weeks later without having issued an opinion on those financial statements. On April 2, 2007, New Century filed for bankruptcy in a U.S. federal court. At the time, New Century was the ninth largest company to file for bankruptcy in U.S. history.[7] In May 2008, company management announced that New Century's audited financial statements for 2005 should no longer be relied upon.

Within a few days of New Century's bankruptcy filing, the company's stock price fell to less than $1 per share, down from more than $30 per share two months earlier—the stock had reached its all-time high of $66 per share in 2004. Not surprisingly, stockholders and other parties were enraged by the company's sudden collapse that mimicked the downfall of Enron and WorldCom a few years earlier. Exhibit 2 presents a sarcastic commentary on New Century's collapse by one of the company's many critics. This commentary was in the form of a fictitious letter addressed to the readers of an online banking forum.

7. The five largest companies to file for bankruptcy in 2007 were mortgage lenders. Four of those five companies were subprime lenders.

"Go-to Auditor"

The New York Times characterized KPMG as the "go-to auditor" for the subprime sector of the mortgage industry.[8] KPMG's audit clients in that sector included the largest subprime lenders, namely, Countrywide, HSBC, New Century, and Wells Fargo. KPMG served as New Century's auditor from the company's inception in 1995 until its resignation in April 2007.

New Century's bankruptcy filing resulted in heated criticism of KPMG. *The New York Times* drew a parallel between Arthur Andersen's audits of Enron Corporation, which had failed to expose the huge energy company's aggressive accounting treatments, and KPMG's audits of New Century. According to the newspaper, KPMG had failed to warn investors that New Century's "mortgage freight train was about to run off the rails."[9]

> *New Century's accounting methods let it prop up profits, charming investors and allowing the company to continue to tap a rich vein of Wall Street cash that it used to underwrite more mortgages. Without the appearance of a strong bottom line, New Century's financial lifeline could have been cut earlier than it was.[10]*

The federal bankruptcy examiner appointed for New Century carried out an exhaustive investigation of the large subprime lender's sudden failure. A major focus of that investigation was KPMG's 2005 audit of New Century and the accounting firm's reviews of the financial statements included in the company's Form 10-Qs for the first three quarters of 2006. KPMG was required to provide the bankruptcy examiner with nearly 2 million pages of documents relating to those engagements. Exhibit 3 presents KPMG's audit report on New Century's 2005 financial statements.

In his 560-page report, the bankruptcy examiner alleged that KPMG had failed to perform its New Century engagements "in accordance with professional standards." The examiner's specific allegations included charges that the 2005 New Century audit was improperly staffed and that the independence of certain KPMG auditors may have been impaired. The examiner also maintained that KPMG failed to adequately consider serious internal control problems evident in New Century's accounting and financial reporting system and failed to properly audit the company's critically important loan repurchase loss reserve.

Staffing Issues on the New Century Engagement

In the spring of 2005, shortly after KPMG completed the 2004 audit of New Century, an almost entirely new team of auditors, approximately 15 KPMG employees in total, was assigned to that client. The only two members of the 2004 audit engagement team "held over" for the 2005 audit were two first-year associates. The two key members of the 2005 audit team, the audit engagement partner and the senior manager, had just joined the Los Angeles office of KPMG, the practice office responsible for servicing New Century.

John Donovan, the engagement partner for the 2005 New Century audit, had served for 17 years as an audit partner with Arthur Andersen prior to that firm being forced to disband in 2002. After Andersen's demise, Donovan became an audit partner with E&Y, which he left in early 2005 to take a similar position with KPMG.

---

8. Bajaj and Creswell, "A Lender Failed."

9. *Ibid.*

10. *Ibid.*

EXHIBIT 3

New Century
Financial
Corporation and
Subsidiaries
Report of
Independent
Registered
Certified Public
Accounting Firm

KPMG's 2005 Audit Report on New Century's Financial Statements

The Board of Directors

New Century Financial Corporation

We have audited the accompanying consolidated balance sheets of New Century Financial Corporation and subsidiaries as of December 31, 2005, and 2004, and the related consolidated statements of income, comprehensive income, changes in stockholders' equity, and cash flows for each of the years in the three-year period ended December 31, 2005. These consolidated financial statements are the responsibility of Company's Management. Our responsibility is to express an opinion on these consolidated financial statements based on our audits.

We conducted our audit in accordance with the standards of the Public Company Accounting Oversight Board (United States). Those standards require that we plan the audit to obtain reasonable assurance about whether the financial statements are free of material misstatement. An audit includes examining, on a test basis, evidence supporting the amounts and disclosures in the financial statements. An audit also includes assessing the accounting principles used and significant estimates made by management, as well as evaluating the overall financial statement presentation. We believe that our audits provide a reasonable basis for our opinion.

In our opinion, the consolidated financial statements referred to above present fairly, in all material respects, the financial position of New Century Financial Corporation and subsidiaries as of December 31, 2005 and 2004, and the results of their operations and their cash flows for each of the years in the three-year period ended December 31, 2005, in conformity with U.S. generally accepted accounting principles.

We have also audited, in accordance with the standards of the Public Company Accounting Oversight Board (United States), the effectiveness of the Company's internal control over financial reporting as of December 31, 2005, based on criteria established in Internal Control—Integrated Framework issued by the Committee of Sponsoring Organizations of the Treadway Commission (COSO), and our report dated March 15, 2006 expressed an unqualified opinion on management's assessment of, and the effective operation of, internal control over financial reporting.

KPMG LLP
Los Angeles, California
March 15, 2006

Source: New Century's 2005 10-K.

New Century's audit committee was unhappy with KPMG's decision to appoint Donovan as the audit engagement partner for the 2005 audit. Members of the audit committee believed that Donovan's lack of experience with the mortgage industry made him a poor choice to supervise that audit and asked KPMG to appoint another partner to oversee the engagement. When KPMG refused, the audit committee considered dismissing KPMG and retaining a different audit firm. "Ultimately, the Audit Committee determined that a switch to a new accounting firm would be tremendously disruptive and would send a bad signal to its lenders."

Mark Kim accepted a position with KPMG in May 2005, shortly before being assigned to serve as the senior manager on the 2005 New Century audit engagement. Kim had several years of prior experience as an auditor and had served for three years as the assistant controller of a small mortgage lending company.

During his tenure on the New Century audit team, Mark Kim complained to John Donovan that it was difficult to recruit a "good team" of auditors to work on the engagement. In an e-mail to Donovan, an exasperated Kim remarked, "We will never get a good team out here because of the reputation that the engagement has." Another e-mail sent by a New Century accountant to the company's controller, David Kenneally, seemed to corroborate Kim's opinion. This latter e-mail noted that KPMG had not assigned the "A team" to the New Century audit.

In fact, Kenneally, a former KPMG employee, was apparently the key reason that the New Century engagement had a negative reputation within KPMG's Los Angeles office. Evidence collected by the New Century bankruptcy examiner suggested that the company's accounting function was "weak" and was overseen by Kenneally who was "domineering" and "difficult, condescending, and quick-tempered." One KPMG subordinate on the New Century audit team testified that Kenneally often berated Donovan and Kim. In another e-mail sent by Kim to Donovan, the KPMG senior manager indicated that "Dave [Kenneally] seems to know the answers for everything and anything and the rest of the accounting department is on almost the same boat as the audit team is—little knowledge of what's going on. This intimidates everyone on the engagement team."

The tense relationship between the KPMG audit engagement team and New Century's management, particularly Kenneally, worsened as the 2005 audit neared completion. Two individuals with KPMG's FDR (Financial Derivatives Resource) Group were brought in to review New Century's accounting for certain hedges and other financial derivatives during the final phase of the audit. They requested various documents from New Century that were needed to complete their review of the aforementioned items. When New Century failed to provide that documentation, the two specialists refused to "sign off" on the company's relevant accounting decisions. This refusal prevented Donovan from releasing the opinion on New Century's financial statements that were to be included in the company's 2005 Form 10-K.

Hours before the SEC filing deadline for New Century's 2005 10-K, an angry Donovan e-mailed one of the FDR specialists: "I am very disappointed we are still discussing this. As far as I am concerned, we are done. The client thinks we are done. All we are going to do is p___ everybody off." Later that same day, a high-ranking KPMG partner in the firm's New York headquarters office told Donovan to release the unqualified opinion on New Century's 2005 financial statements. Donovan was instructed to release the opinion even though the two FDR specialists had not approved the company's accounting decisions for its financial derivatives.[11]

The following day, New Century's audit committee called a meeting with Donovan and Kim. In that meeting, members of the audit committee reportedly "yelled" and "screamed" at the two KPMG auditors. Later, Kenneally told the New Century bankruptcy examiner that he had been "furious" over the "near-disaster"—that is, the fact that New Century's filing of its 2005 10-K with the SEC had almost been delayed. Because of the incident, New Century's audit committee deferred the decision of whether or not to reappoint KPMG as the company's auditor for the 2006 fiscal year.

---

11. The FDR specialists were allowed to dissociate themselves from the decision to issue the audit opinion on New Century's 2005 financial statements in a "disagreement memorandum" included in the 2005 workpapers. The following month, New Century finally provided the documentation that had been requested by those specialists. A review of that documentation revealed that New Century had improperly accounted for certain of its derivatives, resulting in "a misstatement of several million dollars." However, KPMG ruled that those errors were immaterial, meaning that it was not necessary to restate the 2005 financial statements.

Donovan later testified that he had been concerned that the audit committee would dismiss KPMG.

Over the following two months, Donovan assured New Century's audit committee that "a situation like this will never happen again." After receiving that assurance, the audit committee reappointed KPMG as New Century's audit firm.

The bankruptcy examiner speculated that the 2005 10-K incident impaired KPMG's independence during the remainder of the firm's tenure with New Century. "In particular, it is possible that Donovan and Kim were not as skeptical as they might otherwise have been with regard to critical assumptions [underlying New Century's accounting decisions]." The examiner went on to suggest that "Donovan and Kim may have looked for ways to add unique value in order to salvage KPMG's reputation, such as by providing proactive (though erroneous) advice in connection with the repurchase reserve calculation methodology."

In a subsequent interview with *The New York Times*, the bankruptcy examiner further questioned KPMG's independence when he maintained that the New Century auditors had been eager to please the company's management team. "They acquiesced overly to the client, which in the post-Enron era seems mind-boggling."[12] In another interview with the Reuters news agency, the examiner expressed a similar point of view. "In the post-Enron era, one of the lessons should have been that accountants need to be skeptical, strong, and independent. You didn't have any of those attributes here."[13]

Inadequate Consideration of Internal Control Problems

Section 404 of the Sarbanes-Oxley Act requires auditors of public companies to audit the effectiveness of their clients' internal controls over financial reporting.[14] In both 2004 and 2005, KPMG concluded that New Century maintained effective internal control over its financial reporting function.

During the 2004 internal control audit, the KPMG auditors identified five "significant deficiencies" in internal controls that they reported to New Century's audit committee. Since the KPMG auditors concluded that those deficiencies did not qualify as "material weaknesses," the audit firm was able to issue an unqualified opinion on New Century's internal controls for 2004. No significant deficiencies or material weaknesses in internal controls were identified by KPMG during the 2005 internal control audit.

New Century's bankruptcy examiner challenged KPMG's conclusion that the company's internal controls over financial reporting were effective during 2004 and 2005. The examiner pointed out that throughout its existence New Century did not have an "effective mechanism for tracking, processing and handling [loan] repurchase claims." This internal control weakness prevented the company from determining the magnitude of loan repurchase requests at any point in time, which, in turn, prevented the company from properly considering those requests in arriving at the period-ending balances of the loan repurchase loss reserve.

---

12. Bajaj, "Report Assails Auditor."

13. A. Beck, "KPMG Allowed Fraud at New Century, Report Says," *Reuters.com*, 27 March 2008.

14. KPMG's 2004 and 2005 audits of New Century were completed while PCAOB *Auditing Standard No. 2*, "An Audit of Internal Control Over Financial Reporting Performed in Conjunction with an Audit of Financial Statements" was in effect. That standard has subsequently been replaced by PCAOB *Auditing Standard No. 5*, "An Audit of Internal Control Over Financial Reporting That Is Integrated with an Audit of Financial Statements." The two standards are very similar.

A related internal control weakness was New Century's failure to adopt "formal policies and procedures" for calculating the loan repurchase loss reserve at the end of each accounting period. The lower-level accountants who were assigned the task of computing the reserve balance each reporting period testified that they simply followed the instructions passed down to them by the individual who had previously been responsible for the reserve computation.

During both the 2004 and 2005 audits, the KPMG auditors discovered the internal control weaknesses related to New Century's loan repurchase loss reserve. The bankruptcy examiner noted that those control weaknesses had particularly critical implications for New Century in 2005 when the volume of loan repurchase requests was increasing rapidly. Despite those implications, KPMG characterized those weaknesses as "inconsequential" during the 2005 audit. Since the internal control problems were not deemed significant deficiencies or material weaknesses, KPMG did not communicate them to New Century's audit committee.

The bankruptcy examiner insisted that for at least the 2005 audit, the inadequate accounting procedures for loan repurchase requests qualified as a material weakness in internal control, which should have caused KPMG to issue an adverse opinion on New Century's internal controls. In fact, New Century's management reached a similar conclusion in early 2007.

> The material weaknesses identified [by New Century's management in early 2007] were: (1) the failure to maintain effective controls over the interpretation and application of the accounting literature relating to the Company's critical accounting policies (specifically as to the calculation of repurchase reserves); and (2) the failure to maintain effective controls to provide reasonable assurances that the Company collected, analyzed, and used information relating to outstanding purchase claims when establishing the allowance for repurchase losses.

Debbie Biddle was the KPMG audit senior principally responsible for the 2005 internal control audit. Similar to John Donovan and Mark Kim, Biddle had joined KPMG's Los Angeles office shortly before the 2005 New Century audit began. Biddle transferred to the Los Angeles office from a KPMG affiliate in the United Kingdom. Prior to being assigned responsibility for the 2005 New Century internal control audit, Biddle had "virtually no experience auditing U.S. clients and no prior SOX experience."

The bankruptcy examiner reported that Biddle and her colleagues failed to thoroughly review the 2004 audit workpapers for New Century. As a result, they may have been unaware of the internal control problems discovered by KPMG auditors the prior year and thus failed to properly consider those problems in planning and carrying out the 2005 audit.

> The Examiner found no evidence that the KPMG [2005] engagement team engaged in a formal process to compare year over year deficiency findings in connection with the 2005 SOX 404 audit. Conducting this analysis would have been prudent given the wholesale turnover in the KPMG engagement team. This failure is significant, as it impacted the planning for the 404 audit in 2005, the evaluation of findings in 2005, and the planning for the year-end audits.

Failure to Properly Audit New Century's Loan Repurchase Loss Reserve

In early 2005, the quality of New Century's loan portfolio, as measured by such objective criteria as delinquency and default rates, began declining rapidly. Internal data collected by New Century revealed that the delinquency rate on loans originated during 2005 was approximately double that of loans originated during the previous year. The delinquency rate continued to rise throughout 2006 as conditions within the housing market deteriorated.

The increasing delinquency and default rates on loans originated by New Century caused a large increase in the number of loan repurchase claims filed by investors that had purchased large blocks of those loans. Because of the inadequate accounting procedures and internal controls for loan repurchase claims, New Century's accounting staff failed to record the needed increases in the loan repurchase loss reserve throughout 2005 and beyond. For example, despite the large increase in loan repurchase requests in 2005, New Century's loan repurchase loss reserve actually declined from the end of 2004 to the end of 2005.

New Century's bankruptcy examiner estimated that the understatement of the loan repurchase loss reserve and errors in related accounts inflated New Century's reported pre-tax earnings for fiscal 2005 by 14.3 percent or approximately $64 million. The examiner determined that errors in those same accounts overstated New Century's reported pre-tax earnings for the first three quarters of 2006 by approximately $200 million or 59 percent.

New Century's accountants used a 90-day "look-back" period in determining the adequacy of the loan repurchase loss reserve each financial reporting period. That is, only repurchase requests for loans sold in the 90 days immediately preceding the balance sheet date were considered in arriving at the reserve balance. In fact, the company often received repurchase requests for loans sold more than three months earlier.

The bankruptcy examiner criticized KPMG for not insisting that New Century use a longer than 90-day "window" in computing the loan repurchase loss reserve. In fact, a KPMG workpaper suggested that policy was reasonable. "Based on the review of the Company's repurchase log and discussions with management, it appears reasonable that the most recent 3 months sales are at risk for repurchase." The bankruptcy examiner contested the assertion that KPMG had reviewed the log of loan repurchase requests since that accounting record indicated that loans were being reacquired by New Century as long as three years after the date they were sold. The examiner also uncovered evidence suggesting that a New Century executive had informed a KPMG auditor that a significant number of loans older than 90 days were being repurchased by the company.

KPMG's audit workpapers documented the ominous increase in loan repurchase requests received by New Century beginning in late 2004. In 2005, New Century repurchased $332 million of loans, compared with $135 million the prior year. Despite this large increase, the bankruptcy examiner reported that KPMG "failed to perform any increased procedures or testing of New Century's repurchase reserves" during the 2005 audit.

A secondary factor that contributed to the understatement of New Century's loan repurchase loss reserve was the company's failure to consider an "interest recapture" element in computing that reserve each reporting period. The bankruptcy examiner found this obvious oversight by the company's accountants "perplexing."

> The failure to include Interest Recapture in the repurchase reserve calculation from the outset is perplexing because the Examiner understands that it was a long time requirement under loan repurchase agreements for New Century to pay investors the amount of interest that the borrower had failed to pay.

A workpaper memorandum that summarized the audit tests KPMG applied during the 2005 audit to the loan repurchase loss reserve indicated that interest recapture was a component of the reserve.

A KPMG workpaper from January 2006 notes that estimated losses on future repurchases "include accrued interest the investor [loan purchaser] would have collected from the borrower, if the loan had performed, that New Century must pay to the investor at the time of repurchase."

The evidence that KPMG relied on to reach that erroneous conclusion was a statement made by David Kenneally. The bankruptcy examiner criticized the KPMG auditors for not corroborating Kenneally's assertion with other audit evidence. "If KPMG had performed adequate tests and calculations, it would have determined that Interest Recapture was omitted from the repurchase reserve calculation."

During early 2006, New Century changed the method used to compute the period-ending balance of the loan repurchase loss reserve.[15] This change resulted in large increases in the understatements of that account at the end of each subsequent quarterly reporting period—by the third quarter of 2006 the reserve was understated by approximately 1000 percent.

Kenneally testified that the change in accounting for the reserve account was recommended by Mark Kim, the KPMG senior audit manager. Kim would later testify that he did not explicitly remember making that recommendation. Nevertheless, evidence collected by the bankruptcy examiner caused him to conclude that a KPMG auditor "almost certainly" recommended the change in accounting for the reserve account.

At a time when KPMG was aware, as evidenced by its own workpapers, that market conditions were worsening and repurchases were increasing, KPMG made a recommendation to New Century to remove a component of the repurchase reserve that had the effect of decreasing the reserve ... and then failed to inform the Audit Committee of the change in this critical accounting policy.

In November 2006, New Century hired a new chief financial officer (CFO) who had 30 years of prior experience in the mortgage industry. The CFO immediately questioned the adequacy of the company's loan repurchase loss reserve and asked KPMG to provide him with a written statement that the reserve was properly stated. KPMG refused to provide that written assurance.

As a result of the new CFO's persistent inquiries, New Century's accounting staff eventually recognized that the accounting change made in early 2006 for the loan repurchase loss reserve had been improper and had materially understated the reserve for each of the first three quarterly reporting periods of 2006. That realization led to the February 7, 2007, 8-K filing in which New Century reported those understatements. That 8-K disclosure triggered the series of events that resulted in New Century filing for bankruptcy less than two months later.

In Defense of KPMG

Representatives of KPMG responded forcefully to the allegations against their firm in the report prepared by New Century's bankruptcy examiner. Particularly galling to the large accounting firm was the suggestion that KPMG auditors had "deferred excessively"[16] to client executives during the course of the New Century engagements.

---

15. The change in the method of computing the loss reserve involved deleting the "inventory severity" component of that reserve. That component involved those losses expected to be incurred by New Century on loans that had already been reacquired as of the given balance sheet date. Kim allegedly suggested dropping this component because he believed that it was considered by New Century in arriving at the balance of a related valuation account for the company's portfolio of outstanding loans. In fact, that was not the case.

16. Bajaj, "Report Assails Auditor."

In response to that allegation, a KPMG spokesperson told a reporter with *The New York Times*, "There is absolutely no evidence to support that contention."[17] In a subsequent interview with the *Times*, that same individual suggested that the bankruptcy examiner's report was unfair and "one-sided."

> *The examiner was appointed by the court to identify potential lawsuits in a bankruptcy case. Consistent with that charge, he has prepared an advocacy piece, which has many one-sided statements and significant omissions. In the end, the examiner concluded that the bankruptcy estate may be able to file a lawsuit against KPMG for negligence—a claim we strongly dispute—and a claim even the examiner notes in his report for which KPMG has strong defenses.*[18]

Several other parties also came to KPMG's defense. An accounting professor at the University of Chicago maintained that KPMG was not at fault in the New Century case and instead attributed the company's bankruptcy to its high-risk business model. "The business model of New Century depended on real estate values that would continue to go up and certainly not go down. The economic model here is what is at fault. It's the cause of what happened, not anything that KPMG did."[19]

At a minimum, the New Century bankruptcy report served to sustain a string of embarrassing public relations incidents for KPMG. In 2005, KPMG had faced potential criminal charges for a series of questionable tax shelters that it had marketed to well-heeled tax clients. In that same year, KPMG had agreed to pay the SEC $22.5 million to settle charges that audits of one of its largest clients, Xerox, had been flawed. Subsequent to that announcement, KPMG paid $80 million to settle civil litigation stemming from its Xerox audits.

Even before the New Century bankruptcy report was released, KPMG had been linked to the ongoing crises and scandals in the mortgage industry. Charges of large-scale earnings manipulation by Fannie Mae called into question the quality of KPMG's audits of that organization, which for decades had played such a large role in the mortgage industry. Finally, in early January 2008, KPMG had been named a co-defendant in a large class-action lawsuit that charged Countrywide, another KPMG audit client, with perpetrating an accounting fraud.

EPILOGUE

In August 2008, Ed McMahon revealed that he had finally found a buyer for his Beverly Hills mansion that would allow him to pay off his large mortgage.[20] Most individuals snared by the financial crisis that overwhelmed the mortgage industry and housing market in the United States did not share McMahon's good fortune.

By the end of 2008, more than 1.5 million Americans would face foreclosure proceedings on their homes, easily the largest number of residential foreclosures in U.S. history.

In an effort to thwart the nationwide financial panic caused by the meltdowns in the mortgage and housing industries, the U.S. Congress passed

---

17. *Ibid.*

18. Bajaj and Creswell, "A Lender Failed."

19. *Ibid.*

20. Unfortunately, Mr. McMahon passed away in June 2009.

a massive bailout plan in October 2008. The price tag for that plan was measured in hundreds of billions of dollars. Despite that massive effort to shore up the nation's crumbling financial infrastructure, most experts expected that the U.S. economy, as well as the global economy, would suffer adverse lingering effects for years, if not decades, to come.

New Century's collapse resulted in numerous criminal investigations by regulatory and law enforcement authorities as well as a barrage of civil litigation. In July 2010, the SEC announced that it had reached a settlement to resolve fraud charges that it had filed against three former New Century officers including Brad Morrice and David Kenneally. In addition to monetary sanctions of approximately $750,000 for Morrice and $160,000 for Kenneally, each was barred from serving as an officer of a public company for five years. Among the civil lawsuits decided to date, KPMG reportedly agreed to contribute $45 million to a settlement pool in late 2010 to resolve a class-action lawsuit filed by New Century's former stockholders.

Questions

1. KPMG served as the independent audit firm of several of the largest subprime mortgage lenders. Identify the advantages and disadvantages of a heavy concentration of audit clients in one industry or sub-industry.

2. As noted in the case, there was an almost complete turnover of the staff assigned to the New Century audit engagement team from 2004 to 2005. What quality control mechanisms should accounting firms have in such circumstances to ensure that a high-quality audit is performed?

3. Section 404 of the Sarbanes-Oxley Act requires auditors of a public company to analyze and report on the effectiveness of the client's internal controls over financial reporting. Describe the responsibilities that auditors of public companies have to discover and report (a) *significant deficiencies* in internal controls and (b) *material weaknesses* in internal controls. Include a definition of each item in your answer. Under what condition or conditions can auditors issue an unqualified or clean opinion on the effectiveness of a client's internal controls over financial reporting?

4. One of New Century's most important accounts was its loan repurchase loss reserve. Each accounting period, New Century was required to estimate the ending balance of that account. What general principles or procedures should auditors follow when auditing important "accounting estimates"?

5. New Century's bankruptcy examiner charged that KPMG did not comply with applicable "professional standards" while auditing the company. List specific generally accepted auditing standards (GAAS) that you believe KPMG may have violated on its New Century engagements. Briefly defend each item you list.

6. Mortgage-backed securities (MBS) produced by New Century and other major subprime lenders have been a focal point of attention during the recent financial crisis. Many parties have maintained that the mark-to-market rule for securities investments such as MBS has contributed significantly to that crisis and that the rule should be modified, suspended, or even eliminated. Briefly summarize the principal arguments of those parties opposed to the mark-to-market rule. Do you believe that those arguments are legitimate? Why or why not?

7. Identify what you consider to be the three most important "take-aways" or learning points in this case. Rank these items in order of importance (highest to lowest). Justify or defend each of your choices.

Madoff Securities

Bernie wanted to be rich; he dedicated his life to it.

John Maccabee, longtime friend of Bernie Madoff

Bernard Lawrence Madoff was born on April 29, 1938, in New York City. Madoff spent his childhood in a lower middle-class neighborhood in the Borough of Queens. After graduating from high school, Madoff enrolled in the University of Alabama but transferred to Hofstra College on Long Island, now known as Hofstra University, at the beginning of his sophomore year. Three years later in 1960, he graduated with a political science degree from Hofstra.

According to a longtime friend, the driving force in Madoff's life since childhood was to become wealthy. "Bernie wanted to be rich; he dedicated his life to it."[1] That compelling force no doubt accounted for Madoff's lifelong fascination with the stock market. As a teenager, Madoff frequently visited Wall Street and dreamed of becoming a "major player" in the world of high finance. Because he did not have the educational training or personal connections to land a prime job on Wall Street after he graduated from college, Madoff decided that he would set up his own one-man brokerage firm.

While in college, Madoff had accumulated a $5,000 nest egg by installing sprinkler systems during the summer months for wealthy New Yorkers living in the city's affluent suburbs. In the summer of 1960, Madoff used those funds to establish Bernard L. Madoff Investment Securities LLC, which was typically referred to as Madoff Securities. Madoff operated the new business from office space that was provided to him by his father-in-law, who was a partner in a small accounting firm. For nearly five decades, Madoff served as the senior executive of Madoff Securities. During that time, the shy New Yorker who had an occasional stammer and several nervous tics would accumulate a fortune estimated at more than one billion dollars.

Taking on Wall Street

Madoff's brokerage firm initially traded only securities of small over-the-counter companies, securities commonly referred to as "penny stocks." At the time, the securities of most large companies were traded on the New York Stock Exchange (NYSE). The rules of that exchange made it extremely difficult for small brokerage firms such as Madoff's to compete with the cartel of large brokerage firms that effectively controlled Wall Street. Madoff and many other small brokers insisted that the NYSE's rules were anticompetitive and inconsistent with a free market economy. Madoff was also convinced that the major brokerage firms kept securities transaction costs artificially high to produce windfall profits for themselves to the detriment of investors, particularly small investors.

Because of Madoff's resentment of the major Wall Street brokerage firms, he made it his mission to "democratize" the securities markets in the United States while at the same time reducing the transaction costs of trading securities. "Bernie was the king of democratization. He was messianic about this. He pushed to automate the [securities trading] system, listing buyers and sellers on a computer that anyone could access."[2]

---

1. J. Maccabee, "Mom and Dad and Ruth and Bernie," *New York Magazine* (nymag.com), 22 February 2009.
2. S. Fishman, "The Monster Mensch," *New York Magazine* (nymag.com), 22 February 09.

In fact, Madoff Securities was one of the first brokerage firms to utilize computers to expedite the processing of securities transactions. Bernie Madoff is also credited as one of the founders of the NASDAQ stock exchange that was organized in 1971. The NASDAQ was destined to become the world's largest electronic stock exchange and the largest global stock exchange in terms of trading volume. In the late 1980s and early 1990s, Madoff served three one-year terms as the chairman of the NASDAQ.

Madoff's leadership role in the development of electronic securities trading contributed significantly to his firm's impressive growth throughout the latter decades of the twentieth century. By the early years of the twenty-first century, Madoff Securities was the largest "market maker" on the NASDAQ, meaning that the firm accounted for more daily transaction volume on that exchange than any other brokerage.[3] By that time, the firm was also among the largest market makers for the New York Stock Exchange, accounting for as much as 5 percent of its daily transaction volume. This market-making service was lucrative with low risk for Madoff Securities and reportedly earned the firm, which was privately owned throughout its existence, annual profits measured in the tens of millions of dollars.

In 1962, Madoff had expanded his firm to include investment advisory services. For several years, most of the individuals who set up investment accounts with Madoff Securities were referred to him by his father-in-law. Although the firm was a pioneer in electronic trading and made sizable profits from its brokerage operations, investment advisory services would prove to be its most important line of business. By late 2008, the total value of customer accounts managed by Madoff Securities reached $65 billion.

The key factor that accounted for the incredible growth in the amount of money entrusted to Madoff's firm by investors worldwide was the impressive rates of return that the firm earned annually on the funds that it managed. For decades, those funds earned an average annual rate of return generally ranging from 10 to 15 per cent. Although impressive, those rates of return were not spectacular. What *was* spectacular was the consistency of the returns. In 2001, *Barron's* reported that some of the Madoff firm's largest investment funds had never experienced a losing year despite significant stock market declines in several individual years.[4] Even when the stock market collapsed in late 2008, individual Madoff funds continued to report net gains for the year-to-date period.

Although Madoff would eventually serve as an investment adviser to dozens of celebrities, professional athletes, and other wealthy individuals, most of the money he managed came from so-called "feeder firms," which were large hedge funds, banks, and other investment companies. The individuals who had committed their funds to these feeder firms were typically unaware that those funds had been turned over to Madoff.

The reclusive Madoff and his subordinates disclosed as little as possible about the investment strategy responsible for their firm's success in the stock market. On one occasion, Madoff told an executive of a feeder firm, "It's no one's business what goes on here."[5] The *Wall Street Journal* reported that Madoff commonly "brushed

---

3. *Investopedia,* an online encyclopedia of business terms, provides the following description of a "market maker": "Broker-dealer firm that accepts the risk of holding a certain number of shares of a particular security in order to facilitate trading in that security. Each market maker competes for customer order flow by displaying buy and sell quotations for a guaranteed number of shares. Once an order is received, the market maker immediately sells from its own inventory or seeks an offsetting order."

4. *Barron's* (online), "What We Wrote About Madoff," 12 December 2008.

5. *Ibid.*

off" skeptics who questioned his firm's investment results by pointing out that those results had been audited and by insisting that his investment strategy "was too complicated for outsiders to understand."[6]

The only substantive information Madoff Securities provided regarding its investment policies was that it employed a "split-strike conversion" investment model. In simple terms, this strategy involved purchasing several dozen blue-chip stocks and then simultaneously selling both put options and call options on those securities. Supposedly, this strategy ensured a positive rate of return on those investments whether the stock market went up or went down.

Competitors, financial analysts, and academics repeatedly attempted to replicate the success of Madoff Securities' investment strategy. None of those attempts were successful, which only added to Bernie Madoff's stature and mystique on Wall Street. As one industry insider noted in 2001, "Even knowledgeable people can't really tell you what he's doing."[7] A CNN reporter observed that by the turn of the century Madoff was widely regarded as a stock market wizard and that "everyone" on Wall Street, including his closest competitors, was "in awe of him."[8]

The Bubble Bursts

On December 10, 2008, Bernie Madoff asked his two sons, Andrew and Mark, who worked at Madoff Securities, to meet him at his apartment that evening. In this meeting, Madoff reportedly told his sons that the impressive returns earned for clients of his firm's investment advisory division over the previous several decades had been fraudulent. Those returns had been produced by an elaborate Ponzi scheme engineered and overseen by Madoff without the knowledge of any of his employees or family members.[9] The following day, an attorney representing Madoff's sons notified the SEC of their father's confession. That evening, FBI agents came to Madoff's apartment. One of the agents asked Madoff "if there was an innocent explanation"[10] for the information relayed to the SEC from his sons. Madoff replied, "There is no innocent explanation."[11] The agents then placed Madoff under arrest and within hours filed securities fraud charges against him.

The public announcement of Madoff's fraudulent scheme in December 2008 stunned investors worldwide. That announcement further undercut the stability of global stock markets that were already reeling from the subprime mortgage crisis in the United States, which had "frozen" the world's credit markets, caused stock prices to drop precipitously, and threatened to plunge the global economy into a deep depression. Politicians, journalists, and everyday citizens were shocked to learn that a massive investment fraud, apparently the largest in history, could go undetected for decades within the capital markets of the world's largest economic power. Even more disconcerting was the fact that the Madoff fraud went undetected for several

---

6. G. Zuckerman, "Fees, Even Returns and Auditor All Raised Flags," *Wall Street Journal* (online), 13 December 2008.

7. *Ibid.*

8. A. Chernoff, "What Drove Bernie Madoff," *CNNMoney.com*, 5 January 2009.

9. *Investopedia* provides the following description of a "Ponzi scheme": "A fraudulent investing scam promising high rates of return with little risk to investors. The Ponzi scheme generates returns for older investors by acquiring new investors. This scam actually yields the promised returns to earlier investors, as long as there are more new investors. These schemes usually collapse on themselves when the new investments stop."

10. Fishman, "The Monster Mensch."

11. *Ibid.*

years after the implementation of the far-reaching regulatory reforms mandated by the U.S. Congress in the wake of the Enron and WorldCom debacles.

News of the Madoff fraud caused a wide range of parties to angrily demand that the federal government and law enforcement authorities determine why the nation's "watchdog" system for the capital markets had failed once again. The accounting profession was among the first targets of the public's anger. On the day that Madoff's fraud was publicly reported, Floyd Norris, a *New York Times* reporter acquainted with Madoff, asked a simple question that was on the minds of many people, namely, "Who were the auditors?"[12]

"Rubber-stamped" Financial Statements

Business journalists quickly determined that the auditor of Madoff Securities was Friehling & Horowitz, an accounting firm located in the small New York City suburb of New City. Friehling & Horowitz had issued unqualified opinions on the financial statements of Madoff's firm since at least the early 1990s. Madoff had paid Friehling & Hororwitz nearly $200,000 in annual audit fees.

Further investigation revealed that Friehling & Horowitz had only one active accountant, one non-professional employee (a secretary), and operated from a tiny office occupying approximately 200 square feet. The active accountant was David Friehling who had performed the annual audits of Madoff's firm and signed off on the firm's unqualified audit opinions. Accounting and auditing experts interviewed by the Associated Press insisted that it was "preposterous" to conceive that any one individual could complete an audit of a company the size of Madoff Securities by himself.[13]

Friehling and his firm were members of the American Institute of Certified Public Accountants (AICPA). A spokesperson for that organization revealed that Friehling had reported to the AICPA each year that he did not perform any audits. As a result, Friehling's firm was not required to submit to the AICPA's peer review program for CPA firms. Friehling's firm was also not required to have a periodic peer review at the state level. At the time, New York was one of six states that did not have a mandatory peer review program for accounting firms.

In March 2009, *The New York Times* reported that Friehling had maintained dozens of investment accounts with Madoff Securities, according to documents obtained by the court-appointed trustee for that firm. Those same documents indicated that Friehling & Horowitz had another 17 investment accounts with Madoff's firm. In total, Friehling, his accounting firm, and his family members had nearly $15 million invested in funds managed by Madoff. Federal prosecutors noted that these investments had "flouted" the accounting profession's auditor independence rules and "disqualified" Friehling from serving as the auditor of Madoff Securities.[14]

David Friehling would be the second person arrested by federal law enforcement authorities investigating Madoff's fraud. Among other charges, federal prosecutors indicted Friehling for securities fraud, aiding and abetting an investment fraud, and obstructing the IRS. The prosecutors did not allege that Friehling was aware of Madoff's fraudulent scheme but rather that he had conducted "sham audits" of Madoff Securities that had "helped foster the illusion that Mr. Madoff legitimately invested his clients' money."[15]

12. F. Norris, "Bernie Madoff," *New York Times* (online), 12 December 2008.

13. *Associated Press* (online), "Questions Surround Madoff Auditor," 17 December 2008.

14. New York State Society of Certified Public Accountants, "Madoff Auditor Charged for Role in Massive Fraud," 19 March 2009 (www.nysscpa.org/ezine/ETPArticles/ML31909a.htm).

15. L. Neumeister, "Federal Appeals Court to Hear Madoff Jail Argument," *Associated Press* (online), 19 March 2009.

News reports of Friehling's alleged sham audits caused him to be berated in the business press. A top FBI official observed that Friehling's "job was not to merely rubber-stamp statements that he didn't verify" and that Friehling had betrayed his "fiduciary duty to investors and his legal obligation to regulators."[16] An SEC official maintained that Friehling had "essentially sold his [CPA] license for more than 17 years while Madoff's Ponzi scheme went undetected."[17] Many parties found this and other denigrating remarks made by SEC officials concerning Friehling ironic since the federal agency was itself the target of scornful criticism for its role in the Madoff fiasco.

Sir Galahad and the SEC

On at least eight occasions, the SEC investigated alleged violations of securities laws by Madoff Securities during the two decades prior to Bernie Madoff's startling confession. In each case, however, the investigation concluded without the SEC charging Madoff with any serious infractions of those laws. Most of these investigations resulted from a series of complaints filed with the SEC by one individual, Harry Markopolos.

On the March 1, 2009, edition of the CBS news program *60 Minutes*, investigative reporter Steve Croft observed that until a few months earlier Harry Markopolos had been an "obscure financial analyst and mildly eccentric fraud investigator from Boston." Beginning in 1999, Markopolos had repeatedly told the SEC that Bernie Madoff was operating what he referred to as the "world's largest Ponzi scheme." Between May 2000 and April 2008, Markopolos mailed or hand delivered documents and other evidence to the SEC that purportedly proved that assertion. Although SEC officials politely listened to Markopolos's accusations, they failed to vigorously investigate them.

One lengthy report that Markopolos sent to the SEC in 2005 identified 29 specific "red flags" suggesting that Madoff was perpetrating a massive fraud on his clients. Among these red flags was Madoff's alleged refusal to allow the Big Four auditor of an investment syndicate to review his financial records. Another red flag was the fact that Madoff Securities was audited by a one-man accounting firm, namely, Friehling & Horowitz. Also suspicious was the fact that Madoff, despite his firm's leadership role in electronic securities trading, refused to provide his clients with online access to their accounts, providing them instead with monthly account statements by mail.

Among the most credible and impressive evidence Markopolos gave to the SEC were mathematical analyses and simulations allegedly proving that Madoff's split-strike conversion investment strategy could not consistently produce the investment results that his firm reported. Markopolos noted that if such an investment strategy existed, it would be the "Holy Grail" of investing and eventually be replicated by other Wall Street investment advisors. Even if Madoff had discovered this "Holy Grail" of investing, Markopolos demonstrated there was not sufficient transaction volume in the options market to account for the huge number of options that his investment model would have required him to buy and sell for his customers' accounts.

In the months following the public disclosure of Madoff's fraud, Harry Markopolos reached cult hero status within the business press. Markopolos was repeatedly asked to comment on and explain the scope and nature of Madoff's scheme. Markopolos's

---

16. W. K. Rashbaum and D. B. Henriques, "Accountant for Madoff Is Arrested and Charged With Securities Fraud," *New York Times* (online), 18 March 2009.

17. *Ibid.*

dissection of Madoff's fraud suggested that three key factors accounted for it continuing unchecked for decades.

First, Madoff targeted investors who were unlikely to question his investment strategy. According to Markopolos, a large number of "smart" investors had refused to invest with Madoff despite his sterling record. "Smart investors would stick to their investment discipline and walk away, refusing to invest in a black-box strategy they did not understand. Greedy investors would fall over themselves to hand Madoff money."[18]

The second factor that allowed Madoff's fraud to continue for decades was his impeccable credentials. Even if his impressive investment results were ignored, Madoff easily qualified as a Wall Street icon. He was a pioneer of electronic securities trading and throughout his career held numerous leadership positions within the securities industry, including his three stints as NASDAQ chairman. Madoff's stature on Wall Street was also enhanced by his well-publicized philanthropy. He regularly contributed large sums to several charities.

The final and most important factor that allowed Madoff to sustain his fraudulent scheme was the failure of the regulatory oversight function for the stock market. In testimony before Congress and media interviews, Harry Markopolos insisted that the Madoff debacle could have been avoided or at least mitigated significantly if federal regulators, particularly the SEC, had been more diligent in fulfilling their responsibilities. According to Markopolos, Madoff knew that the SEC's accountants, attorneys, and stock market specialists were "incapable of understanding a derivatives-based Ponzi scheme,"[19] such as the one he masterminded. That knowledge apparently emboldened Madoff and encouraged him to continually expand the scope of his fraud.

Even after Markopolos explained the nature of Madoff's fraud to SEC officials, they apparently did not understand it. "I gift-wrapped and delivered the largest Ponzi scheme in history to them . . . [but the SEC] did not understand the 29 red flags that I handed them."[20] The outspoken SEC critic went on to predict that "If the SEC does not improve soon, they risk being merged out of existence in the upcoming rewrite of the nation's regulatory scheme."[21]

Markopolos's pointed criticism of the SEC and additional harsh criticism by several other parties forced the agency's top officials to respond. An embarrassed SEC Chairman Christopher Cox admitted that he was "gravely concerned"[22] by the SEC's failure to uncover the fraud.

> In an extraordinary admission that the SEC was aware of numerous red flags raised about Bernard L. Madoff Investment Securities LLC, but failed to take them seriously enough, SEC Chairman Christopher Cox ordered a review of the agency's oversight of the New York securities-trading and investment management firm.[23]

---

18. D. Carrozza, "Chasing Madoff," *Fraud Magazine*, May/June 2009, 39.

19. *Ibid*, 57.

20. J. Chung and B. Masters, "SEC 'Illiteracy' to Blame for Madoff Affair," *Financial Times* (online), 4 February 2009.

21. Carozza, "Chasing Madoff," 58.

22. A. Lucchetti, K. Scannell, and A. Efrati, "SEC to Probe Its Ties to Madoffs," *Wall Street Journal* (online), 17 December 2008.

23. *Ibid*.

EPILOGUE

On March 12, 2009, Bernie Madoff appeared before Judge Denny Chin in a federal courthouse in New York City. After Judge Chin read the 11 counts of fraud, money laundering, perjury and theft pending against Madoff, he asked the well-dressed defendant how he pled. "Guilty," was Madoff's barely audible one-word reply. Judge Chin then told Madoff to explain what he had done. "Your honor, for many years up until my arrest on December 11, 2008, I operated a Ponzi scheme through the investment advisory side of my business."[24] Madoff then added, "I knew what I did was wrong, indeed criminal. When I began the Ponzi scheme, I believed it would end shortly and I would be able to extricate myself and my clients . . . [but] as the years went by I realized this day, and my arrest, would inevitably come."[25]

Despite allegations that his two sons, his brother, and his wife were at least knowledgeable of his fraud and possibly complicit in it, Madoff refused to implicate any of them or any of his other subordinates. Madoff claimed that he alone had been responsible for the fraud and that the brokerage arm of his business, which had been overseen by his brother and his two sons, had not been affected by his Ponzi scheme. On June 29, 2009, Madoff appeared once more in federal court. After reprimanding Madoff for his actions, Judge Chin sentenced him to 150 years in federal prison, meaning that the 71-year-old felon would spend the rest of his life incarcerated.[26]

David Freihling, Madoff's longtime auditor, pleaded guilty in November 2009 to the nine-count indictment filed against him by federal prosecutors. Freihling's sentencing hearing was delayed while he cooperated with the ongoing investigations of the Madoff fraud. In 2009, the AICPA had announced that it had expelled Freihling for not cooperating with its investigation of his audits of Madoff Securities; one year earlier, Freihling had been stripped of his CPA license by the state of New York. The controversy over the failure of Freihling's firm to undergo any peer reviews persuaded the New York state legislature to pass a law in December 2008 requiring New York accounting firms that provide attest services to be peer reviewed every three years.[27]

Although none of the Big Four accounting firms were directly linked to Madoff Securities, legal experts speculated that those firms would face civil lawsuits in the wake of Madoff's fraud. That potential liability stemmed from the Big Four's audits of the large "feeder firms" that entrusted billions of dollars to Madoff. Lynn Turner, a former chief accountant of the SEC, contended that the auditors of the feeder firms had a responsibility to check out Madoff's auditor. "If they didn't, then investors will have to hold the auditors [of the feeder firms] accountable."[28]

In February 2009, KPMG became the first of the Big Four firms to be named as a defendant in a civil lawsuit triggered by the Madoff fraud. A California charity sued the prominent accounting firm to recover the millions of dollars it lost due to Madoff's scheme. KPMG had served as the independent auditor of a large

---

24. D. B. Henriques and J. Healy, "Madoff Goes to Jail After Guilty Plea," *New York Times* (online), 13 March 2009.

25. *Ibid.*

26. In August 2009, Frank DiPascali, Madoff Securities' former chief financial officer, pleaded guilty to complicity in Madoff's fraudulent scheme. During an appearance in federal court, DiPascali testified that "It was all fake; it was all fictitious. It was wrong and I knew it at the time" (C. Bray and T. Lauricella, "'All Fake': Key Madoff Executive Admits Guilt," *Wall Street Journal* (online), 11 August 2009.)

27. Ironically, the New York law exempts accounting firms that have fewer than three professional accountants, meaning that Friehling & Horowitz would not have been required to undergo a peer review if the law had been in place during the time span covered by Madoff's fraud.

28. I. J. Dugan and D. Crawford, "Accounting Firms That Missed Fraud at Madoff May Be Liable," *Wall Street Journal* (online), 18 February 2009.

hedge fund that had hired Madoff to invest the charity's funds. A legal expert commented on the allegations pending against KPMG:

> The suit alleges that the [hedge] fund's auditor, KPMG, missed numerous red flags that should have alerted the auditor to Madoff's scheme. From financial returns that were too good to be true, to the fact that Madoff's multi-billion dollar operation was utilizing bookkeepers headquartered in an upstate strip mall, KPMG truly missed the elephant in the room.[29]

Over the following years, several other major international accounting firms would be named as defendants in civil lawsuits prompted by the Madoff fraud. Those firms included BDO Seidman, Ernst & Young, and PricewaterhouseCoopers.

In early 2009, President Obama appointed Mary Schapiro to replace Christopher Cox as the chairperson of the SEC. In the aftermath of the Madoff fraud, Schapiro reported that her agency would revamp its oversight policies and procedures for investment advisers having physical custody of customer assets. Among the proposals announced by Schapiro were annual "surprise audits" of such firms to ensure that customer funds were being properly safeguarded. Schapiro also recommended that those firms be required to have internal control audits by independent accounting firms to determine whether they have "the proper controls in place."[30] Finally, Schapiro pledged that the SEC would implement specific measures to ensure that credible whistle-blowing allegations, such as those made by Harry Markopolos regarding Madoff's firm, would be investigated on a thorough and timely basis.

Regulatory and law enforcement authorities predict that it will be years before the total losses suffered by Madoff investors are known. Most estimates put those losses in the tens of billions of dollars. The large asset management firm Fairfield Greenwich Advisers alone had more than one-half of its investment portfolio of $14 billion invested with Madoff. Other companies and organizations that had significant funds in the custody of Madoff Securities include the large Dutch bank Fortis Bank, the large British bank HSBC, the International Olympic Committee, Massachusetts Mutual Life Insurance Company, New York University, Oppenheimer Funds, and Yeshiva University.

One media outlet reported that the list of individuals who had investments with Madoff reads like a lineup from "Lifestyles of the Rich and Famous," a popular television program of the 1980s. Those individuals include award-winning actors and actresses, Hollywood directors and screenwriters, media executives, prominent journalists, professional athletes, a Nobel Prize winner, and high-profile politicians. Among these individuals are Kevin Bacon, Zsa Zsa Gabor, Jeffrey Katzenberg, Henry Kaufman, Larry King, Ed Koch, Sandy Koufax, Senator Frank Lautenberg, John Malkovich, Stephen Spielberg, Elie Wiesel, and Mort Zuckerman.[31]

By early 2011, Irving Picard, the court-appointed trustee charged with recovering the billions of dollars stolen or misused by Madoff, had recouped nearly $10 billion. At the time, nearly 17,000 individuals or entities had filed legal claims to share in the distribution of those funds. Civil lawsuits filed by Picard that are still pending include a nearly $9 billion claim lodged against HSBC and a $6.4 billion claim that names JPMorgan Chase & Co., a global securities and investment banking firm headquartered in New York City, as the principal defendant.

---

29. *USLaw.com*, "The Madoff Saga Continues as Pomerantz Files the First Derivative Suit Against an Auditor," 11 February 2009.

30. S. N. Lynch, "SEC to Consider Surprise Audits of Advisers," *Wall Street Journal* (online), 14 May 2009.

31. To date, several suicides have been attributed to Madoff's massive fraud. One of those victims was Mark Madoff. Bernie Madoff's oldest son took his life on December 11, 2010, two years to the date that his father admitted that he had masterminded a huge investment fraud.

Questions

1. Research recent developments involving this case. Summarize these developments in a bullet format.

2. Suppose that a large investment firm had approximately 10 percent of its total assets invested in funds managed by Madoff Securities. What audit procedures should the investment firm's independent auditors have applied to those assets?

3. Describe the nature and purpose of a "peer review." Would peer reviews of Friehling & Horowitz have likely resulted in the discovery of the Madoff fraud? Why or why not?

4. Professional auditing standards discuss the three key "conditions" that are typically present when a financial fraud occurs and identify a lengthy list of "fraud risk factors." Briefly explain the difference between a fraud "condition" and a "fraud risk factor," and provide examples of each. What fraud conditions and fraud risk factors were apparently present in the Madoff case?

5. In addition to the reforms mentioned in this case, recommend other financial reporting and auditing-related reforms that would likely be effective in preventing or detecting frauds similar to that perpetrated by Madoff.

SECTION 2

AUDITS OF HIGH-RISK ACCOUNTS

2

Jack Greenberg, Inc.

Auditors commonly find themselves facing situations in which they must persuade client executives to do something they absolutely and resolutely do not want to do. When all else fails, auditors may be forced to use a tactic that clinical psychologists, marriage counselors, parents of toddlers, and other interpersonal experts typically frown upon; namely, the old-fashioned "if-you-don't-cooperate, I-will-punish-you" threat. In the mid-1990s, an exasperated team of Grant Thornton auditors resorted to threatening a stubborn client executive to goad him into turning over key documents that had significant audit implications. The executive eventually capitulated and turned over the documents—which resulted in even more problems for the Grant Thornton auditors.

The Brothers Greenberg

For decades, Jack Greenberg oversaw a successful wholesale meat company, a company that he eventually incorporated and named after himself.[1] Jack Greenberg, Inc., marketed a variety of meat, cheese, and other food products along the eastern seaboard of the United States from its Philadelphia headquarters. Jack Greenberg's failing health in the early 1980s prompted him to place his two sons in charge of the company's day-to-day operations. After their father's death, the two brothers, Emanuel and Fred, became equal partners in the business. Emanuel assumed the title of company president, while Fred became the company's vice president. The two brothers and their mother made up the company's three-person board of directors. Several other members of the Greenberg family also worked in the business.

Similar to many family-owned and family-operated businesses, Jack Greenberg, Inc. (JGI), did not place a heavy emphasis on internal control. Like their father, the two Greenberg brothers relied primarily upon their own intuition and the competence and integrity of their key subordinates to manage and control their company's operations. By the mid-1980s, when the privately owned business had annual sales measured in the tens of millions of dollars, Emanuel realized that JGI needed to develop a more formal accounting and control system. That realization convinced him to begin searching for a new company controller who had the expertise necessary to revamp JGI's outdated accounting function and to develop an appropriate network of internal controls for the growing company. In 1987, Emanuel hired Steve Cohn, a CPA and former auditor with Coopers & Lybrand, as JGI's controller. Cohn, who had extensive experience working with a variety of different inventory systems, immediately tackled the challenging assignment of creating a modern accounting and control system for JGI.

Among other changes, Cohn implemented new policies and procedures that provided for segregation of key responsibilities within JGI's transaction cycles. Cohn also integrated computer processing throughout most of JGI's operations, including the payroll, receivables, and payables modules of the company's accounting function.

---

1. The facts of this case and the quotations included in it were taken from the following court opinion: *Larry Waslow, Trustee for Jack Greenberg, Inc., v. Grant Thornton LLP*; United States Bankruptcy Court for the Eastern District of Pennsylvania, 240 B.R. 486; 1999 Bankr. LEXIS 1308.

One of the more important changes that Cohn implemented was the development of an internal reporting system that produced monthly financial statements the Greenbergs could use to make more timely and informed decisions for their business. Cohn's new financial reporting system also allowed JGI to file more timely financial statements with the three banks that provided the bulk of the company's external financing. By the early 1990s, JGI typically had a minimum of $10 million in outstanding loans from those banks.

One area of JGI's operations that Cohn failed to modernize was the company's accounting and control procedures for prepaid inventory. Since the company's early days, imported meat products had accounted for a significant portion of JGI's annual sales. Because foreign suppliers required JGI to prepay for frozen meat items, the company maintained two inventory accounts, Prepaid Inventory and Merchandise Inventory. Prepayments for imported meat products were charged to the Prepaid Inventory account, while all other merchandise acquired by the company for resale was debited to the Merchandise Inventory account. Prepaid inventory typically accounted for 60 percent of JGI's total inventory and 40 percent of the company's total assets.

Long before Cohn became JGI's controller, Jack Greenberg had given his son Fred complete responsibility for the purchasing, accounting, control, and other decisions affecting the company's prepaid inventory. Following their father's death, the two brothers agreed that Fred would continue overseeing JGI's prepaid inventory. When Cohn attempted to restructure and computerize the accounting and control procedures for prepaid inventory, Fred refused to cooperate. Despite frequent and adamant pleas from Cohn over a period of several years, Emanuel refused to order his younger brother to cooperate with Cohn's modernization plan for JGI's accounting system.

Accounting for Prepaid Inventory

Fred Greenberg processed the purchase orders for meat products that JGI bought from foreign vendors. The items purchased were inspected by the appropriate authority in the given country and then loaded into refrigerated lockers to be transported by boat to the United States. When a vendor provided documentation to JGI that a shipment was in transit, Fred Greenberg approved payment of the vendor's invoice. These payments, as noted earlier, were charged or debited to JGI's Prepaid Inventory account. Fred Greenberg maintained a handwritten accounting record known as the prepaid inventory log to keep track of the items included in the Prepaid Inventory account at any point in time.

When a shipment of imported meat products arrived at a U.S. port, a customs broker retained by JGI arranged for the individual items to be inspected and approved for entry into the United States by customs officials. After a shipment had cleared customs, the customs broker sent a notification form to that effect to Fred Greenberg. When the product arrived by truck at JGI's warehouse, a U.S. Department of Agriculture (USDA) official opened and inspected the items included in the order. The USDA official completed a document known as Form 9540-1 to indicate that the items had passed inspection. Each Form 9540-1 also indicated the date that the given products had arrived at JGI's warehouse.

Upon completion of the USDA inspection process, the prepaid inventory items were turned over to the manager of JGI's warehouse. The warehouse manager stamped the items to indicate that they had passed the USDA inspection and then completed a document known as a delivery receipt that listed the date of arrival, the vendor, the type of product, and the quantity of the product. The warehouse manager sent the delivery receipt form to Fred Greenberg, who matched the form with the appropriate vendor invoice. Fred then deleted the given inventory items from the prepaid inventory log and forwarded the matched invoice and delivery receipt to Steve Cohn, who processed an accounting entry that transferred the product from the Prepaid Inventory account to the Merchandise Inventory account. At the end of each year, JGI took a physical inventory of the company's warehouse and adjusted the balance of the Merchandise Inventory account to agree with the results of the physical inventory.

Because of the accounting procedures used for JGI's two inventory accounts, there was some risk that certain inventory items would be "double-counted" at year-end. That is, certain inventory items might be included in both the Prepaid Inventory and Merchandise Inventory accounts if there was any delay in processing the delivery receipt forms. For example, suppose that a shipment of imported meat products arrived at JGI's warehouse on December 29, two days before the close of the company's fiscal year. If Fred Greenberg failed to delete the items in the shipment from the prepaid inventory log and failed to forward the delivery receipt and invoice for the shipment to Steve Cohn on a timely basis, the items in the shipment would be included in both inventory accounts at the end of the year.[2] To reduce the risk of such errors, Cohn reconciled the prepaid inventory log maintained by Fred to the year-end balance of the Prepaid Inventory account. Cohn also asked Fred to allow him to review any delivery receipts that arrived during the last few days of the fiscal year.

Fred's Fraud

Steve Cohn realized that the accounting procedures for prepaid inventory increased the risk that JGI's year-end inventory would be misstated. In early 1992, Cohn, who by this time had been given the title of chief financial officer, designed a computerized accounting system for JGI's prepaid inventory. Cohn then called a meeting with the two Greenberg brothers to illustrate the system and demonstrate the important information and control advantages that it would provide over the "sloppy" manual system that Fred had used for years to account for prepaid inventory. Several years later, Cohn would recount how the Greenberg brothers reacted to his proposal.

> I told Fred how this was a great idea and how I believed that this would be a big step forward in being able to monitor the [prepaid] inventory and determine what was open. . . . And I showed it to Fred, looked at it and said, "Isn't this great? We can do this." And I said, "Don't you want to do this?" And he looked at me and said, "No."

> I was flabbergasted. I looked over to Manny [Emanuel]. He just sat there. And I was furious. I didn't talk to Fred for weeks. I was–I was having a hard time dealing with it. I couldn't imagine why he wouldn't want me to do this. It was such a good thing for the company. And he didn't want to do it.

Later in 1992, the persistent Cohn decided to personally collect the information needed to maintain a computerized accounting system for JGI's prepaid inventory. Cohn would watch for delivery trucks arriving at JGI's warehouse, which was adjacent to the company's administrative offices. When a truck arrived, either he or a subordinate would go to the shipping dock and make copies of the delivery receipt and other documents for each shipment of imported meat products. "We used to run back and forth trying to get these receivings [delivery receipts] that [the warehouse manager] was preparing and it became a game. I became a laughingstock because it was a joke that I was trying to get this information." After several weeks, an exasperated Cohn gave up his futile effort.

---

2. Because such items would be present during the year-end physical inventory of JGI's warehouse, the book-to-physical inventory adjustment would cause them to be included in the December 31 balance of the Merchandise Inventory account.

Fred Greenberg had reason not to cooperate with Cohn's repeated attempts to overhaul the accounting and control procedures for JGI's prepaid inventory. Since the mid-1980s, Fred had been intentionally overstating the company's prepaid inventory. Those overstatements had materially understated JGI's annual cost of goods sold as well as overstated the company's gross profit and net income each year. In subsequent court testimony, Fred reported that his father's failing health had compelled him to begin manipulating JGI's reported operating results. "To avoid aggravating his illness, I started the practice [inflating prepaid inventory] so he would feel better about his business."

Fred also testified that following his father's death "significant changes occurring in the market which adversely affected us" caused him to continue his fraudulent scheme. During the late 1980s and early 1990s, Fred and his brother found it increasingly difficult to compete with larger wholesalers that were encroaching on their company's market. To compete with these larger companies, JGI was forced to reduce the gross margins on the products that it sold. To mitigate the impact of this competitive pressure on JGI's operating results, Fred routinely overstated prepaid inventory to produce gross margins that approximated those historically realized by the company.

Fred manipulated the dates upon which the prepaid inventory was received in order to make it appear that the company's operations generated the same general financial performance from period to period. He did this by determining how much inventory needed to be prepaid inventory so that the percentages of gross profit and net income would remain consistent.

To overstate prepaid inventory, Fred destroyed delivery receipts forwarded to him by JGI's warehouse manager and neglected to update the prepaid inventory log for the given shipments. Weeks or even months later, he would prepare new delivery receipts for those shipments, delete the items in the shipments from the prepaid inventory log, and then forward the receipts along with the corresponding vendor invoices to Cohn. This practice resulted in inventory items being included in the Prepaid Inventory account well after they had arrived at JGI's warehouse.

Auditing Prepaid Inventory

Grant Thornton served as JGI's independent audit firm from 1986 through 1994. Because prepaid inventory was JGI's largest asset and because it posed significant audit risks, the engagement audit team allocated a disproportionate amount of audit resources to that item. Several weeks before the end of each fiscal year, Grant Thornton provided Steve Cohn with an "Engagement Compliance Checklist" that identified the documents and other information needed by the audit engagement team to complete the audit. Many of these requested items involved JGI's prepaid inventory, including "government forms, bills of lading, insurance information, and the delivery receipts prepared by the warehouse personnel evidencing the date upon which the [prepaid] inventory was received at the warehouse." Each year, Grant Thornton also requested a copy of Fred Greenberg's prepaid inventory log and Cohn's reconciliation of the information in that record to JGI's general ledger controlling account for prepaid inventory.

One key item that Grant Thornton did not request from Cohn was the Form 9540-1 prepared for each shipment of imported meat products delivered to JGI's warehouse. Grant Thornton auditors later testified that they became aware in 1988 that a Form 9540-1 was prepared for each prepaid inventory shipment received by JGI. However, the audit team did not learn until 1993 that the USDA official who completed the 9540-1 gave a copy of that document to a JGI warehouse clerk.

Each year, Cohn diligently collected the information requested by Grant Thornton and gave it to the accounting firm well before the date the audit was to begin, with one exception. Because Fred Greenberg failed to give the prepaid inventory log, delivery receipts, and other information he maintained for JGI's prepaid inventory to Cohn on a timely basis, Grant Thornton received that information well after the audit had begun each year.

Grant Thornton audited all of JGI's prepaid inventory transactions each year. "Grant Thornton tested 100 percent of the prepaid inventory transactions which meant that Grant Thornton examined every invoice for prepaid inventory and reviewed the delivery receipts to confirm if and when a delivery had been made." By examining the invoices and delivery receipts, the auditors could determine which prepaid inventory purchases were apparently "still open" at year-end, that is, the prepaid inventory shipments that were properly included in JGI's year-end Prepaid Inventory account.

Because Fred Greenberg had destroyed many of the delivery receipts prepared by the warehouse manager, the Grant Thornton auditors failed to discover that much of JGI's year-end prepaid inventory was "double-counted." A critical issue in subsequent litigation stemming from this case was whether Grant Thornton was justified in relying on the delivery receipts to audit JGI's year-end prepaid inventory. Members of the audit engagement team maintained that because JGI's warehouse manager prepared the delivery receipts independently of the company's accounting function for prepaid inventory, those documents provided sufficient competent evidence to corroborate prepaid inventory. "Grant Thornton believed it was acceptable to rely on the Delivery Receipt to verify the date of delivery because JGI's internal control procedures for inventory were based on a system of 'segregation of duties.'" A Grant Thornton representative provided the following explanation of exactly what was implied by the phrase "segregation of duties."

Question: *You speak of segregation of duties. What do you mean by that?*

Answer: *Somebody is separate–you know, the purchasing function is separate from the receiving function and the approval function is different from the person who executes the transactions.*

Question: *Does that mean that there are separate people that do these different functions?*

Answer: *Yes. Separate people or departments.*

1993 and 1994 JGI Audits

During the 1992 JGI audit, members of the Grant Thornton audit team told Steve Cohn and Emanuel Greenberg they were concerned by the large increase in prepaid inventory over the previous three years.[3] The auditors also expressed concern regarding the haphazard accounting procedures applied to prepaid inventory. These concerns caused the auditors to include the following comments in a report entitled "Internal Control Structure Reportable Conditions and Advisory Comments," which was submitted to Emanuel Greenberg at the conclusion of the 1992 audit. "Prepaid inventory should be set up on a personal computer and updated daily from purchases. This would identify a problem much sooner and reduce the risk of loss should such a problem occur." Cohn later testified that he had encouraged Grant Thornton to include this recommendation in the report filed with Emanuel Greenberg. Despite this

---

3. The dollar value of JGI's prepaid inventory increased by 303 percent from the end of 1989 to the end of 1992.

recommendation, Emanuel would not pressure his brother to cooperate with Cohn's effort to strengthen the accounting procedures for prepaid inventory.

Grant Thornton auditors had access to the notification forms JGI's customs broker sent to Fred Greenberg when a prepaid inventory shipment arrived in a U.S. port. During the 1993 audit, a Grant Thornton auditor noticed that for several prepaid inventory shipments an abnormally long period of time had elapsed between the date the customs broker inspected the merchandise and the date that merchandise arrived at JGI's warehouse. When asked about this issue, Fred Greenberg explained that "floods in the Midwest" had slowed down many shipments en route to the East Coast from ports on the West Coast. A Grant Thornton auditor contacted JGI's customs broker regarding Fred's explanation. The customs broker told the auditor that Fred's explanation was valid.

Near the end of the 1993 audit, a Grant Thornton auditor stumbled across a large stack of Form 9540-1 documents in the receiving office of JGI's warehouse. Following this discovery, the Grant Thornton audit team attempted to match individual delivery receipts with the corresponding Form 9540-1 documents to verify the dates reported on the delivery receipts. Because the latter documents were in no particular alphabetical, chronological, or numerical order, the "task proved insurmountable and was abandoned." In explaining why the auditors did not insist on JGI providing those forms in a usable condition, a Grant Thornton representative noted that the 1993 audit program did not require the delivery receipts to be matched with the Form 9540-1 documents. "However, Grant Thornton decided that since JGI had access to the forms, it wanted them produced for the 1994 audit so that it could use them to verify the date recorded on the delivery receipts."

Following the completion of the 1993 audit, Grant Thornton once again submitted a report entitled "Internal Control Structure Reportable Conditions and Advisory Comments" to Emanuel Goldberg. In this report, Grant Thornton included several specific recommendations regarding improvements needed in the accounting procedures applied to prepaid inventory. One of these recommendations was to maintain an orderly file of the Form 9540-1 documents that could be used for internal control purposes and during the annual independent audit. A second recommendation called for JGI to begin using a specific set of computer-based accounting and internal control procedures and documents for prepaid inventory. These latter items were the same procedures and documents that Steve Cohn had developed and presented to the Greenberg brothers in 1992.

Throughout 1994, Fred Greenberg continued to refuse to adopt Grant Thornton's recommendations for improving the accounting for, and control over, prepaid inventory. In the fall of 1994, Cohn contacted Grant Thornton and told members of the audit engagement team that Fred had not complied with their recommendations. A Grant Thornton representative then met with Fred and told him that, at a minimum, JGI would have to provide the Form 9540-1 documents to Grant Thornton if the accounting firm was to complete the 1994 audit. Still, Fred refused to comply.

Shortly after Grant Thornton began the 1994 audit, a senior member of the audit engagement team advised Fred that unless the Form 9540-1 documents were provided, the accounting firm would likely resign as JGI's independent auditor. Within a few days, Fred turned over the documents to Grant Thornton. "However, before he did so, he altered the dates on them. Apparently, the alterations were so obvious that after reviewing the forms for only 10 seconds, Grant Thornton knew there was a problem. Grant Thornton informed Emanuel and Cohn that the dates were falsified and terminated the audit." When Emanuel confronted his brother regarding the altered documents, the suddenly remorseful Fred "admitted everything."

Following Fred's confession, JGI retained Grant Thornton to determine the impact of the fraudulent scheme on the company's prior financial statements and to develop a set of current financial statements that were reliable. The Greenbergs provided this information to their company's three banks. Within six months, JGI filed for bankruptcy and ceased operations.

EPILOGUE

JGI's sudden collapse sparked a spate of lawsuits. In February 1997, JGI's court-appointed bankruptcy trustee filed a civil action that contained eight specific charges against Grant Thornton. These charges included, among others, breach of contract, negligence, and fraud. A primary defense Grant Thornton used in attempting to rebut those allegations was contributory negligence on the part of JGI and its management.

Grant Thornton argued that JGI had a responsibility to implement internal controls that would have been effective in uncovering Fred Greenberg's fraudulent scheme. In particular, Grant Thornton contended that Emanuel Greenberg should have required his brother to adopt the computer-based accounting and control procedures initially proposed by Steve Cohn in 1992. The accounting firm also maintained that Emanuel Greenberg had been negligent in failing to discover Fred's subterfuge since he had never taken any steps to check or verify his brother's work for the all-important Prepaid Inventory account.

The federal judge who presided over the lawsuit filed against Grant Thornton by JGI's bankruptcy trustee responded to the firm's contributory negligence defense by first suggesting that the accounting firm, rather than JGI's management, had more "leverage" to force Fred Greenberg to adopt Cohn's recommendations. "Cohn could not insist that Fred implement tighter controls over the prepaid inventory, but Grant Thornton, as JGI's auditor, could. Indeed, that is how the fraud was finally discovered in 1994." Additionally, the judge pointed out that Grant Thornton had failed to present any compelling evidence that Emanuel Greenberg had suspected his brother was misrepresenting JGI's prepaid inventory. "Accordingly, Emanuel had no reason to check or verify his brother's work in matching up the delivery receipts with the other prepaid inventory documentation." The judge went even further in absolving Emanuel of responsibility for his brother's misconduct by suggesting that independent auditors are the parties primarily responsible for discovering such schemes.

> Given Fred's equal ownership in the company and his apparent control, not only is there no evidence that Emanuel was "slipshod," there is no evidence that he could have prevented Fred's wrongful acts. Rather, in the unique circumstances where a corporation is owned and operated by family members, the goal of deterring wrongdoing is best served by subjecting the auditors to potential liability, thereby encouraging greater diligence by them in such situations in the future.

After responding to Grant Thornton's arguments, the federal judge criticized several aspects of the firm's JGI audits. Although Grant Thornton identified the large increase in prepaid inventory during the late 1980s and early 1990s as an audit risk factor, the judge suggested that the accounting firm did not thoroughly investigate the underlying cause of that dramatic increase. Likewise, the judge maintained that during the 1993 audit Grant Thornton did not adequately investigate the abnormally long time lag between the date that certain imported meat shipments arrived at a U.S. port and the date they were delivered to JGI's warehouse.[4] The judge also referred to criticism of Grant

---

4. Recall that JGI's customs broker had confirmed Fred Greenberg's assertion that floods in the Midwestern states during 1993 were responsible for this time lag. Apparently, that assertion was not valid.

Thornton that was included in a report prepared by an expert witness retained by JGI's bankruptcy trustee. Among other issues, this report criticized Grant Thornton for not discovering until 1993 that JGI had copies of the Form 9540-1 documents. According to the expert witness, if the auditors had performed a routine "walk-through" audit procedure to document their understanding of JGI's important accounting and control procedures, they would have immediately discovered that "third party documentation [Form 9540-1] existed to verify the arrival dates of the inventory."

The federal judge was most critical of Grant Thornton's decision near the end of the 1993 audit to continue relying on the internally generated delivery receipts when the firm had access to externally generated documentation to vouch the prepaid inventory transactions and year-end balance. In the judge's opinion, that decision could be construed as "reckless."

According to Grant Thornton, although it now knew that third party verification of the delivery dates existed, it considered it unnecessary to have the USDA forms for the 1993 audit because of its reliance on JGI's segregation of duties. Yet, Grant Thornton refused to rely upon JGI's segregation of duties for its 1994 audit. Rather, it demanded that JGI produce the USDA forms for the 1994 audit. . . . If Grant would not issue an unqualified opinion in 1994 relying solely upon JGI's segregation of duties, then why did it do so in 1993?

In October 1999, the federal judge issued a 36-page opinion weighing the merits of the allegations filed by JGI's trustee against Grant Thornton and the validity of the accounting firm's rebuttals of those allegations. After striking down one of the charges filed against Grant Thornton, the judge ruled that the other charges would be addressed in a subsequent trial. Since no further mention of this case can be found in public records, Grant Thornton and JGI's bankruptcy trustee apparently settled the case privately.

Questions

1. Identify important audit risk factors common to family-owned businesses. How should auditors address these risk factors?

2. In your opinion, what primary audit objectives should Grant Thornton have established for JGI's (a) Prepaid Inventory account and (b) Merchandise Inventory account?

3. Assess Grant Thornton's decision to rely heavily on JGI's delivery receipts when auditing the company's prepaid inventory. More generally, compare and contrast the validity of audit evidence yielded by internally prepared versus externally prepared client documents.

4. Describe the general nature and purpose of a "walk-through" audit procedure. Are such tests required by generally accepted auditing standards?

5. Identify audit procedures, other than a walk-through test, that might have resulted in Grant Thornton discovering that Fred Greenberg was tampering with JGI's delivery receipts.

6. Once an audit firm has informed client management of important internal control weaknesses, what further responsibility, if any, does the audit firm have regarding those items? For example, does the audit firm have a responsibility to insist that client management correct the deficiencies or address them in some other way?

Golden Bear Golf, Inc.

Jack Nicklaus electrified sports fans worldwide in 1986 when he won the prestigious Masters golf tournament at the ripe old age of 46. Over the previous several years, the "Golden Bear" had been struggling to remain competitive with the scores of talented young players who had earned the right to play in the dozens of golf tournaments sponsored each year by the Professional Golfers' Association (PGA).

Regaining his golden touch on the golf course was not the only challenge that Nicklaus faced during the mid-1980s. In 1985, Richard Bellinger, an accountant employed by Golden Bear International, Inc. (GBI), the private company that oversaw the famous golfer's many business interests, mustered the courage to approach his employer. Bellinger told Nicklaus that his company was on the verge of bankruptcy. Nicklaus, who had allowed subordinates to manage his company's operations, was startled by the revelation. In a subsequent interview with *The Wall Street Journal,* Nicklaus admitted that after a brief investigation he realized that he had allowed his company to become a tangled knot of dozens of unrelated businesses. "We were an accounting nightmare . . . I didn't know what any of them did and neither did anyone else."[1]

Nicklaus immediately committed himself to revitalizing his company. The first step that he took to turn around his company was naming himself as its chief executive officer (CEO). Nicklaus then placed Bellinger in charge of GBI's day-to-day operations. Within a few years, the two men had returned GBI to a profitable condition by focusing its resources on lines of business that Nicklaus knew best, such as golf course design, golf schools, and the licensing of golf equipment.

In the late 1990s, Jack Nicklaus, however, once again found himself coping with an "accounting nightmare." This time, Nicklaus could not blame himself for the predicament he faced. Instead, the responsibility for the new crisis rested squarely on the shoulders of two of Nicklaus's key subordinates who had orchestrated a fraudulent accounting scheme that jeopardized their employer's corporate empire.

Player of the Century

Jack Nicklaus began playing golf as a young boy and had mastered the game by his mid-teens. After graduating from high school, the golf prodigy accepted a scholarship to play collegiately for Ohio State University in his hometown of Columbus. At the age of 21, Nicklaus joined the professional golf tour and was an instant success, racking up more than one dozen victories within a few years.

Shortly after joining the professional golf tour, the business-minded Nicklaus realized that winning golf tournaments was not the most lucrative way to profit from his enormous skills. At the time, the undisputed "king" of golf was Arnold Palmer, who endeared himself to the golfing public with his easy smile and affable manner on the golf course. Adoring legions of fans known as "Arnie's Army" tracked Palmer's every move during a tournament. Palmer's popularity with the public translated into

---

1. R. Lowenstein, "A Golfer Becomes an Executive: Jack Nicklaus's Business Education," *The Wall Street Journal,* 27 January 1987, 34.

a series of high-profile and profitable endorsement deals. On the other hand, golf fans generally resented Nicklaus's no-nonsense approach on the golf course. Those same fans resented Nicklaus even more when it became evident that the burly Ohioan with the trademark crew cut would likely replace Palmer as the world's best golfer, which he did. Nicklaus would ultimately win a record 18 major golf championships and edge out Palmer for the "Player of the Century" award in the golfing world.

With the help of a professional sports agent, Nicklaus worked hard to develop a softer, more appealing public image. By the mid-1970s, Nicklaus's makeover was complete and his popularity rivaled that of Palmer. As his popularity with the public grew, Nicklaus was able to cash in on endorsement deals and other business opportunities. Eventually, Nicklaus founded GBI to serve as the corporate umbrella for his business interests.

In 1996, Nicklaus decided to expand his business operations by spinning off a subsidiary from GBI via an initial public offering (IPO). Nicklaus named the new public company Golden Bear Golf, Inc. (Golden Bear). One of Golden Bear's principal lines of business would be the construction of golf courses. GBI would remain a privately owned company that would continue to manage Nicklaus's other business ventures. Because Nicklaus planned to retain more than 50 percent of Golden Bear's common stock, he and his subordinates would be able to completely control the new company's operations.

Nicklaus chose his trusted associate Richard Bellinger to serve as Golden Bear's CEO. Bellinger then appointed John Boyd and Christopher Curbello as the two top executives of Paragon International, Golden Bear's wholly owned subsidiary that would be responsible for the company's golf course construction business. Boyd became Paragon's president and principal operating officer, while Curbello assumed the title of Paragon's vice president of operations. On August 1, 1996, Golden Bear went public. The company's stock traded on the NASDAQ exchange under the ticker symbol JACK.

Triple Bogey for Golden Bear

Shortly after Golden Bear's successful IPO, Paragon International's management team was inundated with requests to build Jack Nicklaus–designed golf courses. In a few months, the company had entered into contracts to build more than one dozen golf courses. Wall Street analysts, portfolio managers, and individual investors expected these contracts to translate into sizable profits for Golden Bear. Unfortunately, those profits never materialized.

Less than one year after Golden Bear's IPO, Boyd and Curbello realized that they had been much too optimistic in forecasting the gross profit margins Paragon would earn on its construction projects. Instead of earning substantial profits on those projects, Paragon would incur large losses on many of them. To avoid the embarrassment of publicly revealing that they had committed Paragon to a string of unprofitable construction projects, the two executives instructed Paragon's accounting staff to embellish the subsidiary's reported operating results.

A key factor that may have contributed to Boyd and Curbello's decision to conceal Paragon's financial problems was the incentive compensation package each had received when they signed on with the company. The two executives could earn sizable bonuses if Paragon met certain operating benchmarks. In addition, Boyd had been granted a large number of Golden Bear stock options.

Because Paragon's construction projects required considerably more than one year to complete, the company used percentage-of-completion accounting to recognize the revenues associated with those projects. Initially, Paragon applied the widely used "cost-to-cost" percentage-of-completion method, which requires a company to determine the percentage of a project's total estimated construction costs incurred in a given accounting period. Then, the same percentage of the total revenue (and gross profit) to be earned on the project is booked that period.

During the second quarter of fiscal 1997, Boyd and Curbello determined that Paragon would have a large operating loss if the cost-to-cost method was used to recognize revenue on the golf course construction projects. At that point, the two executives instructed Paragon's controller to switch to what they referred to as the "earned value" percentage-of-completion accounting method. "In developing its percentage-of-completion estimates under the earned value method, Paragon relied not on objective criteria, such as costs incurred, but instead relied on management's subjective estimates as to its [a project's] progress."[2]

Throughout the remainder of fiscal 1997 and into fiscal 1998, Paragon's management routinely overstated the percentage-of-completion estimates for the company's golf course construction projects each quarter. To further enhance Paragon's operating results, the company's accounting staff inflated the contractual revenue amounts for most of the company's construction projects. These increased revenue amounts were allegedly attributable to "change orders" that amended the original construction contracts between Paragon and the company's clients. A final window-dressing scheme used by Paragon involved recording revenue for *potential* construction projects.

> *In some cases, Paragon recognized revenue in connection with potential projects that Paragon had identified while looking for new work, even though Paragon had no agreements in connection with these projects. In other cases, Paragon recognized revenue in connection with projects where the project's owners were either entertaining bids from Paragon and other contractors or were negotiating with Paragon regarding a project yet to be awarded.*[3]

During the spring of 1998, John Boyd and several of his top subordinates, including Christopher Curbello, attempted to purchase Paragon International from Golden Bear. When that effort failed, Boyd and Curbello resigned their positions with Paragon. After their departure, Paragon's new management team quickly discovered that the subsidiary's operating results had been grossly misrepresented.

A subsequent investigation carried out jointly by Arthur Andersen & Co. (Paragon's audit firm), PricewaterhouseCoopers, and Golden Bear's external legal firm resulted in Golden Bear issuing restated financial statements in October 1998 for fiscal 1997 and for the first quarter of fiscal 1998. For fiscal 1997, Golden Bear had initially reported a $2.9 million net loss and golf course construction revenues of $39.7 million; the restated amounts included a $24.7 million net loss for fiscal 1997 and golf course construction revenues of only $21.8 million. For the first quarter of fiscal 1998, Golden Bear had reported an $800,000 net loss and golf course construction revenues of $16.0 million. Those amounts were restated to a net loss of $7.2 million and golf course construction revenues of $8.3 million.

"Audit Failures"

The Securities and Exchange Commission (SEC) launched its own investigation of Golden Bear shortly after the company issued the restated financial statements. A primary target of the SEC investigation was Michael Sullivan, the Arthur Andersen

---

2. Securities and Exchange Commission, *Accounting and Auditing Enforcement Release No. 1604*, 1 August 2002.

3. Securities and Exchange Commission, *Accounting and Auditing Enforcement Release No. 1603*, 1 August 2002.

audit partner who served as the Golden Bear engagement partner. Sullivan had been employed by Andersen since 1970 and had been a partner in the firm since 1984.

The SEC enforcement release that disclosed the results of its investigation of Andersen's Golden Bear audits included a section entitled "Sullivan's Audit Failures." According to the SEC, Sullivan was well aware that the decision to use the earned value method "accelerated revenue recognition by material amounts" for Paragon.[4] In fact, Sullivan was very concerned by Paragon's decision to switch from the cost-to-cost method to the "new and untested" earned value method. This concern prompted him to warn Paragon's management that he expected the earned value method to produce operating results approximately in line with those that would have resulted from the continued application of the cost-to-cost method. To monitor the impact of the earned value method on Paragon's operating results, Sullivan required the client's accounting staff to "provide detailed schedules showing Paragon's project-by-project results under both methods for each reporting period from the second quarter of 1997 through the first quarter of 1998."

By the end of fiscal 1997, the comparative schedules prepared by Paragon's accountants clearly revealed that the earned value method was allowing Paragon to book much larger amounts of revenue and gross profit on its construction projects than it would have under the cost-to-cost method. When Sullivan questioned Paragon's executives regarding this issue, those executives maintained that "uninvoiced" construction costs had caused the cost-to-cost method to significantly understate the stages of completion of the construction projects. To quell Sullivan's concern, in early fiscal 1998, Paragon's management recorded $4 million of uninvoiced construction costs in a year-end adjusting entry for fiscal 1997. These costs caused the revenue that would have been recorded under the cost-to-cost method to approximate the revenue that Paragon actually recorded by applying the earned value method. Unknown to Sullivan, the $4 million of uninvoiced construction costs booked by Paragon were fictitious.[5]

The SEC criticized Sullivan and his subordinates for failing to adequately investigate the $4 million of uninvoiced construction costs that materialized at the end of fiscal 1997. According to the SEC, Sullivan relied almost exclusively on management's oral representations to corroborate those costs.

Sullivan knew that Paragon booked costs for which no invoices had been received and which were not reflected in the company's accounts payable system, and that recording these uninvoiced costs would have substantially reduced the gap between the results produced by the two estimation methods . . . While procedures with respect to invoiced and paid costs were performed, Sullivan did not employ any procedures to determine whether the uninvoiced costs had actually been incurred as of year-end.

Paragon's scheme to overstate its reported revenues and profits by applying the earned value method resulted in a dramatic increase in unbilled revenues by the end of 1997. Approximately 30 percent of the revenues reported in Golden Bear's 1997 income statement had not been billed to its customers. When Paragon's executives switched to the earned value method, they had assured Sullivan that they would

---

4. The remaining quotations in this case were taken from Securities and Exchange Commission, *Accounting and Auditing Enforcement Release No. 1676*, 26 November 2002.

5. Recognize that the $4 million of uninvoiced construction costs that were accrued in the adjusting entry did not reduce Golden Bear's gross profit that it had recognized for fiscal 1997 under the earned value method. The $4 million of construction costs simply replaced an equal amount of expenses that had been recorded to produce the "proper" amount of gross profit under the earned value method.

bill their customers on that basis. Despite that commitment, Paragon continued to bill their customers effectively on a cost-to-cost basis. (Paragon could not bill customers for the full amount of revenue that it was recording on the construction projects since those customers were generally aware of the *actual* stages of completion of those projects.)

The SEC maintained that Sullivan and his subordinates should have rigorously tested Paragon's large amount of unbilled revenues at the end of 1997. "A significant unbilled revenue balance requires adequate testing to determine the reason that the company is not billing for the work it reports as complete and whether unbilled amounts are properly recognized as revenue." Instead, the SEC charged that Sullivan relied "excessively" on oral representations from Paragon management to confirm the unbilled revenues and corresponding receivables.

In at least one case, the SEC reported that members of the Golden Bear audit team asked the owner of a Paragon project under construction to comment on the reasonableness of the $2 million unbilled receivable that Paragon had recorded for that project at the end of 1997. The owner contested that amount, alleging that Paragon had overestimated the project's stage of completion. "Despite this significant evidence that a third party with knowledge of the project's status disputed Paragon's estimated percentage-of-completion under the contract, the audit team did not properly investigate this project or otherwise expand Andersen's scope of testing of Paragon's unbilled revenue balances." According to the SEC, Sullivan did not believe the unbilled revenue posed major audit issues but instead thought it was a "business issue" that Paragon had to resolve with its clients.

A second tactic Paragon used to inflate its reported profits was to overstate the total revenues to be earned on individual construction projects. During the 1997 audit, Andersen personnel selected 13 of Paragon's construction projects to corroborate the total revenue figures the company was using in applying the earned value percentage-of-completion accounting method to its unfinished projects. For 11 of the 13 projects selected, the Andersen auditors discovered that the total revenue being used in the percentage-of-completion computations by Paragon exceeded the revenue figure documented in the construction contract. Paragon's management attributed these differences to unsigned change orders that had been processed for the given projects "but could not produce any documents supporting these oral representations." Sullivan accepted the client's representations that the given revenue amounts were valid. "In each instance, Sullivan failed to properly follow up on a single undocumented amount; instead, Sullivan relied solely on Paragon management's oral representations that the estimated revenue amounts accurately reflected the economic status of the jobs."

Another scam used by Paragon to inflate its revenues and profits was to record revenue for nonexistent projects. In the enforcement release that focused on Sullivan's role in the Paragon scandal, SEC officials pointed out that the publication *AICPA Audit and Accounting Guide–Construction Contracts* is clearly relevant to the audits of construction companies such as Paragon. This publication recommends that auditors visit construction sites and discuss the given projects with project managers, architects, and other appropriate personnel. The purpose of these procedures is to assess "the representations of management (for example, representations about the stage of completion and estimated costs to complete)." Despite this guidance, the Andersen auditors did not visit any project sites during the 1997 audit.[6] Such visits may

---

6. As a point of information, most of Paragon's golf construction projects were outside of the United States. During 1996, auditors employed by foreign affiliates of Andersen visited some of these sites.

have resulted in Andersen discovering that some of Paragon's projects were purely imaginary. In addition, Andersen would likely have determined that Paragon was overstating the stages of completion of most of its existing projects.

The SEC reprimanded Andersen for not visiting any of Paragon's job sites or discussing those projects with knowledgeable parties. "Failing to discuss project status, including percentage-of-completion estimates, with project managers and other on-site operating personnel was, under the circumstances, a reckless departure from GAAS."

The SEC also criticized Sullivan for not insisting that Golden Bear disclose in its 1997 financial statements the change from the cost-to-cost to the earned value method of applying percentage-of-completion accounting. Likewise, the SEC contended that Sullivan should have required Golden Bear to disclose material related-party transactions involving Paragon and Jack Nicklaus, Golden Bear's majority stockholder.

Finally, the SEC noted that Sullivan failed to heed his own concerns while planning the 1997 Golden Bear audit. During the initial planning phase of that audit, Sullivan had identified several factors that prompted him to designate the 1997 Golden Bear audit a "high-risk" engagement. These factors included the subjective nature of the earned value method, Paragon's large unbilled revenues, the aggressive revenue recognition practices advocated by Golden Bear management, and severe weaknesses in Paragon's cost accounting system. Because of these factors, the SEC maintained that Sullivan and his subordinates should have been particularly cautious during the 1997 Golden Bear audit and employed a rigorous and thorough set of substantive audit procedures.

EPILOGUE

In August 1998, angry Golden Bear stockholders filed a class-action lawsuit against the company, its major officers, and its principal owner, Jack Nicklaus. That same month, the NASDAQ delisted the company's common stock, which was trading for less than $1 per share, dramatically below its all-time high of $20. Richard Bellinger resigned as Golden Bear's CEO two months later to "pursue other interests." In December 1999, Golden Bear announced that it had reached an agreement to settle the class-action lawsuit. That settlement required the company to pay its stockholders $3.5 million in total and to purchase their shares at a price of $0.75. In 2000, Golden Bear, by then a private company, was folded into Nicklaus Companies, a new corporate entity that Jack Nicklaus created to manage his business interests.

In November 2002, Michael Sullivan was suspended from practicing before the SEC for one year. Sullivan's employer, Andersen, had effectively been put out of business a few months earlier when a federal jury found it guilty of obstruction of justice for destroying audit documents pertaining to its bankrupt client Enron Corporation.[7] In August 2002, Paragon's former controller received a two-year suspension from practicing before the SEC. At the same time, the SEC sanctioned three former Golden Bear executives by ordering them to "cease and desist" from any future violations of the federal securities laws. One of those executives was Richard Bellinger. The SEC maintained that Bellinger approved Paragon's change from the cost-to-cost to the earned value method. Additionally, the SEC charged that Bellinger knew the change would materially increase Golden Bear's reported revenues and gross profit but failed to require that the change be disclosed in the company's financial statements.

---

7. As discussed in Case 1.1, Andersen's conviction was subsequently overturned by the U.S. Supreme Court.

Finally, in March 2003, a federal grand jury indicted John Boyd and Christopher Curbello on charges of securities fraud and conspiracy to commit securities fraud. Curbello was arrested in San Antonio, Texas, on March 14, 2003, while Boyd was apprehended in Bogota, Columbia, a few days later by Secret Service and FBI agents who immediately flew him to the United States. In June 2003, Curbello pleaded guilty to conspiracy to commit securities fraud and was sentenced to three-and-a-half years in prison. A few months later, Boyd pleaded guilty to similar charges and was given a five-year prison sentence.

Questions

1. Professional auditing standards identify the "management assertions" that commonly underlie a set of financial statements. Which of these assertions were relevant to Paragon's construction projects? For each of the assertions that you listed, describe an audit procedure that Arthur Andersen could have employed to corroborate that assertion.

2. The SEC referred to several "audit failures" that were allegedly the responsibility of Michael Sullivan. Define what you believe the SEC meant by the phrase "audit failure." Do you believe that Sullivan, alone, was responsible for the deficiencies that the SEC noted in Andersen's 1997 audit of Golden Bear? Defend your answer.

3. Sullivan identified the 1997 Golden Bear audit as a "high-risk" engagement. How do an audit engagement team's responsibilities differ, if at all, on a high-risk engagement compared with a "normal" engagement? Explain.

4. The AICPA has issued several *Audit and Accounting Guides* for specialized industries. Do auditors have a responsibility to refer to these guides when auditing clients in those industries? Do these guides override or replace the guidance included in *Statements on Auditing Standards*?

5. Was the change that Paragon made in applying the percentage-of-completion accounting method a "change in accounting principle" or a "change in accounting estimate"? Briefly describe the accounting and financial reporting treatment that must be applied to each type of change.

Happiness Express, Inc.

Executives in the multibillion-dollar toy industry constantly search for the next big "hit," a magical toy that will trigger a nationwide frenzy among youngsters comparable to the mania sparked in recent decades by the Cabbage Patch Kids and Tickle Me Elmo. In more "ancient" times, the Silly Putty, the Slinky, and the Hoola Hoop prompted shouting matches and elbow-to-elbow combat among small armies of short-tempered parents intent on acquiring the latest must-have and hard-to-find toy as a birthday gift or Christmas present for little Suzie or tiny Tommy.

During the mid-1990s, the popular television program that featured the Mighty Morphin Power Rangers produced a windfall of revenues and profits for Happiness Express, Inc., a small New York–based company. Happiness Express had purchased licensing rights that allowed the company to market a wide range of Mighty Morphin Power Rangers toys and other merchandise. Unfortunately, similar to most toy fads, the Power Rangers craze soon subsided. To find a replacement source of revenue for his company, Joseph Sutton, Happiness Express's chief executive officer (CEO), turned to a member of the British royal family, Sarah Ferguson, the Duchess of York.

Following her divorce from Prince Andrew, the second son of Queen Elizabeth II, the Duchess decided to try her hand at writing children's books. Among the characters she created was Budgie the Little Helicopter. Joseph Sutton acquired U.S. licensing rights for toys and other merchandise featuring Budgie. Sutton believed that Budgie would be a huge hit in the United States and generate large sales of toys and related merchandise linked to him and his small squadron of friends. In announcing his company's relationship with Sarah Ferguson, the ever-optimistic and buoyant Sutton proclaimed that "Happiness is proud to represent Budgie the Little Helicopter and to help him make his flight to America."[1]

"In Kids We Trust"

Joseph Sutton and his older brother, Isaac, worked for years as sales representatives for various toy manufacturers. In 1989, the two brothers organized their own toy company, which they named Happiness Express, Inc. Joseph assumed the title of CEO, while his brother became the company's chief operating officer (COO). Despite an initial investment of only $10,000, the Sutton brothers' company quickly gained a toehold in the fiercely competitive toy industry. Happiness Express catapulted from a few hundred thousand dollars of sales in its first year of operation to total revenues of more than $40 million for its fiscal year ended March 31, 1994.

The Suttons' business model involved identifying trendy characters introduced to children in the United States by television programs, major movies, books, and other publications. The brothers then purchased merchandise-licensing rights for those characters from Disney, Nickelodeon, Universal Studios, Warner Brothers, and major publishing companies. Licensed merchandise manufactured by Happiness Express included plastic figurines, stuffed dolls, shoelaces, battery-operated toothbrushes,

---

1. *Business Wire* (online), "Happiness Express Gets Product License for Her Royal Highness the Duchess of York's 'Budgie the Little Helicopter,'" 14 February 1994.

night-lights, bedside lamps, and a wide range of "back-to-school" items such as pencils, notebooks, and binders. Happiness Express marketed its merchandise to FAO Schwartz, J.C. Penney, Kmart, Target, Toys "R" Us, Wal-Mart, and other major retailers. Central to the early success of Happiness Express was the Suttons' heavy reliance on market research that tracked children's interest in new media characters and toys. In fact, Joseph Sutton coined the motto "In Kids We Trust" to express his company's commitment to the results of that research.

The Little Mermaid and Barney, the Purple Dinosaur, were two of the earliest characters for which the Suttons obtained licensing rights. The impressive sales spawned by those two lines of merchandise allowed Happiness Express to establish itself in the toy industry. To acquire the capital needed to expand the company's operations, the Suttons took Happiness Express public in July 1994 with an initial public offering (IPO) that was well received by Wall Street and individual investors. Within a few months, the company's stock price nearly doubled from its initial selling price of $10. In the spring of 1995, *Business Week* named Happiness Express the "#1 Hot Growth Company" in the United States and featured the company on its front cover. According to *Business Week*, over the previous three years Happiness Express had realized annual growth rates in sales, profits, and return on capital of 112 percent, 439 percent, and 68 percent, respectively.

For fiscal 1994, merchandise linked to Barney accounted for approximately 55 percent of Happiness Express's total revenues. In fiscal 1995, Barney-related revenues evaporated, accounting for less than five percent of the company's sales that year. Fortunately, the Mighty Morphin Power Rangers stepped into the vacuum created by the sudden decline in children's affection for Barney–or, at least, Barney-related merchandise. For fiscal 1995, Power Rangers merchandise produced 75 percent of Happiness's revenues.

Despite the gaudy financial results posted by Happiness Express during the mid-1990s, many Wall Street analysts questioned whether the company could sustain that level of financial performance. Those analysts doubted that the Sutton brothers could continue their phenomenal winning streak of identifying the next "hot" children's character. One financial analyst and self-appointed critic of Happiness Express asked Joseph Sutton, "What will replace Power Rangers when they fade?"[2] The self-assured Sutton replied: "We've proved to the industry that we know how to go where the action is."[3] In Sutton's mind, the coming "action" in the toy industry would revolve around Budgie the Little Helicopter and Dudley the Dragon, a Barney-type character that had his own children's television program. Sutton's enthusiasm for those two characters did not placate his critic, who pointed out that toy companies that become heavily dependent on one or a few lines of merchandise often experience severe financial problems due to sudden and unexpected shifts in children's taste for toys.

Budgie Crashes, Dudley Is a Dud

In the spring of 1995, shortly before the close of Happiness Express's 1995 fiscal year, a Wall Street investment firm projected a "precipitous" drop in the company's earnings during fiscal 1996.[4] The firm predicted that declining interest in the Mighty Morphin Power Rangers television program would quickly translate into falling sales of

---

2. L. Bongiorno, "Happiness Is a Hot Toy," *Business Week,* 22 May 1995, 70.

3. *Ibid.*

4. *Business Wire* (online), "Happiness Express 'Comfortable' with Fiscal 1995, '96 Projections," 7 March 1995.

licensed merchandise featuring those characters. Joseph Sutton responded to that grim prediction by referring to another earnings forecast for Happiness Express released at approximately the same time by Donaldson, Lufkin & Jenrette (DLJ), a major investment banking firm. This latter forecast projected a sizable increase in revenues and profits for Happiness Express during fiscal 1996.

To support this second forecast, Sutton revealed that his firm's backlog of toy orders in the spring of 1995 was nearly three times larger than the company's backlog 12 months earlier. While admitting that sales of Power Rangers merchandise would likely decline in fiscal 1996, Sutton insisted that the company's new products would more than make up for those lost sales. Bolstering Sutton's point of view regarding his company's future were the record operating results that Happiness Express reported in the late spring of 1995 for the fiscal year ended March 31, 1995. The company's net income for fiscal 1995 of $7.5 million was nearly double the figure reported the previous year, while its 1995 revenues rose to $60 million, a 50 percent increase over the previous 12 months. Approximately one-half of the latter increase was attributable to Happiness Express's fourth-quarter sales. During the fourth quarter of fiscal 1994, the company reported sales of $2.3 million; that figure was dwarfed by the $12.8 million of sales the company reported for the fourth quarter of fiscal 1995.

Despite Joseph Sutton's rosy outlook for his company, fiscal 1996 proved to be a difficult year for Happiness Express. By the fall of 1995, sales of Power Rangers merchandise had fallen off drastically. Making matters worse for Happiness Express, Budgie the Little Helicopter failed to capture the imagination of children in the United States despite intense promotional efforts by the company and the Duchess of York. Likewise, children's response to Dudley the Dragon was underwhelming. In early September 1995, the price of Happiness Express common stock plunged when Joseph Sutton publicly admitted that DLJ's earnings forecast for fiscal 1996 had been too optimistic. The day following that announcement, the company was rocked by the filing of a large class-action lawsuit that named Happiness Express and its key officers as defendants. The lawsuit charged that Happiness Express's previous financial statements had been distorted by fraudulent misrepresentations and that certain company executives had engaged in "insider trading." As those executives were touting the company's promising prospects earlier in the year, they were allegedly selling large blocks of the company's stock that they owned.

As the end of fiscal 1996 approached, Happiness Express's sales continued to sag, which caused management to issue an earnings release indicating that the company would report a loss of $14 to $17 million for the year. That news sent the company's stock price plummeting to less than $2 per share. A few days later, a company spokesperson revealed that federal authorities, including representatives of the Securities and Exchange Commission (SEC), had seized certain accounting records and documents of Happiness Express and were launching an investigation of financial irregularities within the company. More bad news arrived on May 31, 1996, when Happiness Express's audit firm, Coopers & Lybrand, withdrew the audit opinion it had issued a few weeks earlier on the company's 1996 financial statements. Exhibit 1 presents the letter Coopers & Lybrand sent to Joseph Sutton to notify him of that decision.

Throughout the summer of 1996, the financial condition of Happiness Express worsened. On September 25, the company's board of directors filed for bankruptcy and fired Isaac Sutton; two days later, Joseph Sutton resigned as CEO. In May 1999, the SEC filed a criminal complaint against Joseph Sutton, Isaac Sutton, and Happiness Express's former chief financial officer (CFO), Michael Goldberg. The complaint also named Goldberg's close friend and Goldberg's former landlord as defendants.

EXHIBIT 1

COOPERS &
LYBRAND LETTER
RESCINDING 1996
AUDIT OPINION

May 31, 1996

Mr. Joseph Sutton
Chief Executive Officer
Happiness Express, Inc.
One Harbor Park Drive
Port Washington, NY 11050

Dear Mr. Sutton:

In connection with the investigation into the financial irregularities recently discovered with respect to the financial statements and accounting records of Happiness Express, Inc., certain information has come to our attention regarding the Company's financial statements as of and for the year ended March 31, 1996, that indicates a revision of those statements is necessary.

Please notify persons who are known to be relying or who are likely to rely on the financial statements and the related auditors' report that they should not be relied upon, and that revised financial statements and auditors' report will be issued upon completion of the investigation.

Also, you should discuss with the Securities and Exchange Commission, appropriate stock exchanges, and other regulatory authorities the disclosures to be made or other measures to be taken in the circumstances.

Very truly yours,

Coopers & Lybrand L.L.P.

The SEC charged the Suttons and Goldberg with inflating Happiness Express's sales and net income for fiscal 1995 and 1996. For fiscal 1995, the SEC revealed that the company had actually incurred a net loss of $1 million rather than the $7.5 million net income it had reported. Happiness Express's executives had apparently booked phony sales and receivables to conceal the company's deteriorating financial condition and operating results from Wall Street analysts, investors, and other parties. The primary source of the company's financial problems that had prompted the fraudulent scheme was the sudden drop in sales of Mighty Morphin Power Rangers merchandise.

The SEC alleged that Michael Goldberg had sold Happiness Express common stock during 1995 before the fraudulent scheme was revealed, allowing him to earn "illicit" trading profits of approximately $310,000. Additionally, the SEC's investigation indicated that Goldberg had provided "material nonpublic information concerning Happiness Express's poor financial condition" to two other individuals, his close friend and his landlord. Reportedly, the close friend had used this information to earn large trading profits by "shorting" the common stock of Happiness Express. The nonpublic information that the landlord received from Goldberg caused him to sell Happiness Express's common stock that he owned before the company's true financial condition and operating results were publicly reported.

Class-Action Lawsuit Targets Coopers & Lybrand

Coopers & Lybrand was the principal target of the multimillion-dollar, class-action lawsuit filed by Happiness Express's stockholders in the fall of 1995. Plaintiff attorneys in that lawsuit alleged that Coopers & Lybrand had recklessly audited Happiness Express's financial statements for fiscal 1995, which prevented the firm from uncovering millions of dollars of bogus sales and corresponding receivables in the company's accounting records. Approximately $6 million of the bogus revenues involved fictitious sales to Wow Wee International, Ltd. and West Coast Liquidators that had been booked by Happiness Express's accounting staff near the end of fiscal 1995.

The allegations included in the class-action lawsuit focused almost exclusively on the audit procedures Coopers & Lybrand had applied to Happiness Express's 1995 sales and to the company's 1995 year-end receivables. Plaintiff attorneys charged that the Coopers & Lybrand audit team had failed to obtain a thorough understanding of Happiness Express's operations and internal controls and, as a result, failed to properly plan the 1995 audit. For example, the plaintiff attorneys identified several red flags linked to Happiness Express's year-end receivables that the Coopers & Lybrand auditors had apparently overlooked or ignored. These red flags included a significant change in the nature of Happiness Express's accounts receivable between the end of 1994 and the end of 1995.

Historically, Happiness Express had "factored" most of its accounts receivables. A finance company typically approved or authorized Happiness Express's credit sales before shipments were made to given customers and then provided cash advances for the resulting receivables. This practice significantly reduced the credit risk that Happiness Express faced on its outstanding receivables. At the end of fiscal 1994, approximately 88 percent of Happiness Express's receivables were factored. Because of the bogus sales (and corresponding receivables) entered in the company's accounting records near the end of fiscal 1995, only 19 percent of its 1995 year-end receivables were factored. The Coopers & Lybrand auditors apparently never learned of this change in the nature of Happiness Express's accounts receivable, and, consequently, failed to make the appropriate modifications in their planned audit procedures for that important financial statement line item.

> The allegation here is that Coopers was reckless when it relied on a previous year's information without bothering to independently assess the current year's data, which were vastly different. . . . Coopers' [fiscal 1995] workpapers are replete with inaccurate references to conditions which did not exist at March 31, 1995. For example, in assessing Happiness's controls over its revenues, Coopers noted in its workpapers that: "Accounts receivable are predominantly factored (credit risk is not an issue) and the Company obtains credit authorizations from the factor company prior to shipping."[5]

Another red flag Coopers & Lybrand allegedly ignored in planning the 1995 audit was the suspicious nature of the large receivables from Wow Wee and West Coast Liquidators that resulted from credit sales recorded by Happiness Express in late fiscal 1995. In fact, Happiness Express booked $2.4 million of fictitious sales to Wow Wee, alone, on the final day of fiscal 1995. The majority of the bogus sales to West Coast Liquidators were recorded in the final month of fiscal 1995. In their civil complaint, the attorneys for Happiness Express's stockholders pointed out that Coopers & Lybrand's policy and procedures manual alerted the firm's personnel to the risk posed by such transactions. "Unusually large increases in year-end sales to a single or a few customers is an indicator of the risk of potential material misstatements in financial statements."

Plaintiff legal counsel also pointed out that Coopers & Lybrand should have doubted the integrity of *any* credit sales made to Wow Wee since that company

---

5. This and all subsequent quotations, unless indicated otherwise, were taken from the following source: *Jacobs and Sbordone, et al. v. Coopers & Lybrand, et al.*, 1999 U.S. Dist. LEXIS 2102; Fed. Sec. L. Rep. (CCH) P90, 443.

was a toy manufacturer and one of Happiness Express's largest suppliers. An audit procedure performed by Coopers & Lybrand involved obtaining and testing a Happiness Express report listing the company's "Top 25 Customers" for the period April 1, 1994–March 31, 1995. The $3.2 million of sales allegedly made to Wow Wee during fiscal 1995 should have placed that company among Happiness Express's five largest customers. However, Wow Wee did not appear on the "Top 25" list, nor did the Coopers & Lybrand auditors apparently question client personnel regarding this noticeable omission from that report.

During the fiscal 1995 audit, the Coopers & Lybrand auditors performed a sales cutoff test. Included in this test were the $2.4 million of bogus credit sales to Wow Wee recorded by Happiness Express on the final day of fiscal 1995. Plaintiff attorneys contended that carelessness on the part of the auditors caused them to overlook glaring irregularities evident in the accounting documents for those sales.

> *In the performance of the sales cutoff test, Coopers purportedly examined invoices and bills of lading associated with approximately $2.4 million of approximately $3.2 million of phony Wow Wee sales. However, the invoices and bills of lading purportedly examined by Coopers in the performance of this test were highly suspicious on their face. For example, none of these Wow Wee invoices contained customer purchase order numbers. In addition, at least one of the three bills of lading associated with the fictitious Wow Wee sales purportedly examined by Coopers in the performance of the sales cutoff test was, illogically, purportedly signed by the shipping company's representative on March 29, 1995, two days prior to the date of the bill of lading. Obviously, it would have been impossible for someone to sign a bill of lading before it was generated. Yet, Coopers did not question the legitimacy of the bill of lading.*

Coopers & Lybrand mailed accounts receivable confirmations to selected customers of Happiness Express at the end of fiscal 1995. The auditors informed Michael Goldberg that the Wow Wee receivable was included in the accounts chosen for confirmation. Because Goldberg provided the auditors with an incorrect address for Wow Wee, the confirmation was never returned to Coopers & Lybrand. After the auditors discussed this matter with Goldberg, he offered to contact the appropriate individual at Wow Wee to ensure that the confirmation was returned. The auditors accepted Goldberg's offer. Goldberg then forged a confirmation and had it faxed to Coopers & Lybrand. The auditors apparently accepted the confirmation without performing any follow-up procedures.

The large receivable from West Coast Liquidators accounted for approximately 13 percent of Happiness Express's accounts receivable at the end of fiscal 1995.[6] However, that receivable was not among the accounts Coopers & Lybrand selected for confirmation. In the civil complaint they filed against Coopers & Lybrand, plaintiff attorneys also pointed out that Coopers & Lybrand's sales cutoff test did not include any of the bogus sales to West Coast Liquidators during the final month of fiscal 1995. The attorneys maintained that even a cursory investigation of those transactions would have revealed that they were suspicious in nature.

> *In fact, had Coopers even performed the perfunctory procedure of examining Happiness's invoices associated with the year-end receivables from West Coast Liquidators, it would have discovered that they also were highly suspicious on their face. For example, such invoices representing $1,346,598 of purported sales to West Coast Liquidators did not contain any bills of lading or purchase order numbers.*

---

6. Happiness Express had total receivables of almost $11 million at the end of fiscal 1995, accounting for approximately one-third of the company's total assets.

EPILOGUE

Coopers & Lybrand contested each of the allegations included in the class-action lawsuit. At one point, the firm's legal counsel charged that the allegations involved no more than "nitpicking attacks" by the plaintiff attorneys. U.S. District Judge Robert P. Patterson, however, ruled that the allegations were sufficient to allow the case to proceed to trial. In particular, the federal judge ruled that, if proven, the plaintiffs' allegations would support a finding of "scienter" under the federal securities laws.

> Based on the facts as alleged, a trier of fact could find Coopers' audit so reckless that Coopers should have had knowledge of the underlying fraud and acted in blind disregard that there was a strong likelihood that Happiness was engaged in the underlying fraud. Proving this will be plaintiffs' burden at trial, but they have alleged facts sufficient to support a finding of scienter on the part of Coopers and so Coopers' motion to dismiss is denied.

After several years of legal wrangling, an out-of-court settlement was reached to resolve the class-action lawsuit stemming from the Happiness Express fraud. In January 2002, the parties to the lawsuit filed a legal notice describing the details of the proposed settlement with the federal district court in which the case would have been tried. The proposed settlement required Coopers & Lybrand to contribute $1.3 million to a settlement fund. Happiness Express's former stockholders would receive $715,000, or 55 percent, of the settlement fund, while the stockholders' attorneys would receive the remaining $585,000.

In the legal notice filed with the federal court, the plaintiff attorneys were required to state why they supported the settlement. The attorneys noted that a major problem they would have to surmount in pursuing the case was proving that Coopers & Lybrand had a motive to issue a false audit opinion on Happiness Express's financial statements. Additionally, the plaintiff attorneys admitted that they would have to overcome the contention by Coopers & Lybrand that the Happiness Express auditors had no actual knowledge of the falsifications in the company's accounting records and financial statements. Finally, even if the jury ultimately ruled in favor of Happiness Express's former stockholders, the plaintiff attorneys pointed out that the jury might decide that Coopers & Lybrand was responsible for only a small portion of the losses suffered by the stockholders. As a result, the stockholders might receive only a nominal judgment from the accounting firm.[7]

The SEC settled the charges pending against Michael Goldberg by requiring him to pay a $150,000 civil fine and to forfeit the $310,000 of insider trading profits that he had earned while serving as Happiness Express's CFO. Goldberg also agreed not to violate federal securities laws in the future, although under the terms of the SEC settlement he neither admitted nor denied the charges that the SEC had filed against him. In February 2003, the SEC issued a litigation release that reported the settlement of the charges pending against Michael Goldberg's close friend who had received "material nonpublic information" from Goldberg regarding Happiness Express's deteriorating financial condition. Goldberg's friend was required to forfeit the $79,000 of trading profits he had earned by "shorting" Happiness Express's common stock and to pay a civil fine in the same amount. The SEC also announced that it had settled the insider trading claim filed previously against Goldberg's former landlord but did not reveal the nature of that settlement.

In 2003, Joseph Sutton pleaded guilty to conspiracy to commit bank fraud and securities fraud and was sentenced to 30 months in federal prison. His brother, Isaac, refused to plead guilty to similar charges pending against him and instead opted for a jury trial. On September 29, 2004, a New York jury found Isaac Sutton innocent of all the fraud charges filed against him by the SEC.

---

7. No further public comment or report regarding the proposed settlement was found. Most likely, the parties agreed to the proposed settlement. As a point of information, the settlement payment would have been made by the successor firm to Coopers & Lybrand, PricewaterhouseCoopers.

Questions

1. Identify the primary audit objectives that auditors hope to accomplish by (a) confirming a client's year-end accounts receivable, (b) performing year-end sales cutoff tests.

2. Identify and briefly describe any mistakes or errors in judgment that Coopers & Lybrand may have made in its effort to confirm the Wow Wee receivable at the end of fiscal 1995. In your opinion, did these apparent mistakes or errors in judgment involve "negligence" on the part of the given auditors? Would you characterize the mistakes or errors as "reckless" or "fraudulent"? In each case, justify your answer.

3. Should the Coopers & Lybrand auditors have confirmed the receivable from West Coast Liquidators at the end of fiscal 1995? Why or why not? Should the auditors have included one or more sales to West Coast Liquidators in their year-end sales cutoff tests for fiscal 1995?

4. What alternative audit procedures can be applied to a large receivable of an audit client when a confirmation of that receivable cannot be obtained, for whatever reason? Compare and contrast the evidence provided by these procedures with the evidence yielded by a confirmation.

5. The SEC charged certain executives of Happiness Express with "insider trading." Do auditors have a responsibility to consider or investigate the possibility that client executives have engaged in insider trading activities? Defend your answer.

General Motors Company

*As long as the unwritten rule stands that the best way to achieve
success at GM is to be a good finance man, the bad habit of juggling
numbers in order to present the picture people want to see cannot be
broken.*

> Mary Ann Keller,
> analyst for the automotive industry,
> September 1990

The Great Depression dealt a devastating blow to Billy Durant. During the depths of
the Depression in 1936, Durant, a high school dropout who was born a few months
after the outbreak of the Civil War in 1861, was forced to declare bankruptcy. Like millions of Americans, the tough-minded and resilient Durant survived the Depression
by becoming a jack-of-all-trades, a "job" that he had mastered as a young man. During his early twenties, the free-spirited Durant had worked as an itinerant salesman
traveling from town to town peddling patent medicines. During the latter days of the
Depression, Durant, who was in his late seventies by this time, made ends meet by
managing a bowling alley. After suffering a stroke in 1942, he and his wife subsisted
on a pension provided to him by a company that he had once managed. Durant died
a few years later in 1947.

If one considered only the early and later years of Durant's life, his life story would
not be particularly compelling. However, in the 50-year span between working as a
traveling medicine man and managing a bowling alley, William C. "Billy" Durant created an organization that would become the United States' biggest corporation and
have the largest workforce of any company worldwide.

Durant made a fortune in the late 1880s and 1890s manufacturing horse-drawn car-
riages, a business that he had launched in 1886 on $3,000 of borrowed money. In
the early days of the 20th century, Durant realized that the horseless carriage would
soon supplant his company's product. Over the next few years, Durant invested much
of his personal wealth in several automobile manufacturers, most notably the Buick
Motor Company. In 1908, Durant merged those companies to create General Motors
Corporation (GM).

For 77 years, from 1931 through 2008, GM reigned as the number one automobile
manufacturer worldwide. Only a few months after that long run ended, GM, just like Billy
Durant some seven decades earlier, filed for bankruptcy.[1] GM's bankruptcy filing in June
2009 had been foreshadowed by the going-concern audit opinion issued on its 2008
financial statements a few months earlier by Deloitte & Touche, its longtime audit firm.

Pensions & Panic

Similar to many companies, GM was victimized by the economic crisis triggered in
late 2008 by collapsing housing prices and the implosion of the subprime sector of
the mortgage industry. That crisis quickly spread to other sectors of the U.S. economy,

---

1. After losing control of General Motors in the early 1920s, Billy Durant became preoccupied with
"playing" the stock market. The stock market crash of 1929 wiped out Durant's massive wealth and
eventually forced him to file for bankruptcy.

including the large automotive industry. Panic and fear caused millions of distraught U.S. consumers to delay or cancel "big-ticket" discretionary expenditures, such as purchases of new automobiles.

Well before the economic crisis that gripped the country in 2008 and 2009, GM's financial condition had been deteriorating. The generous pensions that the company historically paid to its former workers and executives, such as Billy Durant, were a key factor that contributed to GM's declining health. Wage freezes implemented during World War II by the federal government had prompted many companies, including GM, to establish an employee pension plan–or expand an existing one–to give their employees a legal pay "raise." The retirement benefits provided by those pension plans became increasingly lucrative during the latter half of the twentieth century due largely to the effective negotiation skills of such labor unions as the United Auto Workers (UAW).

The large expenses stemming from GM's pension plan and other postretirement benefit plans added significantly to the company's cost of producing automobiles. Because foreign competitors such as Toyota paid more modest wages and provided their employees with less liberal pension and other postretirement benefits, they could produce automobiles more cheaply than GM. Over time, this economic disadvantage caused the annual sales of GM to shrink as car buyers gravitated to foreign models. In 2009, Toyota finally overtook GM as the world's largest automobile producer.

Easily one of the most controversial issues surrounding GM's financial problems in early 2009 was: What would happen to the company's huge and significantly under-funded pension plan if the company failed. Nearly 500,000 GM retirees or surviving spouses received monthly pension payments financed by the company. The major-ity of those individuals relied on their GM pension as the principal source of their retirement income. Likewise, the approximately 250,000 active GM employees had built their retirement plans around the pension benefits promised to them by their employer. What frightened GM's retirees and employees was that the present value of the liabilities associated with GM's pension plan were estimated to exceed $100 billion while the pension plan had total assets of only $85 billion. As the company tottered on the verge of bankruptcy, it was unclear how, or whether, the pension plan would be salvaged if the company filed for bankruptcy.

Pension Accounting: A Brief History

GM's impending bankruptcy in early 2009 refocused attention on longstanding allega-tions that top management manipulated the company's financial data to conceal its deteriorating financial condition and operating results. The company's critics included Maryann Keller, a longtime analyst of the automotive industry who two decades earlier had published a book entitled *Rude Awakening: The Rise, Fall, and Struggle for Recovery of General Motors* (HarperCollins, 1990). Keller suggested that GM management routinely "juggled" the company's accounting numbers to conceal its serious financial problems. Among the financial statement items that GM management allegedly distorted were the expenses and liabilities associated with the company's enormous pension plan.

In fairness to GM, a large number of companies have faced similar allegations, that is, charges that they "manage" their reported earnings and apparent financial condi-tion by improperly accounting for their employee pension plans. In fact, accounting for pension-related financial statement items has long been one of the most complex and controversial issues facing the accounting profession.

Prior to the mid-1960s, most companies accounted for their pension plan expenses on a pay-as-you-go or cash basis. In addition to simply ignoring the long-term liabili-ties associated with pension plans, a major drawback to this accounting method was that it allowed companies to readily and legally manipulate their reported earnings by varying the amounts they contributed each year to their pension plans. For example, if a company was having a poor year profit-wise, it could simply reduce its pension plan contribution and thus reduce its pension expense for the year.

Accounting for pension plan–related expenses and liabilities did not change dramatically until 1985 when the Financial Accounting Standards Board (FASB) adopted a new accounting standard that moved the profession toward accrual basis accounting for those items. However, this new standard, *Statement on Financial Accounting Standards No. 87 (SFAS No. 87)*, "Employers' Accounting for Pensions," still provided opportunities for companies to window-dress their financial statements.

SFAS No. 87 required companies for the first time to make several key assumptions in accounting for financial statement items associated with a defined-benefit pension plan, similar to the one that GM provided to its employees.[2] Critics of the new standard argued that since these assumptions were "discretionary," they could be easily "manipulated" by corporate executives hoping to make their company's financial statements more impressive.[3] Among the most important of these assumptions was the discount rate used to determine the present value of a company's pension liability. This choice had important financial statement implications, particularly for labor-intensive companies with huge pension plans, such as GM. For example, a company could raise or lower—most likely the latter—the present value of its pension liability by varying the discount rate it applied to those liabilities.[4]

Rate Debates

In late 2002, GM faced an unpleasant predicament. Falling stock market prices were driving down the value of the assets held by its pension plan, while falling interest rates were increasing the present value of its pension liability. These two conditions were causing the unfunded portion of GM's pension liability and the company's projected pension expense under *SFAS No. 87* to increase dramatically.

During the final few months of 2002, several GM executives, including the company's chief financial officer (CFO), chief accounting officer (CAO), and controller, agonized over the decision of which discount rate to apply to the company's pension liability. Those executives recognized that the choice of that discount rate would have a material impact on GM's reported operating results and financial condition. *SFAS No. 87* obligated GM to choose the most reasonable discount rate to apply in computing the present value of its pension liability but did not specify how that discount rate was to be chosen. The mathematical method historically used by the company produced a discount rate of 6 percent. As in years past, the company also asked its actuarial firm to develop an independent estimate of the appropriate discount rate to apply to its pension liability. GM's actuarial firm reported that its mathematical modeling suggested that a 6.18 percent discount rate was appropriate.

---

2. Recognize that a company's pension plan is nearly always a legal entity independent of the company that created it. The issue in this context is not the actual accounting for a pension plan but rather the accounting for pension plan–related financial statement amounts of the given employer or "sponsor" of that plan.

3. Audit Integrity (www.auditintegrity.com), "Pension Liabilities: The Elephant in the Room," March 2009.

4. Addressing the specific features and requirements of pension accounting is beyond the scope of this case. Refer to any intermediate accounting text for a comprehensive treatment of that topic. In 2006, the FASB replaced *SFAS No. 87* with *SFAS No. 158*, "Employers' Accounting for Defined Benefit Pension and Other Postretirement Plans." Following the issuance of *SFAS No. 158*, the FASB has continued to debate and consider additional modifications to its pension accounting guidelines and rules.

Instead of using either a 6.0 percent or 6.18 percent discount rate, GM's executives chose a discount rate of 6.75 percent to apply to the company's pension liability. This latter discount rate was not produced by a rigorous mathematical model but rather by simply averaging the interest rates on a relatively small sample of high-quality corporate bonds tracked by the Moody's investment service. In fact, the actual average interest rate of the sample used by the executives to arrive at the 6.75 percent discount rate was 6.63 percent. (When choosing a discount rate, GM "rounded" the given estimate of that rate to the nearest quarter of a percent.)

By the first week of January 2003, Deloitte's audit of GM's 2002 financial statements was well under way. On January 7, 2003, Deloitte auditors met with representatives of the GM department responsible for developing the discount rate to apply to the company's pension liability. At that meeting, the GM representatives presented the three-point estimates of the discount rate that had been considered and the source of each of those estimates. Their principal justification for choosing the 6.75 percent point estimate was that "most companies"[5] were relying on the Moody's database of interest rates to choose the discount rate to apply to their pension liability. The Securities and Exchange Commission (SEC) subsequently challenged that assertion. The federal agency also maintained that GM officials had made no effort to determine whether the companies actually using the Moody's data were "demographically similar to GM" and thus a valid sample to use in supporting the company's decision to rely on that source.

Following the January 7, 2003, meeting, the Deloitte auditors informed client personnel that they would begin their review of the company's decision to apply the 6.75 percent discount rate. The auditors also informed the client that a second meeting to discuss the issue would be necessary. Finally, the auditors noted that their initial impression was that the 6.75 percent discount rate was too high.

A few days later, the Deloitte auditors asked to meet again with the client to discuss the 6.75 percent discount rate. Deloitte insisted that representatives of GM's actuarial firm attend this second meeting. GM's controller also attended this meeting. Following this second meeting, the controller told GM's CFO and CAO that the Deloitte auditors were "now resigned to our use of 6.75%."

GM personnel at this second meeting apparently convinced the Deloitte auditors to accept the 6.75 percent rate by pledging to include a "sensitivity analysis in the company's 2002 Form 10-K." This supplemental disclosure would supposedly illustrate the impact of an array of discount rates on GM's pension-related financial statement items. In an intercompany communication, GM's controller told the CFO and CAO that a Deloitte audit partner accepted this compromise as a "reasonable although imperfect solution or compromise to his concerns." Despite agreeing to the compromise solution proposed by GM, the Deloitte partner believed that a 6.50 percent discount rate would have been a "better choice." Deloitte subsequently issued an unqualified audit opinion on GM's 2002 financial statements.

GM filed its 2002 Form 10-K with the SEC on March 13, 2003. As the company had pledged to Deloitte, it included a sensitivity analysis in the 10-K, relevant to its choice of the 6.75 percent discount rate. That analysis disclosed what GM's pension expense and total pension liabilities would have been for both a 6.5 percent and 7 percent discount rate. If the 6.5 percent discount rate had been applied, the company's

---

5. The remaining quotes in this case were taken from the following source: *Securities and Exchange Commission v. General Motors Corporation*, Case 1:09-cv-00119, U.S. District Court for the District of Columbia, 22 January 2009.

pension expense for 2002 would have increased by $120 million, which would have lowered its pre-tax earnings by approximately 6 percent. Likewise, the choice of a 6.5 percent discount rate would have increased GM's total pension liability reported on its balance sheet by approximately 10 percent or $1.8 billion and would have reduced the company's stockholders' equity by approximately 16 percent or $1.1 billion.[6]

In a subsequent complaint filed against GM by the SEC in January 2009, the federal agency maintained that the pension-related amounts and disclosures within the company's 2002 financial statements were "materially misleading." The SEC was particularly concerned by GM's lack of candor in the sensitivity analysis that it presented for its selected pension discount rate. Since that analysis disclosed the financial statement impacts of using 6.5 and 7.0 percent discount rates, it implied that the selected discount rate of 6.75 percent was near the midpoint of the discount rates that had been considered by the company, which was not true. The SEC also criticized GM for failing to disclose that an unconventional method had been used to select the 2002 discount rate.

EPILOGUE

In late January 2009, the SEC issued *Accounting and Auditing Enforcement Release No. 3033*, which disclosed a litany of accounting and financial reporting abuses by GM over the previous several years. The principal focus of that document was the improper decisions that the company had made in accounting for its pension-related expenses and liabilities. Without admitting or denying the charges, GM agreed to a consent decree under which the SEC enjoined the company from any future violations of federal securities laws. To date, the SEC has not sanctioned Deloitte for its role in GM's pension accounting debacle.

Six months after being sanctioned by the SEC, GM emerged from bankruptcy as the "new" General Motors or "General Motors Company." Following GM's reorganization, the federal government was its largest stockholder as a result of investing nearly $60 billion in the company through the Troubled Asset Relief Program (TARP).[7] Fortunately for GM's retirees and workforce, the bankruptcy reorganization plan left the company's huge pension plan intact.

Questions

1. Auditing standards don't specifically discuss the audit procedures that should be applied to a client's pension-related financial statement amounts. Identify five audit procedures that would be relevant to those items. For each audit procedure that you list, identify the related audit objective.

2. Under what general circumstances should auditors retain outside experts to assist them in completing an audit? How could an expert be useful in auditing a client's pension-related financial statement items?

---

6. In its 2002 Form 10-K, GM reported total assets of $370.8 billion, total liabilities of $364 billion, and total stockholders' equity of $6.8 billion.

7. On November 17, 2010, General Motors Company went public. On that day, trading in GM's stock accounted for nearly 10 percent of the trading volume on the New York Stock Exchange. Most financial analysts predict that the federal government will eventually recover the full amount of the nearly $60 billion it invested in the company by selling the GM stock that it owns.

3. Do you believe that Deloitte behaved properly by accepting GM's decision to apply a 6.75 percent discount rate to its pension liabilities? What, if any, other steps or measures should Deloitte have taken under the circumstances?

4. Did the choice of the 6.75 percent discount rate in 2002 have a material impact on GM's financial statements? Defend your answer.

Lipper Holdings, LLC

Over the past few decades, hedge funds have become among the most controversial and largest investment vehicles on Wall Street. Critics of hedge funds argue that their high-risk investment strategies contributed significantly to the economic crisis that gripped the world's capital markets beginning in late 2008. Prior to that crisis, the total market value of investments held by hedge funds was estimated to be a staggering $2.5 trillion.

In fact, pegging the total value of hedge funds at any point in time is a difficult task since there is a lack of consensus among even Wall Street experts on exactly which investment funds qualify as "hedge funds." Hedge funds are generally thought of by lay investors as investment funds that use sophisticated risk management techniques to limit the downside risk of the investments that they hold. Many hedge funds, however, do just the reverse. These latter funds employ investment strategies, such as buying and selling a wide range of exotic financial derivatives, that serve to increase, rather than decrease, the overall risk of their investment portfolios.

The two traits that most commonly cause an investment fund to be labeled a "hedge fund" are minimal regulatory oversight and the payment of "performance fees" to the fund managers. Many hedge funds are domiciled in offshore tax havens, such as the Cayman Islands, that impose little regulatory oversight on investment companies, banks, and related entities. Hedge funds headquartered in the United States typically have a legal structure that allows them to avoid intense scrutiny by the Securities and Exchange Commission (SEC) and other federal and state regulatory authorities.

In addition to the annual management fees that most investment fund managers are paid, the managers of hedge funds collect performance fees equal to a certain percentage of their fund's profit each year. These performance fees vary considerably from fund to fund but range as high as 20 percent. Critics of hedge funds, such as renowned investor Warren Buffett, maintain that performance fees encourage fund managers to adopt high-risk, if not reckless, investment strategies, which would explain why many hedge funds specialize in "junk bonds" and "distressed" corporate securities.[1]

Hedge Funds and Hollywood

During the 1990s, Kenneth Lipper emerged as a leader of the rapidly growing hedge fund "industry" in the United States. Born in 1941, Lipper, the son of a shoe salesman, spent his childhood in a modest working-class neighborhood in New York City's South Bronx. As an adolescent, he enjoyed a wide range of interests, including sports, movies, and the stock market. Unlike his childhood friend, Alfredo "Sonny" Pacino, Lipper decided as a young adult to pursue a career on Wall Street rather than in Hollywood—at least initially.

Lipper was a brilliant student who relied on academic scholarships to finance an undergraduate degree at Columbia, a law degree at Harvard, and a master's degree from the New York University School of Law before pursuing postgraduate studies

---

1. Increasing the risk preference of hedge fund managers is the fact that those individuals do not absorb any portion of a net loss suffered in a given year by a fund that they manage.

at the University of Paris. The charismatic Lipper developed an impressive list of wealthy and well-connected friends and acquaintances during his college years.

In 1966, when he was 25 years old, Lipper married the daughter of one of New York's richest philanthropists. That marriage placed Lipper's Wall Street career on the "fast track, according to Business Week."[2] Shortly thereafter, he joined the prestigious Wall Street firm of Lehman Brothers; by the age of 32, Lipper was among that firm's youngest partners.

Lipper left Lehman in 1975 to become a partner and managing director of a competing firm, Salomon Brothers. His bright career was briefly derailed when the SEC accused him of aiding and abetting violations of the federal securities laws in a covert attempt to take over a large public company. Lipper settled those charges without admitting or denying any wrongdoing and escaped with only mild sanctions being imposed on him by the federal agency.

In 1983, one year after settling the SEC charges, Lipper took a sabbatical from the world of high finance to serve as deputy mayor of New York City. After three years in New York City's rough-and-tumble political arena, Lipper became involved in a Hollywood film project being developed by Oliver Stone. The famous movie director tapped Lipper to serve as a technical advisor for the film *Wall Street* that starred Michael Douglas and Charlie Sheen. Following the release of the Academy Award–winning movie, Lipper wrote a novel of the same name based upon the film's screenplay.

Over the next two decades, Lipper lived a high-profile, bicoastal lifestyle, in which he was a mainstay in both the West Coast's glitzy movie industry and Wall Street's economic powerhouse some 3,000 miles away. In Hollywood, Lipper enjoyed a successful career as a screenwriter and film producer and even collaborated with his old friend Al Pacino on a major film project.[3] At the same time, Lipper oversaw a burgeoning financial empire on the East Coast through his investment firm, Lipper Holdings, LLC, that he organized in the late 1980s. Lipper's firm, for which he served as both president and chief executive officer (CEO), would eventually manage investments having a total market value exceeding $4 billion.

Lipper's network of influential friends on both coasts served as a pipeline of clients to his Wall Street firm. Julia Roberts, Sylvester Stallone, and Disney CEO Michael Eisner were among the many Hollywood luminaries for whom Lipper served as a financial advisor. One-time presidential candidate U.S. Senator Fritz Hollings, former Federal Reserve Chairman Paul Volcker, and Lipper's former boss Ed Koch, the longtime and very popular mayor of New York City, were examples of political heavyweights who entrusted much of their wealth to Lipper's firm. As *Business Week* reported, "The flashy pitchman [Kenneth Lipper] with his fancy connections and wealth was a magnet for investors who never questioned his ability to manage their money... these were people who were wowed by his blue-chip Wall Street credentials."[4]

Lipper delegated the day-to-day responsibilities of managing his firm's investment funds to his subordinates. One of his principal subordinates was Edward Strafaci, an executive vice-president of Lipper Holdings. Strafaci served as the portfolio manager for three large hedge funds within the family of Lipper investment funds. Those three

---

2. M. Vickers, "The Fallen Financier," *Business Week* (online), 9 December 2002.

3. In 1999, Lipper received an Oscar for his role as the producer of *The Last Days*, a documentary film focusing on the Holocaust. Al Pacino played the lead role in *City Hall*, a 1996 feature film produced by Lipper.

4. Vickers, "The Fallen Financier."

hedge funds were Lipper Convertibles, Lipper Convertibles Series II, and Lipper Fixed Income Fund. Each of the funds had been legally structured so that they were not required to register with the SEC as investment companies under the Investment Company Act of 1940. Because Lipper Convertibles and Lipper Convertibles Series II were legally "broker-dealers," however, they were required to file annual audited financial statements with the SEC pursuant to the requirements of the Securities Exchange Act of 1934.

Strafaci used financial leverage to enhance the rates of return earned by the investors in the three hedge funds, that is, he arranged for the funds to borrow large amounts of cash that were then invested along with the equity capital of the investors. This financial leverage caused the rates of return earned by investors to be considerably higher than the returns earned on the funds' investment portfolios. Of course, the use of financial leverage also meant that when the funds suffered losses in a given year, the corresponding losses of the funds' investors were magnified.

The marketing materials Lipper's firm used to promote his hedge funds reported that 70 percent of their holdings were high-quality, "investment grade" securities. In fact, the actual percentage of investment grade securities held by the three hedge funds was considerably lower than that figure. To ensure that the funds continued to attract new investors, Strafaci believed it was imperative for them to earn impressive rates of return. Because investment grade securities didn't yield such returns, he invested an increasingly large percentage of the hedge funds' assets in high-risk, high-return securities. These securities were typically convertible bonds and convertible preferred stocks issued by companies experiencing financial problems.

"Recipe for Fraud"

When the volatile securities that Strafaci purchased for Lipper's hedge funds failed to produce the rates of return that he wanted, he began intentionally overstating their reported market values to achieve those desired returns. In January 2002, Strafaci resigned his lucrative position with Lipper Holdings. His unexpected resignation prompted an internal investigation over the following several weeks, which led to the discovery of his fraudulent scheme.

In late February 2002, Lipper Holdings publicly reported that the market values of the investments held by the three hedge funds formerly managed by Strafaci had been overstated. When those investments were reflected at their true market values, the investors in the largest of the three funds, Lipper Convertibles, realized a nearly 50 percent reduction in their equity capital. More modest but still significant losses were suffered by the investors in Lipper's two other hedge funds.

Subsequent investigations by regulatory and law enforcement authorities revealed that Strafaci had personally supervised the "marking to market" of the investments held by the three hedge funds that he managed.[5] This revelation caused a prominent Wall Street money manager to point out that most hedge fund managers use an independent third party to value their investment portfolios and that allowing "insiders" to do so was a "recipe for fraud."[6]

When the overstatements of the Lipper hedge funds' investments were initially reported, Edward Strafaci vehemently denied any involvement in, or knowledge of, them. Instead, Strafaci laid the blame for the misstatements squarely on the shoulders

---

5. Many of these securities were "thinly-traded" securities for which readily determinable market values were not available.

6. Vickers, "The Fallen Financier."

of his former boss, Kenneth Lipper. "We [Strafaci and his subordinates] don't bear any responsibility at all. Clients have to go to Ken Lipper if they're mad—he was the CEO."[7]

In August 2004, Strafaci did a sudden about-face. Strafaci pleaded guilty to fraudulently overstating the collective value of the investments he had managed for Lipper's hedge funds and subsequently received a six-year prison sentence. He was also ordered by a federal judge to pay restitution of nearly $90 million. Despite Strafaci's guilty plea, many parties, including former Lipper investors, maintained that Kenneth Lipper was ultimately responsible for the huge losses suffered by the Lipper hedge funds.

> Lipper most likely knew these traders were mispricing the portfolio and juicing the returns all along. But he was so concerned with his reputation and impressing his celebrity clients that he allowed it, until they just got too deep to recover. It was pure hubris.[8]

Auditors Miss the "Mark"

While federal prosecutors dogged Edward Strafaci and Kenneth Lipper, PricewaterhouseCoopers (PwC), Lipper's longtime audit firm, was being investigated by the SEC for failing to uncover the grossly overstated values of the investments held by the Lipper hedge funds. Particularly galling to the hedge fund investors was the allegation that those overstatements should have been readily apparent to the auditors. Making the situation even less palatable for the investors was the fact that Lipper Holdings had chosen PwC to audit its three hedge funds in part because of that firm's "touted expertise with respect to hedge funds and valuation of hard-to-price securities."[9,10]

The principal focus of the SEC's investigation of PwC was the firm's 2000 audits of the three Lipper hedge funds, the final audits completed by PwC prior to the discovery of the accounting fraud. The primary individual targeted by the federal agency during that investigation was Larry Stoler. Stoler became a partner with PwC's predecessor firm, Price Waterhouse, in 1980 and retired from the firm in 2002, shortly after the Lipper scandal surfaced. With the exception of two years in the mid-1990s, Stoler served as the audit engagement partner for each of the three Lipper hedge funds from 1989 through the collapse of those funds in early 2002. During the two years that he was not the audit engagement partner, Stoler had served as the concurring partner on the audits of those funds.

During its investigation of PwC's 2000 audits, the SEC discovered that Stoler had for several years been aware of internal control weaknesses that should have "heightened [PwC's] scrutiny of the valuation of their [the hedge funds'] investments." Most importantly, Stoler had been aware that Edward Strafaci personally supervised the marking to market of the hedge funds' investments each year and that there was no "formal review" of that process by another credible party.

The most important audit procedures applied by PwC during its 2000 audit of the Lipper hedge funds were the audit tests intended to determine whether the funds' major investments were appropriately valued at year end.[11] According to the SEC,

---

7. *Ibid.*

8. *Ibid.*

9. Lipper actually retained the predecessor firm of PwC, Price Waterhouse, as the auditor of the three hedge funds. In 1998, Price Waterhouse merged with Coopers & Lybrand to create PwC.

10. This and all subsequent quotations, unless indicated otherwise, were taken from the following source: Securities and Exchange Commission, *Accounting and Auditing Enforcement Release No. 2470*, 31 July 2006.

11. These audit procedures were applied to the investments held by the Lipper Convertibles hedge fund, the largest of the three Lipper hedge funds. The investment portfolios of the other two hedge funds consisted of subsets of the securities held by Lipper Convertibles.

the basis for the values assigned to those investments by Strafaci was allegedly December 31, 2000, price quotes that he had received directly from a sample of the brokers that executed securities trades for the three hedge funds. PwC's audit workpapers, however, did not include copies of the documents containing those alleged price quotes or any evidence that the auditors had reviewed those documents.

The initial audit procedure applied to the year-end securities prices of the hedge funds' investments involved a review of the December 31, 2000, statements obtained by the auditors from the brokers actually holding those investments on that date on behalf of the funds. These prices were inconsistent with the market prices that had been applied to the investments by Strafaci. According to the SEC, Stoler did not discuss these inconsistencies "with anyone at Lipper Holdings," nor did the PwC workpapers indicate how these inconsistencies were resolved.

PwC's workpapers documented the fact that the year-end market values of the hedge funds' investments appeared to be overstated given the results of the initial audit test. For Lipper Convertibles the apparent overstatement was approximately 13 percent. However, this amount "ignored the impact of leverage on the portfolio" of that fund. If the auditors had considered the impact of that leverage, they would have determined that the apparent errors made by Strafaci in marking to market Lipper Convertibles' investments had overstated the equity capital of the fund's investors "by approximately 48%."

The PwC auditors also used year-end market prices reported by the Bloomberg investment service "to obtain an independent price for 65% of the total market value positions held at 12/31/00" by the Lipper hedge funds. This audit procedure resulted in the auditors once again discovering apparent overstatements in the year-end market values of the hedge funds' investments. PwC's audit program called for the investigation of any "significant variances" between the year-end Bloomberg prices and the prices applied by Strafaci to those investments.

> Any Bloomberg prices that were "greater than 2% of what Lipper Convertibles has recorded" were to be "independently confirmed" by "directly contacting" the brokers with whom Convertibles traded and from whom Strafaci purportedly obtained the quotes on which he based his values for the securities "so that they may confirm the price of the positions."

This follow-up audit procedure involved a junior auditor assigned to the PwC audit team sending faxes to salespersons at five broker-dealers used by the Lipper hedge funds. These faxes included a schedule of all the securities prices used by Strafaci to mark the hedge funds' investments to market on December 31, 2000. The faxes asked the recipients to "Please verify the attached schedule of broker quotes as of 12/31/00 were [sic] provided by you to Lipper Convertibles." The faxes also instructed the recipients to sign the schedules and fax them back to the auditor.

Representatives of four of the five brokers signed the schedules and faxed them back to the junior auditor "without any notation or comments." PwC considered these four returned faxes to be "clean confirmations" of the year-end market prices applied by Strafaci. The fifth returned fax was unsigned and included notations indicating that several of the market prices were significantly higher than the actual year-end prices of the given securities.

The SEC charged that PwC's confirmation audit procedure was "flawed in several significant respects." For example, the faxed confirmations did not specifically instruct the recipients to "provide quotes for the specified securities or ask them to attest to the reasonableness of the values listed on the schedules." As a result, with the exception of the one broker-dealer representative who questioned several of the market prices included in the confirmation, there was no evidence "that the salespeople who returned signed confirmations had actually ascertained the broker-dealer's quote or valued the security." In fact, in some cases, the given broker-dealers did not make a market in certain securities listed on the confirmation and thus had no basis for attesting to the year-end market prices of those securities.

EPILOGUE

In a July 2006 enforcement release, the SEC reported that "most" of the relevant audit evidence collected by PwC during its 2000 audit of Lipper's hedge funds "indicated that Strafaci's valuation of the Funds' assets were substantially overstated." For that reason, the federal agency ruled that the unqualified audit reports on the funds' financial statements, reports signed by Larry Stoler, were unjustified.

Stoler ignored, discounted, or failed to apprise himself of, the evidence produced by the audit tests... Thus, he failed to obtain sufficient competent evidential matter concerning the valuation of the Funds' assets, and failed to adequately supervise the assistants working on the audit.

Accompanying the 2000 audited financial statements filed with the SEC by the Lipper Convertibles and Lipper Convertibles Series II hedge funds were supplemental reports on their internal controls prepared by PwC, reports mandated at the time for broker-dealers registered with the federal agency. The reports, signed by Stoler, indicated that PwC had uncovered no material weaknesses in the two hedge funds' internal controls. In its 2006 enforcement release, the SEC ruled that the latter conclusion was "inaccurate."

The SEC sanctioned Larry Stoler for failing to comply with generally accepted auditing standards (GAAS) during the 2000 audits of Lipper Holdings' three hedge funds.[12] According to the SEC, Stoler was "a cause" of the funds' violations of the federal securities laws.

The Funds' audited financial statements for the year ended December 31, 2000, were disseminated to investors/clients and prospective investors/clients, along with PwC's unqualified audit reports on those statements. PwC's unqualified audit reports on those statements gave comfort to investors/clients, among others, that the Funds were being properly valued. Investors/clients who received those audited financial statements were solicited to make, and in some cases made, investments or additional investments in the Funds.

The three Lipper hedge funds audited by Stoler and his subordinates were liquidated by Lipper Holdings beginning in 2002. Those forced liquidations resulted in hundreds of millions of dollars of losses for the funds' investors. Numerous civil lawsuits stemming from the Lipper scandal have been filed by the investors or their representatives. One such lawsuit was filed against PwC by a bankruptcy trustee appointed to represent the investors. According to published reports, a preliminary settlement to that lawsuit was reached in 2010. That tentative settlement required PwC to pay $29.9 million to the former Lipper investors.[13,14]

---

12. Although Stoler had retired in 2002, in its 2006 enforcement release the SEC suspended his right to practice before it for one year.

13. Kirby McInerney LLP, "Lipper Convertibles, L.P.," http://kmslaw.us/news.asp?type=cases&id=32.

14. Kenneth Lipper was not sanctioned by the SEC following its investigation of Edward Strafaci's fraudulent scheme nor was he criminally indicted for any role in that scheme.

Questions

1. Identify specific fraud risk factors present during PwC's audits of the Lipper hedge funds. Explain how PwC should have responded to the fraud risk factors that you identified.

2. Provide examples of important audit objectives for complex financial instruments and transactions. For each audit objective that you identify, list one or more audit procedures that could be used to accomplish that objective.

3. Identify the factors that may have contributed to the alleged flaws in the audit procedures that PwC applied in testing the year-end market values of the Lipper hedge funds' investments. Discuss specific measures that audit firms can employ to reduce the likelihood that such factors will undercut the quality of their audits.

CBI Holding Company, Inc.

During the 1980s, CBI Holding Company, Inc., a New York–based firm, served as the parent company for several wholly owned subsidiaries, principal among them Common Brothers, Inc. CBI's subsidiaries marketed an extensive line of pharmaceutical products. The subsidiaries purchased these products from drug manufacturers, warehoused them in storage facilities, and then resold them to retail pharmacies, hospitals, long-term care facilities, and related entities. CBI's principal market area stretched from the northeastern United States into the upper Midwest.

In 1991, Robert Castello, CBI's president and chairman of the board, sold a 48 percent ownership interest in his company to Trust Company of the West (TCW), a diversified investment firm. The purchase agreement between the two parties gave TCW the right to appoint two members of CBI's board; Castello retained the right to appoint the three remaining board members. The purchase agreement also identified several so-called "control-triggering events." If any one of these events occurred, TCW would have the right to take control of CBI. Examples of control-triggering events included CBI's failure to maintain certain financial ratios at a specified level and unauthorized loans to Castello and other CBI executives.

Castello engaged Ernst & Young (E&Y) as CBI's independent audit firm several months before he closed the TCW deal. During this same time frame, Castello was named "Entrepreneur of the Year" in an annual nationwide promotion co-sponsored by E&Y. From 1990 through 1993, E&Y issued unqualified opinions on CBI's annual financial statements.

Accounting Gimmicks

Castello instructed several of his subordinates to misrepresent CBI's reported operating results and financial condition for the fiscal years ended April 30, 1992 and 1993.[1] Those misrepresentations allowed Castello to receive large, year-end bonuses to which he was not entitled. CBI actively concealed the fraudulent activities from TCW's management, from TCW's appointees to CBI's board, and from the company's E&Y auditors because Castello realized that the scheme, if discovered, would qualify as a control-triggering event under the terms of the 1991 purchase agreement with TCW. Several years later in a lawsuit prompted by Castello's fraud, TCW executives testified that they would have immediately seized control of CBI if they had become aware of that scheme.

Understating CBI's year-end accounts payable was one of the methods Castello and his confederates used to distort CBI's 1992 and 1993 financial statements. At any point in time, CBI had large outstanding payables to its suppliers, which included major pharmaceutical manufacturers such as Burroughs-Wellcome, Schering, and FoxMeyer. At the end of fiscal 1992 and fiscal 1993, CBI understated payables due to its large vendors by millions of dollars. Judge Burton Lifland, the federal magistrate who presided over the lawsuit stemming from Castello's fraudulent scheme, ruled that the intentional understatements of CBI's year-end payables were very material to the company's 1992 and 1993 financial statements.

---

1. Due to a change in CBI's fiscal year, the company's 1992 fiscal year was only 11 months.

E&Y's 1992 and 1993 CBI Audits

In both 1992 and 1993, E&Y identified the CBI audit as a "close monitoring engagement." The accounting firm's audit manual defined a close monitoring engagement as "one in which the company being audited presents significant risk to E&Y . . . there is a significant chance that E&Y will suffer damage to its reputation, monetarily, or both."[2] E&Y's workpapers for the 1992 and 1993 audits also documented several "red flags," suggesting that the engagements posed a higher-than-normal audit risk.

Control risk factors identified for the CBI audits by E&Y included the dominance of the company by Robert Castello,[3] the absence of an internal audit function, the lack of proper segregation of duties within the company's accounting department, and aggressive positions taken by management personnel regarding key accounting estimates. These apparent control risks caused E&Y to describe CBI's control environment as "ineffective." Other risk factors identified in the CBI audit workpapers included the possible occurrence of a control-triggering event, an "undue" emphasis by top management on achieving periodic earnings goals, and the fact that Castello's annual bonus was tied directly to CBI's reported earnings.

For both the 1992 and 1993 CBI audits, the E&Y engagement team prepared a document entitled "Audit Approach Plan Update and Approval Form." This document described the general strategy E&Y planned to follow in completing those audits. In 1992 and 1993, this document identified accounts payable as a "high risk" audit area. The audit program for the 1992 audit included two key audit procedures for accounts payable:

a. Perform a search for unrecorded liabilities at April 30, 1992, through the end of field work.

b. Obtain copies of the April 30, 1992, vendor statements for CBI's five largest vendors, and examine reconciliations to the accounts payable balances for such vendors as shown on the books of CBI.

The 1993 audit program included these same items, although that program required audit procedure "b" to be applied to CBI's 10 largest vendors.

During the 1992 audit, the E&Y auditors discovered numerous disbursements made by CBI in the first few weeks of fiscal 1993 that were potential unrecorded liabilities as of April 30, 1992. The bulk of these disbursements included payments to the company's vendors that had been labeled as "advances" in the company's accounting records. CBI personnel provided the following explanation for these advances when questioned by the auditors: "When CBI is at its credit limit with a large vendor, the vendor may hold an order until they receive an 'advance.' CBI then applies the advance to the existing A/P balance."

In truth, the so-called advances, which totaled nearly $2 million, were simply payments CBI made to its vendors for inventory purchases consummated on, or prior to, April 30, 1992. Castello and his confederates had chosen not to record these transactions–their purpose being to strengthen key financial ratios of CBI at the end of fiscal 1992 and otherwise embellish the company's apparent financial condition. The conspirators developed the advances ruse because they feared that E&Y would discover the material understatements of accounts payable at year-end.

Subsequent court testimony revealed that after reviewing internal documents supporting the advances explanation–documents that had been prepared to deceive

---

2. This and all subsequent quotes were taken from the following court opinion: *In re CBI Holding Company, Inc., et al., Debtors; Bankruptcy Services, Inc., Plaintiff–against–Ernst & Young, Ernst & Young, LLP, Defendants;* 247 B.R. 341; 2000 Bankr. LEXIS 425.

3. The CBI audit engagement partner noted during the 1993 audit that the company's CFO appeared to be "afraid of his boss, Castello." When questioned by an auditor regarding an important issue, the CFO typically responded by telling the individual to "ask Castello." In the audit partner's view, this raised an "integrity red flag."

E&Y—the E&Y auditors readily accepted that explanation and chose not to treat the items as unrecorded liabilities. This decision prompted severe criticism of the audit firm by Judge Lifland.

The federal judge pointed out that the auditors had failed to rigorously investigate the alleged advances and to consider the veracity of the client's explanation for them. For example, the auditors did not investigate the "credit limit" feature of that explanation. The E&Y auditors neglected to determine the credit limit that the given vendors had established for CBI or whether CBI had "maxed out" that credit limit in each case as maintained by client personnel. Nor did the auditors attempt to analyze the given vendors' payable accounts or contact those vendors directly to determine if the alleged advances applied to specific invoice amounts, particularly invoice amounts for purchases made on or before April 30, 1992. Instead, the auditors simply chose to record in their workpapers the client's feeble explanation for the advances, an explanation that failed to address or resolve a critical issue. "The advance explanation recorded in E&Y's workpapers, even if it were true, did not tell the E&Y auditor the essential fact as to whether the merchandise being paid for by the advance had been received before or after April 30, 1992."

Because of the lack of any substantive investigation of the advances, the E&Y auditors failed to determine "whether a liability should have been recorded for each such payment as of fiscal year-end, and whether, in fact, a liability was recorded for such payment as of fiscal year-end." This finding caused Judge Lifland to conclude that E&Y had not properly completed the search for unrecorded liabilities. The judge reached a similar conclusion regarding the second major audit procedure for accounts payable included in the 1992 audit program for CBI.

The 1992 audit program required the E&Y auditors to obtain the year-end statements sent to CBI by the company's five largest vendors and to reconcile the balances in each of those statements to the corresponding balances reported in CBI's accounting records. E&Y obtained year-end statements mailed to CBI by five of the company's several hundred vendors and completed the reconciliation audit procedure. However, the vendors involved in this audit test were not the company's five largest suppliers. In fact, E&Y never identified CBI's five largest vendors during the 1992 audit. The federal judge scolded E&Y for this oversight and maintained that the "minimal" amount of testing applied by E&Y to the small sample of year-end vendor statements was "not adequate."

The audit procedures that E&Y applied to CBI's year-end accounts payable for fiscal 1993 suffered from the same flaws evident during the firm's 1992 audit. Similar to the previous year, CBI's management attempted to conceal unrecorded liabilities at year-end by labeling subsequent payments of those amounts as "advances" to the given vendors. Once more, Judge Lifland noted that the "gullible" auditors readily accepted the explanation for these advances that was relayed to them by CBI personnel. As a result, the auditors failed to require CBI to prepare appropriate adjusting entries for approximately $7.5 million of year-end payables that the client's management team had intentionally ignored.

The 1993 audit program mandated that E&Y obtain the year-end statements for CBI's 10 largest vendors and reconcile the balances in those statements to the corresponding accounts payable balances in CBI's accounting records. Again, E&Y failed to identify CBI's largest vendors and simply applied the reconciliation procedure to a sample of 10 CBI vendors.[4]

---

4. The court opinion that provided the background information for this case did not indicate what criteria E&Y used to select the vendor accounts to which the reconciliation procedure was applied in the 1992 and 1993 audits.

One of CBI's 10 largest vendors was Burroughs-Wellcome. If the E&Y auditors had reconciled the balance due Burroughs-Wellcome in its year-end statement with the corresponding account payable balance in CBI's accounting records, the auditors would have discovered that a $1 million "advance" payment made to that vendor in May 1993 was actually for an inventory purchase two weeks prior to April 30, 1993. This discovery would have clearly established that the $1 million amount was an unrecorded liability at year-end.

E&Y Held Responsible for CBI's Bankruptcy

In March 1994, E&Y withdrew its opinions on CBI's 1992 and 1993 financial statements after learning of the material distortions in those statements that were due to Castello's fraudulent scheme. Almost immediately, CBI began encountering difficulty obtaining trade credit from its principal vendors. A few months later in August 1994, the company filed for bankruptcy. In early 2000, Judge Lifland presided over a 17-day trial in federal bankruptcy court to determine whether E&Y would be held responsible for the large losses that CBI's collapse inflicted on TCW and CBI's former creditors. Near the conclusion of that trial, Judge Lifland ruled that E&Y's conduct during the 1992 and 1993 CBI audits was the "proximate cause" of those losses.

> *The demise of CBI was a foreseeable consequence of E&Y's failure to conduct its audits in fiscal 1992 and 1993 in accordance with GAAS, which was the cause of its failure to detect the unrecorded liabilities, which in turn foreseeably caused it to withdraw its opinions in March 1994. As direct and reasonably foreseeable consequences thereof, CBI's vendors restricted the amount of credit available, CBI's inventory and sales declined, its revenues declined, its value as a going concern diminished, and ultimately it filed for bankruptcy and was liquidated.*

Judge Lifland characterized E&Y's conduct as either "reckless and/or grossly negligent" and identified several generally accepted auditing standards that the accounting firm violated while performing the 1992 and 1993 CBI audits. Although the bulk of the judge's opinion dealt with the audit procedures E&Y applied to CBI's accounts payable, his harshest criticism focused on the firm's alleged failure to retain its independence during the CBI engagements.

Several circumstances that arose during E&Y's tenure as CBI's audit firm called into question its independence. For example, Judge Lifland referred to an incident in 1993 when Robert Castello demanded that E&Y remove the audit manager assigned to the CBI engagement. Apparently, Castello found the audit manager's inquisitive and probing nature disturbing. The CBI audit engagement partner "submissively acquiesced" to Castello's request and replaced the audit manager.

Shortly after the completion of the 1993 audit, Castello hired a new chief financial officer (CFO). This individual resigned eight days later. The CFO told members of the E&Y audit team he was resigning because of several million dollars of "grey accounting" he had discovered in CBI's accounting records. Judge Lifland chided E&Y for being slow to pursue this allegation. Nearly five months passed before the CBI audit engagement partner contacted the former CFO. By that point, E&Y had already discovered Castello's fraudulent scheme and withdrawn its 1992 and 1993 audit opinions.

In February 1994, the audit engagement partner met with Castello to discuss several matters. E&Y's unpaid bill for prior services provided to CBI was the first of those matters, while the second issue discussed was E&Y's fee for the upcoming audit. The last topic on the agenda was the allegation by CBI's former CFO regarding the company's questionable accounting decisions. According to Judge Lifland, the audit partner "wanted to speak to [the former CFO] in order to ask him whether his leaving the post of chief financial officer and his allegations of 'grey accounting' had anything to do with the financial statements that E&Y had just certified; however, [the audit partner] obligingly allowed himself to be put off." In Judge Lifland's opinion, the E&Y audit partner was "more concerned about insuring E&Y's fees than he was about speaking to [the former CFO]."

The final matter Judge Lifland discussed in impugning E&Y's independence was the accounting firm's effort to retain CBI as an audit client after discovering that the 1992 and 1993 audits had been deficient. Judge Lifland charged that E&Y officials realized when they withdrew the audit opinions on CBI's 1992 and 1993 financial statements that the CBI audits had been flawed. In the days prior to withdrawing those opinions, two individuals, a former CBI accountant and CBI's controller at the time, informed E&Y that the "advances" discovered during the 1992 and 1993 audits had been for payment of unrecorded liabilities that existed at the end of CBI's 1992 and 1993 fiscal years. After investigating these admissions, E&Y determined that they were true. E&Y also determined that the CBI auditors "had failed to detect the unrecorded liabilities because they had failed to properly perform the search [for unrecorded liabilities]."

E&Y failed to notify CBI's board of directors of the flaws in the 1992 and 1993 audits.[5] According to Judge Lifland, E&Y did not inform the board members of those flaws because the accounting firm realized that doing so would lower, if not eliminate, its chance of landing the "reaudit" engagement for CBI's 1992 and 1993 financial statements. "E&Y's egocentric desire to get the reaudit work is illustrated by the fact that it prepared an audit program for the reaudit two days before E&Y met with the CBI board of directors and one day before they withdrew their opinion."

CBI's board ultimately selected E&Y to reaudit the company's 1992 and 1993 financial statements. Given the circumstances under which E&Y obtained that engagement, Judge Lifland concluded that the accounting firm's independence was likely impaired. "Thus, E&Y knew prior to agreeing to perform the reaudit work that it had not complied with GAAS. E&Y also knew that CBI's board of directors did not know of E&Y's failure to comply with GAAS. It is reasonable to infer that if CBI's board of directors knew of such failure, E&Y and CBI would be in adversarial positions."[6]

Questions

1. Most of Judge Lifland's criticism of E&Y focused on the firm's audit procedures for CBI's accounts payable. Generally, what is the primary audit objective for accounts payable? Do you believe that E&Y's two principal audit tests for CBI's accounts payable would have accomplished that objective if those tests had been properly applied? Why or why not?

2. Do you believe that the E&Y auditors should have used confirmations in auditing CBI's year-end accounts payable? Defend your answer. Briefly explain the differing audit objectives related to accounts receivable and accounts payable confirmation procedures and the key differences in how these procedures are applied.

---

5. At this point, the TCW representatives on CBI's board were apparently the company's principal decision makers.

6. The plaintiffs in this case were initially awarded a judgment of approximately $70 million. E&Y appealed that judgment, an appeal that prompted what one legal expert referred to as a decade-long "epic battle" in the appellate courts. In late 2010, Judge Lifland brokered a settlement to end that court battle. The amount paid by E&Y to the plaintiffs to settle the case was apparently never reported publicly.

3. In early 1994, E&Y officials discovered that the CBI auditors had failed to determine the true nature of the "advances" they had uncovered during the 1992 and 1993 audits. In your view, did E&Y have an obligation to inform CBI management of this oversight prior to seeking the "reaudit" engagement? More generally, does an auditor have a responsibility to inform client management of mistakes or oversights made on earlier audits?

4. Under what circumstances, if any, should an audit engagement partner acquiesce to a client's request to remove a member of the audit engagement team?

5. E&Y officials believed that the CBI audits were high-risk engagements. Under what general circumstances should an audit firm choose not to accept a high-risk engagement?

Geo Securities, Inc.

In 1980, Frank Sinopoli, a 27-year-old accountant, accepted a job offer from a CPA firm based in Dallas, Texas. Four years later, Sinopoli became a partner with the firm. Perkins, Dexter, Sinopoli & Hamm (PDSH) provided accounting and accounting-related services to small- and medium-sized businesses located principally in the Dallas–Fort Worth Metroplex. During his long tenure with PDSH, Sinopoli supervised a wide range of engagements. Those engagements included the 2000 through 2005 audits of a small brokerage firm, Geo Securities, Inc.

Geo Companies of North America (GCNA), a Dallas-based oil and gas exploration company, organized Geo Securities as a wholly-owned subsidiary in June 1996. The sole business purpose of Geo Securities was to market interests in oil and gas properties owned or controlled by GCNA. Similar to GCNA, Geo Securities was not a public company. However, because Geo Securities was a registered broker-dealer with the Securities and Exchange Commission (SEC), its annual financial statements had to be audited by an independent accounting firm.

Throughout the six-year period that Sinopoli supervised the annual audits of Geo Securities, the company was entangled in two civil lawsuits filed in a federal district court in Georgia. The two principal defendants in these lawsuits were GCNA and Geo Securities. The primary allegation filed against the defendants was that they had "fraudulently offered and sold"[1] joint partnership interests in oil and gas properties.

In 2004, the Georgia federal court ordered the defendants to pay a nominal amount of damages, approximately $217,000, to the plaintiffs to settle the two civil lawsuits. The court also appointed an arbitrator to determine whether the plaintiffs would be entitled to recover some or all of their sizable attorneys' fees from the defendants. In April 2005, three months before Geo Securities' 2005 fiscal year-end of July 31, 2005, the arbitrator ruled that GCNA, Geo Securities, and the other defendants in the civil lawsuits—who were individuals affiliated with the two companies—would be required to reimburse the plaintiffs for $949,688 of legal fees they had incurred in pursuing the case. The defendants were jointly and severally liable for those legal fees. GCNA had informed Geo Securities and the other defendants that it would pay the $217,000 settlement but did not make such a commitment regarding the much larger arbitration award.

GCNA, Geo Securities, and the other defendants appealed the 2004 court-ordered settlement and filed a challenge to the 2005 arbitration decision. Because Geo Securities' management believed that GCNA would pay the full amount of the arbitration award, if it was not overturned, the company did not record a contingent liability or loss related to that award in its accounting records. Instead, the company disclosed the arbitration award in a financial statement footnote accompanying its 2005 financial statements (see Exhibit 1).

---

1. This and all subsequent quotes were taken from the following source: Securities and Exchange Commission, *Accounting and Auditing Enforcement Release No. 2979*, 27 May 2009.

EXHIBIT 1

LOSS
CONTINGENCIES
FOOTNOTE
ACCOMPANYING
GEO SECURITIES'
2005 FINANCIAL
STATEMENTS

NOTE EIGHT—LOSS CONTINGENCIES

During 2000 and 2002, two separate lawsuits were filed against the Company (Geo Securities), GCNA, and other related parties by individuals in Georgia. The suits allege that the Company violated applicable security laws. During the fiscal year ended July 31, 2005, the trial judge granted a motion to enforce a contested settlement and ordered the issue of the plaintiffs' attorney fees to be resolved at arbitration. The arbitrator determined that $949,688 in attorney fees should be paid by the Company, GCNA, and the other related parties. The judge construed that a settlement agreement had been reached. This settlement agreement is currently being appealed. Additionally, the Company, GCNA, and other related parties have sued the plaintiffs and their attorneys for unrelated claims not related to the Georgia lawsuits. Management believes that the original suits are without merit and are vigorously defending its position in both lawsuits. The Company, GCNA, and the other related parties feel the original claims have no merit.

Geo Securities reported total assets of $155,183, total liabilities of $12,441, and total stockholder's equity of $142,742 in its July 31, 2005, balance sheet. The company's income statement for the year ended July 31, 2005, reflected total revenues of $551,131 and a net loss of $100,167. The unqualified opinion that PDSH issued on Geo Securities' 2005 financial statements is shown in Exhibit 2.

EXHIBIT 2

AUDIT REPORT
ISSUED BY PDSH ON
GEO SECURITIES'
2005 FINANCIAL
STATEMENTS

To the Board of Directors

GEO SECURITIES, INC.

Dallas, Texas

Independent Auditors' Report

We have audited the accompanying statement of financial condition of GEO SECURITIES, INC. as of July 31, 2005, and the related statements of income, changes in stockholder's equity, and cash flows for the year then ended that you are filing pursuant to Rule 17a-5 under the Securities Exchange Act of 1934. These financial statements are the responsibility of the Company's management. Our responsibility is to express an opinion on these financial statements based on our audit.

We conducted our audit in accordance with auditing standards generally accepted in the United States of America. Those standards require that we plan and perform the audit to obtain reasonable assurance about whether the financial statements are free of material misstatement. An audit includes examining, on a test basis, evidence supporting the amounts and disclosures in the financial statements. An audit also includes assessing the accounting principles used and significant estimates made by management, as well as evaluating the overall financial statement presentation. We believe that our audit provides a reasonable basis for our opinion.

In our opinion, the financial statements referred to above present fairly, in all material respects, the financial position of GEO SECURITIES, INC. at July 31, 2005, and the results of its operations and its cash flows for the year then ended in conformity with accounting principles generally accepted in the United States of America.

Our audit was conducted for the purpose of forming an opinion on the basic financial statements taken as a whole. The supplemental information presented in Schedule

EXHIBIT 2–
continued

AUDIT REPORT
ISSUED BY PDSH ON
GEO SECURITIES'
2005 FINANCIAL
STATEMENTS

1–Computation of Net Capital Pursuant to Rule 15c3-1 and Schedule 2–Exemptive Provision of Rule 15c3-3 is presented for the purposes of additional analysis and is not a required part of the basic financial statements, but is supplementary information required by Rule 17a-5 under the Securities Exchange Act of 1934. Such information has been subjected to the audit procedures applied in the examination of the basic financial statements, and, in our opinion, is fairly stated in all material respects in relation to the basic financial statements taken as a whole.

Perkins, Dexter, Sinopoli & Hamm, PC [signed]

Richardson, Texas

September 30, 2005

In May 2009, the SEC ruled that Geo Securities' 2005 financial statements were materially misstated because they "failed to include a material liability for the Arbitrator's award." The SEC pointed out that generally accepted accounting principles (GAAP) require companies to record a loss and a liability in their accounting records for a loss contingency that is both probable and subject to reasonable estimation. Since the arbitration award met both criteria and since the defendants in the lawsuit were jointly and severally liable, the SEC deemed that Geo Securities should have reported a loss and corresponding liability of $949,688 in its 2005 financial statements.

Compounding this error was Geo Securities' failure to consider the arbitration award when computing its "net capital." Registered broker-dealers must include a "computation of net capital" schedule with their audited financial statements that they file each year with the SEC. The purpose of this schedule is to demonstrate that a broker-dealer has sufficient equity to sustain its operations. In this schedule, broker-dealers must make certain adjustments to the stockholders' equity reported in their audited balance sheets to arrive at a more conservative (lower) net capital figure.[2] In computing its net capital, Geo Securities did not consider the large contingent loss stemming from the arbitration award, which was not surprising given the accounting treatment it applied to that award.[3]

The SEC also sanctioned Frank Sinopoli for failing to properly audit Geo Securities' 2005 financial statements and the net capital schedule that accompanied those statements. According to the SEC, Sinopoli was fully aware of the arbitration award when he planned and performed the 2005 Geo Securities audit. In fact, Sinopoli "assisted" Geo Securities management when it was deciding whether to record the award as a loss and liability in the company's 2005 financial statements or simply disclose the arbitration award in the accompanying financial statement footnotes.

Despite Sinopoli's awareness of Geo Securities' litigation problems, he did not identify "litigation, claims, and assessments as an area of significant risk" while planning the 2005 audit. Sinopoli also did not identify the attorneys representing Geo Securities in those legal matters, nor did he request that Geo Securities "send an audit inquiry letter" to those attorneys.

The SEC also criticized Sinopoli for relying on a representation made by Geo Securities' president that GCNA, Geo Securities' parent company, would ultimately pay

---

2. Among many other items, these adjustments include reductions for "non-allowable" or illiquid assets.

3. Geo Securities did include a supplementary disclosure in its net capital schedule that referred to "contingent indebtedness" equal to the full amount of the arbitration award.

the arbitration award in full if the effort to overturn that award proved unsuccessful. That representation was particularly relevant to Geo Securities' status as a going concern. In fact, the SEC reported that during the 2005 audit Sinopoli did not explicitly consider whether Geo Securities was a going concern. Sinopoli "failed to evaluate GSI's ability to continue as a going concern, failed to obtain additional information about the conditions raising the concerns and failed to evaluate management's plans for dealing with the adverse effects of the conditions raising the concerns, as required by GAAS."

The SEC maintained that, at a minimum, Sinopoli should have corresponded with GCNA to determine whether it intended to pay the arbitration award, as claimed by Geo Securities' president. Since GCNA was also a client of PDSH, Sinopoli could have easily contacted the company regarding that matter. The SEC noted that when Geo Securities subsequently disclosed its net capital deficiency in January 2006, GCNA failed to intervene, resulting in Geo Securities being forced out of business.

A final complaint lodged against Sinopoli by the SEC was his failure to identify the impact of the arbitration award on Geo Securities' net capital computation in the supplemental schedule accompanying its 2005 financial statements. As reflected in Exhibit 2, Sinopoli's 2005 audit opinion indicated that the information in that schedule was "fairly stated in all material respects in relation to the basic financial statements taken as a whole." In contrast to Sinopoli's conclusion, the SEC ruled that Geo Securities' net capital computation was "materially misstated" since it ignored the large contingent loss due to the arbitration award.

In a May 2009 *Accounting and Auditing Enforcement Release*, the SEC summarized its overall conclusions regarding Sinopoli's 2005 audit of Geo Securities.

Sinopoli failed to conduct the 2005 GSI [Geo Securities] audit in accordance with GAAS. Among other things, he failed to exercise professional skepticism and failed to obtain sufficient evidential matter to evaluate adequately and report properly the Arbitrator's award in GSI's financial statements. Furthermore, Sinopoli's work papers fail to evaluate GSI's ability to continue as a going concern. Nonetheless, Sinopoli signed, on behalf of PDSH, an audit report dated September 30, 2005, containing an unqualified opinion incorrectly claiming that PDSH's audit of GSI's July 31, 2005, financial statements had been conducted in accordance with GAAS. The opinion also incorrectly claims that GSI's audited financial statements present fairly, in all material respects, the financial position of GSI in conformity with GAAP.

The sanctions imposed on Sinopoli included a cease and desist order prohibiting him from any future violations of the federal securities laws and a one-year suspension from practicing before the SEC.

Questions

1. When auditing contingent liabilities, which of the management assertions discussed in the professional auditing standards are of primary concern to an auditor? Explain.

2. The SEC criticized Frank Sinopoli for not sending an "audit inquiry letter" to Geo Securities' external legal counsel. Describe the nature and purpose of such a letter. Do you agree with the SEC that Sinopoli should have contacted Geo Securities' external legal counsel?

3. Under what circumstances must audit procedures be applied to supplemental information accompanying a client's financial statements? Describe the responsibilities auditors have when auditing such information.

4. Under what circumstances, if any, are auditors required to assess the going-concern status of an audit client? What procedures should auditors apply when performing such an assessment?

Belot Enterprises

As David Robinson works his way through the large, festive crowd, he keeps bumping into people he knows. All the while, Robinson is hoping that he will avoid the one person he doesn't want to meet face to face.[1]

Belot Enterprises' several hundred employees and their family members are celebrating July the 4th with a corporate picnic. For the occasion, the company reserved a municipal park perched on the bank of the Mississippi River in a Minneapolis suburb. The corporate picnic actually serves two purposes. In addition to celebrating July the 4th, Belot's employees are marking the end of the successful corporate-wide "Nail the Number" campaign.

The campaign was the brain child of Kyle Allen, Belot's chief operating officer (COO) who joined the company six months ago. Allen was handpicked for the COO position by the top management of Helterbrand Associates, Belot's parent company. Helterbrand is a large, publicly-owned conglomerate with five wholly-owned subsidiaries that operate in five diverse industries.

Belot, a consumer products company, accounts for approximately one-third of Helterbrand's annual revenues and consolidated assets. During the previous several years, however, Belot has never accounted for more than 10 percent of Helterbrand's consolidated operating income. Two decades ago, Belot was the flagship of the Helterbrand corporate family. Declining profit margins in Belot's mature and intensely competitive industry have caused the company's profitability to gradually erode despite slow but persistent growth in its annual revenues.

Allen, a 38-year-old Harvard MBA who established himself as a corporate turn-around specialist in the automotive supplies industry, was hired to reinvigorate Belot. After spending several weeks studying all facets of Belot's operations, Allen organized the Nail the Number campaign for the company's second quarter–April 1 through June 30. The goal of the campaign was to increase Belot's year-over-year quarterly operating income by 100 percent. Although that goal seemed impressive, it was not earthshaking since the company had earned a very modest, even by recent historical standards, operating income during the previous year's second quarter.

The tactics employed by Allen during the three-month campaign were also not earthshaking. They included focusing Belot's marketing efforts on products with relatively high profit margins, incentive-based compensation programs for the company's sales staff, and a variety of corporate-wide cost-cutting initiatives.

When David Robinson learned of the details of the Nail the Number campaign, he was not impressed. In his mind, the company should have implemented each of those strategic measures long ago. Then again, as a member of Belot's audit engagement team, Robinson recognized that his responsibilities did not include openly critiquing corporate management or its policies.

Detox and Grizz

In two months, David Robinson will mark his fourth anniversary with the Big Four accounting firm that serves as the independent auditor of Helterbrand Associates

---

1. This case was developed from an actual series of events. Certain background information has been changed to conceal the identities of the individuals involved in the case.

and each of its five subsidiaries, including Belot Enterprises. During the past spring, Robinson completed his fourth busy season assigned to the Belot engagement. Since joining the firm after graduating with bachelor's and master's degrees in accounting from the University of Minnesota, 60 percent of Robinson's chargeable hours have been spent working at Belot.

Robinson has spent so much time at Belot's headquarters office on the northern edge of Minneapolis that he often feels as if he is an employee rather than an independent auditor of the firm. As he surveys the large throng of people attending the company's July 4th picnic, Robinson isn't sure that it is appropriate for him to be there. But the Belot audit engagement partner, R.B. Hansen, insisted that he attend the event.

The person that Robinson is hoping to avoid at the picnic is Belot's accounting general manager, Zachariah Crabtree. As the current in-charge senior on the audit team, Robinson interacts with Crabtree on an almost daily basis. The two men have an excellent relationship. In fact, over the previous few years, Robinson and Crabtree have become good friends, so much so that they regularly refer to each other using the nicknames–Detox and Grizz, respectively, that each was tagged with at the University of Minnesota.

Crabtree is a huge man, six-feet five-inches tall with a sturdy frame and girth. In his early forties, he wears old-fashioned, black plastic-framed glasses that have lenses as thick as the bottom of a Coke bottle and sports an unruly head of bushy, prematurely gray hair. Making Grizz–short for "grizzly bear"–stand out even more in a crowd is his Johnny Cash–like insistence on wearing black. His standard workday attire is a pair of black cowboy boots, black denim jeans, a black button-down shirt, and a garish tie–the maroon and gold colors of the University of Minnesota's Golden Gophers are his favorite hues when it comes to ties.

Topping off Grizz's imposing persona is a dour expression that seems to convey that he is perpetually unhappy, if not chronically sociopathic. In truth, Crabtree is a kind and likable person with a dry sense of humor, who despite his unconventional appearance is well respected by both his superiors and subordinates.

Unlike Crabtree, Robinson could easily be mistaken for a Ralph Lauren model. The audit senior is a tall, handsome, athletically built 27-year-old who wears a stylish suit to work each day along with a starched, white button-down Polo shirt that is accessorized with a matching Polo tie. Robinson has a gregarious, outgoing personality. As for as his nickname, "Detox" is not a reference to any personal shortcomings but simply a jazzed-up version of the initials of his first and middle names given to him by his fraternity brothers.

Despite being so different in appearance and temperament, Robinson and Crabtree share one interest that bind them together. Both are certified sports fanatics. Each is a long-suffering fan of the various athletic teams fielded by the Golden Gophers and the local professional sports franchises, most notably the purple-clad Minnesota Vikings. The two sports aficionados typically start each conversation with the latest sports controversy being fueled by ESPN.

Nailing the Number the Easy Way

During his time at Belot, there have been few disputes between Robinson and Crabtree over accounting matters. Sit-down discussions involving the two accountants have centered on topics such as dollar-value LIFO, foreign currency translations, and impairment of long-lived assets. Robinson is grateful to Crabtree for his patience and willingness to explain the finer points of complex accounting issues despite his busy work schedule.

Robinson and Crabtree recently experienced their first truly unpleasant confrontation over an accounting issue, which explains why Robinson is hoping that he doesn't encounter Crabtree at the picnic. That dispute stemmed from Kyle Allen's Nail the Number campaign.

Crabtree is extremely loyal to Belot. He is concerned that if Belot's operating results don't improve soon, Helterbrand's top management may decide to sell the company outright or, even worse, split it up and sell it on a piecemeal basis. Crabtree once confided in Robinson that if the company is jettisoned by Helterbrand, he will probably lose his job and have difficulty finding a comparable position in the area. Like Robinson, Crabtree has strong family and emotional ties to the state of Minnesota and to the Minneapolis–St. Paul metroplex.

Over the past three months, Crabtree wore one of the promotional stickers for the Nail the Number campaign on his shirt pocket each day. The stickers, which feature a cartoonish icon of a large hammer posed over a dollar sign, were distributed to all of Belot's employees but few actually wore them.

Crabtree came up with his own personal contribution to the Nail the Number campaign by deciding to tighten the company's major discretionary accruals as of June 30. Those accruals include the allowances for bad debts, coupon redemptions, employee vacations, inventory obsolescence, and product warranties. Crabtree defends his decision by pointing out that in the past Belot's controller, Travis Logan, instructed him to err on the side of conservatism in establishing the accruals, meaning that each of them have been routinely overstated by a modest amount. Crabtree maintains that he is simply reducing the accruals to their appropriate levels.

Robinson rarely speaks with Logan who, like Crabtree, has spent his entire professional career with Belot. Only a few years away from retirement, Logan is a straight-laced, no-nonsense accountant who can quote specific passages from key accounting standards. Robinson particularly admires Logan because of his exemplary personal life. Logan spends hundreds of hours each year working as a volunteer and fund raiser for a local charity that operates a private school for disabled children.

Crabtree's decision to record relatively modest June 30th balances for the five discretionary accruals has created a rift between himself and Logan. When he made that decision, Crabtree did something very uncharacteristic for him, namely, bypassing Logan, his immediate superior, and discussing the matter directly with Kyle Allen. Allen responded enthusiastically to Crabtree's proposal and agreed that all of the "fat" should be cut out of the accruals. He then sent an e-mail to Logan telling him that he approved Crabtree's decision.

After receiving the e-mail, Logan immediately met with Allen and voiced his disapproval. At that point, Allen reportedly told Logan point blank that the accruals would be reduced whether he liked it or not. When Logan continued to object, Allen told him that Crabtree would have complete authority for establishing the period-ending balances of the accruals for the foreseeable future. Not surprisingly, Allen's decision made Logan livid. Robinson had heard rumors that Logan is considering submitting his resignation as a result of the incident.

Allen's actions have confirmed Robinson's perception that Belot's new COO is its *de facto* chief executive officer (CEO). Allen apparently has *carte blanche* authority from the top management of Helterbrand Associates to do whatever is necessary to improve Belot's operating results.

The controversy over the period-ending accruals has cast a tense pall over Belot's corporate accounting staff. Each member of that staff has effectively been forced to side with either Logan or Crabtree who are barely speaking to each other. Robinson feels as if he is being forced to make the same choice. Although he seldom interacts with Logan, he does sit down with him during each audit and quarterly review to discuss the major "hot spots" in Belot's financial statements.

Robinson realizes that if Logan resigns, Crabtree will likely be chosen to replace him. He is also convinced that Crabtree's decision to reduce the accruals was not motivated by his desire to replace Logan. Robinson believes that Crabtree is a man of honesty and integrity and that his actions were motivated strictly by his desire to help save Belot.

The most troubling aspect of the accrual controversy for Robinson is its impact on Belot's second-quarter operating results. Kyle Allen's Nail the Number campaign was successful. In fact, just yesterday, the day before the corporate picnic, Allen circulated an e-mail to all Belot employees thanking them for making the campaign an "unmitigated, flabbergasting success"–his exact words. Belot's operating income for the just completed quarter is 140 percent higher than the corresponding figure for the prior year's second quarter. Granted, Allen included a brief caveat in the e-mail indicating that the second-quarter numbers are not yet "official," meaning that the auditors have not yet signed off on them.

Robinson has determined that the reductions in the five discretionary accruals at the end of the second quarter account for approximately 70 percent of the improvement in Belot's year-over-year operating results. If Travis Logan's "conservative" strategy was used in establishing those accruals, Robinson estimates that Belot would post a modest 40 percent increase in its second-quarter operating income, considerably less than the 100 percent goal targeted by Allen for the Nail the Number campaign.

Conservatism vs. Precision

Robinson reviewed Belot's major discretionary accruals while performing analytical procedures on the company's preliminary second-quarter financial statements. It was then that he found that each of the accruals was smaller than expected given the relevant benchmark amount. For example, the allowance for bad debts is a smaller than normal percentage of the period-ending balance of accounts receivable. Robinson immediately went to Crabtree's office to ask him about the unexpectedly modest discretionary accruals. In response to Robinson's inquiry, Crabtree told him of a new "precise point estimate" method that he had used to establish those accruals.

"'Precise point estimate'? What's that?" Robinson had asked.

"Just what it implies. We're using the best available information we have to arrive at a precise point estimate of each of those accruals."

"So Grizz, you're saying that the method you used the previous 419 quarters was wrong?" Robinson had used his normal lighthearted style in posing the question to Crabtree. He was surprised when Crabtree seemed offended.

"Yeah, they were wrong. Just like the rest of the numbers we feed you high and mighty and holier-than-thou auditors constantly," Crabtree had snapped.

"Well, hey Grizz, there's no reason to bite my head off. You know, I have a job to do."

"Detox, I know what your *job* is. Your job is to scan the second-quarter numbers during a coffee break, rack up a few hours of chargeable time, and then call your bosses and tell them that everything looks okay. Right?"

"Well, I think a quarterly review is a little more involved than that." Before Robinson could continue, Crabtree had cut him off.

"There you are. Key word 'review.' All you have to do is 'review' those numbers. You don't have to rip them apart or *audit* them. Right?"

Crabtree's impertinence had caused Robinson to adopt a more professional demeanor. Over the following 10 to 15 minutes, the two men had an even-handed, frank discussion of the method Belot had used in the past to compute the discretionary accruals, the method that had been used to compute them at the end of the just-completed second quarter, and the reason for the change.

During their discussion, Crabtree had repeatedly defied Robinson to prove that the "precise point estimate" method he had used to determine the accruals was improper in any way or resulted in a violation of generally accepted accounting principles. Crabtree insisted that all he had done was eliminate what Travis Logan had always referred to as the "add-ons" to "fudge" those numbers a little higher than they should be. The tone of the discussion became tense when Robinson asked Crabtree about the connection between Kyle Allen's Nail the Number campaign and the more modest accrual balances.

"Allen didn't have anything to do with this. This didn't start with him. This was my idea. Everyone around here has been busting their behind over the past three months to keep this ship from sinking. I thought I should do my part too."

Near the end of his meeting with Crabtree, Robinson had mentioned matter-of-factly that he would have to discuss the accruals with Anna Bledsoe, the audit manager for the Belot engagement, and, ultimately, with R.B. Hansen, both of whom were out of town but would be returning on July 5th. Crabtree had grimaced at that point and shook his head in disgust.

"Come on, Detox. There's no reason to try to score some points for yourself by bringing this up with either of them. Why make trouble for yourself, for them, and for me? This is a non-issue. We haven't done anything wrong. The numbers are okay." When Robinson didn't reply immediately, Crabtree had continued. "Hey, if you pass on these accruals, no one will ever be the wiser. There is no way you can argue that any of them are individually 'wrong' or 'materially inaccurate' or whatever. So, just drop it and go play golf this afternoon." Ironically, the more desperate Crabtree had become in defending the accruals, the more worried Robinson had become that the accruals were a problem.

Crabtree was unaware that his comment regarding "scoring points" had struck close to home for Robinson. Over the past four years, Robinson seldom gave much thought to any career planning initiatives. Instead, he simply plodded along, completing each assignment given to him. Robinson reserved most of his energy and enthusiasm for his principal "outside" interest, namely, sports. When he wasn't rooting for the Golden Gophers or the Vikings, he was playing golf or tennis or managing one of his many fantasy sports teams.

Two recent incidents, however, have made Robinson dwell at length for the first time on his future in the accounting profession. First, he realized that as his four-year anniversary with his employer approached, he was one of the few members of his "start class" still with the firm. Nearly all of his former colleagues have moved on to other jobs, most of them higher-paying positions with clients. The second and more important event that caused him to think of his future was a lunch meeting a few weeks ago with R.B. Hansen.

During that lunch, Hansen encouraged Robinson to become more focused on his career and to devote himself more fully to his job. According to Hansen, Robinson's strong interpersonal skills are just what the firm is looking for in partner candidates. Hansen told Robinson he could use those skills to recruit new clients to the firm, a talent that is highly valued by existing partners, many of whom are not "natural communicators" or "marketing types."

Hansen's pep talk caused Robinson to seriously consider for the first time that he may be partner "material." Robinson has always possessed a remarkable degree of self-confidence. When he commits himself to accomplishing a goal, he always rises to the occasion. In his mind, there is no reason why he cannot become a partner with his firm if he adopts that objective as a personal and career goal.

Prior to his meeting with Hansen, Robinson would very likely have just "gone along" with Zachariah Crabtree's suggestion that he "pass" on the June 30th discretionary accruals. But now that he realizes he is potential partner material, his outlook on his job has changed suddenly and dramatically.

Robinson doesn't want to do anything that would cause R.B. Hansen to perceive that he is "coasting" along as usual. In fact, standing up to Grizz, who Hansen knows he is very close to, would provide Robinson an opportunity to demonstrate to the partner that he has adopted a more professional mindset to his job and responsibilities.

Grizzly Sighting

Prior to the Belot company picnic, Robinson spent much of the two previous days stewing over his dilemma. He eventually settled on a compromise plan that would possibly appease Crabtree while at the same time allowing him to impress R.B. Hansen. His compromise, which he intends to discuss with Hansen before relaying it to Crabtree, involves requiring Belot to increase the June 30th balances of the allowances for bad debts and inventory obsolescence to more normal levels, while allowing the company to use the "precise point estimates" for the other three discretionary accruals. Robinson realizes that Hansen is most concerned with the bad debts and inventory obsolescence accruals since they have a "higher profile" in Belot's financial statements than the other accruals.

Robinson's compromise plan would reduce the year-over-year increase in Belot's operating income for the just-completed quarter from 140 percent to approximately 103 percent–slightly above the target figure that Allen established for the Nail the Number campaign. Although Robinson believes his compromise is reasonable, he is worried that Crabtree will react negatively to it.

Because he wants to avoid discussing the accruals issue with Crabtree at the picnic, Robinson has been scanning the clusters of people in front of him trying to spy Grizz's hulking figure as he works his way across the large park. Suddenly, Robinson feels a large hand clamp down on his shoulder from behind. As he turns around, he finds himself standing face to face with Zachariah Crabtree. Plastered across Grizz's chest are three creased and crinkled Nail the Number stickers.

Questions

1. Is David Robinson's suggested compromise appropriate? Why or why not?

2. Do you believe that Zachariah Crabtree is a person of integrity? What about David Robinson? Defend both of your answers. Does Robinson have an inappropriate relationship with Crabtree? Explain.

3. Identify the primary audit objectives for a client's year-end discretionary expense accruals. Is it permissible for companies to overstate period-ending expense accruals to make their financial statements more "conservative"?

4. Discuss the scope and nature of an auditor's responsibilities during a review of a client's quarterly financial statements.

Regina Company, Inc.

Donald Sheelen was born into a middle-class family in upstate New York in 1946. In high school, the handsome Sheelen was the prototype of the all-American boy, excelling in both academics and athletics. Following graduation, Sheelen attended the University of Dayton, where he was elected president of his senior class and named a Big Man on Campus. After earning an MBA from Syracuse University, Sheelen landed a job with a large Wall Street brokerage firm and then three years later accepted a middle-management position with Johnson & Johnson. In 1980, at the age of 34, Sheelen was hired by Regina Company, Inc., and placed in charge of the company's marketing department.

Regina was a wholly-owned subsidiary of the large conglomerate General Signal Corporation. Founded in Rahway, New Jersey, in 1892, Regina had originally been a music box manufacturer before entering the floor care industry in the early 1900s. Throughout most of its existence, Regina was known as a complacent, slow-growth company and was dominated within the floor care industry by Hoover and Eureka. Donald Sheelen quickly changed Regina's complacent image and tackled the sizable task of moving the company out of the shadows of its two larger competitors.

Cornflakes, Celebrity and Cash for Donald Sheelen

When Sheelen joined Regina, the company had annual sales approaching $60 million. The ambitious Sheelen was not satisfied with Regina's small share of the vacuum cleaner market or the fact that the company depended heavily on one product. He believed that for Regina to challenge Hoover and Eureka, the company had to expand its product line and dramatically increase its annual advertising expenditures. By 1984, Sheelen, who had been promoted to company president the previous year, had introduced a series of new Regina products, including a portable spa and an upright vacuum cleaner. To promote these and other new products, he poured millions of dollars into Regina's advertising budget. Eventually, the company's annual advertising expenditures exceeded 20 percent of its annual sales and eclipsed the combined advertising outlays of Hoover and Eureka.

Shortly after being appointed Regina's president, Sheelen announced that he intended to make Regina the industry's dominant firm by the end of the decade. He repeatedly vowed that Regina would "bomb" Hoover, the number one firm in the industry at the time. The exuberant executive even laid a Hoover doormat outside his office so that each day he could "walk over" his company's major rival.[1]

Sheelen became well known both inside and outside the floor care industry for his so-called cornflake routine that he often performed at trade shows and during news conferences. This routine involved sprinkling crushed cereal on a carpet and then demonstrating that a Regina vacuum cleaner did a much better job of cleaning up the mess than a comparable Hoover product. Sheelen converted this demonstration into a television advertisement and was promptly sued by Hoover. He was forced

---

1. J.A. Byrne, "How Don Sheelen Made a Mess That Regina Couldn't Clean Up," *Business Week*, 12 February 1990, 46–50.

EXHIBIT 1

REGINA COMPANY'S
1986–1988
FINANCIAL
STATEMENTS

Regina Company, Inc.
Balance Sheets 1986–1988 (000s omitted)

	1988	June 30, 1987	1986
Current Assets:			
Cash	$ 885	$ 514	$ 63
Receivables (net)	51,076	27,801	14,402
Inventories	39,135	19,577	9,762
Other Current Assets	3,015	1,449	708
Total Current Assets	94,111	49,341	24,935
Property, Plant and Equipment	21,548	14,788	16,383
Other Assets	2,481	1,112	1,884
Total Assets	$118,140	$65,241	$43,202
Current Liabilities:			
Short-term Borrowings	$ —	$ —	$2,707
Current Portion of Long-term Debt	1,250	900	—
Accounts Payable	13,288	15,072	7,344
Accrued Liabilities	4,710	5,468	3,127
Income Taxes Payable	3,782	2,619	1,554
Total Current Liabilities	23,030	24,059	14,732
Long-term Debt:			
Industrial Revenue Bonds	12,650	13,900	14,800
Mississippi State Debt	1,975	—	—
Bank Debt	47,432	5,941	—
Total Long-term Debt	62,057	19,841	14,800
Deferred Income Taxes	1,881	1,254	685
Stockholders' Equity:			
Common Stock	1	1	1
Additional Paid-in Capital	7,902	7,771	7,774
Retained Earnings	23,269	12,315	5,210
Total Stockholders' Equity	31,172	20,087	12,985
Total Liabilities and Stockholders' Equity	$ 118,140	$ 65,241	$43,202

to withdraw the ad from the airwaves after Hoover proved that the Regina vacuum cleaner used in the commercial had an industrial-strength suction that was not available on the model sold to retail customers.

In mid-1984, Sheelen and several other Regina executives bought a majority interest in the company via a leveraged buyout. Sheelen personally invested only $750,000 in the venture but emerged with more than a 50 percent equity interest in Regina, which had total assets approaching $40 million at the time. The following year, Sheelen and his partners took Regina public. Surging sales and profits quickly landed Regina on the "buy" lists of several large brokerage firms and tagged the company's

EXHIBIT 1–
continued

REGINA COMPANY'S
1986–1988
FINANCIAL
STATEMENTS

Regina Company, Inc.
Balance Sheets 1986–1988 (000s omitted)

	1988	June 30, 1987	1986
Net Sales	$181,123	$128,234	$76,144
Operating Costs and Expenses:			
Cost of Goods Sold	94,934	70,756	46,213
Selling, Distribution, and Administrative	21,870	14,621	10,366
Advertising	39,992	26,449	8,557
Research and Development	2,423	1,530	1,182
Total Operating Costs and Expenses	159,219	113,356	66,318
Operating Income	21,904	14,878	9,826
Interest Expense	3,189	1,584	1,930
Income Before Income Taxes	18,715	13,294	7,896
Income Tax Expense	7,761	6,189	3,807
Net Income	$ 10,954	$ 7,105	$ 4,089
Earnings per Share	$1.21	$.78	$.46

stock as a "can't miss" investment on Wall Street. In commenting on the company, one financial analyst noted, "Regina is not only an earnings play but an investment in a skilled management team that has turned the company around."[2] (Exhibit 1 presents Regina's balance sheets and income statements for 1986 through 1988.)

Within a little more than two years after going public, Regina's stock price had soared by nearly 500 percent and was expected to go much higher by analysts. The spectacular rise in Regina's stock price made Sheelen and the company's other principal stockholders millionaires many times over. Sheelen's stock alone had a market value of almost $100 million by 1988.

Regina's Profits: Just So Much Hot Air

Unfortunately, the too-good-to-be-true story of Regina Company was too good to be true. The sparkling sales and earnings figures released by Regina after it went public had been doctored by Sheelen. For the fiscal year ended June 30, 1988, the company had suffered a multimillion-dollar loss rather than the reported $11 million profit. Instead of a growth company with bright prospects, Regina was a dying company mired in mounting losses.

Regina's financial difficulties stemmed largely from product quality problems. Sheelen and the company's other top executives failed to pay sufficient attention to quality control issues during the manufacturing process for the new products introduced during the early and mid-1980s. These new products were innovative and less expensive than those of the company's competitors. They were also unreliable, having been rushed to the market without being adequately tested. The impressive sales figures registered following the introduction of the new products were negated by

2. G.G. Marcal, "Regina Keeps Cleaning Up," *Business Week*, 12 January 1987, 117.

customer return rates several times greater than those experienced by Regina's competitors. One major retailer subsequently reported that the return rate for a Regina vacuum cleaner was nearly 50 percent, while the comparable models of Hoover and Eureka had return rates of less than 1 percent.

By 1987, Sheelen realized that Regina was in deep trouble. Rather than admitting the problems facing the company, Sheelen chose to conceal them by manipulating Regina's accounting records. In a subsequent investigation, the Securities and Exchange Commission (SEC) charged that maintaining Regina's stock price at a high level was the prime motive underlying the accounting fraud. Colleagues of Sheelen later corroborated this allegation. "Nothing fired Sheelen's emotions like the company's stock price. Even a temporary flutter would cause him to rush to the phone to drum up support. He would pick up the phone himself and say, 'Why don't you [a financial analyst] write something to get the stock up?'"[3]

Sheelen began earnestly manipulating Regina's reported operating results during the second quarter of the company's 1988 fiscal year. Regina had posted steady increases in sales and earnings from 1985 through most of 1987. However, by December 31, 1987, the end of the second quarter of fiscal 1988, Regina's huge sales returns were threatening the company's impressive sales and earnings trends. At that point, Sheelen began establishing target sales and earnings levels that he believed Regina had to reach for the company to sustain "the confidence of the securities markets."[4]

To meet his financial targets for the second quarter of 1988, Sheelen ordered Vincent Golden, Regina's chief financial officer, to understate the company's product returns for that quarter: "With Golden's approval, employees altered Regina's computer system so that products returned by certain large volume customers could be processed through Regina's customer service department but would not be recorded on the company's books." Sheelen and Golden also misrepresented Regina's product returns during the final two quarters of fiscal 1988. According to the SEC, the company understated its sales returns by at least $13 million for the year.

During the fourth quarter of fiscal 1988, Sheelen realized that slashing recorded sales returns alone would not allow Regina to reach the sales and earnings goals he had established for that year. With Golden's help, Sheelen came up with several other accounting schemes to ensure that Regina reached his 1988 target sales and earnings figures of approximately $180 million and $1.20 per share, respectively.

Sheelen instructed Golden to record fictitious sales during the fourth quarter of fiscal 1988: "With Golden's approval, Regina's computer system was programmed to create false invoices in amounts of prior orders from certain large volume customers. Large volume customers were used because Golden and certain members of his staff believed that such customers were less likely than smaller customers to respond to audit confirmations." Golden also made sure that the bogus invoices were not sent to Regina's customers or routed to members of the company's accounting department who were unaware of their fraudulent nature. In total, Golden and his subordinates generated 200 bogus invoices, representing collective sales of more than $5 million.

Another method Sheelen used during 1988 to inflate Regina's revenues involved booking what Golden referred to as "ship-in-place" sales. These items were actually sales orders that Regina had received but not filled as of June 30, 1988. In fact, some of the orders were not due to be shipped for several weeks following Regina's

---

3. Byrne, "How Don Sheelen Made a Mess," 47.

4. This and all subsequent quotations, unless indicated otherwise, were taken from Securities and Exchange Commission, *Accounting and Auditing Enforcement Release No. 215*, 8 February 1989.

fiscal year-end. Golden recorded approximately $6 million of ship-in-place sales in the last few days of fiscal 1988. The SEC charged that the recording of these sales was a blatant violation of generally accepted accounting principles: "The ship-in-place transactions did not qualify for revenue recognition under GAAP because no exchange had taken place, the risks of loss and rights of ownership had not passed from Regina to customers, and there was no substantial business purpose for structuring the transactions as ship-in-place transactions." The last measure that Sheelen and Golden used to ensure that Regina reached its earnings goal for 1988 was to simply understate the company's cost of goods sold for the fourth quarter by more than $3 million.

In the late summer of 1988, Regina released its fiscal 1988 financial statements. Those statements reported net sales of approximately $181 million and earnings per share of $1.21, each of which was slightly higher than the corresponding target figure established months earlier by Sheelen. In Regina's 1988 annual report, Sheelen boasted of the company's financial performance and suggested that the following year it would produce even better operating results. (Exhibit 2 contains excerpts from Sheelen's 1988 letter to Regina's stockholders.)

On September 15, 1988, Sheelen told a group of financial analysts that Regina would be reporting an increase in sales for the first quarter of fiscal 1989. In fact, Sheelen knew that Regina's sales would decline during that quarter. Over the next few days, Sheelen gradually realized that he could no longer conceal Regina's deteriorating financial condition. On September 20, 1988, he called Golden into his office, and the two men agreed to reveal that Regina's prior financial statements were materially misstated. Instead of disclosing the true cause of the inaccurate financial statements, Sheelen and Golden decided to blame the errors on computer malfunctions.

After meeting with Golden, Sheelen issued a press release reporting that Regina's sales would be lower than previously forecast for the first quarter of fiscal 1989. The press release also indicated that the company would suffer a loss for that quarter. Sheelen then notified Peat, Marwick, Mitchell & Company, Regina's audit firm, that the company's 1988 financial statements contained errors resulting from glitches

---

EXHIBIT 2

EXCERPTS FROM DONALD SHEELEN'S 1988 LETTER TO REGINA'S STOCK HOLDERS.

It feels real good to finish Fiscal 1988 and to be thankful that your company achieved its best year ever. I'm sure you can see by looking at the numbers that we have set records in both Sales and Earnings. We are very proud of this, but we are also especially proud of the consistency over the last eight years–Fiscal 1988 was our eighth consecutive year of record Sales and Earnings.

I feel especially good about the significant change in Regina's product mix over the last four years. As early as 1984, virtually 100% of earnings came from one line–Electrikbroom. Now, four years later, we have a broad base with five major lines contributing to our growth. Regina has gone from being the "runt" of the floorcare industry in the United States to being on the verge of taking over the Number 1 spot.

Every year when I look at what our Company has achieved, I ask myself the question what about the future. I have always said to you that there are no guarantees for the future, but my level of confidence has never been greater than today. I feel this way because the number of different programs/products that we are bringing to the market have never been greater. There is no question that we will probably make a few mistakes over the next year–we have in the past–but I also believe that we will set new records in all areas. By the time this report reaches you, we should be on the verge of making public announcements which we believe will very much enhance our growth.

Source: Regina Company's 1988 annual report.

in computer processing. Sheelen asked the audit firm to review Regina's accounting records to determine the magnitude of the errors.

The price of Regina's common stock plunged 60 percent by the close of the financial markets on September 21, 1988, as investors reacted to Sheelen's press release. Over the next few days, Sheelen and Golden resigned their positions with Regina and Peat, Marwick, Mitchell & Company withdrew the unqualified audit, opinion issued several weeks earlier on the company's fiscal 1988 financial statements. In early October, a U.S. attorney initiated a criminal investigation of Regina's financial affairs. During that investigation, Sheelen voluntarily revealed the details of the earnings manipulation schemes used to misrepresent Regina's 1988 operating results.

Aftermath of the Regina Fraud

Donald Sheelen and Vincent Golden pleaded guilty to federal mail and securities fraud charges in February 1989. When the company subsequently filed for bankruptcy, its common stock became essentially worthless. In July 1989, a competitor, Electrolux Corporation, acquired Regina. An Israeli company purchased Regina in 1994 and then sold it the following year to Philips Electronics, N.V., a large Dutch firm. Regina ceased operating as a separate entity after being acquired by Philips.

In May 1989, a federal judge handed Sheelen a one-year prison term, a sentence that he was allowed to serve in a halfway house. Golden received a similar sentence of only six months' duration. The federal judge also fined both men and placed them on probation; Sheelen was assessed a $25,000 fine, while Golden was fined $12,500. According to the judge, the lenient sentences were appropriate because both men had cooperated with authorities investigating the scandal. Before beginning his sentence, Sheelen contacted Regina's new chairman and asked if he could return to the company. The chairman reportedly responded with a question of his own: "Are you _____ crazy?"[5]

One charge leveled at Sheelen and Golden by the SEC was that the former executives had repeatedly and intentionally misled the company's audit firm, Peat Marwick. As an example, the SEC pointed out that during the 1988 audit, Peat Marwick auditors discovered one of the ship-in-place sales transactions and notified Golden. Golden assured the auditors that no similar transactions had been recorded in Regina's accounting records.

In the enforcement release that focused on the Regina scandal, the SEC did not criticize Peat Marwick for failing to uncover the massive fraud masterminded by Sheelen and Golden. Nevertheless, several articles appearing in the financial press were critical of the audit firm. A Peat Marwick partner responded to such criticism by noting that "We're only human and prefer to trust the people we're auditing."[6]

Questions

1. Prepare common-sized financial statements for Regina for the period 1986 to 1988. Also, compute key liquidity, solvency, activity, and profitability ratios for the years 1987 and 1988. Given these data, identify what you believe were the high-risk financial statement line items for the 1988 Regina audit.

---

5. Byrne, "How Don Sheelen Made a Mess," 50.

6. L. Berton, "Battle of the Books: Audit Firms Are Hit by More Investor Suits for Not Finding Fraud," *The Wall Street Journal,* 24 January 1989, A1, A12.

2. Identify audit procedures that might have resulted in Peat Marwick discovering (a) the $5 million of bogus sales recorded by Regina executives during fiscal 1988 and (b) the intentional understatement of the company's sales returns for that same period.

3. Identify and discuss the principal audit objectives associated with the performance of year-end sales cutoff tests. Which of the fraudulent errors in Regina's accounting records would such tests have likely uncovered? Explain.

4. Were the Peat Marwick auditors justified in relying on Golden's assertion that the ship-in-place sales transaction they discovered was an isolated item? If not, what additional audit procedures do you believe Peat Marwick should have performed at that point?

5. As noted in this case, one Peat Marwick partner stated that his firm preferred to trust the people it was auditing. Should auditors trust their clients? If so, under what circumstances and to what extent?

SECTION 3

INTERNAL CONTROL ISSUES

3

The Trolley Dodgers

In 1890, the Brooklyn Trolley Dodgers professional baseball team joined the National League. Over the following years, the Dodgers would have considerable difficulty competing with the other baseball teams in the New York City area. Those teams, principal among them the New York Yankees, were much better financed and generally stocked with players of higher caliber.

After nearly seven decades of mostly frustration on and off the baseball field, the Dodgers shocked the sports world by moving to Los Angeles in 1958. Walter O'Malley, the flamboyant owner of the Dodgers, saw an opportunity to introduce professional baseball to the rapidly growing population of the West Coast. More important, O'Malley saw an opportunity to make his team more profitable. As an inducement to the Dodgers, Los Angeles County purchased a goat farm located in Chavez Ravine, an area two miles northwest of downtown Los Angeles, and gave the property to O'Malley for the site of his new baseball stadium.

Since moving to Los Angeles, the Dodgers have been the envy of the baseball world: "In everything from profit to stadium maintenance . . . the Dodgers are the prototype of how a franchise should be run."[1] During the 1980s and 1990s, the Dodgers reigned as the most profitable franchise in baseball with a pretax profit margin approaching 25 percent in many years. In late 1997, Peter O'Malley, Walter O'Malley's son and the Dodgers' principal owner, sold the franchise for $350 million to media mogul Rupert Murdoch. A spokesman for Murdoch complimented the O'Malley family for the longstanding success of the Dodgers organization: "The O'Malleys have set a gold standard for franchise ownership."[2]

During an interview before he sold the Dodgers, Peter O'Malley attributed the success of his organization to the experts he had retained in all functional areas: "I don't have to be an expert on taxes, split-fingered fastballs, or labor relations with our ushers. That talent is all available."[3] Edward Campos, a longtime accountant for the Dodgers, was a seemingly perfect example of one of those experts in the Dodgers organization. Campos accepted an entry-level position with the Dodgers as a young man. By 1986, after almost two decades with the club, he had worked his way up the employment hierarchy to become the operations payroll chief.

After taking charge of the Dodgers' payroll department, Campos designed and implemented a new payroll system, a system that only he fully understood. In fact, Campos controlled the system so completely that he personally filled out the weekly payroll cards for each of the 400 employees of the Dodgers. Campos was known not only for his work ethic but also for his loyalty to the club and its owners: "The Dodgers trusted him, and when he was on vacation, he even came back and did the payroll."[4]

---

1. R. J. Harris, "Forkball for Dodgers: Costs Up, Gate Off," *The Wall Street Journal*, 31 August 1990, B1, B4.

2. R. Newhan, "Dodger Sale Heads for Home," *Los Angeles Times*, 5 September 1997, C1, C12.

3. Harris, "Forkball for Dodgers," B1.

4. P. Feldman, "7 Accused of Embezzling $332,583 from Dodgers," *Los Angeles Times*, 17 September 1986, Sec. 2, 1, 6.

Unfortunately, the Dodgers' trust in Campos was misplaced. Over a period of several years, Campos embezzled several hundred thousand dollars from his employer. According to court records, Campos padded the Dodgers' payroll by adding fictitious employees to various departments in the organization. In addition, Campos routinely inflated the number of hours worked by several employees and then split the resulting overpayments fifty-fifty with those individuals.

The fraudulent scheme came unraveled when appendicitis struck down Campos, forcing the Dodgers' controller to temporarily assume his responsibilities. While completing the payroll one week, the controller noticed that several employees, including ushers, security guards, and ticket salespeople, were being paid unusually large amounts. In some cases, employees earning $7 an hour received weekly paychecks approaching $2,000. Following a criminal investigation and the filing of charges against Campos and his cohorts, all the individuals involved in the payroll fraud confessed.

A state court sentenced Campos to eight years in prison and required him to make restitution of approximately $132,000 to the Dodgers. Another of the conspirators also received a prison sentence. The remaining individuals involved in the payroll scheme made restitution and were placed on probation.

Questions

1. Identify the key audit objectives for a client's payroll function. Comment on objectives related to tests of controls and substantive audit procedures.

2. What internal control weaknesses were evident in the Dodgers' payroll system?

3. Identify audit procedures that might have led to the discovery of the fraudulent scheme masterminded by Campos.

Howard Street Jewelers, Inc.

Lore Levi was worried as she scanned the most recent monthly bank statement for the Howard Street Jewelers.[1] For decades, she and her husband, Julius, had owned and operated the small business that they had opened after fleeing Nazi Germany during World War II. Certainly the business had experienced ups and downs before, but now it seemed to be in a downward spiral from which it could not recover. In previous times when sales had slackened, the Levis had survived by cutting costs here and there. But now, despite several measures the Levis had taken to control costs, the business's cash position continued to steadily worsen. If a turnaround did not occur soon, Lore feared that she and her husband might be forced to close their store.

Lore had a theory regarding the financial problems of Howard Street Jewelers. On more than one occasion, she had wondered whether Betty the cashier, a trusted and reliable employee for nearly 20 years, might be stealing from the cash register. To Lore, it was a logical assumption. Besides working as a part-time sales clerk, Betty handled all of the cash that came into the business and maintained the cash receipts and sales records. If anybody had an opportunity to steal from the business, it was Betty.

Reluctantly, Lore approached her husband about her theory. Lore pointed out to Julius that Betty had unrestricted access to the cash receipts of the business. Additionally, over the previous few years, Betty had developed a taste for more expensive clothes and more frequent and costly vacations. Julius quickly dismissed his wife's speculation. To him, it was preposterous to even briefly consider the possibility that Betty could be stealing from the business. A frustrated Lore then raised the subject with her son, Alvin, who worked side by side with his parents in the family business. Alvin responded similarly to his father and warned his mother that she was becoming paranoid.

Near the end of each year, the Levis met with their accountant to discuss various matters, principally taxation issues. The Levis placed considerable trust in the CPA who served as their accountant; for years he had given them solid, professional advice on a wide range of accounting and business matters. It was only natural for Lore to confide in the accountant about her suspicions regarding Betty the cashier. The accountant listened intently to Lore and then commented that he had noticed occasional shortages in the cash receipts records that seemed larger than normal for a small retail business. Despite Julius's protestations that Betty could not be responsible for any cash shortages, the accountant encouraged the Levis to closely monitor her work.

Embezzlements are often discovered by luck rather than by design. So it was with the Howard Street Jewelers. Nearly two years after Lore Levi had suggested that Betty might be stealing from the business, a customer approached the cash register and told Alvin Levi that she wanted to make a payment on a layaway item. Alvin, who was working the cash register because it was Betty's day off, searched the file of layaway sales tickets and the daily sales records but found no trace of the customer's layaway purchase. Finally, he apologized and asked the customer to return the next day when Betty would be back at work.

---

1. Most of the facts of this case were reconstructed from information included in several legal opinions. The following two articles served as additional sources for this case: *Securities Regulation and Law Report*, "Accounting & Disclosure: Accounting Briefs," Vol. 23, No. 21 (24 May 1991), 814; *Securities Regulation and Law Report*, "Accounting & Disclosure: Accounting Briefs," Vol. 24, No. 19 (8 May 1992), 708.

The following day, Alvin told Betty that he was unable to find the layaway sales ticket. Betty expressed surprise and said she would search for the ticket herself. Within a few minutes, Betty approached Alvin, waving the sales ticket in her hand. Alvin was stumped. He had searched the layaway sales file several times and simply could not accept Betty's explanation that the missing ticket had been there all along. Suspicious, as well, was the fact that the sale had not been recorded in the sales records–a simple oversight, Betty had explained.

As Alvin returned to his work, a troubling and sickening sensation settled into the pit of his stomach. Over the next several weeks, Alvin studied the daily sales and cash receipts records. He soon realized that his mother had been right all along. Betty, the trusted, reliable, longtime cashier of the Howard Street Jewelers, was stealing from the business. The estimated embezzlement loss suffered by Howard Street Jewelers over the term of Betty's employment approached $350,000.

Questions

1. Identify the internal control concepts that the Levis overlooked or ignored.

2. When Lore Levi informed the CPA of her suspicions regarding Betty, what responsibilities, if any, did the CPA have to pursue this matter? Alternately, assume that, in addition to preparing tax returns for Howard Street Jewelers, the CPA (a) *audited* the business's annual financial statements, (b) *reviewed* the annual financial statements, and (c) *compiled* the annual financial statements.

3. Assume that you have a small CPA firm and have been contacted by a husband and wife, John and Myrna Trubey, who are in the final stages of negotiating to purchase a local jewelry store. John will prepare jewelry settings, size jewelry for customers, and perform related tasks, while Myrna will be the head salesclerk. The Trubeys intend to retain four of the current employees of the jewelry store–two salesclerks, a cashier, and a college student who cleans the store, runs errands, and does various other odd jobs. They inform you that the average inventory of the jewelry store is $200,000 and that annual sales average $800,000, 30 percent of which occur in the six weeks prior to Christmas.

   The Trubeys are interested in retaining you as their accountant should they purchase the store. They know little about accounting and have no prior experience as business owners. They would require assistance in establishing an accounting system, monthly financial statements for internal use, annual financial statements to be submitted to their banker, and all necessary tax returns. John and Myrna are particularly concerned about control issues–given the dollar value of inventory that will be on hand in the store and the significant amount of cash receipts that will be processed daily.

   You see this as an excellent opportunity to acquire a good client. However, you have not had a chance to prepare for your meeting with the Trubeys because they came in without an appointment. You do not want to ask them to come back later, since that may encourage them to check out your competitor across the street.

   Required: Provide the Trubeys with an overview of the key internal control issues they will face in operating a jewelry store. In your overview, identify at least five control activities you believe they should implement if they acquire the store. You have never had a jewelry store as a client, but you have several small retail clients. Attempt to impress the Trubeys with your understanding of internal control issues for small retail businesses.

United Way of America

In 1887, several of Denver's community and religious leaders established the Charity Organization Society. During its first year of operation, the organization raised a little more than $20,000, which it then distributed to several local charities. The charity-of-charities fundraising concept spread across the United States over the following decades. After several name changes, the original Denver-based organization adopted the name United Way in 1963.

United Way grew rapidly during the latter decades of the twentieth century, eventually becoming the nation's largest charitable organization. In 2006, United Way raised four billion dollars, more than double the charitable donations received that year by the Salvation Army, the nation's second largest charitable organization. Each year, approximately 40,000 charities across the United States receive cash distributions from United Way.

Football & Fraud

For more than two decades beginning in the early 1970s, William Aramony served as the president of United Way of America. The Virginia-based United Way of America serves as the umbrella organization for the almost 1,400 local United Way chapters scattered across the United States. An alliance that Aramony negotiated with the National Football League (NFL) resulted in huge nationwide exposure for the United Way during every Sunday afternoon and Monday night NFL game. That exposure was largely responsible for the explosive growth that United Way realized during Aramony's tenure as president.

In recent years, United Way has faced two major challenges that threaten its leadership position in the charitable sector. Over the past several decades, the number of charitable and other not-for-profit organizations in the United States has skyrocketed. Currently, there are nearly two million registered tax-exempt organizations in the United States, the majority of which are charities. Collectively, these organizations employ one of every ten working Americans. Registered charities alone raise more than $300 billion each year in donations from the public and private sector. The intense and growing competition for Americans' charitable donations has made it increasingly difficult for United Way to sustain the impressive growth that it realized under William Aramony's leadership.

The second major challenge facing United Way is a loss of credibility suffered by the organization due to a series of embarrassing and highly publicized embezzlement schemes. In the early 1990s, federal prosecutors indicted William Aramony for allegedly embezzling and otherwise misusing millions of dollars of United Way funds. In 1995, a federal jury found Aramony guilty of more than two dozen of the individual fraud charges that had been filed against him. Aramony was later sentenced to serve seven years in federal prison. Testimony during Aramony's trial revealed that he had squandered United Way funds on lavish trips to Las Vegas, Europe, Africa, and other destinations. The 68-year-old Aramony reportedly used United Way funds to finance multiple romantic relationships as well.

Shortly before Aramony went to trial, another United Way executive in Westchester, New York, admitted to embezzling several hundred thousand dollars of her chapter's funds. This individual, Evol Sealy, who oversaw the Westchester chapter's accounting and finance functions, was later sentenced to a three-year prison term. In 2003, Jacquelyn Allen-MacGregor, the former vice president of finance of a United Way chapter in East Lansing, Michigan, pleaded guilty to stealing $1.9 million from the organization. Allen-MacGregor revealed that she had used the stolen funds to support her hobby, namely, horses—over the course of her embezzlement scheme she purchased more than seventy quarter horses. In June 2004, Allen-MacGregor was sentenced to four years in prison to be followed by three years of supervised probation.

In 2004, Aramony's friend and former associate, Oral Suer, who served for almost three decades as the president of a large United Way chapter in Washington, D.C., pleaded guilty to embezzling $1.5 million of United Way funds. The evidence collected by federal prosecutors against Suer included testimony documenting that Suer and Aramony had spent time together at a local racetrack. That evidence also documented that Suer used cash taken from his chapter to make good on the generous and well-publicized personal contribution pledges that he made during annual United Way fundraising campaigns. At his sentencing hearing, a contrite Suer told the presiding judge, "This is a very sad day for me, for the community and for the United Way. What I feel is embarrassment, shame and guilt."[1] The judge then handed Suer a three-year prison sentence, the maximum permissible under federal sentencing guidelines.

United Way's reported theft losses have had a chilling effect on the organization's fundraising efforts nationwide in recent years. Not surprisingly, individual chapters impacted directly by the embezzlement losses have experienced dramatic declines in their annual receipts. For example, adverse publicity resulting from the embezzlement loss at the United Way chapter in the Washington, D.C., area caused that chapter's annual donations to plummet from $45 million to $18 million.

In recent years, many large charities in addition to United Way have suffered large losses due to embezzlements and other fraudulent activities perpetrated by organizational insiders. In 1989, former television evangelist Jim Bakker was sentenced to 18 years in federal prison. Bakker was convicted of diverting millions of dollars for his personal use from the PTL Club, a religious broadcasting network that he and his wife, Tammy Faye, founded in the 1970s. The Bakkers had used passionate and persistent televised fundraising campaigns to convince the faithful and mostly shallow-pocketed viewers of their network to send them donations.

In 1997, John G. Bennett, the founder of the New Era Philanthropy Foundation, was sentenced to 12 years in prison after embezzling an estimated $8 million from that charitable organization. In California, seven employees of Goodwill Industries, all of whom were related, operated a large-scale "fencing" operation from the early 1970s through 1998 in which they sold furniture, clothing, and other goods donated to that charity. Law enforcement authorities estimate that the seven relatives stole more than $25 million from that organization over the course of the fraudulent scheme.

To date, the largest fraud impacting a charity was a Ponzi scheme that involved the Baptist Foundation of Arizona. In 2006, William Crotts, the chief executive of that charitable religious organization, received an eight-year prison sentence for defrauding an estimated 10,000 individuals of nearly $160 million. Making matters worse, most of the victims of Crotts' fraud were elderly individuals, many of whom lost a sizable portion of their retirement nest eggs as a result of the fraud.

---

1. J. Markon, "Ex-Chief of Local United Way Sentenced," *Washington Post* (online), 15 May 2004.

Empirical research has confirmed that fraud is a major problem plaguing the charitable sector. A recent study by four accounting professors estimates that approximately one of every eight dollars contributed to charitable organizations in the United States is stolen each year, resulting in annual losses to those organizations of $40 billion.[2] That study found that 95 percent of the losses suffered by charities result from the theft of cash and that the culprits are typically involved in the charity's financial functions. "They're usually done by someone in the financial area–the treasurer, the bookkeeper, the signer of checks–who knows how to avoid getting caught."[3]

Recipe for Theft: Weak Controls and Ineffective Regulatory Oversight

A common theme of the frauds that have plagued charities in recent years has been inadequate or nonexistent internal controls. Understandably, charitable organizations make every effort to minimize their administrative expenses, including their accounting and control-related expenditures. For example, an internal study by United Way of America in 2002 found that fewer than 15 percent of the organization's local chapters had invested the time and other resources to develop written policies to address fundamental accounting and control issues.[4] No doubt, the porous nature of charities' internal control systems not only encourages opportunistic individuals to take advantage of those organizations but also makes it difficult to detect ongoing frauds.

In 2004, PricewaterhouseCoopers released a 200-page report that detailed the results of a seven-month investigative audit of the embezzlement loss suffered by the East Lansing, Michigan, chapter of United Way. That report castigated United Way for failing to implement some of the most rudimentary control procedures intended to prevent thefts by organizational insiders. "The audit, more than seven months in the making, gives a scathing review, depicting the charity as a place where top managers were permitted to dip into the millions of dollars in public donations with little or no oversight."[5]

According to *The New York Times*, the individual who embezzled the funds from the East Lansing chapter "did not need to be a criminal mastermind to succeed in the theft."[6] Instead, that individual took advantage of the chapter's lack of proper internal controls and stole the funds at will. "She simply wrote checks to herself, forging the signatures of the required co-signers and destroying the canceled checks when the bank mailed them back. No one noticed this because she also kept the organization's books."[7]

Similar to the other United Way fraudsters, the executive who embezzled several hundred thousand dollars from the Westchester, New York, United Way chapter used a simple scam to "rip off" her organization. The executive endorsed checks made payable to United Way from local donors and then deposited those checks in her personal bank account. The fraud was uncovered when a bank teller reported her to local authorities. In commenting on the embezzlement scheme, the local district

---

2. S. Strom, "Report Sketches Crime Costing Billions: Theft From Charities," *The New York Times* (online), 29 March 2008.

3. *Ibid.*

4. S. Strom, "Questions Arise on Accounting at United Way," *The New York Times* (online), 19 November 2002.

5. J. Salmon and P. Whoriskey, "Audit Excoriates United Way Leadership," *Washington Post* (online), 25 June 2004.

6. S. Strom, "Guilty Plea Due Today in Big United Way Theft," *The New York Times* (online), 6 February 2003.

7. *Ibid.*

attorney noted, "There was most certainly a total lack of supervision which permitted this to occur."[8] The president of that chapter expressed a different point of view. "As in the case of virtually any organization, our system of internal control procedures, no matter how strong, is based on trust."[9]

Compounding the weakness of the internal control systems of charities such as United Way is the absence of strong regulatory oversight for the charitable sector. The regulatory infrastructure for charities is weak and enforcement is inconsistent. Unlike public companies that are overseen by the Securities and Exchange Commission (SEC), charitable organizations are not subject to direct oversight by a federal agency. Federal oversight of charities involves principally an annual information filing with the Internal Revenue Service (IRS).

Similar to other tax-exempt organizations, most charities are required to submit a Form 990 to the IRS each year. Among many other required disclosures in Form 990, charities must report their total annual revenues and the principal sources of those revenues, fundraising expenses, the salaries of highly paid executives, and losses due to theft, embezzlement, and other fraudulent activities. The latter disclosure was added to Form 990 beginning in 2008 as a direct consequence of the mounting theft losses being incurred by charities. A searchable database of the approximately two million Form 990s filed each year with the IRS is available at www.guidestar.org.

Although there is no federal agency with a direct responsibility to regulate charities, many states have established such an agency. Nevertheless, these state agencies tend to be underfunded and are ineffectual as a result. "While most states have agencies [overseeing charitable organizations], most are inactive, ineffective or significantly understaffed."[10]

Bring in the Auditors?

Following the passage of the Sarbanes-Oxley Act in 2002, some charities adopted internal control reforms and other provisions included in that federal statute. Not satisfied, prominent members of the philanthropic community have lobbied state and federal legislators to pass legislation that would require charities to implement a comprehensive reform agenda similar to that mandated by Sarbanes-Oxley. "The American government can no longer make a plausible argument that charities don't deserve the type of scrutiny that the for-profit sector warrants. Quite simply, the charitable sector is much too large to warrant the continued disinterest our government has shown it."[11]

One proponent of regulatory reform has suggested that charities be required to obtain a "seal of approval" of some type to reassure donors that their contributions are not being misused.[12] In fact, a common measure included in proposed regulatory reforms for charities is a requirement that they be subject to an annual independent audit by an accounting firm.

> *Only a few states currently require annual financial audits of nonprofit corporations . . . Independent financial audits have become such a fundamental and essential test of the financial soundness of any corporate enterprise that all best practice codes of nonprofit*

8. J. Steinberg, "United Way Accountant Admits $282,500 Theft," *The New York Times* (online), 19 May 1992.

9. *Ibid.*

10. A. Rothschild, "Public Scrutiny of Exempt Organizations," www.abanet.org/rppt/publications/estate/2004/2/Rothschild-PublicScr.pdf.

11. T. Stamp, "Why Does Our Government Ignore Charities?" *Charity Navigator* (online), 14 October 2002.

12. W. Muller, "Charities and Anti-Money Laundering: Is a 'Seal of Approval' the answer?" *Trusts and Trustees* 14 (May 2008): 259–271.

governance require that every nonprofit corporation with substantial assets or annual revenue should be audited annually by an independent auditing firm.[13]

California and Massachusetts are examples of states that have passed legislation in recent years to require certain charities to be audited annually. California's Nonprofit Integrity Act of 2004 requires charities with annual gross revenues exceeding $2 million to be audited. The comparable state statute in Massachusetts requires charities with annual revenues exceeding $500,000 or total assets greater than $5 million to be audited. These same charities are also required by the Massachusetts law to establish an audit committee.

Not all charity reform advocates believe that mandatory independent audits would remedy the problems facing the charitable sector. These parties point out that several of the charities that suffered large losses due to embezzlement and other fraudulent schemes had been audited by accounting firms. One such charity was United Way of America, which was audited by Arthur Andersen during the time frame that Aramony was embezzling from the organization. Andersen was widely criticized for failing to detect Aramony's fraud. The managing partner of the Andersen office that audited the organization responded to that criticism by insisting that United Way officials had intentionally concealed the fraudulent activities from the auditors.[14]

The auditors of the East Lansing, Michigan, United Way chapter that suffered an embezzlement loss of $1.9 million were also criticized for failing to uncover that fraud. The audit partner who supervised the annual audits of that chapter staunchly defended himself and his subordinates. "This [embezzlement scheme] went on prior to our being engaged in 1999, and when you have fraud going on a long time, it's hard to find because it has become the norm [within the organization]."[15]

Questions

1. Identify and briefly describe fundamental and cost-effective internal controls that charitable organizations could implement to reduce their exposure to theft losses.

2. Do CPA firms have a responsibility to perform audits of charitable organizations for reduced or lower-than-normal audit fees? Defend your answer. Other than audit fees, what other benefits do accounting firms accrue by auditing a charity?

3. Identify unique or uncommon audit risk factors posed by a charity. How should accounting firms modify their audits to address these risk factors?

---

13. T. Silk, "Good Governance Practices for 501 (c)(3) Organizations: Should the IRS Become Further Involved?" *International Journal of Not-for-Profit Law*, 2007 (Vol. 10), 40.

14. J. Garnatz, "United Way Cleaning House Nationally, Doing Well Locally," *St. Petersburg Times*, 17 April 1992, 11.

15. Strom, "Guilty Plea Due Today," *The New York Times*.

First Keystone Bank

A Japanese bank introduced the concept of around-the-clock access to cash in the 1960s when it installed the world's first cash-dispensing machine. In 1968, the first networked ATM appeared in Dallas, Texas.[1] Two generations later, there are more than two million "cash-points," "bancomats," and "holes-in-the-wall" worldwide, including one in Antarctica.

Not surprisingly, ATMs have been a magnet for thieves since their inception. In 2009, an international gang of racketeers used a large stash of counterfeit ATM cards to steal $9 million from hundreds of ATMs scattered around the globe in a well-planned and coordinated 30-minute crime spree. Several high-tech thieves have hacked into the computer networks of banks and modified their ATM software. One such miscreant reprogrammed a network of ATMs to change the denomination of bills recognized by the brainless machines–the ATMs treated $20 bills as if they were $5 bills. High-powered video cameras and miniature electronic devices attached to ATMs have been used to steal personal identification numbers (PINs) from a countless number of unsuspecting bank customers.

A variety of low-tech schemes have also been used to rip off banks and their cus-tomers via ATMs, including forced withdrawals and post-withdrawal armed rob-beries. "Ram-raiding" involves using heavy-duty equipment to rip an ATM from its shorings. The ram-raiders then haul the ATM to a remote location and blast it open with explosives. The most common and lowest-tech type of ATM pilfering involves the aptly named tactic of "shoulder-surfing."

Many banks have suffered losses from their ATM operations due to embezzle-ment schemes perpetrated by employees. One such bank was the Swarthmore, Pennsylvania, branch of First Keystone Bank. Swarthmore, a quiet suburb of Phila-delphia, is best known for being home to one of the nation's most prestigious liberal arts colleges. In 2008, *Forbes Magazine* ranked Swarthmore College as the fourth best institution of higher learning in the United States–Princeton, CalTech, and Har-vard claimed the top three spots in that poll.

In January 2010, three tellers of First Keystone's Swarthmore branch were arrested and charged with stealing more than $100,000 from its ATM over the previous two years. The alleged ringleader was Jean Moronese, who had worked at the branch since 2002 and served as its head teller since 2006. According to media reports, Moronese told law enforcement authorities that she initially began taking money from the branch's ATM in 2008 to pay her credit card bills, rent, and day care expenses.

No doubt emboldened by the ease with which she could steal the money, Moro-nese reportedly began taking cash from the ATM "just to spend" because she "got greedy."[2] Prior to taking a vacation in the fall of 2008, a tearful Moronese approached one of her subordinates and fellow tellers, Kelly Barksdale, and confessed that she had been stealing from the ATM. Moronese "begged" Barksdale to help her conceal her thefts "because she didn't want her children to see her go to jail."[3] Barksdale was

---

1. In the United States, "ATM" generally refers to an "automated teller machine" or "automated transac-tion machine." In some English-speaking countries, however, "ATM" refers to "all-time-money."

2. C. Scharr, "Bank Employees Charged in Embezzlement Scheme," *The Delaware County Daily Times* (online), 12 January 2010.

3. M. Schaefer, "Ex-tellers at Swarthmore Bank Charged in Theft," www.philly.com, 12 January 2010.

apparently persuaded by Moronese's tearful plea and agreed to help her cover up the embezzlement scheme.

In fact, the cover-up was easily accomplished. According to the local police, Moronese and Barksdale simply changed the ledger control sheets that were supposed to report the amount of cash stored in the ATM and in the locked vault within the ATM. First Keystone's internal control procedures mandated that two employees be involved in resupplying the ATM and its locked vault and in maintaining the ATM ledger control sheets. However, either Moronese or Barksdale completed those tasks by themselves.

In early 2009, a third teller, Tyneesha Richardson, overheard Moronese and Barksdale discussing the embezzlement scheme. Richardson then reportedly asked Moronese for money to pay off her car loan. Moronese agreed to give Richardson the money and told her that she shouldn't worry because "the bank had a lot of money and they would never miss it."[4,5] After telling Barksdale that she had given money to Richardson, Moronese told Barksdale that if she ever needed any money "to let her know."[6] Not long thereafter, Barksdale allegedly asked Moronese for $600 to pay her rent.

An internal audit eventually uncovered the embezzlement scheme at First Keystone's Swarthmore branch. That internal audit revealed that $40,590 was missing from the branch's ATM, while another $60,000 was missing from the locked vault within the ATM's interior.

While being interrogated by law enforcement authorities, Barksdale reportedly confessed that she and her colleagues had also stolen money from the local municipality. City employees periodically dropped off at the First Keystone branch large bags of coins collected from Swarthmore's parking meters. Tellers at the branch were supposed to feed the coins into a coin-counting machine and then deposit the receipts printed by the machine into the city's parking account. According to Barksdale, she and her two fellow conspirators diverted money from Swarthmore's parking funds and split it among themselves. The police estimated that the three tellers stole approximately $24,000 of the parking funds.

In January 2010 when the three tellers were arrested, they did not have to go far since the Swarthmore police station was across the street from the First Keystone branch where they worked. In commenting on the case, the local district attorney observed that Barksdale and Richardson had a choice to make when they learned of Moronese's embezzlement scheme and that each had made the wrong choice. "So, the lesson is you can either be a witness or you can be a defendant. These two chose to be defendants."[7]

The district attorney also commented on the branch's failure to require employees to comply with internal control procedures. "The case is yet another example of the importance of not only implementing internal accounting safeguards, but ensuring that those safeguards are being followed by all employees at all levels of the business."[8,9]

---

4. Scharr, "Bank Employees Charged."

5. While at work, the three coworkers reportedly used the code word "Todd" to refer to "their friend" when they needed or wanted to take money from the ATM.

6. Scharr, "Bank Employees Charged."

7. Schaefer, "Ex-tellers at Swarthmore Bank."

8. Press release issued January 11, 2010, by G. Michael Green, District Attorney, Delaware County, Media, Pennsylvania. (http://www.delcoda.com/documents/FirstKeystoneStatement byMikeGreen.pdf)

9. In March 2010, an employee of First Keystone's branch in Berwick, Pennsylvania, pleaded guilty to embezzling $750,000 over the 17 years that she had worked for that branch. According to published reports, the employee routinely "skimmed" money received by the bank and deposited the stolen funds into bank accounts that she controlled.

Questions

1. Prepare a list of internal control procedures that banks and other financial institutions have implemented, or should implement, for their ATM operations.

2. What general conditions or factors influence the audit approach or strategy applied to a bank client's ATM operations by its independent auditors?

3. Identify specific audit procedures that may be applied to ATM operations. Which, if any, of these procedures might have resulted in the discovery of the embezzlement scheme at First Keystone's Swarthmore branch? Explain.

Goodner Brothers, Inc.

"Woody, that's $2,400 you owe me. Okay? We're straight on that?"

"Yeah, yeah. I got you."

"And you'll pay me back by next Friday?"

"Al. I said I'd pay you back by Friday, didn't I?"

"Just checkin'."

Borrowing money from a friend can strain even the strongest relationship. When the borrowed money will soon be plunked down on a blackjack table, the impact on the friendship can be devastating.

Woody Robinson and Al Hunt were sitting side by side at a blackjack table in Tunica, Mississippi. The two longtime friends and their wives were spending their summer vacation together as they had several times. After three days of loitering in the casinos that line the banks of the Mississippi River 20 miles south of Memphis, Woody found himself hitting up his friend for loans. By the end of the vacation, Woody owed Al nearly $5,000. The question facing Woody was how he would repay his friend.[1]

Two Pals Named Woody and Al

Woodrow Wilson Robinson and Albert Leroy Hunt lived and worked in Huntington, West Virginia, a city of 60,000 tucked in the westernmost corner of the state. The blue-collar city sits on the south bank of the Ohio River. Ohio is less than one mile away across the river, while Kentucky can be reached by making a 10-minute drive westward on Interstate 64. Woody and Al were born six days apart in a small hospital in eastern Kentucky, were best friends throughout grade school and high school, and roomed together for four years at college. A few months after they graduated with business management degrees, each served as the other's best man at their respective weddings.

Following graduation, Al went to work for Curcio's Auto Supply on the western outskirts of Huntington, a business owned by his future father-in-law. Curcio's sold lawnmowers, bicycles, and automotive parts and supplies, including tires and batteries, the business's two largest revenue producers. Curcio's also installed the automotive parts it sold, provided oil and lube service, and performed small engine repairs.

Within weeks of going to work for Curcio's, Al helped Woody land a job with a large tire wholesaler that was Curcio's largest supplier. Goodner Brothers, Inc., sold tires of all types and sizes from 14 locations scattered from southern New York to northwestern South Carolina and from central Ohio to the Delaware shore. Goodner concentrated its operations in midsized cities such as Huntington, West Virginia; Lynchburg, Virginia; Harrisburg, Pennsylvania; and Youngstown, Ohio, home to the company's headquarters.

Founded in 1979 by two brothers, T. J. and Ross Goodner, nearly three decades later Goodner Brothers' annual sales approached $40 million. The Goodner family dominated the company's operations. T. J. served as the company's chairman of the

---

1. The central facts of this case were drawn from a legal opinion. The names of the actual parties involved in the case and the relevant locations and dates have been changed. Additionally, certain of the factual circumstances reported in this case are fictionalized accounts of background material disclosed in the legal opinion.

board and chief executive officer (CEO), while Ross was the chief operating officer (COO). Four second-generation Goodners also held key positions in the company.

Goodner purchased tires from several large manufacturers and then sold those tires at wholesale prices to auto supply stores and other retailers that had auto supply departments. Goodner's customers included Sears, Wal-Mart, Kmart, and dozens of smaller retail chains. The company also purchased discontinued tires from manufacturers, large retailers, and other wholesalers and then resold those tires at cut-rate prices to school districts, municipalities, and to companies with small fleets of automobiles.

Goodner Brothers hired Woody to work as a sales representative for its Huntington location. Woody sold tires to more than 80 customers in his sales region that stretched from the west side of Huntington into eastern Kentucky and north into Ohio. Woody, who worked strictly on a commission basis, was an effective and successful salesman. Unfortunately, a bad habit that he acquired during his college days gradually developed into a severe problem. A gambling compulsion threatened to wreck the young salesman's career and personal life.

Woody bet on any and all types of sporting events, including baseball and football games, horse races, and boxing matches. He also spent hundreds of dollars each month buying lottery tickets and lost increasingly large sums on frequent gambling excursions with his friend Al. By the summer of 2006 when Woody, Al, and their wives visited Tunica, Mississippi, Woody's financial condition was desperate. He owed more than $50,000 to the various bookies with whom he placed bets, was falling behind on his mortgage payments, and had "maxed out" several credit cards. Worst of all, two bookies to whom Woody owed several thousand dollars were demanding payment and had begun making menacing remarks that alluded to his wife, Rachelle.

Woody Finds a Solution

Upon returning to Huntington in early July 2006, Woody struck upon an idea to bail himself out of his financial problems: He decided to begin stealing from his employer, Goodner Brothers. Other than a few traffic tickets, Woody had never been in trouble with law enforcement authorities. Yet, in Woody's mind, he had no other reasonable alternatives. At this point, resorting to stealing seemed the lesser of two evils.

One reason Woody decided to steal from his employer was the ease with which it could be done. After several years with Goodner, Woody was very familiar with the company's sloppy accounting practices and lax control over its inventory and other assets. Goodner's executives preached one dominant theme to their sales staff: "Volume, volume, volume." Goodner achieved its ambitious sales goals by undercutting competitors' prices. The company's dominant market share in the geographical region it served came at a high price. Goodner's gross profit margin averaged 17.4 percent, considerably below the mean gross profit margin of 24.1 percent for comparable tire wholesalers. To compensate for its low gross profit margin, Goodner scrimped on operating expenses, including expenditures on internal control measures.

The company staffed its 14 sales outlets with skeletal crews of 10 to 12 employees. A sales manager supervised the other employees at each outlet and also worked a sales district. The remaining staff typically included two sales representatives, a receptionist who doubled as a secretary, a bookkeeper, and five to seven employees who delivered tires and worked in the unit's inventory warehouse. Goodner's Huntington location had two storage areas, a small warehouse adjacent to the sales office and a larger storage area two miles away that had previously housed a discount grocery store. Other than padlocks, Goodner provided little security for its tire inventory, which typically ranged from $300,000 to $700,000 for each sales outlet.

Instead of an extensive system of internal controls, T. J. and Ross Goodner relied heavily on the honesty and integrity of the employees they hired. Central to the company's employment policy was never to hire someone unless that individual could provide three strong references, preferably from reputable individuals with some connection to Goodner Brothers. Besides following up on employment references, Goodner Brothers obtained thorough background checks on prospective employees from local detective agencies.

For almost three decades, Goodner's employment strategy had served the company well. Fewer than 10 of several hundred individuals employed by the company had been terminated for stealing or other misuse of company assets or facilities.

Each Goodner sales outlet maintained a computerized accounting system. These systems typically consisted of an "off-the-shelf" general ledger package intended for a small retail business and a hodgepodge of assorted accounting documents. Besides the Huntington facility's bookkeeper, the unit's sales manager and two sales representatives had unrestricted access to the accounting system.

Because the large volume of sales and purchase transactions often swamped the bookkeeper, sales representatives frequently entered transactions directly into the system. The sales reps routinely accessed, reviewed, and updated their customers' accounts. Rather than completing purchase orders, sales orders, credit memos, and other accounting documents on a timely basis, the sales reps often jotted the details of a transaction on a piece of scrap paper. The sales reps eventually passed these "source documents" on to the bookkeeper or used them to enter transaction data directly into the accounting system.

Sales reps and the sales manager jointly executed the credit function for each Goodner sales outlet. Initial sales to new customers required the approval of the sales manager, while the creditworthiness of existing clients was monitored by the appropriate sales rep. Sales reps had direct access to the inventory storage areas. During heavy sales periods, sales reps often loaded and delivered customer orders themselves.

Each sales office took a year-end physical inventory to bring its perpetual inventory records into agreement with the amount of inventory actually on hand. One concession that T. J. and Ross Goodner made to the policy of relying on their employees' honesty was mandating one intra-year inventory count for each sales office. Management used these inventories, which were taken by the company's two-person internal audit staff, to monitor inventory shrinkage at each sales outlet.

Goodner's inventory shrinkage significantly exceeded the industry norm. The company occasionally purchased large shipments of "seconds" from manufacturers; that is, tires with defects that prevented them from being sold to major retailers. The tires in these lots with major defects were taken to a tire disposal facility. A sales office's accounting records were not adjusted for these "throwaways" until the year-end physical inventory was taken.

Selling Tires on the Sly

Within a few days after Woody hatched his plan to pay off his gambling debts, he visited the remote storage site for the Huntington sales office. Woody rummaged through its dimly lit and cluttered interior searching for individual lots of tires that apparently had been collecting dust for several months. After finding several stacks of tires satisfying that requirement, Woody jotted down their specifications in a small notebook. For each lot, Woody listed customers who could potentially find some use for the given tires.

Later that same day, Woody made his first "sale." A local plumbing supply dealer needed tires for his small fleet of vehicles. Woody convinced the business's owner that Goodner was attempting to "move" some old inventory. That inventory would be sold on a cash basis and at prices significantly below Goodner's cost. The owner agreed to purchase two dozen of the tires. After delivering the tires in his large pickup, Woody received a cash payment of $900 directly from the customer.

Over the next several months, Woody routinely stole inventory and kept the proceeds. Woody concealed the thefts in various ways. In some cases, he would charge merchandise that he had sold for his own benefit to the accounts of large volume customers. Woody preferred this technique since it allowed him to reduce the inventory balance in the Huntington facility's accounting records. When customers complained to him for being charged for merchandise they had not purchased, Woody simply apologized and corrected their account balances. If the customers paid the improper charges, they unknowingly helped Woody sustain his fraudulent scheme.

Goodner's customers frequently returned tires for various reasons. Woody completed credit memos for sales transactions voided by his customers, but instead of returning the tires to Goodner's inventory, he often sold them and kept the proceeds. Goodner occasionally consigned tires to large retailers for promotional sales events. When the consignees returned the unsold tires to Goodner, Woody would sell some of the tires to other customers for cash. Finally, Woody began offering to take throwaways to the tire disposal facility in nearby Shoals, West Virginia, a task typically assigned to a sales outlet's delivery workers. Not surprisingly, most of the tires that Woody carted off for disposal were not defective.

The ease with which he could steal tires made Woody increasingly bold. In late 2006, Woody offered to sell Al Hunt tires he had allegedly purchased from a manufacturer (by this time, Al owned and operated Curcio's Tires). Woody told Al that he had discovered the manufacturer was disposing of its inventory of discontinued tires and decided to buy them himself. When Al asked whether such "self-dealing" violated Goodner's company policy, Woody replied, "It's none of their business what I do in my spare time. Why should I let them know about this great deal that I stumbled upon?"

At first reluctant, Al eventually agreed to purchase several dozen tires from Woody. No doubt, the cut-rate prices at which Woody was selling the tires made the decision much easier. At those prices, Al realized he would earn a sizable profit on the tires.

Over the next 12 months, Woody continued to sell "closeout" tires to his friend. After one such purchase, Al called the manufacturer from whom Woody had reportedly purchased the tires. Al had become suspicious of the frequency of the closeout sales and the bargain basement prices at which Woody supposedly purchased the tires. When he called the manufacturer, a sales rep told Al that his company had only one closeout sale each year. The sales rep also informed Al that his company sold closeout merchandise directly to wholesalers, never to individuals or retail establishments.

The next time Al spoke to Woody, he mentioned matter-of-factly that he had contacted Woody's primary supplier of closeout tires. Al then told his friend that a sales rep for the company indicated that such merchandise was only sold to wholesalers.

"So, what's the point, Al?"

"Well, I just found it kind of strange that, uh, that . . ."

"C'mon, get to the point, Al."

"Well, Woody, I was just wondering where you're getting these tires that you're selling."

"Do you want to know, Al? Do you really want to know, Buddy? I'll tell you if you want to know," Woody replied angrily.

After a lengthy pause, Al shrugged his shoulders and told his friend to "just forget it." Despite his growing uneasiness regarding the source of the cheap tires, Al continued to buy them and never again asked Woody where he was obtaining them.

Internal Auditors Discover Inventory Shortage

On December 31, 2006, the employees of Goodner's Huntington location met to take a physical inventory. The employees treated the annual event as a prelude to their New Year's Eve party. Counting typically began around noon and was finished within three hours. The employees worked in teams of three. Two members of each team climbed and crawled over the large stacks of tires and shouted out their counts to the third member who recorded them on preformatted count sheets.

Woody arranged to work with two delivery workers who were relatively unfamiliar with Goodner's inventory since they had been hired only a few weeks earlier. He made sure that his team was one of the two count teams assigned to the remote storage facility. Most of the inventory he had stolen over the previous six months had been taken from that site. Woody estimated that he had stolen approximately $45,000 of inventory from the remote storage facility, which represented about 10 percent of the site's book inventory. By maintaining the count sheets for his team, Woody could easily inflate the quantities for the tire lots that he and his team members counted.

After the counting was completed at the remote storage facility, Woody offered to take the count sheets for both teams to the sales office where the total inventory would be compiled. On the way to the sales office, he stopped in a vacant parking lot to review the count sheets. Woody quickly determined that the apparent shortage remaining at the remote site was approximately $20,000. He reduced that shortage to less than $10,000 by altering the count sheets prepared by the other count team.

When the year-end inventory was tallied for Goodner's Huntington location, the difference between the physical inventory and the book inventory was $12,000, or 2.1 percent. That percentage exceeded the historical shrinkage rate of approximately 1.6 percent for Goodner's sales offices. But Felix Garcia, the sales manager for the Huntington sales office, did not believe that the 2006 shrinkage was excessive. As it turned out, neither did the accounting personnel and internal auditors at Goodner's corporate headquarters.

Woody continued "ripping off" Goodner throughout 2007. By midyear, Woody was selling most of the tires he stole to Al Hunt. On one occasion, Woody warned Al not to sell the tires too cheaply. Woody had become concerned that Curcio's modest prices and its increasing sales volume might spark the curiosity and envy of other Huntington tire retailers.

In October 2007, Goodner's internal audit team arrived to count the Huntington location's inventory. Although company policy dictated that the internal auditors count the inventory of each Goodner sales outlet annually, the average interval between the internal audit inventory counts typically ranged from 15 to 20 months. The internal auditors had last counted the Huntington location's inventory in May 2006, two months before Woody Robinson began stealing tires. Woody was unaware that the internal auditors periodically counted the entire inventory of each Goodner operating unit. Instead, he understood that the internal auditors only did a few test counts during their infrequent visits to the Huntington sales office.

After completing their inventory counts, the two internal auditors arrived at an inventory value of $498,000. A quick check of the accounting records revealed a book inventory of $639,000. The auditors had never encountered such a large difference between the physical and book inventory totals. Unsure what to do at this point, the auditors eventually decided to take the matter directly to Felix Garcia, the Huntington sales manager.

The size of the inventory shortage shocked Garcia. He insisted that the auditors must have overlooked some inventory. Garcia, the two internal auditors, and three delivery workers spent the following day recounting the entire inventory. The resulting physical inventory value was $496,000, $2,000 less than the original value arrived at by the auditors.

Following the second physical inventory, the two internal auditors and Garcia met at a local restaurant to review the Huntington unit's inventory records. No glaring trends were evident in those records to either Garcia or the auditors. Garcia admitted to the auditors that the long hours required "just to keep the tires coming and going" left him little time to monitor his unit's accounting records. When pressed by the auditors to provide possible explanations for the inventory shortage, Garcia erupted. "Listen. Like I just said, my job is simple. My job is selling tires. I sell as many tires as I can, as quickly as I can. I let you guys and those other suits up in Youngstown track the numbers."

The following day, the senior internal auditor called his immediate superior, Goodner's chief financial officer (CFO). The size of the inventory shortage alarmed the CFO. Immediately, the CFO suspected that the inventory shortage was linked to the Huntington unit's downward trend in monthly profits over the past two years.

Through 2005, the Huntington sales office had consistently ranked as Goodner's second or third most profitable sales outlet. Over the past 18 months, the unit's slumping profits had caused it to fall to the bottom one-third of the company's sales outlets in terms of profit margin percentage. Tacking on the large inventory shortage would cause the Huntington location to be Goodner's least profitable sales office over the previous year and one-half.

After discussing the matter with T. J. and Ross Goodner, the CFO contacted the company's independent audit firm and arranged for the firm to investigate the inventory shortage. The Goodners agreed with the CFO that Felix Garcia should be suspended with pay until the investigation was concluded. Garcia's lack of a reasonable explanation for the missing inventory and the anger he had directed at the internal auditors caused Goodner's executives to conclude that he was likely responsible for the inventory shortage.

Within a few days, four auditors from Goodner's independent audit firm arrived at the Huntington sales office. Goodner's audit firm was a regional CPA firm with six offices, all in Ohio. Goodner obtained an annual audit of its financial statements because one was demanded by the New York bank that provided the company with a line of credit. Goodner's independent auditors had never paid much attention to the internal controls of the client's sales offices. Instead, they performed a "balance sheet" audit that emphasized corroborating Goodner's year-end assets and liabilities.

During their investigation of the missing inventory, the auditors were appalled by the Huntington unit's lax and often nonexistent controls. The extensive control weaknesses complicated their efforts to identify the source of the inventory shortage. Nevertheless, after several days, the auditors' suspicions began settling on Woody Robinson.

A file of customer complaints that Felix Garcia kept in his desk revealed that over the past year an unusually large number of customer complaints had been filed against Woody. During that time, 14 of his customers had protested charges included on their monthly statements. Only two customers serviced by the other sales rep had filed similar complaints during that time frame.

When questioned by the auditors, Garcia conceded that he had not discussed the customer complaints with Woody or the other sales rep. In fact, Garcia was unaware that a disproportionate number of the complaints had been filed against Woody. When Garcia received a customer complaint, he simply passed it on to the appropriate sales rep and allowed that individual to deal with the matter. He maintained a file of the customer complaints only because he had been told to do so by the previous sales manager whom he had replaced three years earlier.

After the independent auditors collected other incriminating evidence against Woody, they arranged for a meeting with him. Also attending that meeting were Goodner's CFO and Felix Garcia. When the auditors produced the incriminating evidence, Woody disclaimed any knowledge of, or responsibility for, the inventory shortage. Woody's denial provoked an immediate and indignant response from Goodner's CFO. "Listen, Robinson, you may have fooled the people you've been working with, but you're not fooling me. You'd better spill the beans right now, or else." At this point, Woody stood, announced that he was retaining an attorney, and walked out of the meeting.

EPILOGUE

Goodner Brothers filed a criminal complaint against Woody Robinson two weeks after he refused to discuss the inventory shortage at the Huntington sales office. A few weeks later, Woody's attorney reached a plea bargain agreement with the local district attorney. Woody received a five-year sentence for grand larceny, four years of which were suspended. He eventually served seven months of that sentence in a minimum-security prison. A condition of the plea bargain agreement required Woody to provide a full and candid written summary of the fraudulent scheme that he had perpetrated on his employer.

Woody's confession implicated Al Hunt in his theft scheme. Over the 15 months that Woody had stolen from Goodner, he had "fenced" most of the stolen inventory through Curcio's Tires. Although the district attorney questioned Al Hunt extensively, he decided not to file criminal charges against him.[2]

Goodner Brothers filed a $185,000 insurance claim to recoup the losses resulting from Woody's thefts. The company's insurer eventually paid Goodner $130,000, which equaled the theft losses that Goodner could document. After settling the claim, the insurance company sued Curcio's Tires and Al Hunt to recover the $98,000 windfall that Curcio's allegedly realized due to Al Hunt's involvement in the theft ring. The case went to federal district court where a judge ordered Hunt to pay $64,000 to Goodner's insurer. Al Hunt then sued Woody Robinson to recover that judgment. The judge, who had presided over the earlier case, quickly dismissed Al Hunt's lawsuit. According to the judge, Al Hunt's complicity in the fraudulent scheme voided his right to recover the $64,000 judgment from his former friend.

Questions

1. List what you believe should have been the three to five key internal control objectives of Goodner's Huntington sales office.

2. List the key internal control weaknesses that were evident in the Huntington unit's operations.

3. Develop one or more control policies or procedures to alleviate the control weaknesses you identified in responding to Question 2.

4. Besides Woody Robinson, what other parties were at least partially responsible for the inventory losses Goodner suffered? Defend your answer.

---

2. Ironically, Woody's confession also implicated his wife, Rachelle. After Woody revealed that Rachelle had typically deposited the large checks written to him by Al Hunt, the district attorney reasoned that Rachelle must have been aware of Woody's fraudulent scheme and was thus an accessory to his crime. However, Woody insisted that he had told his wife the checks were for gambling losses owed to him by Al. After interrogating Rachelle at length, the district attorney decided not to prosecute her.

Buranello's Ristorante

In 1983, Marta Giordano inherited the restaurant that her grandfather, Alberto Buranello, had established shortly after returning to his hometown of Boston after serving in World War I.[1] For nearly a century, the restaurant, Buranello's Ristorante, has been a landmark and favorite gathering spot for generations of families in Boston's historic North End neighborhood.

Over the years, the large corner restaurant that has a staff of approximately 40 employees, most of whom are part-time workers, has been essentially recession-proof. But Giordano's business recently faced two major challenges. Three local, formerly family-owned restaurants that Giordano considers to be her primary competitors were purchased by private investors who then renovated their interiors and facades and refurbished their kitchens. Although Buranello's breakfast and lunchtime traffic were largely unaffected by the competitors' upgrades, its dinner traffic fell by 20 percent. Making matters worse for Giordano during this same time span was another problem that was plaguing the restaurant, namely, abnormally large cash shortages apparently resulting from employee theft. These shortages were typically discovered at the close of business when the daily sales reconciliation worksheet was prepared.

The Suspect

Michael Barnes, Buranello's general manager, was just as frustrated by the cash shortages as his boss, Marta Giordano. Barnes has worked at Buranello's for more than 20 years and is practically a member of the Giordano family. His first position with the restaurant was as a busboy when he was 14-years-old. During college he worked as a waiter at the restaurant. When he graduated from Northeastern University with a management degree, Barnes turned down an offer from Giordano to become a member of Buranello's management staff, choosing instead to work for a large, nationally franchised restaurant chain that had an extensive management trainee program. Five years later, though, Barnes returned to Buranello's when Giordano offered him the position of general manager.

Barnes eventually called a meeting of the restaurant's management staff–himself, three shift managers, three assistant managers, and the chef–to address the cash shortages being experienced by Buranello's. At the meeting, which Giordano also attended, Barnes informed his subordinates that the cash shortages were becoming larger and more frequent. He pledged that he would catch the culprit or culprits and prosecute them to the fullest extent of the law. Barnes did not discuss specific measures that he planned to take to determine the source of the cash shortages. Why? Because he suspected that the thief was a member of the management staff. The prime suspect in Barnes mind was Aaron O'Neil, one of the three shift managers.

Barnes rotates the work assignments for the shift managers so that each of them works the closing shift, which is 3 p.m. to 11 p.m., only twice per week.[2] Buranello's

---

1. This case was developed from a recent legal opinion. The names of the actual parties involved in the case and the location have been changed. In addition, certain of the background details presented in the case are fictionalized accounts of information disclosed in the legal opinion.

2. The opening shift runs from 7 a.m. to 3 p.m. Shift managers supervise four eight-hour shifts each week. During their fifth eight-hour shift each week, they serve as an assistant manager to the shift manager on duty.

is closed on Sundays when it often hosts private parties such as family reunions and wedding receptions. One of the responsibilities of the shift manager at closing is to prepare the daily sales reconciliation. To perform this task the shift manager completes one of the standard reconciliation templates used for that purpose within the restaurant industry. The final task of the closing shift manager is to prepare the bank deposit for that day's sales. The day's receipts along with the completed deposit slip are left overnight in the restaurant's safe. The following morning, the shift manager who opens the restaurant recounts the receipts, traces the resulting total to the deposit slip, and then takes both to Buranello's bank a few blocks away.

The purpose of the daily sales reconciliation is to reconcile the day's sales reflected by the cash register printout to the total cash and cash items in the cash register at the close of business. The final line item on the reconciliation worksheet is entitled "Variance." A negative variance reflects a cash shortage, while a positive variance indicates a cash overage. Similar to most restaurants and retail businesses, Buranello's typically has a modest cash shortage at the end of each business day.

After Buranello's began experiencing abnormally large cash shortages, Barnes retained the business's accounting firm to analyze the restaurant's daily sales reconciliations. The accounting firm attempted to correlate the cash shortages with the shifts worked by the management staff and the cashiers, but the results of that analysis were inconclusive.[3] The accounting firm also attempted to determine whether the cash shortages were correlated with the presence of a specific shift manager during the closing shifts–Barnes believed that cash was most likely being stolen during the nightly closing procedures. Again, the results were inconclusive. There was no definite trend that linked the shortages to the closing shifts worked by specific shift managers. In Barnes's mind, the results of the accounting firm's analyses suggested that the thief or thieves were sufficiently clever to make it difficult for the cash shortages to be traced directly to them.

The only evidence that linked Aaron O'Neil to the cash shortages was the fact that they began occurring within a few weeks of the date that he began working at Buranello's. But there was another reason that Barnes suspected O'Neil. During the 20 years prior to accepting a position with Buranello's, O'Neil had been employed by seven different restaurants or restaurant chains. That unstable employment history had concerned Barnes when he interviewed him. The reference letters provided by O'Neil's former employers had also posed some degree of concern since they had been generally lukewarm, at best, in their endorsement of him. Despite the fact that O'Neil had been a marginal job candidate, Barnes had hired him because Buranello's management team was chronically understaffed. Similar to most restaurants, management and employee turnover is a constant problem faced by Buranello's.

The Opportunity

The cash shortages infuriated Barnes not only because of the adverse financial impact they had on the restaurant but also because they reflected poorly on his management style and overall performance as the caretaker of the business for the Giordano family. Barnes much prefers "pressing the flesh" with customers and the restaurant's wait staff rather than taking care of his back office responsibilities. He often allows his paperwork, which includes health inspection reports, tax reporting schedules, and the daily sales reconciliation worksheets, to pile up on his desk.

---

3. Five individuals have access to Buranello's cash register during each shift: the cashier, the shift manager, the assistant manager, Barnes, and Giordano, who typically spends a few hours each day in the restaurant.

Barnes finds the daily sales reconciliation worksheets particularly wearisome. He would never admit as much to Marta Giordano or any of his subordinates, but even after having completed hundreds of daily sales reconciliations, it is still a challenging task for him on the infrequent occasions when he closes the restaurant.

The objective of a daily sales reconciliation is obvious to Barnes, but the task itself is tedious and frustrating. The process of completing the worksheet at the end of a busy day requires properly analyzing a wide array of nonstandard transactions. These items may include a variety of coupons redeemed by customers, discounted meals purchased by employees, unpaid meal tickets of "deadbeat" customers who slipped out of the restaurant without paying, duplicate meal tickets issued to replace lost or misplaced tickets, refunds for overcharges, purchases or redemptions of meal cards given as gifts, petty cash expenditures such as modest charitable contributions, discounts or rain checks given to unhappy patrons whose pasta was not cooked to order, and so on and so forth. Each time that he completes a daily sales reconciliation worksheet, Barnes is reminded why he switched his major from accounting to management during his sophomore year of college.

Barnes also finds the task of reviewing completed daily sales reconciliation worksheets unpleasant, which is why he often has a stack of them sitting on his desk. Ironically, despite his accounting "dyslexia," he is the person responsible for the final approval of the reconciliations. The most challenging facet of reviewing the reconciliations is deciphering, comprehending, and then clearing the numerous comments printed or scrawled haphazardly in the margins of the worksheet form. On a typical day, there are six to eight "problem" reconciling items that the closing shift manager must explain in a written comment on the worksheet form—the template used by Buranello's does not have a "comments" section.

The intricate nature of the reconciliation worksheets has convinced Barnes that an unscrupulous shift manager could easily use them as a tool to conceal amounts embezzled from the daily sales receipts. This ever-present opportunity, if not invitation, to steal from the restaurant means that the larger than normal cash shortages recently experienced by Buranello's may have been significantly understated.

The Sting

The day following the management meeting in which he addressed Buranello's recurring cash shortages, Barnes met with Marta Giordano. He had developed a plan to address the problem, and he wanted her approval before he went forward with it. Barnes told Giordano that he wanted to carry out a "sting" operation to test the honesty of Aaron O'Neil—Giordano was aware that Barnes considered O'Neil to be the most likely source of the cash shortages.

The plan called for Barnes to replace the closing shift manager on an evening before O'Neil was scheduled to open the restaurant the following day. During the closing procedures, Barnes would prepare a deposit slip that understated the amount of cash receipts by several hundred dollars—Giordano would be present to verify the understatement. Barnes expected, actually hoped, that O'Neil would steal the excess cash prior to making the morning bank deposit. Barnes then planned to contact the police and file theft charges against O'Neil. Giordano reluctantly approved Barnes's plan, although she thought it smacked of entrapment and considered it to be distasteful.

Barnes executed his plan the following week and it seemed to work to perfection. Neither O'Neil nor the bank reported the difference between the cash receipts and the dollar amount reflected on the given deposit slip. In Barnes's mind that meant that O'Neil had stolen the excess cash in the deposit, which amounted to $360.

The following day, Barnes contacted the police and reported the incident. He and Giordano met the police detective assigned to investigate the apparent embezzlement. Barnes told the officer that he believed O'Neil had stolen the $360 and wanted to press charges against him on behalf of Buranello's. Barnes also told the detective that he suspected O'Neil was responsible for the rash of abnormally large cash shortages experienced by the restaurant over the past several months. The detective informed Barnes that it would be necessary for him to provide evidence to support that allegation.

That afternoon, the detective went to O'Neil's apartment with two uniformed officers–O'Neil had not been scheduled to work that day. After the detective explained the circumstances of the alleged embezzlement, O'Neil indicated that he wanted to contact his attorney. The uniformed officers then arrested O'Neil, handcuffed him, and marched him through the large courtyard of his apartment complex on the way to the patrol car.

O'Neil's attorney arrived at the police station to consult with his client later that afternoon. At approximately 5 p.m., the attorney arranged a meeting involving himself, O'Neil, and the detective in charge of the case. During this meeting, the attorney told the detective that O'Neil had not stolen the $360. When counting the cash before making the deposit, O'Neil had discovered that the cash receipts exceeded the amount reported on the deposit slip by $360. O'Neil had then taken that amount and placed it in Buranello's safe in an envelope marked to the attention of Michael Barnes.

The detective telephoned Michael Barnes, passed along the information provided by O'Neil, and asked him to search the safe. Barnes and Giordano went through the safe but could not find the envelope. When the detective told O'Neil that the envelope could not be found, O'Neil asked to be taken to the restaurant to search for it himself. The detective refused to do that.

O'Neil then asked the detective to send a police officer to search the safe. After the detective agreed to send an officer to the restaurant, O'Neil told the detective exactly where the envelope containing the $360 could be found. According to O'Neil, he had placed the letter-sized envelope containing the $360 in a larger envelope that was labeled "Equipment Leases." When the detective asked O'Neil why he had hidden the cash so well, he replied that he believed he was being "set up" by Barnes. O'Neil explained that he had been hoping to "buy some time" to figure out exactly what to do, which also explained why he had not called Barnes immediately and reported the excess cash.

The police officer sent to Buranello's found the hidden cash in a matter of minutes. The charges filed against O'Neil were immediately dropped, and he was released from police custody.

The Lawsuit

Aaron O'Neil never returned to Buranello's, choosing instead to resign immediately, but Michael Barnes and Marta Giordano had not heard the last of him.[4] One month later, O'Neil filed a "malicious prosecution" civil lawsuit that named Buranello's, Barnes, and Giordano as defendants. Following a brief trial, the jury ruled in O'Neil's favor and awarded him a judgment of $66,000. The defendants immediately appealed the jury's ruling. One year later, an appellate court overturned the jury's decision and voided the judgment. The appellate court ruled that because Barnes and Giordano

---

4. The abnormally large cash shortages experienced by Buranello's ended abruptly when O'Neil terminated his employment.

had "probable cause" to file theft charges against O'Neil they could not be accused of "malicious prosecution."

Questions

1. Identify internal control weaknesses evident in Buranello's operations. What risks are posed by these internal control problems?

2. For each internal control weakness you listed in responding to the previous question, identify a measure that Buranello's could implement to remedy that weakness. Indicate whether these measures would be cost effective.

3. Prepare a list of internal control procedures for a restaurant other than the controls referred to in this case. For each control that you list, identify its underlying objective.

4. Do you believe that Barnes's plan to test Aaron O'Neil's honesty was appropriate? Was it ethical? What ethical responsibilities does a business's senior management or owner have when an employee is suspected of theft?

Foamex International Inc.

In 1937, Otto Bayer, a research scientist for the large German chemical company IG Farben, discovered a new chemical compound that would become known as polyurethane. During World War II, polyurethane was used principally in the manufacture of military equipment and supplies. Following the war, IG Farben was dismantled by the Allied Forces as punishment for its collaboration with the Nazis. Certain of the company's products had been used by the Nazis to perpetrate unconscionable atrocities on innocent civilians.

During the latter one-half of the twentieth century, polyurethane was used in the manufacture of a wide range of consumer goods, including automotive trims and moldings, batteries, carpet padding, and diapers. Among the most important polyurethane derivatives was a compound initially referred to as "imitation Swiss cheese." Polyurethane foam was "invented" in a research laboratory in the early 1950s when water was accidentally added during the production process for polyurethane.

One of the initial manufacturers of polyurethane foam was the Firestone Tire and Rubber Company. The Firestone division that produced the product would eventually become a freestanding company, Foamex International, Inc. Foamex became the United States' largest producer of polyurethane foam due to an ambitious acquisition program initiated by the company's management during the 1980s. By 2001, Foamex owned and operated more than 50 manufacturing and distributing facilities in the United States, Canada, and Mexico.

An unanticipated by-product of Foamex's acquisition program was a chaotic accounting system. The companies acquired by Foamex continued to use the accounting systems that they had previously employed. As a result, by the year 2000, Foamex's corporate accounting system was an amalgamation of dozens of geographically dispersed "legacy" systems that relied on a haphazard assortment of computer hardware and software components.

Foamex's failure to develop a coherent, integrated corporate accounting system complicated the annual audits of the company. In August 1999, PricewaterhouseCoopers (PwC), Foamex's independent audit firm, notified the company's audit committee that Foamex needed to improve its internal controls. "The auditor reported that Foamex's systems for the preparation of interim financial information did not provide an adequate basis for the auditor to complete, prior to certain filing deadlines, its reviews of Foamex's interim financial statements."[1] In May 2000, following the completion of the 1999 Foamex audit—the company's fiscal year coincided with the calendar year—PwC issued a "Report to Management." This report identified several serious internal control problems or "reportable conditions"[2] and

---

1. This and all subsequent quotes, unless indicated otherwise, were taken from the following source: Securities and Exchange Commission, *Accounting and Auditing Enforcement Release No. 2274*, 11 July 2005.

2. At the time, professional auditing standards defined "reportable conditions" as "matters coming to the auditor's attention that, in his judgment, should be communicated to the audit committee because they represent significant deficiencies in the design or operation of internal control, which could adversely affect the organization's ability to initiate, record, process, and report financial data consistent with the assertions of management in the financial statements." (AU Section 325.02 [superseded])

recommended that Foamex take the following specific actions to remedy these problems:

(1)   *make significant improvements in the control environment and reporting practices of Foamex's foreign operations;*

(2)   *conduct a comprehensive analysis of financial results on a quarterly basis;*

(3)   *improve inventory reporting; and*

(4)   *develop a comprehensive information technology strategy, including an enterprise-wide security program.*

During the 2000 audit of Foamex, PwC informed the company's audit committee on multiple occasions of reportable conditions similar to those included in the Report to Management issued in May 2000. After completing the 2000 audit, PwC resigned in June 2001. The following month, Foamex retained Deloitte & Touche as its independent audit firm.

Foamex's management informed the SEC in 2002 that the company was in the process of resolving the internal control problems previously identified by PwC. Nevertheless, in early 2003, during its 2002 audit, Deloitte identified five reportable conditions that it communicated to Foamex's audit committee.[3] These conditions involved the following areas of concern:

(1)   *oversight of financial reporting by international subsidiaries;*

(2)   *inventory procedures, processes, and systems;*

(3)   *integration of IT systems;*

(4)   *access and security for IT systems; and,*

(5)   *process for reviewing and approving journal entries.*

In January 2004, Foamex restated the financial statements included in its Form 10-Qs filed with the SEC for the first three quarterly reporting periods of 2003. These restatements were necessary because of a major glitch discovered in the processing of inventory transactions. After completing its 2003 audit of Foamex in March 2004, Deloitte notified the company's audit committee of four reportable conditions. Three of these items involved control issues identified in Deloitte's 2003 report to the audit committee. The fourth reportable condition concerned control weaknesses in Foamex's quarterly financial reporting system.

After receiving Deloitte's internal control report in March 2004, Foamex's audit committee dismissed Deloitte and retained KPMG as the company's new audit firm. Over the following few months, Foamex made several changes in its senior management. One of those changes involved appointing a former Ernst & Young partner to the company's board of directors and audit committee. Foamex's new management team also hired a "special consultant on internal accounting controls" to remedy the company's pervasive internal control problems.

Foamex's efforts in 2004 to improve its internal controls were "too little and too late" to satisfy the SEC. In 2005, Foamex became the first SEC registrant to be sanctioned by the federal agency solely for having inadequate internal controls. In the *Accounting and Auditing Enforcement Release* summarizing its investigation of Foamex, the SEC defended the decision to sanction the company despite its belated attempt to improve its internal controls.

> *The repeated observations of the auditors and Foamex's history of restating its interim financial reports show that Foamex did not devote the appropriate managerial effort*

---

3. The SEC enforcement release for this case did not reveal whether Deloitte discovered reportable conditions in Foamex's internal controls during its 2001 audit.

and other resources to remediate its deficient internal controls, which were identified as reportable conditions in 1999.

The cease and desist order issued to Foamex by the SEC included a road map for the company to follow to improve its internal controls. During the 2005 audit, the SEC ordered Foamex to "cooperate fully" with KPMG's review and evaluation of the company's internal controls pursuant to Section 404 of the Sarbanes-Oxley Act of 2002. Following the 2005 audit, the SEC instructed KPMG to issue a "Section 404 Report" to Foamex's audit committee. That report would document any "significant deficiencies" in Foamex's internal controls. The audit committee would then forward the report to Foamex's special consultant on internal controls.

Within 90 days, the special consultant would issue a report to Foamex's audit committee and the SEC that identified specific recommendations for eliminating the internal control deficiencies. The SEC mandated that Foamex adopt those recommendations or propose alternative measures that would be equally as effective. The special consultant was also instructed to issue quarterly reports to Foamex's audit committee and the SEC until all of the reported internal control deficiencies were eliminated.

The SEC's decision to sanction Foamex was interpreted as a "message"[4] being sent by the federal agency to public companies. The intended message was that the SEC would rigorously enforce the new internal control initiatives included in the Sarbanes-Oxley Act. Ironically, absent the SEC's specific directive that required KPMG to perform a Section 404 review and evaluation of Foamex's internal controls, the company would have been exempt from that requirement because it was a "non-accelerated filer."[5] Due to widespread concern that Section 404 audit and internal control remediation costs would be onerous for small public companies, the SEC had delayed the implementation of the principal Section 404 requirements for those registrants. In late 2010, Congress passed a law that permanently exempted non-accelerated filers from being required to obtain Section 404 reports on their internal controls.

Questions

1. Who has the final responsibility for the integrity of an SEC registrant's internal controls: its audit committee, its management team, or its independent auditors? Explain.

2. Under the professional standards currently in effect, what responsibility do auditors have to identify internal control problems within their clients' accounting systems? To whom must auditors communicate such problems? In responding to these questions, indicate how auditors' responsibilities differ, if at all, between public and nonpublic clients.

3. Under what conditions is a public company allowed to dismiss its independent audit firm? Under what conditions is an independent audit firm allowed to resign as the auditor of a public company? What disclosures, if any, does the SEC mandate when a public company experiences a change in its independent auditors?

4. Should the SEC selectively prosecute companies, organizations, or individuals to encourage compliance with legal or professional standards? Defend your answer.

---

4. P.J. Martinek, "SEC Probe Into Foamex Internal Controls Won't Be Last," *Compliance Week* (online), 12 April 2006.

5. Non-accelerated filers are generally SEC registrants that have a market capitalization of $75 million or less.

ETHICAL RESPONSIBILITIES OF ACCOUNTANTS

4

Creve Couer Pizza, Inc.

Imagine this scenario. A few years after graduating from College of William & Mary, Xavier University, or Youngstown State University with an accounting degree, you find yourself working as an audit senior with an international accounting firm. Your best friend, Rick, whom you have known since kindergarten, is a special agent with the Internal Revenue Service (IRS). Over lunch one day, Rick mentions the IRS's informant program.

"You know, Jess, you could pick up a few hundred dollars here and there working as a controlled informant for us. In fact, if you would feed us information regarding one or two of those large corporate clients of yours, you could make a bundle."

"That's funny, Rick. Real funny. Me, a double agent, spying on my clients for the IRS? Have you ever heard of the confidentiality rule?"

Sound farfetched? Not really. Since 1939, the IRS has operated an informant program. Most individuals who participate in this program provide information on a one-time basis; however, the IRS also retains hundreds of "controlled informants" who work in tandem with one or more IRS special agents on a continuing basis. Controlled informants provide the IRS with incriminating evidence regarding individuals and businesses suspected of cheating on their taxes. In the early 1990s, the IRS revealed that more than 40 of these controlled informants were CPAs.

Now consider this scenario. You, the audit senior, are again having lunch with your friend Rick, the IRS special agent. Rick knows that the IRS is investigating you for large deductions taken in recent years on your federal income tax returns for a questionable tax shelter scheme. The additional tax assessments and fines you face significantly exceed your net worth. Your legal costs alone will be thousands of dollars. To date, you have been successful in concealing the IRS investigation from your spouse, other family members, and your employer, but that will not be possible much longer.

"Jess, I know this investigation is really worrying you. But I can get you out of this whole mess. I talked to my supervisor. She and three other agents are working on a case involving one of your audit clients. I can't tell you which one right now. If you agree to work with them as a controlled informant and provide them with information that you can easily get your hands on, they will close the case on you. You will be off the hook. No questions. No fines or additional taxes. Case closed . . . permanently."

"Rick, come on, I can't do that. What if my firm finds out? I'd lose my job. I would probably lose my certificate."

"Yeah, but face these facts. If the IRS proves its case against you, you are going to lose your job and your certificate . . . and probably a whole lot more. Maybe even your marriage. Think about it, Jess. Realistically, the agency is looking at a maximum recovery of $50,000 from you. But if you cooperate with my supervisor, she can probably squeeze several million out of your client."

"You're sure they would let me off . . . free and clear?"

"Yes. Free and clear. Come on, Jess, we need you. More important, you need us. Plus, think of it this way. You made one mistake by becoming involved in that phony tax shelter scam. But your client has been ripping off the government, big time, for years. You would be doing a public service by turning in those crooks."

Returning to reality, consider the case of James Checksfield. In 1981, Checksfield, a Missouri CPA, became a controlled informant for the IRS. The IRS special agent who recruited Checksfield had been his close friend for several years and knew that Checksfield was under investigation by the IRS. Reportedly, Checksfield owed back taxes of nearly $30,000 because of his failure to file federal income tax returns from 1974 through 1977.

At the same time the IRS recruited Checksfield, the federal agency was also investigating a Missouri-based company, Creve Couer Pizza, Inc. The IRS believed that the owner of this chain of pizza restaurants was "skimming receipts" from his business– that is, failing to report on his federal income tax returns the total sales revenue of his eight restaurants. Checksfield had served as Creve Couer's CPA for several years, although both the IRS and Checksfield denied that he was recruited specifically to provide information regarding that company.

From 1982 through 1985, Checksfield funneled information to the IRS regarding Creve Couer Pizza. Based upon this information, federal prosecutors filed a six-count criminal indictment against the owner of that business in 1989. This indictment charged the owner with underreporting his taxable income by several hundred thousand dollars. The owner faced fines of nearly $1 million and a prison term of up to 24 years if convicted of the charges. Meanwhile, the IRS dropped its case against Checksfield. Both the IRS and Checksfield maintained that there was no connection between the decision to drop the case against him and his decision to provide the IRS with information regarding Creve Couer Pizza.

Following the indictment filed against the owner of Creve Couer Pizza, the owner's attorneys subpoenaed the information that the IRS had used to build its case against him. As a result, the owner discovered the role played by his longtime friend and accountant in the IRS investigation. Quite naturally, the owner was very upset. "What my accountant did to me was very mean and devious. He sat here in my home with me and my family. He was like a member of the family. On the other hand, he was working against me."[1] In another interview, the owner observed, "A client has the right to feel he's getting undivided loyalty from his accountant."[2] Contributing to the owner's anger was the fact that he had paid Checksfield more than $50,000 in fees for accounting and taxation services during the time the CPA was working undercover for the IRS.

The print and electronic media reported the case of the "singing CPA" nationwide, prompting extensive criticism of the IRS. The case also caused many clients of CPAs to doubt whether they could trust their accountants to protect the confidentiality of sensitive financial information. When questioned concerning the matter, the IRS expressed no remorse for using Checksfield to gather incriminating evidence regarding the owner of Creve Couer Pizza. An IRS representative also rejected the contention that communications between accountants and their clients should be "privileged" under federal law similar to the communications between attorneys and their clients.

> The IRS says the claim of a privileged [accountant-client] relationship is nonsense. "To the contrary," says Edward Federico of the IRS's criminal-investigation division in St. Louis, "the accountant has a moral and legal obligation to turn over information."[3]

---

1. "Accountant Spies on Client for IRS," *Kansas City Star*, 18 March 1992, 2.

2. "The Case of the Singing CPA," *Newsweek*, 17 July 1989, 41.

3. *Ibid.*

The accounting profession was appalled by the Checksfield case and tried to minimize the damage it had done to the public's trust in CPAs. In particular, the profession condemned the actions of the IRS.

> *Rarely has there been such a case of prosecutorial zeal that violated rudimentary standards of decency. . . . Turning the client–accountant relationship into a secret tool for government agents is an abominable practice. It demeans the service. It erodes trust in the accounting profession.*[4]

EPILOGUE

In August 1990, the Missouri State Board of Accountancy revoked James Checksfield's CPA license for violating a state law that prohibits CPAs from disclosing confidential client information without the client's permission. In November 1991, the U.S. Department of Justice suddenly announced that it was dropping the tax evasion charges against the owner of Creve Couer Pizza, although pretrial arguments had already been presented for the case. The Justice Department had little to say regarding its decision. Legal experts speculated that federal prosecutors dropped the charges because the judge hearing the case was expected to disallow the evidence that the IRS had collected with the assistance of Checksfield.

Despite the negative publicity produced by the Creve Couer case, the IRS continues to use accountants both in public practice and private industry as informants. In the late 1990s, *Forbes* magazine reported a case in which a disgruntled controller of a retail electronics chain got even with his boss.[5] Shortly before leaving the firm, the controller copied accounting and tax records documenting a large-scale tax fraud perpetrated by the chain's owner. Thanks to this information, the IRS collected a nearly $7 million fine from the owner and sent him to jail for 10 months. The former controller received a significant but undisclosed "finder's fee" from the IRS for his "cooperation."[6]

Questions

1. Do CPAs who provide accounting, taxation, and related services to small businesses have a responsibility to serve as the "moral conscience" of those clients? Explain.

2. In a 1984 opinion handed down by the U.S. Supreme Court, Chief Justice Warren Burger noted that "the independent auditor assumes a public responsibility transcending any employment relationship with the client." If this is true, do auditors have a moral or professional responsibility to turn in clients who are cheating on their taxes or violating other laws?

3. Assume that you were Jess in the second hypothetical scenario presented in this case. How would you respond to your friend's suggestion that you become a controlled informant for the IRS? Identify the parties that would be affected by your decision and the obligations you would have to each.

---

4. "IRS Oversteps with CPA Stoolies," *Accounting Today*, 6 January 1992, 22.

5. J. Novack, "Boomerang," *Forbes*, 7 July 1997, 42–43.

6. In 2007, the IRS Whistleblower Office was established. This office administers a provision of a 2006 federal law that guarantees individuals who report significant tax deficiencies owed by other parties a minimum payment equal to 15 percent of the delinquent taxes collected.

F&C International, Inc.

Alex Fries emigrated to the United States from Germany in the early nineteenth century.[1] The excitement and opportunities promised by the western frontier fascinated thousands of new Americans, including the young German who followed his dreams and the Ohio River west to Cincinnati. A chemist by training, Fries soon found a job in the booming distillery industry of southern Ohio and northern Kentucky. His background suited him well for an important need of distilleries, namely, developing flavors to make their products more palatable for the public. Alex Fries eventually established his own flavor company. Thanks largely to Fries, Cincinnati became the home of the small but important flavor industry in the United States. By the end of the twentieth century, the flavor industry's annual revenues approached $5 billion.

Alex Fries' success in the flavor industry became a family affair. Two of his grandsons created their own flavor company, Fries & Fries, in the early 1900s. Several decades later, another descendant of Alex Fries, Jon Fries, served as the president and CEO of F&C International, Inc., a flavor company whose common stock traded on the NASDAQ stock exchange. F&C International, also based in Cincinnati, reigned for a time during the 1980s as Ohio's fastest-growing corporation. Sadly, the legacy of the Fries family in the flavor industry came to a distasteful end in the early 1990s.

The Fraud

Jon Fries orchestrated a large-scale financial fraud that led to the downfall of F&C International. At least 10 other F&C executives actively participated in the scam or allowed it to continue unchecked due to their inaction. The methods used by Fries and his cohorts were not unique or even innovative. Fries realized that the most effective strategy for embellishing his company's periodic operating results was to inflate revenues and overstate period-ending inventories. Throughout the early 1990s, F&C systematically overstated sales revenues by backdating valid sales transactions, shipping customers product they had not ordered, and recording bogus sales transactions. To overstate inventory, F&C personnel filled barrels with water and then labeled those barrels as containing high-concentrate flavor products. The company also neglected to write off defective goods and included waste products from manufacturing processes in inventory. Company officials used F&C's misleading financial statements to sell equity securities and to obtain significant bank financing.

As F&C's fraud progressed, Jon Fries and his top subordinates struggled to develop appropriate sales and inventory management strategies since the company's accounting records were unreliable. To help remedy this problem, F&C created an imaginary warehouse, Warehouse Q.

---

1. The facts in this case were taken from several SEC enforcement releases and a series of articles that appeared in the *Cincinnati Enquirer.* The key parties in this case neither admitted nor denied the facts reported by the SEC. Those parties include Jon Fries, Catherine Sprauer, Fletcher Anderson, and Craig Schuster.

Warehouse Q became the accounting repository for product returned by customers for being below specification, unusable or nonexistent items, and items that could not be found in the actual warehouses.[2]

Another baffling problem that faced Fries and his confederates was concealing the company's fraudulent activities from F&C's independent auditors. The executives continually plotted to divert their auditors' attention from suspicious transactions and circumstances uncovered during the annual audits. Subversive measures taken by the executives included creating false documents, mislabeling inventory counted by the auditors, and undercutting subordinates' attempts to expose the fraud.

The size and complexity of F&C's fraud eventually caused the scheme to unravel. Allegations that the company's financial statements contained material irregularities triggered an investigation by the Securities and Exchange Commission (SEC). The investigation revealed that F&C had overstated its cumulative pretax earnings during the early 1990s by approximately $8 million. The company understated its pretax net loss for fiscal 1992 alone by nearly 140 percent or $3.8 million.

The Division Controller

Catherine Sprauer accepted an accounting position with F&C International in July 1992, shortly after the June 30 close of the company's 1992 fiscal year. Sprauer, a CPA, drafted the Management's Discussion and Analysis (MD&A) section of F&C's 1992 Form 10-K registration statement. In October 1992, the 28-year-old Sprauer became the controller of F&C's Flavor Division. Following that promotion, Sprauer continued to help prepare the MD&A sections of F&C's periodic financial reports submitted to the SEC.

In early January 1993, an F&C employee told Sprauer that he saw company employees filling inventory barrels with water in the final few days of June 1992. This individual also advised Sprauer that he had documentation linking two F&C executives to that incident, which was apparently intended to overstate the company's year-end inventory for fiscal 1992. According to the SEC, Sprauer abruptly ended the conversation with this employee and did not discuss his allegations with anyone.

Later that same day, another F&C employee approached Sprauer and confessed that he was involved in the episode recounted to her earlier in the day. This individual told Sprauer that he had acted under the direct instructions of Jon Fries. The employee then attempted to hand Sprauer a listing of inventory items affected by the fraud. Sprauer refused to accept the list. The persistent employee placed the list in Sprauer's correspondence file. The document detailed approximately $350,000 of nonexistent inventory in F&C's accounting records. Sprauer reportedly never showed the list of bogus inventory to her superiors, to other F&C accountants, or to the company's independent auditors. However, she subsequently warned F&C's chief operating officer (COO), Fletcher Anderson, that the company had "significant inventory problems."

The Chief Operating Officer

Fletcher Anderson became the COO of F&C International in September 1992 and joined the company's board of directors a few days later. On March 23, 1993, Anderson succeeded Jon Fries as F&C's president and CEO. During the fall of 1992, Anderson stumbled across several suspicious transactions in F&C's accounting records. In

---

2. Securities and Exchange Commission, *Accounting and Auditing Enforcement Release No. 605*, 28 September 1994. All subsequent quotations are taken from this source.

late September 1992, Anderson discovered sales shipments made before the given customers had placed purchase orders with F&C. He also learned that other sales shipments had been delivered to F&C warehouses rather than to customers. Finally, in early October 1992, Anderson uncovered a forged bill of lading for a customer shipment. The bill of lading had been altered to change the reported month of shipment from October to September. Each of these errors inflated F&C's reported earnings for the first quarter of fiscal 1993, which ended September 30, 1992.

More direct evidence that F&C's financial data were being systematically distorted came to Anderson's attention during the second quarter of 1993. In November, a subordinate told Anderson that some of the company's inventory of flavor concentrate was simply water labeled as concentrate. The following month, Anderson learned of Warehouse Q and that at least $1.5 million of the inventory "stored" in that warehouse could not be located or was defective.

Catherine Sprauer submitted her resignation to Fletcher Anderson in late January 1993. Among the reasons Sprauer gave for her resignation were serious doubts regarding the reliability of the company's inventory records. Anderson insisted that Sprauer not tell him why she believed those records were unreliable because he wanted to avoid testifying regarding her concerns in any subsequent litigation.

In February 1993, shortly before Anderson replaced Jon Fries as F&C's top executive, an F&C cost accountant warned him that the company had an inventory problem "in the magnitude of $3-4 million." Anderson later told the SEC that although the cost accountant had access to F&C's inventory records and its actual inventory, he believed the accountant was overstating the severity of the company's inventory problem.

The Chief Financial Officer

Craig Schuster served as the chief financial officer (CFO) of F&C International during the early 1990s. As F&C's CFO, Schuster oversaw the preparation of and signed the company's registration statements filed with the SEC, including the company's Form 10-K reports for fiscal 1991 and 1992. Throughout 1992, Schuster became aware of various problems in F&C's accounting records, most notably the existence of Warehouse Q. In March 1992, Schuster learned that his subordinates could not locate many items listed in F&C's perpetual inventory records. A few months later, Schuster discovered that customer shipments were being backdated in an apparent attempt to recognize sales revenue prematurely. In late 1992, Schuster determined that approximately $1 million of F&C's work-in-process inventory was classified as finished goods.

On December 17, 1992, a frustrated Schuster prepared and forwarded to Fletcher Anderson a 23-page list of $1.5 million of inventory allegedly stored in Warehouse Q. The memo indicated that the inventory could not be located or was defective. The SEC's enforcement releases focusing on the F&C fraud did not reveal how or whether Anderson responded to Schuster's memo.

Because he supervised the preparation of F&C's financial reports filed with the SEC, Schuster knew that those reports did not comment on the company's inventory problems. On January 1, 1993, Craig Schuster resigned as the CFO of F&C International. The final F&C registration statement Schuster signed was the company's Form 10-Q for the first quarter of fiscal 1993, which ended September 30, 1993.

The Rest of the Story

In a September 28, 1994, enforcement release, the SEC criticized Catherine Sprauer, Fletcher Anderson, and Craig Schuster for failing to ensure that F&C's financial reports "filed with the Commission and disseminated to the investing public were accurate."

The federal agency also chastised the three individuals for not disclosing in F&C's financial reports "significant accounting problems of which they were aware." Finally, the SEC scolded Anderson and Schuster for not establishing adequate internal controls to provide for the proper recognition of revenue and the proper valuation of inventory. In an agreement reached with the SEC to settle the allegations pending against them, the three former F&C executives pledged to "permanently cease and desist" from committing or causing violations of federal securities laws.

A second enforcement release issued by the SEC on September 28, 1994, contained a series of allegations directed at Jon Fries and seven other senior F&C executives. The SEC charged that these executives were primarily responsible for F&C's fraudulent earnings scheme. To settle these charges, each executive pledged not to violate federal securities laws in the future. The settlement agreement permanently banned Jon Fries from serving as an officer or director of a public company. Several of the individuals agreed to forfeit proceeds received from earlier sales of F&C securities. Fries relinquished more than $2 million he had realized from the sale of F&C common stock. Finally, the SEC imposed civil fines on four of the executives that ranged from $11,500 to $20,000.

F&C International filed for bankruptcy in April 1993 shortly after the fraud became public. The following year, a competitor purchased F&C's remaining assets. In March 1995, Jon Fries began serving a 15-month sentence in a federal prison for his role in the F&C fraud.

Questions

1. Jon Fries (CEO), Fletcher Anderson (COO), Craig Schuster (CFO), and Catherine Sprauer (division controller) were the four central figures in this case. Identify the key responsibilities associated with the professional roles these individuals occupied. Briefly describe the type and extent of interaction each of these individuals likely had with F&C's independent auditors.

2. Using the scale shown below, evaluate the conduct of the four key individuals discussed in this case. Be prepared to defend your answers.

−100 . . . . 0 100

Highly   Highly

Unethical   Ethical

3. For a moment, step into the shoes of Catherine Sprauer. What would you have done during and following each of the confrontations she had with the two employees who insisted that F&C executives were involved in a fraudulent scheme to misrepresent the company's financial statements?

4. Craig Schuster resigned as F&C's CFO on January 1, 1993. Apparently, Schuster did not reveal to any third parties the concerns he had regarding F&C's accounting records and previous financial statements. In your opinion, did Schuster have a responsibility to inform someone of those concerns following his resignation? Defend your answer.

5. Assume that you, rather than Fletcher Anderson, were F&C's COO in December 1992. What would you have done upon receiving the list of Warehouse Q inventory from Craig Schuster?

Suzette Washington, Accounting Major

Suzette Washington financed her college education by working as an inventory clerk for Bertolini's, a clothing store chain located in the southeastern United States.[1] Bertolini's caters primarily to fashion-conscious young men and women. The company's stores carry a wide range of clothing, including casual wear, business suits, and accessories. The Bertolini's store for which Suzette worked is located a few blocks from the campus of the large state university that she attended. Except for management personnel, most of Bertolini's employees are college students. Suzette's best friend and roommate, Paula Kaye, worked for Bertolini's as a sales clerk. Paula majored in marketing, while Suzette was an accounting major.

During Suzette's senior year in college, Bertolini's began experiencing abnormally high inventory shrinkage in the store's three departments that stocked men's apparel. Suzette's supervisor, an assistant store manager, confided in her that he believed one or more of the sales clerks were stealing merchandise. Over lunch one day in the student union, Suzette casually mentioned the inventory problem to Paula. Paula quickly changed the subject by asking Suzette about her plans for the weekend.

"Paula, rewind for just a second. Do you know something that I don't?"

"Huh? What do you mean?"

"Missing inventory . . . shrinkage . . . theft?"

After a few awkward moments, Paula stopped eating and looked squarely into her friend's eyes. "Suzette, I don't know if it's true, but I've heard a rumor that Alex and Matt are stealing a few things each week. Polo shirts, silk ties, jeans. Occasionally, they take something expensive, like a hand-knit sweater or sports jacket."

"How are they doing it?"

"I've heard---and don't repeat any of this now--I've heard that a couple of times per week, Alex stashes one or two items at the bottom of the trash container beneath the number two cash register. Then Matt, you know he empties the trash every night in the dumpster out in the alley, takes the items out and puts them in his car."

"Paula, we can't let them get away with this. We have to tell someone."

"No 'we' don't. Remember, this is just a rumor. I don't know that it's true. If you tell a manager, there will be questions. And more questions. Maybe the police will be brought in. You know that eventually someone's going to find out who told. And then . . . slashed tires . . . phone calls in the middle of the night."

"So, don't get involved? Don't do anything? Just let those guys keep stealing?"

"Suze, you work in inventory. You know the markup they put on those clothes. They expect to lose a few things here and there to employees."

"Maybe the markup wouldn't be so high if theft wasn't such a problem."

Now, there was no doubt in Paula's mind that Suzette was going to report the alleged theft scheme to management. "Two months, Suze. Two months till we graduate.

---

1. This case was developed from information provided by a former college student who is now a CPA. The names, location, and certain other background facts have been changed.

Can you wait till then to spill the beans? Then we can move out of state before our cars are spray-painted."

One week following Suzette and Paula's conversation, a Bertolini's store manager received an anonymous typed message that revealed the two-person theft ring rumored to be operating within the store. Bertolini's immediately retained a private detective. Over a four-week period, the detective documented $500 of merchandise thefts by Alex and Matt. After Bertolini's notified the police, the local district attorney filed criminal charges against the two young men. A plea bargain agreement arranged by their attorneys resulted in suspended prison sentences for Alex and Matt. The terms of that agreement included making restitution to Bertolini's, completing several hundred hours of community service, and a lengthy period of probation.

Questions

1. What would you do if you found yourself in a situation similar to that faced by Suzette in this case?

2. Do you believe that it was appropriate for Suzette to report the alleged theft ring to a store manager? Would it have been unethical for Suzette *not* to report the rumored theft ring?

3. Accounting majors are preparing to enter a profession recognized as having one of the strongest and most rigorously enforced ethical codes. Given this fact, do you believe that accounting majors have a greater responsibility than other business majors to behave ethically?

4. Briefly discuss internal control activities that might have prevented the theft losses suffered by Bertolini's.

Freescale Semiconductor, Inc.

Who will guard the guardians?

Juvenal

During the summer of 2006, a syndicate of investors led by The Blackstone Group, one of Wall Street's largest private equity investment firms, initiated a secret plan to acquire Freescale Semiconductor. Based in Austin, Texas, Freescale is among the world's largest producers of semiconductors and for decades was a subsidiary of Motorola, Inc., the large electronics company. In July 2004, Motorola spun off Freescale in one of that year's largest initial public offerings.

Blackstone retained Ernst & Young (E&Y) to serve as a consultant for the planned buyout of Freescale. Among other services, Blackstone wanted E&Y to review Freescale's human resource functions and to make recommendations on how to streamline and strengthen those functions following the acquisition. James Gansman, a partner in E&Y's Transaction Advisory Services (TAS) division, was responsible for overseeing that facet of the engagement.

Similar to the other Big Four accounting firms, E&Y became involved in the investment banking industry during the 1990s. In fact, by the late 1990s, the small fraternity of accounting firms could boast of having two of the largest investment banking practices in the world, at least in terms of the annual number of consulting engagements involving merger and acquisition (M&A) deals. In 1998, KPMG consulted on 430 M&A transactions, exactly one more than the number of such engagements that year for PricewaterhouseCoopers (PwC). Despite those impressive numbers, KPMG and PwC had not established themselves as dominant firms in the investment banking industry.

In 1998, the total dollar volume of the M&A engagements on which KPMG and PwC consulted was $1.65 billion and $1.24 billion, respectively. Those numbers paled in comparison to the annual dollar value of M&A transactions for industry giants such as Goldman Sachs, which was involved in M&A deals valued collectively at nearly $400 billion in 1998. At the time, Goldman Sachs, Lehman Brothers, Morgan Stanley, and the other major investment banking firms consulted exclusively on "mega" or multibillion-dollar M&A engagements. By contrast, the "low end" of the M&A market–in which the Big Four firms competed–typically involved transactions measured in a few million dollars.

E&Y's involvement in the huge Freescale M&A deal was a major coup for the Big Four firm. When the transaction was consummated in December 2006, the price paid for the company by the investment syndicate led by The Blackstone Group approached $18 billion. That price tag made it the largest private takeover of a technology company to that point in time as well as one of the ten largest corporate takeovers in U.S. history.

Not surprisingly, Blackstone demanded strict confidentiality from E&Y and the other financial services firms that it retained to be involved in the planned acquisition of Freescale. James Gansman, for example, was told that Blackstone wanted the transaction to be "super confidential" and was instructed in an internal E&Y e-mail to "not breathe the name of the target [Freescale] outside of the [engagement] team."[1]

---

1. U.S. Department of Justice, "Former Ernst & Young Partner and Investment Banker Charged in Insider Trading Scheme," 29 May 2008, (http://newyork.fbi.gov).

During June and July 2006 while he was working on the Freescale engagement, Gansman passed "inside information about the pending transaction"[2] to Donna Murdoch, a close friend who worked in the investment banking industry. An FBI investigation revealed that Gansman and Murdoch "communicated over 400 times via telephone and text messages"[3] in the weeks leading up to the September 11, 2006, announcement that the Blackstone investment syndicate intended to acquire Freescale. In that time span, Murdoch purchased hundreds of Freescale stock options, which she cashed in on September 11–12, 2006, realizing a windfall profit of $158,000.

The FBI also determined that between May 2006 and December 2007 Gansman provided Murdoch with information regarding six other M&A transactions on which E&Y consulted. In total, Murdoch used that inside information to earn nearly $350,000 in the stock market. Murdoch gave that information to three other individuals, including her father, who also used it to produce significant stock market profits.

Published reports indicate that Murdoch became involved in the insider trading scheme to help make the large monthly payments on a $1.45 million subprime mortgage on her home. The funds she initially used to "play the market" were provided to her by one of the individuals to whom she disclosed the inside information given to her by James Gansman. In addition, Gansman at one point loaned her $25,000.

The Securities and Exchange Commission (SEC) uses sophisticated software programs to detect suspicious trading activity in securities listed on stock exchanges. In early 2007, the SEC placed Murdoch on its "watch list" of individuals potentially involved in insider trading and began scrutinizing her stock market transactions. Information collected by the SEC resulted in criminal charges being filed against Murdoch. In December 2008, she pleaded guilty to 15 counts of securities fraud and two related charges.

In May 2009, Murdoch served as one of the prosecution's principal witnesses against Gansman in a criminal trial held in a New York federal court. During the trial, Gansman testified that he had been unaware that Murdoch was acting on the information he had supplied her. Defense counsel also pointed out that Gansman had not personally profited from any of the inside information that he had been privy to during his tenure with E&Y. Nevertheless, the federal jury convicted Gansman of six counts of securities fraud. A federal judge later sentenced him to a prison term of one year and one day.

EPILOGUE

In October 2007, the surging stock market produced an all-time high of 14,164.53 for the Dow Jones Industrial Average. One year later, stock prices began plummeting in the face of an economic crisis triggered by the collapsing housing and subprime mortgage markets in the United States. The frenzied stock market over this time frame produced a record number of insider trading cases as unprincipled investors either attempted to make a "fast buck" when stock prices were trending ever higher or attempted to mitigate their losses when stock prices began nosediving.

Personnel at all levels of the Big Four accounting firms routinely gain access to highly confidential inside information, information that can

2. *Ibid.*
3. *Ibid.*

be used to gain an unfair advantage over other stock market investors. Unfortunately for the accounting profession, James Gansman is not the only partner or employee of one of those firms who has been implicated recently in a major insider trading scandal.

In January 2008, the SEC charged two former PwC employees with using confidential client information to earn large profits in the stock market. One of the individuals was on PwC's audit staff, while the other was assigned to PwC's Transaction Services group, the PwC division comparable to E&Y's TAS department.[4] The individual in the Transactions Services group accessed the confidential information while working on several M&A consulting engagements for PwC. He then provided that information to his friend on PwC's audit staff, who relied on it to purchase securities of companies that were acquisition targets. This latter individual's name was recognized by a PwC audit partner when he was reviewing a list of securities transactions for a client that another company was attempting to acquire. The audit partner informed the SEC, which then filed insider trading charges against the two friends.

In November 2010, the U.S. Department of Justice filed insider trading charges against a former Deloitte tax partner and his wife, who had also been employed by that firm.[5] The couple allegedly obtained confidential information regarding seven Deloitte clients that were involved in M&A transactions. According to the SEC, the couple communicated that information to family members living in Europe who then engaged in securities involving the companies that were parties to those transactions. The SEC reported that the former Deloitte partner and his wife netted more than $3 million in stock market gains between 2006 and 2008 from the insider trading scheme, while their British relatives netted more than $20 million

in profits.[6] In investigating this case, the Justice Department and SEC sought and received the cooperation of the Financial Services Authority, the British agency charged with regulating Great Britain's securities markets.

To date, the most publicized case of insider trading directly linked to the accounting profession involved Thomas Flanagan, a former vice chairman of Deloitte who spent 38 years with that firm. In October 2008, Deloitte announced that it was suing Flanagan for allegedly trading in the securities of at least 12 Deloitte audit clients for which he had served as an "advisory"[7] partner.

Deloitte claims that Flanagan held and traded securities of his own clients for the past three years. The firm alleges he bought one of his client's stock one week before it announced an acquisition of a public company. He is also accused of violating the firm's independence and conflict-of-interest policies and hiding his personal securities holdings from Deloitte. In his role as an advisory partner, he attended the audit committee meetings of seven of the twelve clients affected.[8]

Press reports indicated that the clients linked to the allegations surrounding Flanagan included Allstate, Best Buy, Motorola, Sears, and Walgreens.

In August 2010, the SEC announced that it had settled insider trading charges that it had filed against Flanagan. The terms of the settlement required Flanagan to pay more than $1 million in fines and penalties. Flanagan consented to the settlement without admitting or denying the SEC's allegations. Flanagan's son, who had allegedly made securities trades based upon inside information given to him by his father, reached a similar settlement with the SEC and paid fines and penalties of approximately $120,000. Other litigation cases linked to Flanagan's alleged indiscretions are still ongoing, including the lawsuit that Deloitte filed against him.

---

4. A. Rappeport, "Ex-PwC Pals were Inside Traders, SEC Says," *CFO.com*, 15 January 2009.

5. P. Lattman, "Couple Accused of Trading Insider Tips," *The New York Times* (online), 30 November 2010.

6. E. Stevens, "Pacific Heights Socialites Charged in Elaborate Insider-Trading Scheme," *Bay Citizen* (online), 9 January 2010.

7. A Deloitte "advisory" partner is typically a senior audit partner who has significant industry expertise relevant to a given client. In addition to consulting with members of an audit engagement team on important issues arising during an audit, an advisory partner typically reviews the audit workpapers before the engagement is completed.

8. S. Johnson, "Deloitte Insider Case Sparked Doubts About Audits," *CFO.com*, 10 November 2008.

Questions

1. Identify the specific circumstances under which auditors are allowed to provide confidential client information to third parties.

2. Suppose that you and a close friend are employed by the same accounting firm. You are assigned to the firm's audit staff, while your friend is a consultant who works on M&A engagements. What would you do under the following circumstances: (1) your friend discloses to you highly confidential "market-moving" information regarding a soon-to-be announced merger; (2) your friend not only discloses such information to you but also informs you that he or she plans to use it to make a "quick" profit in the stock market? In your responses, comment on your ethical responsibilities in each scenario.

3. E&Y was providing a consulting service to The Blackstone Group in connection with its planned acquisition of Freescale Semiconductor. Explain how a CPA's professional responsibilities differ between consulting engagements and audit engagements.

Wiley Jackson, Accounting Major

Wiley Jackson spent three months as an audit intern with a local practice office of a major accounting firm while he was earning an undergraduate accounting degree at the University of Wisconsin–Milwaukee.[1] Wiley thoroughly enjoyed the three-month internship. He made several friends and, more importantly, gained valuable work experience and insight into the nature and work environment of independent auditing. On the final day of his internship, Wiley had an exit interview with the office managing partner (OMP). The OMP told Wiley that he had impressed his superiors and co-workers. Wiley's performance reviews indicated that he had strong technical and interpersonal skills and always conducted himself in a professional and ethical manner. At the end of the exit interview, the OMP offered Wiley a full-time position with the firm once he completed his master's degree in accounting at UWM. Wiley was thrilled by the offer and accepted it immediately.

While working on his graduate degree, Wiley received a packet of documents from his future employer that he was to complete and return. The packet contained standard insurance forms, 401-K elections, a W-4 form, a personal investments worksheet for independence-compliance purposes, and a "Statement of Arrests and Convictions" form. Wiley recalled having completed an earlier version of the latter document before beginning his internship. Among the questions included in this form was the following:

Have you ever been convicted of a misdemeanor (excluding minor traffic violations) or a felony, or driving while intoxicated in this or any other state, or are criminal charges currently pending against you?

The form required a full explanation if this question was answered "Yes." Wiley had previously responded "No" to this question because, at the time, he had had a "clean" record, except for a few parking tickets and one speeding violation. But now, as he sat at his desk staring at the form, he was not sure how to respond to the question.

After completing his internship, Wiley had been invited to a graduation party at an off-campus location. Although he was not a "party animal," Wiley had decided to accept the invitation since it would likely be his final opportunity to see many of his friends who were graduating from UWM. When he arrived at the site of the party, Wiley was surprised by the large number of people there. In fact, because the older, two-story home could not accommodate all the partygoers, several dozen of them were congregated in the front yard and on the residential street on which the house was located.

As he made his way through the boisterous crowd, Wiley suddenly came face to face with Sally Jones. Sally, a UWM alumna, had been the audit senior assigned to Wiley's largest client during his internship. While Wiley was talking to Sally, an acquaintance thrust a cold beer into his hand and slapped him on the shoulder. "No talking business

---

1. This case was written by Brian Daugherty, Assistant Professor at the University of Wisconsin–Milwaukee. The facts of this case were developed from an actual series of events. Certain background information has been changed to conceal the identities of the individuals involved in the case.

here, Dude. It's party time!" As luck would have it, just a few minutes later, the party was "busted" by the local police. Before Wiley realized exactly what was happening, a policeman approached him and asked for his I.D. As he handed over his driver's license, Wiley, who was three days short of his 21st birthday, realized that he was in trouble. Moments later, the stone-faced policeman began writing out a minor-in-possession citation. The citation ordered Wiley to appear before a local judge the following month.

Wiley was distraught and had a difficult time sleeping that night. The next morning, he called an attorney and told him what had happened. The attorney informed Wiley that he had dealt with many similar situations involving college students and that Wiley should not be "stressed out" by the incident. For first-time offenders, like Wiley, the attorney had always been successful in persuading a judge to approve "deferred adjudication." As long as Wiley stayed out of trouble over the following two years, the minor-in-possession charge would be expunged from his record, "just like it never happened," according to the attorney.

Questions

1. Place yourself in Wiley's position. How would you respond to the "Arrests and Convictions" question? Before responding, identify the decision alternatives available to you.

2. Suppose that Wiley does not disclose the citation he received. A few weeks after going to work for his new employer, Wiley is called into the OMP's office. The OMP tells Wiley that he recently learned of the minor-in-possession citation that Wiley had been given. The OMP then hands Wiley a copy of the Arrest and Convictions form that he completed after receiving the job offer from the firm. How should the OMP deal with this matter? How, if at all, should Wiley be disciplined? Defend your answer.

3. Assume that Sally Jones was the individual who told the OMP that Wiley had been given a police citation at the graduation party. Do you believe Sally had a moral or ethical responsibility to inform the OMP of that matter? Why or why not?

Arvel Smart, Accounting Major

Arvel Ray Smart was born in Lebanon, Missouri, and grew up in the small town of Bolivar, 40 miles west of Lebanon in southeastern Missouri.[1] Arvel's mother and father graduated from the University of Missouri with accounting degrees in the mid-1970s. The Smarts spent three years working on the tax staff of a Big Eight practice office in Kansas City before deciding to establish their own accounting firm in Bolivar. Arvel helped out in his parents' office during high school, especially when they were facing tax deadlines. He enjoyed the work, which is why he decided to major in accounting when he enrolled at the University of Missouri following graduation from high school. Arvel realized that he would most likely have the opportunity to take over his parents' accounting firm when they retired. His only sibling, an older sister, was a performing arts major at Washington University in St. Louis and had no interest in becoming involved in the family business.

During his junior year at Mizzou, Arvel was admitted into the five-year program in the School of Accountancy. Arvel would receive Bachelor of Science and Master of Accountancy degrees when he completed the 150-hour program. After completing his junior year, Arvel accepted an internship with a Big Four practice office in Kansas City. Because he wanted to gain a better understanding of auditing, Arvel chose to intern on the audit staff of that office. Arvel was surprised by the number of interesting assignments he was given that summer. In fact, by the end of the summer he was reconsidering the decision he had made earlier to choose the tax track of Mizzou's five-year accounting program.

On the final day of Arvel's internship, the office managing partner met with him and offered him an entry-level auditing position. Arvel thanked the partner for the job offer and told him that he would seriously consider accepting it. He explained to the partner that he had not made a final decision about whether to focus on auditing or taxation early in his career. The partner was very understanding and told Arvel that he had plenty of time to make up his mind and then added that the job offer would remain open for 12 months, until the end of the following summer.

Arvel enrolled in the undergraduate auditing course during the spring semester of his fourth year in college. He enjoyed the course so much that he made up his mind to begin his career as an auditor and to accept the job offer from the firm with which he had interned the previous summer. He planned to delay accepting that offer, however, until the end of the summer. Arvel's girlfriend, who was also an accounting major at Mizzou, had accepted an offer for a summer internship with a Big Four practice office in St. Louis. Arvel was hoping to spend the summer in St. Louis, so he had interviewed earlier in the year with two regional accounting firms based in that city. Both of the firms had offered him an internship.

During the final week of the spring semester of his fourth year, Arvel accepted an internship offer from one of the two St. Louis–based accounting firms. Arvel realized that both regional and national accounting firms use internships as a tool to recruit permanent employees and that they typically offer internships to students

---

1. This case is based on factual circumstances involving a recent accounting graduate. Key facts, including the individual's name and relevant locations, have been changed to obscure his or her identity.

who they believe have an interest in eventually accepting a permanent position with them. That realization caused Arvel to experience some degree of guilt when he called and accepted the internship with the St. Louis firm. He quickly cleared his guilty conscience by convincing himself that there was some remote chance he would change his mind and accept a job with the St. Louis accounting firm. In fact, in Arvel's mind, that firm had a responsibility to prove to him that it offered more opportunities than the Big Four accounting firm from which he had already received a job offer.

Questions

1. Before interviewing with the two St. Louis accounting firms, did Arvel have an obligation to inform them that he had an outstanding job offer from a Big Four practice office in Kansas City? Why or why not?

2. Did Arvel Smart behave unethically by accepting the internship with the St. Louis accounting firm when he intended to accept the outstanding job offer from the Big Four accounting firm at the completion of that internship? Defend your answer.

David Quinn, Tax Accountant

We have all had *that* friend, an individual who attaches himself or herself to us without our encouragement–or approval, for that matter.[1] For Debbie Woodruff, *that* friend was David Quinn. Debbie met David in the very first college accounting class that either of them took at the large public university they attended. Shortly before the instructor entered the room, David had rushed in and taken the seat to Debbie's left. Moments later, an out-of-breath David had leaned over and asked Debbie, "Is this Accounting 201?" That question was the beginning of a relationship that would last for decades.

Debbie had little trouble grasping the revenue recognition rule, accrual accounting, straight-line depreciation, and the other fundamental concepts and topics in the introductory financial accounting course. David, on the other hand, struggled to earn a "B" in the course. Debbie never questioned David's intelligence. The problem was that David simply had too many outside interests–campus politics, his social fraternity, and weekend parties–to devote sufficient time to studying for the rigorous departmental exams in ACCT 201.

Before each exam, David would ask Debbie if they could study together. Debbie was not particularly fond of David, but she agreed to tutor him while she prepared for each exam because explaining an accounting concept or principle to someone else made the given item "gel" in her own mind. During two of these tutoring sessions, David asked Debbie for a date. The second time, Debbie told him that she did not mind studying together but that their "chemistry" made dating out of the question. David's outspoken and opinionated manner was the principal source of the chemistry problem between the two accounting majors. On most subjects–politics and economics, in particular–David had an opinion, an expert opinion, which he was more than willing to share with anyone who would listen. Debbie was much more reserved and preferred to spend her time focusing on her studies rather than debating whatever happened to be the front- page issue of the day.

Over the remainder of their college careers, Debbie and David sat side by side in most of their accounting courses and several other business courses, as well. Eventually, Debbie came to accept David's brash personality and considered him a friend–just not a close friend. Debbie maintained a near-perfect 3.9 GPA in her accounting courses, while David finished with a 3.2 GPA in his accounting major. During her final year of college, Debbie accepted an audit staff position with a nearby office of a Big Eight accounting firm. As fate would have it, David accepted a job on the tax staff of that same office.

Debbie wasn't thrilled by the fact that she and David would be working for the same firm. She expected, however, that they would seldom see each other since she would be working primarily at client locations, while David would likely be "stuck" in the office completing tax returns and doing tax research. Debbie was right. During their first year in public accounting, she saw David only on the rare occasions that she was in the office, which was typically during the wrap-up phase of an audit to which she had been assigned.

---

1. The key facts of this case were provided by a former public accountant who is now an accounting professor. The names of all parties and locations have been changed.

Each time she was in the office, David would ask Debbie to go to lunch with him. Debbie always accepted. She didn't like to admit it, but the lunches served a useful purpose, namely, catching up on all the office scuttlebutt. David seemingly made it his business to know everyone else's business. He would joyfully tell Debbie which tax manager had not received a recommendation for promotion, which audit senior was interviewing for a position on a client's accounting staff, and which intra-office relationship was not "working out."

One Friday in early April, Debbie and David met for lunch to celebrate the end of her second busy season. Debbie was in the office tying up loose ends on the soon-to-be-completed audit of her largest client. She was looking forward to the lunch because she hadn't spoken to David since the office Christmas party almost four months earlier.

On their way to a nearby restaurant, David told Debbie that three of his friends on the tax staff of another Big Eight accounting firm would be meeting them for lunch. Debbie realized that the presence of those individuals would likely divert David's attention and deprive her of the latest news from the office grapevine. So, she resigned herself to a having a boring lunch. She could not have been more wrong.

During lunch, the four tax professionals swapped war stories regarding the latest returns on which they had worked. Debbie found the topic of the conversation inappropriate. In her mind, it was best to never discuss professional engagements, audit or otherwise, over lunch in a public setting. You just never knew who might be eavesdropping at an adjoining table. Debbie became particularly uncomfortable when David began discussing the tax return of a wealthy local businessman who had previously served several terms on the city council.

"Yeah, you wouldn't believe the investments this guy has," David said to the friend on his left. "The guy is loaded. And I mean . . . loaded!" Debbie cringed. Anyone within 20 feet could have heard David's emphatic pronouncement. She attempted to change the subject of the conversation, but David refused to yield the floor.

"No, wait, Debbie, I gotta tell these guys about the latest racket this dude is running." Debbie cringed once more. "You wouldn't believe what he wants us to do. He wants to write off the cost of his daughter's wedding as an entertainment expense. And, you know what? I think we are going to let him do it!"

Debbie couldn't take it anymore. "David, you shouldn't be talking about this at lunch. You don't know who is listening."

"Come on, Debbie. No one's listening."

"David. I'm serious. This is inappropriate."

"What?" David was obviously surprised that his normally meek friend was challenging him. Over the five years that he had known Debbie, she had never behaved in this manner. He was not only surprised but also somewhat miffed that Debbie was running the risk of embarrassing him in front of three fellow tax professionals. "Look around us, Debbie. These people aren't listening to us. Besides, they are all strangers."

"David, that's the point. These people are strangers. And how do you know that they aren't listening? Isn't it possible that one of them might call up your client and tell him what they heard?"

David leaned back in his chair and shook his head. "Oh yeah, I'm sure Grandma over there wrote down every word I just said."

Debbie was flabbergasted at her friend's flippant attitude toward what she considered a very important topic. "David, does the phrase 'client confidentiality' mean anything to you? Surely you tripped across it when studying for the CPA exam?"

"Oh, so you are going to bring up the CPA exam? I guess you *are* trying to embarrass me in front of my friends. Just because you passed that stupid thing the first time and I am still working on it doesn't make you an expert on ethics issues."

"David. You know that's not what I meant," Debbie responded indignantly. "Even if 'Grandma' isn't listening, you are talking about sensitive issues regarding a tax client with three guys from a competing office."

"Oh, I see. My buddies here are going back to their office to report me to the state board, right?" David was no longer miffed; he was angry. "Now, you've gone too far, Debbie. My friends would never do anything to get me into trouble." He then added in a sarcastic tone, "If anyone 'reports me,' it will be you, Miss Self-Righteous."

Debbie reached into her purse and counted out the money for her part of the bill. She then laid the cash on the table in front of her and, without speaking to David or his friends, left the restaurant.

David and Debbie did not speak again until their office's annual July Fourth golf tournament. To his credit, David approached Debbie and said that he hoped they could put their unpleasant encounter behind them.

"I'm sorry it happened. Why don't we just forget it, Debbie? We've been friends for a long time. There's no reason we can't get over this."

Debbie stepped forward and gave David a light hug and told him that they could be friends once more. Despite the nice overture by David, in the future Debbie made every effort to avoid him when she was working in the office.

EPILOGUE

Debbie sat waiting in the college placement office to meet the managing partner of the practice office where she had worked as a staff accountant and senior auditor. After almost five years in that office, Debbie had decided that public accounting was not for her. Instead, she had decided to pursue a Ph.D.–with the eventual career objective of becoming an accounting professor. Debbie subsequently spent five years earning her doctoral degree, including a stressful 18 months fretting over her dissertation. Ten years later, after accumulating an impressive portfolio of publications, she returned to her alma mater to accept a tenured position in its accounting department. After 15 years at her alma mater, Debbie was a full professor and just a few years away from retirement.

Each fall semester, representatives of the major accounting firms came to Debbie's campus to interview the latest crop of soon-to-be accounting graduates. Today was her former employer's opportunity to attempt to impress her students. Debbie realized that she had a responsibility to interact with the recruiters who came to campus–but she always dreaded meeting with the recruiters from her former employer. She knew that throughout lunch David Quinn, her old friend who was now the managing partner of the office in which she had worked, would tell story after story of their college and co-worker days, stories that she had heard repeatedly, stories that became more embellished each year.

In Debbie's mind, the annual lunch with David and his subordinates was a small price to pay to help her students land a job with her former employer. Besides, this year, she had a course to teach immediately after lunch, so she had an excuse to leave early. As she sat waiting for David, she suddenly realized that her course that afternoon was in the same classroom where she had met him for the first time more than 30 years earlier.

Questions

1. Explain the meaning of the phrase "client confidentiality" in the context of a CPA's ethical responsibilities. In your opinion, did David Quinn violate the accounting profession's client confidentiality rule?

2. Assume the role of Debbie Woodruff. How would you have handled the situation that arose in the restaurant?

3. Did Debbie have a responsibility to report David's behavior to a superior in her practice office or to anyone else? Why or why not? Did Debbie have a responsibility to determine whether her firm's tax department was providing appropriate professional advice regarding the deductibility of the entertainment expenses being claimed by David's client?

ETHICAL RESPONSIBILITIES OF INDEPENDENT AUDITORS

5

Cardillo Travel Systems, Inc.

If virtue is not its own reward,
I don't know any other stipend attached to it.

Lord Byron

Act 1

Russell Smith knew why he had been summoned to the office of A. Walter Rognlien, the 74-year-old chairman of the board and chief executive officer (CEO) of Smith's employer, Cardillo Travel Systems, Inc.[1] Just two days earlier, Cardillo's in-house attorney, Raymond Riley, had requested that Smith, the company's controller, sign an affidavit regarding the nature of a transaction Rognlien had negotiated with United Airlines. The affidavit stated that the transaction involved a $203,000 payment by United Airlines to Cardillo but failed to disclose why the payment was being made or for what specific purpose the funds would be used. The affidavit included a statement indicating that Cardillo's stockholders' equity exceeded $3 million, a statement that Smith knew to be incorrect. Smith also knew that Cardillo was involved in a lawsuit and that a court injunction issued in the case required the company to maintain stockholders' equity of at least $3 million. Because of the blatant misrepresentation in the affidavit concerning Cardillo's stockholders' equity and a sense of uneasiness regarding United Airlines' payment to Cardillo, Smith had refused to sign the affidavit.

When Smith stepped into Rognlien's office on that day in May 1985, he found not only Rognlien but also Riley and two other Cardillo executives. One of the other executives was Esther Lawrence, the firm's energetic 44-year-old president and chief operating officer (COO) and Rognlien's wife and confidante. Lawrence, a long-time employee, had assumed control of Cardillo's day-to-day operations in 1984. Rognlien's two sons by a previous marriage had left the company in the early 1980s following a power struggle with Lawrence and their father.

As Smith sat waiting for the meeting to begin, his apprehension mounted. Although Cardillo had a long and proud history, in recent years the company had begun experiencing serious financial problems. Founded in 1935 and purchased in 1956 by Rognlien, Cardillo ranked as the fourth-largest company in the travel agency industry and was the first to be listed on a national stock exchange. Cardillo's annual revenues had steadily increased after Rognlien acquired the company, approaching $100 million by 1984. Unfortunately, the company's operating expenses had increased more rapidly. Between 1982 and 1984, Cardillo posted collective losses of nearly $1.5 million. These poor operating results were largely due to an aggressive franchising strategy implemented by Rognlien. In 1984 alone that strategy more than doubled the number of travel agency franchises operated by Cardillo.

Shortly after the meeting began, the overbearing and volatile Rognlien demanded that Smith sign the affidavit. When Smith steadfastly refused, Rognlien showed

---

1. The events discussed in this case were reconstructed principally from information included in Securities and Exchange Commission, *Accounting and Auditing Enforcement Release No. 143*, 4 August 1987. All quotations appearing in this case were taken from that document.

him the first page of an unsigned agreement between United Airlines and Cardillo. Rognlien then explained that the $203,000 payment was intended to cover expenses incurred by Cardillo in changing from American Airlines' Sabre computer reservation system to United Airlines' Apollo system. Although the payment was intended to reimburse Cardillo for those expenses and was refundable to United Airlines if not spent, Rognlien wanted Smith to record the payment immediately as revenue.

Not surprisingly, Rognlien's suggested treatment of the United Airlines payment would allow Cardillo to meet the $3 million minimum stockholders' equity threshold established by the court order outstanding against the company. Without hesitation, Smith informed Rognlien that recognizing the United Airlines payment as revenue would be improper. At that point, "Rognlien told Smith that he was incompetent and unprofessional because he refused to book the United payment as income. Rognlien further told Smith that Cardillo did not need a controller like Smith who would not do what was expected of him."

Act 2

In November 1985, Helen Shepherd, the audit partner supervising the 1985 audit of Cardillo by Touche Ross, stumbled across information in the client's files regarding the agreement Rognlien had negotiated with United Airlines earlier that year. When Shepherd asked her subordinates about this agreement, one of them told her of a $203,000 adjusting entry Cardillo had recorded in late June. That entry, which follows, had been approved by Lawrence and was apparently linked to the United Airlines–Cardillo transaction:

Dr Receivables–United Airlines	$203,210	
Cr Travel Commissions and Fees		$203,210

Shepherd's subordinates had discovered the adjusting entry during their second-quarter review of Cardillo's Form 10-Q statement. When asked, Lawrence had told the auditors that the entry involved commissions earned by Cardillo from United Airlines during the second quarter. The auditors had accepted Lawrence's explanation without attempting to corroborate it with other audit evidence.

After discussing the adjusting entry with her subordinates, Shepherd questioned Lawrence. Lawrence insisted that the adjusting entry had been properly recorded. Shepherd then requested that Lawrence ask United Airlines to provide Touche Ross with a confirmation verifying the key stipulations of the agreement with Cardillo. Shepherd's concern regarding the adjusting entry stemmed from information she had reviewed in the client's files that pertained to the United Airlines agreement. That information suggested that the United Airlines payment to Cardillo was refundable under certain conditions and thus not recognizable immediately as revenue.

Shortly after the meeting between Shepherd and Lawrence, Walter Rognlien contacted the audit partner. Like Lawrence, Rognlien maintained that the $203,000 amount had been properly recorded as commission revenue during the second quarter. Rognlien also told Shepherd that the disputed amount, which United Airlines paid to Cardillo during the third quarter of 1985, was not refundable to United Airlines under any circumstances. After some prodding by Shepherd, Rognlien agreed to allow her to request a confirmation from United Airlines concerning certain features of the agreement.

Shepherd received the requested confirmation from United Airlines on December 17, 1986. The confirmation stated that the disputed amount was refundable through 1990 if certain stipulations of the contractual agreement between the two parties were not fulfilled.[2] After receiving the confirmation, Shepherd called Rognlien and asked him to explain the obvious difference of opinion between United Airlines and Cardillo regarding the terms of their agreement. Rognlien told Shepherd that he had a secret arrangement with the chairman of the board of United Airlines. "Rognlien claimed that pursuant to this confidential business arrangement, the $203,210 would never have to be repaid to United. Shepherd asked Rognlien for permission to contact United's chairman to confirm the confidential business arrangement. Rognlien refused. In fact, as Rognlien knew, no such agreement existed."

A few days following Shepherd's conversation with Rognlien, she advised William Kaye, Cardillo's vice president of finance, that the $203,000 amount could not be recognized as revenue until the contractual agreement with United Airlines expired in 1990. Kaye refused to make the appropriate adjusting entry, explaining that Lawrence had insisted that the payment from United Airlines be credited to a revenue account. On December 30, 1985, Rognlien called Shepherd and told her that he was terminating Cardillo's relationship with Touche Ross.

In early February 1986, Cardillo filed a Form 8-K statement with the Securities and Exchange Commission (SEC) notifying that agency of the company's change in auditors. SEC regulations required Cardillo to disclose in the 8-K statement any disagreements involving accounting, auditing, or financial reporting issues with its former auditor. The 8-K, signed by Lawrence, indicated that no such disagreements preceded Cardillo's decision to dismiss Touche Ross. SEC regulations also required Touche Ross to draft a letter commenting on the existence of any disagreements with Cardillo. This letter had to be filed as an exhibit to the 8-K statement. In Touche Ross's exhibit letter, Shepherd discussed the dispute involving the United Airlines payment to Cardillo. Shepherd disclosed that the improper accounting treatment given that transaction resulted in misrepresented financial statements for Cardillo for the six months ended June 30, 1985, and the nine months ended September 30, 1985.

In late February 1986, Raymond Riley, Cardillo's legal counsel, wrote Shepherd and insisted that she had misinterpreted the United Airlines-Cardillo transaction in the Touche Ross exhibit letter filed with the company's 8-K. Riley also informed Shepherd that Cardillo would not pay the $17,500 invoice that Touche Ross had submitted to his company. This invoice was for professional services Touche Ross had rendered prior to being dismissed by Rognlien.

Act 3

On January 21, 1986, Cardillo retained KMG Main Hurdman (KMG) to replace Touche Ross as its independent audit firm. KMG soon addressed the accounting treatment Cardillo had applied to the United Airlines payment. When KMG personnel discussed the payment with Rognlien, he informed them of the alleged secret arrangement with United Airlines that superseded the written contractual agreement. According to Rognlien, the secret arrangement precluded United Airlines from demanding a refund of the $203,000 payment under any circumstances. KMG refused to accept this explanation. Roger Shlonsky, the KMG audit partner responsible for the Cardillo

---

2. Shepherd apparently never learned that the $203,000 payment was intended to reimburse Cardillo for expenses incurred in switching to United Airlines' reservation system. As a result, she focused almost exclusively on the question of when Cardillo should recognize the United Airlines payment as revenue. If she had been aware of the true nature of the payment, she almost certainly would have been even more adamant regarding the impropriety of the $203,000 adjusting entry.

engagement, told Rognlien that the payment would have to be recognized as revenue on a pro rata basis over the five-year period of the written contractual agreement with United Airlines.[3]

Cardillo began experiencing severe liquidity problems in early 1986. These problems worsened a few months later when a judge imposed a $685,000 judgment on Cardillo to resolve a civil suit filed against the company. Following the judge's ruling, Raymond Riley alerted Rognlien and Lawrence that the adverse judgment qualified as a "material event" and thus had to be reported to the SEC in a Form 8-K filing. In the memorandum he sent to his superiors, Riley discussed the serious implications of not disclosing the settlement to the SEC: "My primary concern by not releasing such report and information is that the officers and directors of Cardillo may be subject to violation of rule 10b-5 of the SEC rules by failing to disclose information that may be material to a potential investor."

Within ten days of receiving Riley's memorandum, Rognlien sold 100,000 shares of Cardillo stock in the open market. Two weeks later, Lawrence issued a press release disclosing for the first time the adverse legal settlement. However, Lawrence failed to disclose the amount of the settlement or that Cardillo remained viable only because Rognlien had invested in the company the proceeds from the sale of the 100,000 shares of stock. Additionally, Lawrence's press release underestimated the firm's expected loss for 1985 by approximately 300 percent.

Following Lawrence's press release, Roger Shlonsky met with Rognlien and Lawrence. Shlonsky informed them that the press release grossly understated Cardillo's estimated loss for fiscal 1985. Shortly after that meeting, KMG resigned as Cardillo's independent audit firm.

EPILOGUE

In May 1987, the creditors of Cardillo Travel Systems, Inc., forced the company into involuntary bankruptcy proceedings. Later that same year, the SEC concluded a lengthy investigation of the firm. The SEC found that Rognlien, Lawrence, and Kaye had violated several provisions of the federal securities laws. These violations included making false representations to outside auditors, failing to maintain accurate financial records, and failing to file prompt financial reports with the SEC. In addition, the federal agency charged Rognlien with violating the insider trading provisions of the federal securities laws. As a result of these findings, the SEC imposed permanent injunctions on each of the three individuals that prohibited them from engaging in future violations of federal securities laws. The SEC also attempted to recover from Rognlien the $237,000 he received from selling the 100,000 shares of Cardillo stock in April 1986. In January 1989, the two parties resolved this matter when Rognlien agreed to pay the SEC $60,000.

---

3. Cardillo executives also successfully concealed from the KMG auditors the fact that the United Airlines payment was simply an advance payment to cover installation expenses for the new reservation system.

Questions

1. Identify the accountants in this case who faced ethical dilemmas. Also identify the parties who would be potentially affected by the outcome of each of these dilemmas. What responsibility did the accountant in each case owe to these parties? Did the accountants fulfill these responsibilities?

2. Describe the procedures an auditor should perform during a review of a client's quarterly financial statements. In your opinion, did the Touche Ross auditors who discovered the $203,000 adjusting entry during their 1985 second-quarter review take all appropriate steps to corroborate that entry? Should the auditors have immediately informed the audit partner, Helen Shepherd, of the entry?

3. In reviewing the United Airlines–Cardillo agreement, Shepherd collected evidence that supported the $203,000 adjusting entry as booked and evidence that suggested the entry was recorded improperly. Identify each of these items of evidence. What characteristics of audit evidence do the profession's technical standards suggest auditors should consider? Analyze the audit evidence that Shepherd collected regarding the disputed entry in terms of those characteristics.

4. What are the principal objectives of the SEC's rules that require Form 8-K statements to be filed when public companies change auditors? Did Shepherd violate the client confidentiality rule when she discussed the United Airlines–Cardillo transaction in the exhibit letter she filed with Cardillo's 8-K auditor change statement? In your opinion, did Shepherd have a responsibility to disclose to Cardillo executives the information she intended to include in the exhibit letter?

5. Do the profession's technical standards explicitly require auditors to evaluate the integrity of a prospective client's key executives? Identify the specific measures auditors can use to assess the integrity of a prospective client's executives.

American International Group, Inc.

Cornelius Vander Starr wanted to see the world. In 1918, the 26-year-old Californian emptied his bank account to purchase a one-way ticket to the Far East on a steamship. After "bumming around" Japan for several months, Vander Starr traveled to Shanghai, China, where he landed a job working for an insurance company. Within a short period of time, Vander Starr realized that selling insurance was a low overhead business that was ideally suited for a young entrepreneurial type like himself so he quit his job and set up his own insurance agency, American Asiatic Underwriters. Vander Starr's business grew rapidly. By the time of his death in the late 1960s, Starr's one-man firm had become a multi-billion dollar international conglomerate with operating units in Europe, Latin America, the Middle East, and the United States. The Starr Foundation that he created before his death ranks among the world's largest philanthropic organizations.

In 1948, the Chinese civil war forced Vander Starr to relocate his company's headquarters from Shanghai to New York City. As he neared retirement, Vander Starr chose his protégé, Maurice "Hank" Greenberg, to replace him as his company's chief executive officer. During the early 1960s, Greenberg had revamped the company's business model. Instead of focusing on selling life insurance and other insurance products for individuals, Greenberg convinced Starr that the company's principal line of business should be insurance and other financial services products designed for large corporations. In 1969, Greenberg took the company, which had been renamed American International Group, Inc. (AIG), public by listing its stock on the New York Stock Exchange.

Greenberg would serve as AIG's top executive for nearly four decades. Under his leadership, the company became known worldwide for the new and innovative financial services products that it continually developed and the aggressive methods that it used to market those products. These efforts produced impressive financial results for the company. By the turn of the century, AIG was one of the ten largest companies in the United States and among the 20 largest companies worldwide.

In early 2001, a group of AIG executives came up with an idea for a new financial service that they believed would appeal to a wide range of large corporations. This service would involve AIG creating customized "special purpose entities" or SPEs for such companies. An SPE is typically a limited partnership that two or more companies join together to form. Since an SPE is an unconsolidated subsidiary, a company can download or transfer underperforming assets and related liabilities to that entity to improve its apparent financial condition. This "balance sheet management feature" of SPEs was the principal selling point that AIG intended to use in marketing its new service.

In fact, many large corporations were already using SPEs "to perform cosmetic surgery on their balance sheets."[1] Enron Corporation, a large Houston-based energy company, was among the most prolific users of SPEs.[2] Enron had significantly improved its apparent financial condition by "hiding" distressed assets and much of

---

1. J. Kahn, "Off Balance Sheet–And Out of Control," *Fortune,* 18 February 2002, 84.

2. See *Enron Corporation*, Case 1.1.

its outstanding debt in hundreds of SPEs that it had created. AIG's management was convinced that, unlike Enron, most companies did not have the in-house expertise to develop their own SPEs.

AIG's executives realized that their new SPE service, which was effectively an accounting mechanism, would be more credible if one of the major accounting firms was involved in its development and marketing. For that reason, AIG retained Michael Joseph, a partner in the national office of Ernst & Young (E&Y) and a "nationally recognized expert on the accounting for structured financial vehicles and SPEs,"[3] to help develop and market the new service. "To assist AIG in its marketing" of the new SPE service "Joseph caused E&Y to issue reports pursuant to *Statement on Auditing Standards No. 50*, 'Reports on the Application of Accounting Principles.'"[4] These *SAS No. 50* reports indicated that the "nonconsolidation accounting treatment" for the assets and liabilities transferred to an SPE that had been designed by AIG "was an appropriate application of GAAP." In promoting its new SPE service, "AIG referred to E&Y's advice in its marketing materials and referred potential buyers directly to Joseph to answer accounting-related questions."

Among the first companies to express an interest in purchasing AIG's SPE service was PNC Financial Services Group, Inc. (PNC), a large financial services firm that operated the fifth-largest bank in the United States. During the negotiations with AIG, PNC consulted with its independent auditors to determine whether the accounting treatment for AIG's SPE product complied with GAAP. In fact, PNC's audit firm was E&Y, which meant that the company's auditors contacted Joseph to determine whether PNC's proposed SPE would be GAAP-compliant.

Joseph gave the PNC auditors a copy of a *SAS No. 50* report that he had written for AIG. The auditors relied on that report "without performing any meaningful separate analysis" in deciding that the accounting treatment for the proposed SPE was acceptable. Joseph billed the time that he spent interacting with the PNC auditors to the PNC audit engagement.

During July 2001, PNC transferred nearly $100 million of nonperforming loans to an SPE that was created by AIG. A few months later, the company downloaded more than $100 million of additional nonperforming loans to another AIG-created SPE. In an earnings press release in late 2001, PNC reported that it had $361 million of nonperforming loans. That figure did not include the more than $200 million of such loans that had been transferred to its SPEs.

Federal Reserve officials contacted PNC in November 2001 and inquired regarding the company's nonperforming loans. When those officials reviewed the transactions that had resulted in $207 million of PNC's nonperforming loans being transferred to SPEs, they questioned whether those transfers were appropriate. At this point, PNC executives asked Michael Joseph to intercede on their behalf with the Federal Reserve. Joseph discussed the matter with the Federal Reserve and defended the accounting and financial reporting treatment for the loans that had been transferred to SPEs. The Federal Reserve disagreed with Joseph and in January 2002 ordered PNC to reverse the SPE transactions and include the $207 million of nonperforming loans in the company's consolidated financial statements.

---

3. Securities and Exchange Commission, *Accounting and Auditing Enforcement Release No. 2523*, 11 December 2006. Unless indicated otherwise, subsequent quotes in this case were taken from this source.

4. Accounting firms typically prepare *SAS No. 50* reports to provide a third party, other than an audit client, with technical guidance on how "existing accounting principles apply to new transactions and financial products" (AU 625.01).

The Federal Reserve's decision to force PNC to reverse its SPE transactions triggered an investigation of the company by the Securities Exchange Commission (SEC). In reviewing PNC's SPE transactions, the SEC discovered that they were not in compliance with GAAP. GAAP dictates that for a company to treat an SPE as an unconsolidated subsidiary, an external entity must have a minimum capital investment of 3 percent in the SPE. The external entity that had invested in PNC's SPEs was AIG. However, AIG's investments in the SPEs had not met the required 3 percent threshold, meaning that the financial data for PNC's SPEs should have been included in the company's consolidated financial statements.

EPILOGUE

In July 2002, PNC executives agreed to cease and desist from any future violations of federal securities laws to settle charges pending against the company by the SEC. One year later, PNC agreed to pay $115 million to settle related fraud charges filed against the company by the U.S. Justice Department.

In December 2006, the SEC issued an accounting and auditing enforcement release focusing on Michael Joseph's role in PNC's SPE transactions. In this release, the SEC reported that "Joseph was a cause of PNC's violations" of federal securities laws. The SEC maintained that Joseph should have known that PNC's SPE transactions were not in compliance with GAAP. In this same enforcement release, the SEC alleged that Joseph's dual role with AIG and PNC had been improper and had posed a conflict of interest for him.

> Joseph was involved in the development and marketing of the AIG [SPE] accounting product. He advised AIG on the structure, he prepared several SAS 50 letters used in marketing the product, he participated in conference calls with potential purchasers . . . Consequently, Joseph was invested both financially and reputationally in the success of the [SPE] product and therefore had a conflict of interest when he later evaluated the accounting for the product by E&Y's audit client, PNC.

The SEC went on to observe that Joseph's conduct was "highly unreasonable" and undermined the independence of E&Y's PNC audit engagement team. An accounting professor interviewed by the *Los Angeles Times* used an analogy to describe the likely impact that Joseph's conduct had on the PNC audit engagement team. "Did it bias the individual auditors in this particular case? It's like asking whether 40 years of smoking led to someone's lung cancer."[5]

The SEC suspended Joseph for three years from being involved with audits of public companies. In March 2007, the SEC fined E&Y $1.6 million for the firm's independence violations stemming from Joseph's conduct. The following month, E&Y agreed to pay approximately $9 million to settle a class-action lawsuit filed against it for its role in the PNC accounting scandal.

In late 2004, AIG agreed to pay $126 million in fines and restitution for its involvement in PNC's improper SPE accounting. That amount would be dwarfed by the $1.6 billion fine that AIG agreed to pay in late 2005 to settle charges that it had intentionally misrepresented its own accounting records. Among many other allegations, AIG had reportedly recorded bogus sales of insurance policies to inflate its earnings and understated its loss reserves. In addition to the huge fine, Hank Greenberg was forced to resign as AIG's chief executive as a result of the massive accounting fraud.[6]

AIG was front and center in news headlines once more in late 2008 when the largest

---

5. *Los Angeles Times* (online), "Ernst & Young in SEC Probe of PNC's Books," 8 December 2004.

6. In August 2009, Greenberg agreed to pay a $15 million fine to settle civil fraud charges filed against him by the SEC. The settlement also prohibited Greenberg from serving as an officer of a public company for three years.

economic crisis, since the Great Depression, erupted in the United States and quickly spread around the globe. In September 2008, the federal government seized control of AIG to prevent the company from collapsing. The company had such an extensive role in global credit and insurance markets that financial experts maintained that its collapse would cause a worldwide economic calamity. In exchange for approximately $85 billion of capital, the federal government received an 80 percent equity interest in the company. In the following months, tens of billions of dollars of additional federal "bailout" money was invested in AIG to keep the company afloat. AIG would ultimately receive more federal bailout funds than any other U.S. company.

Questions

1. Is it ethical for a CPA or CPA firm to help companies "manage" their reported earnings and financial condition? In responding to this question, first assume that the CPA or CPA firm is serving as a consultant, and then assume that the CPA or CPA firm is serving as the given entity's independent auditor. Defend your answers.

2. When a dispute arises between an audit client and its auditor regarding the proper accounting treatment for a transaction or other item, the audit client will sometimes retain another accounting firm to issue a *SAS No. 50* report on the proper accounting treatment for the given item. Identify the potential ethical dilemmas that may result from allowing accounting firms to issue *SAS No. 50* reports to non-audit clients.

The North Face, Inc.

Executives of The North Face, Inc., faced a troubling dilemma during the 1990s.[1] For decades, those executives had struggled to develop and maintain an exclusive brand name for their company's extensive line of outdoor apparel and sporting equipment products. By positioning those products for the "high-end" segment of the retail market, North Face's management had consciously chosen to ignore the much larger and more lucrative mainstream market. This decision kept the company's primary customers happy. Those customers, principally small, independent specialty sporting goods stores, did not want North Face to market its merchandise to major discount retailers such as Wal-Mart and Costco.

Economic realities eventually forced North Face's executives to begin selling the company's products to the mainstream market via backdoor marketing channels. Unfortunately, the company's relatively high-priced merchandise did not compete effectively with the mass-market brands sold by the major discount retailers. Making matters worse, as the company's merchandise began appearing on the shelves of discount retailers, those products quickly lost their exclusive brand name appeal, which caused North Face's sales to its principal customers to drop sharply.

North Face's change in marketing strategies, the company's decision to spend millions of dollars to relocate its headquarters from northern California to Colorado, and other gaffes by its management team caused *Chief Executive* magazine to include North Face among the nation's five "worst-managed" corporations. A short time later, North Face's public image and reputation on Wall Street would be damaged even more by public revelations that the company's reported operating results had been embellished with various accounting and marketing gimmicks.

Adventurers, Inc.

Hap Klopp founded North Face in the mid-1960s to provide a ready source of hiking and camping gear that he and his many free-spirited friends and acquaintances needed to pursue their "back to nature" quest. Initially, the business operated from a small retail store in San Francisco's North Beach neighborhood. The company quickly added a mail-order sales operation. In 1970, North Face began designing and manufacturing its own line of products after opening a small factory in nearby Berkeley.

Over the next decade, North Face endeared itself to outdoor enthusiasts by sponsoring mountain-climbing expeditions across the globe, including successful attempts to scale Mount Everest, Mount McKinley, China's K-2, and the highest peaks in South America. The name recognition and goodwill generated by these expeditions allowed North Face to establish itself as the premier supplier of top-quality parkas, tents, backpacking gear, and other apparel and equipment demanded by "professional" mountain climbers. Adding even more credibility to North Face's merchandise was the lifetime warranty that Hal Klopp attached to each item his company sold and the fact that the United States Marine Corps purchased tents and other bivouac supplies from North Face.

---

1. The development of this case was funded by Glen McLaughlin. I would like to thank Mr. McLaughlin for his generous and continuing support of efforts to integrate ethics into business curricula.

North Face's sterling reputation for rugged and durable hiking, camping, and mountaineering gear prompted company management to begin marketing related lines of apparel and sporting equipment for skiers, whitewater daredevils, and other outdoor types. Among the most popular items marketed by the company were its Mountain Jacket, Snow Leopard Backpack, and Tadpole Tent. The company's expanding product line triggered rapid sales growth during the 1970s and 1980s. Similar to the management teams of many growth companies, North Face's executives confronted several imposing challenges that could undermine their company's financial success. The most critical of those challenges was maintaining quality control in North Face's cramped production facilities.

Company executives prided themselves on producing only the highest quality outdoor sporting equipment and apparel. To maintain the quality of that merchandise, they insisted on manufacturing all of North Face's products in-house, rather than outsourcing some of the company's manufacturing operations to third parties. By the mid-1980s, North Face's overburdened manufacturing facilities could not satisfy the steadily growing demand for the company's merchandise or maintain the high-quality production standards established by management. North Face's limited production capacity and mounting quality control problems caused the company to routinely deliver merchandise to retail stores after the peak selling seasons for its highly seasonal products. The quality control problems also caused North Face to accumulate a large inventory of "seconds," that is, merchandise items having minor flaws.

In the late 1980s, North Face's management made a decision it would soon regret. The company opened several outlet stores to dispose of obsolete and second-grade merchandise. This decision angered the specialty sporting goods stores that had been North Face's primary customers since the company's inception. To pacify those customers, North Face did a quick about-face and closed the outlet stores.

Over the next several years, North Face continued to struggle with maintaining its image as the leading producer of high-quality outdoor apparel and sporting equipment, while at the same attempting to gradually ease into the mainstream retail market. By this time, Hap Klopp had left the company to become an author—one of his books was entitled *The Complete Idiot's Guide to Business Management*. In fact, the company experienced several changes in company management and ownership during the late 1980s and throughout the 1990s.

In July 1996, a new management team took North Face public, listing the company's common stock on the NASDAQ exchange. Sold initially at $14 per share, the company's stock price peaked at nearly $30 per share in February 1998, fueled by the company's steadily increasing sales and profits. In fiscal 1994, North Face reported total sales of $89 million; four years later in fiscal 1998, the company's sales had nearly tripled, rising to approximately $250 million.

Despite the company's strong operating results, by early 1999 North Face's stock price had plunged from its all-time high. Persistent rumors that North Face's management had enhanced the company's reported revenues and profits by "channel stuffing" and other questionable, if not illegal, practices caused the sharp decline in the stock price. To squelch those rumors, North Face's board of directors attempted to purchase the company in a leveraged buyout underwritten by a large investment banking firm. That effort failed in March 1999 when NASDAQ officials halted public trading of North Face's stock following an announcement that the company would be restating its previously reported operating results due to certain "bad bookkeeping."[2]

---

2. D. Blount, "Shares of Colorado-Based Outdoor Clothing Maker Slump," *Denver Post* (online), 11 May 1999.

In May 1999, North Face officials publicly revealed that their company's audited financial statements for 1997 and the company's pre-audited operating results for 1998, which had been released in January 1999, had been distorted by fraudulent accounting schemes. The principal schemes involved violations of the revenue recognition principle. For 1997, North Face's reported revenues of $208.4 million had been overstated by approximately $5 million, while the company's net income of $11.2 million had been overstated by $3.2 million. In January 1999, the company had reported unaudited revenue and net income of $263.3 million and $9.5 million, respectively, for fiscal 1998. The company's actual 1998 revenues were $247.1 million, while the company's actual net income for the year was $3.6 million.

Bartering for Success at North Face

The management team that took over North Face in the mid-1990s established a goal of reaching annual sales of $1 billion by 2003. Many Wall Street analysts believed North Face could reach that goal, given the company's impressive operating results over the previous several years. When the actual revenues and profits of North Face failed to meet management's expectations, the company's chief financial officer (CFO) and vice president of sales took matters into their own hands, literally.

In December 1997, North Face began negotiating a large transaction with a barter company. Under the terms of this transaction, the barter company would purchase $7.8 million of excess inventory North Face had on hand near the end of fiscal 1997. In exchange for that inventory, North Face would receive $7.8 million of trade credits that were redeemable only through the barter company. Historically, companies have used such trade credits to purchase advertising or travel services.

Before North Face finalized the large barter transaction, Christopher Crawford, the company's chief financial officer (CFO), asked North Face's independent auditors how to account for the transaction. The auditors referred Crawford to the appropriate authoritative literature for nonmonetary exchanges. That literature generally precludes companies from recognizing revenue on barter transactions when the only consideration received by the seller is trade credits. To circumvent the authoritative literature, Crawford restructured the transaction. The final agreement with the barter company included an oral "side agreement" that was concealed from North Face's independent auditors.

> Crawford, however, structured the transaction to recognize a profit on the trade credits. First, he required the barter company to pay a portion of the trade credits in cash. Crawford agreed that The North Face would guarantee that the barter company would receive at least 60 percent recovery of the total purchase price when it resold the product. In exchange for the guarantee, the barter company agreed to pay approximately 50 percent of the total purchase price in cash and the rest in trade credits. This guarantee took the form of an oral side agreement that was not disclosed to the auditors.[3]

To further obscure the true nature of the large barter transaction, Crawford split it into two parts. On December 29, 1997, two days before the end of North Face's fiscal 1997 fourth quarter, Crawford recorded a $5.15 million sale to the barter company. For this portion of the barter deal, North Face received $3.51 million in cash and trade credits of $1.64 million. Ten days later, during North Face's first quarter of fiscal 1998, the company's accounting staff booked the remaining $2.65 million portion of

---

3. U.S. District Court, Northern District of California, *Securities and Exchange Commission v. Christopher F. Crawford and Todd F. Katz*, February 2003.

the barter transaction. North Face received only trade credits from the barter company for this final portion of the $7.8 million transaction. North Face recognized its normal profit margin on each segment of the barter transaction.

Crawford, who was a CPA, realized that Deloitte & Touche, North Face's auditors, would not challenge the $3.51 million portion of the barter transaction recorded during the fourth quarter of fiscal 1997. There was no reason for the auditors to challenge that component of the transaction since North Face was being paid in cash. Crawford also realized that Deloitte would disagree with the company's decision to recognize revenue for the $1.64 million component of the barter transaction for which North Face would be paid exclusively in trade credits. However, Crawford was aware of the materiality thresholds that Deloitte had established for North Face's key financial statement items during the fiscal 1997 audit. He knew that the gross profit of approximately $800,000 on the $1.64 million component of the barter transaction fell slightly below Deloitte's materiality threshold for North Face's collective gross profit. As a result, he believed that Deloitte would propose an adjustment to reverse the $1.64 million item but ultimately "pass" on that proposed adjustment since it had an immaterial impact on North Face's financial statements. In fact, that is exactly what Deloitte did.

In early January 1998, North Face recorded the remaining $2.65 million portion of the $7.8 million barter transaction. Again, Crawford instructed North Face's accountants to record the full amount of profit margin on this "sale" despite being aware that accounting treatment was not consistent with the authoritative literature. Crawford did not inform the Deloitte auditors of the $2.65 million portion of the barter transaction until after the 1997 audit was completed.

The barter company ultimately sold only a nominal amount of the $7.8 million of excess inventory that it purchased from North Face. As a result, in early 1999, North Face reacquired that inventory from the barter company.

In the third and fourth quarters of fiscal 1998, Todd Katz, North Face's vice president of sales, arranged two large sales to inflate the company's revenues, transactions that were actually consignments rather than consummated sales. The first of these transactions involved $9.3 million of merchandise "sold" to a small apparel wholesaler in Texas. During the previous year, this wholesaler had purchased only $90,000 of merchandise from North Face. The terms of this transaction allowed the wholesaler to return any of the merchandise that he did not resell and required North Face to pay all of the storage and handling costs for that merchandise. In fact, North Face arranged to have the large amount of merchandise stored in a warehouse near the wholesaler's business. Katz negotiated a similar $2.6 million transaction with a small California wholesaler a few months later.

During a subsequent internal investigation, North Face's audit committee questioned the validity of the large transaction with the Texas wholesaler. North Face paid for the Texas customer to fly to North Face's new corporate headquarters in Aspen, Colorado, to discuss that transaction with members of the audit committee and the company's CEO, who were not aware of the true nature of the transaction. The night before the customer met with North Face officials, Katz went to his hotel room and had him sign a fake purchase order for the $9.3 million transaction—a purchase order had not been prepared for the bogus sale when it was originally arranged by Katz.

Several months later, Katz instructed a North Face sales representative to ask the Texas customer to sign an audit confirmation letter sent to him by Deloitte. By signing that letter, the customer falsely confirmed that he owned the $9.3 million of merchandise as of December 31, 1998, North Face's fiscal year-end. The California wholesaler involved in the bogus $2.6 million sale signed a similar confirmation after having been asked to do so by a North Face sales representative. In May 1999, following the completion of North Face's 1998 audit, the Texas customer returned the $9.3 million of merchandise that he had supposedly purchased from North Face.

Erasing the Past

Richard Fiedelman served for several years as the Deloitte "advisory" partner assigned to the North Face audit engagements. Within Deloitte, an advisory partner is typically a senior audit partner who has significant industry expertise relevant to a given audit client. Fiedelman was the advisory partner on the North Face engagement team because he was in charge of Deloitte's "consumer retail group" in the firm's northern California market area. In addition to consulting with members of an audit engagement team on important issues arising during an audit, an advisory partner typically reviews the audit workpapers before the engagement is completed.[4]

Pete Vanstraten was the audit engagement partner for the 1997 North Face audit.[5] Vanstraten proposed the adjusting entry near the end of the 1997 audit to reverse the $1.64 million barter transaction that North Face had booked in the final few days of fiscal 1997. Vanstraten proposed that adjustment because he was aware that the authoritative literature generally precludes companies from recognizing revenue on barter transactions when the only consideration received by the seller is trade credits. Vanstraten was also the individual who "passed" on that adjustment after determining that it did not have a material impact on North Face's 1997 financial statements. Richard Fiedelman reviewed and approved those decisions by Vanstraten.

Shortly after the completion of the 1997 North Face audit, Pete Vanstraten was transferred from the office that serviced North Face. In May 1998, Will Borden was appointed the new audit engagement partner for North Face.[6] In the two months before Borden was appointed the North Face audit engagement partner, Richard Fiedelman functioned in that role.

Fiedelman supervised the review of North Face's financial statements for the first quarter of fiscal 1998, which ended on March 31, 1998. While completing that review, Fiedelman became aware of the $2.65 million portion of the $7.8 million barter transaction that Christopher Crawford had instructed his subordinates to record in early January 1998. Recall that North Face received only trade credits from the barter company for this final portion of the large barter transaction. Despite being familiar with the authoritative literature regarding the proper accounting treatment for barter transactions involving trade credits, Fiedelman did not challenge North Face's decision to record its normal profit margin on the January 1998 "sale" to the barter company. As a result, North Face's gross profit for the first quarter of 1998 was overstated by more than $1.3 million, an amount that was material to the company's first-quarter financial statements. In fact, without the profit margin on the $2.65 million transaction, North Face would have reported a net loss for the first quarter of fiscal 1998 rather than the modest net income it actually reported that period.

In the fall of 1998, Will Borden began planning the 1998 North Face audit. An important element of that planning process was reviewing the 1997 audit workpapers.

---

4. The information regarding the nature and role of a Deloitte advisory partner was obtained from a senior audit manager with that firm.

5. "Pete Vanstraten" is a fictitious name assigned to the 1997 North Face audit engagement partner. The SEC enforcement releases issued in this case and other available sources did not identify that partner's actual name.

6. "Will Borden" is also a fictitious name.

While reviewing those workpapers, Borden discovered the audit adjustment that Pete Vanstraten had proposed during the prior-year audit to reverse the $1.64 million barter transaction. When Borden brought this matter to Fiedelman's attention, Fiedelman maintained that the proposed audit adjustment should not have been included in the prior-year workpapers since the 1997 audit team had *not* concluded that North Face should *not* record the $1.64 million transaction with the barter company. Fiedelman insisted that, despite the proposed audit adjustment in the 1997 audit workpapers, Pete Vanstraten had concluded that it was permissible for North Face to record the transaction and recognize the $800,000 of profit margin on the transaction in December 1997.

Fiedelman could not offer any viable explanation to Borden as to why the 1997 workpapers included the proposed audit adjustment for the $1.64 million transaction. Borden could have easily addressed that issue by simply contacting Vanstraten; however, he apparently chose not to do so. Nor did he refer to the authoritative literature to determine whether North Face was entitled to record that transaction. Instead, Borden simply accepted Fiedelman's assertion that North Face was entitled to recognize profit on a sales transaction in which the only consideration received by the company was trade credits. Borden also relied on this assertion during the 1998 audit. As a result, Borden and the other members of the 1998 audit team did not propose an adjusting entry to require North Face to reverse the $2.65 million sale recorded by the company in January 1998.

After convincing Borden that the prior-year workpapers misrepresented the decision that Pete Vanstraten had made regarding the $1.64 million barter transaction, Fiedelman "began the process of documenting this revised conclusion in the 1997 working papers."[7] According to a subsequent investigation by the Securities and Exchange Commission (SEC), Deloitte personnel "prepared a new summary memorandum and adjustments schedule reflecting the revised conclusion about profit recognition, and replaced the original 1997 working papers with these newly-created working papers." The Deloitte personnel who revised the 1997 workpapers did not document the revisions in those workpapers. "In the end, the 1997 working papers, as revised, did not indicate that the 1997 audit team had originally reached a different conclusion concerning the company's accounting for the 1997 barter transaction."

The SEC requires that a partner not assigned to an engagement team review the audit workpapers for an SEC registrant. The Deloitte "concurring" partner who reviewed the 1998 workpapers questioned Will Borden's decision to allow North Face to recognize revenue on a sales transaction for which it had been paid exclusively in trade credits. The partner then referred to the prior-year workpapers and discovered that the workpapers pertaining to the December 1997 transaction with the barter company had been altered.

Because of concerns raised by the concurring partner, Deloitte investigated the 1997 and 1998 North Face transactions with the barter company. The concurring partner's concerns also prompted North Face's audit committee to retain a second accounting firm to investigate the company's 1997 and 1998 accounting records. These investigations ultimately revealed the true nature of the transactions with the barter company, including the previously undisclosed "side agreement" that Christopher Crawford had made with officials of that company. The investigations

---

7. This and all remaining quotes in this case were taken from the following source: Securities and Exchange Commission, *Accounting and Auditing Enforcement Release No. 1884*, 1 October 2003, 2.

also led to the discovery of the two bogus consignment sales that Crawford had arranged during 1998.

EPILOGUE

The SEC sanctioned Richard Fiedelman for failing to document the changes that his subordinates had made in the 1997 North Face workpapers. In commenting on the North Face case, the federal agency stressed the important function of audit workpapers and the need for any *ex post* changes in those workpapers to be clearly and fully documented.

> *The auditor's working papers provide the principal support for the auditor's report, including his representation regarding the observance of the standards of field work, which is implicit in the reference in his report to generally accepted auditing standards. It therefore follows that any addition, deletion, or modification to the working papers after they had been finalized in connection with the completion of the audit may be made only with appropriate supplemental documentation, including an explanation of the justification for the addition, deletion, or modification.*

The SEC also criticized Fiedelman for failing to exercise due professional care while reviewing North Face's financial statements for the first quarter of 1998. According to the SEC, Fiedelman allowed North Face to record the January 1998 barter transaction "directly contrary to the conclusion reached by Deloitte in its 1997 year-end audit." In October 2003, the SEC imposed a three-year suspension on Fiedelman prevented him from being involved in the audits of SEC clients.

In February 2003, the SEC suspended Christopher Crawford for five years, which prohibited him from serving as an officer or director of a public company or being associated with any financial statements filed with the federal agency over that time frame. The SEC also fined Crawford $30,000 and required him to disgorge approximately $30,000 of trading profits he had earned on the sale of North Face stock. The SEC also denied Todd Katz, the former vice president of sales who had helped Crawford manipulate North Face's reported operating results, the privilege of serving as an officer of a public company for five years and fined him $40,000. The two former North Face customers involved in the bogus consignment sales arranged by Katz were reprimanded by the SEC.

In May 2000, VF Corporation, the world's largest apparel company, more commonly known as Vanity Fair, made North Face a wholly owned subsidiary by purchasing the company's outstanding common stock for $2 per share. VF immediately installed a new management team to take over North Face's operations. Under the leadership of that new management team, North Face quickly returned to profitability and reestablished itself as one of the nation's premier suppliers of outdoor equipment and apparel.

Questions

1. Should auditors insist that their clients accept all proposed audit adjustments, even those that have an "immaterial" effect on the given financial statements? Defend your answer.

2. Should auditors take explicit measures to prevent their clients from discovering or becoming aware of the materiality thresholds used on individual audit engagements? Would it be feasible for auditors to conceal this information from their audit clients?

3. Identify the general principles or guidelines that dictate when companies are entitled to record revenue. How were these principles or guidelines violated by the $7.8 million barter transaction and the two consignment sales discussed in this case?

4. Identify and briefly explain each of the principal objectives that auditors hope to accomplish by preparing audit workpapers. How were these objectives undermined by Deloitte's decision to alter North Face's 1997 workpapers?

5. North Face's management teams were criticized for strategic blunders that they made over the course of the company's history. Do auditors have a responsibility to assess the quality of the key decisions made by client executives? Defend your answer.

Waverly Holland, Audit Senior

Waverly Edward Holland, III, grew up in sunny Tucson, Arizona, but his heart was always in the mountains of Colorado. From the age of three, "Dutch" spent at least one week each winter at Aspen, Breckenridge, Vail, or some other Colorado ski resort with his family. He loved the weather and the quaint atmosphere of the small mountain resort towns, but mostly he loved to ski. By the age of 16, Dutch had decided that he would pursue a career that would allow him the opportunity to indulge the sport that he loved. Thanks to his pragmatic parents and a thoughtful high school counselor, Dutch's career objective eventually evolved from being a "ski bum" to becoming involved in the management of a ski resort.[1]

During his annual ski excursions while in high school, Dutch discussed his career goal with several management personnel at major ski resorts. With those individuals' help, Dutch developed a master plan for accomplishing that goal. Since one of the ski resort managers he interviewed had convinced him that a thorough knowledge of accounting would be extremely helpful in managing any business, including a ski resort, Dutch decided to major in accounting at the University of Arizona. Making that decision even easier was the fact that occupational aptitude tests he took in high school indicated he was well suited for accounting.

Dutch planned to take a one-semester "sabbatical" during his undergraduate program to work as an intern or "gopher" at a ski resort. After completing his accounting degree, Dutch would work for a few years in the accounting profession before returning to college to earn an MBA specializing in resort or hotel management. With that background, Dutch believed that he could obtain a management trainee position with a major ski resort.

"Class-action" Headache

By the age of 26, Dutch was well on his way to completing his master plan. After earning an undergraduate degree in accounting at the U of A, Dutch accepted a staff auditor position with a major accounting firm. Dutch chose auditing because he believed it would give him a thorough understanding of "real world" accounting and internal control issues that he would need as a future business manager. During his third year in public accounting, Dutch took the GMAT exam and applied to several universities that had MBA programs tailored to his specific career interest. After being admitted to the program that was his top choice, Dutch gave his employer notice that he would be leaving the firm a few months later.

Midway through his first semester of graduate school, Dutch was elated when he learned that he had been accepted for a management internship program at a large ski resort he had visited several times in the past. Dutch realized that he would likely be offered a full-time job with the resort when he finished the three-month internship program the following summer. That full-time position would begin when he completed his MBA degree the following spring.

---

1. The key facts presented in this case were provided by a former public accountant who is now an accounting professor. Dates, locations, and other background information have been changed to conceal the identities of the individuals and entities involved in the case.

We have all known individuals who seem to lead charmed existences in which their lives unfold as they have scripted them. Dutch Holland was one of those individuals. But Dutch's charmed life suddenly became more complex and less predictable a few months after he left public accounting. One late November afternoon Dutch's phone rang while he was studying in his apartment. The caller identified himself as Robert Chope, an attorney for a law firm in a nearby metropolitan area. Chope told Dutch that his firm was representing the plaintiffs in a class-action securities lawsuit to be filed in a matter of days against Padova & Vicenza, a large public company involved in the apparel industry. The lawsuit would allege that Padova & Vicenza had intentionally and materially misrepresented its financial condition and operating results over the past three years. Dutch was well aware of Padova & Vicenza since the manufacturing company was one of the largest audit clients of his former employer. In fact, Dutch had spent three years assigned to the audit engagement team for Padova & Vicenza. The final year, Dutch had served as the principal audit senior on that team.

When Chope used the phrase "class-action," Dutch winced in pain. Among the greatest fears of an auditor is for a client or former client to be the target of a class-action lawsuit predicated on material financial statement misrepresentations. If the company's audit firm is named as a co-defendant in such a lawsuit, the audits of that client will be subjected to painstaking scrutiny by both plaintiff and defense attorneys.

Dutch had enjoyed the three years that he spent in public accounting. Unlike many of his college friends who had accepted entry-level positions in other fields following graduation, Dutch had seldom been bored as an auditor. He had found the wide range of businesses, accounting and control systems, and technical issues that he had been exposed to stimulating and rewarding. Granted, on many occasions he had felt as if he was "in over his head" given the challenging assignments that his firm continually gave him. He had subdued those brief anxiety attacks with the realization that his firm had an impressive support network that included both extensive technical resources and helpful, sympathetic, and encouraging colleagues and superiors. Dutch had enjoyed the challenges and camaraderie of public accounting so much that he had briefly reconsidered his planned career path as he neared completion of his three-year stint as an auditor. But the lure of Colorado's ski trails had prevailed and kept him from extending his time in public accounting.

The only major downside of public accounting, at least in Dutch's mind, had been the ever-present fear of "screwing up" by overlooking material errors in a client's financial statements. That concern had loomed over every audit to which Dutch had been assigned. In looking back on his three years in public accounting, Padova & Vicenza was the only former client that Dutch had some lingering questions regarding the material accuracy or fairness of its periodic financial statements. Those lingering questions immediately flooded back into Dutch's mind that November afternoon when Robert Chope mentioned the lawsuit to be filed against Padova & Vicenza.

During the three years that Dutch had served on the Padova & Vicenza audit engagement team, the company had been in chronically poor financial condition. For more than a decade, the company's operating results had been deteriorating in the face of stiff competition from foreign companies. Those foreign competitors had a lower cost structure than Padova & Vicenza due to the considerably lower wages they paid to their non-union workers—each of Padova & Vicenza's four production facilities was unionized.

As Padova & Vicenza's profitability and liquidity steadily worsened each year, the company had made increasingly aggressive accounting decisions. Among other accounts, those decisions had affected the company's allowances for bad debts and inventory obsolescence and discretionary year-end expense accruals. In Dutch's final year on the Padova & Vicenza engagement, management had also made several dubious operating decisions to improve the company's apparent financial condition. Management had slashed the company's advertising and promotional budget, laid off dozens of salaried employees including two-thirds of the internal audit staff, and deferred periodic maintenance expenditures on production line equipment. The questionable accounting and operating decisions had been necessary because the company was dangerously close to violating several long-term debt covenants tied to key financial measures. If Padova & Vicenza had violated those debt covenants, the long-term debt would have become immediately due and payable, which would have forced the company to either obtain waivers of those covenants from its lenders or file for bankruptcy.

Dutch had spent his final few months in public accounting supervising the field work on the Padova & Vicenza audit–the company had a June 30 fiscal year-end and Dutch had completed his work on that audit the weekend before he began his MBA program in early September. During the nearly three months that had elapsed since completing that engagement, Dutch had not spoken to any of his former colleagues who had been assigned to the audit. So, the information that Robert Chope relayed to him during their phone conversation was the first update he had received regarding Padova & Vicenza's financial health since completing that audit.

Chope told Dutch that Padova & Vicenza would issue a press release within one week that would recall the company's audited financial statements for the past three years. According to Chope, management planned to announce that those financial statements would be restated due to several material but allegedly inadvertent misstatements. When Dutch asked which specific accounts had been misstated, Chope had refused to provide any additional details. By this point in the conversation, Dutch had gone from feeling stressed to feeling physically sick. He realized that if there were material errors in Padova & Vicenza's financial statements, he had probably signed off on workpapers relevant to the accounts affected by those errors.

The "Go-to-Guy"

Near the end of their conversation, Chope finally told Dutch why he had called. Chope wanted to meet with Dutch and discuss several "unresolved issues" that he and his team of subordinates hoped to clarify before filing the class-action lawsuit on behalf of Padova & Vicenza's stockholders and former stockholders. Chope believed that Dutch could quickly explain those issues given the "in-depth knowledge" of the company he had acquired while auditing it for three years.

The fact that Chope knew exactly how long Dutch had worked on the Padova & Vicenza engagement was troubling to him. He wondered what else the articulate and self-assured attorney knew of his involvement in those audits. Dutch was aware that it was highly unlikely Chope's firm had copies of all the Padova & Vicenza workpapers since his former employer would not turn over those workpapers to a third party unless ordered to do so by a court.

Dutch could not overcome the temptation to ask Chope if his former employer would be named as a defendant in the lawsuit. The attorney's reply, "Not at the present time," was less than reassuring to Dutch. According to Chope, the principal defendants in the lawsuit would be the company itself, three senior company executives–the chief executive officer, the chief operating officer, and the chief financial officer, and several current and former board members.

Dutch reluctantly asked one final question of Chope, a question for which he already knew the answer. "Why did you call *me*? A lot of other people worked on that audit."

"Waverly, you can understand that your former colleagues are not willing to speak to us."

Dutch hated to be called "Waverly," but even more so he hated to be tabbed as the "go-to-guy" in a major class-action lawsuit. With the exception of the tough final exams that he faced over the next two weeks, his life was perfect. He had no interest whatsoever in rehashing the details of the Padova & Vicenza audits, especially with a team of attorneys whose intentions were at best unclear. He simply wanted to be left alone. In his mind, he had no responsibility to become involved in the pending lawsuit—on either side. He had completed all of the procedures that he had been assigned on the Padova & Vicenza audits to the best of his ability. That was what had been expected of him and that was exactly what he had done.

When Dutch failed to respond to Chope's previous statement, the attorney continued, "We will be more than happy to meet you at a time and place that is most convenient with you. Can we arrange that meeting now?"

Upset and flustered, Dutch responded with a stammering reply. "Well, uh, you see, I . . . I'm really busy right now. I'm in the middle of a couple of big projects and then I have final exams coming up. You know, I would like to help you, but I . . . I just don't have the time." Notwithstanding the white lie that he had slipped in, Dutch was pleased with his off-the-cuff, under-pressure response. But he wasn't pleased with Chope's comeback.

"I understand your hesitance to meet with us. But you should understand that you will have to meet with us sooner or later. It would be much better for you to meet with us now. If you cooperate with us, we assure you that you have nothing to worry about from us."

Suddenly, Dutch felt very lonely and extremely apprehensive. He felt as if he was trying to hold off a man-eating tiger with a paper sword. Chope was not going to accept a wishy-washy response. Before he could muster the courage and brainpower to construct a more substantive reply, Chope spoke once more.

"Mr. Holland, you have my word. If you cooperate with us now, we will never name you as a defendant in the lawsuit that we are going to file."

Chope's pledge was both frightening and heartening to Dutch. There was no longer any need to wonder if he might be named in the lawsuit. He was certain that he would be named if he didn't, at a minimum, agree to meet with Chope.

Without giving any more thought to the matter, Dutch heard the words "okay, I will meet you" come out of his mouth.

"With Friends Like These . . ."

The telephone conversation between Dutch and Robert Chope occurred on a Thursday afternoon. Dutch had agreed to meet with Chope the following Monday afternoon. By Sunday evening, Dutch was having second thoughts regarding that decision. Finally, he came up with what seemed to be a great idea. He would call Clayton Morris, an audit partner with his former employer, and ask for his advice.

Morris had served as the audit engagement partner for each of the three Padova & Vicenza audits to which Dutch had been assigned. Although Dutch did not have a close relationship with Morris, he trusted the partner's judgment. Morris was well respected within the practice office in which Dutch had worked. He was a young partner with a brash, outgoing personality who was the office's principal "rainmaker"—he brought in more new clients than any other partner in the office.

Before Dutch could finish relaying all of the details of his conversation with Robert Chope to Clayton Morris, the partner cut him off.

"The nerve of that guy! Calling you out of the blue. Who does he think he is?"

The tone of Morris's interjection made Dutch hesitant to proceed. He realized now that Morris would almost certainly be upset that he had agreed to meet with Chope.

When Dutch failed to continue, Morris prodded him, "Go ahead, Dutch. Tell me how you told this guy off."

"Well . . . actually . . . actually, I didn't know what to tell him." Dutch paused once more to muster the strength to blurt out the words that he didn't want to say and that Morris certainly didn't want to hear. "So, I told him that I would meet with him. Tomorrow. At 5:00 P.M. In my apartment."

For several awkward moments, the other end of the line was silent. But, in his mind's eye, Dutch could picture Morris sitting there dazed and dumbfounded and becoming angrier with each passing moment. Finally, Morris spoke.

"You did what?"

"Well, I didn't know what to . . . he was just so persistent, that I—"

"You agreed to meet with him? Are you out of your mind?"

"Clayton, I didn't know what to do. I've never been in a situation like that." Dutch wasn't angry but he was indignant by this point. The change in his tone prompted a change in Morris's tone as well.

"Dutch. I understand. Those plaintiff attorneys are shock jocks. They can put you on the spot and keep applying the pressure. But now listen to me. Listen to me closely. I want you to call this guy back and tell him that you are not going to meet with him." Morris paused, expecting Dutch to respond. When Dutch didn't, Morris continued. "When he starts applying the pressure, just tell him courteously that he is to call T.J. Gillette in our headquarters office. Gillette is one of our best in-house attorneys. He will deal with this guy. I promise you that you won't hear from him again."

"How do you know that he won't contact me again? How do you know that he won't include me as a defendant in the lawsuit?"

"Come on Dutch, he was just trying to bluff you into cooperating. Let's get real here. There's no doubt that we [Dutch's former employer] will be named as a defendant eventually. We're the ones with the deep pockets. Will they name you? Of course not. You know whose name will be in the spotlight. Mine, not yours. They don't go after the staff or seniors or managers in these cases. It's only the partners that they're interested in. They want to talk to you because they hope to squeeze information out of you that they might be able to use in building a case against the firm and me."

By this point, Dutch felt some sense of relief. He now had a more complete understanding of the circumstances he faced.

"Okay, Clayton. I will call him. I guess I will tell him that I won't meet with him tomorrow." Dutch had used the term "guess" loosely. In fact, he meant to convey that he would definitely not meet with Chope. Unfortunately, Morris didn't read the same meaning into Dutch's response.

"You 'guess'? You 'guess' that you won't meet with him?" Morris's tone was now derisive and angry. "Let me tell you this. And, I am only going to say it once. If you meet with Chope, we, and I mean myself and the entire firm, are going to expect you to testify on behalf of the plaintiffs. You make that decision and we will go after you. We will tie you up in depositions and interrogatories for the next two years. I can guarantee you that you won't be finishing that graduate degree any time soon."

Morris's response caused the normally good-natured Dutch to become angry. He had been bullied by Chope, but he certainly hadn't expected Morris to treat him in the same manner. Dutch realized that nothing would be gained by becoming involved in an angry exchange, so he abruptly ended the conversation by telling Morris that he appreciated his input and then said a hasty "good-bye." A moment before he hung up the phone, he heard Morris anxiously say, "Dutch, wait a minute."

Decision Time

The following morning, Dutch was awakened by a phone call. The caller was T.J. Gillette, the in-house attorney for his former employer. Gillette was civil but his message was the same as Morris's: Don't even consider cooperating with the plaintiff attorneys in the Padova & Vicenza case. Surprisingly to Dutch, Gillette did not ask him whether he still intended to meet with Chope later that day. Gillette ended the brief conversation with a terse "Good luck young man" before hanging up the phone.

For the next several minutes, Dutch sat on the side of his bed wondering what he should do. Should he call Robert Chope and cancel their five o'clock meeting? Should he call Clayton Morris once more? Finally, Dutch got up slowly from the bed and trudged to the kitchen to make his morning cup of coffee.

Questions

1. How do you believe that Dutch Holland resolved the dilemma that he faced? Do you believe that he met with Robert Chope? Why or why not? Place yourself in Dutch's position. What would you have done? Explain.

2. Identify the ethical issues that Dutch faced. How should he have addressed or dealt with those issues?

3. Do you believe that Clayton Morris dealt appropriately with Dutch during their telephone conversation? Defend your answer.

Phillips Petroleum Company

Bill Grant sat in the middle of a large jail cell with 12 other inmates as the long October night dragged on.[1] To pass the time, Grant and several other inmates played cards and talked about their hopes of being reunited with their families. The accommodations of the Tulsa County Jail were not unlike those of most jails: dirty, no lid on the toilet, and 12 beds for 13 inmates. What made this scene unusual was not the less-than-glamorous, overcrowded condition of the jail cell, but rather the presence of Grant, a Big Eight audit partner and graduate of the Harvard Business School. At the time, Grant served as the managing partner of the Tulsa office of Arthur Young & Company, but he was destined to become Arthur Young's co-managing partner in 1988 shortly before that firm merged with Ernst & Whinney to form Ernst & Young.

Earlier that day, Grant had appeared in a Tulsa federal courthouse at a hearing presided over by Judge Allan Barrow. Judge Barrow had ordered Grant to produce certain audit workpapers that had been subpoenaed by a federal grand jury. Those workpapers had been prepared during an audit of the large oil company, Phillips Petroleum Company, a client of Arthur Young's Tulsa office. When Grant respectfully denied the judge's request, he was cited for civil contempt, handcuffed, and led away to jail. Apparently, the judge hoped that an overnight stay in a crowded jail cell would convince Grant to change his mind.

The federal grand jury's interest in the Arthur Young workpapers stemmed from an ongoing investigation of Phillips. That investigation focused on possible tax fraud related to a secret, multimillion-dollar fund that Phillips' executives had established to make political contributions. One contribution made from the secret fund, which was maintained in a Swiss bank account, was an illegal donation of $100,000 to what became known during the Watergate era as CREEP–the Committee to Reelect the President (Richard Nixon). Under the terms of an earlier plea bargain agreement with Watergate, special prosecutor Archibald Cox, Phillips' chairman of the board, had admitted to the $100,000 contribution to Nixon's 1972 reelection campaign and pleaded guilty to one misdemeanor.[2] Following that plea bargain agreement, a seven-count indictment was filed against Phillips that charged the company with filing false federal tax returns for failing to report interest revenue earned on the secret Swiss bank account.

Prior to Bill Grant's appearance before Judge Barrow, Arthur Young had turned over to the federal grand jury approximately 12,000 pages of Phillips's audit workpapers. Arthur Young, however, had refused to give the grand jury several workpapers relating to two key items: (1) certain tax accruals made by Phillips and (2) attorneys'

---

1. The facts of this case were drawn principally from the following articles: "Arthur Young Aide Cited for Contempt and Jailed in Tulsa," *The Wall Street Journal*, 8 October 1975, 10; F. Andrews, "Arthur Young Faces Test on Protecting Client Audit Secrets," *The Wall Street Journal*, 14 October 1975, 23; "Arthur Young & Co. Gives Grand Jury Data On Phillips Petroleum," *The Wall Street Journal*, 15 October 1975, 28; "Pleas by Phillips Petroleum Filed On U.S. Charges," *The Wall Street Journal*, 23 November 1977, 2.

2. Phillips's chairman also revealed that he had delivered $50,000 to Nixon in a New York City apartment during the 1968 presidential campaign in which Nixon eventually defeated Senator Hubert Humphrey.

letters that Arthur Young had obtained from Phillips's law firms. Among other topics, these attorneys' letters were known to include discussions of "unasserted claims" by Phillips's attorneys. The federal grand jury believed that both sets of workpapers might provide important insight on the allegations involving Phillips.

Arthur Young had refused to provide the contested workpapers to the grand jury on the grounds that they contained confidential information that, if disclosed, would be potentially damaging to Phillips. Tax accrual audit workpapers, for example, typically contain an audit firm's analysis of tax-related decisions made by their clients. Access to such workpapers would make it much easier for the Internal Revenue Service (IRS) to "build a case" against a given company.

Bill Grant was released from the Tulsa County Jail on October 7, 1975, but was ordered to make an appearance the following week before Judge Barrow. If Grant again refused to produce the workpapers subpoenaed by the grand jury, he faced the risk of being cited for criminal contempt and receiving a 17-month jail term. During the week between Grant's two court appearances, Arthur Young's attorneys worked out a compromise with Judge Barrow. Under the terms of the agreement, Arthur Young turned over copies of the requested tax accrual workpapers. All matters other than those specifically identified by the subpoena were masked in the copies of the workpapers given to the grand jury. Judge Barrow also granted Arthur Young the right to contest any subsequent court order to provide the original "unmasked" tax accrual workpapers to the grand jury.

Judge Barrow did not relent with respect to the contested attorneys' letters. He ordered Arthur Young to provide copies of those letters to the grand jury. Phillips filed a motion to appeal this order, but that appeal was denied.

EPILOGUE

The Watergate-related problems of Phillips Petroleum continued to plague the company following the resolution of the dispute involving the Arthur Young workpapers. In early 1976, Phillips's executives temporarily turned over control of the company to its outside directors. This decision was spurred by the filing of a large class-action lawsuit against Phillips linked to the charges of illegal campaign contributions. In November 1977, Phillips settled these charges by pleading guilty to engaging in a conspiracy to make illegal campaign contributions, pleading no contest to four related tax evasion charges, and paying a fine of $30,000.

Ironically, Arthur Young's tax accrual workpapers for another audit client, the large oil company Amerada Hess, became the focal point of another major litigation case. The issue in this case was whether the IRS had the right to review copies of auditors' tax accrual workpapers. In 1984, the Supreme Court decided the case by unanimously ruling that the IRS has the right to review tax accrual workpapers prepared during an independent audit.

Questions

1. Do you believe that Bill Grant was justified in refusing to provide the requested workpapers to the grand jury? Explain.

2. What responsibility, if any, does a public accounting firm have to its partners and employees when they are subpoenaed to testify regarding a client?

3. What is the purpose of "attorneys' letters" obtained during the course of an audit? If attorneys are aware that these letters can be routinely subpoenaed, how does this fact likely affect the quality of the audit evidence yielded by these letters?

4. Do you believe the documentation included in tax accrual audit workpapers is likely affected by auditors' knowledge that those workpapers can be obtained by the IRS? Explain.

American Fuel & Supply Company, Inc.

Consider this scenario. You are the audit manager responsible for supervising the fieldwork for a major audit client. After hundreds of hours of hard work, the audit is successfully completed, the client receives a clean opinion, and you and your colleagues go on to your next assignment. Now, the bad news. Several months later, you discover that the client's financial statements contain a material error, an error not revealed by the audit. What should you do at this point? What will you do? An audit manager with Touche Ross faced these difficult circumstances in 1986.

In the mid-1980s, Wisconsin-based American Fuel & Supply Company, Inc. (AFS), was a wholesale distributor of automotive supplies, lawn and garden supplies, and related products.[1] AFS purchased merchandise from several vendors. One of the company's largest suppliers was Chevron Chemical Company, a division of Chevron Corporation. Products that AFS purchased from Chevron included insecticides and weedkillers bearing the Ortho brand label. AFS's president and sole shareholder directed the company's day-to-day operations.

AFS prepared comparative financial statements for its fiscal year ending December 31, 1985, which were accompanied by an unqualified audit opinion issued by Touche Ross on February 28, 1986. The company distributed 100 copies of the financial statements, principally to creditors such as Chevron Chemical.

Several months following the completion of the 1985 AFS audit, Touche Ross personnel discovered that the company's 1985 financial statements contained a material error. AFS had billed certain of its customers twice for merchandise they had purchased. This error caused the company's 1985 revenues to be overstated by nearly $1 million. More important, the error had converted the net loss actually suffered by AFS that year to a reported net income. Chevron Chemical and other creditors of AFS later testified that they relied on the erroneous financial statements in deciding to continue extending credit to the company.

During August and September 1986, members of the AFS audit engagement team wrestled with the question of what they should do given the dilemma they faced. A central figure in these deliberations was James Wagner, the audit manager who had supervised the field work on the 1985 AFS audit. In late August 1986, Wagner bluntly summarized the situation for his superiors: "There is a set of financial statements out being used by [AFS's] vendors and lenders that has an error in it." Two weeks later, Wagner, a Touche Ross audit partner, and the accounting firm's assistant legal counsel held a conference call to discuss the matter. During this conference call, these individuals agreed on the course of action Touche Ross would take to resolve the matter.

Unless AFS notified its creditors and vendors of the existence of the error in the financial statements, Touche would withdraw their opinion and give notice to its creditors

---

1. The principal facts of this case and the quotations appearing within it were drawn from the following legal opinion: *Chevron Chemical v. Deloitte & Touche*, 483 N.W. 2d 314 (Wis. App. 1992).

and vendors whom they knew were relying upon the financial statements that their opinion had been withdrawn.

Following the conference call, Touche Ross representatives met with AFS officials and attempted to persuade them to recall the company's 1985 financial statements. The AFS officials refused to do so. Touche Ross then advised the client that it intended to withdraw its audit report on AFS's 1985 financial statements and to inform all parties known to be relying on those financial statements that the audit report had been withdrawn.

A few days later, Touche Ross personnel met again with AFS's management. The company's legal counsel also attended this meeting. AFS's attorney insisted that Touche Ross would violate the confidentiality of its contractual relationship with AFS by withdrawing its audit opinion and notifying third parties of that decision. The client's attorney then threatened legal action against Touche Ross if the accounting firm carried through on its planned course of action. Eventually, AFS and Touche Ross hammered out a compromise. This compromise permitted Touche Ross to notify AFS's sole secured creditor (lender) that the firm's audit opinion on AFS's 1985 financial statements had been withdrawn. However, Touche Ross could not notify AFS's unsecured creditors of its decision to withdraw the audit report. These unsecured creditors included Chevron Chemical and AFS's other suppliers.

James Wagner believed the compromise was unacceptable. In a confidential memo apparently intended for his superiors, Wagner maintained that Touche Ross had an obligation to the other parties relying on the audit opinion issued on AFS's 1985 financial statements. Wagner suggested that Touche Ross should "send a letter to the vendors or creditors that we know have received the financial statements telling them that . . . the opinion should no longer be relied upon."

EPILOGUE

AFS filed for bankruptcy in April 1987. The company's president filed for personal bankruptcy approximately two years later. In early 1989, Chevron Chemical sued Touche Ross, alleging that the accounting firm negligently audited AFS's 1985 financial statements. Chevron Chemical also claimed that Touche Ross had a responsibility to notify it after learning of the error in AFS's 1985 financial statements.

A Wisconsin state court rejected the allegation that Touche Ross negligently audited AFS in 1985. However, the court ruled, and a Wisconsin state appellate court later agreed, that Touche Ross "was negligent as a matter of law in failing to notify plaintiff [Chevron Chemical] of the withdrawal of their opinion." The original state court awarded damages of $1.6 million to Chevron Chemical.

Questions

1. A major focus of the lawsuit that Chevron Chemical filed against Touche Ross was the auditing profession's rules regarding the "subsequent discovery of facts existing at the date of the auditor's report." Those rules distinguish between situations in which a client cooperates with the auditor in making all necessary disclosures and situations involving uncooperative clients. Briefly summarize the differing responsibilities that auditors have in these two sets of circumstances.

2. Given your previous answer, do you believe that Touche Ross complied with the applicable professional standards after learning of the error in AFS's 1985 financial statements? Explain.

3. Do you agree with the assertion of AFS's legal counsel that Touche Ross would have violated the profession's client confidentiality rule by withdrawing its 1985 audit opinion and notifying all relevant third parties of that decision? Why or why not?

4. Suppose that Touche Ross had resigned as AFS's auditor following the completion of the 1985 audit but prior to the discovery of the error in the 1985 financial statements. What responsibility, if any, would Touche Ross have had when it learned of the error in AFS's 1985 financial statements?

PROFESSIONAL ROLES

6

Leigh Ann Walker, Staff Accountant

Leigh Ann Walker graduated from a major state university with a bachelor's degree in accounting.[1] During her college career, Walker earned a 3.9 grade point average and participated in several extracurricular activities, including three student business organizations. Her closest friends often teased her about the busy schedule she maintained and the fact that she was, at times, a little too "intense." During her final year of college, Walker interviewed with several public accounting firms and large corporations and received six job offers. After considering those offers, she decided to accept an entry-level position on the auditing staff of a major international accounting firm. Walker was not sure whether she wanted to pursue a partnership position with her new employer. But she believed that the training programs the firm provided and the breadth of experience she would receive from a wide array of client assignments would get her career off to a fast start.

Walker's "start date" was June 4th, exactly one month following her graduation date. She spent the first two weeks on her new job at her firm's regional audit staff training school. On returning to her local office in mid-June, she was assigned to work on the audit of Saint Andrew's Hospital, a large sectarian hospital with a June 30 fiscal year-end. Walker's immediate superior on the Saint Andrew's engagement was Jackie Vaughn, a third-year senior. On her first day on the Saint Andrew's audit, Walker learned that she would audit the hospital's cash accounts and assist with accounts receivable. Walker was excited about her first client assignment and pleased that she would be working for Vaughn. Vaughn had a reputation as a demanding supervisor who typically brought her engagements in under budget. She was also known for having an excellent rapport with her clients, a thorough knowledge of technical standards, and for being fair and straightforward with her subordinates.

Like many newly hired staff auditors, Walker was apprehensive about her new job. She understood the purpose of independent audits and was familiar with the work performed by auditors but doubted that one auditing course and a two-week staff-training seminar had adequately prepared her for her new work role. After being assigned to work under Vaughn's supervision, Walker was relieved. She sensed that although Vaughn was demanding, the senior would be patient and understanding with a new staff auditor. More important, she believed that she could learn a great deal from working closely with Vaughn. Walker resolved that she would work hard to impress Vaughn and had hopes that the senior would mentor her through the first few years of her career.

Early in Walker's second week on the Saint Andrew's engagement, Jackie Vaughn casually asked her over lunch one day whether she had taken the CPA examination in May. After a brief pause, Walker replied that she had not but planned to study intensively for the exam during the next five months and then take it in November.[2]

---

1. This case is based upon a true set of facts; however, the names of the parties involved have been changed. An employee of a job placement firm provided much of the information incorporated in this case. This firm had been retained by the student identified in this case as Leigh Ann Walker.

2. At the time, the CPA examination was offered twice annually, in November and May. In most states, including Leigh Ann's home state, an individual who sat for the exam for the first time was required to take all four parts.

Vaughn indicated that was a good strategy and offered to lend Walker a set of CPA review manuals–an offer Walker declined. In fact, Walker had returned to her home state during the first week of May and sat for the CPA exam, but she was convinced that she had failed it. Fear of failure or, rather, fear of admitting failure, caused Walker to decide not to tell her co-workers that she had taken the exam. She realized that most of her peers would not pass all sections of the exam on their first attempt. Nevertheless, Leigh Ann wanted to avoid the embarrassment of admitting throughout the remainder of her career that she had not been a "first timer."

Walker continued to work on the Saint Andrew's engagement throughout the summer. She completed the cash audit within budget, thoroughly documenting the results of the audit procedures she applied. Vaughn was pleased with Walker's work and frequently complimented and encouraged her. As the engagement was winding down in early August, Walker received her grades on the CPA exam in the mail one Friday evening. To her surprise, she had passed all parts of the exam. She immediately called Vaughn to let her know of the impressive accomplishment. To Walker's surprise, Vaughn seemed irritated, if not disturbed, by the good news. Walker then recalled having earlier told Vaughn that she had not taken the exam in May. Walker immediately apologized and explained why she had chosen not to disclose that she had taken the exam. Following her explanation, Vaughn still seemed annoyed, so Walker decided to drop the subject and pursue it later in person.

The following week, Vaughn spent Monday through Wednesday with another client, while Walker and the other staff assigned to the Saint Andrew's engagement continued to wrap up the hospital audit. On Wednesday morning, Walker received a call from Don Roberts, the office managing partner and Saint Andrew's audit engagement partner. Roberts asked Walker to meet with him late that afternoon in his office. She assumed that Roberts simply wanted to congratulate her on passing the CPA exam.

The usually upbeat Roberts was somber when Walker stepped into his office that afternoon. After she was seated, Roberts informed her that he had spoken with Jackie Vaughn several times during the past few days and that he had consulted with the three other audit partners in the office regarding a situation involving Walker. Roberts told Walker that Vaughn was very upset by the fact that she (Walker) had lied regarding the CPA exam. Vaughn had indicated that she would not be comfortable having a subordinate on future engagements whom she could not trust to be truthful. Vaughn had also suggested that Walker be dismissed from the firm because of the lack of integrity she had demonstrated.

After a brief silence, Roberts told a stunned Walker that he and the other audit partners agreed with Vaughn. He informed Walker that she would be given 60 days to find another job. Roberts also told Walker that he and the other partners would not disclose that she had been "counseled out" of the firm if they were contacted by employers interested in hiring her.

Questions

1. In your opinion, did Vaughn overreact to Walker's admission that she had been untruthful regarding the CPA exam? If so, how would you have dealt with the situation if you had been in Vaughn's position? How would you have dealt with the situation if you had been in Roberts' position?

2. Vaughn obviously questioned Walker's personal integrity. Is it possible that one can fulfill the responsibilities of a professional role while lacking personal integrity? Why or why not?

Bill DeBurger,
In-Charge Accountant

"Bill, will you have that inventory memo done by this afternoon?"

"Yeah, Sam, it's coming along. I should have it done by five, or so."

"Make it three . . . or so. Okay, Bub?"

Bill responded with a smile and a nod. He had a good relationship with Sam Hakes, the partner supervising the audit of Marcelle Stores.[1]

Bill DeBurger was an in-charge accountant who had 18 months experience with his employer, a large national accounting firm. Bill's firm used the title "in-charge" for the employment position between staff accountant and audit senior. Other titles used by accounting firms for this position include "advanced staff" and "semi-senior." Typically, Bill's firm promoted individuals to in-charge after one year. An additional one to two years experience and successful completion of the CPA exam were usually required before promotion to audit senior. The title "in-charge" was a misnomer, at least in Bill's mind. None of the in-charges he knew had ever been placed in charge of an audit, even a small audit. Based upon Bill's experience, an in-charge was someone a senior or manager expected to work with little or no supervision. "Here's the audit program for payables. Go spend the next five weeks completing the 12 program steps . . . and don't bother me," seemed to be the prevailing attitude in making work assignments to in-charges.

As he turned back to the legal pad in front of him, Bill forced himself to think of Marcelle Stores' inventory—all $50 million of it. Bill's task was to summarize it in a two-page memo, 900 hours of work that he, two staff accountants, and five internal auditors had done over the past two months. Not included in the 900 hours was the time spent on eight inventory observations performed by other offices of Bill's firm.

Marcelle Stores was a regional chain of 112 specialty stores that featured a broad range of products for do-it-yourself interior decorators. The company's most recent fiscal year had been a difficult one. A poor economy, increasing competition, and higher supplier prices had slashed Marcelle's profit to the bone over the past 12 months. The previous year, the company had posted a profit of slightly less than $8 million; for the year just completed, the company's pre-audit net income hovered at an anemic $500,000.

Inventory was the focal point of each audit of Marcelle's financial statements. This year, inventory was doubly important. Any material overstatement discovered in the inventory account would convert a poor year profit-wise for Marcelle into a disastrous year in which the company posted its first-ever loss.

Facing Bill on the small table that served as his makeshift desk were two stacks of workpapers, each two feet tall. Those workpapers summarized the results of extensive price tests, inventory observation procedures, year-end cutoff tests, an analysis of the reserve for inventory obsolescence, and various other audit procedures. Bill's

---

1. The source for this case was a former public accountant who is now a college instructor. The names of the parties involved in the case and certain other background facts have been changed.

task was to assimilate all of this audit evidence into a conclusion regarding Marcelle's inventory. Bill realized that Sam Hakes expected that conclusion to include the key catch phrase "presented fairly, in all material respects, in conformity with generally accepted accounting principles."

As Bill attempted to outline the inventory memo, he gradually admitted to himself that he had no idea whether Marcelle's inventory dollar value was materially accurate. The workpaper summarizing the individual errors discovered in the inventory account reflected a net overstatement of only $72,000. That amount was not material even in reference to Marcelle's unusually small net income. However, Bill realized that the $72,000 figure was little better than a guess.

The client's allowance for inventory obsolescence particularly troubled Bill. He had heard a rumor that Marcelle intended to discontinue 2 of the 14 sales departments in its stores. If that were true, the inventory in those departments would have to be sold at deep discounts. The collective dollar value of those two departments' inventory approached $6 million, while the client's allowance for inventory obsolescence had a year-end balance of only $225,000. Earlier in the audit, Bill had asked Sam about the rumored closing of the two departments. The typically easygoing partner had replied with a terse "Don't worry about it."

Bill always took his work assignments seriously and wanted to do a professional job in completing them. He believed that independent audits served an extremely important role in a free market economy. Bill was often annoyed that not all of his colleagues shared that view. Some of his co-workers seemed to have an attitude of "just get the work done." They stressed form over substance: "Tic and tie, make the workpapers look good, and don't be too concerned with the results. A clean opinion is going to be issued no matter what you find."

Finally, Bill made a decision. He would not sign off on the inventory account regardless of the consequences. He did not know whether the inventory account balance was materially accurate, and he was not going to write a memo indicating otherwise. Moments later, Bill walked into the client office being used by Sam Hakes and closed the door behind him.

"What's up?" Sam asked as he flipped through a workpaper file.

"Sam, I've decided that I can't sign off on the inventory account," Bill blurted out.

"What?" was Sam's stunned, one-word reply.

Bill stalled for a few moments to bolster his courage as he fidgeted with his tie. "Well . . . like I said, I'm not signing off on the inventory account."

"Why?" By this point, a disturbing crimson shade had already engulfed Sam's ears and was creeping slowly across his face.

"Sam . . . I just don't think I can sign off. I mean, I'm just not sure whether the inventory number is right."

"You're . . . *just not sure?*" After a brief pause, Sam continued, this time pronouncing each of his words with a deliberate and sarcastic tone. "You mean to tell me that you spent almost 1,000 hours on that account, and you're just not sure whether the general ledger number is right?"

"Well . . . yeah. Ya know, it's just tough to . . . to reach a conclusion, ya know, on an account that large."

Sam leaned back in his chair and cleared his throat before speaking. "Mr. De-Burger, I want you to go back into that room of yours and close the door. Then you sit down at that table and write a nice, neat, very precise and to-the-point inventory memo. And hear this: I'm not telling you what to include in that memo. But you're going to write that memo, and you're going to have it on my desk in two hours. Understood?" Sam's face was entirely crimson as he completed his short speech.

"Uh, okay," Bill replied.

Bill returned to the small conference room that had served as his work area for the past two months. He sat in his chair and stared at the pictures of his two-year-old twins, Lesley and Kelly, which he had taped to the wall above the phone. After a few minutes, he picked up his pencil, leaned forward, and began outlining the inventory memo.

Questions

1. What conclusion do you believe Bill DeBurger reached in his inventory memo? Put yourself in his position. What conclusion would you have expressed in the inventory memo? Why?

2. Would you have dealt with your uncertainty regarding the inventory account differently than Bill did? For example, would you have used a different approach to raise the subject with Sam Hakes?

3. Evaluate Sam Hakes' response to Bill's statement that he was unable to sign off on the inventory account. In your view, did Sam deal with the situation appropriately? Was Sam's approach "professional"? Explain.

4. Is it appropriate for relatively inexperienced auditors to be assigned the primary responsibility for such critical accounts as Marcelle Stores' inventory? Explain.

Hamilton Wong, In-Charge Accountant

After spending much of the previous three months working elbow-to-elbow with as many as six colleagues in a cramped and poorly ventilated conference room, Hamilton Wong was looking forward to moving on to his next assignment.[1] Wong was an in-charge accountant on the audit staff of the San Francisco office of a large international accounting firm, the firm that had offered him a job two years earlier as he neared completion of his accounting degree at San Jose State University. His current client, Wille & Lomax, Inc., a public company and the second largest client of Wong's office, owned a chain of retail stores in the western United States that stretched from Seattle to San Diego and as far east as Denver and Albuquerque.

Although Wille & Lomax's stores operated under different names in different cities, each stocked the same general types of merchandise, including briefcases and other leather goods, luggage and travel accessories, and a wide range of gift items such as costume jewelry imported from Pacific Rim countries. The company also had a wholesale division that marketed similar merchandise to specialty retailers throughout the United States. The wholesale division accounted for approximately 60 percent of the company's annual sales.

A nondescript building in downtown San Francisco, just one block from bustling Market Street, served as Wille & Lomax's corporate headquarters. The company's fiscal year-end fell on the final Saturday of January. With the end of March just a few days away, Hamilton and his fellow "Willies"–the nickname that his office assigned to members of the Wille & Lomax audit engagement team–were quickly running out of time to complete the audit. Wong was well aware that the audit was behind schedule because he collected, coded, and input into an electronic spreadsheet the time worked each week by the individual Willies. He used the spreadsheet package to generate a weekly time and progress report that he submitted to Angela Sun, the senior who supervised the field work on the Wille & Lomax audit.

In addition to Wong and Sun, another in-charge accountant, Lauren Hutchison, and four staff accountants had worked on the Wille & Lomax audit since early January. Wong and Hutchison knew each other well. They shared the same start date with their employer and the past two summers had attended the same weeklong staff and in-charge training sessions at their firm's national education headquarters. Hutchison's primary responsibility on the current year's audit was the receivables account but she also audited the PP&E (property, plant, and equipment) and leases accounts. Besides his administrative responsibilities, which included serving as the engagement timekeeper and maintaining the correspondence file for the audit, Wong supervised and coordinated the audit procedures for inventory, accounts payable, and a few smaller accounts.

---

1. This case is based upon the experiences of an individual previously employed by one of the major accounting firms. The names of the parties involved in this case and other background information, such as locations, have been changed.

Hamilton was thankful that it was late Friday afternoon. In recent weeks, with the audit deadline looming, Angela Sun had required the Willie & Lomax crew to work until at least 7 P.M. each weekday except Friday, when she allowed them to leave "early" at 5 P.M. The engagement team had spent three consecutive Saturdays in the client's headquarters and would be spending both Saturday and Sunday of the coming weekend hunched over their workpapers. Wong had just completed collecting and coding the hours worked during the current week by the other members of the engagement team. Now it was time for him to enter in the electronic spreadsheet his chargeable hours, which he dutifully recorded at the end of each work day in his little "black book."

Before entering his own time, Wong decided to walk across the hall and purchase a snack in the employees' break room. In fact, he was stalling, trying to resolve a matter that was bothering him. Less than 30 minutes earlier, Lauren Hutchison had told him that during the current week, which included the previous weekend, she had spent 31 hours on the receivables account, 18 hours on the leases account, and 3 hours on PP&E. What troubled Wong was the fact that he knew Hutchison had worked several additional hours on the Wille & Lomax audit during the current week.

This was not the first time Hutchison had underreported her hours worked. On several occasions, Wong had noticed her secretively slipping workpaper files into her briefcase before leaving for home. The next morning, those files included polished memos or completed schedules that had not existed the previous day. Wong was certain that Hutchison was not reporting the hours she spent working at home on her audit assignments. He was just as certain that each week she consciously chose to shave a few hours off the total number she had spent working at the client's headquarters. Collectively, Wong estimated that Hutchison had failed to report at least 80 hours she had worked on the audit.

"Eating time" was a taboo subject among auditors. Although the subject was not openly discussed, Wong was convinced that many audit partners and audit managers subtly encouraged subordinates to underreport their time. By bringing their jobs in near budget, those partners and managers enhanced their apparent ability to manage engagements. The most avid time-eaters among Wong's peers seemed to be the individuals who had been labeled as "fast-track" superstars in the office.

After Hutchison had reported her time to Wong that afternoon, he had nonchalantly but pointedly remarked, "Lauren, who are you trying to impress by eating so much of your time?" His comment had caused the normally mild-mannered Hutchison to snap back, "Hey, Dude, you are the timekeeper, not the boss. So just mind your own ___ business." Immediately, Wong regretted offending Hutchison, whom he considered his friend. But she stomped away before he could apologize.

Wong knew who Hutchison was trying to impress. Angela Sun would almost certainly be promoted to audit manager in the summer and then become the audit manager on the Wille & Lomax engagement, meaning that there would be a vacancy in the all-important senior position on the engagement team. Both Hutchison and Wong also anticipated being promoted during the summer. The two new seniors would be the most likely candidates to take over the job of overseeing the field work on the Wille & Lomax audit.

The in-charge accountant who handled the administrative responsibilities on the Wille & Lomax engagement was typically the person chosen to take over the senior's role when it came open. But Wong worried that the close friendship that had developed between Lauren Hutchison and Sun might affect his chances of landing the coveted assignment. Almost every day, Hutchison and Sun went to lunch together without extending even a token invitation to Wong or their other colleagues to join them. John Berardo, the audit engagement partner, would choose the new senior for the Wille & Lomax engagement, but Angela Sun would certainly have a major influence on his decision.

There was little doubt in Wong's mind that Hutchison routinely underreported the time she worked on the Wille & Lomax audit to enhance her standing with Sun and Berardo. Not that Hutchison needed to spruce up her image. She had passed the CPA exam shortly after joining the firm, had a charming personality that endeared her to her superiors and client executives, and, like both Sun and Berardo, was a Stanford graduate. Wong, on the other hand, had struggled to pass the CPA exam, was shy by nature, and had graduated from a public university.

What irritated Wong the most about his subtle rivalry with Hutchison was that during the past two weekends he had spent several hours helping her research contentious technical issues for Wille & Lomax's complex lease contracts on its retail store sites. Earlier in the engagement, Hutchison had also asked him to help analyze some tricky journal entries involving the client's allowance for bad debts. In each of those cases, Wong had not charged any time to the given accounts, both of which were Hutchison's responsibility.

Before entering his time for the week, Wong checked once more the total hours that he had charged to date to his major accounts. For both inventory and accounts payable, he was already over budget. By the end of the audit, Wong estimated that he would "bust" the assigned time budgets for those two accounts by 20 to 25 percent each. On the other hand, Hutchison, thanks to her superior "time management" skills, would likely exceed the time budget on her major accounts by only a few hours. In fact, she might even come in under budget on one or more of her accounts, which was almost unheard of, at least on the dozen or so audits to which Wong had been assigned.

After finishing the bag of chips he had purchased in the snack room, Wong reached for the computer keyboard in front of him. In a few moments, he had entered his time for the week and printed the report that he would give to Angela Sun the following morning. After briefly glancing at the report, he slipped it into the appropriate work-paper file, turned off the light in the empty conference room, and locked the door behind him as he resolved to enjoy his brief 16-hour "weekend."

Questions

1. Place yourself in Hamilton Wong's position. Would you report all of your time worked on the Wille & Lomax audit? Why or why not? Do you believe that Lauren Hutchison behaved unethically by underreporting the time she worked on that engagement? Defend your answer.

2. Academic research suggests that underreporting time on audit engagements is a common practice. What are the key objectives of tracking hours worked by individual accounts or assignments on audit engagements? What implications does the underreporting of time have for individual auditors, their colleagues, and the overall quality of independent audits?

3. What measures can accounting firms take to ensure that time budgets do not interfere with the successful completion of an audit or become dysfunctional in other ways?

4. What measures can accounting firms take to reduce the likelihood that personal rivalries among auditors of the same rank will become dysfunctional?

Tommy O'Connell, Audit Senior

Tommy O'Connell had been a senior with one of the major international accounting firms for less than one month when he was assigned to the audit engagement for the Altamesa Manufacturing Company.[1] Tommy worked out of his firm's Fort Worth, Texas, office, while Altamesa was headquartered in Amarillo, the "capital" of the Texas Panhandle. The young senior realized that being assigned to the tough Altamesa engagement signaled that Jack Morrison, the Altamesa audit partner and the office managing partner, regarded his work highly. Serving as the audit senior on the Altamesa job would allow Tommy to become better acquainted with Morrison. Despite the challenges and opportunities posed by his new assignment, Tommy did not look forward to spending three months in Amarillo, a five-hour drive from Fort Worth. This would be his first assignment outside of Fort Worth since his marriage six months earlier. He dreaded breaking the news to his wife, Suzie, who often complained about the long hours his job required.

Altamesa manufactured steel girders used in the construction and renovation of bridges in West Texas, New Mexico, Colorado, and Oklahoma. The company's business was very cyclical and linked closely to the funding available to municipalities in Altamesa's four-state market area. To learn more about the company and its personnel, Tommy arranged to have lunch with Casi McCall, the audit senior on the Altamesa job the two previous years. According to Casi, Altamesa's management took aggressive positions regarding year-end expense accruals and revenue recognition. The company used the percentage-of-completion method to recognize revenue since its sales contracts extended over two to five years. Casi recounted several disputes with the company's chief accountant regarding the estimated stage of completion of jobs in progress. In an effort to "front-load" as much of the profit on jobs as possible, the chief accountant typically insisted that jobs were further along than they actually were.

Speaking with Casi made Tommy even more apprehensive about tackling the Altamesa engagement. But he realized that the job gave him an excellent chance to strengthen his fast-track image within his office. To reach his goal of being promoted to manager by his fifth year with the firm, Tommy needed to prove himself on difficult assignments such as the Altamesa engagement.

An Unpleasant Surprise for Tommy

It was late May, just two weeks before Tommy would be leaving for Amarillo to begin the Altamesa audit—the company had a June 30 fiscal year-end. Tommy, Jack Morrison, and an audit manager were having lunch at the Cattleman's Restaurant in the Cowtown district of north Fort Worth.

"Tommy, I've decided to send Carl with you out to Amarillo. Is that okay?" asked Jack Morrison.

"Uhh . . . sure, Jack. Yeah, that'll be fine," Tommy replied.

---

1. This case is based upon an actual series of events. Names and certain background information have been changed to conceal the identities of the individuals involved in the case.

"Of all people," Tommy thought to himself, "he would send Carl Wilmeth to Amarillo with me." Carl was a staff accountant with only a few months' experience, having been hired in the middle of the just-completed busy season. Other than being auditors and approximately the same age, the two young men had little in common. Tommy was from Lockettville, a small town in rural West Texas, while Carl had been raised in the exclusive Highland Park community of north central Dallas. Texas Tech, a large state-supported university, was Tommy's alma mater. Carl had earned his accounting degree from a small private college on the East Coast.

Tommy did not appreciate Carl's cocky attitude, and his lack of experience made him a questionable choice in Tommy's mind for the Altamesa engagement. As he tried to choke down the rest of his prime rib, Tommy recalled the complaints he had heard about Carl's job performance. Over the past three months, Carl had worked on two audits. In both cases, he had performed admirably–too admirably, in fact, coming in well under budget on his assigned tasks. On one engagement, Carl had completed an assignment in less than 60 hours when the audit budget allotted 100 hours; the previous year, 110 hours had been required to complete that same task. Both seniors who had supervised Carl suspected that he had not completed all of his assigned audit procedures, although he signed off on those procedures on the audit program. The tasks assigned to Carl had been large-scale tests of transactions that involved checking invoices, receiving reports, purchase orders, and other documents for various attributes. Given the nature of the tests, the seniors would have had difficulty confirming their suspicions.

"Boss" Tommy

Six weeks later, in early July, the Altamesa audit was in full swing. Carl had just finished his third assigned task on the job, in record time, of course. "Boss, here's that disbursements file," Carl said as he plopped a large stack of workpapers in front of Tommy. "Anything else you want me to do this afternoon? Since I'm way ahead of schedule, maybe I should take off and work on my tan out on the golf course."

"No, Carl. I think we have plenty to keep you busy right here." Tommy was agitated but he tried not to let it show. "Why don't you pull out the contracts file and then talk to Abby Littleton in the sales office. Get copies of any new contracts or proposals over the past year and put them in the contracts file."

At this point, Tommy simply did not have time to review Carl's cash disbursements workpapers. He was too busy trying to untangle Altamesa's complex method of allocating overhead costs to jobs in process. Later that afternoon, he had an appointment to meet with the chief accountant and a production superintendent to discuss the status of a large job. Tommy and the chief accountant had already butted heads on two occasions regarding a job's stage of completion. Casi had been right: The chief accountant clearly meant to recognize profit on in-progress jobs as quickly as possible. With four decades of experience, Scrooge–a nickname Casi had pinned on the chief accountant–obviously considered the young auditors a nuisance and did not appreciate their probing questions. Each time Tommy asked him a question regarding an important issue, the chief accountant registered his disgust by pursing his lips and running his hand through his thinning hair. He then responded with a rambling, convoluted answer intended to confuse rather than inform.

To comprehend Altamesa's accounting decisions for its long-term contracts, Tommy spent several hours of nonchargeable time each night in his motel room flipping through copies of job order worksheets and contracts. Occasionally, he referred to prior-year workpapers, his firm's policy and procedures manual, and even his tattered cost accounting textbook from his college days. Carl spent most of his evenings in the motel's club being taught the Texas Two-step and Cotton-eyed Joe by several new friends he had acquired.

During July and August, Tommy and Carl worked 50 to 60 hours per week on the Altamesa engagement. Several times Tommy wondered to himself whether it was worthwhile to work so hard to earn recognition as a "superstar" senior. He was also increasingly concerned about the impact of his fast-track strategy on his marriage. When he tried to explain to Suzie that the long hours and travel would pay off when he made partner, she was unimpressed. "Who cares if you make partner? I just want to spend more time with my husband," was her stock reply.

To Tell or Not to Tell

Finally, late August rolled around and the Altamesa job was almost complete. Jack Morrison had been in Amarillo for the past three days combing through the Altamesa workpapers. Nothing seemed to escape Morrison's eagle eye. Tommy had spent 12 hours per day since Morrison had arrived, tracking down missing invoices, checking on late confirmations, and tying up dozens of other loose ends. Carl was already back in Fort Worth, probably working on his golf swing. Morrison had allowed Carl to leave two days earlier after he had finished clearing the review comments in his workpaper files.

"Tommy, I have to admit that I was a little concerned about sending a light senior out to run this audit. But, by golly, you have done a great job." Morrison did not look up as he signed off on the workpapers spread before him on Altamesa's conference table. "You know, this kid Carl does super work. I've never seen cleaner, more organized workpapers from a staff accountant."

Tommy grimaced as he sat next to Morrison at the conference table. "Yeah, right. They should look clean, since he didn't do half of what he signed off on," Tommy thought to himself. Here was his opportunity. For the past several weeks, Tommy had planned to sit down with Morrison and talk to him regarding Carl's job performance. But now he was reluctant to do so. How do you tell a partner that you suspect much of the work he is reviewing may not have been done? Besides, Tommy realized that as Carl's immediate supervisor, he was responsible for that work. Tommy knew that he was facing a no-win situation. He leaned back in his chair and remained silent, hoping that Morrison would hurry through the last few workpaper files so they could make it back to Fort Worth by midnight.

EPILOGUE

Tommy never informed Jack Morrison of his suspicions regarding Carl's work. Thankfully, no problems—of a legal nature—ever arose on the jobs to which Carl was assigned. After passing the CPA exam on his first attempt, Carl left the accounting firm and enrolled in a prestigious MBA program. Upon graduation,

Carl accepted a job on Wall Street with one of the large investment banking firms. Tommy reached his goal of being promoted to audit manager within five years. One year later, he decided that he was not cut out to be a partner and resigned from the firm to accept a position in private industry.

Questions

1. Compare and contrast the professional roles of an audit senior and a staff accountant. In your analysis, consider the different responsibilities assigned to each role, the job-related stresses that individuals in the two roles face, and how each role contributes to the successful completion of an audit engagement. Which of these two roles is (a) more important and (b) more stressful? Defend your choices.

2. Assume that you are Tommy O'Connell and have learned that Carl Wilmeth will be working for you on the Altamesa audit engagement. Would you handle this situation any differently than Tommy did? Explain.

3. Again, assume that you are Tommy. Carl is badgering you for something to do midway through the Altamesa job. You suspect that he is not completing all of his assigned procedures, but at the time you are wrestling with an important accounting issue facing the client. What would you do at this point? What could you do to confirm your suspicions that Carl is not completing his assignments?

4. Now, assume that Jack Morrison is reviewing the Altamesa workpapers. To date, you (Tommy) have said nothing to Morrison about your suspicions regarding Carl. Do you have a professional responsibility to raise this matter now with Morrison? Explain.

5. Assume that at some point Tommy told Morrison that he suspected Carl was not completing his assigned tasks. The only evidence Tommy had to support his theory was the fact that Carl had come in significantly under budget on every major task assigned to him over a period of several months. If you were Jack Morrison, how would you have handled this matter?

Avis Love, Staff Accountant

"Oh no, not Store 51," Avis Love moaned under her breath. For the third time, Avis compared the dates listed in the cash receipts journal with the corresponding dates on the bank deposit slips. Avis shook her head softly and leaned back in her chair. There was no doubt in her mind now. Mo Rappele had definitely held open Store 51's cash receipts journal at the end of October.[1]

Avis Love was a staff accountant with the Atlanta office of a large international accounting firm. Several months earlier, Avis had graduated with an accounting degree from the University of Alabama at Birmingham. Although she did not plan to pursue a career in public accounting, Avis had accepted one of the several offers she had received from major accounting firms. The 22-year-old wanted to take a two-or three-year "vacation" from college, while at the same time accumulating a bankroll to finance three years of law school. Avis intended to practice law with a major firm for a few years and then return to her hometown in eastern Alabama and set up her own practice.

For the past few weeks, Avis had been assigned to the audit engagement for Lowell, Inc., a public company that operated nearly 100 retail sporting goods stores scattered across the South. Avis was nearing completion of a year-end cash receipts cutoff test for a sample of 20 Lowell stores. The audit procedures she had performed included preparing a list of the cash receipts reported in each of those stores' accounting records during the last five days of Lowell's fiscal year, which ended October 31. She had then obtained the relevant bank statements for each of the stores to determine whether the cash receipts had been deposited on a timely basis. For three of the stores in her sample, the deposit dates for the cash receipts ranged from three to seven days following the dates the receipts had been entered in the cash receipts journal. The individual store managers had apparently backdated cash receipts for the first several days of the new fiscal year, making it appear that the receipts had occurred in the fiscal year under audit by Avis's firm.

Avis had quickly realized that the objective of the store managers was not to overstate their units' year-end cash balances. Instead, the managers intended to inflate their recorded sales. Before Avis began the cutoff test, Teddy Tankersley, the senior assigned to the Lowell audit and Avis's immediate superior, had advised her that there was a higher-than-normal risk of cash receipts and sales cutoff errors for Lowell this year. The end of Lowell's fiscal year coincided with the end of a three-month sales promotion. This campaign to boost Lowell's sagging sales included bonuses for store managers who exceeded their quarterly sales quota. This was the first time that Lowell had run such a campaign and it was a modest success. Fourth-quarter sales for the fiscal year just ended topped the corresponding sales for the previous fiscal year by 6 percent.

When Avis uncovered the first instance of backdated cash receipts, she had felt a noticeable surge of excitement. In several months of tracing down invoices and receiving reports, ticking and tying, and performing other mundane tests, the young

---

1. This case was developed from an actual series of events. Names, locations, and certain other background information have been changed to conceal the identities of the individuals involved in the case.

accountant had occasionally found isolated errors in client accounting records. But this was different. This was fraud.

Avis had a much different reaction when she uncovered the second case of backdated cash receipts. She had suddenly realized that the results of her cutoff test would have "real world" implications for several parties, principally the store managers involved in the scheme. During the past few months, Avis had visited six of Lowell's retail stores to perform various interim tests of controls and to observe physical inventory procedures. The typical store manager was in his or her early 30s, married, with one or two small children. Because of Lowell's miserly pay scale, the stores were chronically understaffed, meaning that the store managers worked extremely long hours to earn their modest salaries.

No doubt, the store managers who backdated sales to increase their bonuses would be fired immediately. Clay Shamblin, Lowell's chief executive officer (CEO), was a hard-nosed businessman known for his punctuality, honesty, and work ethic. Shamblin exhibited little patience with subordinates who did not display those same traits.

When Avis came to the last store in her sample, she had hesitated. She realized that Mo Rappelle managed Store 51. Three weeks earlier, Avis had spent a long Saturday afternoon observing the physical inventory at Store 51 on the outskirts of Atlanta. Although the Lowell store managers were generally courteous and accommodating, Mo had gone out of his way to help Avis complete her tasks. Mo allowed Avis to use his own desk in the store's cramped office, shared a pizza with her during an afternoon break, and introduced her to his wife and two small children who dropped by the store during the afternoon.

"Mo, what a stupid thing to do," Avis thought to herself after reviewing the workpapers for the cutoff tests a final time. "And for just a few extra dollars." Mo had apparently backdated cash receipts for only the first two days of the new year. According to Avis's calculations, the backdated sales had increased Mo's year-end bonus by slightly more than $100. From the standpoint of Lowell, Inc., the backdated sales for Mo's store clearly had an immaterial impact on the company's operating results for the year just ended.

After putting away the workpapers for the cutoff test, a thought dawned on Avis. The Lowell audit program required her to perform cash receipts cutoff tests for 20 stores . . . any 20 stores she selected. Why not just drop Store 51 from her sample and replace it with Store 52 or 53 or whatever?

EPILOGUE

Avis brooded over the results of her cutoff test the remainder of that day at work and most of that evening. The following day, she gave the workpaper file to Teddy Tankersley. Avis reluctantly told Teddy about the backdated cash receipts and sales she had discovered in three stores: Store 12, Store 24, and Store 51. Teddy congratulated Avis on her thorough work and told her that Clay Shamblin would be very interested in her findings.

A few days later, Shamblin called Avis into his office and thanked her for uncovering the backdated transactions. The CEO told her that the company's internal auditors had tested the year-end cash receipts and sales cutoff for the remaining 72 stores and identified seven additional store managers who had tampered with their accounting records. As Avis was leaving the CEO's office, he thanked her once more and assured her that the store managers involved in the scam "would soon be looking for a new line of work . . . in another part of the country."

Questions

1. Would it have been appropriate for Avis to substitute another store for Store 51 after she discovered the cutoff errors in that store's accounting records? Defend your answer.

2. Identify the parties potentially affected by the outcome of the ethical dilemma faced by Avis Love. What obligation, if any, did Avis have to each of these parties?

3. Does the AICPA's *Code of Professional Conduct* prohibit auditors from developing friendships with client personnel? If not, what measures can auditors take to prevent such friendships from interfering with the performance of their professional responsibilities?

4. Identify the key audit objectives associated with year-end cash receipts and sales cutoff tests.

5. What method would you have recommended that Avis or her colleagues use in deciding whether the cutoff errors she discovered had a material impact on Lowell's year-end financial statements? Identify the factors or benchmarks that should have been considered in making this decision.

CASE 6.6

Charles Tollison, Audit Manager

"No, that's okay, Bea. I'll write that memo this weekend and send it to Mr. Fielder. You go on home."[1]

"Are you sure, Chuck? I don't mind staying a while longer."

"Thanks, Bea, but you've already put in too much overtime this week."

After he sent his secretary home, Charles Tollison spent several minutes shuffling through the audit workpapers and correspondence stacked on his desk, trying to decide what work he would take home over the weekend. Finally, only one decision remained. Tollison couldn't decide whether to take the inventory file with him. Compulsive by nature, Tollison knew that if he took the inventory file home, he would have to complete his review of that file, which would increase his weekend workload from 6 hours to more than 12 hours. As he stewed over his decision, Tollison stepped to the window of his office and idly watched the rush-hour traffic on the downtown streets several stories below.

It was nearly 6:30 on a Friday evening in early August. Charles Tollison, an audit manager for a large international accounting firm, had suffered through a tough week. His largest audit client was negotiating to buy a smaller company within its industry. For the past two months, Tollison had supervised the fieldwork on an intensive acquisition audit of the competitor's accounting records. The client's chief executive officer (CEO) suspected that the competitor's executives had embellished their firm's financial data in anticipation of the proposed buyout. Since the client was overextending itself financially to acquire the other firm, the CEO wanted to be sure that its financial data were reliable. The CEO's principal concern was the valuation of the competitor's inventory, which accounted for 45 percent of its total assets.

The client's CEO had requested that Tollison be assigned to the acquisition audit because she respected Tollison and the quality of his work. Normally, an audit manager spends little time "in the trenches" supervising day-to-day audit procedures. Because of the nature of this engagement, however, Tollison had felt it necessary to spend 10 hours per day, six and seven days per week, poring over the accounting records of the takeover candidate with his subordinates.

As Tollison stared at the gridlocked streets below, he was relieved that the acquisition audit was almost complete. After he tied up a few loose ends in the inventory file, he would turn the workpapers over to the audit engagement partner for a final review.

Tollison's tough week had been highlighted by several contentious meetings with client personnel, a missed birthday party for his eight-year-old daughter, and an early breakfast Thursday morning with his office managing partner, Walker Linton. During that breakfast, Linton had notified Tollison that he had been passed over for promotion—for the second year in a row. The news had been difficult for Tollison to accept.

For more than 13 years, Tollison had been a hardworking and dedicated employee of the large accounting firm. He had never turned down a difficult assignment, never complained about the long hours his work required, and made countless personal

---

1. This case was developed from information obtained from a CPA employed for many years with a large international accounting firm.

sacrifices, the most recent being the missed birthday party. After informing Tollison of the bad news, Linton had encouraged him to stay with the firm. Linton promised that the following year he would vigorously campaign for Tollison's promotion and "call in all favors" owed to him by partners in other offices. Despite that promise, Tollison realized that he had only a minimal chance of being promoted to partner. Seldom were two-time "losers" ticketed for promotion.

Although he had been hoping for the best, Tollison had not expected a favorable report from the Partner Selection Committee. In recent weeks, he had gradually admitted to himself that he did not have the profile for which the committee was searching. Tollison was not a rainmaker like his friend and fellow audit manager, Craig Allen, whose name appeared on the roster of new partners to be formally announced the following week. Allen was a member of several important civic organizations and had a network of well-connected friends at the local country club. Those connections had served Allen well, allowing him to steer several new clients to the firm in recent years.

Instead of a rainmaker, Tollison was a technician. If someone in the office had a difficult accounting or auditing issue to resolve, that individual went first to Tollison, not to one of the office's six audit partners. When a new client posed complex technical issues, the audit engagement partner requested that Tollison be assigned to the job. One reason Tollison was a perfect choice for difficult engagements was that he micromanaged his jobs, insisting on being involved in every aspect of them. Tollison's management style often resulted in his "busting" time budgets for audits, although he seldom missed an important deadline. To avoid missing deadlines when a job was nearing completion, Tollison and the subordinates assigned to his engagements would work excessive overtime, including long weekend stints.

Finally, Tollison turned away from his window and slumped into his chair. As he sat there, he tried to drive away the bitterness that he was feeling. "If Meredith hadn't left the firm, maybe I wouldn't be in this predicament," Tollison thought to himself. Three years earlier, Meredith Oliveti, an audit partner and Tollison's closest friend within the firm, had resigned to become the chief financial officer (CFO) of a large client. Following Oliveti's resignation, Tollison had no one within the firm to sponsor him through the tedious and political partner selection process. Instead, Tollison had been "lost in the shuffle" with the dozens of other hardworking, technically inclined audit managers within the firm who aspired to a partnership position.

Near the end of breakfast Thursday morning, Walker Linton had mentioned to Tollison the possibility that he could remain with the firm in a senior manager position. In recent years, Tollison's firm had relaxed its "up or out" promotion policy. But Tollison was not sure he wanted to remain with the firm as a manager with no possibility of being promoted to partner. Granted, there were clearly advantages associated with becoming a permanent senior manager. For example, no equity interest in the firm meant not absorbing any portion of its future litigation losses. On the other hand, in Tollison's mind accepting an appointment as a permanent senior manager seemed equivalent to having "career failure" stenciled on his office door.

Ten minutes till seven, time to leave. Tollison left the inventory file lying on his desk as he closed his bulging briefcase and then stepped toward the door of his office. After flipping off the light switch, Tollison paused momentarily. He then grudgingly turned and stepped back to his desk, picked up the inventory file, and tucked it under his arm.

Questions

1. Do you believe Charles Tollison was qualified for a partnership position with his firm? Explain.

2. Did Tollison's firm treat him "fairly"? Why or why not?

3. Identify the criteria you believe large international accounting firms should use when evaluating individuals for promotion to partner. In your opinion, which of these criteria should be most heavily weighted by these firms? Should smaller accounting firms establish different criteria for evaluating individuals for promotion to partner? Explain.

4. Discuss the advantages and disadvantages of the "up or out" promotion policy followed by many accounting firms.

PROFESSIONAL ISSUES

7

Ligand Pharmaceuticals

In the late 1990s, James Fazio reached what many CPAs consider the pinnacle of success in the accounting profession, namely, partnership in one of the Big Four public accounting firms. For more than a decade, Fazio served as an audit partner with Deloitte & Touche in that firm's San Diego, California, practice office. Similar to his colleagues within Deloitte and the other major accounting firms, Fazio's professional life was disrupted by the Enron and WorldCom debacles. The sudden collapse of those two large companies following the turn of the century prompted a public outcry to impose more rigorous regulatory controls over the financial reporting function for publicly owned companies. The federal government's response to that outcry would further complicate the already complex and stressful nature of James Fazio's professional role as an audit partner with a Big Four accounting firm.

Peek-A-Boo

In the summer of 2002, the U.S. Congress hurriedly passed the Sarbanes-Oxley Act (SOX). The SOX legislation contained the most far-reaching financial reporting reforms at the federal level since the passage of the Securities Act of 1933 and the Securities Exchange Act of 1934. These reforms included a requirement that public companies have their internal controls over financial reporting audited by an independent accounting firm. That requirement, which became effective for most companies in 2004, forced U.S. companies to spend billions of dollars to rethink and, in many cases, completely overhaul their internal control systems.

The SOX legislation was an economic boon for Deloitte and the other Big Four accounting firms since those firms were ideally suited to provide the thousands of internal control audits mandated by SOX. To take full advantage of this large new revenue stream, these firms redesigned their audit processes, retooled their organizational structures, and hired a large number of new employees.

SOX also established a new regulatory structure for the independent audit function that had far-reaching implications for the major accounting firms. The role of the new Public Company Accounting Oversight Board (PCAOB) was to strengthen and improve the independent audit function for public companies and thereby minimize the likelihood of "audit failures." Many parties have alleged that the Enron and World-Com fiascoes could have been avoided or at least mitigated if those companies' financial statements had been audited more rigorously.

Based in Washington, D.C., the PCAOB, commonly referred to as "Peek-a-boo" by auditing practitioners, falls under the regulatory purview of the Securities and Exchange Commission (SEC). The PCAOB's operations are overseen by five board members appointed by the SEC, has several hundred employees, and an annual operating budget exceeding $100 million. The agency's regulatory mandate includes registering and monitoring accounting firms that audit public companies required to file periodic financial statements with the SEC. Other responsibilities of the PCAOB include establishing auditing, ethical, and quality control standards for those firms and carrying out disciplinary investigations.

The years immediately following the passage of SOX presented exciting and profitable opportunities for the Big Four accounting firms but posed enormous challenges for them as well. No one knew exactly how the new regulatory agenda and infrastructure would impact the nature of financial reporting and the independent audit function in the United States. Despite the uncertainty they faced, James Fazio and other Big Four audit partners had more pressing concerns at the time, namely, the everyday "business" of, and professional responsibilities associated with, supervising the audits of their clients.

Deloitte's 2003 Ligand Audit

In early 2004, the 43-year-old Fazio was overseeing the 2003 audit of Ligand Pharmaceuticals, a San Diego-based company whose stock was traded on the NASDAQ exchange. As the audit engagement partner for Ligand, Fazio had a wide range of responsibilities. The following excerpts from Deloitte's *Accounting and Auditing Practice Manual* at the time addressed the role and responsibilities of an audit engagement partner.

> *It is the responsibility of the Engagement Partner to form the audit opinion, or to disclaim an opinion, on the financial statements.*
>
> *The Engagement Partner has the final responsibility for the planning and performance of the audit engagement, including the assignment, on-the-job training, and audit work of professional staff, and the implementation of the decisions concerning matters that have been the subject of consultation . . .*
>
> *The knowledge and skills of an Engagement Partner should be matched with the needs and characteristics of the engagement.*

For several years, James Fazio had been involved in his office's "High Technology Group." Because of his experience with emerging growth companies, Fazio seemed well suited to serve as the audit engagement partner for Ligand, which was still in a developmental stage. In company press releases, Ligand described itself as an "emerging R&D and royalty-driven biotechnology company." The company's principal products included a painkiller and several cancer treatment drugs. The company also had several new products under development. Rising expectations for the company's future prospects had caused its stock price to soar from under $4 per share in early 2003 to nearly $24 per share in early 2004 despite the company never having reported an operating profit.

Deloitte requires each audit engagement team to assess the degree of "engagement risk" posed by a given audit.[1] Fazio and his subordinates concluded that the 2003 Ligand audit posed a "greater than normal" degree of engagement risk due to questions surrounding Ligand's accounting for sales returns. Ligand's distribution channel consisted principally of three large drug wholesalers. These wholesalers purchased Ligand's products and then marketed them to pharmacies and other healthcare facilities throughout the United States. Ligand recorded product shipments made to the three wholesalers as consummated sales transactions although the wholesalers had the right to return any products that they did not "sell through" to their customers. Because of this revenue recognition policy, Ligand was required to record a reserve (allowance) for expected future sales returns at the end of each accounting period.

By early 2004 when Deloitte was auditing Ligand's 2003 financial statements, the company had been marketing its major products for only a short period of time, which meant that Ligand's accountants had limited historical experience on which

---

1. The three levels of engagement risk that can be assigned to a given audit include normal, greater than normal, and much greater than normal.

to base their estimates of future sales returns. Complicating matters was the difficulty Ligand had in obtaining sales and inventory data from its three wholesalers.

Ligand typically shipped product to those wholesalers twelve months before the expiration date of the given product. The wholesalers generally had the right to return product received from Ligand in a twelve-month window that extended six months on either side of a product's expiration date. To properly assess the quantity of future sales returns, Ligand's accounting staff needed up-to-date "sell-through" data from its wholesalers. However, the three wholesalers frequently failed to provide that data on a timely basis. In fact, Ligand often received large and unexpected shipments of product returns from the three wholesalers.

The limited sales returns data available to Ligand during 2003 suggested that the company was significantly underestimating its rate of product returns. For example, one product had experienced rates of return ranging from 13 percent to as high as 20 percent on "open lots."[2] Company management was convinced that those return rates were not representative of the overall return rate that product would eventually experience. As a result, management instructed the company's accountants to apply a much more modest 2.5 percent return rate when determining the product's 2003 year-end allowance for future sales returns.

Shortly before Deloitte completed the 2003 Ligand audit in early March 2004, Ligand received additional information from its wholesalers regarding the return rates being experienced by its major products. Although this information was available from the company's accounting staff, the Deloitte auditors did not review it. The updated sales returns data, similar to the earlier data that had been reviewed by the Deloitte auditors, indicated that the December 31, 2003, allowance for future sales returns was inadequate. In some cases, the returns received in early 2004 for products sold in 2003 exceeded those products' total 2003 year-end provision for sales returns.

Fazio was aware of the difficulty Ligand had in estimating its future sales returns and the fact that the projected return rates being applied by the company appeared insufficient given the actual sales returns data available from the company's wholesalers. Despite this knowledge, Fazio authorized the issuance of an unqualified opinion on Ligand's 2003 financial statements on March 10, 2004.

The following month, Fazio supervised Deloitte's interim review of Ligand's financial statements for the first quarter of 2004. During that engagement, Fazio and his subordinates obtained Ligand's sales returns data for the first two months of fiscal 2004.

Those data alone demonstrated that the year-end allowance for sales returns was significantly understated. However, Ligand's accounting staff also provided forecast data to the auditors indicating that the company would experience a large amount of additional product returns from fiscal 2003 sales during the remaining months of 2004. Despite the considerable evidence that Ligand's 2003 year-end allowance for sales returns was materially understated, Fazio failed to recommend that the company recall and restate its 2003 financial statements.

The Trials and Tribulations of James Fazio

The contentious accounting issues posed by Ligand were not the only challenges that James Fazio faced during the 2003 audit of that company. Several months before that audit began, Fazio's immediate superior, the partner in charge of Deloitte's San Diego audit

---

2. Ligand used the term "lot" in reference to a given quantity of items of the same product that were manufactured at the same time and had the same expiration date. The term "open lot" referred to a product shipment for which the given wholesaler still had a right to return the unsold inventory from that shipment.

practice, asked to meet with him. During that meeting, Fazio was told that concerns were being expressed about his job performance. In fact, members of Deloitte's management had suggested that Fazio no longer be allowed to supervise audits of public companies.

In February 2004, during the course of the 2003 Ligand audit, Fazio's immediate superior met with him once more. During this meeting, Fazio was told that he was perceived as a "quality risk" and was "counseled to resign from the firm."[3] Several of Deloitte's top partners had been involved in the decision to ask for Fazio's resignation. These partners included the director of Deloitte's Risk Management Program, the Regional Audit Managing Partner for Deloitte's Pacific Southwest Region, and Deloitte's National Audit Managing Partner.

On March 5, 2004, the San Diego Audit Managing Partner and the Regional Audit Managing Partner met with Fazio. Following that meeting, the Regional Audit Managing Partner sent an e-mail to the National Audit Managing Partner that summarized the discussions that took place during the meeting. The e-mail documented the reasons why Fazio was being asked to resign from Deloitte.

> Among the reasons given were the views of certain members of Deloitte's management that the Engagement Partner [Fazio] did not have the skills to adequately supervise public company engagements and other engagements with above-average risk profiles and that the Engagement Partner [Fazio] was not suited to handling complex or risky engagements.[4]

Five days later, on March 10, 2004, Fazio signed the unqualified audit opinion issued by Deloitte on Ligand's 2003 financial statements. Fazio remained the audit engagement partner for Ligand following the issuance of that audit report.

On August 5, 2004, Deloitte resigned as Ligand's independent auditor. The price of Ligand's stock declined sharply following Deloitte's abrupt and unexpected resignation. From its high-water mark of nearly $24 per share in April 2004, the stock would eventually fall to under $1.50 per share by late 2008.

EPILOGUE

In May 2005, Ligand's management announced that the company would be restating its financial statements for 2002, 2003, and the first three quarters of 2004. Management reported that a joint investigation by the company's audit committee and new audit firm, BDO Seidman, had revealed material errors in those financial statements. The errors resulted principally from "improperly recognizing revenue on product shipments to distributors."[5] The financial restatement released by Ligand later in 2005 reduced the company's previously reported revenues for 2003 by 52 percent or $59 million in total. The company also increased its reported operating loss for 2003 by 250 percent.

Ligand insisted that the joint investigation by its audit committee and BDO Seidman had "found no evidence of improper or fraudulent actions or practices by any member of management or that management acted in bad faith in adopting and administering the company's historical revenue recognition policies."[6] The company also

---

3. PCAOB, "Order Instituting Disciplinary Proceedings, Making Findings and Imposing Sanctions: In the Matter of Deloitte & Touche LLP," *PCAOB Release No. 105-2007-005*, 10 December 2007, 7.

4. *Ibid.*

5. J. McEntee, "Ligand to Restate Financials Back to 2002," *sandiego.com*, 20 May 2005.

6. *Ibid.*

reported that it intended to adopt a new revenue recognition model based upon sell-through accounting under which revenue would not be recognized until the company's wholesalers had sold Ligand's products to their customers.

On December 10, 2007, the PCAOB issued joint disciplinary releases announcing sanctions imposed on James Fazio and Deloitte & Touche, stemming from Fazio's involvement in the 2003 Ligand audit.[7] The PCAOB barred James Fazio from being associated with a PCAOB-registered public accounting firm for two years. In a PCAOB press release also issued on December 10, 2007, an agency spokesperson reported that Fazio had violated several professional auditing standards during the 2003 Ligand audit.

> *Mr. Fazio failed to perform appropriate and adequate audit procedures related to Ligand's reported revenue from sales of products for which a right of return existed and failed to supervise others adequately to ensure the performance of such procedures.*

> *Mr. Fazio neither performed nor ensured the performance of procedures that adequately took into account the existence of factors indicating that Ligand's ability to make reasonable estimates of product returns may have been impaired.*

> *Mr. Fazio neither performed nor ensured the performance of procedures that adequately took into account the extent to which Ligand had consistently and substantially underestimated its product returns.*

> *In auditing Ligand's reported revenues, Mr. Fazio failed to [exercise] . . . the due care and professional skepticism required under the circumstances.*

> *He also failed to identify and appropriately address issues concerning Ligand's policy*

of excluding certain types of returns from its estimates of future returns and the adequacy of Ligand's disclosure of this accounting policy.[8]

The PCAOB publicly censured Deloitte and fined the firm $1 million for failing to take "meaningful steps to assure the quality of the audit work"[9] on the 2003 Ligand audit engagement. According to the PCAOB spokesperson, prior to and during the 2003 Ligand audit, "Certain members of Deloitte's management concluded that Mr. Fazio should be removed from public company audits" and that "he should be asked to resign from the firm."[10] The spokesperson went on to note that despite the grave concerns expressed regarding Mr. Fazio's competence, he was allowed to continue as the engagement partner for the 2003 Ligand audit.

The PCAOB's Director of Enforcement and Investigations issued a separate statement on the responsibility of registered accounting firms to ensure that their partners are competent to perform public company audits.

> *Registered public accounting firms must take reasonable steps to assure that their audit partners and other audit professionals are competent to conduct public audits. When concerns about an auditor's competency rise, a firm must act with dispatch to protect audit quality. The firm [Deloitte] failed to meet the Board's auditing standards in the audit led by Mr. Fazio.*[11]

The sanctions imposed on Deloitte were the first levied on a Big Four accounting firm by the PCAOB. A former SEC official noted that the Ligand case was a milestone in the new agency's short regulatory history. "It shows that the PCAOB's Enforcement Division is fully mature and also that we should expect to see within

---

7. Although the PCAOB issued the disciplinary reports in this case, SEC and PCAOB personnel were involved in the related investigations. In 2005, the SEC had announced that it was launching an independent investigation of Ligand. The federal agency apparently completed that investigation without imposing sanctions on Ligand or any Ligand executive or employee.

8. PCAOB, "PCAOB Issues Disciplinary Orders Against Deloitte & Touche LLP and a Former Audit Partner," www.pcaobus.org/News_and_Events/2007/12-10.aspx, 10 December 2007.

9. *Ibid.*

10. *Ibid.*

11. *Ibid.*

a short period of time additional cases against not only other Big Four firms, but against the so-called second four firms as well."[12]

Deloitte issued a public statement responding to the sanctions imposed on it by the PCAOB. In that statement, a Deloitte official reported that the firm had "established and implemented changes to its quality-control policies that directly address the PCAOB's concerns."[13] The Deloitte spokesperson went on to insist that the firm was "confident that its audit policies and procedures were among the very best in the profession and that they meet or exceed all applicable standards."[14]

Questions

1. Describe what you believe is implied by the term "engagement risk." What are the key factors likely considered by Deloitte and other audit firms when assessing engagement risk? How, if at all, are auditors' professional responsibilities affected when a client poses a higher than normal degree of engagement risk?

2. What quality control mechanisms should major accounting firms have in place to ensure that audit partners have the proper training and experience to supervise audit engagements?

3. Identify the accounting standards and concepts that dictate the proper accounting treatment for sales returns. How were these standards and concepts violated by Ligand?

4. During the review of Ligand's first-quarter financial statements for 2004, the Deloitte auditors learned that the company had significantly underestimated its future sales returns at the end of 2003. What responsibility, if any, did this discovery impose on the Deloitte auditors?

5. Since its inception, the PCAOB has been criticized by many parties. Summarize the principal complaints that have been directed at the PCAOB. Do you believe this criticism is justified? Explain. What measures could the PCAOB take to improve its effectiveness and efficiency as a regulatory body?

12. C. Johnson, "Deloitte Settles in Key Case Over Faulty Audit," *Washington Post*, 11 December 2007, D01.

13. F. Norris, "Deloitte Agrees to Pay $1 Million Fine," *The New York Times* (online), 11 December 2007.

14. *Ibid.*

CASE 7.2

Sarah Russell, Staff Accountant

Sarah Russell grew up in a small town in the flatlands of western Kansas where she was born.[1] In high school, she was homecoming queen, valedictorian of her graduating class, point guard on her basketball team for two years, and a candy striper (volunteer) at the local hospital. Since her parents had attended the University of Kansas, Sarah was off to Lawrence at age 18.

After spending her freshman year posting straight A's in 30 hours of college courses, Sarah settled on accounting as her major after seriously considering journalism, pre-law, and finance. Although Sarah had yet to take any courses in accounting, she had been impressed by a presentation that a female partner of a large accounting firm had made at a career fair. Sarah was excited by the challenges and opportunities presented by public accounting, as described by the partner. Here was a field in which she could learn a great deal in a short period of time and advance rapidly to a position where she had important responsibilities. Plus, public accounting provided a wide range of career paths. If she really enjoyed public accounting, she could pursue a partnership position with a large accounting firm. Then again, she might "hang out her shingle" in her hometown, see the world on the internal audit staff of a large corporation, or return to college after a couple of years of real-world experience to earn an MBA.

Sarah completed the tough accounting courses at the University of Kansas with only two small blemishes on her transcript–B's in individual and corporate taxation. During the fall semester of her senior year, Sarah accepted a position as a staff accountant with a Big Eight accounting firm. Sarah considered staying in her home state but decided instead to request an assignment in her new employer's Chicago office. She believed that exposure to big-city life would allow her to arrive at a more informed decision when it was time to make a long-term commitment to a career path and a lifestyle.

During her first year on the job, Sarah served on six audit engagements. Her clients included a pipeline company, a religious foundation, and a professional sports team. She worked hard on those assignments and earned impressive performance appraisals from each of her immediate supervisors. Somehow Sarah also squeezed a CPA review course into her hectic schedule that first year. And she was glad she did. She was among the few rookies in her large office to pass each section of the CPA exam on her first attempt. With that barrier out of the way, Sarah focused her energy on being promoted to audit senior as quickly as possible.

Several individuals provided Sarah with much-needed moral support during her first year, including R. J. Bell, an audit partner. Bell was 40 years old and had been a partner for eight years. According to the office grapevine, he was in line to become the new office managing partner within the next year or so. Bell tried to get to know the new staff accountants assigned to the audit staff and to help them adjust to their jobs in any way he could. Several times during the year, Bell invited small groups of staff accountants to his home to have dinner with him and his family. Recognizing

1. This case was authored by Carol Knapp, an assistant professor at the University of Oklahoma. This case is based upon experiences related by a young woman previously employed by a large accounting firm. The names of the individuals involved in this case and other background facts, such as locations, have been changed.

that Sarah was new to Chicago, he made a special effort to include her in such social gatherings and to give her complimentary tickets to cultural and sporting events. When Sarah's old car from college died, Bell arranged for her to obtain a loan from a local bank. Sarah appreciated Bell's help and guidance. She considered the firm to be very lucky to have an audit partner so supportive of staff accountants.

Shortly after her first anniversary with the firm, Sarah received a telephone call from Bell at home one Saturday afternoon. At first, Sarah thought there must be a client emergency that required her assistance, but Bell did not bring up any client business during the conversation. Instead, he told Sarah that he had just called to chat. Sarah felt mildly uncomfortable with the situation but spoke with Bell for a few minutes before making up an excuse to get off the phone.

The following day, Sarah, an avid jogger, had just completed a four-mile run on her regular jogging trail in a city park when Bell pulled up as she was walking toward her car. "Hi, Sarah. How was your run?" Bell asked nonchalantly. "I was just driving by and thought you might like to get a Coke after your workout."

As Sarah approached Bell's car she felt awkward but tried to act natural, as if his unexpected appearance was only a coincidence. "Thanks, R. J. But I really need to get back to my apartment. I've got several errands to run and phone calls to make."

"You sure? I'm buying."

"Yeah, I'd better get home."

"Well, okay."

Over the next several weeks, Bell made a concerted effort to develop a personal relationship with Sarah. Eventually, Bell, who was known for working long hours, was calling her nearly every evening from his office just "to chat." Once or twice per week, he invited her to get a drink with him after work. On a couple of occasions, she accepted, hoping that by doing so he would stop asking her. No such luck. Finally, she began avoiding him in the office and stopped answering her home phone when she thought it was him calling. Twice, Bell dropped by her apartment in the evening. Panic-stricken both times, Sarah refused to answer the door, hoping he would quickly decide that she was not home.

Bell's persistence caused Sarah to feel increasing levels of stress and powerlessness. She did not know what to do or to whom she could turn. She was reluctant to discuss the matter with her friends in the office since she did not want to start a rumor mill. Embarrassment prevented her from discussing the matter with her parents or other family members. Worst of all, Sarah began wondering whether she had somehow encouraged Bell's behavior. She racked her brain to recall each time that she had spoken or met with him during her first year on the job. She could not remember saying anything that could have been misconstrued by him. But maybe she had inadvertently said something that had given him the wrong impression. Maybe he had mistaken the sense of respect and admiration she had for him as affection. Maybe she had asked him an inappropriate question. Maybe . . .

EPILOGUE

After more than six weeks of enduring Bell's advances, Sarah summoned the courage to make an appointment with him one Friday afternoon in his office. When Sarah informed Bell that she wanted to keep their relationship on a strictly professional level, he failed to respond for several tense moments. Finally, he remarked that Sarah must have misinterpreted his actions over the past several weeks. He was simply trying to make her feel more comfortable with her job. "I go out of my way to be as friendly and sociable with as many members of the audit staff as I can." Bell then told Sarah that, given the circumstances, he would see to it that she was not assigned to any of his engagements in the future. After another few moments of tense silence, he tersely asked, "Is there anything else I can do for you, Miss Russell?" Sarah shook her head softly and then got up and left his office.

Sarah had no further contact or conversations with Bell following that Friday afternoon meeting. A few months later, she decided to return to Kansas to be closer to her family. At last report, Sarah was the chief financial officer (CFO) of a charitable organization.

Questions

1. In your opinion, how should Sarah have handled this matter? Identify the factors that Sarah should have considered in dealing with the situation. Also, identify the professional and personal responsibilities of Sarah, R. J. Bell, and other relevant individuals in this matter.

2. What were the costs and potential costs to Sarah's employer in this case? How should accounting firms attempt to prevent these types of situations from occurring? Assume that rather than speaking to Bell, Sarah had told the office managing partner about the problem she faced. How should the office managing partner have dealt with the matter?

3. This case took place several years ago. Do you believe that events similar to those that took place in this case could occur now? Explain.

Bud Carriker, Audit Senior

Since childhood, Louis Armstrong Carriker had been known simply as "Bud," a nickname given to him by his paternal grandmother.[1] Bud's father, a New Orleans native, was a lifelong fan of the famous blues musician after whom he named his only son. After graduating from high school, Elliot Carriker joined the military. In April 1951, Elliot, an African American, married Bud's mother, a Mexican American, while he was stationed at a military base in Texas. Two years later, Bud arrived. Sadly, Bud's mother died during childbirth. As a result, Bud spent most of his childhood in New Orleans being raised by his grandmother.

When he was a young teenager, Bud was reunited with his father in Dallas, Texas. Bud's new family included a stepmother and one-year old twin sisters. In high school, Bud excelled in both academics and athletics and earned a scholarship to play basketball at a small Division 1 school. Bud realized that his athletic career would end after college, so he dedicated himself to obtaining a degree that would provide him with an opportunity to earn a good livelihood following graduation. After leaving the military, Elliot Carriker had relied on the GI Bill to earn a college degree in finance. Because of his experience in the business world as a senior loan officer for a major metropolitan bank, Elliot encouraged his son to consider majoring in either accounting or finance. After several sessions with his high school career counselor, Bud decided to take his father's advice and pursue an accounting degree in college.

During his senior year in college, Bud interviewed with several of the international accounting firms and with two large Houston-based oil companies. After discussing his job offers with his father, Bud decided to begin his career in the public accounting profession. Bud realized that a few years experience on the audit staff of a major accounting firm would provide him with a strong background in financial accounting. He intended to use that background to obtain a mid-level position on the accounting staff of a bank with an eventual career goal of becoming either a corporate controller or chief financial officer (CFO) in the financial services industry.

Bud launched his career in public accounting in June 1975 and was promoted to audit senior in the late fall of 1977, just prior to the beginning of his third busy season. By the time that his fifth busy season arrived in late 1979, Bud had decided that he would begin searching for a job in the private sector when he was promoted to audit manager, which he expected would be sometime during the following 18 months. Although he enjoyed public accounting, Bud was anxious to get his "real" career started.

In mid-November 1979, Alex Saunders, the managing partner of the practice office that Bud had been assigned to throughout his career, asked Bud to meet with him one afternoon. Saunders informed Bud that the firm had unexpectedly acquired a new client. The new client was a privately owned bank in a midsized city in central Texas. Since accepting a position with his employer, Bud had made it known that he wanted to be assigned to a client in the banking or financial services industries. The acquisition of the new client provided Saunders an opportunity to finally grant Bud's request.

---

1. This case is based upon factual circumstances. Although the key events occurred in the approximate time frame identified in the case, the names of all parties and the locations have been changed.

"Bud, when we picked up this client, I immediately thought of you since you have expressed an interest in gaining some experience in the banking industry. Plus, this is one of those clients where we really need an experienced audit senior to run the engagement."

"Thank you, sir. I am looking forward to this opportunity." Bud's practice office was quite large. As a result, he did not have a close relationship with Alex Saunders. Nevertheless, Bud had considerable respect for Saunders. Saunders, a native of Lubbock, was an imposing man physically, towering well over six feet. He spoke with a distinctive west Texas twang and often wore a bolo tie and cowboy boots to work. Saunders had spent his entire 35-year career in the practice office that he now managed and was well known and respected within the business community. Bud particularly appreciated Saunders' blunt, no-nonsense management style. He had a reputation for candor with his subordinates and with clients. You always knew where you stood with "Big Alex," as he was often referred to by his subordinates.

"Eric Jones will be the audit engagement partner. But I am going to shadow Eric on this job. Just like you, Eric doesn't have any past experience with a bank client. Since I have had a slew of bank clients, he can use me as a sounding board if problems develop. K. T. Wilson will be the audit manager. He's worked on a couple of savings and loan audits."

"Okay. Of course, I have worked with Eric and K. T. on a couple of audits in the past."

"Let me give you a little background on this client," Saunders said as he leaned back in his chair and folded his arms across his chest. This guy, Jim Charles, who owns the bank, is one of those 'self-made' millionaires who is more than happy to tell you his success story. He prides himself on being a 'good ol' boy' from west Texas." Alex paused. "Kind of like me, I guess," he added with a smile. "Ya know, he doesn't have a college degree."

"That's interesting."

"Well, that's what he claims, at least. He got lucky about 15 years ago and brought in a couple of wildcat wells in the Permian Basin. He used that money to buy a small bank in his hometown. In the past few years, the bank has grown by leaps and bounds because of the deregulation of the banking industry. I have reviewed his loan portfolio and it seems to me that he specializes in funding commercial real estate projects and high-risk oil and gas ventures." Bud listened intently as Saunders continued. "That's why I want an experienced audit senior running this engagement. I want you to spend a lot of time in the field. Ya know, in the past, bank clients were always considered extremely low risk. But that has totally changed in the past few years with the new legislation."

"Well sir, I will do my best."

"I know you will, Bud. What I would like you to do is meet with Eric this afternoon. As luck would have it, the firm has a three-day seminar on bank auditing next week in Houston. I want you and Eric to attend that seminar. K. T.'s schedule won't allow him to make it."

"Okay. Sir, what about the Garrett audit? Will I continue to work on that job?" For the past three years, Bud had spent the majority of the winter months assigned to the audit engagement team for Garrett Manufacturing, a local prefabricated housing company.

"No. You're gonna be too busy with this new client. I have already made arrangements to have Zach Payne take your spot on that job."

When Bud left Saunders' office, he felt a surge of excitement. This was just the type of assignment he had been hoping to land. Given the nature of the engagement and his required hands-on role, he would learn a great deal about the banking industry in a short time. Bud realized that this experience would position him well to obtain the type of job he wanted in the banking industry when he left public accounting.

In the two weeks following his meeting with Alex Saunders, Bud attended the banking seminar with Eric Jones and spent several days reviewing copies of the new client's prior-year workpapers that had been obtained from the previous auditor. On a Monday morning in early December, Bud made his first trip to the client's headquarters. He and K. T. Wilson planned to introduce themselves to key client personnel and to do some preliminary internal control work.

The meetings with client personnel went well, at least until they met with Jim Charles, who was not only the principal owner of the bank but also its chief executive officer (CEO). During that meeting, Charles seemed annoyed for some reason. In fact, the meeting lasted no more than a few minutes. Charles told the two auditors that he had several important phone calls to make and rushed them out of his office. Although Charles had been less than cordial, Bud quickly dismissed the episode. He realized that as the audit senior he would have little interaction with Charles.

Bud and K. T. Wilson completed their initial work at the client's headquarters and returned to their firm's office late on Tuesday afternoon. Over the next three days, Bud planned to draft a preliminary copy of the audit program and have it ready for a meeting that he and K.T. had scheduled with Eric Jones and Alex Saunders the following Monday afternoon.

Just as Bud was completing a draft of the audit program on Friday afternoon, Alex Saunders unexpectedly dropped by the cubicle in which he was working. Alex asked Bud to come to his office. "Do you want me to bring the draft of the audit program? It's almost done."

"No. That won't be necessary," Saunders replied.

As they walked silently down the hall together, Bud suspected that something was wrong. Although he didn't know Saunders well, Bud sensed that the partner was upset. Bud's suspicions were heightened when Saunders turned and closed the door behind them after they entered his office.

"Please sit down, Bud," Saunders said quietly as he motioned to the chair positioned directly in front of his desk. After sitting down himself, Saunders fumbled with a couple of overstuffed workpaper files on his desktop and then spent several moments reviewing a small stack of handwritten telephone messages. Finally, he spoke.

"Bud, I have decided to place you back on the Garrett audit. I have already spoken with Zach Payne. Zach will be taking your place on the bank engagement."

Bud was stunned, too stunned to speak. The sudden and unexpected announcement was both startling and extremely disappointing. Here was the assignment that he had literally coveted and now it was being taken away from him. For several awkward moments, Bud sat facing Saunders, who refused to look at him. Not making eye contact with whomever he was speaking to was very uncharacteristic of Saunders.

When Bud realized that Saunders did not intend to provide an explanation for removing him from the bank engagement, he took the initiative. "Sir, I don't understand. I was really looking forward to this assignment. I'm not sure why you believe Zach Payne is more qualified than me to run this job."

Saunders cleared his throat as he turned to the right and gazed out the large plate window that overlooked a busy street several blocks below. Saunders then turned back and faced Bud. "This is not about Zach Payne, Bud. I have decided that you are not the right person for this engagement. I'm sorry, but that's my decision." Saunders paused momentarily and then added, "Thanks for your time, Bud," signaling that the brief meeting had ended.

Still in shock, Bud rose slowly from the chair in which he had been sitting and turned toward the door. After taking a few steps, Bud turned back toward Saunders. "Mr. Saunders, I consider myself a professional. I work hard, I enjoy my work, and I believe I do a good job. I typically don't challenge the decisions of those above me. But I believe that I deserve an explanation for why you are taking me off this job." After speaking, Bud stood his ground, staring directly at Saunders who was once again nervously shuffling papers on his desktop.

After more awkward silence, Saunders rose to his feet and made direct eye contact with Bud as he spoke. "You're right, young man. You deserve an explanation. I'm sorry that I wasn't more to the point. Avoiding issues is not my style." Saunders paused and cleared his throat again before speaking. "Jim Charles called me Wednesday afternoon and told me that he wanted a different senior assigned to the audit. He said that he wouldn't be comfortable working with you." After one final pause, Saunders continued. "That's why we are taking you off the job."

"Comfortable? What does that mean?" Bud blurted out.

Saunders shoved his hands into the pockets of his trousers and shrugged his shoulders in exasperation. "You know what I mean. Charles . . . Charles wants another . . . another type of person assigned to the audit."

Now, Bud understood. He had a crystal clear understanding of why he was being removed from the bank audit. As he stood there staring at Saunders, Bud felt several emotions, principally anger. He wanted to respond to Saunders, but he wasn't sure exactly what to say. Bud had always been aware that he was different from his colleagues. He was one of a handful of non-Caucasians in his office. In fact, it had been that way throughout his career. But he had never considered his race to be an issue of any kind. At least, not until this moment.

Finally, after an extended period of silence, Saunders turned away from Bud and walked over to his window and stared down at the Friday afternoon traffic. Bud shook his head in disgust, let out a deep breath, and then left Saunders' office. It was the last time that Bud would speak to, or meet with, Alex Saunders.

EPILOGUE

Bud Carriker spent his final busy season with his employer supervising the fieldwork on the Garrett Manufacturing engagement. Shortly after that engagement was completed, he received a brief letter from Alex Saunders congratulating him on his promotion to audit manager that would take effect a few months later on July 1. However, Bud never officially became an audit manager with the firm. In June of that year, Bud resigned from the firm and accepted a position as an assistant controller with a large healthcare facility in Dallas.

The banking empire of Jim Charles collapsed suddenly in the early 1980s. Charles' bank was one of hundreds that regulatory authorities closed down during that time period for operating in an "unsafe and unsound" manner. Charles' equity in the bank, along with that of the bank's other investors, was wiped out by huge losses in the bank's loan portfolio.

Questions

1. How do you believe Alex Saunders should have reacted when Jim Charles insisted that Bud be removed from the bank's audit engagement team? What would you have done under similar circumstances if you had been Saunders?

2. In your opinion, did Saunders' decision to comply with Charles' request violate any professional or ethical standards? Defend your answer.

3. How do you believe that Bud should have reacted when Saunders told him why he had been removed from the audit engagement team?

4. The key events in this case transpired during the late 1970s. Do you believe that such a series of events could occur now? Explain.

Hopkins V. Price Waterhouse

In 1978, at the age of 34, Ann Hopkins faced a dilemma that a growing number of professional women are being forced to confront. Hopkins had to make a difficult choice involving her family and her career. Although comfortable with her position at Touche Ross & Company, for which she had worked several years, Hopkins realized that either she or her husband, also a Touche Ross employee, had to leave the firm because of its nepotism rules. Otherwise, neither would be considered for promotion to partner. Hopkins chose to make the personal sacrifice. She resigned from Touche Ross and within a few days accepted a position in the consulting division of Price Waterhouse.

Four years later, Hopkins was among the 88 individuals nominated for promotion to partner with Price Waterhouse. Hopkins, a senior manager in the firm's Washington, D.C., office, was the only woman in that group. Hopkins stood out from the other nominees in another respect. She had generated the most business for Price Waterhouse of all the partner candidates. Over the previous four years, clients obtained by Hopkins had produced $40 million of revenues for the firm. Because client development skills generally rank as the most important criterion in partnership promotion decisions, Hopkins appeared to be a shoo-in for promotion.

Strengthening Hopkins' case even more was the unanimous and strong backing her nomination received from the seven partners in the Washington, D.C., office. The extent of home office support for a candidate's nomination was another key factor Price Waterhouse considered in evaluating individuals for promotion to partner.

Much to her surprise, Hopkins was not awarded a partnership position. Instead, the senior manager was told that she would be considered for promotion the following year. A few months later, Hopkins was surprised again when her office managing partner informed her that she was no longer considered a viable candidate for promotion to partner. The firm's top executives did invite her to remain with Price Waterhouse in a nonpartner capacity. Disenchanted and somewhat bitter, Hopkins resigned from Price Waterhouse in January 1984 and accepted a position with the World Bank in Washington, D.C. Eventually, nagging uncertainty regarding her failure to make partner caused Hopkins to file a civil lawsuit against Price Waterhouse.

Prior Criticism of Personnel Practices of Big Eight Firms

The lawsuit Ann Hopkins filed against Price Waterhouse drew attention to an issue simmering within the public accounting profession for years. During a 1976 investigation of the profession by a U.S. Senate subcommittee, several parties charged that Big Eight firms' personnel practices discriminated against females and minorities.[1] At one point during its hearings, the Senate subcommittee requested each of the Big Eight firms to disclose the average compensation of their partners and the number of females and nonwhite males in their partner ranks.

---

1. U.S. Congress, Senate Subcommittee on Reports, Accounting and Management of the Committee on Government Operations, *The Accounting Establishment* (Washington, DC: U.S. Government Printing Office, 1977).

The Senate subcommittee's request evoked uncooperative responses from several of the Big Eight firms. Exhibit 1 presents two of those responses. Exhibit 2 contains a letter that Senator Lee Metcalf, chairman of the investigative subcommittee, wrote to Ernst & Ernst after that firm questioned the Senate's authority to investigate the personnel practices of private partnerships. Eventually, six of the Big Eight firms provided the requested information regarding the number of females and minority males among their partners. Collectively, these firms had seven female partners and four partners who were African-American males out of a total of more than 3,500 partners.

EXHIBIT 1

SELECTED
RESPONSES TO
U.S. SENATE
REQUEST FOR
INFORMATION
REGARDING BIG
EIGHT FIRMS'
PERSONNEL
PRACTICES

June 11, 1976

The Honorable Lee Metcalf, Chairman
Subcommittee on Reports, Accounting, and Management
Committee on Government Operations
United States Senate
Washington, D.C. 20510

Dear Senator Metcalf:

I acknowledge receipt of your letter of June 7, 1976. As you know, this firm has responded and in considerable detail to the Committee's earlier requests. However, we consider the information sought in this letter to exceed the scope of the Committee's investigative authority. Moreover, the information sought includes data proprietary to this firm and its individual members. As a result, we respectfully decline to provide the requested data.

Very truly yours,

Russell E. Palmer
Managing Partner and
Chief Executive Officer
Touche Ross & Company

June 30, 1976

The Honorable Lee Metcalf, Chairman
Subcommittee on Reports, Accounting,
and Management
United States Senate
Washington, D.C. 20510

Dear Senator Metcalf:

This will acknowledge your letter of June 7 which was received during the period I was away from my office.

We find it difficult to understand why the compensation of our partners is a matter of valid interest to a subcommittee of the Committee on Government Operations. We are even more perplexed with the suggestion that this could be a matter of importance in an assessment of our professional performance.

Along with these reservations we also confess to a deep-rooted belief that members of a private partnership have a right to maintain privacy over such matters if they wish to do so. Therefore, absent an understanding of its justification, we respectfully decline to furnish the compensation information you have requested.

Two partners (.5% of the total number of our partners) are female. None of our partners are blacks.

Yours very truly,

William S. Kanaga
Arthur Young & Company

EXHIBIT 2

U.S. Senate
Response to
Ernst & Ernst's
Reluctance to
Provide Requested
Personnel
Information

June 28, 1976

Mr. R.T. Baker
Managing Partner
Ernst & Ernst
Union Commerce Building
Cleveland, Ohio 64115

Dear Mr. Baker:

In your letter of June 24, you question the authority of this subcommittee to request information from your firm on various subjects. You note that our authority is primarily directed to the accounting practices of Federal departments and agencies.

Our requests for information from your firm are based on the unusual and substantial relationship which has developed between certain Federal agencies and influential segments of the accounting profession. This relationship has led to official recognition by Federal agencies of judgments on binding standards which have been made entirely within the private sector. The Securities and Exchange Commission has even formalized its acceptance of private decision-making through Accounting Series Release 150. The Moss amendment to the Energy Policy and Conservation Act also contemplates Federal recognition of private decisions on the manner of uniform accounting to be developed for the oil and gas industry.

The substantial reliance by Federal agencies upon decisions made in the private sector represents a significant delegation of the statutory authority vested in those agencies. This arrangement involves important decisions affecting the policies of the Federal government and other segments of our society.

Decisions made by Federal agencies are subject to review by Congress and the public. Much progress has been made both in Congress and the Federal government in opening the processes of decision-making to public scrutiny. The public has a right to know the identity and interests of those who act under the public's authority to determine the directions which this nation shall take.

When public decision-making authority is delegated to the private sector, the public has an even greater interest in knowing who is directing important national policies. As you are well aware, little information is available to Congress or the public concerning the activities of accounting firms. That is why it is necessary for this subcommittee to request information on various activities of accounting firms.

Your firm is substantially involved in the private decision-making process which develops accounting standards that are recognized by Federal agencies. The information which has so far been requested by this subcommittee is only a small fraction of the information that is publicly available regarding the identity and interests of Federal officials, or even major corporate officials. Yet, the decision-making area in which your firm is involved influences public policy as much or more than do many companies for which the requested information is publicly available.

This subcommittee has a responsibility to ensure that Federal accounting practices are responsive to the public interest. We must be informed on matters which are relevant to Federal accounting practices. That is why your firm has been requested to provide information to this subcommittee.

Very truly yours,

Lee Metcalf, Chairman
Subcommittee on Reports,
   Accounting, and Management

The criticism of the Big Eight firms' personnel practices spawned by the 1976 Senate investigation spurred academic researchers and the business press to begin monitoring the progress of women and minorities within Big Eight firms. By the late 1980s, when the Hopkins suit against Price Waterhouse was working its way through the courts, neither group had made significant inroads into the top hierarchy of the Big Eight firms. For instance, in 1988, women held approximately 3.5 percent of the partnership positions with Big Eight firms, although those firms had been hiring women in considerable numbers since the mid-1970s.[2]

Continued concern regarding the progress of women and minorities within Big Eight firms focused the accounting profession's attention on Ann Hopkins' civil suit against Price Waterhouse. Although the Hopkins case provides only anecdotal evidence regarding the personnel practices of large international accounting firms, it is noteworthy for several reasons. First, the case yielded revealing insights into the partnership selection process employed by large accounting firms. Second, the case pointed to the need to rid performance appraisal methods of gender-based criteria in all disciplines, including professional fields. Finally, *Hopkins v. Price Waterhouse* stimulated discussion of measures that professional firms could take to facilitate the career success of their female employees.

Price Waterhouse's Consideration of Ann Hopkins for Promotion to Partner

During the 1980s, the partners of Price Waterhouse annually identified and then nominated for promotion to partner those senior managers whom they considered to be partner "material." Price Waterhouse's admissions committee collected these nominations and then provided a list of the nominees to each partner in the firm. The admissions committee invited partners to provide either a "long form" or "short form" evaluation of the individual candidates.

Typically, a partner well acquainted with a nominee provided a long form evaluation. Partners having had little or no contact with a given nominee submitted a short form evaluation or no evaluation at all. Both forms required the partners to assess the partnership potential of the nominees on several scaled dimensions, including client development abilities, interpersonal skills, and technical expertise. After responding to the scaled items, the partners indicated whether the given individual should be promoted, whether he or she should be denied promotion, or whether the promotion decision should be deferred for one or more years. The partners also provided a brief written explanation documenting the key reasons for their overall recommendation for each candidate.

After studying and summarizing the evaluations, the admissions committee prepared three lists of candidates: those recommended for admission to partnership, those not recommended for promotion, and those who had received a "hold" recommendation. These latter candidates typically included individuals having partner potential but also one or more weaknesses that needed to be addressed before they were considered again for promotion. The admissions committee submitted its recommendations to the firm's policy board, which reviewed them and selected the final slate of candidates to be voted on by the entire partnership.[3]

2. E. Berg, "The Big Eight," *The New York Times*, 17 December 1977, D1; "Women Comprise Half of 1986–87 Graduates," *Public Accounting Report*, 1 February 1988, 7.

3. This description of Price Waterhouse's partnership selection process was summarized from information presented in the 1985 court opinion *Hopkins v. Price Waterhouse*, 618 F. Supp. 1109 (D.C.D.C. 1985).

The admissions committee received 32 evaluation forms commenting on Ann Hopkins' nomination for partner. Thirteen partners submitted positive recommendations, eight recommended she not be promoted, three suggested she be held over for consideration the following year, and eight did not include a recommendation in their evaluation forms.

The most common criticism of Hopkins by partners who recommended she not be promoted was that she had poor interpersonal skills and an abrasive personality. These individuals criticized her for being too demanding of her subordinates, for using profanity, and for being generally harsh and overly aggressive. Two partners used gender-specific terms when commenting on Hopkins. One partner referred to her as "macho," while another observed that "she may have overcompensated for being a woman."[4]

After reviewing Hopkins' evaluations, the admissions committee recommended that she be held over for consideration, a recommendation accepted by the policy board. The admissions committee decided that her interpersonal skills needed to be strengthened to allow her to function effectively as a partner.

To improve her chances of promotion the following year, Hopkins agreed to undergo a "quality control review" to help her identify specific interpersonal and other job-related skills needing improvement. Subsequent to the quality control review, several partners indicated they would give her opportunities to demonstrate that she was remedying the deficiencies in her interpersonal skills. These partners never followed through on their commitments. Four months after Hopkins completed the quality control review, her office managing partner informed her that she would not be nominated for partner that year. Hopkins was also told that she probably would never be considered again for promotion to partner.

Ann Hopkins' Civil Suit against Price Waterhouse

Ann Hopkins learned of the "hold" recommendation given to her nomination for partner in mid-1983. At that time, her office managing partner discussed with her some of the reservations partners expressed regarding her nomination. In particular, he told Hopkins that several partners believed her appearance and interpersonal manner were overtly masculine and that these traits caused her to be less appealing as a partner candidate.

The office managing partner suggested that she could improve her chances for promotion if she would "walk more femininely, wear make-up, have her hair styled, and wear jewelry." Following her resignation from Price Waterhouse, Hopkins recalled these suggestions and began to question why she had been denied promotion to partner. She began to suspect that Price Waterhouse had denied her promotion not because she was perceived as unqualified to be a partner with the firm but, rather, because she was perceived as unqualified to be a *female* partner with the firm.

Eventually, Hopkins concluded that Price Waterhouse, in fact, did apply different standards for promoting females and males to partner. This issue became the focal point of the civil trial in the *Hopkins v. Price Waterhouse* case. Hopkins included the following four specific allegations in the lawsuit she filed against Price Waterhouse:

1. The criticisms of her interpersonal skills were fabricated by the Price Waterhouse partners.

---

4. This and all subsequent quotations, unless indicated otherwise, were taken from *Hopkins v. Price Waterhouse*, 618 F. Supp. 1109 (D.C.D.C. 1985).

2. Even if the criticisms of her interpersonal skills were valid, Price Waterhouse had promoted male candidates to partner having similar deficiencies in their interpersonal skills.

3. The criticisms of her interpersonal skills resulted from sexual stereotyping by Price Waterhouse partners.

4. Price Waterhouse's partnership selection process did not discount the sexually discriminatory comments made regarding her candidacy.

The judge who presided over the civil trial dismissed Hopkins' first allegation. According to the judge, the defense counsel clearly proved that Hopkins did have poor interpersonal skills, particularly when dealing with subordinates. The judge ruled that Price Waterhouse was well within its rights to deny an individual a partnership position who did not possess adequate interpersonal skills. However, the judge then pointed to court testimony documenting that Price Waterhouse had previously promoted male partner candidates described as "crude, abrasive, and overbearing." These comments were very similar to criticisms of Hopkins' interpersonal skills made during the partner selection process.

A review of the firm's past promotion decisions also revealed that two earlier female partner candidates may have been denied admission to the partnership for reasons identical to those that cost Hopkins her promotion. Evaluation comments made for those candidates criticized them for acting like "Ma Barker" or for trying to be "one of the boys."

An earlier legal case established the precedent that an employer who evaluates a woman with an aggressive or abrasive personality differently than a man with similar personality traits is guilty of sex discrimination. After reviewing all of the evidence presented during the trial, the judge ruled that Price Waterhouse had evaluated Hopkins as a candidate for becoming a female partner rather than simply a partner with the firm.

> [Female] candidates were viewed favorably if partners believed they maintained their femininity while becoming effective professional managers. To be identified as a "women's libber" was regarded as a negative comment. Nothing was done to discourage sexually biased evaluations. One partner repeatedly commented that he could not consider any woman seriously as a partnership candidate and believed that women were not capable of functioning as senior managers—yet the firm took no action to discourage his comments and recorded his vote in the overall summary of the evaluations.

Although Hopkins was found to have been the victim of sex discrimination, the judge deemed that the discrimination was not overt or intentional. In fact, Hopkins freely admitted during the trial that she never perceived she was being discriminated against because of her gender while employed with Price Waterhouse. Instead, sexually discriminatory attitudes latent within the culture of Price Waterhouse victimized Hopkins' candidacy for partner. That is, the partners who made the sexually biased remarks regarding Hopkins were unaware that they were evaluating her unfairly relative to male candidates for partner. Nevertheless, the judge ruled that Price Waterhouse perpetuated an evaluation system that allowed sexual stereotypes to undermine the promotion opportunities of female employees.

> There is no direct evidence of any determined purpose to maliciously discriminate against women but plaintiff appears to have been a victim of "omissive and subtle" discriminations created by a system that made evaluations based on "outmoded" attitudes. . . . Price Waterhouse should have been aware that women being evaluated by male partners might well be victims of discriminatory stereotypes. Yet the firm made no efforts . . . to discourage comments tainted by sexism or to determine whether they were influenced by stereotypes.

EPILOGUE

In May 1990, six years after Ann Hopkins filed suit against Price Waterhouse, a federal judge ordered the firm to pay her $400,000 of compensatory damages. More important, the judge ordered the CPA firm to offer Hopkins a partnership position. During a party to celebrate the court's decision, Hopkins maintained that she had no reservations joining a firm that had unfairly rejected her for partnership seven years earlier. She also joked with her male co-workers at the World Bank regarding several less-than-complimentary remarks made regarding her during the trial. In particular, she questioned the assertion of one Price Waterhouse partner that she needed to enroll in charm school. Moments later, Hopkins took a long and noisy slug of champagne—straight from the bottle.

In 1996, five years after rejoining Price Waterhouse, Ann Hopkins documented her difficult road to becoming a partner in a book published by the University of Massachusetts Press that was entitled "So Ordered: Making Partner the Hard Way." Despite the ordeal that she experienced, Hopkins insists that she has no "hard feelings" toward her fellow partners. In fact, Hopkins' daughter joined PricewaterhouseCoopers (PwC), the successor firm to Price Waterhouse, when she graduated from college in 1998.

Growing numbers of women have obtained partnership positions with the large international accounting firms since the resolution of the *Hopkins* case. But women still remain significantly underrepresented in the partnership ranks of those firms.[5] That fact was a key issue raised by Melissa Page, a former PwC tax manager, when she filed a lawsuit against PwC in July 2004 that was reminiscent of Ann Hopkins' lawsuit two decades earlier. In her complaint, Page alleged that the firm was guilty of "systematically discriminating" against women and suggested that an "old boy network" still pervaded PwC's culture.

> [Page] claims her career was derailed by a corporate culture that kept women away from the very opportunities that led to partnership—including informal networking events, golf outings, and other activities that would have given her more access to clients and company executives.[6]

Page's lawsuit prompted other women in the profession to speak out. One of those individuals was Barbara Hufsmith, who reported that she had chosen to establish her own accounting firm after being a victim of gender discrimination in a male-dominated accounting firm.

> I too have been discriminated against in an old boys CPA firm. It has forced me to start my own firm, for which I am grateful, but it should not have been such a painful and expensive experience. I truly believe that only a couple of partners from my old firm knew what they were doing to me was not fair. The rest of the partners were blind, stupid, and arrogant. Hopefully, a case like Ms. Page will help change the industry to be more female-partner friendly.[7]

Questions

1. Do public accounting firms have a responsibility to facilitate the career success of female employees? Why or why not? Identify policies accounting firms could implement to increase the retention rate of female employees.

---

5. The results of a survey released by the *Public Accounting Report* in June 2009 indicated that approximately 18 percent of Big Four partners were women.

6. *AccountingWEB.com*, "PricewaterhouseCoopers Faces Discrimination Suit," 29 July 2004.

7. *Ibid.*

2. In business circles, one frequently hears references to the "old boy network." Many women in professional firms complain that their gender precludes them from becoming a member of the old boy network within their firm. Define, in your own terms, the phrase *old boy network*. Should professional firms attempt to break down these networks?

3. Suppose that an audit client objects to a given auditor because of his or her gender or race. Identify the alternative courses of action the auditor's employer should consider taking in such a case. Which of these alternatives do you believe the accounting firm should take? Defend your answer.

4. The nepotism rules of many professional firms pose a major inconvenience for married couples who work for, or would like to work for, those firms. Discuss the costs and benefits of these rules in a public accounting setting. In practice, do you believe these rules are equally fair (or unfair) to both sexes?

Fred Stern & Company, Inc.
(Ultramares Corporation v. Touche et al.)

In the business world of the Roaring Twenties, the scams and schemes of flimflam artists and confidence men were legendary. The absence of a strong regulatory system at the federal level to police the securities markets–the Securities and Exchange Commission was not established until 1934–aided, if not encouraged, financial frauds of all types. In all likelihood, the majority of individuals involved in business during the 1920s were scrupulously honest. Nevertheless, the culture of that decade bred a disproportionate number of opportunists who adopted an "anything goes" approach to transacting business. An example of a company in which this self-serving attitude apparently prevailed was Fred Stern & Company, Inc. During the mid-1920s, Stern's executives duped three of the company's creditors out of several hundred thousand dollars.

Based in New York City, Stern imported rubber, a raw material demanded in huge quantities by many industries in the early twentieth century. During the 1920s alone, industrial demand for rubber in the United States more than tripled. The nature of the rubber importation trade required large amounts of working capital. Because Stern was chronically short of funds, the company relied heavily on banks and other lenders to finance its day-to-day operations.

In March 1924, Stern sought a $100,000 loan from Ultramares Corporation, a finance company whose primary line of business was factoring receivables. Before considering the loan request, Ultramares asked Stern's management for an audited balance sheet. Stern had been audited a few months earlier by Touche, Niven & Company, a prominent accounting firm based in London and New York City. Touche had served as Stern's independent auditor since 1920. Exhibit 1 presents the unqualified opinion Touche issued on Stern's December 31, 1923, balance sheet. Stern's management obtained 32 serially numbered copies of that audit report. Touche knew that Stern intended to use the audit reports to obtain external debt financing but was unaware of the specific banks or finance companies that might receive the audit reports.

After reviewing Stern's audited balance sheet, which reported assets of more than $2.5 million and a net worth of approximately $1 million, and the accompanying audit report, Ultramares granted the $100,000 loan requested by the company. Ultramares later extended two more loans to Stern totaling $65,000. During the same time frame, Stern obtained more than $300,000 in loans from two local banks after providing them with copies of the December 31, 1923, balance sheet and accompanying audit report.

Unfortunately for Ultramares and the two banks that extended loans to Stern, the company was declared bankrupt in January 1925. Subsequent courtroom testimony revealed that the company had been hopelessly insolvent at the end of 1923 when its audited balance sheet reported a net worth of $1 million. An accountant with Stern, identified only as Romberg in court records, concealed Stern's bankrupt status from the Touche auditors. Romberg masked Stern's true financial condition by making several false entries in the company's accounting records. The largest of these

EXHIBIT 1

TOUCHE, NIVEN &
COMPANY'S AUDIT
OPINION ON STERN'S
DECEMBER 31,
1923, BALANCE
SHEET

February 26, 1924

Touche, Niven & Co.
Public Accountants
Eighty Maiden Lane,
New York

Certificate of Auditors

We have examined the accounts of Fred Stern & Co., Inc., for the year ended December 31, 1923, and hereby certify that the annexed balance sheet is in accordance therewith and with the information and explanations given us. We further certify that, subject to provision for federal taxes on income, the said statement in our opinion, presents a true and correct view of the financial condition of Fred Stern & Co., Inc., as at December 31, 1923.

entries involved a debit of more than $700,000 to accounts receivable and an offsetting credit to sales.

Following Stern's bankruptcy, Ultramares sued Touche to recover the $165,000 loaned to Stern. Ultramares alleged that the audit firm had been both fraudulent and negligent in auditing Stern's financial records. *The New York Times* noted that the negligence claim in the *Ultramares* suit was "novel" and would likely serve as a major "test case" for third parties hoping to recover losses from audit firms.[1] The novel aspect of the negligence claim stemmed from the absence of a contractual relationship between Touche and Ultramares. Touche's contract to audit Stern's December 31, 1923, balance sheet was made solely with Stern's management. At the time, a well-entrenched legal doctrine dictated that only a party in privity with another–that is, having an explicit contractual agreement with another–could recover damages resulting from the other party's negligence.

Another interesting facet of the *Ultramares* lawsuit involved the founder of Touche, Niven & Company, Sir George Alexander Touche. George Touche, who served for two years as the sheriff of London during World War I, merged his accounting practice in the early 1900s with that of a young Scottish accountant, John B. Niven, who had immigrated to New York City. The new firm prospered, and George Touche, who was knighted in 1917 by King George V, eventually became one of the most respected leaders of the emerging public accounting profession. John Niven also became influential within the profession. Ironically, Niven was serving as the president of the American Institute of Accountants, the predecessor of the American Institute of Certified Public Accountants, when Fred Stern & Company was declared insolvent. An issue posed by the *Ultramares* lawsuit was whether George Touche and his fellow partners who were not involved in the Stern audit could be held personally liable for any improper conduct on the part of the Touche auditors assigned to the Stern engagement. Ultramares raised that issue by naming each of the Touche partners as co-defendants.

Ultramares Corporation v. Touche et al.: A Protracted Legal Battle

The *Ultramares* civil suit against Touche was tried before a jury in a New York state court. Ultramares' principal allegation was that the Touche auditors should have easily discovered the $700,000 overstatement of receivables in Stern's December 31, 1923,

---

1. "Damages Refused for Error in Audit," *The New York Times*, 27 June 1929, 50.

balance sheet. That error, if corrected, would have slashed Stern's reported net worth by nearly 70 percent and considerably lessened the likelihood that Ultramares would have extended the company a sizable loan.

A young man by the name of Siess performed most of the field work on the Stern audit. When Siess arrived at Stern's office to begin the audit in early February 1924, he discovered that the company's general ledger had not been posted since the prior April. He spent the next few days posting entries from the client's journals to its general ledger. After Siess completed that task, Stern's accounts receivable totaled approximately $644,000. Stern's accountant, Romberg, obtained the general ledger the day before Siess intended to prepare a trial balance of the company's accounts. After reviewing the ledger, Romberg booked an entry debiting receivables and crediting sales for approximately $706,000. Beside the entry in the receivables account, he entered a number cross-referencing the recorded amount to the company's sales journal.

The following day, Romberg notified Siess of the entry he had recorded in the general ledger. Romberg told Siess that the entry represented Stern's December sales that had been inadvertently omitted from the accounting records. Without questioning Romberg's explanation for the large entry, Siess included the $706,000 in the receivables balance. In fact, the receivables did not exist and the corresponding sales never occurred. To support the entry, Romberg or one of his subordinates hastily prepared 17 bogus sales invoices.

In a subsequent testimony, Siess initially reported that he could not recall whether he reviewed any of the 17 invoices allegedly representing Stern's December sales. Plaintiff counsel then demonstrated that "a mere glance" at the invoices would have revealed that they were forged. The invoices lacked shipping numbers, customer order numbers, and other pertinent information. Following this revelation, Siess admitted that he had not examined any of the invoices.[2] Touche's attorneys attempted to justify this oversight by pointing out that audits involve "testing and sampling" rather than an examination of entire accounting populations.[3] Thus, it was not surprising or unusual, the attorneys argued, that none of the fictitious December sales invoices were among the more than 200 invoices examined during the Stern audit.

The court ruled that auditing on a sample basis is appropriate in most cases. But, given the suspicious nature of the large December sales entry recorded by Romberg, the court concluded that Touche should have specifically reviewed the December sales invoices.

> Verification by test and sample was very likely a sufficient audit as to accounts regularly entered upon the books in the usual course of business. . . . [However], the defendants were put on their guard by the circumstances touching the December accounts receivable to scrutinize with special care.[4]

Ultramares' attorneys noted during the trial that Touche had even more reason than just the suspicious nature of Romberg's December sales entry to question the integrity of the large year-end increase in receivables. While auditing the company's inventory, Touche auditors discovered several errors that collectively caused the inventory account to be overstated by more than $300,000, an overstatement of 90 percent. The auditors also uncovered large errors in Stern's accounts payable and discovered that the company had improperly pledged the same assets as collateral for several bank

---

2. *Ultramares Corporation v. Touche et al.*, 255 N.Y. 170, 174 N.E. 441 (1930), 449.
3. *Ibid.*
4. *Ibid.*

loans. Given the extent and nature of the problems revealed by the Touche audit, the court ruled that the accounting firm should have been particularly skeptical of the client's accounting records. This should have been the case, the court observed, even though Touche had not encountered any reason in previous audits to question the integrity of Stern's management.

> No doubt the extent to which inquiry must be pressed beyond appearances is a question of judgment, as to which opinions will often differ. No doubt the wisdom that is born after the event will engender suspicion and distrust when old acquaintance and good repute may have silenced doubt at the beginning.[5]

The jury in the *Ultramares* case dismissed the fraud charge against Touche. The jurors ruled that the company's attorneys failed to establish that the audit firm had intentionally deceived Ultramares–intentional deceit being a necessary condition for fraud. Regarding the negligence charge, the jury ruled in favor of Ultramares and ordered Touche to pay the company damages of $186,000.

The judge who presided over the *Ultramares* case overturned the jury's ruling on the negligence charge. In explaining his decision, the judge acknowledged that Ultramares' attorneys had clearly established that Touche had been negligent during its 1923 audit of Stern. Nevertheless, the judge ruled that the jury had overlooked the long-standing legal doctrine that only a party in privity could sue and recover damages resulting from a defendant's negligence.

> Negligence is not actionable unless there is a breach of duty owing by defendants to the plaintiff. To hold that the defendants' duty extended to not only Stern but to all persons to whom Stern might exhibit the balance sheet, and who would act in reliance thereon, would compel the defendants to assume a potential liability to practically the entire world.[6]

Ultramares' attorneys quickly appealed the trial judge's decision. The appellate division of the New York Supreme Court reviewed the case. In a 3 to 2 vote, the appellate division decided that the trial judge erred in reversing the jury's verdict on the negligence charge. As appellate Justice McAvoy noted, the key question in the case centered on whether Touche had a duty to Ultramares "in the absence of a direct contractual relation."[7] Justice McAvoy concluded that Touche did have an obligation to Ultramares, and to other parties relying on Stern's financial statements, although the accounting firm's contract was expressly and exclusively with Stern.

> One cannot issue an unqualified statement [audit opinion] . . . and then disclaim responsibility for his work. Banks and merchants, to the knowledge of these defendants, require certified balance sheets from independent accountants, and upon these audits they make their loans. Thus, the duty arises to these banks and merchants of an exercise of reasonable care in the making and uttering of certified balance sheets.[8]

Justice McAvoy and two of his colleagues were unwavering in their opinion that Touche had a legal obligation to Ultramares. Nevertheless, the remaining two judges on the appellate panel were just as strongly persuaded that no such obligation existed. In the dissenting opinion, Justice Finch maintained that holding Touche responsible to a third party that subsequently relied upon the Stern financial statements was patently unfair to the accounting firm.

---

5. *Ibid.*, 444.

6. "Damages Refused for Error."

7. *Ultramares Corporation v. Touche et al.*, 229 App. Div. 581, 243 N.Y.S. 179 (1930), 181.

8. *Ibid.*, 182.

> *If the plaintiff [Ultramares] had inquired of the accountants whether they might rely upon the certificate in making a loan, then the accountants would have had the opportunity to gauge their responsibility and risk, and determine with knowledge how thorough their verification of the account should be before assuming the responsibility of making the certificate run to the plaintiff.[9]*

Following the appellate division's ruling in the *Ultramares* case, Touche's attorneys appealed the decision to the next highest court in the New York state judicial system, the Court of Appeals. That court ultimately handed down the final ruling in the lengthy judicial history of the case. The chief justice of New York's Court of Appeals, Benjamin Cardozo, was a nationally recognized legal scholar whose opinions were given great weight by other courts.

Justice Cardozo and his six associate justices ruled unanimously that the judge who presided over the *Ultramares* trial had properly reversed the jury's decision on the negligence claim. Justice Cardozo reiterated the arguments made by Justice Finch. He maintained that it would be unfair to hold Touche legally responsible to a third party, unknown to Touche when its audit was performed, that happened to obtain and rely upon Stern's audited balance sheet. However, Justice Cardozo went on to suggest that had Ultramares been clearly designated as a beneficiary of the Stern-Touche contract, his ruling would have been different.

Unfortunately for the accounting profession, Justice Cardozo's opinion did not end with his commentary on the negligence question in the *Ultramares* case. After resolving that issue, he sharply criticized Touche's audit of Stern. The judge implied that Ultramares might have been successful in suing Touche on the basis of gross negligence: "Negligence or blindness, even when not equivalent to fraud, is none the less evidence to sustain an inference of fraud. . . . At least this is so if the negligence is gross. . . . [In the *Ultramares* case] a jury might find that . . . [the Touche auditors] closed their eyes to the obvious, and blindly gave assent."[10]

The Ultramares Decision: Implications for the Accounting Profession

In retrospect, the *Ultramares* decision had two principal implications for the public accounting profession. First, Justice Cardozo's opinion established the precedent that certain direct beneficiaries of an audit, generally referred to as primary beneficiaries, are entitled to recover damages from a negligent auditor. Subsequent to the *Ultramares* ruling, very few plaintiffs were successful in establishing themselves as primary beneficiaries of an audit.[11] Consequently, this "expansion" of the auditor's legal exposure proved to be fairly insignificant.

The second key implication of the *Ultramares* case was that it provided a new strategy for plaintiff counsel to use in suing auditors on behalf of nonprivity parties. Following the *Ultramares* ruling, attorneys representing such plaintiffs began predicating lawsuits against auditors on allegations of gross negligence. Before that ruling, nonprivity third parties faced the heavy burden of proving fraud if they wanted to recover losses resulting from auditor misconduct. Because establishing gross negligence is much easier than proving intent to defraud, the *Ultramares* decision significantly increased auditors' legal exposure to nonprivity third parties.

---

9. *Ibid.*, 186.

10. *Ultramares Corporation v. Touche et al.*, 255 N.Y. 170, 174 N.E. 441 (1930), 449.

11. Decades later, the *Credit Alliance* case established several restrictive conditions that third parties must satisfy to qualify as primary beneficiaries. See: *Credit Alliance Corporation v. Arthur Andersen & Company*, 483 N.E. 2d 110 (N.Y. 1985).

A secondary issue addressed by Justice Cardozo in the *Ultramares* case was whether or not Sir George Touche and his fellow partners who had no direct connection with the Stern engagement could be held liable for the deficient Stern audit. This issue was moot regarding the negligence allegation since that charge had already been dismissed. But, the issue was still pertinent to the fraud charge since Justice Cardozo ruled that Ultramares was entitled to a retrial to determine whether Touche's negligence was severe enough to infer fraudulent conduct or gross negligence.[12] Because the auditors assigned to the Stern engagement were acting as agents of the accounting firm's partners, Justice Cardozo ruled that all of Touche's partners were legally responsible for the actions of those individuals.

EPILOGUE

In the years following the *Ultramares* case, the legal exposure of public accountants to third-party financial statement users was gradually extended. The first extension came on the heels of the *Ultramares* case with the passage of the Securities Act of 1933. That federal statute imposed on auditors a very significant legal obligation to initial purchasers of new securities marketed on an interstate basis.

Under the 1933 Act, plaintiffs do not have to prove fraud, gross negligence, or even negligence on the part of auditors. Essentially, plaintiffs must only establish that they suffered investment losses and that the relevant financial statements contain material errors or omissions. If a plaintiff establishes those elements of proof, the defendant accounting firm assumes the burden of proving that its employees were "duly diligent" in performing the audit.[13] To sustain a due diligence defense, an accounting firm must show that, following a "reasonable investigation," it had "reasonable ground to believe and did believe" that the audited financial statements were materially accurate. Federal courts have not been receptive to the due diligence defense if the plaintiffs have clearly established that the financial statements in question contain material errors.[14]

Auditors' legal exposure has also expanded under the common law over the past several decades. In 1965, the American Law Institute issued *Restatement of Torts*, a legal compendium relied on heavily in many jurisdictions. This source suggests that "foreseen" beneficiaries, in addition to primary beneficiaries, should have a right to recover damages from negligent auditors.[15] Foreseen beneficiaries are members of a limited group or class of third-party financial statement users. Auditors are typically aware of this distinct group of potential financial statement users but unaware of the specific individuals or entities who make up that group.

The 1983 *Rosenblum* ruling went beyond the boundary established by the *Restatement of Torts*. That judicial ruling suggested that even "reasonably foreseeable" or "ordinary"

---

12. For whatever reason, Ultramares chose not to file an amended lawsuit against Touche that was predicated upon an allegation of gross negligence.

13. Accounting firms have other defenses available to them when sued under the Securities Act of 1933. These defenses include, among others, expiration of the statute of limitations, establishing that the plaintiff knew the relevant financial statements were misleading when he or she purchased the securities, and proving that the plaintiff's damages were not caused by the misleading financial statements.

14. Case 7.6, "First Securities Company of Chicago (*Ernst & Ernst v. Hochfelder et al.*)," examines the legal implications posed for public accounting firms by the Securities Exchange Act of 1934, which is the "sister" statute to the 1933 Act.

15. American Law Institute, *Restatement of the Law, Second: Torts* (Philadelphia: American Law Institute, 1965).

third-party financial statement users should be allowed to recover damages from negligent auditors.[16] Reasonably foreseeable third parties include a much larger population of potential financial statement users than "foreseen" third parties. The most liberal definition of "reasonably foreseeable third parties" includes individual investors who happen to obtain a copy of audited financial statements and make a decision based upon them.

Questions

1. Observers of the accounting profession suggest that many courts attempt to "socialize" investment losses by extending auditors' liability to third-party financial statement users. Discuss the benefits and costs of such a policy to public accounting firms, audit clients, and third-party financial statement users, such as investors and creditors. In your view, should the courts have the authority to socialize investment losses? If not, who should determine how investment losses are distributed in our society?

2. Auditors' legal responsibilities differ significantly under the Securities Exchange Act of 1934 and the Securities Act of 1933. Briefly point out these differences and comment on why they exist. Also comment on how auditors' litigation risks differ under the common law and the 1934 Act.

3. The current standard audit report differs significantly from the version issued during the 1920s. Identify the key differences in the two reports and discuss the forces that accounted for the evolution of the audit report into its present form.

4. Why was it common in the 1920s for companies to have only an audited balance sheet prepared for distribution to external third parties? Comment on the factors that, over a period of several decades, resulted in the adoption of the financial statement package that most companies presently provide to external third parties.

5. When assessing audit risk, should auditors consider the type and number of third parties that may ultimately rely on the client's financial statements? Should auditors insist that audit engagement letters identify the third parties to whom the client intends to distribute the audited financial statements? Would this practice eliminate auditors' legal liability to nonprivity parties not mentioned in engagement letters?

---

16. *H. Rosenblum, Inc. v. Adler*, 461 A. 2d 138 (N.J. 1983).

First Securities Company of Chicago (*Ernst & Ernst v. Hochfelder et al.*)

Ladislas Nay immigrated to the United States from Hungary in 1921 at the age of 18. The opportunities offered by his new land excited the industrious young immigrant and he promised himself that he would make the most of them. Shortly after arriving in the United States, Nay made his way to Chicago and landed a job in the booming securities industry with a small brokerage firm. For the next several years, Nay worked long and hard hours learning the brokerage business.

Unfortunately for Nay, the Great Depression hit the securities industry particularly hard. Young stockbrokers like him were the first to be laid off by their firms when personnel cuts were necessary. During the bleak 1930s, Nay, who by this time had Americanized his first name to Leston, endured several job changes and two failed marriages. In 1942, as World War II began to pull the United States out of the Depression, Nay landed a permanent job with the brokerage firm of Ryan-Nichols & Company.

Within two years of joining Ryan-Nichols, Nay was promoted to president. He eventually became the firm's principal stockholder, accumulating more than 90 percent of its outstanding common stock. In 1945, the firm successfully applied for membership to the Midwest Stock Exchange and was renamed First Securities Company of Chicago. Over the next two decades, Nay's career and personal life flourished. Nay and his wife, Elizabeth, participated in a wide range of community affairs, including serving on several prominent civic boards, and eventually purchased a home in the upper-class neighborhood of Hyde Park. Nay made numerous friends among the faculty and staff of nearby University of Chicago. In fact, many of his best customers were associated with the prestigious school.

Nay's personal attention to the financial needs of his customers earned him their respect and admiration. One of his customers described him as a kind and considerate man, much "like an old-fashioned English solicitor who took care of a family's affairs."[1] His conservative investment strategies particularly appealed to his retired clients and those nearing retirement. Nay offered many of these customers an opportunity to invest in a lucrative fund that he personally managed. This fund was not an asset of First Securities, nor were any other First Securities personnel aware it existed. Nay referred to this fund as the "escrow syndicate."

Nay loaned funds invested in the escrow syndicate to blue chip companies that developed sudden and unexpected working capital shortages. These companies paid interest rates well above the prevailing market rates. Individuals who invested in the escrow syndicate earned 7 to 12 percent on their investments, considerably more than the interest rates paid at the time by banks on savings accounts.

One of Nay's closest friends, Arnold Schueren, entrusted him with more than $400,000 over three decades and granted him a power of attorney to make investment decisions regarding those funds. Nay invested a large portion of Schueren's

---

1. J. M. Johnston, "How Broker Worked $1 Million Swindle," *Chicago Daily News*, 13 December 1968, 42, 43.

savings in the escrow syndicate. Another individual who relied heavily on Nay for investment advice was the widow of a close associate of the famed University of Chicago scientist Enrico Fermi. This woman later testified that Nay had managed her family's investments for many years but did not offer her the opportunity to invest in the escrow syndicate until after her husband's death. Nay told her that he only offered this investment opportunity to his "nearest and dearest friends."[2] Following the death of another of his customers, Norman Moyer, Nay convinced Moyer's widow to invest her husband's estate of $90,000 in the escrow syndicate. In total, 17 of Nay's friends and/or their widows invested substantial sums in the escrow syndicate.

Dr. Jekyll and Mr. Hyde: A Tragic Ending

On the morning of June 4, 1968, Leston Nay drove to St. Luke's Hospital in Chicago to pick up his wife, who had fallen and broken her hip the previous week. Earlier that morning, Nay had telephoned his secretary to tell her that he would not be in the office that day because he had a stomach virus. Shortly before noon, as his wife, who was still on crutches, made her way to the kitchen of their apartment, Nay retrieved his 12-gauge shotgun and shot her in the upper back from close range. Nay then laid a suicide note on a dressing table in his bedroom, sat down on his bed, put the muzzle of the gun in his mouth, and pulled the trigger.

News of the murder-suicide shocked the Nays' friends and associates. These same people were shocked again when the Chicago police released the contents of Nay's suicide note. The note revealed that the kindly stockbroker had led a Dr. Jekyll-Mr. Hyde existence for decades. In the note, addressed "To whom it may concern," Nay admitted stealing from his customers for more than 30 years. The escrow syndicate in which his closest friends had invested did not exist–police speculated that Nay had lost the investors' funds in the stock market. Nay had successfully concealed the missing funds for as long as he did because he periodically mailed the investors checks for interest supposedly earned by the escrow syndicate. These periodic interest payments deterred the victims of the scam from questioning the safety of their investments.

In the suicide note, Nay displayed some remorse when he referred to the 80-year-old Mrs. Moyer, who was penniless as a result of his actions. He also explained why he had decided to take his life. After Arnold Schueren died in 1967, the executor of his estate had demanded that Nay return Schueren's investment in the escrow syndicate. Nay indicated in the suicide note that he had "stalled" as long as he could but that the executor would not be put off any longer. So he took his life. Most likely, Nay murdered his wife to "save" her from the shame she would feel when his fraudulent scheme, of which she was apparently unaware, was disclosed.

Defrauded Customers Sue to Recover Their Investments

The investors in Nay's escrow syndicate filed civil lawsuits against several parties in an effort to recover their collective investments of more than $1 million. Initially, the investors sued the Midwest Stock Exchange. In that suit, the investors alleged that the stock exchange failed to adequately investigate Nay's background before admitting his firm to membership. According to the investors, a more thorough investigation might have revealed that Nay had a history, although well concealed, of unscrupulous business practices. The investors suggested that the discovery of Nay's past unethical conduct would have forced the exchange to deny his firm's membership application

---

2. *Ibid.*

and possibly prevented him from engaging in the escrow syndicate fraud. The court hearing the suit quickly dismissed the investors' claims, concluding that the stock exchange had sufficiently investigated Nay's background before approving his firm's membership application.

Nay's 17 escrow participants or their estates also sued First Securities Company of Chicago. The court ruled that the brokerage firm had clearly facilitated Nay's fraudulent activities. But, since the brokerage firm was bankrupt, the escrow investors found themselves thwarted again.

Finally, Nay's former customers filed suit against Ernst & Ernst, the accounting firm that audited First Securities Company for more than two decades. The lawsuit alleged that Ernst & Ernst's negligence had prevented the firm from detecting what became known throughout the lengthy judicial history of the *First Securities* case as Nay's "mail rule." According to the plaintiffs' legal counsel, "Nay had forbidden anyone other than himself to open mail addressed to him, and in his absence all such mail was simply allowed to pile up on his desk, even if it was addressed to First Securities for his attention."[3] Nay's mail rule allowed him to conceal the escrow syndicate scam from his subordinates at First Securities and from the brokerage's independent auditors. Had Ernst & Ernst discovered the mail rule, the plaintiffs alleged, an investigation would have been warranted. Such an investigation would very likely have led to the discovery of Nay's escrow investment scam.

Ernst & Ernst v. Hochfelder et al.

The defrauded investors filed their lawsuit against Ernst & Ernst under the Securities Exchange Act of 1934. That federal statute does not expressly provide civil remedies to stockholders of companies registered with the Securities and Exchange Commission (SEC). However, since the adoption of the 1934 Act, federal courts have allowed stockholders to use the statute as a basis for civil suits against company officers, investment brokers, auditors, and other parties associated with false financial statements filed with the SEC. Most of these suits allege one or more violations of Rule 10b-5 of the 1934 Act, shown in Exhibit 1.

In the *First Securities* case, the plaintiffs charged that Ernst & Ernst's alleged negligence in failing to discover Nay's mail rule constituted a violation of Rule 10b-5.

> The premise [of the investors' suit] was that Ernst & Ernst had failed to utilize "appropriate auditing procedures" in its audits of First Securities. . . . Respondents [investors]

EXHIBIT 1

RULE 10b-5 OF THE SECURITIES EXCHANGE ACT OF 1934

Employment of manipulative and deceptive devices. It shall be unlawful for any person, directly or indirectly, by the use of any means or instrumentality of interstate commerce, or of the mails or of any facility of any national securities exchange,

(a) To employ any device, scheme, or artifice to defraud,
(b) To make any untrue statement of a material fact or to omit to state a material fact necessary in order to make the statements made, in the light of the circumstances under which they were made, not misleading, or
(c) To engage in any act, practice, or course of business which operates or would operate as a fraud or deceit upon any person, in connection with the purchase or sale of any security.

---

3. *Securities and Exchange Commission v. First Securities Company of Chicago*, 463 F.2d 981 (1972), 985.

contended that if Ernst & Ernst had conducted a proper audit, it would have discovered this "mail rule." The existence of the rule then would have been disclosed to the Exchange [Midwest Stock Exchange] and to the Commission [SEC] by Ernst & Ernst as an irregular procedure that prevented an effective audit.[4]

To support their claim that the mail rule qualified as a critical internal control weakness having important audit implications, the escrow investors submitted affidavits from three expert witnesses with impressive credentials in the accounting profession. Exhibit 2 lists a portion of one of those affidavits.

The federal district court that initially presided over the *Hochfelder et al. v. Ernst & Ernst* case quickly dismissed the lawsuit.[5] This court deemed that there was no substantive evidence to support the allegation that Ernst & Ernst had negligently audited First Securities. When the investors appealed this decision, the U.S. Court of Appeals reversed the lower court decision and ordered that the case go to trial. In its decision, the appeals court ruled that sufficient doubt existed regarding the negligence claim against Ernst & Ernst to have the case heard. The appeals court also suggested that if the plaintiffs established negligence on the part of Ernst & Ernst, the accounting firm could be held civilly liable to the defrauded investors under Rule 10b-5 of the 1934 Act.

Before the *Hochfelder* case went to trial in a federal district court, Ernst & Ernst appealed the ruling of the U.S. Court of Appeals to the U.S. Supreme Court. Ernst & Ernst argued before the Supreme Court that the negligence allegation of the escrow investors was insufficient, even if proved, to constitute a violation of Rule 10b-5. This issue had surfaced in many previous civil cases filed under the Securities Exchange Act of 1934. In these earlier cases, the federal courts had generally ruled or suggested that negligence constituted a violation of Rule 10b-5. That is, fraud or gross negligence, either of which is much more difficult for a plaintiff to prove than ordinary negligence, did *not* have to be established for a defendant to be held civilly liable to a plaintiff under Rule 10b-5.

Ernst & Ernst contested these earlier rulings by arguing that Rule 10b-5, as worded, could not be construed to encompass negligent behavior. Given the longstanding controversy surrounding this issue, the Supreme Court decided to rule on the issue

EXHIBIT 2

EXCERPT FROM
EXPERT WITNESS
TESTIMONY
REGARDING NAY'S
MAIL RULE

Expert Witness No. 3:

If I had discovered in making an audit of a security brokerage business that its president had established an office rule that mail addressed to him at the business address, or to the company for his attention should not be opened by anyone but him, even in his absence; and that whenever he was away from the office such mail would remain unopened and pile up on his desk I would have to raise the question whether such rule or practice could possibly have been instituted for the purpose of preventing discovery of irregularities of whatever nature; would, at a minimum, have to undertake additional audit procedures to independently establish a negative answer to the latter question; also failing such an answer either withdraw from the engagement or decline to express an opinion on the financial statements of the enterprise.

---

4. *Ernst & Ernst v. Hochfelder et al.*, 425 U.S. 185 (1976), 190. (One of the investors defrauded by Nay was Olga Hochfelder.)

5. *Hochfelder et al. v. Ernst & Ernst*, 503 F.2d 1100 (1974).

in the Hochfelder case. This ruling would then establish a precedent for future law-suits filed under Rule 10b-5.

Before the Supreme Court heard Ernst & Ernst's appeal, the SEC filed a legal brief with the Court. This brief supported the defrauded investors' argument that Rule 10b-5 encompassed both fraudulent and negligent conduct. The SEC pointed out that the end result of investors' acting on false financial statements is the same whether the errors in the statements result from fraud or negligence. Because a central purpose of the federal securities laws is to ensure that investors receive reliable information, the SEC argued that the ambiguity in Rule 10b-5 should be resolved in favor of investors.

Surprisingly, the bulk of the Supreme Court's opinion in the *Hochfelder* case responded to the SEC's legal brief rather than the arguments of the defrauded investors or those of Ernst & Ernst. The Court rejected the SEC's largely philosophical argument and instead focused on the question of whether the authors of Rule 10b-5 intended it to encompass both negligent and fraudulent behavior. In addressing this issue, the Court reviewed the legislative history of the 1934 Act and did a painstaking analysis of the semantics of Rule 10b-5.

The Supreme Court eventually concluded that the key signal to the underlying meaning of Rule 10b-5 was the term *manipulative*. As shown in Exhibit 1, the heading of the rule clearly indicates that it pertains to "manipulative and deceptive" devices. According to the Court, negligence on the part of independent auditors or other parties associated with false financial statements could not be construed as manipulative behavior. The Court suggested that, in most cases, for behavior to qualify as manipulative, intent to deceive–the legal term being *scienter*–had to be present.

> When a statute speaks so specifically in terms of manipulation and deception, and of implementing devices and contrivances–the commonly understood terminology of intentional wrongdoing–and when its history reflects no more expansive intent, we are quite unwilling to extend the scope of the statute to negligent conduct.[6]

Two of the nine Supreme Court justices dissented to the *Hochfelder* decision, while one justice abstained. In disagreeing with the majority decision, Justice Harry Blackmun sided with the view expressed by the SEC. He noted that although the decision was probably consistent with the semantics of the Securities Exchange Act of 1934, the decision clashed with the underlying intent of that important federal statute. He wrote: "It seems to me that an investor can be victimized just as much by negligent conduct as by positive deception, and that it is not logical to drive a wedge between the two, saying that Congress clearly intended the one but certainly not the other."[7] Justice Blackmun went on to comment on the "critical importance" of the independent auditor's role and the ultimate responsibility of the auditor to serve the "public interest."[8] Given this societal mandate, Justice Blackmun argued, negligent auditors should be held accountable to investors who rely to their detriment on false financial statements.

---

6. *Ernst & Ernst v. Hochfelder et al.*, 214. A particularly troublesome issue for the Supreme Court to resolve was the underlying meaning of Subsection b of Rule 10b-5. Subsections a and c of that rule refer explicitly to fraud, implying that negligence is not a severe enough form of misconduct to constitute a violation of Rule 10b-5. However, Subsection b contains no explicit reference to fraudulent conduct. The SEC construed this omission to suggest that Subsection b covers both fraudulent and negligent misconduct. The Supreme Court rejected this argument, maintaining instead that the explicit references to fraud in Subsections a and c signaled that fraudulent conduct was the implied, although unstated, culpability standard in Subsection b as well.

7. *Ernst & Ernst v. Hochfelder et al.*, 216.

8. *Ibid.*, 218.

An Unresolved Issue

At first reading, the Supreme Court's *Hochfelder* opinion appeared to establish, once and for all, the culpability standard for determining Rule 10b-5 violations. Unfortunately, the opinion is not as precise or definitive as it first appeared. A footnote to the opinion suggests that in certain cases, scienter, or intent to deceive, may not be a necessary element of proof for a plaintiff to establish in a civil suit alleging a Rule 10b-5 violation. The Court noted that some jurisdictions equate scienter with willful or reckless disregard for the truth or, more simply, "recklessness."[9] When engaging in reckless behavior, a party does not actually possess conscious intent to deceive; that is, scienter is not present. For whatever reason, the Court refused to rule on the question of whether reckless behavior would be considered equivalent to scienter and thus constitute a violation of Rule 10b-5. This omission caused subsequent plaintiffs to predicate alleged Rule 10b-5 violations by independent auditors on reckless behavior, since that type of professional misconduct is much easier to prove than actual scienter.

EPILOGUE

Congressional critics of the Supreme Court's decision in the *Hochfelder* case insisted that the alleged "flaw" in Rule 10b-5 should be corrected legislatively. In late 1978, legislators introduced a bill in the U.S. House of Representatives to hold negligent auditors civilly liable to investors who relied on false financial statements filed with the SEC. Fortunately for independent auditors, Congress rejected that bill.

Questions

1. Under present technical standards, would auditors be required to disclose a company policy similar to Nay's mail rule that they discover during an audit? Explain. Assuming such disclosure had been required at the time this case took place, would that disclosure have resulted in the mail rule being discontinued?

2. Ernst & Ernst argued that the mail rule was not relevant to its audits of First Securities since that rule only involved personal transactions of Nay and the escrow investors. Do you agree? Why or why not?

3. Define *negligence* as that term has been used in legal cases involving independent auditors. What is the key distinction between negligence and fraud? Between recklessness and fraud? For all three types of professional misconduct, provide an example of such behavior in an audit context.

4. Assume that the investors defrauded by Nay could have filed their lawsuit against Ernst & Ernst under the Securities Act of 1933. How, if at all, do you believe the outcome of their suit would have been affected?

5. The *Restatement of Torts* is a legal compendium issued by the American Law Institute. This compendium is relied on by courts in many jurisdictions as the basis for legal rulings. Under the *Restatement of Torts*, courts have ruled that negligent auditors can be held liable to unknown third parties if those parties belonged to a known group of financial statement users who the auditors were aware would likely rely on the audited financial statements. If this legal principle had been invoked in the *Hochfelder* case, would the defrauded investors have been successful in pursuing a negligence claim against Ernst & Ernst under the common law? Why or why not?

---

9. *Ibid.*, 194.

SECTION 8

INTERNATIONAL CASES

8

Livent, Inc.

The structure of a play is always the story of how the birds came home to roost.

Arthur Miller

In 1995, Canadian native Maria Messina achieved one of the most sought-after career goals in the public accounting profession when she was promoted to partner with Deloitte & Touche, Chartered Accountants, the Canadian affiliate of the U.S.-based Deloitte & Touche, LLP. In an interview she granted to an accounting trade publication shortly after receiving that promotion, Ms. Messina noted that "Becoming a partner is exciting because you are a part of everything."[1] Messina's promotion earned her the respect and admiration of her family, her friends, and her colleagues and catapulted her to a much higher tax bracket and a more comfortable standard of living. But another opportunity soon arose, an opportunity that promised even more intrinsic and extrinsic rewards for Messina.

Throughout the 1990s, Livent, Inc., was the only publicly owned company whose primary line of business was live theatrical productions. Livent's co-founder and the individual recognized as the creative genius responsible for the company's impressive string of Tony Award-winning shows was Garth Drabinsky. Livent's audit firm was Deloitte & Touche, Chartered Accountants. Maria Messina served as the engagement partner for the 1996 audit, after having been the audit manager on several prior audits of the company. Following the completion of the 1996 Livent audit, Drabinsky asked Messina to leave Deloitte & Touche and become Livent's chief financial officer (CFO). After carefully weighing the challenges, opportunities, and potential drawbacks of making the job change, Messina gave up the partnership position with Deloitte & Touche that she had coveted for years in exchange for a "back office" but high-paying and high-profile position in the glitzy and glamorous world of show business.

Within a few weeks of signing on with Livent, Maria Messina was questioning the wisdom of her decision. Time budgets, out-of-town travel, inexperienced subordinates, and an array of other common "stressors" faced by partners of major accounting firms had complicated Messina's professional and personal life when she was at Deloitte. But, at Livent, the pressures she faced were much more intense, much more difficult to manage and control, even physically debilitating at times. Each passing month imposed a heavier emotional burden on Messina. By the late summer of 1998, Messina's life was in complete disarray. A few months later, in January 1999, Messina pleaded guilty to a felony for her role in a massive financial fraud. Following that plea, the single mother of a ten-year-old daughter faced up to five years in prison and a $250,000 fine.

There Is No Business Like Show Business

The entertainment industry had fascinated Garth Drabinsky from an early age. Unlike many of his colleagues in the industry, Drabinsky did not benefit from a network of family members and friends in show business. Instead, Drabinsky relied on his own drive, inspiration, and indomitable work ethic to claw his way to the top of the volatile and fickle entertainment industry. Born in Toronto in 1947, Drabinsky was struck

---

1. T. Frank, "Opportunity Knocks," *CA Magazine*, March 1997, 27.

down by polio at age three, leaving him with a severe limp for the remainder of his life. The young Canadian refused to allow his physical limitations to prevent him from reaching his goals. In fact, Drabinsky freely admits that his physical problems and his modest upbringing—his father sold air conditioners—were key factors that motivated him to "aim for the stars."

During his college years, Drabinsky made his first foray into show business by publishing a free magazine that provided critiques of movies appearing in local theaters. After graduating from law school, where he concentrated his studies on the entertainment industry, Drabinsky became involved in real estate development. The young attorney hoped to accumulate a nest egg that he could use to begin producing movies and live plays. A successful condominium project provided him with the funds he needed to begin dabbling in motion pictures and Broadway productions. By age 30, Drabinsky had produced three feature-length movies and one Broadway musical, none of which were particularly well received by critics or the ticket-buying public.

In 1979, Drabinsky and a close friend, Myron Gottlieb, decided to enter the show business world via the "back door." The two young entrepreneurs persuaded a prominent Toronto businessman to invest nearly $1 million in a "cinema complex" project they had conceived.[2] This project involved converting the basement of a large shopping mall into a multiscreen theater. The design for the "cineplex" included plush interiors for each theater, luxurious seats, and cappuccino bars in the lobby. Drabinsky intended to make a trip to the local movie theater the captivating experience it had been several decades earlier in the halcyon days of Hollywood.

Most industry insiders predicted that Drabinsky's blueprint for his cineplex concept would fail, principally because the large overhead for his theaters forced his company to charge much higher ticket prices than competitors. But the critics were wrong. Toronto's moviegoers were more than willing to pay a few extra dollars to watch a film in Drabinsky's upscale theaters. Over the next several years, Drabinsky and Gottlieb expanded their company with the help of well-heeled investors whom they convinced to pony up large sums to finance the development of multiscreen theater complexes throughout Canada and the United States. By the mid-1980s, their company, Cineplex Odeon, controlled nearly 2,000 theaters, making it the second-largest theater chain in North America.

Several major investors in Cineplex Odeon eventually began complaining of Drabinsky's unrestrained spending practices. The company's rapid expansion and the increasingly sumptuous designs Drabinsky developed for new theaters required Cineplex Odeon to borrow enormous amounts from banks and other lenders. An internal investigation in 1989 uncovered irregularities in the company's accounting records that wiped out a large profit for the year and resulted in Cineplex Odeon reporting a significant loss instead. The controversy sparked by the discovery of the accounting irregularities gave Cineplex Odeon's major investors the leverage they needed to force Drabinsky and Gottlieb to resign. During the negotiations that led to their departure from the company, Drabinsky and Gottlieb acquired the Pantages Theatre, a large live production theater in Toronto, as well as the Canadian rights to certain Broadway plays.

Within a few weeks after severing their ties with Cineplex Odeon, Drabinsky and Gottlieb had organized Live Entertainment Corporation to produce Broadway-type shows in their hometown of Toronto. Drabinsky's concept for this new company, which he coaxed several large investors and lenders to bankroll, was to bring "corporate

---

2. The key financial amounts reported in this case are expressed in Canadian dollars.

management" to the notoriously freewheeling and undisciplined show business industry. Following a series of widely acclaimed productions, the company–renamed Livent, Inc.–went public in 1993.[3] In May 1995, Livent filed an application with the Securities and Exchange Commission (SEC) to sell its stock in the United States. The SEC approved that application, and Livent's stock began trading on the NASDAQ stock exchange. Within two years, U.S. investors controlled the majority of Livent's outstanding stock.

By early 1998, Livent owned five live production theaters in Canada and the United States, including a major Broadway theater in New York. The company's productions, among them *Fosse, Kiss of the Spider Woman, Ragtime, Show Boat,* and *The Phantom of the Opera*, had garnered a total of more than 20 Tony Awards. Show business insiders attributed Livent's rapid rise to prominence to Garth Drabinsky. After organizing Livent, Drabinsky quickly developed a keen sense of the types of shows that would appeal to the public. Even more important, he was able to identify and recruit talented directors, actors, set designers, and the array of other skilled artisans needed to produce successful Broadway shows. The single-minded and domineering Drabinsky micromanaged not only the creative realm of Livent's operations but every other major facet of the company's operations as well, although he relied heavily on his friend and confidant, Myron Gottlieb–who had an accounting background–to help him oversee the company's accounting and financial reporting functions.

Despite the artistic success enjoyed by several Livent productions and the company's increasing stature in the entertainment industry, Garth Drabinsky was dogged by critics throughout the 1990s. The enigmatic Drabinsky had a well-deserved reputation as flamboyant and charming with Wall Street analysts, metropolitan bankers, and fellow corporate executives. But critics were prone to point out that Drabinsky also had a darker side to his personality. "He is–by his own admission–complex and difficult, cranky and litigious, breathtakingly ambitious, singled-minded and self-centered."[4] According to company insiders, Drabinsky could be "tyrannical and abusive"[5] to his subordinates, berating them when they failed to live up to his perfectionist standards or when they questioned his decisions. Maria Messina subsequently revealed that Livent's accountants were common targets of verbal abuse by Drabinsky and other Livent executives. "They [Livent's accountants] were told on a very regular basis that they are paid to keep their [expletive] mouths shut and do as they are [expletive] told. They are not paid to think."[6]

Critics also charged that Drabinsky failed to live up to his pledge of bringing a disciplined style of corporate management to Broadway. In reality, Drabinsky was anything but disciplined in managing Livent's finances. Because he demanded that the company's live productions be "motion-picture perfect," most of Livent's shows,

---

3. Drabinsky and Gottlieb's company was not affiliated with the California-based Live Entertainment, Inc. Jose Menendez organized the latter company in 1988 but was murdered along with his wife, Kitty, in August 1989. In one of the many "trials of the century," the Menendez's sons, Lyle and Erik, were subsequently convicted of murdering their parents.

4. K. Noble, "The Comeback King: Garth Drabinsky Is Back, and Creating a Lot of Showbiz Buzz," *MacLean's* (online), 4 June 2001.

5. M. Potter and T. Van Alphen, "Livent Charges $7.5 Million Kickback Scam," *The Toronto Star* (online), 19 November 1998.

6. *Profit*, "Backstage at Livent," May 1999, 29.

particularly those that were box-office successes, incurred huge cost overruns. By 1998, Livent was buckling under the huge load of debt Drabinsky had incurred to finance the company's lavish productions. In early 1998, Roy Furman, a Wall Street investment banker and close friend, persuaded Drabinsky to accept a $20 million investment from former Disney executive Michael Ovitz to alleviate Livent's financial problems. A condition of Ovitz's investment was that he be granted sufficient common stock voting rights to allow him to control the company's board of directors.

During the 1980s, Ovitz had reigned as Hollywood's top talent agent. When he became chairman of the Creative Artists Agency, show business periodicals tagged him with the title of "Hollywood's most powerful man." In late 1995, Disney chief executive officer (CEO) Michael Eisner chose Ovitz to serve as his top lieutenant and gave him the title of company president. A little more than one year later, repeated personality clashes between the two Hollywood heavyweights resulted in Eisner dismissing Ovitz. No doubt, Ovitz hoped that Livent would provide him with an opportunity to refurbish his reputation in the entertainment industry, a reputation that had been tarnished during his brief and turbulent stint with Disney. Just as important, taking control of Livent would allow Ovitz to compete head-to-head with his former boss. At the time, Disney's *The Lion King* was a colossal hit on Broadway.

Before agreeing to invest in Livent, the cautious Ovitz retained the Big Five accounting firm KPMG to scrutinize the company's accounting records. After KPMG's "due diligence" investigation yielded a clean bill of health for Livent, Ovitz became the company's largest stockholder in early June of 1998 and took over effective control of the company. Ovitz took a seat on the company's board and became chairman of the board's executive committee, while Furman assumed Drabinsky's former titles of chairman of the board and CEO. Drabinsky was given the titles of vice chairman and chief creative director. In the latter role, Drabinsky continued to oversee the all-important creative facets of Livent's operations. To provide a second opinion on artistic matters, Ovitz appointed the noted producer and songwriter Quincy Jones to Livent's board.

Ovitz also demoted Myron Gottlieb to a vice president position. A former Disney executive who left that company along with Ovitz assumed Gottlieb's former position as Livent's president. Among other changes that Ovitz made in Livent's corporate management structure was the hiring of former KPMG audit partner Robert Webster to serve as an executive vice president of the company. Webster, who had supervised KPMG's due diligence investigation of Livent's accounting records, was given a broad range of responsibilities, but his principal role was to monitor Livent's accounting and finance functions for Ovitz's new management team.

Webster's Summer of Discontent

Like Maria Messina, Robert Webster quickly discovered that the work environment within Livent was much less than ideal. After joining Livent in the early summer of 1998, Webster found that the accounting staff, including Messina, who remained Livent's CFO, was reluctant to discuss accounting matters with him. Webster later testified that some of the Livent accountants "told him that Mr. Drabinsky had warned them not to provide certain financial information until [Drabinsky] had reviewed and approved it."[7] Even more troubling to Webster was Drabinsky's management style. Webster testified, "I had never before experienced anyone with Drabinsky's abusive

7. M. Petersen, "The Roar of the Accountants: The Strange Last Days of a Theater Impresario's Reign," *The New York Times* (online), 10 October 1998.

and profane management style."[8] He was shocked to find that Livent's executives often screamed and swore at the company's accountants. Webster reported that after meeting with Drabinksy, Livent's accountants were often in tears or even nauseous. Following one such meeting, Webster recalled Messina "shaking like a leaf."[9]

When Webster demanded that Livent's accountants provide him with unrestricted access to the company's accounting records, the former KPMG partner became the target of Drabinsky's wrath. Drabinsky accused Webster of attempting to "tear the company" apart with his persistent inquiries and told him that he was there to "service his [Drabinsky's] requirements."[10] Webster refused to be deterred by Drabinsky's bullying tactics. In early August 1998, after Webster began asking questions regarding a suspicious transaction he had uncovered, Messina and four of her subordinates secretly met with him. The five accountants admitted to Webster that Livent's accounting records had been distorted by a series of fraudulent schemes initiated and coordinated by Drabinsky and other top Livent executives.

Webster relayed the disturbing revelations to Livent's board. On August 11, 1998, Roy Furman issued a press release announcing that "significant financial irregularities" adversely affecting Livent's financial statements for the past three years had been discovered. The press release also indicated that Drabinsky and Gottlieb had been indefinitely suspended pending the outcome of a forensic investigation by KPMG. During the fall of 1998, company officials issued successive press releases suggesting that the impact of the accounting irregularities would be more severe than initially thought. Adding to Livent's problems was the suspension of all trading in the company's stock and a series of large class-action lawsuits filed against the company and its officers. In August 1998 alone, 12 such lawsuits were filed.

On November 18, 1998, Livent's board announced that KPMG's forensic investigation had revealed "massive, systematic, accounting irregularities that permeated the company."[11] The press release issued by Livent's board also disclosed that Deloitte & Touche had withdrawn its audit opinions on the company's 1995-1997 financial statements. Finally, the press release reported that Drabinsky and Gottlieb had been dismissed and that Livent had simultaneously filed for bankruptcy in Canada and the United States. A few weeks later, a federal grand jury in New York issued a 16-count fraud indictment against Drabinsky and Gottlieb. When the former Livent executives failed to appear for a preliminary court hearing, a U.S. federal judge issued arrest warrants for the two Canadian citizens and initiated extradition proceedings.

A "Pervasive and Multi-faceted" Fraud

Details of the fraud allegedly conceived by Garth Drabinsky and Myron Gottlieb were eventually revealed to the public by the SEC, the Ontario Securities Commission—a Canadian agency comparable to the SEC—and publicly available records of various court proceedings in civil lawsuits. In numerous enforcement and litigation releases, SEC officials repeatedly used the descriptive phrase "pervasive and multi-faceted" when referring to the Livent fraud. One of the earliest elements of the fraud was a large kickback scheme.

---

8. A. Clark, "An Epic from Livent: Executive Accuses Drabinsky of Bullying Tactics," *MacLean's* (online), 1 March 1999.

9. *Ibid.*

10. *Ibid.*

11. *In re Livent, Inc. Noteholders Securities Litigation*, 151 F. Supp. 2d 371 (2001).

"As early as 1990, and continuing through 1994, Drabinsky and Gottlieb operated a kickback scheme with two Livent vendors designed to siphon millions of dollars from the company directly into their own pockets."[12] Gottlieb reportedly instructed the two vendors to include in the invoices that they submitted to Livent charges for services that they had not provided to the company. After Livent paid the inflated invoice amounts, Drabinsky and Gottlieb received kickbacks equal to the payments for the bogus services. According to the SEC, over a four-year period in the 1990s, Drabinsky and Gottlieb received approximately $7 million in kickbacks from the two Livent vendors. The fake charges billed to Livent by the vendors were capitalized in "preproduction" cost accounts for the various shows being developed by the company. Legitimate costs charged to those accounts included expenditures to produce sets and costumes for new shows, costs that were amortized over a maximum period of five years.

By the mid-1990s, the kickback scheme and large losses being registered by several of Livent's plays made it increasingly difficult for the company to achieve quarterly earnings targets that Drabinsky and Gottlieb had relayed to Wall Street analysts. The two conspirators realized that if Livent failed to reach those earnings targets, the company's credit rating and stock price would fall, jeopardizing the company's ability to raise the additional capital needed to sustain its operations. Faced with these circumstances, the SEC reported that beginning in 1994 Drabinsky and Gottlieb directed Livent's accounting staff to engage in an array of "accounting manipulations" to obscure the company's financial problems.

These manipulations included such blatant subterfuges as simply erasing from the accounting records previously recorded expenses and liabilities at the end of each quarter. A particularly popular accounting scam within Livent involved the transfer of preproduction costs from a show that was running to a show still in production. Such transfers allowed the company to defer, sometimes indefinitely, the amortization of those major cost items. To further reduce the periodic amortization charges for preproduction costs, Livent's accountants began charging such costs to various fixed asset accounts. These assets were typically depreciated over 40 years, compared with the five-year amortization period for preproduction costs. Eventually, the company's accountants began debiting salary expenses and other common operating expenses to long-term fixed asset accounts.

The SEC estimated that the accounting manipulations understated Livent's expenses by more than $30 million in the mid-1990s. Despite the resulting favorable impact on Livent's financial statements, Drabinsky and Gottlieb eventually realized that additional efforts were needed to embellish the company's financial data. So, beginning in 1996, Drabinsky and Gottlieb organized and carried out what the SEC referred to as a "fraudulent revenue-generating" scheme.

This new scam involved several multimillion-dollar transactions arranged by Drabinsky and Gottlieb. The specific details of these transactions varied somewhat, but most of them involved the sale of production rights owned by Livent to third parties. For example, Livent sold the rights to produce *Ragtime* and *Show Boat* in various U.S. theaters to a Texas-based company. The contract for this transaction indicated that the $11.2 million fee paid to Livent by the Texas company was not refundable under any circumstances. However, a secret side agreement arranged by Livent's executives shielded the Texas company from any loss on this deal and, in

---

12. Securities and Exchange Commission, *Accounting and Auditing Enforcement Release No. 1095*, 19 May 1999.

fact, guaranteed it a reasonable rate of return on its large investment. Despite the considerable uncertainty regarding the actual profit, if any, that would ultimately be earned on this and similar transactions, Livent's accounting staff included at least $34 million of revenues on those transactions in the company's 1996 and 1997 income statements.

A final Livent scam documented by the SEC involved inflating reported box-office results for key productions. In late 1997, Livent opened *Ragtime* in a Los Angeles theater. The agreement with that theater allowed it to close the show if weekly ticket sales fell below $500,000. Livent's executives planned to open *Ragtime* on Broadway in January 1998. Those executives realized that if the show fared poorly in Los Angeles, its Broadway opening could be jeopardized. To inflate *Ragtime's* ticket sales during its Los Angeles run, Livent executives arranged to have two of the company's vendors–the same individuals involved in the fraudulent kickback scheme alluded to previously–purchase several hundred thousand dollars of tickets to the show. Livent reimbursed the vendors for these ticket purchases and charged the payments to various fixed asset accounts.

The fraudulent schemes engineered by Livent's executives caused the company's periodic financial statements to be grossly misrepresented. For example, in 1992, the company reported a pretax profit of $2.9 million when the actual figure was approximately $100,000. Four years later, Livent reported a pretax profit of $14.2 million when it actually incurred a loss of more than $20 million. By 1997, the company's total fixed assets of $200.8 million were overstated by nearly $24 million due to the various accounting schemes.

SEC officials found two features of the Livent fraud particularly disturbing. As the scope of the fraud steadily grew throughout the 1990s, the company's accounting staff found it increasingly difficult to provide meaningful financial data to top management. "Because of the sheer magnitude and dollar amount of the manipulations, it became necessary for senior management to be able to track both the real and the phony numbers."[13] Gordon Eckstein, the company's senior vice president of finance and administration and Maria Messina's immediate superior, allegedly instructed a subordinate to develop computer software that would solve this problem. This software could be used to filter the bogus data out of the company's accounting records. The secret software also served a second purpose, namely, allowing Livent's accountants to record fraudulent transactions "without leaving a paper trail that Livent's outside auditors might stumble across."[14] The accountants processed in a batch mode the fraudulent changes in the accounting records demanded by Livent's executives. When these so-called "adjustments" were processed, they replaced the initial journal entries for the given transactions, making the adjustments appear as if they were the original transactions, thus duping the company's Deloitte auditors.

The second extremely troubling feature of the Livent fraud, according to the SEC, was the matter-of-fact manner in which the company's management team organized and carried out the fraud. Reportedly, Drabinsky, Gottlieb, and Robert Topol, Livent's chief operating officer (COO), regularly met with Eckstein, Messina, and other members of the company's accounting staff to discuss the details of the fraud. At these meetings, the three top executives reviewed preliminary financial reports prepared by the accounting staff and instructed the accountants on the "adjustments" needed to improve or embellish those reports. As suggested earlier, Livent's

13. *Ibid.*

14. M. A. Hiltzik and J. Bates, "U.S. Indicts Stage Producer Drabinsky," *Los Angeles Times* (online), 14 January 1999.

top executives relied on coercion and intimidation to browbeat their accountants, including Messina, into accepting these illicit changes. Once the adjustments were processed, "the bogus numbers were presented to Livent's audit committee, the auditors, investors, and eventually filed with the Commission [SEC]."[15]

Keeping the Auditors in the Dark

Press reports of a large accounting fraud involving a public company often prompt scathing criticism of the company's independent audit firm. The disclosure of the Livent fraud in the late summer and fall of 1998 caused Deloitte & Touche to become a target of such criticism. A Canadian financial analyst observed that investors depend on auditors to clamp down on their clients and force them to prepare reliable financial reports. "They [auditors] are the only ones in a position to question the policies, to question the numbers, to make sure they're right."[16]

Critics could readily point to several red flags or fraud risk factors during Deloitte's tenure with Livent that should have placed the accounting firm on high alert regarding the possible existence of financial statement misrepresentations. Among those factors were an extremely aggressive, growth-oriented management team; a history of prior financial reporting indiscretions by Drabinsky and Gottlieb; a constant and growing need for additional capital; and the existence of related-party transactions. Regarding the latter factor, several of Livent's fraudulent "revenue-generating transactions" that were documented by the SEC involved companies or corporate executives affiliated with Livent or its management team.

In Deloitte's defense, a massive collusive fraud that involves a client's top executives and the active participation of its accountants is extremely difficult to detect. Making matters worse for Deloitte was the contemptuous attitude that Livent's executives had toward independent auditors. At one point, a top Livent officer told a subordinate that independent auditors were a "necessary evil and that it was no one's business how they [Livent's executives] ran their company."[17] Also complicating the Livent audits for Deloitte was the fact Maria Messina and Christopher Craib, two former members of the Livent audit engagement team, had accepted key accounting positions with the company. The personal relationships the auditors had with Messina and Craib may have impaired their objectivity during the Livent engagements.

Christopher Craib replaced Maria Messina as the audit manager assigned to the Livent audit engagement team following Messina's promotion to partner in 1995. After the 1996 audit was completed, Drabinsky hired Craib to serve as Livent's senior controller for budgeting. Not long after joining Livent, Craib, a chartered accountant, became involved in the ongoing effort to segregate Livent's "real" accounting data from its bogus data. In subsequent testimony, Craib recalled meeting with Gordon Eckstein to discuss Livent's schizoid accounting system. Eckstein explained to Craib why it was imperative to track both the real and bogus accounting data: "I have to keep all the lies straight. I have to know what lies I'm telling these people [outside auditors]. I've told so many lies to different people I have to make sure they all make sense."[18]

---

15. Securities and Exchange Commission, *Accounting and Auditing Enforcement Release No. 1095.*

16. J. McCarten, "Auditors Taking the Heat after Financial Scandals," *The Toronto Star* (online), 18 August 1998.

17. Securities and Exchange Commission, *Accounting and Auditing Enforcement Release No. 1096*, 19 May 1999.

18. *Ibid.*

Like Craib, Maria Messina realized that concealing the Livent fraud from the Deloitte auditors was among her primary responsibilities. During a meeting shortly after Messina joined Livent, she became aware of the adversarial attitude that Livent's top executives had toward the company's independent auditors. During this meeting, Topol became angry when Messina raised an issue involving what documents to turn over to Deloitte. Topol responded with an angry outburst. "[Expletive] you and your auditors . . . I don't care what they see or don't see."[19]

Despite the efforts of Livent officials to sabotage their independent audits, the company's Deloitte auditors focused considerable attention on several suspicious transactions that they uncovered. The Deloitte auditors became increasingly skeptical of Livent's accounting records in 1996 and 1997 when Drabinsky and his colleagues were scrambling to conceal the deteriorating financial condition of their company while, at the same time, attempting to raise much needed debt and equity capital.

Near the end of the 1996 audit, Deloitte & Touche, LLP, the U.S.-based branch of the firm, initially refused to allow its Canadian affiliate to issue an unqualified audit opinion on Livent's financial statements filed with the SEC. Deloitte's top technical partners in the United States believed that Livent had been much too aggressive in recognizing revenue on a few large transactions–transactions that, unknown to partners of both the firm's Canadian and U.S. affiliates, included fraudulent elements. After a series of meetings between Livent officials and representatives of Deloitte & Touche, LLP, a compromise was reached. Livent agreed to defer the recognition of revenue on one of the two large transactions in question until 1997. In return, Deloitte allowed the company to record the full amount of the revenue for the other disputed transaction.

During 1997, a major transaction with a real estate firm triggered another conflict between Deloitte and Livent management. In the second quarter of that year, the real estate firm purchased for $7.4 million the development rights to a valuable parcel of land owned by Livent. The contract between the two companies included a stipulation or "put agreement" allowing the real estate firm to cancel the transaction prior to the date that it began developing the property. When the Deloitte audit engagement partner learned of the put agreement, he insisted that no revenue could be recorded for the transaction. Complicating matters was the fact that the transaction involved a related party since Myron Gottlieb served on the board of directors of the real estate firm's parent company.

To quell the audit partner's concern, Gottlieb arranged to have an executive of the real estate firm send the partner a letter indicating that the put agreement had been cancelled–which it had not. After receiving the letter, the Deloitte partner told Gottlieb that the revenue resulting from the transaction could be recorded during Livent's third quarter when the put agreement had allegedly been cancelled. At this point, a frustrated Gottlieb ignored the partner's decision and included the disputed revenue in Livent's earnings press release for the second quarter of 1997.

When Deloitte officials learned of the press release, they demanded a meeting with Livent's board of directors. At this meeting, Deloitte threatened to resign. After considerable discussion, Livent's board and the Deloitte representatives reached a compromise. According to a subsequent legal transcript, the board agreed to reverse the journal entry for the $7.4 million transaction in the second quarter, recording it instead during the third quarter. The board also agreed to issue an amended earnings release for the second quarter. In exchange for these concessions, Deloitte officials

---

19. Securities and Exchange Commission, *Accounting and Auditing Enforcement Release No. 1097,* 19 May 1999.

purportedly agreed to allow Livent to reverse certain accrued liabilities that had been recorded at the end of the second quarter. The reversal of those accrued liabilities and the corresponding expenses reduced by approximately 20 percent the profit "correction" reported by Livent in the amended earnings press release for the second quarter.[20]

Another serious disagreement arose between Livent executives and Deloitte auditors shortly after the dispute just described was resolved. During the third quarter of 1997, Livent's management arranged to sell for $12.5 million the naming rights for one of its existing theaters and a new theater that the company was planning to build. Neither Maria Messina nor the Deloitte auditors assigned to the Livent engagement believed that the $12.5 million payment should be recorded immediately as revenue since the contract between Livent and the other party, AT&T, was strictly an oral agreement at the time and since one of the theaters was yet to be built. Gottlieb retained Ernst & Young (E&Y) to review the matter.

The report E&Y submitted to Gottlieb did not take a firm position on the revenue recognition issue. Instead, E&Y's report simply suggested that the $12.5 million payment for the naming rights could be "considered" for recording during the third quarter. After receiving a copy of E&Y's report, Deloitte hired Price Waterhouse to review the transaction. When Price Waterhouse reached the same conclusion as E&Y, Deloitte allowed Livent to book the $12.5 million as revenue during the third quarter.

Don't Blame Me, Blame . . .

Resolving the legal implications of a major accounting and financial reporting fraud can require years. However, one Canadian journalist suggested that in the Livent case the legal wrangling could continue even longer, possibly for decades.[21] From its inception, a key factor complicating the resolution of this case was its "cross-border" nature.

Beginning in late 1998, officials from several federal agencies in Canada and the United States became embroiled in a tedious and often contentious struggle to determine which agency would be the first to prosecute the key parties involved in the Livent fraud. Those agencies included the Royal Canadian Mounted Police, the Ontario Securities Commission, the SEC, and the U.S. Department of Justice, among others. Law enforcement authorities in the United States failed to win the cooperation of their Canadian counterparts in attempting to extradite Garth Drabinsky and Myron Gottlieb to face a series of federal fraud charges filed against them in U.S. courts. Even more frustrating to U.S. authorities was the snail's pace at which Canadian authorities moved in pursuing legal action against the two alleged fraudsters.

While Canadian and U.S. law enforcement authorities tangled over jurisdictional matters, the leading actors in the final Livent "production" waged a public relations war against each other in major metropolitan newspapers and in the courts. Drabinsky and Gottlieb were the most vocal of these individuals. They repeatedly insisted that they were not responsible for the various fraudulent schemes that had been uncovered within Livent. At a press conference held in early 1999, Drabinsky suggested that he had been too busy overseeing Livent's creative operations to become involved in any creative bookkeeping.[22] In his typical Shakespearean manner,

---

20. *In re Livent, Inc. Noteholders Securities Litigation*. As a point of information, this legal transcript did not include any commentary from Deloitte's perspective regarding the nature and outcome of these negotiations.

21. Noble, "The Comeback King."

22. M. Lewyckyj, "Livent's Accounting Designed to Deceive," *Toronto Sun* (online), 15 January 1999.

Drabinsky declared: "The final act of this tragedy has yet to be played out and, when it is, Myron Gottlieb and I have complete confidence that we will be vindicated."[23]

In January 1999, Myron Gottlieb filed a civil lawsuit against Maria Messina, Christopher Craib, Gordon Eckstein, and three other former Livent accountants; the lawsuit charged those six individuals with responsibility for the Livent accounting fraud. In court documents filed with this lawsuit, Gottlieb alleged that he was not "an expert on accounting practices" and that he had relied on Livent's accounting staff to ensure that the company's financial statements were accurate.[24] In responding to that lawsuit, the six named defendants, with the exception of Eckstein, claimed that they had been coerced into participating in the fraud by its principal architects.[25] These defendants also rejected Gottlieb's assertion that he was unfamiliar with accounting practices. "Gottlieb was and remains an experienced businessman with a sophisticated and comprehensive grasp of accounting and auditing issues and intimate knowledge of the details of Livent's accounting practices."[26]

When Eckstein eventually responded to Gottlieb's lawsuit, he charged the Livent co-founder with being a key architect of the accounting fraud. "Gottlieb's denial of responsibility or knowledge of the accounting irregularities at Livent is in complete disregard to the facts as they existed. . . . [He] had the requisite expertise and business acumen to create and help foster the corporate culture at Livent, which ultimately resulted in the alteration of the books and records."[27] Eckstein also claimed that he was not involved in altering Livent's accounting records, although he did admit to relaying the changes demanded by Drabinsky and Gottlieb in those records to Livent's accounting staff. Finally, Eckstein maintained that Maria Messina had played an important role in the fraudulent scheme. "Messina relied on her former position as a partner at Deloitte in dealing with the field audit team . . . to ensure that the financial statements of Livent, as presented to the auditors, were approved."[28]

Messina answered Eckstein and other critics by maintaining that she had attempted to dissuade Livent's executives from using accounting gimmicks to boost the company's revenues and profits. She insisted that she had "begged" her former colleagues at Deloitte to crack down on the aggressive revenue recognition policies being used by Livent's management.[29] To support her claim that she had not been a willing member of the Livent conspiracy, Messina pointed out that she had refused to sign the letters of representations for the 1996 and 1997 audits, each of which indicated that there were no material inaccuracies in Livent's financial statements. In fact, near the end of the 1997 audit, Messina had redrafted Deloitte's pre-formatted letter of representations to remove her name from it.[30]

---

23. C. Brodesser and M. Peers, "U.S. Indicts Duo in Liventgate," *Variety*, 18 January 1999, 137.

24. *The Gazette* (online), "Livent Co-Founder Sues 6 Employees," 19 February 1999.

25. V. Menon, "Livent Whistle-Blowers File Defence," *The Toronto Star* (online), 1 April 1999.

26. B. Bouw, "Livent Employees Fight Back: 'Gottlieb to Blame,'" *National Post* (online), 1 April 1999.

27. B. Shecter, "Drabinsky's Assertions Refuted," *National Post* (online), 26 June 1999.

28. *Ibid.*

29. *Profit*, "Backstage at Livent." In a deposition filed in one of the many lawsuits triggered by the Livent fraud, Messina described Deloitte's audits of the company as "inadequate." See D. Francis, "Livent: A Bean Counter Scandal," *National Post* (online), 10 May 2001.

30. In a court document, Messina reported that she did not reveal the various Livent fraudulent schemes prior to August 1998 because she feared Drabinsky and Gottlieb and because she believed that she would be "implicated by association." See B. Bouw, "Livent Employees Fight Back: 'Gottlieb to Blame,'" *National Post* (online), 1 April 1999.

After firing Drabinsky and Gottlieb, Michael Ovitz and the members of the new management team he installed at Livent in June 1998 sued the company's co-founders for $325 million for their alleged role in the fraudulent accounting schemes. That lawsuit prompted Drabinsky and Gottlieb to file a $200 million defamation-of-character lawsuit against Ovitz and his colleagues.

In September 1998, Drabinsky sued KPMG, the accounting firm that Ovitz had retained to perform a due diligence investigation earlier in the year and the firm retained by Livent's board of directors in August 1998 to investigate the charges of accounting irregularities revealed by Maria Messina and her subordinates. That lawsuit, which requested damages of more than $26 million, was predicated on the fact that Drabinsky had been a client of KPMG over the past two decades. Drabinksy charged that by agreeing to perform the forensic audit requested by Livent's board in August 1998, KPMG had placed itself in a conflict of interest between two clients.[31]

Deloitte & Touche was a primary target of the various plaintiffs attempting to hold someone responsible for the Livent debacle and the resulting financial losses. In December 1999, a U.S. federal judge dismissed Deloitte as a defendant in one of those lawsuits filed by Livent's former stockholders. The judge concluded that the plaintiffs had not made a reasonable argument that Deloitte was at least "reckless" in auditing Livent. For lawsuits filed under the Securities and Exchange Act of 1934, as amended by the Private Securities Litigation Reform Act (PSLRA) of 1995, plaintiffs must allege or "plead" that the given defendant was at least "reckless."

In another class-action lawsuit filed by Livent creditors, a federal judge ruled in June 2001 that the plaintiffs had met the pleading standard of recklessness, meaning that the lawsuit could proceed. This judge observed that Livent's "accounting manipulations" were so flagrant that there was a reasonable likelihood Deloitte was reckless in failing to discover them. "Deloitte & Touche's actions and omissions in connection with Livent's manipulations of its books and records display acquiescence and passivity that, in this Court's reading of the pleadings, cross over the boundary of ordinary breaches of reasonable care into the zone of recklessness."[32] Published reports indicate that Deloitte & Touche was dropped as a defendant in this case after it agreed to pay $5.5 million to a restitution fund established for Livent's former creditors.

EPILOGUE

In July 1999, SFX Entertainment purchased the remaining assets of Livent, ending the company's dramatic and turbulent existence after only ten years. In June 2000, the disciplinary committee of the Institute of Chartered Accountants of Ontario (ICAO) sanctioned the former Livent accountants who had publicly admitted some degree of involvement in the Livent fraud. Maria Messina, who pleaded guilty to three charges of professional misconduct, was fined $7,500 and suspended from practicing as a chartered accountant for two years. Christopher Craib received a six-month suspension and a $1,000 fine.

In 2007, the ICAO found three of the Deloitte auditors who had been assigned to the 1997 Livent audit engagement team guilty of professional misconduct, publicly reprimanded them, and levied fines against them and Deloitte totaling $1.55 million. In early 2010, a Canadian

31. Drabinsky and KPMG ultimately settled this lawsuit out of court. Although the settlement's financial terms were not disclosed, KPMG acknowledged that it had breached its "fiduciary duty" to Drabinsky by agreeing to perform the forensic audit requested by Livent's board.

32. *In re Livent, Inc. Noteholders Securities Litigation.*

appellate court overturned those sanctions. The court ruled that the ICAO had failed to prove that the Deloitte auditors were guilty of a "significant departure" from professional standards during the 1997 Livent audit.

The SEC sanctioned Craib and three other Livent accountants who had confessed to some role in the Livent accounting fraud. Craib received a three-year suspension from practicing before the SEC. The SEC has not yet formally sanctioned Maria Messina for her role in the Livent fraud. Likewise, federal prosecutors in the United States have yet to make a sentencing recommendation following Messina's guilty plea to one felony count of violating U.S. federal securities laws. A key factor that federal authorities in the United States will consider in determining Messina's punishment will be whether she continues cooperating with Canadian and U.S. authorities prosecuting the key architects of the fraud.

As predicted, Canadian law enforcement authorities were extremely methodical in pursuing their investigation and prosecution of Garth Drabinsky, Myron Gottlieb, and the other key individuals involved in the Livent scandal. In late 2002, the Royal Mounted Canadian Police finally filed a fraud indictment against Drabinsky and Gottlieb that contained 19 individual charges. Five years later, Gordon Eckstein pleaded guilty to one count of fraud and agreed to testify against Drabinsky and Gottlieb. Eckstein's and Maria Messina's testimony would prove to be pivotal evidence in the 11-month long criminal trial of Drabinsky and Gottlieb.[33] That trial ended in late March 2009 with both Drabinsky and Gottlieb being convicted of fraud and forgery.

The Canadian judge who presided over the lengthy trial rejected Drabinsky and Gottlieb's principal argument that they had been unaware of the massive accounting fraud and that it had been orchestrated by their subordinates. In handing down her verdict, the judge concluded that the two executives "had initiated the improper accounting system" that had "systemically manipulated" Livent's reported operating results and financial condition.[34, 35] In August 2009, the judge sentenced Drabinsky and Gottlieb to prison sentences of seven years and six years, respectively.

The 2009 criminal convictions of Drabinsky and Gottlieb did not end the long-running Livent legal ordeal. Both men immediately appealed the convictions, appeals that would likely take several years to work their way through the Canadian courts. In addition, the two men still faced securities fraud charges in Canada and the unhappy prospect of eventually being extradited to face the litany of criminal charges pending against them for more than a decade in the United States.

Questions

1. Identify common inherent risk factors that companies involved in the entertainment industry pose for their independent auditors. List and briefly describe specific audit procedures that would not be used on "typical" audit engagements but would be required for audits of companies involved in live theatrical productions, such as Livent.

---

33. Defense attorneys in this case revealed that Messina was being paid $325,000 annually by Livent's bankruptcy receiver to testify in the various Livent-related lawsuits. Those attorneys also alleged that law enforcement authorities in the United States had privately agreed to drop all charges against Messina if Drabinsky and Gottlieb were ultimately sent to prison.

34. *Reuters* (online), "Former Broadway Impresario Drabinsky Found Guilty," 25 March 2009.

35. Robert Topol, Livent's former COO, had faced charges similar to those for which Drabinsky and Gottlieb were prosecuted. However, those charges were dismissed in 2008 when his attorneys convinced the judge that he had been denied his right to a speedy trial.

2. Compare and contrast the responsibilities of an audit partner of a major accounting firm with those of a large public company's CFO. Which work role do you believe is more important? Which is more stressful? Which role would you prefer and why?

3. Explain why some corporate executives may perceive that their independent auditors are a "necessary evil." How can auditors combat or change that attitude?

4. When auditor–client disputes arise during an audit engagement, another accounting firm is sometimes retained by the client and/or the existing auditor to provide an objective report on the issue at the center of the dispute–as happened during Deloitte's 1997 audit of Livent. Discuss an accounting firm's responsibilities when it is retained to issue such a report.

5. Do you believe Deloitte & Touche should have approved Livent's decision to record the $12.5 million "naming rights" payment as revenue during the third quarter of 1997? Defend your answer. What broad accounting concepts should be considered in determining the proper accounting treatment for such transactions?

6. Maria Messina testified that when she learned of the accounting irregulari-ties at Livent shortly after becoming the company's CFO she felt "guilty by association," which prevented her from revealing the fraud to regulatory or law enforcement authorities. Explain what you believe she meant by that statement. Place yourself in Messina's position. What would you have done after discovering the fraudulent schemes affecting Livent's accounting records?

7. What professional standards apply to "due diligence" investigations performed by accounting firms?

Parmalat Finanziaria, S.p.A.

In late December 2003, Claudio Pessina, a financial accountant for the large Italian food conglomerate Parmalat, was given an unusual order by his immediate superior, the company's chief accounting officer (CAO). Luciano Del Soldato told Pessina to destroy his laptop computer.[1] When Pessina reacted with surprise to the request, an animated Del Soldato repeated the order, telling Pessina that he wanted him to use a large hammer to pound the computer into hundreds of small pieces.

A few days later, on Christmas Eve 2003, Parmalat filed for bankruptcy. New Year's Eve proved to be even more unpleasant for Del Soldato and seven other Parmalat executives. Italian law enforcement authorities arrested the executives and charged each of them with being involved in what would prove to be the largest accounting fraud in European history. At the time, Parmalat accounted for 1.5 percent of Italy's annual gross national product (GNP), which meant that the company had a much larger impact on the Italian economy than either Enron or WorldCom had on the U.S. economy before those two companies collapsed in spectacular fashion a few years earlier.

Parmalat's financial statements had grossly misrepresented the company's financial condition and operating results for more than 15 years. Subsequent investigations revealed that Parmalat had overstated its assets by more than $16 billion and understated its liabilities by more than $10 billion. Included in the company's fictitious assets was nearly $5 billion of cash supposedly on deposit with Bank of America.

Del Soldato had ordered Pessina to destroy his computer because it contained files that documented many of the important details of the fraud, including a mysterious intercompany account, Account 999. Investigators would discover that Account 999 had been used as a virtual garbage dump by the company's accounting staff for the billions of dollars of fictitious assets that accumulated on Parmalat's balance sheet over the course of the long-running fraud.

Fausto Tonna, Parmalat's former chief financial officer (CFO) and a close friend and confidant of the company's founder, was one of the masterminds of the massive fraud. Tonna was less than contrite after being arrested by members of Italy's federal police force, the *carabinieri*. While being escorted by the police to his arraignment, Tonna was peppered with questions by a frenzied throng of journalists. On the steps of the courthouse, Tonna paused and addressed his antagonists in an angry and deliberate tone. "I wish you and your families a slow and painful death."[2]

"The Coca-Cola of Milk"

Collecchio is a picturesque village strategically located in northwestern Italy. Nearby is Milan, the world's fashion capital; Verona, the setting that Shakespeare chose for *Romeo and Juliet*; "Fat Bologna," the gastronomic capital of Italy; and Cinque Terre,

---

1. I would like to acknowledge a former student of mine, Meredith Oliveti, for her excellent research that contributed to this case. I would also like to thank Mr. Glen McLaughlin for his generous and continuing support of efforts to develop experiential instructional materials for accounting and auditing courses.

2. J. Stewart, "Parmalat: A Slow and Painful Death," www.financialdirector.co.uk, 4 February 2004.

a string of five quaint fishing villages, which has become one of Europe's favorite tourist destinations. After World War II decimated Italy's economy, Melchiorre Tanzi, a longtime resident of Collecchio, supported his family by peddling preserved meats door to door with the help of Calisto, his oldest son, who was born in 1938. When he graduated from the local *liceo* or high school, Calisto left Collecchio to earn a university degree. Although he enjoyed working with his father, he had bigger dreams than being a small-town merchant. Calisto planned to become a professional accountant and work for a major Italian corporation.

Unfortunately, Melchiorre Tanzi died before Calisto could finish his college degree. Following his father's premature death, Calisto did what is common under such circumstances within Italian culture; he returned home to replace his father as the patriarch of his family, a role that included taking over the family business. Despite returning to Collecchio, Calisto did not give up his dream of becoming involved in big business.

The determined young Italian quickly expanded his father's business. By the mid-1960s, it sold a wide range of food products, including dairy products. In 1966, Tanzi learned of a new milk pasteurization process that had been developed in Sweden. Tanzi recognized that the new process, referred to as ultra-high-temperature (UHT) pasteurization, provided an opportunity to consolidate Italy's large but highly fragmented milk market. Within a short time, UHT milk became the primary product marketed by Tanzi's business. Tanzi would later rename his company Parmalat[3] to reflect the fact that his company was based in the Parma region of northwestern Italy and that the company's primary product was milk–the Italian term for milk is *latte*. (The most famous product of the Parma region is Parmesan cheese.)

Over the next quarter of a century, Parmalat grew rapidly. Although milk remained the company's principal product, Parmalat eventually began producing and selling fruit juices, baked goods, and many other food items. (Parmalat's best known brand in the United States was Archway Cookies.) In 1988, Tanzi successfully fought off a takeover attempt of Parmalat by the U.S.-based Kraft Foods. Two years later, he took the company public by listing its stock on the Milan Stock Exchange, Italy's largest securities market.

During the 1990s, Tanzi committed Parmalat to an aggressive acquisition program intended to make his company a major international food distributor. The program was successful. By 2003, the company had more than 36,000 employees and operations in more than 30 countries. Soon after he began marketing UHT milk, Tanzi had commented that he wanted his company to become the "Coca-Cola of milk" and that's exactly what the company became. By the turn of the century, an estimated 12 billion glasses of Parmalat milk were being consumed annually across the globe.

Parmalat's success made Tanzi one of the most recognized and respected individuals within Italy. Although he never ran for public office, Tanzi was an important leader and financial supporter of the Christian Democratic Party (*Democrazia Cristiana*) that dominated Italian politics for nearly five decades following World War II. Tanzi's principal political rival was Silvio Berlusconi. After the Christian Democratic Party collapsed amid a political scandal in the early 1990s, Berlusconi was

---

3. Parmalat Finanziaria S.p.A. was the umbrella name for the Parmalat organization. The company's principal operating subsidiary was Parmalat S.p.A., which was responsible for producing and distributing milk and dairy products. The "S.p.A." suffix identifies Italian corporations that are "joint stock companies," meaning that they are publicly owned.

chosen to serve as prime minister. The billionaire businessman and media magnate would eventually serve three non-consecutive terms as the nation's prime minister.[4]

Despite becoming a large, international conglomerate, Parmalat effectively remained a family-controlled business throughout the 40-plus years that Calisto Tanzi served as its top executive.[5] When Parmalat went public in 1990, Tanzi retained a 51 percent ownership interest in the company so that he and his family could control its operations.

Family-controlled businesses have long dominated Italy's economy. A prominent British publication suggests that the importance of the family unit in Italian society explains many unique features of Italian culture, including why "dynastic capitalism" is prevalent within the nation's economy. "The [family is the] enduring unit of Italian society. It explains the lack of public spirit in Italy. It explains the Mafia, the biggest family of them all. It also explains the pattern of business."[6]

Most of Parmalat's executives were members of Tanzi's extended family or, like Fausto Tonna, close friends of Tanzi from Collecchio that he had known most of his life. Parmalat's board of directors included his son Stefano, a brother, and a nephew. During his career with Parmalat, Stefano also held several senior management positions with the company.

Another method used by Calisto Tanzi to maintain control over Parmalat was to create what *The Wall Street Journal* referred to as a "secretive and labyrinthine"[7] organizational structure. By 2003, the company was an intricate web of more than 200 interlocking corporations and subsidiaries—including 20 finance companies—scattered around the globe. Parmalat's complex organizational structure served to thwart governmental oversight, which Tanzi, like most Italian entrepreneurs, deeply resented. *TIME Magazine*, for example, reported that Parmalat's "chaotic" organizational structure helped keep the "tax man at bay."[8]

To finance Parmalat's international expansion program during the 1990s and beyond, the company raised billions of dollars by selling bonds and by obtaining large bank loans. Between 1995 and 2003, the company floated 35 bond issues, including several that were marketed exclusively in the United States. By early 2003, many institutional investors and large investment firms, most notably Lehman Brothers and Merrill Lynch, were questioning why Parmalat needed to continue borrowing funds when its periodic balance sheets reported billions of dollars of unrestricted cash. In November 2003, Parmalat officials made the mistake of admitting to representatives of several Italian banks that their company would have difficulty paying off a small bond issue that was coming due. That candid admission triggered even more questions and rumors regarding the integrity of Parmalat's financial statements.

As Parmalat's liquidity crisis deepened, Calisto Tanzi swallowed his pride and traveled to Rome to pay a visit to his longtime nemesis, Prime Minister Berlusconi. During the private meeting, Tanzi apparently asked Berlusconi to intercede on Parmalat's

4. Berlusconi and Tanzi were also rivals in another arena. Berlusconi owned A.C. Milan, one of Italy's most successful professional soccer teams, while Tanzi's family owned Parma F.C., another popular Italian soccer team.

5. During most of his tenure at Parmalat, Tanzi was the chairman of the company's board of directors as well as its managing director, which is equivalent to being the chief executive officer (CEO) of a U.S. company.

6. P. Popham, "Calisto Tanzi: The Family Man Who Milked His Own Dairy Empire," *The Independent* (www.independent.co.uk), 3 January 2004.

7. A. Galloni and D. Reilly, "How Success Story at Parmalat Got A Very Sour Final Chapter," *The Wall Street Journal* (online), 21 December 2003.

8. P. Gumbel and J. Israely, "Enron, Italian Style," *TIME Magazine* (online), 12 January 2004.

behalf and arrange for emergency government loans or loan guarantees to keep the company afloat. Tanzi returned from his visit with Berlusconi empty handed. One month later, the worst fears of Parmalat's stockholders and creditors were realized when a Bank of America spokesperson revealed that $5 billion of cash that a Parmalat subsidiary supposedly had on deposit with the large bank was totally fictitious. That revelation caused Parmalat to file for bankruptcy and to be placed under the control of a government-appointed management team. A few days later, on December 27, 2003, Tanzi was indicted for fraud and arrested.

Parmalat's sudden downfall stunned Italian citizens and the world's investment community. Around the globe, the business press compared the company's implosion to that of U.S.-based Enron Corporation almost exactly two years earlier. Like Parmalat, Enron was a large and high-profile company whose senior executives were known for pioneering innovative business practices. An observation by a disillusioned Parmalat employee could have been made by one of Enron's thousands of employees who lost their jobs in late 2001 when their company disintegrated. "What is most incredible is to find out that a company you thought was so great was really a castle of cards."[9]

"An Amateurish Fraud"

In the late 1980s, Parmalat suffered large losses on an ill-planned and brief foray into television broadcasting. Tanzi failed miserably in his attempt to create an Italian television network that would compete with the networks controlled by Silvio Berlusconi. During this same period, Parmalat also sustained large operating losses on one of its earliest international ventures, a Brazilian subsidiary that it had established in the mid-1970s. Tanzi and Tonna realized that these losses, if reported, would make it difficult for Parmalat to raise the funds needed to finance its international expansion program. That realization goaded the two executives to conceal the losses by manipulating Parmalat's accounting records. Increasingly large losses by Parmalat's Brazilian subsidiary throughout the 1990s forced the conspirators to steadily expand the scope and magnitude of their fraudulent scheme.

The lynchpin of Parmalat's fraud was what became known in the business press as the "double-billing scheme." Tanzi, Tonna, and their co-conspirators used this ruse to generate billions of dollars of fictitious sales and receivables. Parmalat's accounting staff routinely processed two accounting entries for certain domestic (Italian) sales of dairy products. One of those entries recorded the legitimate sales revenue and account receivable produced by the given transaction, which typically involved a sale of milk to a supermarket or another retail outlet. The second accounting entry recorded a bogus sale to, and receivable from, the trucking or another distribution company that delivered the goods to the customer.

The secret to the success of the double-billing scheme was the fact that Parmalat owned many of the distribution companies that delivered its dairy products to customers—the subterfuge was not used when an independent distribution company delivered sales items. Parmalat's distribution companies were owned by subsidiaries that were shell corporations without any actual business operations. These shell corporations had been established for the express purpose of producing the bogus sales and receivables. The legal "nexus" or location of these corporate subsidiaries was typically a small offshore tax haven that had strict bank secrecy laws and lax regulatory oversight for corporations domiciled within its jurisdiction. These sites included, among others, the Cayman Islands, Malta, and the Netherlands Antilles.

---

9. Galloni and Reilly, "How Success Story at Parmalat Got a Very Sour Final Chapter."

The fictitious sales and receivables produced by the double-billing scheme significantly enhanced Parmalat's reported operating results and financial condition, which helped the company raise large amounts of debt capital through dozens of bond issues. Company management also used the bogus receivables as collateral for large bank loans. A Parmalat accountant subsequently testified that as many as 300 company employees either participated directly in the double-billing scheme or were aware of its existence.

Parmalat's fraudsters eventually began booking totally fictitious sales through the company's offshore subsidiaries. Among the most notorious of these transactions was a "sale" of more than 300,000 tons of powdered milk to the Cuban federal agency responsible for purchasing and distributing food imports in that Communist country. The conspirators also used an assortment of other accounting charades to window-dress Parmalat's financial statements. These gimmicks included processing bogus repurchases of outstanding debt to improve Parmalat's apparent solvency and liquidity, recording borrowed funds as equity investments, treating outstanding bank loans as intercompany loans that were then eliminated in period-ending consolidated financial statements, and simply failing to record the liabilities arising from bank loans.

Similar to Enron Corporation, Parmalat also created numerous special purpose entities or SPEs. Parmalat's executives used SPEs to "store" some of the company's fictitious assets in offshore subsidiaries. The company's most notorious SPE was entitled *Buconero*, which translates to "black hole" in Italian. The fraudsters chose that tongue-in-cheek name apparently as a light-hearted jab at Italian regulatory authorities that failed to uncover their colossal swindle.

In addition to the fraudulent accounting, Tanzi and his subordinates embezzled large sums from Parmalat. Prosecutors estimated that the conspirators stole more than one billion dollars of company assets over the course of the fraud. Most of those thefts involved simple transfers of cash to the conspirators from Parmalat bank accounts.

Parmalat's accounting staff diverted most of the bogus accounting data produced by the various fraudulent schemes to Account 999. The accountants then used that data during the consolidation process at the end of each accounting period to manufacture a set of consolidated financial statements that made Parmalat appear to be a thriving company. By late 2003, the majority of Parmalat's reported assets were a product of Account 999. One participant in the long-running fraud testified that the account served as a "trash bin for the fake revenues, assets, and profits that Parmalat had accumulated over the years."[10]

Although the Parmalat fraud was enormous in scope, involved hundreds of employees, and continued unabated for 15 years or more, many third parties found that its most shocking feature was its simplicity. Because the tactics used by the fraudsters to manipulate Parmalat's financial statements were neither innovative nor particularly complex, the business press maintained that the fraud should have been exposed easily and quickly. *TIME Magazine* captured this sentiment when it posed the simple question, "Why wasn't such an amateurish fraud detected earlier?"[11]

Within days of the Parmalat fraud being revealed, business journalists and other critics began suggesting that the scandal confirmed a widely held belief within the global investment community, namely, that Italy's system of corporate oversight was grossly deficient. Those same critics also derided the two international accounting

---

10. *In Re Parmalat Securities Litigation*, U.S. District Court, Southern District of New York, 18 October 2004, 12.

11. Gumbel and Israely, "Enron, Italian Style."

firms that had audited Parmalat's financial statements during most of the time the fraud went unchecked. Despite Italy's inadequate corporate oversight system, those critics insisted that had the two firms performed thorough audits of Parmalat and candidly reported the results of those audits, the fraud would have been uncovered years earlier.

Corporate Oversight, Italian Style

Shortly after the end of World War II, the monarchy that had ruled Italy since the nineteenth century was dissolved when King Umberto II was forced to abdicate.[12] A national referendum resulted in the creation of a new democracy, *Repubblica Italiana*, on January 1, 1948. Social unrest and economic problems plagued the new Italian republic over its first several decades. During that time frame, there was only limited federal oversight of the nation's economic system. That minimal government oversight, widespread corruption by government officials, and the pervasive influence of organized crime syndicates throughout the Italian economy undermined the confidence of domestic and foreign investors in the nation's capital markets.

During the 1970s, Italy placed a high priority on strengthening the credibility of its capital markets. Increasing foreign direct investment (FDI) was a primary objective of that initiative. Government officials realized that the Italian economy would prosper only if foreign companies invested considerable debt and equity capital in domestic businesses. In 1974, the Italian parliament created a new federal regulatory agency comparable to the Securities and Exchange Commission (SEC) in the United States. This agency, *Commissione Nazionale per le Societa e la Borsa,* is commonly referred to in Italy and elsewhere as Consob. Another important market reform was implemented in 1975. A new Italian law mandated that public companies have their annual financial statements audited by an independent accounting firm. Most of these companies had never been audited. Consob oversees the independent audit function within Italy and other facets of the financial reporting process for public companies.

Most large Italian companies must also have a "board of statutory auditors" or a similar oversight body. According to an Italian academic, statutory auditors are a "particularly Italian device" that serves as the "fundamental monitor inside the company." [13] The primary responsibilities of statutory auditors include monitoring the compliance of a company's executives with the organization's corporate bylaws and governmental regulations as well as periodically reviewing the adequacy of the company's internal controls—including its accounting system. Statutory auditors are in many ways analogous to audit committees within the United States. In fact, an Italian law that took effect in 2004 allows public companies to establish an audit committee in lieu of a board of statutory auditors. One responsibility of statutory auditors that is not shared with U.S. audit committees is issuing an annual audit report that is included in the given company's annual financial report. This audit report is in addition to that issued by the company's independent auditors.

Independent auditors within Italy have essentially the same responsibilities as independent auditors within the United States. One minor difference is that Italian auditors must determine whether client financial statements have been prepared

---

12. Although technically a monarchy, Italy was effectively ruled by the fascist military leader Benito Mussolini from 1922 through 1943. Mussolini plunged Italy into World War II when he aligned the country with Nazi Germany and declared war against the Allied Forces.

13. A. Melis, "Corporate Governance Failures: To What Extent Is Parmalat A Particularly Italian Case?" *Corporate Governance* 13 (July 2005), 480.

in accordance with International Financial Reporting Standards (IFRS) rather than U.S. generally accepted accounting principles (GAAP). Since January 1, 2005, Italian companies have been required to apply IFRS.

Italy was the first country in the European Union (EU) to require companies to rotate their auditors. An Italian company can appoint an independent audit firm for a maximum of three three-year terms. Once an independent auditor has been appointed, neither the auditor nor the client can terminate the relationship before the completion of the three-year term except under extraordinary circumstances, such as professional misconduct by the auditor.

To serve as the independent auditor of a publicly owned Italian company, an accounting firm must first register with Consob. The federal agency is charged with monitoring the quality of independent audits performed by registered accounting firms. If Consob determines that an accounting firm's audits are deficient, the agency can prohibit that firm from auditing public companies in the future or can impose other sanctions or remedies on the firm that it deems appropriate. Following the Parmalat scandal, critics claimed that Consob's oversight of Italy's independent audit function was inadequate. Those critics suggested that if Consob had rigorously exercised its oversight responsibilities, it would have discovered that Parmalat's independent auditors had been derelict in auditing the company's annual financial statements.

Independent Audits, Italian Style

The audit market for large public companies in Italy is controlled by the Big Four accounting firms. The Italian affiliates of those firms audit more than 95 percent of all Italian companies that are required to be audited by Consob or by other governmental mandates.[14] When Parmalat went public in 1990, the company retained the Italian affiliate of Grant Thornton, an international accounting firm but not a Big Four firm, to serve as its independent auditor.[15]

Because Italy's auditor rotation rule limits the tenure of an auditor to a maximum of nine years with any given client, Parmalat management was forced to appoint an accounting firm to replace Grant Thornton in 1999. At that point, the company chose the Italian affiliate of Deloitte & Touche to serve as its independent auditor. Deloitte was Parmalat's auditor when the company's accounting fraud was exposed in late December 2003. In 2004, Parmalat's new government-appointed management team chose PricewaterhouseCoopers (PwC) to serve as the company's independent auditor.

The need to change auditors in 1999 posed a major inconvenience and potentially serious problem for Tanzi and Tonna. Why? Because they realized it was unlikely that the replacement auditor would be as accommodating as Grant Thornton. During a subsequent criminal trial, a senior member of Parmalat's Grant Thornton audit team confessed that as early as 1997 he was aware that there was a large "hole"[16] in the company's accounting records. That hole was a large amount of non existent assets being reported in the company's periodic balance sheets. When the auditor brought this matter to the attention of Tonna, the CFO convinced him that the "hole would be filled in three years"[17] by Parmalat's profitable operations. Tonna's argument apparently persuaded the Grant Thornton auditor not to pull the plug on the fraud.

14. "Italy Survey: Recession Strikes Profession," *World Accounting Intelligence* (www.worldaccountingintelligence.com), April 2009.

15. In 1990, there were actually six major international accounting firms known at the time as the "Big Six." A subsequent merger and the demise of Andersen & Co. created the "Big Four."

16. S. Taub, "'I Warned Parmalat CFO': Ex-Auditor," *CFO.com*, 25 January 2008.

17. *Ibid.*

As the 1999 deadline for Parmalat to replace Grant Thornton approached, Tonna approved a plan to conceal the ongoing accounting fraud from the new auditor by exploiting a loophole in the auditor rotation rule. That rule requires Italian companies to rotate their primary auditor every nine years but allows them to retain the former primary auditor in a secondary role. The new primary auditor must issue the audit opinion on the client's consolidated financial statements, but the former primary auditor–or any other audit firm for that matter–can audit up to 49 percent of the consolidated entity's reported assets and related financial statement amounts. Tonna's plan was to retain Grant Thornton as the auditor for Parmalat's offshore subsidiaries that were the source of nearly all the fraudulent accounting data, while the new auditor would audit Parmalat's real operations.[18]

During a criminal trial in which he was a primary defendant, Fausto Tonna testified that Parmalat's Grant Thornton auditors not only were aware of the company's accounting fraud but actively participated in it. According to Tonna, Grant Thornton had helped Parmalat organize several of the offshore subsidiaries that played a major role in the fraud and had been aware of the large bogus transaction involving the sale of powdered milk to a Cuban federal agency. Likewise, senior members of the Grant Thornton audit team had supposedly warned Tonna that Parmalat's replacement auditor would uncover the fraudulent schemes being perpetrated through the offshore subsidiaries. The Grant Thornton auditors allegedly helped Tonna develop the plan to conceal those scams from the replacement auditor and to conceal their (Grant Thornton's) involvement in them.

Despite the measures taken to prevent the new Deloitte audit team from discovering Parmalat's huge fraud, several parties believed that Deloitte quickly uncovered the fraud after being appointed the company's primary auditor in 1999. The parties most vocal in claiming that Deloitte auditors had promptly uncovered the fraud were attorneys representing plaintiffs that had filed civil lawsuits against Deloitte. Those attorneys claimed that once Deloitte detected the fraud, the firm failed to take the appropriate steps to end it, which would have included reporting the matter to Consob.[19] Criminal prosecutors also charged that the Deloitte auditors were aware of the fraud well before late 2003 when it was publicly disclosed.

Critics of the Deloitte auditors contended that even if they had not been explicitly aware of the Parmalat fraud, Deloitte had been reckless in auditing the company. One of Parmalat's subsidiaries that frequently posed contentious accounting and financial reporting issues was the large and financially troubled Brazilian subsidiary that Parmalat had established in the mid-1970s. Shortly after Deloitte became Parmalat's primary auditor, the accounting firm's Brazilian affiliate that audited that subsidiary began questioning the accuracy of its accounting records. In particular, Deloitte's affiliate questioned the authenticity of a $500 million intercompany receivable owed to the Brazilian subsidiary by Parmalat's Cayman Islands subsidiary.[20]

---

18. Tonna initially asked PwC to replace Grant Thornton as Parmalat's primary auditor in 1999. However, PwC officials refused to accept the engagement. Those officials later reported that although they realized the arrangement suggested by Tonna would comply with Italy's auditor rotation rule, they believed it would be difficult to coordinate the large audit with Grant Thornton.

19. During early 2003, Consob inquired of Deloitte regarding several suspicious items in Parmalat's financial statements. Allegedly, Deloitte was less than candid in responding to the regulatory agency regarding those matters.

20. Criminal investigators would later determine that this subsidiary, which was one of Parmalat's many offshore shell corporations, played a central role in the long-running fraud.

Near the conclusion of the 2002 Parmalat audit, the audit engagement partner for the Brazilian affiliate threatened to issue a qualified opinion on the Brazilian subsidiary's financial statements, a threat he had also made the previous year. Parmalat's top management was very concerned by the possibility that the Brazilian subsidiary would receive a qualified opinion. Near the end of the 2002 audit, the audit engagement partner for the Brazilian subsidiary was removed from that engagement. Subsequent testimony suggested that a top official of Deloitte's global firm, Deloitte Touche Tohmatsu (DTT), reassigned that individual after being pressured to do so by Parmalat executives.

Deloitte vigorously defended itself from the allegations that its audits of Parmalat had been reckless or worse. Deloitte's primary defense was that it had relied almost exclusively on Grant Thornton to audit the Parmalat subsidiaries through which the bulk of the fraudulent schemes were perpetrated. "In relation to the above-mentioned amounts [the fraudulent financial statement data for Parmalat's offshore subsidiaries] Deloitte & Touche stated that their opinion was based solely upon other auditors' [Grant Thornton's] reports."[21]

The tangled knot of criminal and civil lawsuits spawned by the disclosure of the Parmalat fraud was comparable in most respects to the litigation prompted by major accounting frauds in the United States. However, a legal issue that is critically important to international accounting firms but that does not surface in most litigation cases involving those firms did become a major focus of attention in the Parmalat litigation. This issue was whether or not each member of those firms' global practice networks could be held liable for the malfeasance of any one of their members. This issue is particularly important to the U.S. affiliates of international accounting firms since they are easily the most financially robust of those firms' global practice units. These U.S. affiliates would face potentially devastating legal exposure if they were routinely held liable for the malfeasance of the other affiliates of their firms' global practice networks. In the Parmalat case, one lawsuit alone sought damages exceeding more than $10 billion from both Deloitte and Grant Thornton, a huge amount for even the most deep-pocketed members of the fraternity of international accounting firms.

Global Partners? Maybe, Maybe Not

The origin of each of the major international accounting firms can be traced to a single practice office in the United Kingdom or the United States. Deloitte was founded in London in 1845 by 27-year-old William Welch Deloitte, who is believed to be the first individual ever retained to serve as a company's independent auditor.[22] In 1924, 26-year-old Alexander Richardson Grant created Alexander Grant & Co. in Chicago, the accounting firm that would evolve into Grant Thornton. These two firms along with the predecessors of the other prominent international accounting firms developed large and profitable professional practices in their home countries that specialized in providing accounting, auditing, taxation, and business consulting services. During the early to mid-twentieth century, these firms expanded their operations into other countries, most notably Canada and several nations in Western Europe.

Following World War II, a market for the professional services offered by the multinational accounting firms developed in every major country of the world, including China, India, Japan, and Russia. As the global economy expanded and third-world countries began engaging in international commerce, these firms moved into those markets as well. By the turn of the century, the professional practices of all the Big

---

21. Melis, "Corporate Governance Failures," 483.

22. In 1849, the Great Western Railway Company retained Deloitte to audit its accounting records.

Four firms as well as Grant Thornton were truly international in scope. Each of these firms currently operates in more than 100 countries.

International accounting firms typically dominate the markets that they have entered. In fact, there are only a few examples where domestic accounting firms have market shares that rival those of the international accounting firms that have made a significant commitment to establishing a professional practice in their countries.

Two key factors allowed a handful of accounting firms to come to dominate the global market for accounting and related professional services. Arguably the most important of these factors was the brand name and accompanying reputation for competence and professionalism that each of these firms had developed in the United States and/or the United Kingdom. This factor gave Deloitte, the other Big Four firms, and a few non-Big Four firms, most notably Grant Thornton, a critical advantage when competing against "home-grown" or domestic accounting firms. In addition, these firms enjoyed economies of scale that allowed them to deliver high-quality professional services at a more reasonable cost than smaller domestic firms in individual countries.

In their global marketing campaigns, the major accounting firms presented themselves as unitary organizations that provided the same quality and types of professional services worldwide. To reinforce their image as unified, worldwide firms and to promote cooperation between and among their individual national practice units, Deloitte, Grant Thornton, and their peers established umbrella global entities. At the time that the Parmalat scandal surfaced, Grant Thornton International (GTI) was the entity representing Grant Thornton's global practice network, while DTT was the global entity that tied together the worldwide practice network of Deloitte.

The efforts of international accounting firms to present themselves as unified worldwide organizations have backfired in one respect. A growing number of plaintiffs in civil lawsuits filed against those firms have named the given firm's entire global organization as a defendant. In such cases, the plaintiff legal counsel attempts to hold the accounting firm's global entity and each of its national practice units jointly and severally liable for any legal judgment awarded by the court. This legal tactic is most commonly employed when the relevant audit client is a multinational company and when the national practice unit that is the primary defendant does not have sufficient resources to cover the potential judgment.

Until recently, most courts quickly dismissed an international accounting firm's global organization as a defendant in civil lawsuits involving specific practice units of those firms. According to a legal scholar, the global organizations of accounting firms have been dismissed as defendants in such cases principally because the plaintiff attorneys did not fully develop their "one firm" arguments.[23] That is, those attorneys failed to convince the given court that the defendant accounting firm was, in fact, a unified global entity.

Many of the Parmalat civil lawsuits were filed in U.S. courts because some of the fraudulent misconduct took place in the United States and/or because Parmalat, Deloitte, and Grant Thornton each had a legal nexus within the United States. Plaintiffs in certain of these lawsuits named not only the Italian practice units of Deloitte and Grant Thornton as defendants but those firms' entire global organizations as well. Ostensibly, this decision was made because the Italian affiliates of Deloitte and Grant Thornton were relatively small and faced potential legal judgments in Parmalat-related lawsuits that could easily bankrupt them. Unlike earlier cases, the plaintiff attorneys

---

23. L. E. Delo, "In Re Parmalat Securities Litigation: The Dawn of 'One Firm' International Accounting Liability," Delo & Bowers, LLP, Portland, Oregon, 13 February 2006.

in these lawsuits laid out comprehensive and coherent "one firm" arguments as to why the global organizations of both Deloitte and Grant Thornton were properly included as defendants.

In contesting these lawsuits, attorneys for both Deloitte and Grant Thornton faced the awkward task of arguing that the firms were not unified global businesses. This was an awkward assignment because for decades the two firms had included statements in promotional materials and other documents claiming that they were integrated global organizations. While largely ignoring such statements, the two firms' legal defense teams attempted to convince the courts that the firms were loosely knit worldwide confederations, the individual practice units of which were "all legally separate and independent companies."[24]

The two firms' attorneys also used a second and relatively novel argument in their efforts to have the Deloitte and Grant Thornton global organizations dismissed as defendants in the U.S.-based Parmalat civil lawsuits. This largely philosophical argument was based upon a utilitarian point of view. The firms' attorneys maintained that holding international accounting firms jointly and severally liable for the misdeeds of their individual practice units could eventually "imperil the capital markets"[25] by driving those firms out of business. Because only the international accounting firms have the resources and expertise to properly audit large multinational companies, the confidence of investors and creditors worldwide in those companies' financial statements would be undermined, which, in turn, would destabilize global capital markets.

Plaintiff legal counsel insisted that Deloitte and Grant Thornton were, in fact, unitary global businesses and should be treated as such by the courts. Among the most obvious indications that each firm was a single global entity was the fact that they issued annual consolidated financial reports for their global organizations.

The plaintiff attorneys also presented evidence that Deloitte and Grant Thornton had worldwide "integrated professional structures"[26,27] that required each national practice unit to adopt uniform operating policies and procedures. For example, in a document filed with the SEC, the CEO of DTT described a new global ethics and compliance program that would be imposed throughout DTT's global organization. In referring to the implementation of that program, the CEO noted that "[this] is a vast effort for an organization with 120,000 people in 150 nations."[28] The plaintiff legal counsel also presented evidence that DTT and GTI routinely made important decisions for individual national practice units involving risk management issues and legal matters. DTT, for example, requires each national practice unit to purchase a specified amount of professional liability insurance and prohibits individual practice units from suing each other.

Among the strongest evidence used to establish that DTT and GTI exercised an important measure of control over their individual practice units was the manner in

---

24. *Ibid.*

25. *Ibid.*

26. *Ibid.*

27. The umbrella global entities of the international accounting firms have different legal structures. DTT, for example, for decades was organized as a Swiss *verein*. "*Verein*" is a German term for "union." Essentially, a Swiss *verein* is (supposedly) a voluntary association of individual businesses or not-for-profit organizations. DTT was arguably the best known *verein* worldwide. In late 2010, DTT reorganized its global legal structure. The organization is no longer a Swiss *verein* but now operates as a "private company" under the laws of the United Kingdom.

28. *In Re Parmalat Securities Litigation*, U.S. District Court, Southern District of New York, 18 October 2004, 54.

which each responded to the initial reports of the Parmalat fraud. Shortly after the fraud was revealed, DTT reported that it planned to "vigorously defend"[29] the individual auditors of its Italian practice unit that faced criminal charges for their role in the fraud. On the other hand, GTI expelled its Italian practice unit within two weeks following the first public report of the fraud. Although DTT and GTI responded very differently in dealing with their Italian practice units, the reaction of each suggested that they had a strong agency relationship with those units and a dominating influence on their operations.

In 2005 and 2009, Judge Lewis Kaplan, a federal judge in a Manhattan U.S. District Court, issued separate rulings addressing the "one firm" arguments made by attorneys representing plaintiffs that had filed Parmalat-related lawsuits against Deloitte and Grant Thornton. In each of his rulings, Judge Kaplan concluded that the plaintiffs' arguments were reasonable and that the global organizations of the two firms would remain defendants in the given lawsuits. A legal scholar suggested that Judge Kaplan's 2005 ruling might very well serve as the "dawn" of "one firm international accounting liability."[30] Judge Kaplan's comparable ruling in 2009 prompted another legal commentator to observe that "In essence, Judge Kaplan has said that the parent can't hide from the misdeeds of its children."[31]

Following Judge Kaplan's initial ruling in 2005, the senior executives of Deloitte, Grant Thornton, and four other international accounting firms issued a joint report entitled "Serving Global Markets and the Global Economy." In that report, the senior executives warned, "Our firms are not and can never be the insurers of last resort for the capital markets."[32] The executives went on to suggest that their firms needed to be able to enforce consistent policies within their global networks without facing the enormous legal risks that would be posed by "making all the firms in a network liable"[33] for errors made by one of the member firms.

EPILOGUE

Claudio Pessina refused to destroy his computer as his superior had ordered. Prosecutors would later use many of the files on that computer, particularly those files relating to Account 999, to reconstruct key details of the Parmalat fraud and to develop the evidence they needed to file criminal charges against dozens of individuals involved in the fraud.

Three criminal trials were held in Italy for the defendants indicted for having some role in the Parmalat fraud. The most common charges filed against the defendants included false accounting, market rigging, obstructing an investigation of a government agency (Consob), and conspiring to issue false information to investors. Because of Italy's extremely lenient criminal sentencing guidelines, most of the Parmalat defendants avoided prison sentences after being convicted. Under Italian law, prison sentences of two years or less are suspended, while a defendant who receives a sentence of two to three years is placed on probation and

---

29. D. Reilly, "Deloitte Touche Vows to Defend Partners in Parmalat Case," *Dow Jones Business News* (online), 2 March 2004.

30. Delo, *In Re Parmalat Securities Litigation.*

31. A. Longstreth, "Auditors Beware: Judge Kaplan Allows Parmalat Suit Against Deloitte to Move Forward," *The AM Law Litigation Daily* (www.law.com), 28 January 2009.

32. F. Norris, "A Report by the World's Largest Auditors Urges Relaxed Standards for Liability," *The New York Times* (online), 8 November 2006.

33. *Ibid.*

required to do community service. If a criminal defendant is lucky enough to be 70 years old or older when he or she is convicted, the individual's sentence is typically waived.

In 2005, Fausto Tonna, Parmalat's former CFO, was convicted and given a 30-month prison sentence, meaning that the prison sentence would be converted to community service. Three years later, in December 2008, Calisto Tanzi was sentenced to 10 years for his role in the Parmalat fraud. Because Tanzi had reached the "lucky" age of 70 one month earlier, it was very unlikely that he would serve that sentence even if the appeal of his conviction was denied. In commenting on Italy's leniency toward individuals convicted of financial crimes, a British journalist questioned what incentive Italian business executives have to be honest. "All right to cheat? In Italy, it seems, you'd be crazy not to."[34]

Two of the senior Deloitte auditors assigned to the Parmalat engagements received 18-month prison sentences for their roles in the scandal, while the senior member of Parmalat's board of statutory auditors received a 20-month prison sentence. One of the harshest penalties handed down to a criminal defendant in the Parmalat case was a nine-year sentence given to a Grant Thornton partner who had been involved in several of the Parmalat audits during the 1990s. An Italian court also fined Grant Thornton's former Italian affiliate €240,000.

Similar to the civil litigation prompted by other accounting frauds, most of the civil lawsuits stemming from the Parmalat fraud were settled out of court. In January 2007, a Deloitte spokesperson announced that the firm had agreed to pay $149 million to settle a lawsuit filed against it by Parmalat's former bondholders. Ironically, two years later, Judge Kaplan dismissed those same bondholders' claims against Grant Thornton when he ruled that the bondholders' losses were due principally to the misconduct of Parmalat's management rather than any malfeasance by Grant Thornton auditors.

In late 2009, DTT and GTI agreed to pay a total of $15 million to settle lawsuits pending against them by U.S. citizens who had suffered losses on investments in Parmalat securities. An attorney for the plaintiffs observed, "It is very rare that worldwide coordinating audit networks enter into settlements like what we have."[35] These settlements only added to the perception that the global organizations of international accounting firms are facing an increased risk of joint and several liability for the wrongdoing of their individual practice units.

Recall that Prime Minister Silvio Berlusconi had refused to intercede on Parmalat's behalf when asked to do so by Calisto Tanzi. When Parmalat faced almost certain bankruptcy in late December 2003, however, Berlusconi publicly stated that he would not allow the iconic company to be liquidated. A government bailout plan and a new management team headed up by the individual originally appointed to serve as Parmalat's bankruptcy administrator saved the company from that fate. The new management team sold off many of Parmalat's foreign subsidiaries and refocused most of the company's resources and strategic initiatives on its line of dairy products. By 2006, the reincarnated Parmalat was posting modest operating profits and had listed its common stock for trading on the Milan Stock Exchange.

Questions

1. Identify key factors or circumstances that complicate an independent audit of a multinational company.

2. What audit procedures would likely have been the most effective for detecting Parmalat's fraudulent double-billing scheme? Defend your choices.

---

34. *The Economist* (online), "Why Not Let Everyone Off? Italy and the Law," 29 July 2006.

35. J. Stempel, "Ex-Parmalat Auditors Settle U.S. Investor Lawsuit," *Reuters* (online), 19 November 2009.

3. Identify the fraud risk factors that were present during the Parmalat audits. Rank order these risk factors from the most important to the least important. Be prepared to defend your rank ordering.

4. According to generally accepted auditing standards (GAAS), how should the responsibility for performing "shared audits" be allocated to the accounting firms involved in such engagements?

5. Do you believe that the individual national practice units of international accounting firms' global networks should face joint and several liability? Defend your answer.

6. Cultural norms and nuances affect the operations of large companies worldwide. Identify examples of distinctive cultural norms and nuances specific to three countries. Explain how these cultural traits likely impact the independent audits of companies in each of those countries.

7. Identify the advantages and disadvantages of mandatory audit firm rotation. What, if any, auditor rotation rules are in effect in the United States?

8. Both Deloitte and Grant Thornton were named as defendants in a class-action lawsuit filed by Parmalat's bondholders. Deloitte agreed to pay $149 million to settle the lawsuit, while Grant Thornton chose to contest the lawsuit and was ultimately dismissed as a defendant. Identify the factors that accounting firms should consider in deciding how to deal with a pending lawsuit.

Kansayaku

Kokai saki ni tatazu [repentance never comes first]

Japanese proverb

Satoshi Hirata served on the audit staff of Asahi, one of Japan's four largest public accounting firms.[1] Like its three principal rivals, Asahi was affiliated with one of the Big Four international accounting firms, namely, KPMG. Throughout the spring of 2003, Hirata had been assigned to the audit of Resona, a large metropolitan bank. The bank was being audited jointly by Asahi and Shin Nihon, the Japanese affiliate of Ernst & Young. On April 24, 2003, after completing his work for the day on the Resona engagement, Satoshi Hirata returned to his 12-story apartment building in central Tokyo, went to the roof of that building, and leaped to his death.

Disloyal Auditors

Although Satoshi Hirata did not leave a note explaining his decision to take his life, law enforcement authorities subsequently learned that the young auditor was distressed by his job. At the time, Resona and Japan's other major banks were experiencing major financial problems. For well over a decade, Japan's handful of "megabanks" had routinely embellished their reported financial health by, among other means, refusing to provide adequate reserves for their expected loan losses. In the spring of 2003, Resona's financial condition had deteriorated to the point that its independent auditors doubted the bank could survive without a large infusion of capital from another bank or the federal government.

Hirata, one of the subordinate auditors on Resona's joint team of Asahi and Shin Nihon auditors, knew that Resona was technically insolvent and had been for years despite the fact the bank had received unqualified audit opinions each year on its annual financial statements. Hirata was apparently concerned that his superiors would issue a similar opinion at the conclusion of the audit to which he was assigned. According to one newspaper report, Mr. Hirata's suicide was intended as a "dramatic gesture to persuade his seniors that Japan could no longer afford to keep covering over the cracks."[2] The "cracks" referred to in this quotation were the huge and unreported financial problems facing Resona and Japan's other major banks.

Following Mr. Hirata's death, Asahi withdrew from the Resona audit engagement. Asahi's resignation meant that Shin Nihon would be forced to decide the large bank's future. Resona's president, Yasuhisa Katsuta, a prominent political power broker in Japan, never doubted that Shin Nihon would give his bank a clean bill of health. But he was wrong. When the Shin Nihon auditors insisted that the bank seek outside financing to remedy its financial problems, Katsuta accused them of "betraying" his firm.[3] A few days after the auditors refused to give Resona an unqualified audit opinion, Japan's federal government announced that an emergency infusion of government funds equivalent to $17 billion was necessary to rescue the bank from

---

1. *"Kansayaku"* is a generic term for "inspector" or "auditor" in the Japanese language.
2. M. Nakamoto and D. Pilling, "Resona's Downfall," *Financial Times*, 13 June 2003, 11.
3. *Ibid.*

imminent bankruptcy. To fully understand Mr. Katsuta's reaction to Shin Nihon's decision, it is necessary to study the history of Japan's banking system and its independent audit function.

Okurasho

By the end of World War II, Japan's economy was practically destroyed. Over the following five years, General Douglas MacArthur of the U. S. Army supervised the post-war occupation of Japan by the Allied Powers. In carrying out his mission to convert the Japanese nation into a democracy and to establish a free market economic system within the country, General MacArthur largely succeeded in his attempt to dismantle Japan's ancient political and economic infrastructure. But one important feature of that infrastructure, the secretive and powerful Okurasho, was left largely unscathed by General MacArthur's purge.

From the seventh century A.D. through World War II, the Okurasho or "great storehouse ministry" was responsible for overseeing the economic development and well-being of the Japanese nation. Often referred to by political insiders as the "ministry of ministries," the Okurasho was a tightly knit group of powerful and wealthy individuals who advised the Japanese emperor on all major economic decisions facing the country and who effectively controlled the nation's banking system. In the Japanese economy, the banking system has historically been very powerful because the principal source of funds for private businesses has been debt rather than equity capital. The Okurasho also played a major role in overseeing Japan's stock market when it became a significant factor in the Japanese economy during the twentieth century.

Because senior members of the Okurasho chose each successive generation of the organization's leaders, the organization was self-perpetuating. In fact, the individuals who controlled the organization pressured their children to marry only members of other Okurasho families. Because General MacArthur was unaware of the Okurasho's far-reaching influence within Japan's social structure and economic system, members of the clandestine organization resurfaced following World War II and quickly took control of the Ministry of Finance (MOF), the government agency that would be responsible for managing the country's economy when the post-war occupation of Japan ended.

Despite the democratic political system imposed on Japan by General MacArthur, the country's elected officials had only minimal input into the post-war economic policies established by the MOF. Few of those officials ever questioned the MOF's heavy-handed, if not authoritarian, policies since those policies were responsible for the rapid modernization and recovery of the Japanese economy following World War II. Within four decades, the MOF's policies created the second-largest economy in the world and produced a level of economic prosperity surpassed only by the U.S. economy.

During the 1990s, President Clinton frequently criticized the MOF for its protectionist international trade policies that resulted in the United States having a huge and unfavorable trade imbalance with Japan. President Clinton charged that the secretive agency prevented Japan from becoming a "fully modern state with fair and open trade."[4] A *Business Week* report provided a similarly blunt assessment of the MOF's role in Japan's economy. "Japan's Ministry of Finance is much more than an office of

---

4. *BusinessWeek* (online), "The Ministry: How Japan's Most Powerful Institution Endangers World Markets," 25 September 2006.

government. It is a political, economic, and intellectual force without parallel in the developed world. It enjoys a greater concentration of powers, formal and informal, than any comparable body in any other industrialized democracy. In Japan, there is no institution with more power."[5]

By the early 1990s, Japan faced its first major financial crisis since World War II. Various economic factors and conditions prevented Japan from sustaining the impressive growth that it had experienced over the previous decades. Suddenly, Japan's economy faced many of the same problems that have frequently plagued the U.S. economy over the past century: volatile interest rates, inflation, and surging unemployment. These problems caused Japan's stock market to decline sharply and eventually led to a startling number of business failures.

The large number of business failures during the 1990s produced huge losses in the loan portfolios of the major metropolitan banks that were the principal source of Japan's investment capital. However, the extent of the loan losses was not reported in the audited financial statements released periodically by those banks. Pressure applied by MOF officials on the auditors of Japan's large banks resulted in those banks receiving clean audit opinions despite their massive financial problems. Eventually, both the MOF and the nation's major accounting firms would be held responsible for the huge government bailouts that were necessary to rescue Resona and other large Japanese banks.

Japan's Independent Audit Function

A small number of large accounting firms have dominated Japan's accounting profession and independent audit function since World War II. In turn, the MOF effectively controlled those large accounting firms over most of that time frame, wielding power over them similar to the power that it wielded over the nation's major banks. In 1998, the founder of one of Japan's major accounting firms told a U.S. journalist that the large government agency "really controls the accounting profession in Japan."[6] So complete was the MOF's control of the accounting profession that it reportedly hand-picked the individuals who were to serve in key executive positions at the country's largest accounting firms. In the late 1990s, the chief executives of four of Japan's six largest accounting firms had previously worked in some capacity with the MOF. The close ties between the MOF and the major accounting firms meant that the top executives of those firms routinely kowtowed to the wishes and demands of MOF officials.

Japan's public accounting profession is much smaller than that of the United States. In the United States, there is one CPA for approximately every 800 citizens, while in Japan there is one CPA for approximately every 9,600 citizens. In fact, Japan has fewer CPAs per capita by far than any other major industrialized country. The relatively small number of CPAs in Japan is due, in large part, to the historically onerous requirements for becoming a CPA in that nation. Until 2006, CPA candidates in Japan were required to pass three rigorous examinations and serve a three-year internship with an accounting firm before they could become a CPA.

The large accounting firms in Japan that dominate the nation's accounting profession also audit the great majority of the country's public companies, large private companies, and other important organizations in the private and public sector. Approximately 10,000 Japanese companies must be audited each year, including the approximately

5. *Ibid.*

6. L. Berton, "Japanese Accounting Bites Back," *Accounting Today* (online), 9 November 1998.

4,000 companies that have securities listed on public stock exchanges. The remaining companies that must be audited include unlisted corporations that have total capital exceeding 500 million yen and corporations that receive government subsidies.

Similar to the United States, the number of major accounting firms within Japan has been declining in recent years, principally due to mergers. By 2006, Japan's Big Four included ChuoAoyama–an affiliate of PricewaterhouseCoopers, Deloitte Touche Tohmatsu, Ernst & Young Shin Nihon, and KPMG AZSA & Co. The latter firm was created in 2004 when Asahi, the firm that employed Satoshi Hirata, merged with another large Japanese accounting firm.

The nature, purpose, and structure of independent audits are generally very similar in Japan and the United States. However, there is one significant difference. Audit fees in Japan are dramatically lower than in the United States. The audit fee for a large Japanese company is generally one-tenth of the fee for a similar U.S. company. The much smaller audit fees charged by Japanese accounting firms impose severe restraints on the scope of independent audits and result in audit services being considerably less profitable for Japanese accounting firms than for their U.S. counterparts.

In the United States, the business press, financial analysts, and regulatory authorities maintain that an absence of auditor independence was a key factor that contributed to the series of high-profile audit failures of such companies as Enron, WorldCom, and Adelphia Communications, among others. Allegedly, the long tenure of auditors with their clients, personal relationships between individual auditors and client personnel, and the large consulting fees that clients paid their auditors for nonaudit services made it difficult for audit firms to objectively report on major clients' financial statements. However, parties familiar with auditing practices and norms around the world insist that Japanese auditors have historically had much closer ties to their clients than auditors in any other country, including the United States.

The cordial relationship between Japanese auditors and their clients is at least partially a cultural phenomenon because the Japanese business community "emphasizes relationships and harmonious working practices."[7] A critic of the Japanese public accounting profession suggested that this cultural norm results in Japanese auditors subordinating their judgment to the wishes or demands of their clients. "Even when corporate clients ask the auditors to do something that isn't allowed under the law, they just do it."[8]

By the late 1990s, Japan's independent audit function faced a growing credibility crisis. "In the late 1990s, problems with the current audit system started coming to light–exposed by a series of deplorable events at many corporations, including fraudulent accounting and the abrupt failure of financial institutions once considered healthy."[9] Worsening that credibility crisis was the fact that the principal regulatory authority for the public accounting profession, the MOF, rarely imposed sanctions of any kind on auditors who had failed to fulfill their professional responsibilities. In 1999, the MOF revoked a CPA's license to practice for the first time in more than 20 years.

Mounting frustration with the MOF's failure to take measures to strengthen Japan's independent audit function was one of several factors that resulted in the powerful agency being stripped of much of its regulatory authority near the turn of the century. The MOF lost even more of its authority following the election of Junichiro Koizumi as Japan's prime minister in 2001. The reform-minded Koizumi hoped to revitalize

---

7. D. Reilly and A. Morse, "Japan Leans On Auditors to Be More Independent," *post-gazette.com*, 18 May 2006.

8. *Ibid.*

9. *The Yomiuri Shimbun* (online), "CPA–Client Collusion Must Be Severed," 10 August 2006.

Japan's stagnant economy by enhancing the "transparency" of the nation's capital markets. To accomplish that objective, Koizumi realized that the arcane regulatory structure for those markets had to be overhauled.

Under Prime Minister Koizumi's leadership, a new federal agency, the Financial Services Agency (FSA), assumed most of the responsibility for monitoring Japan's capital markets–including the nation's banking and financial reporting systems. To assist the FSA in overseeing the independent audit function and accounting profession, the new federal agency was placed in charge of the newly created Certified Public Accountants and Auditing Oversight Board (CPAAOB), which is comparable to the Public Company Accounting and Oversight Board (PCAOB) in the United States. To police the securities markets, another new federal agency, the Securities and Exchange Surveillance Commission, was established and placed under the FSA's control.

In 2004, Japan's federal legislative body, the Diet, rewrote the Certified Public Accountants Law. A major purpose of revising this law was to increase the number of CPAs in Japan. Among other changes, the revised law requires CPA candidates to pass only one examination rather than three to become a CPA. The national organization of CPAs, the Japanese Institute of Certified Public Accountants (JICPA), also adopted a series of measures to strengthen the profession, many of which focused on the independent audit function. Among these latter measures was prohibiting independent auditors from having any direct financial interest in a public client. Previously, auditors of public companies had been allowed to own a limited number of shares of a public client's outstanding stock.

The first major test of Japan's new regulatory structure for the accounting profession and independent audit function was posed by a financial scandal involving a large manufacturing company, Kanebo, Ltd. The nation's business press often refers to the Kanebo fiasco as "Japan's Enron."[10]

Kanebo, Ltd: Japan's Enron

The Tokyo Cotton Trading Company was founded in 1887 on the banks of the Sumida River that flows through Tokyo. Over the following decades, the company became a large and prosperous textile and apparel manufacturer–only to have its operating facilities totally destroyed during World War II. With the help of significant bank loans, the company, renamed Kanebo, Ltd., resumed operations on a much smaller scale in the late 1940s. By the late 1990s, the company ranked among Japan's largest public corporations. Kanebo's principal operations included the manufacture and sale of a long line of cosmetics, apparel, textiles, pharmaceuticals, toiletries, and food products.

In July 2005, Japanese law enforcement authorities arrested three former Kanebo executives, including Takashi Hoashi, the company's former president. The three individuals were charged with violating the Securities and Exchange Law, the principal federal statute that established the regulatory framework for Japan's securities markets, a statute comparable to the federal securities laws passed by the U.S. Congress in the early 1930s. Allegedly, the former Kanebo executives conspired to conceal their company's deteriorating financial health beginning in the 1990s. Throughout the time frame that the fraud was being perpetrated, Kanebo's audited financial statements indicated that the company was in reasonably good financial condition. However, a criminal investigation revealed that the company was hopelessly insolvent from 1995 through 2004.

---

10. *Accountancy* (accountancymagazine.com), "ChuoAoyama faces £100m Revenue Hit," 31 May 2005.

According to a representative of Tokyo's Public Prosecutor's Office, Hoashi ordered Kanebo's accounting staff to falsify the company's accounting records. Hoashi reportedly told the accountants that if they did not cooperate, the company would fail and its employees would lose their jobs. Hoashi's two subordinates (who were also indicted) gave the company's accountants specific instructions on how to distort Kanebo's reported financial data. The accountants were told to record fictitious sales and to understate various expenses to improve Kanebo's operating results and to make the company appear solvent.

In March 2006, Takashi Hoashi and one of his subordinates pleaded guilty to falsifying Kanebo's financial statements.[11] In commenting on the fraud, the judge who would ultimately sentence the two former executives noted, "It was a vicious and organizational crime committed by the leaders of a major Japanese company. It was also unprecedentedly cleverly devised."[12] Despite the judge's harsh remarks, he gave the two former executives suspended prison sentences.

ChuoAoyama, the second-largest CPA firm in Japan, served for decades as the audit firm of Kanebo Ltd. Tokyo's Public Prosecutor's Office filed fraud charges against three ChuoAoyama auditors who had been assigned to the Kanebo audit engagements. Each of those auditors had worked on the annual audits of that company for more than 15 years. One of the defendants had been assigned to the Kanebo engagement team for more than 30 years. In fact, it was common in post-World War II Japan for the same team of auditors to be assigned to an audit client indefinitely. According to the prosecutors, the three ChuoAoyama auditors had not only been aware of Kanebo's true financial condition but had also recommended additional methods for concealing the company's poor financial health. Among these methods was "de-consolidating" certain Kanebo subsidiaries that were posting large operating losses each year. The defendants never admitted as much, but the prosecutors speculated that the three auditors learned of this scheme from reading published reports of the Enron accounting fraud in the United States.

In the summer of 2006, the case against the ChuoAoyama auditors went to trial in Tokyo District Court. As one journalist noted, Japan's public accounting profession was "turned on its head"[13] by the case because it represented the first time in the country's history that auditors from a major CPA firm had faced criminal charges for allegedly falsifying or helping to falsify a client's financial statements. A few years earlier, ChuoAoyama had been involved in a precedent-setting civil lawsuit in Japan. ChuoAoyama had been the longtime auditor for Yamaichi Securities, a large brokerage firm that unexpectedly collapsed in late 1997. The following year, Yamaichi's former stockholders sued ChuoAoyama, charging that the firm had negligently audited Yamaichi. The lawsuit was the first of its kind filed by Japanese stockholders against an audit firm. In 2003, ChuoAoyama settled the lawsuit by agreeing to pay the Yamaichi bankruptcy administrator an amount equal to the total audit fees it had received for its final five annual audits of Yamaichi. Despite the settlement, ChuoAoyama officials insisted that the firm had properly performed those audits.

During the criminal trial of the three ChuoAoyama auditors, the defendants testified that shortly before the Kanebo fraud was uncovered by law enforcement authorities they had pleaded with Hoashi and his subordinates to make the proper correcting entries in the company's accounting records. According to the three auditors, the client executives refused to make those entries. When the auditors pressed the issue,

---

11. No published report could be found regarding the resolution of the criminal charges filed against the third Kanebo executive.

12. *Associated Press* (online), "Ex-Kanebo Executives Sentenced for False Information," 27 March 2006.

13. *International Accounting Bulletin* (online), "Japan Confronts Its Audit Problem," 12 August 2006.

the Kanebo executives "secured their cooperation by pointing out that ChuoAoyama had long overlooked the company's window dressing and said it was pointless to start complaining after taking a complacent stance for so long."[14]

In August 2006, the three ChuoAoyama auditors were convicted of the charges filed against them. Before sentencing the three individuals, the presiding judge noted that they had "damaged the social trust of certified public accountants" and that their "crimes deserve to be severely criticized."[15] The judge also observed, "It is shameful that they have failed to realize the high professional morality as certified accountants and lost the true aim of auditing, which is to protect investors."[16] After berating the three convicted auditors, the judge gave each of them suspended sentences ranging from one year to 18 months. The judge defended the suspended sentences by pointing out that Kanebo's executives, not the three auditors, were primarily responsible for the fraudulent scheme. The suspended prison sentences for the three auditors meant that no one involved in the large-scale Kanebo fraud would serve any time in prison for their misdeeds.

In May 2006, the FSA announced that the three ChuoAoyama auditors involved in the Kanebo fraud would have their CPA qualifications revoked. The FSA also announced that ChuoAoyama would be forced to suspend its operations for the two-month period July 1–August 31, 2006. The announcement of the suspension stunned Japan's public accounting profession. Japan's Securities and Exchange Law requires each listed company to have an independent audit firm at all times. The suspension of ChuoAoyama meant that the firm's approximately 800 clients that had securities listed on a stock exchange would be forced to either retain a temporary auditor for the two-month suspension period or dismiss ChuoAoyama and retain a new audit firm.

EPILOGUE

To prevent Kanebo, Ltd. from being forced to liquidate, the Japanese federal government placed the company in a "rehabilitation" program under the direction of the Industrial Revitalization Corporation of Japan (IRCJ). The government-sponsored and government-funded IRCJ had been created in April 2003 to help financially distressed companies obtain the capital they needed to survive and to provide them with "turnaround" advice from professional business consultants. Under the leadership of the IRCJ, Kanebo sold off its large cosmetics subsidiary and received more than $1 billion in government-guaranteed loans and waivers of

outstanding loans. In 2006, a large investment fund purchased a majority of Kanebo's stock and took over control of the company from the IRCJ.

ChuoAoyama lost approximately one-third of its audit clients, including more than 200 publicly listed clients, during the two-month suspension imposed by the FSA. These companies included ChuoAoyama's two most high profile audit clients, Sony Corporation and Toyota Motor Corporation. While serving the suspension, ChuoAoyama underwent an extensive internal review to strengthen its quality control functions and changed its name to the Misuzu Audit Corporation.[17]

---

14. *Japan Economic Newswire* (online), "Japanese Editorial Excerpts," 11 August 2006.

15. J. Hong, "CPAs in Kanebo Fraud Avoid Prison," *Japan Times* (online), 10 August 2006.

16. *Agence France Presse* (online), "Ex-Accountants Found Guilty in Japanese Fraud Case," 9 August 2006.

17. In February 2007, Misuzu announced that it was disbanding. The remaining three members of Japan's former Big Four hired the majority of Misuzu's employees.

EXHIBIT 1

EXCERPT FROM
THE BUSINESS
IMPROVEMENT
ORDER ISSUED TO
CHUOAOYAMA BY
THE FSA

As a result of inspecting ChuoAoyama PricewaterhouseCoopers, the firm-wide management to ensure audit quality control was deemed insufficient . . .

Specifically, its [measures for ensuring] compliance with laws/regulations and its implementation of auditors' independence [mandates] were found to be insufficient, and its system [for] training, etc. was deemed partially insufficient.

In addition, its risk assessments at the time of engagement acceptance/continuance, the performance of audit work by each audit team and the documentation/retention of audit working papers were deemed partially insufficient. In terms of internal reviews of audits, although a multi-tiered review system has been implemented, reviews rely on those [provided] by review partners and some are deemed to lack depth. In this context, its internal review system [for identifying problematic] issues of each audit and [for confirming] the appropriateness of the judgments and dispositions [with regard] to such issues were partially insufficient. Its monitoring of the quality control system was deemed partially insufficient, and joint audits were deemed insufficient.

Furthermore, its control system for branch offices was deemed insufficient.

Source: Financial Services Agency (www.fsa.go.jp).

Shortly after the FSA announced that it was suspending ChuoAoyama's operations for two months, the accounting firm's U.S. affiliate, PricewaterhouseCoopers, revealed that it would be creating a new Japanese accounting firm known as Aarata, a name that means "new and fresh" in Japanese. Aarata commenced operations on July 1, 2006, and in the subsequent weeks acquired dozens of ChuoAoyama's former clients, including Sony and Toyota. In addition, nearly one-fourth of ChuoAoyama's employees left that firm to join Aarata.

The Kanebo audit failure prompted the FSA to investigate the audit practices of each of Japan's four large accounting firms. These investigations were carried out by the newly created CPAAOB that had been placed under the authority of the FSA. The stated purpose of the investigations was to "regain public trust in certified public accountants damaged by ChuoAoyama auditors' involvement in Kanebo's falsification of its financial statements."[18] The CPAAOB issued a report on the six-month long investigations in July 2006. That report criticized the operating policies and procedures of the four accounting firms. As a result of the CPAAOB's report, the FSA issued "business improvement orders" to each of the four firms. Exhibit 1 includes an excerpt of the business improvement order issued to ChuoAoyama.

In the aftermath of the Kanebo audit failure, leaders of the Japanese accounting profession spoke out about the need for additional reforms to strengthen the nation's independent audit function. One such individual was Tsuguoki Fujinuma, the chairman and president of the JICPA. Fujinuma issued a public statement in which he compared the Kanebo incident to the Enron debacle in the United States.

The Enron affair was not an isolated problem of one accounting firm. To the contrary, it was regarded as a failure of the entire CPA system and provoked a barrage of criticism against audits and auditors in the U.S. public. This affair ultimately led to the passage of the Sarbanes-Oxley Act, legislation imposing severe controls on CPAs. I urge all JICPA members engaged in

18. *Japan Economic Newswire* (online), "FSA to Inspect 4 Biggest Auditing Firms," 25 October 2005.

audits to make efforts to ensure the public confidence in auditing practices, together with the JICPA itself. As they do so, I further urge them not to regard the Enron affair as a distant or unrelated failure to the accounting system, nor to regard the Kanebo incident as an isolated problem involving only one auditing firm.[19]

Despite such statements and the actions of the FSA and other regulatory authorities in response to the Kanebo affair, many third parties doubted that there would be major changes in Japan's independent audit function. As one skeptic noted, "cultural mores" will likely prove to be "sand in the gears of change."[20]

Questions

1. Research online news services to identify recent developments impacting the accounting and auditing profession in Japan. Briefly summarize these developments in a bullet format.

2. As noted in this case, Japanese companies typically rely more heavily on debt capital than U.S. companies. Explain how this fact may cause the independent audit functions in the two countries to differ.

3. The much higher barriers to enter the public accounting profession in Japan (as compared with other major industrialized countries) has resulted in a relatively small number of CPAs in that nation. Identify and briefly discuss the comparative advantages and disadvantages of high barriers to entry for a given profession.

4. In both Japan and the United States, a small number of accounting firms audit the great majority of large public companies. Identify the advantages and disadvantages of this "market structure" for independent audit services.

5. In both Japan and the United States, external auditors have frequently been accused of failing to maintain a proper degree of independence from their clients. What measures have and should be taken to promote the independence of auditors from their clients?

---

19. T. Fujinuma, "On the Alleged Fraudulent Accounting at Kanebo," website of Japanese Institute of Certified Public Accountants (www.hp.jicpa.or.jp/), 16 September 2005.

20. Reilly and Morse, "Japan Leans On Auditors."

Registered Auditors, South Africa

Where the cattle stand together, the lion lies down hungry.

African Proverb

After earning a law degree from the University of Capetown in 1988, 24-year-old Brett Kebble accepted an entry-level position with a prestigious Capetown law firm. The gregarious and impetuous Kebble soon realized that it would take years, if not decades, to achieve his personal goal of "making a name for himself" if he remained in the staid legal profession. So, Kebble decided to quit practicing law and join his father in the mining industry that has dominated the Republic of South Africa's economy throughout that nation's existence. Kebble's father, a successful mining engineer, had raised his family in the mining town of Springs in northwestern South Africa, 40 miles south of Pretoria, the nation's capital.

In 1991, Kebble and his father purchased a controlling interest in a small gold mining company. Three years later, Kebble, with the financial backing of his father and several other major investors, orchestrated the takeover of Randgold & Exploration Company Limited, one of South Africa's leading mining companies. Over the following decade, Brett Kebble would become the chief executive of Randgold and two other mining companies, all three of which were publicly owned firms.

By the turn of the century, Brett Kebble had accomplished his ultimate personal goal. Thanks to his role as the self-appointed spokesperson for South Africa's all-important mining industry, Kebble easily ranked among the nation's highest-profile corporate executives. Besides his prominent position in the South African business community, Kebble had close associations with several of South Africa's leading politicians and was a strong supporter of the arts. In 2002, Kebble, a large, heavyset man known for his quick wit and humor (and lack of modesty), established and funded the annual Brett Kebble Art Awards to recognize and reward leading South African artists, sculptors, and photographers.

A Career Cut Short

Kebble's reputation and business career were severely damaged in 2004 when Randgold & Exploration Company Limited, the crown jewel of his large business empire, reported a huge cash shortage. The missing funds were equivalent to several hundred million U.S. dollars. Stockholder revolts forced Kebble to resign in August 2005 as the chief executive of Randgold and the other two public companies for which he served in that position. One month later, in September 2005, the 41-year-old Kebble was gunned down in a wealthy section of Johannesburg while on his way to a dinner engagement in his silver Mercedes.

Johannesburg police immediately concluded that Kebble's murder had been a well-planned "hit." The widely publicized murder of the controversial businessman reinforced Johannesburg's reputation as the murder capital of the world and served to bolster the prevailing view in the international business community that South Africa was a high-risk and dangerous place to do business. Even more damaging to the reputation of South Africa's business community were subsequent revelations of the underhanded and illegal methods that Kebble had used to build his massive empire. One journalist characterized the late Kebble as a "cheat, manipulator, corrupter, briber, and swindler."[1] South Africa's largest newspaper would add to that sentiment: "Brett Kebble was not a good South African. He was the great corrupter, a dirty businessman who had little respect for the law or codes of good business practice."[2]

South African law enforcement authorities were investigating Kebble and his business and political allies well before he was murdered in September 2005. Those investigations continued on a larger scale following his death. Among the parties targeted by the investigations was PricewaterhouseCoopers (PwC), the audit firm of Randgold & Exploration Company Limited. Throughout Kebble's tenure as Randgold's chief executive, PwC had issued clean opinions on the company's annual financial statements even as a huge amount of the company's funds were being siphoned off by Kebble and several of his top subordinates. Randgold's board of directors dismissed PwC and retained KPMG as the company's independent audit firm shortly after the public was apprised of the missing funds.

After Brett Kebble's death, Randgold's new management team hired a consulting firm to carry out a forensic investigation of the company's accounting records and financial affairs over the previous decade. Two dozen forensic auditors from the consulting firm spent months unraveling a series of complex and multilayered "Enron-style transactions" that Kebble and his subordinates had used to divert Randgold assets into related entities that they controlled.[3] In a lengthy report issued in November 2005, the consulting firm recommended that Randgold's new management team file civil and criminal charges against PwC. The consulting firm suggested that proper audits of Randgold would have led to the discovery and termination of the massive fraud engineered by Kebble.

Doing Business, South Africa Style

In many ways, Brett Kebble's life and death epitomizes the turbulent nature of South Africa's business world following the collapse of apartheid in the early 1990s. In 1990, the South African federal government succumbed to immense international and domestic pressure when it lifted the ban on the African National Congress (ANC), the political party that had struggled for decades to eliminate apartheid in the country. The ANC drew its support from blacks who accounted for more than three-fourths of the nation's total population. The National Party, the political party of the nation's white minority that controlled most of South Africa's economic resources (including its crucial mining industry), had dominated South Africa's federal government since the 1940s. Shortly after World War II, the National Party had implemented the segregationist social and economic policies that formed the basis for what became known as apartheid.

When the first truly multiracial elections were held in South Africa in 1994, Nelson Mandela was elected the nation's president. Mandela, the leader of the ANC, had been imprisoned by the South African government from 1963 through 1990. The democratic elections also resulted in the ANC assuming control of South Africa's parliament. After decades of a bitter and often extremely bloody struggle, South Africa's black majority had finally taken control of the country.

Since the collapse of apartheid and the takeover of the federal government by the ANC, South Africa's economy has been characterized by uncertainty and volatility.

---

1. S. Ulys, "The Mysterious Murder of Brett Kebble," www.ever-fasternews.com, 2 October 2005.

2. A. Meldrum, "Brett Kebble, Controversial Business Leader from the New South Africa," *The Guardian* (online), 7 October 2005.

3. "Massive Fraud Revealed at Randgold & Exploration," www.randgold.co.za, press release issued by Randgold & Exploration Company Limited, 1 November 2005.

Major institutional investors around the world have been reluctant to commit significant investment capital to South African business ventures because of that uncertainty and volatility. A related factor that has inhibited direct foreign investment in the South African economy has been corruption. An Ernst & Young survey of corporate executives from nearly 70 countries around the world identified "corruption" as the principal factor that made them hesitant to do business in South Africa.[4] According to the Ernst & Young study, the corruption in South Africa's economy has been manifested in widespread bribery, payroll fraud, inventory theft, and unauthorized expenditures by corporate executives, among other abuses.

South Africa's economy and capital markets have also suffered a loss of credibility as a result of a series of high-profile financial reporting scandals that have occurred in recent years. Those scandals have involved companies such as LeisureNet, MacMed, Regal Treasury, Saambou, and, most notably, Randgold & Exploration Company Limited. Critics of South Africa's accounting profession insist that much of the responsibility for these scandals should be borne by the accounting firms that audited those companies' financial statements and failed to uncover the fraudulent schemes carried out by Brett Kebble and other self-interested corporate executives.

Numerous journalists and political adversaries of Brett Kebble maintain that he used assets stolen from Randgold not only for his personal enrichment but also to buy political favors from leaders of the ANC. Since the early 1990s, Kebble, who was of western European descent, had been among the most vocal supporters of the black empowerment movement in South Africa and a leading figure in the ANC. One of his closest associates was Jacob Zuma who served for several years as South Africa's deputy president (vice president) before being forced to resign in June 2005 amid allegations of abuse of power. (Zuma resurrected his political career in 2009 when he was elected president of South Africa, thanks to the support of the ANC.) The published reports of the missing funds within Randgold as well as Kebble's close ties and financial dealings with Zuma ignited the stockholder revolts that forced him to resign as the chief executive of Randgold and of the other two mining companies that he and his family had controlled since the mid-1990s.

South Africa's business press has referred to the financial scandal at Randgold & Exploration Company Limited as that nation's "Enron." Like the actual Enron debacle in the United States, the highly publicized Randgold scandal persuaded the South African Parliament to pass major legislation to combat financial fraud and strengthen the nation's financial reporting system. This new legislation was intended to convince the international investment community that South Africa's capital markets would be characterized by integrity in the future. The lynchpin of the legislative reforms was a new federal law that had pervasive implications for the nation's accounting profession.

Overview of South Africa's Accounting Profession

South Africa's accounting discipline has several professional organizations. The two most important of these organizations are the South African Institute of Professional Accountants (SAIPA), which until recently was known as the Institute of Certified Public Accountants, and the South African Institute of Chartered Accountants (SAICA). Members of the SAIPA are certified public accountants (CPAs) who typically

---

4. M.S. Bayat, "Curbing Corruption in the Republic of South Africa," *Public Manager*, Summer 2005, 15. The results of a study by PricewaterhouseCoopers that was published in late 2007 identified South Africa as the "white-collar crime capital" of the world (*Africa News* [online], "South Africa: Country is White-Collar Crime Capital," 16 October 2007.)

provide tax and bookkeeping services to small South African businesses. The most prominent organization in the South African accounting profession is the SAICA, which issues the Chartered Accountant (CA) professional designation. The CA designation is equivalent to the CPA designation in the United States.

Unlike the United States, the accounting profession in South Africa is regulated almost exclusively at the federal level. Until recently, the federal agency overseeing that profession was the Public Accountants' and Auditors' Board (PAAB). PAAB delegated much of the responsibility for overseeing the South African accounting profession to the SAICA. The working relationship between the PAAB and the SAICA was analogous to the relationship that exists in the United States between state boards of accountancy and the American Institute of Certified Public Accountants (AICPA). For example, until recently, an internal SAICA committee developed and issued South Africa's professional auditing standards, which were then routinely endorsed by the PAAB. Similarly, the PAAB adopted a condensed version of the code of professional ethics developed by the SAICA.

The abrupt change of control in South Africa's federal government in the early 1990s presented major challenges for the nation's federal agencies, such as the PAAB, and its professional organizations, among them the SAICA. Throughout its history, South Africa's accounting profession, like other professions, had been dominated by the nation's white minority–principally white males. The ANC's takeover of the South African government in 1994 resulted in federal mandates calling for the integration of the nation's professions. Since that time, the SAICA and the nation's major accounting firms have spent considerable time and resources attempting to recruit black South Africans into the profession. Those efforts have produced discouraging results. In 2009, fewer than 5 percent of South Africa's 29,000 CAs were blacks.

In the post-apartheid era, a large percentage of South Africa's white professionals have immigrated to other countries, including an estimated 20 to 25 percent of the nation's CAs. The emigration of white CAs and the continuing underrepresentation of blacks have resulted in a significant shortage of professional accountants within South Africa. In the United States, there is roughly one CPA for every 500 citizens. South Africa, on the other hand, has approximately one resident CA for every 2,500 citizens.

In April 2006, three Big Four firms–Deloitte, KPMG and PwC–asked the South African federal government to relax its restrictive immigration laws to make it easier for those firms to recruit accounting professionals from other countries. The three firms maintained that the significant shortage of skilled accountants within South Africa had made it increasingly difficult for the nation's accounting profession to provide the accounting, auditing, tax, and related services needed by South African citizens and businesses. The South African government never responded to that request. The federal government's position is that allowing skilled accounting professionals to immigrate to South Africa–even if those individuals are black–will only serve to continue the underrepresentation of native South African blacks within the profession.

The most significant challenge facing South Africa's accounting profession in the post-apartheid era has been the rash of accounting and financial reporting scandals involving major companies. Many parties internal and external to the profession have suggested that the most effective way to mitigate that problem is to strengthen the nation's professional accounting and auditing standards. After considerable debate, South Africa's accounting profession decided to adopt, as of January 1, 2005, the International Financial Reporting Standards (IFRS) issued by the International Accounting Standards Board (IASB). On that same date, the South African profession also adopted the International Standards on Auditing (ISAs) issued by the International Federation of Accountants (IFAC).

The adoption of international accounting and auditing standards did not placate the most vocal critics of South Africa's accounting profession. Those critics became even more strident as the Randgold accounting and financial reporting scandal unfolded during 2005 and 2006. That scandal provided the impetus for South Africa's Parliament to pass a federal statute in 2006 that had been placed on the legislative agenda ten years earlier. The Auditing Profession Act made sweeping changes to South Africa's financial reporting system, particularly the nation's independent audit function.

Auditing Profession Act

South Africa's Auditing Profession Act (APA) went into effect on April 1, 2006. The new federal law eliminated the PAAB and replaced it with the Independent Regulatory Board for Auditors (IRBA). The term "independent" was included in the new agency's name because, unlike its predecessor, a majority of its governing board would not be accountants. Likewise, unlike the PAAB that had been financed exclusively by the accounting profession, the APA mandated that the IRBA be funded jointly by the profession and the federal government. These two stipulations were a direct response to criticism that the PAAB had been an ineffective oversight body for South Africa's accounting profession because it had been "captured" by that profession. In particular, critics suggested that the PAAB had been overly sensitive to the interests and demands of the Big Four international accounting firms, each of which has a strong presence in South Africa.

The APA also established a new professional designation in South Africa's accounting profession: Registered Auditor (RA). Under the APA, only CAs who also hold the RA credential can perform independent audits in South Africa. According to an official of the IRBA, the new RA designation was necessary because of the large number of audit failures and alleged audit failures that had occurred in South Africa over the previous several years. "Auditors have taken a huge knock in the past few years and we need to establish a brand locally that will restore integrity."[5]

The creation of the new professional designation was generally not welcomed by the SAICA and individual CAs who realized that the RA credential would almost certainly impair the prestige and prominence of the CA credential. In fact, officials of the IRBA candidly admitted that they hoped the public would impute more credibility to the new RA designation. "We're trying to tell people [existing CAs] that if you're an RA, it will have higher regard than a CA in South Africa because of the stringent new laws and examination. We want people to strive to be RAs not CAs."[6]

Prior to the passage of the APA, the SAICA had administered the CA examination. Under the APA, the SAICA continues to administer that examination; however, to become an RA a CA candidate must successfully complete a second examination administered by the IRBA. Before receiving the CA or RA credential, candidates must complete a minimum three-year internship or "training program" within the accounting profession. This requirement had existed for CA candidates prior to the passage of the APA and the creation of the IRBA.

---

5. S. Naidoo, "Auditors' Brand Set to Rival That of a CA," *Sunday Times* (online), 1 October 2006.
6. *Ibid.*

EXHIBIT 1

MISSION
STATEMENTS OF THE
SAICA AND THE
IRBA

SAICA's mission is to serve the interests of the Chartered Accountancy profession and society, by upholding professional standards and integrity, and the pre-eminence of South African CAs nationally and internationally, through delivering competent entry level members, providing services to assist members to maintain and enhance their professional competence thereby enabling them to create value for their clients and employers, enhancing the quality of information used in the private and public sectors for measuring and enhancing organizational performance, running and facilitating programmes to transform the profession and to facilitate community upliftment and fulfilling a leadership role regarding relevant business related issues and providing reliable and respected public commentary.

The mission of the IRBA, on the other hand, is to protect the financial interest of the South African public and international investors in South Africa, through the effective regulation of audits conducted by registered auditors, and in accordance with internationally recognized standards and processes. This is achieved by providing the means and the regulatory framework for the education and training of adequate numbers of competent and disciplined accountants and auditors, to serve the needs of South Africa. The Board [IRBA] strives constantly toward the maintenance and improvement of standards of registered auditors. The Board protects the public who rely on the services of registered auditors and supports registered auditors who carry out their duties competently, fearlessly, and in good faith.

Source: SAICA website (www.saica.co.za).

Leaders of the South African accounting profession were concerned that the creation of the IRBA and the new RA designation would lead to confusion on the part of the public regarding the nature of the CA and RA designations and the roles and responsibilities of the IRBA and the SAICA. To alleviate such confusion, the two organizations issued mission statements clarifying their roles and responsibilities and their relationship to the CA and RA credentials. Exhibit 1 presents summaries of those mission statements that were posted to the SAICA website.

The APA also made major changes in the regulatory infrastructure for South Africa's independent audit function. Under this new federal statute, the IRBA has far-reaching oversight responsibilities for that function. Individual RAs as well as accounting firms providing independent audits are required to register with the IRBA. Registered accounting firms must undergo an extensive quality review of their professional audit practices by the IRBA every three years.

The IRBA also has the statutory responsibility to establish ethical standards and rules for RAs. The APA required the IRBA to establish a "committee for auditor ethics" that will "determine what constitutes improper conduct by registered auditors by developing rules and guidelines for professional ethics, including a code of professional conduct."[7] The IRBA also requires RAs to engage in continuing professional development (CPD) each year. Organizations offering CPD courses or programs must be accredited by the IRBA.

By far, the most controversial and important change in the nature of independent audits and auditors' professional responsibilities brought about by the APA was a requirement that RAs immediately inform the IRBA of any "reportable irregularities" relating to an audit client that come to their attention.

---

7. *Government Gazette, The Republic of South Africa,* "Auditing Profession Act, 2005," Vol. 487, No. 28406 (16 January 2006), 26.

Reportable irregularities are defined by the APA as

any unlawful act or omission committed by any person responsible for the management of an entity, which:

–has caused or is likely to cause material financial loss to the entity or any partner, member, shareholder, creditor or investor of the entity in respect of his/her or its dealings with that entity; or

–is fraudulent or amounts to theft; or

–represents a material breach of any fiduciary duty owed by such person to the entity or any partner, member, shareholder, creditor or investor of the entity under any law applying to the entity or the conduct or management thereof.[8]

RAs must disclose a reportable irregularity (RI) "without delay" to the IRBA, meaning that these matters are not to be discussed with client management before they are communicated to the federal agency. After an RI report has been submitted to the IRBA, an RA must discuss that report with client management within three days. Over the following 30 days, client management must be given an opportunity to respond to the report. At the end of this 30-day period, the RA must send a second report to the IRBA regarding the RI. In this second report, the RA must indicate whether in his or her opinion an actual irregularity has taken place or is taking place.

Reportable irregularities have extensive implications for the audit reports prepared by South African RAs. The APA provides specific guidance for auditors to follow in determining whether and/or how to modify their audit reports for a wide range of circumstances involving RIs. For example, if an auditor reports a potential RI to the IRBA but then determines that an actual irregularity did not take place, no modification of the audit report is necessary. Management's failure to disclose an RI, whether or not the matter has been appropriately addressed, may require the auditor to issue an adverse opinion on the client's financial statements. If at the audit report date an auditor has not determined whether a potential RI is an actual RI, then the potential RI, at a minimum, must be disclosed in the audit report.

The APA mandates that RAs have a responsibility to report RIs regardless of how they became aware of them. For example, anonymous tips, statements made by disgruntled former employees, or confidential communications to the auditor by client employees could each trigger an RI report to the IRBA. Likewise, an RI discovered during the course of a nonaudit services engagement for a client must be disclosed to the IRBA. Under the APA, the reporting responsibility for RIs falls on individual RAs, not accounting firms. The RA on the engagement team who has the ultimate responsibility for the successful completion of the audit–typically, the audit engagement partner–has the obligation to report an RI to the IRBA. This stipulation of the law is very important given the serious criminal penalties for willfully choosing not to report an RI. An RA who has a responsibility to report an RI and fails to do so faces a large fine and a prison sentence of up to ten years.

In addition to exposing RAs to criminal sanctions, the APA mandates that RAs who fail to fulfill their RI-related responsibilities will be subject to civil liability as well. This civil liability extends to any "partner, member, shareholder, creditor or investor of an entity" for which an RA fails to report an RI.[9] One of South Africa's leading corporate law firms reported that this provision of the APA "has potentially enormous consequences for auditors' liability claims."[10]

---

8. *Ibid.*, 10.

9. *Ibid.*, 48.

10. K. Gawith, "Reportable Irregularities," www.deneysreitz.co.za.

The stated purpose of the RI provisions of the APA was to "eradicate" the large-scale frauds, such as the Randgold & Exploration Company Limited scandal, that had undermined the integrity of South Africa's capital markets within the international community and resulted in large diversions of assets by dishonest corporate executives. Although certain parties, particularly South Africa's business press, welcomed the RI provisions of the APA, many corporate executives and members of the nation's accounting profession were startled, if not shocked, by those provisions. An audit partner with one of the Big Four accounting firms maintained that the RI disclosure rule would undermine the "relationship of confidentiality between auditor and client" and create an "atmosphere in which clients will be reluctant to discuss problems with their auditors."[11]

To minimize any confusion regarding the RI disclosure requirements imposed on auditors by the APA, the SAICA recommended that accounting firms send each of their audit clients a letter describing in detail the nature of those requirements. Exhibit 2 includes a draft of such a letter prepared by the SAICA and distributed to its members.

EXHIBIT 2

DRAFT OF LETTER THAT THE SAICA SUGGESTED RAS SEND TO THEIR AUDIT CLIENTS REGARDING THE REPORTABLE IRREGULARITIES DISCLOSURE RULE

Dear Client:

You may be aware from press and other reports that new legislation regulating auditors has been enacted during 2006.

I have a statutory obligation to report matters to a regulatory oversight body or other person, such as the Independent Regulatory Board for Auditors (IRBA). Where permissible I shall endeavor to bring such circumstances to your attention.

Without detracting from the generality of such requirements, I am writing to you to provide a brief overview of the new reporting obligations imposed by the Auditing Profession Act 2005 (Act 26 of 2005).

The new legislation brings into existence a new regulator in the form of the IRBA which supersedes the Public Accountants' and Auditors' Board (PAAB).

Section 45 of the Auditing Profession Act places a legal requirement on the auditor to report to the IRBA, without delay, details of any reportable irregularity which comes to our attention, which we are satisfied or have reason to believe has taken place or is taking place in respect of [entity name].

The Auditing Profession Act defines a reportable irregularity as "any unlawful act or omission committed by any person responsible for the management of an entity, which:

–has caused or is likely to cause material financial loss to the entity or any partner, member, shareholder, creditor or investor of the entity in respect of his/her or its dealings with that entity; or
–is fraudulent or amounts to theft; or
–represents a material breach of any fiduciary duty owed by such person to the entity or any partner, member, shareholder, creditor or investor of the entity under any law applying to the entity or the conduct or management thereof."

---

11. *Africa News* (online), "Auditors Generally Welcome New Law despite Concerns about Education Roles," 7 April 2006.

EXHIBIT 2—
continued

DRAFT OF LETTER
THAT THE SAICA
SUGGESTED RAS
SEND TO THEIR
AUDIT CLIENTS
REGARDING THE
REPORTABLE
IRREGULARITIES
DISCLOSURE RULE

Matters which come to my attention and meet the definition above are clearly of a serious nature. In addition to reporting such matters to you and to those charged with governance of [entity name], I am obliged to report such matters to the IRBA.

Accordingly, the South African Institute of Chartered Accountants, of which I am a member, has advised its members who practice as auditors to write to their audit clients informing them of the requirements of the section dealing with reportable irregularities and what the implications can be.

What must the auditor do?

1. In terms of the legislation, if an auditor or an entity is satisfied, or has reason to believe that a reportable irregularity has taken place or is taking place, he or she must, without delay, send a written report to the IRBA.
2. The report must give particulars of the alleged irregularity.
3. The auditor must notify the members of the management board of the entity in writing within three (3) days of sending the report.
4. The auditor must take all reasonable measures to discuss the report with the management board of the entity.
5. The auditor must afford the members of the management board an opportunity to make representations in respect of the report. The auditor must send another report to the IRBA within 30 days of the initial report to the IRBA stating in his or her opinion whether or not a reportable irregularity has taken place or is taking place. This report should also deal with whether adequate steps have been taken for the prevention or recovery of any loss.
6. The auditor may carry out such investigations he or she may consider necessary to comply with the above requirements.
7. The auditor must refer to the alleged irregularity in his or her audit report attached to the annual financial statements.
8. It is important to note that the procedure described above must be carried out regardless of how the auditor came to know of the irregularity.

What the regulator must do?

The IRBA has a responsibility to report a reportable irregularity to the appropriate regulator (which includes any government agency) e.g. South African Revenue Services, South African Police Services, or the Financial Services Board.

Possible Penalties

I need to draw your attention to the fact that if the auditor fails to report a reportable irregularity, he or she may be guilty of an offense and may be liable to a fine of R10 million or imprisonment for a term not exceeding 10 years, or both a fine and imprisonment.

Conclusion

As mentioned previously, the auditors' responsibility with regard to reportable irregularities are well defined and can have serious consequences on the auditor if not followed appropriately.

(continued)

EXHIBIT 2—
continued

DRAFT OF LETTER
THAT THE SAICA
SUGGESTED RAs
SEND TO THEIR
AUDIT CLIENTS
REGARDING THE
REPORTABLE
IRREGULARITIES
DISCLOSURE RULE

While I am certain that you are committed to ensuring that such reportable irregularities do not exist, or if they do arise they are dealt with appropriately within applicable legal requirements, you may wish to further discuss the reporting obligations with me.

Yours Sincerely,
Registered Auditor, CA

Source: SAICA website (www.saica.co.za).

EPILOGUE

Within the first five months that the APA was in effect, the IRBA received more than 200 RI reports from auditors. By 2010, the IRBA reported that it was receiving more than 1,000 such reports annually. The majority of RIs involve alleged violations of South African tax laws, apparent violations of the nation's federal securities laws, and a wide range of questionable accounting practices.[12] The regulatory agency has also received informal reports from auditors that clients have threatened to dismiss them if they made an RI disclosure. These informal reports tend to confirm that the RI reporting rule has created tension between auditors and their clients. In an interview with a newspaper reporter, the IRBA's senior executive, Kariem Hoosain, admitted that the new requirement had resulted in a "strained relationship" between auditors and their clients.[13] But Hoosain quickly added that was simply "tough luck." In the same article in which Hoosain was quoted, an officer of the SAICA indicated that the RI rule was "onerous" for auditors and expressed his opinion that the criminal sanctions auditors faced under that rule were unfair.[14] The officer went on to note that "there's not much we can do now. It is the law and our members have to abide by [it]."[15]

As the details of the Randgold fraud were reported to the public, PwC, Randgold's former audit firm, became the target of increasing criticism for its role in that scandal. One reporter observed that "When the full tale of Brett Kebble's larceny is finally told, it would be something of a crime in itself if his auditors came off unscathed."[16] In October 2006, Karien Hoosain revealed that his agency was initiating an investigation of PwC's Randgold audits. Hoosain indicated that such an investigation was warranted given the report of the forensic consulting firm that had been retained by Randgold's board to scrutinize Kebble's fraudulent schemes. That report indicated that Randgold's fiscal 2003 financial statements (on which PwC had issued an unqualified opinion) "grossly misrepresented" the company's financial condition.[17] Hoosain reported that because of the "complexities and sensitivities" of the Randgold case, the investigation of PwC's audits would likely take years to complete.[18]

12. *Africa News* (online), "Auditors Reporting Dubious Clients," 29 August 2006.

13. Naidoo, "Auditors' Brand Set to Rival That of a CA."

14. *Ibid.*

15. *Ibid.*

16. B. Rose, "What About PwC's Role in Kebble Saga?" www.resourceinvestor.com, 13 March 2006.

17. Naidoo, "Auditors' Brand Set to Rival That of a CA."

18. *Ibid.* In 2008, Randgold management filed a large civil lawsuit against PwC. Shortly thereafter, IRBA announced that it was suspending its investigation of PwC's Randgold audits pending the outcome of that lawsuit. The lawsuit was still unresolved in early 2011.

In November 2006, South African police arrested a businessman on suspicion of involvement in the murder of Brett Kebble. The businessman, who was subsequently charged with murder and conspiracy to commit murder, was a close personal friend of the South African Police Commissioner and also reportedly a member of a South African crime syndicate. Several months after his arrest, the murder suspect confessed that he had been involved in Kebble's death *at Kebble's request*. According to the suspect, Kebble had arranged to have his "assisted suicide" appear as a murder so that his family could collect large sums on life insurance policies that he had purchased. A lengthy criminal trial ended in November 2010 with the suspect being acquitted.

Adding even more suspense to the unresolved murder case of Brett Kebble was an unconfirmed sighting of him on a remote Caribbean island by several South African citizens—Kebble's body, or what was allegedly Kebble's body, was cremated shortly after his apparent murder. In any event, given the complexity of the case, South African law enforcement authorities believe that it may be years before it is ultimately solved.

Questions

1. Research online and hardcopy databases to identify important recent developments within the South African accounting profession. Summarize these developments in a bullet format.

2. Over the history of the global accounting profession, political forces have often played a major role in the development of individual nations' independent audit function. Explain how political forces have influenced the development and evolution of the independent audit function in the United States.

3. Identify the advantages and disadvantages of having a professional credential or designation for independent auditors in addition to a professional credential for accountants.

4. In your opinion, should the United States adopt a rule similar to South Africa's "reportable irregularities" rule? Defend your answer. How do you believe such a requirement would affect the independent audit function and capital markets in the United States?

5. Identify strategies that the South African accounting profession could use to encourage young black men and women in that country to choose accounting as a career. In your opinion, what party or parties should take the lead in such recruiting efforts?

Zuan Yan

Let China sleep, for when it wakes, it will shake the world.

Napoleon

Every four years, the International Federation of Accountants (IFAC) organizes the World Congress of Accountants.[1] Accountants from across the globe attend this meeting to share their views on major issues and challenges facing their profession. In November 2002, the People's Republic of China hosted the World Congress of Accountants for the first time in the nation's history. Premier Zhu Rongji, the second-highest ranking official in the Chinese government, delivered the welcoming speech during the opening ceremonies. In his remarks, Premier Zhu, long known for his candid, if not blunt, manner, spoke openly of the embarrassing series of financial scandals that had created a major credibility crisis for the worldwide accounting profession over the previous decade. Premier Zhu pointed out that many of those accounting scandals had involved Chinese firms, a fact that Western journalists had largely ignored.

Similar to political leaders in many Western countries in recent years, Premier Zhu called on the accounting profession to reform itself and restore its credibility with the investing and lending public. He reminded the participants in the conference that "honesty and trustworthiness" are the lifeblood of the accounting profession.[2] Premier Zhu also assured those present that China was committed to "the cultivation of professional ethics among accountants" and, even more importantly, to creating a modern and transparent financial reporting system.[3]

Then, Mao, and Now

For several millennia, a series of family dynasties ruled China; these included most notably the Han, Ming, and Qing Dynasties. The collapse of the Qing Dynasty in 1912 led to the creation of the Republic of China that was dominated by a political party known as the Kuomintang or National Party. For four years following the end of World War II, a bloody civil war ensued between forces loyal to Chiang Kai-shek, the leader of the National Party, and the increasingly popular Communist Party led by Mao Zedong and his top subordinate, Zhou Enlai. In 1949, the Communist Party gained control of the country, forcing Chiang Kai-shek and his followers into exile on the island of Taiwan. On October 1, 1949, the Communist country was renamed the People's Republic of China.

Mao immediately installed a Marxist regime in China under which the central government controlled practically all of the nation's economic resources. To revitalize China's economy that had been decimated by World War II and the Chinese civil war, Mao implemented a series of economic programs, most notably the "Great Leap Forward," that were intended to convert the nation's largely agricultural economy into a modern industrial economy. These programs were dismal failures, leaving China's economy in disarray and the country's citizens with a miserable standard of living.

---

1. *Zuan yan* is a Chinese phrase meaning "to search for the truth and hold fast to it."

2. *People's Daily*, "Cherish Integrity of Accounting Profession: Chinese Premier," http://english.peopledaily.com.cn, 21 November 2002.

3. *Ibid.*

In 1966, Mao launched the "Great Proletarian Cultural Revolution," more commonly referred to by historians as the "Cultural Revolution."[4] This sweeping set of social and economic reforms was intended to rid China of the "liberal bourgeoisie" that was allegedly undermining Mao's efforts to establish a utopian, Communistic society controlled by the working class. In reality, the Cultural Revolution was a desperate attempt by Mao to divert attention from his failed economic policies, while at the same time reaffirming his position as China's supreme leader. From 1966 through 1976, an estimated 500,000 Chinese citizens were executed and millions more exiled and persecuted at the hands of Mao's supporters.

Following Mao's death in 1976, several political figures wrestled for control of the country. Eventually, Deng Xiaoping established himself as China's unchallenged new leader, although he never officially held the top position in China's central government. Deng renounced the economic and social policies implemented by Mao during the Great Leap Forward and the Cultural Revolution. To raise China's standard of living, Deng replaced the nation's Soviet-style "command economy" with a "socialistic market economy."

Under China's new economic system, the nation's central government, which was still controlled by the Communist Party, would allow private enterprises to compete with state-owned enterprises (SOEs) across many sectors of the economy. Another critical element of Deng's economic blueprint was the encouragement given to foreign companies to invest in China, a complete reversal of Mao's "closed door" policy. Deng especially encouraged large multinational corporations based in the United States and other Western countries to finance joint business ventures with Chinese SOEs.

In 1980, Deng emphatically endorsed his new economic plan for China, while at the same time shocking Communist allies and democratic societies around the world, when he proclaimed that "to be rich is to be glorious." Over the next three decades, Deng's economic policies, which remained in effect after his death in 1997, triggered an explosion of economic activity within China. By 2005, state-controlled enterprises accounted for only one-third of the nation's annual gross domestic product (GDP). Although still "poor" relative to common economic benchmarks, most Chinese citizens experienced a dramatic improvement in their standard of living under their nation's new "mixed" economy, which surpassed Japan in 2010 as the world's second largest economy. Economists predict that before the midpoint of the twenty-first century, China's GDP will surpass that of the United States, making the Chinese economy the largest in the world.

Deng Xiaoping's economic policies have impacted every facet of Chinese society, including the nation's professions, which had been largely discredited and debased during the three decades that Mao Zedong imposed his Marxist ideology on the country. Among the professional groups that have benefited the most from Deng's "revolution" is China's accounting profession. In recent years, China's political leaders have come to recognize that for their country to sustain its economic revival, a wide range of parties need reliable and comprehensive financial data regarding the nation's SOEs and other business enterprises. That data can only be provided if China develops a modern financial reporting system and an army of skilled accountants and auditors.

---

4. Wikipedia, "Cultural Revolution," http://en.wikipedia.org/wiki/Cultural_Revolution.

Accounting for Profits

To fully appreciate the accounting and financial reporting issues facing the Chinese economy, it is first necessary to identify the major types of business organizations within China. Prior to 1980, SOEs were the overwhelmingly dominant form of business organization within China in terms of annual economic output. As a result of the economic reforms introduced by Deng Xiaoping, three additional types of business organizations have become well established within China: collectively owned enterprises (COEs), individually owned enterprises (IOEs), and enterprises with foreign investments (FOEs).[5] COEs are typically local cooperatives organized by the members of a small community, while IOEs are principally small businesses owned and operated by individual entrepreneurs. Because most COEs and IOEs do not obtain significant investment capital from third-party investors and lenders, external financial reporting is not a major concern or regulatory requirement of these two types of organizations.

FOEs are either joint business ventures involving Chinese companies–typically SOEs–and foreign multinational corporations, or China-based businesses that are wholly owned by foreign multinational corporations. As a result, the financial data of most FOEs are eventually integrated into the consolidated financial statements of a foreign multinational corporation domiciled in the United States, a member nation of the European Union, or another developed country, meaning that FOEs typically employ "Western-style" accounting and financial reporting systems.

Over the past three decades, the efforts to develop a modern accounting and financial reporting system within China have centered on SOEs. Although the annual economic output of SOEs as a percentage of China's GDP has been steadily decreasing over the past three decades, these organizations remain the most important business units in China. In recent years, the Chinese government has sold minority ownership interests in many SOEs to private investors, ownership interests that are traded on either the Shanghai or Shenzhen Stock Exchanges, China's two major stock exchanges. China's political leaders apparently have no intention of completely "privatizing" the large petrochemical, iron and steel, and other manufacturing enterprises that continue to make up the backbone of the nation's economic infrastructure.[6]

Despite the fact that SOEs remain under the control of China's central government, the organizational structure of these entities and their internal operating policies and procedures have changed dramatically under the economic system installed by Deng Xiaopeng. Likewise, the role of SOEs' accounting and financial reporting systems has changed radically.

> *Prior to 1978 . . . SOEs were essentially production units (factories). The managers of SOEs in the pre-reform era had little or no managerial autonomy. The state provided all financing to the factories and controlled virtually all the investment and operating decisions. . . . The factories simply served the purpose of fulfilling the production quota stipulated by the government. Consequently, the managers of these factories had neither the incentive nor the managerial authority to reduce costs and generate profits. In such a command economy, the main role of accounting was to assist the government in planning and controlling decisions.*[7]

---

5. X. Bing, "Institutional Factors Influencing China's Accounting Reforms and Standards," *Accounting Horizons*, June 1998, 107.

6. *Ibid.,* 109.

7. *Ibid.*

In China's present economic system, the central government has transferred the responsibility for the day-to-day operations and long-term strategic planning for most SOEs to professional management teams. So, despite being ultimately accountable to the central government, most SOEs "now significantly resemble modern corporations in the West in that they are characterized by a high degree of managerial autonomy and a separation of ownership from control."[8]

The dramatic change in the nature of SOEs over the past three decades has created a need for Western-style accounting systems for these organizations. Such accounting systems produce the data necessary to properly evaluate the operating decisions of professional management teams. Likewise, under China's new economic system, there is an explicit recognition on the part of the country's political leaders that individual SOEs are competing for a finite quantity of economic resources. Consequently, there is a need to regularly assess the extent to which individual SOEs are contributing to the overall economic productivity of the nation. Finally, the central government realizes that for SOEs to raise investment capital from external sources, they must provide those parties relevant financial data.

The Ministry of Finance (MOF) is the government agency responsible for overseeing China's economy, including the nation's financial reporting system. In 1993, the MOF adopted an accounting framework for China analogous to the "Conceptual Framework" developed by the U.S. accounting profession in the late 1980s. This framework was entitled "The Accounting Standards for Business Enterprises" (ASBE). Throughout the 1980s, the MOF and other Chinese government agencies had taken steps to revamp the outmoded accounting and financial reporting systems being used by SOEs. However, those measures had been largely ineffectual. The adoption of the ASBE suggested that China's central government was intent on requiring SOEs to adopt Western-style accounting and financial reporting practices. "The introduction of ASBE was considered the most significant achievement of China's accounting reforms since the 1980s in that it signaled the end of traditional accounting in China and brought China's accounting practices into close conformity with international standards."[9]

The ASBE required most SOEs and other large Chinese enterprises to adopt the fundamental accounting principles and financial reporting formats used in Western democracies. "Among the accounting characteristics specified in the standards [ASBE] are double-entry accrual records, consistency, conservatism, comparative financial statements . . . and explanatory disclosures."[10] Although the ASBE principally dealt with broad accounting and financial reporting issues, the pronouncement also introduced such specific accounting methods as LIFO/FIFO, the allowance method of accounting for bad debts, the percentage-of-completion approach to revenue recognition, accelerated depreciation methods, and consolidated financial statements. Following the issuance of the ASBE, the MOF retained Deloitte Touche Tohmatsu as a consultant to assist in developing a comprehensive set of accounting standards for the Chinese economy. Over the following decade, the MOF approved several dozen accounting standards proposed by Deloitte. These new standards were generally referred to as Chinese Accounting Standards (CAS).

---

8. *Ibid.*, 111.

9. T. Tang, B. Cooper, and P. Leung, "Accounting in China: Developments and Opportunities," in *Perspectives on Accounting and Finance in China*, edited by J.B. Black and S. Gao (London: Routledge, 1995).

10. G. M. Winkle, H. Fenwick, and X. Chen, "Accounting Standards in the People's Republic of China: Responding to Economic Reforms," *Accounting Horizons*, September 1994, 55.

As one would expect, there was almost no opposition to, or criticism of, the decision by China's authoritarian central government to adopt Western-style accounting standards. However, the MOF and other government agencies faced considerable challenges in executing that decision. The most intractable of these challenges stemmed from the fact that China's accounting profession had been dismantled under Mao Zedong's regime. As one journalist noted recently, "Grey hair and experience [in China's domestic accounting profession] are scarce because the Cultural Revolution wiped out the profession."[11]

Within Mao's Soviet-style economy, professional accountants who understood complex accounting and financial reporting issues were no longer needed and, in fact, were considered part and parcel of the "liberal bourgeoisie" that had to be eliminated. Instead of skilled accountants and auditors, China's state-controlled enterprises required only the services of bookkeepers and "bean counters" to accumulate production statistics and related data, which were then funneled to the proper authorities.

To help organize and promote China's accounting profession, the MOF created the Chinese Institute of Certified Public Accountants (CICPA) in 1988. This new government agency immediately began licensing CPAs; three years later, the agency began administering a CPA examination. In 1993, the "CPA Law" issued by China's central government provided a more coherent regulatory infrastructure for the new profession by documenting in detail the specific responsibilities of the CICPA. Although this law designated the CICPA as the principal regulatory body for the accounting profession, the powerful MOF retained the authority to override any decisions made by the CICPA.

Presently, China has approximately 150,000 CPAs; however, many of these individuals are retired government bureaucrats with minimal or even no formal training or experience in accounting. These latter individuals were granted CPA designations by the CICPA because they had administrative experience of some kind with an SOE or other significant government-related organization. Leaders of China's accounting profession estimate that the nation has fewer than 100,000 professional accountants who have formal accounting training of any kind. That figure is in contrast with the approximately 650,000 CPAs in the United States, which has approximately one-fourth the population of China. Making matters worse, the educational programs completed by China's accountants are considerably less rigorous than the educational programs completed by professional accountants in Western economies. In fact, in 2000, fewer than 20 percent of China's CPAs held a university degree of any kind.[12]

Most of China's accounting firms were quickly organized in the early 1980s when the need for accounting services within the nation's new economy became evident. However, these new accounting firms were not equivalent to accounting firms in the United States and other developed economies. The largest and most prominent of China's new generation of accounting firms were created by various government agencies and, in reality, were simply appendages of those agencies. These "accounting firms" typically provided accounting services exclusively to the SOEs and other entities that were overseen by the agencies that had created the firms.

---

11. *The Asian Banker Journal* (online), "In Search of a Reliable Auditor," 31 August 2006.

12. Y. Tang, "Bumpy Road Leading to Internationalization: A Review of Accounting Development in China," *Accounting Horizons*, March 2000, 99.

Because the MOF and the CICPA recognized that the quality of services provided by the government agency–affiliated accounting firms was suspect, the two organizations launched a "clean-up" program in 1997 to force those firms to sever their relationships with the agencies that had created them. The MOF and CICPA also reviewed the operating policies and procedures of all Chinese accounting firms, including those not affiliated with government agencies. Over the course of the two-year clean-up program, approximately 10 percent of China's estimated 4,000 accounting firms were forced to disband, while another 30 percent were sanctioned and required to implement remedial measures of some kind.

Another principal objective of this clean-up program was to make accounting firms and individual accountants aware of their ethical responsibilities. One Chinese scholar observed that China's new accounting profession was created in a "moral vacuum" devoid of any consideration of ethical principles or issues.[13] In 1999, the CICPA issued a new authoritative pronouncement entitled "Professional Ethics" that identified the fundamental ethical responsibilities of Chinese CPAs, particularly their responsibility to perform accounting services with objectivity and integrity.

Big Four Lead the Way in Chinese Audits

During the early 1980s, the major international accounting firms recognized that the robust economy emerging in China was creating a new and potentially huge market for professional accounting services. Over the following two decades, each of the major international accounting firms established a network of practice offices in China. PricewaterhouseCoopers (PwC) invested $200 million to staff 12 offices in China with a workforce of 5,500 accountants, while Deloitte spent approximately the same amount to establish 10 China-based offices with a staff of 3,000 accountants.[14] KPMG and Ernst & Young established China practice units of comparable size to those of PwC and Deloitte. As one Chinese news service noted, the Big Four firms suddenly developed an "insatiable interest" in the Chinese market.[15] Ernst & Young's global chief operating officer seemed to confirm that point of view when he observed, "There is no greater opportunity in the world than in China in terms of our business."[16]

By 2005, the Big Four accounting firms were operating the four largest accounting practices in China. The largest domestic firm, Shu Lun Pan Certified Public Accountants, based in Shanghai, had annual revenues equal to less than one-third of KPMG's China practice, which was the smallest of the Big Four accounting practices in terms of annual revenues. As could be expected, China's major domestic accounting firms felt threatened by the Big Four's rapid growth in their country.[17] Instead of choosing to compete with the Big Four, many of the large domestic firms developed working relationships with one or more Big Four firms.

Independent auditing was a principal focus of the Big Four's practice development activities in China. Prior to Deng Xiaoping's economic reforms, there was little need for an independent audit function in China similar to that of Western economies. The

---

13. *Ibid.*

14. *SinoCast China Financial Watch* (online), "Accounting Giants Load Up on China," 28 June 2005.

15. *Ibid.*

16. W. Davies, "China Accounting Sector Makes Gains amid IPO Drive," *Global News Wire–Asia Africa Intelligence Wire*, 6 February 2007.

17. T. LeeMaster, "Cleaner Regime for China Auditors," *Global News Wire–Asia Africa Intelligence Wire*, 18 April 2005.

SOEs that dominated China's economy did not prepare periodic financial reports comparable to those prepared by large corporations in the United States and other free market economies. In addition, the principal users of the financial data prepared by SOEs were government bureaucrats that had access to the accounting systems of SOEs and could "audit" that data directly if they questioned its authenticity.

As China's new economy began emerging, the need for an independent audit function became readily apparent. The large FOEs that were developing in China were typically required to have their financial data audited since those data would be consolidated into another reporting entity's financial statements. Likewise, China's political leaders quickly recognized that SOEs needed annual audits to encourage foreign investors to purchase minority ownership interests in them. Those officials also realized that annual audits of SOEs would establish an important measure of accountability for their professional management teams.

China's domestic independent audit function developed slowly and haphazardly during the 1980s. Unlike in the United States and other Western economies, China's accounting firms did not initially provide audit services. In the early 1980s, organizations offering audit-type services began appearing in China's major metropolitan areas. Similar to China's first-generation accounting firms, most of the nation's early audit firms were affiliated with, or sponsored by, a government agency. These audit firms—which were overseen by the State Audit Administration (SAA)—provided principally operational, compliance, and "social" audit services. Full-scope financial statement audits were rare and when they were performed, they were not oriented around the rigorous professional standards used in Western economies. Eventually, many of China's larger domestic accounting firms began providing services similar to those provided by audit firms, resulting in significant competition between the two types of firms.

By the early 1990s, the Chinese audit market was a mishmash of various types of audit-type services and service providers. Adding to the confusion was an array of often conflicting auditing rules and regulations issued by the CICPA, MOF, SAA, and other government agencies that claimed some degree of regulatory oversight for the audit services market. This chaos was a contributing factor to several large-scale accounting and auditing scandals within China during the 1990s. Among the most notorious of these scandals was the Great Wall Fundraising fraud involving the Great Wall Electrical Engineering Science and Technology Company. This company's executives used financial statements "certified" by a local accounting firm to raise a large amount of funds from private investors across China, much of which they embezzled. A subsequent investigation revealed that the accounting firm had spent only one day auditing the company's financial statements. China's central government dealt quickly and harshly with the parties involved in the fraud. The chief architect of the fraud, the company president, was executed, while the company's accounting firm was disbanded.

The Great Wall Fundraising scandal and mounting criticism of China's chaotic audit services market by various parties, including the major international accounting firms, were key factors that persuaded the central government to issue the 1993 CPA Law. That statute consolidated the nation's accounting and auditing professions and placed them under the regulatory supervision of the CICPA, which remained ultimately accountable to the MOF. The CPA Law also mandated that the CICPA develop independent auditing standards that would be subject to the approval of the MOF.

In late 1994, the CICPA formed a task force to begin drafting Chinese Independent Auditing Standards (CIAS). Over the next several years, the CICPA issued auditing standards dealing with such topics as materiality, internal control risks, application of analytical procedures, computer-based auditing procedures, fraud detection, and "special considerations in the audit of state-owned companies."[18] Despite the promulgation of these standards, the quality of independent audits provided by domestic firms remained questionable. Many of China's domestic firms treated the new standards as guidelines rather than mandatory rules. Even more troubling, many audit clients routinely pressured their auditors to help them conceal material errors and fraudulent misrepresentations in their accounting records. "Some clients . . . expected their auditors to help them conceal their frauds. Many companies would not reappoint their auditors if the latter were unwilling to help them cover up their wrongdoings."[19]

As the Chinese audit discipline continued to evolve in the late 1990s and into the new century, the Big Four firms became increasingly important participants in that market. According to one Asian business publication, the Big Four's growing prominence in China's audit services market was due to those firms' reputation for "professionalism, technical ability, and their independence from clients."[20]

By 2006, the Big Four firms audited a large majority of China's major business organizations. A Hong Kong brokerage firm surveyed 150 large companies listed on Chinese stock exchanges and found that only six did not employ Big Four auditors. The brokerage firm referred to those companies as the "suspicious six,"[21] implying that their financial statements were suspect. A manager of a Hong Kong hedge fund expressed a similar point of view: "I don't think I'm comfortable with local [audit] firms. It's the professionalism of the people. It seems like they like to twist the rules. That bothers me."[22]

The most prized of all audit clients in China are the "Big Four" banks that serve as the cornerstones of the nation's economy. These banks include the Agricultural Bank of China, the Bank of China, the China Construction Bank, and the Industrial and Commercial Bank of China. Over the past several years, China's central government has used initial public offerings (IPOs) to sell minority ownership interests in these formerly wholly owned SOEs. For each of those IPOs, government officials retained a Big Four accounting firm to audit the given bank's financial statements. This "vote of confidence" in the Big Four accounting firms by China's political leaders suggested that those firms would likely play a significant role in the future development of the Chinese economy.

EPILOGUE

In 2005, the MOF announced that it was working with the International Accounting Standards Board (IASB) to converge CAS with International Financial Reporting Standards (IFRS). The deadline for completing this convergence process was extended on multiple occasions, but the process was ultimately expected to be completed no later than 2012. Most Chinese business organizations were required to adopt the revised CAS. The IASB reported that it would help Chinese officials develop IFRS-consistent CAS to meet the special needs of China's economic system, including an accounting standard addressing the controversial issue of disclosing material related-party transactions.

---

18. J. Z. Xiao, Y. Zhang, and Z. Xie, "The Making of Independent Auditing Standards in China," *Accounting Horizons*, March 2000, 77.

19. *Ibid.*

20. *The Asian Banker Journal*, "In Search of a Reliable Auditor."

21. *Ibid.*

22. *Ibid.*

This is a sound principle in general and particularly appropriate for companies in countries where the government owns a piece of everything, and presses companies to take steps that may be bad for them (such as buying from troubled suppliers to protect jobs). But because overlapping ownership is so common in China (the government still owns shares in almost every large company), detailing each [related-party] transaction would overwhelm the financial report.[23]

At the same time that the MOF announced the plan to converge CAS with IFRS, the government agency also announced that as of January 1, 2007, CIAS would be converged with International Standards on Auditing (ISAs). These latter standards are issued by the International Auditing and Assurance Standards Board (IAASB), an entity sponsored by the IFAC.

The decision by the MOF to converge Chinese accounting and auditing standards with international standards enhanced the already strong competitive position that the Big Four firms had established within the Chinese accounting and auditing services market. Because each of those firms had global accounting practices, they had extensive expertise in helping companies implement IFRS as well as significant experience in applying ISAs. As a result, the firms were ideally suited to help Chinese companies make the transition to the new accounting and auditing standards.

Despite the Big Four's bright prospects in China, the firms still face significant challenges in that market. These challenges include acquiring sufficient skilled accountants and auditors to staff their rapidly growing Chinese practices and coping with the nation's regulatory infrastructure that continues to be a cluttered maze of often-conflicting regulations issued by several layers of the Communist bureaucracy. Two more serious and difficult-to-resolve problems facing Big Four firms are an increasing litigation risk within China and the need to deal with an authoritarian central government that influences every facet of the Chinese society and economy.

Since the 1970s, arguably the most important challenge faced by the Big Four accounting firms in the United States has been the large number of civil lawsuits filed against them. In recent years, the Big Four firms have begun experiencing litigation problems in China. Numerous accounting frauds, embezzlement schemes, and related scams have been perpetrated by opportunists hoping to take advantage of China's new economic system. Many private investors, institutional investors, government agencies, and other parties adversely affected by these subterfuges have begun adopting a Western-style strategy to recover their losses and/or mend their wounded pride, namely, filing lawsuits against parties even remotely associated with the fraudulent activities. At least in part because of their "deep pockets" and high public profiles, Big Four firms have increasingly found themselves targets of such lawsuits.

In 2003, KPMG became the first of the Big Four accounting firms to be named as a defendant in a major securities lawsuit filed by Chinese investors. The accounting firm issued a series of unqualified opinions on the financial statements of Jinzhou Port Company Limited, a company sanctioned by the MOF for intentionally overstating its revenues over the five-year period 1996–2000. The other Big Four firms have been ensnared in similar financial scandals involving Chinese companies: Deloitte (Guangdong Kelon Electrical Holdings Company), PwC (Shanghai Waigaoqiao Free Trade Zone Development Company Limited), and Ernst & Young (Global Trend Intelligent Technologies).

The Big Four firms insist that the complaints filed against them in these and other cases are unwarranted and that the engagements in question were completed with due professional care. Nevertheless, critics suggest that the quality of independent audits in China is generally weaker than in Western countries, an allegation seemingly confirmed by a Deloitte partner. "Auditing is easier in an environment where all your clients have 25 accountants, internal controls, and independent boards. The audit process is the same in this part of the world; we follow the same methodology

---

23. *The Economist* (online), "Cultural Revolution: New Accounting Rules Have Replaced the Little Red Book as China's Guide to Self-improvement; Can the State Handle the Truth?" 11 January 2007.

and document it in the same way. But, the material you're dealing with is different."[24] A KPMG partner voiced a similar opinion when he noted that within China "the public expects too much of auditors. Audit work is one thing. The most important thing is the integrity of the owners and managers."[25]

An even more serious challenge than the increasing risk of civil litigation facing the Big Four accounting firms in China is how they will deal with their ultimate "client" in that market, namely, the authoritarian central government. No doubt, executives of the Big Four firms recognize that conflicts with officials of the Chinese government could damage their future opportunities in the lucrative Chinese market. These executives also realize that their credibility in other markets around the globe could be damaged if their firms are perceived as kowtowing to Chinese governmental officials.

Ernst & Young was the first of the Big Four firms to have a highly publicized confrontation with China's Communist central government. In 2006, a Chinese government agency hired Ernst & Young to prepare a report on the "nonperforming loans" held by China's Big Four banks. Over the previous several years, the magnitude of China's nonperforming loans had become a major international issue. "The size of China's bad loans is a figure of immense importance, as it serves as a measure of the banking sector's financial health."[26] At the time, many economists maintained that governmental officials routinely embellished the health of the Chinese economy by refusing to disclose that a significant proportion of the Big Four banks' loan portfolios were uncollectible. Allegedly, those officials refused to recognize the magnitude of this problem because doing so would have damaged China's credit rating in international markets, discouraged much-needed foreign investment, and undercut the

impressive economic trends that the central government regularly touted in the global press.

In May 2006, Ernst & Young reported that China's Big Four banks had total nonperforming loans of more than $900 billion. That figure was several times higher than the $133 billion figure being reported by the Chinese government. Chinese officials reacted quickly and fiercely to the E&Y report, referring to it as "ridiculous and barely understandable."[27] Those officials went on to point out that if the nonperforming loans figure reported by E&Y was accurate, then the "clean" opinion E&Y had issued on a Big Four bank's financial statements was almost certainly wrong.

Within a few days of the harsh criticism by Chinese officials, Ernst & Young retracted its report. In the retraction, Ernst & Young stated that "Upon further research, Ernst & Young Global finds that this number cannot be supported, and believes it to be factually erroneous."[28] The retraction went on to note that Ernst & Young believed that the nonperforming loans figure of $133 billion reported by the Chinese government was accurate. Skeptics immediately accused E&Y of capitulating to the Chinese government. Many economic analysts chimed in as well, insisting that the Chinese government's figure was only a fraction of the actual bad loans held by the Big Four banks.

The E&Y incident raised two concerns within the global investment and business community. First, the incident only added to widespread speculation that China's impressive economic data had been intentionally inflated by the nation's Communist government. "It has become an article of faith over the past quarter of a century of China's economic opening up that numbers issued by the Beijing government are at best rose-tinted, and at worst politically motivated fabrications."[29] Second, the incident suggested that China's central

---

24. *The Asian Banker Journal,* "In Search of a Reliable Auditor."

25. *Ibid.*

26. *Agence France Presse* (online), "Ernst & Young Withdraws 'Erroneous' Report on Bad Loans in China," 15 May 2006.

27. J. Manthorpe, "Accountants Backtrack on China Bad-Debt Report," *The Vancouver Sun,* 23 May 2006, E5.

28. *Ibid.*

29. *Ibid.*

government would not hesitate to use its authoritarian powers to stifle dissent or honest differences of opinion, even an objective opinion expressed by a respected international accounting firm.

Ernst & Young's unpleasant encounter with Chinese governmental officials angered many Western journalists. In commenting on that encounter, one such journalist suggested that those officials had not internalized the slogan adopted by Deng Xiaoping when he attempted to resurrect the Chinese economy after nearly 30 years of the failed policies of Mao Zedong. "'Truth from facts' was the slogan adopted by the Chinese government after Mao's death to strip away the lies that left China a wallowing giant. Thirty years on, this remains an elusive goal."[30]

Questions

1. Research relevant databases to identify important recent developments within China's accounting profession, including the nation's independent audit function. Summarize these developments in a bullet format.

2. Since ethical and moral values vary from culture to culture and nation to nation, does this mean that a global profession, such as the accounting profession, cannot have a uniform ethical code? Explain.

3. How, if at all, do financial reporting objectives differ between a free market economy and a "socialistic market economy"? Explain. Are there specific accounting concepts or principles that are more or less relevant in a free market economy than in a socialistic market economy? If so, identify those concepts or principles and briefly explain your rationale.

4. Consider two organizations that require annual independent audits. Organization A is a Chinese SOE with a minority ownership interest of 20 percent, while Organization B is a U.S. company of similar size operating in the same industry. The common stock of both entities is traded on a domestic stock exchange, and each is audited by a Big Four firm. List specific differences that you might expect in the independent audits of these two organizations. *Ceteris paribus*, would you expect more "audit failures" for SOE audit clients than for similar U.S. audit clients? Defend your answer.

5. What recommendations would you make to Big Four firms to help them (1) avoid confrontations with governmental officials in an authoritarian society and (2) deal effectively with such confrontations that do arise?

---

30. *The Economist*, "Truth from Facts," 13 January 2007, 14.

Kaset Thai Sugar Company

The black Toyota minivan made slow but steady progress down the narrow, unpaved road as it approached the village of Takhli in south central Thailand, approximately 150 miles north of Bangkok. On either side of the bumpy road were fields of sugarcane, dense thickets of scrub brush, and an occasional rice paddy. Seated in a rear window seat of the minivan was Michael Wansley, a senior partner with Deloitte Touche Tohmatsu, who was based in that firm's Melbourne, Australia, practice office. The vehicle's four other occupants were Thai nationals and employees of the Kaset Thai Sugar Company. No doubt, the five weary travelers who had spent several hours in the cramped minivan were overjoyed when they finally caught a glimpse of the large sugar mill in the distance that was their final destination. The sugar mill was one of many owned and operated by the Kaset Thai Sugar Company.

For the past several weeks, Michael Wansley had been supervising a debt-restructuring engagement for the company's banks and other lenders. Kaset Thai Sugar had defaulted on nearly $500 million of loans to those lenders. Wansley and the 14 subordinates on his engagement team were to study the company's accounting records and business operations and then make recommendations about how the lenders should proceed in attempting to collect all—or, at least, a significant portion—of the outstanding loans.

Wansley, a well-known debt-restructuring expert, had become all too familiar with remote Thailand communities, such as Takhli, over the previous several months because the services of debt-restructuring specialists were much in demand within Thailand during the late 1990s. In March 1999 when Wansley visited the sugar mill on the outskirts of Takhli, the nation of Thailand was mired in a financial crisis. From 1985 through 1995, Thailand had boasted the highest economic growth rate in the world, averaging almost 9 percent annually over that time span. That trend prompted billions of dollars of foreign direct investment in Thailand companies, the bulk of which was in the form of loans.

Thailand's impressive economic growth came to a jarring halt in 1997, undercut by speculative investments, mismanagement, and extensive fraud on the part of business owners and corporate executives. According to one critic of Thailand's free-wheeling economic system, "cronyism, collusion, corruption, and complacency" had long been the "four modern horsemen of the apocalypse" in that economy.[1] By the late 1990s, hundreds of Thai companies faced bankruptcy, unable to pay back the loans they had secured over the previous decade. In 1999, nearly one-half of the $150 billion in outstanding loans to large Thai companies was classified as "nonperforming"—and it was estimated that $50 billion of that total would never be collected."[2]

As Thailand's financial crisis deepened, the foreign banks and other lenders that had pumped billions of dollars of debt capital into Thai companies began retaining

---

1. U. Parpart, "Restructuring East Asia: A Progress Report," *The Milken Institute Review*, Third Quarter 1999, 42.

2. *Ibid.*, 40.

debt-restructuring specialists in Australia, the United States, and other developed countries to help them determine how best to deal with their mounting portfolios of nonperforming loans. Among the major providers of these debt-restructuring services were the large international accounting firms, including Deloitte, Michael Wansley's firm.

The nature of debt-restructuring services varies significantly but such engagements often begin with an intense study or "audit" of the given entity's accounting records. This examination is intended to uncover any evidence of embezzlement or other malfeasance by management or other parties. These engagements also commonly include an in-depth analysis of the debtor company's business model to determine whether the entity appears to be economically viable. A debt-restructuring engagement typically concludes with the engagement team developing a series of recommendations intended to help the lenders of the financially troubled company minimize their loan losses. These recommendations may involve replacing the existing management team, having the lender or lenders forgive their outstanding loans in exchange for equity interests in the given company, or liquidating the company to raise funds that can be used to repay or partially repay its outstanding loans.

Not surprisingly given their nature and purpose, debt-restructuring engagements can be rife with tension. *Business Week* noted that Thailand's financial crisis spawned "Debt Wars" in that country that pitted representatives of the large international accounting firms, such as Michael Wansley, against Thai business owners and executives.[3] Thai business owners and executives resented the probing and relentless investigations of the "farangs" (foreigners) who did not appreciate or fully understand the informal and low-key culture of the Thai business community, a culture in which "handshake" contracts were common, disagreements were considered impolite, and face-to-face confrontations were rare. Making matters worse, Thai companies were not accustomed to having their financial records and business operations scrutinized by third parties since the nation's independent audit function was still evolving and was not nearly as rigorous as in developed countries around the world.

The investigative work of debt-restructuring specialists was particularly galling to members of the wealthy Thai families that had long dominated their nation's economy. Until the late 1990s, 15 Thai families controlled networks of businesses that accounted for more than one-half of Thailand's annual gross domestic product.[4] Among these families was the Siriviriyakul family that owned the Kaset Thai Sugar Company. For centuries, these families had operated their business empires with only minimal oversight or regulation from the Thai government or other parties. Suddenly, these prominent families found themselves being forced to respond to embarrassing questions and accusations posed by a small army of foreign accountants.

In January 1999, *Business Week* interviewed the 58-year-old Wansley regarding the difficult and stressful nature of his work in Thailand. Wansley noted that the most frustrating facet of debt-restructuring engagements in Thailand was the belligerent attitude of company owners. "Once you become grossly insolvent you're not supposed to be in a position of great strength, but here they think they are."[5] In a subsequent interview, Wansley also admitted that the hostile nature of the debt-restructuring engagements caused him to sometimes question his and his subordinates' safety. That concern was not unwarranted.

---

3. F. Balfour, "Fixing Thailand's Debt Mess," *Business Week* (www.businessweek.com), 12 February 2001.

4. Parpart, "Restructuring East Asia," 41.

5. R. Corben, M. Clifford, and B. Einhorn, "Thailand: Bring Your Spreadsheet–and Bulletproof Vest," *Business Week* (www.businessweek.com), 29 March 1999.

As the black minivan carrying Wansley and the four employees of Kaset Thai Sugar Company rolled to a stop outside the firm's Takhli sugar mill, two men on a motorcycle pulled up beside the vehicle. The man sitting on the rear of the motorcycle leaped off and within a matter of seconds fired eight bullets from an automatic pistol into the interior of the minivan. The bullets struck Michael Wansley in the head, killing him instantly. The four other passengers in the minivan were left unharmed as the gunman and his confederate sped away on the motorcycle.

The murder of Michael Wansley triggered outrage in Australia and the international business community. Australian government officials demanded that Thailand law enforcement authorities vigorously investigate the crime and apprehend those responsible. Eventually, six individuals would face criminal charges for Wansley's murder. These individuals included the gunman, the motorcyclist, the owner of the motorcycle, two employees of Kaset Thai Sugar Company who had allegedly been involved in the conspiracy to kill Wansley, and the owner of the Takhli sugar mill who was a member of the powerful Siriviriyakul family. This latter individual was charged with masterminding Wansley's murder.

The motorcyclist, who was arrested shortly after the incident, was convicted for his role in the crime and given a life sentence. A human resources manager of Kaset Thai Sugar and the owner of the motorcycle, a retired policeman, were convicted of conspiring to murder Wansley and received death sentences. The brother of the human resources manager, who was also a Kaset Thai Sugar employee, was convicted of conspiracy to commit murder but received a life sentence. In July 2008, the individual who allegedly shot Wansley was acquitted of that crime by a Thai court. The only witnesses who identified that individual as the gunman were two of his alleged co-conspirators; however, those witnesses' testimony was dismissed by the court. The court ruled that those witnesses were not credible since they were convicted felons.

The most controversial outcome in the criminal cases emanating from Wansley's death was the acquittal of the owner of the Takhli sugar mill despite seemingly strong evidence linking him to the crime. During this individual's trial, a witness testified that the defendant had paid him approximately $1,000 to dispose of the motorcycle used in the Wansley murder. Another individual, a senior law enforcement official, revealed that the sugar mill owner had offered him $4 million in exchange for not filing charges against him in the case. Phone records introduced as evidence during the trial documented that prior to the shooting the defendant had frequent telephone conversations with the three individuals convicted of conspiring to kill Wansley.

Court testimony also revealed that shortly before his death, Michael Wansley discovered that approximately $150 million loaned to the Kaset Thai Sugar Company had been secretly transferred to small companies controlled by the sugar mill owner and other members of his family. This testimony established that the defendant had a strong motive to harm Wansley. In fact, a Kaset Thai Sugar employee testified that following Wansley's death, the sugar mill owner had told him, "It's very good the farang is dead; now we can all live comfortably."[6] Despite such evidence, the three-judge tribunal that presided over the trial handed down a "not guilty" verdict, clearing the sugar mill owner of any involvement in Wansley's murder.[7,8]

---

6. J. Pollard, "Death Penalty for Aussie Auditor's Killers," *The Australian* (www.theaustralian.news.com.au), 6 September 2006.

7. One of the judges initially assigned to the case had been replaced when allegations surfaced that he had been paid a large bribe by the defendant's family.

8. The Siriviriyakul family maintained control of the Kaset Thai Sugar Company following Michael Wansley's death. When the debt-restructuring plan eventually developed by Deloitte was rejected by the company's creditors, a Thai court refused to liquidate the company and instead allowed the Siriviriyakul family to continue operating it.

The six individuals who faced criminal charges stemming from the murder of Michael Wansley were not the only parties blamed for his death. A journalist suggested that Wansley's employer, Deloitte, should shoulder some of the blame for his untimely death. Deloitte officials "should have known that they were sending the locally inexperienced Wansley into a dangerous situation without taking precautions."[9] The journalist pointed out that among the major international accounting firms, Deloitte had established a reputation as a leader in risk assessment and risk management. "These days, expertise in risk assessment–on which D. T. T. [Deloitte Touche Tohmatsu] prides itself–cannot be prudently limited to financial risk."[10]

Deloitte apparently did not respond directly to such criticism. However, several years later, Keith Skinner, the chief operating officer (COO) of Deloitte Touche Tohmatsu and a close friend of Michael Wansley, agreed to be interviewed regarding Wansley's death. In that interview, Skinner indicated that Wansley's murder "has had a lasting impact" on Deloitte's operations in regions of the world that are "culturally different."[11] When asked what specific changes Deloitte had made in response to the incident, Skinner reported that Deloitte was placing a higher priority on "security" issues for professional services engagements in high-risk countries. During this same interview, Skinner noted that his friend had not only been a well-respected professional but also an individual who was known for his extraordinary personal integrity and for being a devoted humanitarian. In particular, Wansley had devoted considerable time to working with the International Red Cross.

Questions

1. Suppose in the future you are assigned to an audit engagement that requires you to travel to a foreign country openly hostile to the United States. Because of that hostility, you are uncomfortable with the assignment. What would you do? Before responding, identify the alternatives you have.

2. Do you believe it is appropriate for a professional services firm to ask employees to serve on engagements in which their personal safety is at risk? Defend your answer.

---

9. Parpart, "Restructuring East Asia," 39.

10. *Ibid.*

11. A. Caldwell, "Murdered Accountant's Son Welcomes Sentences," www.abc.net.au, 5 September 2006.

Republic of Somalia

Accounting has a reputation as a fairly unexciting line of work. That won't be the case in Mogadishu.

Frank James, National Public Radio

The Horn of Africa has long played an important role in world history. Most historians believe that the large triangular peninsula that juts into the Indian Ocean along the east coast of Africa was the home of the legendary Kingdom of Punt, an important trading partner of ancient Egypt during the time of the pharaohs. Centuries later, the tribes that occupied the Horn of Africa played a pivotal role in the development of a strategic trade route linking the East and West. Those tribes patrolled the narrow mouth of the Red Sea that served as a passageway for merchant ships transporting goods to and from the Far East and Eurasia.

In modern times, the Horn of Africa has been home to the Republic of Somalia, a country that gained its independence from Italy and Great Britain in 1960. For most of the past five decades, the arid country with approximately ten million residents has been plagued by a bloody civil war. In 1991, the nation's central government collapsed, resulting in Somalia being carved up into lawless fiefdoms controlled by tribal warlords. In addition to being ravaged by civil war, Somalia has suffered greatly due to frequent military raids launched within its borders by neighboring Ethiopia and Kenya, each of which views the anarchy in Somalia as a threat to its own political and economic stability. Humanitarian organizations estimate that more than one million Somalis have been displaced by the two decades of warfare since Somalia plunged into anarchy. One-third of those Somalis who have not fled their homeland live in abject poverty without access to clean water or the most basic healthcare services.

Somalia has been in the news in recent years because of the gangs of pirates that operate from several camps along its long coastline. Following the turn of the century, these pirates began commandeering commercial ships that must skirt the coast of Somalia on their way to and from the Red Sea. *The New York Times* reported that during 2009 Somali pirates attacked 214 ships and successfully hijacked 47 of them.[1] According to the *Boston Globe*, the pirates received approximately $200 million in ransom payments from private companies and other organizations in a period of less than 15 months in 2008 and 2009. These payments were made in exchange for the release of the cargo and crews of the hijacked ships.[2]

The most pressing international concern posed by the civil unrest in Somalia has been the growing influence of the terrorist organization al Qaeda within the country. Al Qaeda has established training bases in Somalia and actively recruits large numbers of Somali youths who have few, if any, other employment opportunities. Because of Somalia's strategic importance to ocean trade routes and the Middle Eastern oil fields, the United States and other western powers have attempted to blunt the growing influence of al Qaeda in the country.

---

1. M. McDonald, "Record Number of Somali Pirate Attacks in 2009," *New York Times* (online), 29 December 2009.

2. A. Taylor, "Pirates of Somalia," *Boston Globe* (online), 16 March 2009.

In 2004, the United Nations and the African Union, with the financial support of the United States, organized the Transitional Federal Government (TFG) for Somalia. This new governmental entity was intended to re-establish some degree of civil law and rudimentary social functions, such as an educational system, within Somalia with a long-range objective of mediating the differences among the nation's warring tribes. The bulk of the financial support for the TFG was to be provided by foreign countries and by wealthy Somalis who had fled the country and settled elsewhere, principally in Canada, Great Britain, and the United States. In the first few years following its creation, the TFG received an estimated one billion dollars of foreign aid annually from Somali expatriates and other sources.

Shortly after the TFG was created, it faced a troublesome and largely unanticipated problem. When Somalia's central government disintegrated in 1991, the nation's banking system collapsed. The absence of a banking system made it difficult for the TFG to perform some of the most basic administrative functions necessary to sustain its operations, such as purchasing equipment and supplies and distributing payroll funds. (A security force of approximately 10,000 officers and soldiers is the largest component of the TFG's workforce.) The absence of a banking system when coupled with the TFG's failure to establish reliable accounting and control functions resulted in much of the foreign aid pouring into Somalia each year being embezzled. In turn, the reports of rampant embezzlement made it increasingly difficult for the TFG to raise funds from foreign sources.

To establish financial accountability for the TFG, representatives of a UN agency were stationed in Mogadishu, the country's capital. This UN team was to provide banking and related administrative functions for the TFG. Within a short time, however, the UN withdrew those individuals due to enormous safety concerns posed by the frequent street-to-street fighting, mortar attacks, and suicide bombings within Mogadishu.

In 2009, with the TFG in dire financial straits, the UN brokered a private agreement to have an outside organization manage the TFG's financial affairs. That organization was the world's largest accounting firm, PricewaterhouseCoopers (PwC). In a brief press release issued in July 2009, a PwC spokesperson confirmed that the firm had been "appointed to hold and manage the pledged and allocated funds for institutional capacity building and development [in Somalia]."[3] Citing client confidentiality and security concerns, PwC refused to divulge any more information regarding the unusual engagement or the nature of its contract with the TFG.[4]

Additional details of PwC's contractual agreement with the TFG were eventually leaked to the press. PwC reportedly had made a commitment to station 20 professional accountants and consultants in Nairobi, Kenya, to staff the engagement. (Nairobi is located approximately 600 miles east of Mogadishu—Kenya and Somalia share a long border.) These PwC staffers were charged with developing orderly cash receipts and disbursements functions for the foreign aid funneled to the TFG each year. Before releasing funds requisitioned by a TFG agency, PwC personnel would audit the requisition and establish that the funds were to be used for a legitimate purpose. After funds were disbursed to an agency, PwC would perform post-audit procedures to ascertain whether the funds had been used for their designated purpose.

Since the PwC staff would be stationed in Nairobi, Somali nationals living in the small sector of Mogadishu controlled by the TFG would be hired and trained by the

---

3. *BBC* (online), "Somalia Appoints Accountancy Firm," 8 July 2009.

4. *Ibid.*

firm to perform day-to-day administrative duties. PwC apparently agreed, however, that members of the Nairobi-based engagement team would occasionally travel to Mogadishu and remain there for short periods of time.

According to published reports, PwC was to be compensated on a commission basis for its services. The commissions earned by the firm would be equal to 2 to 4 percent of the funds that were ultimately spent for their designated purpose. Although PwC stood to earn tens of millions of dollars annually on the engagement, the firm's compensation was considerably more modest than the 10–14 percent commission charged by the UN agency that had previously performed similar services for the TFG.

TFG officials maintained that the services provided by PwC would help them rebuild a social and economic infrastructure for Somalia, as well as strengthen their organization's credibility around the globe. "This is a big step in reconstructing Somalia. In addition, this will enhance transparency and accountability."[5] Despite those expectations, the TFG's decision to hire PwC proved to be very controversial for both parties.

One prominent TFG critic suggested that despite public reports that the UN had brought together PwC and the TFG, the agreement between the two parties had been secretly orchestrated by Kenyan and Ethiopian government officials who were acting in the best interests of their countries, not those of Somalia.[6] This same critic also chided the TFG for choosing PwC rather than one of the other international accounting firms. "Of all the international accounting firms that your government could have hired, PwC should have been the last to be considered for the job. Take a look at how many scandals and lawsuits they have been involved in."[7] This individual then identified ten high-profile incidents that documented PwC's recent legal troubles, including the firm's role in the Satyam fraud in India.

Several other parties provided less emotional and thus more credible critiques of the TFG's decision to retain PwC. These parties' most common complaint involved the lack of transparency surrounding the decision by the TFG to hire PwC and its failure to publicly disclose the specific nature of PwC's responsibilities. One critic observed that since TFG officials had been involved in previous "illegal agreements," it was inappropriate for them to engage in confidential contracts that could provide them an opportunity to once again use foreign donations for their own personal benefit.[8] "The PwC contract will most likely generate windfalls for personal benefit [of TFG officials]. Client confidentiality is a very handy defense for any abuse of power and misappropriation of funds."[9] This same critic noted that Transparency International, a highly regarded organization committed to leading the global fight against corruption, insists that secret contracts such as the TFG-PwC agreement effectively shield corrupt governmental officials from prosecution.[10] (In 2009, Somalia topped Transparency International's list of the most corrupt nations worldwide.)

---

5. *Somalialand Times* (online), "Somalia Hires UK Accountancy Firm," 11 July 2009.

6. *Hiiraan* (online), "There Is No Circular Logic in Honesty," 21 January 2010. (Note: Hiiraan is an online Somali news and information service.)

7. *Ibid.*

8. M. M. Uluso, "PwC's Contract Empowers 'The Smartest Guys in the Room,'" *Somaliatalk.com*, 2 August 2009.

9. *Ibid.*

10. *Ibid.*

Certain parties also questioned the judgment of PwC in accepting the Somalia engagement. One concern voiced repeatedly was how the firm could ensure the safety of the individuals assigned to the engagement, particularly when those individuals found it necessary to travel to war-torn Mogadishu. In response to that concern, PwC officials noted that their firm had previously carried out similar but less-publicized engagements in both Afghanistan and Sudan. On its website, PwC disclosed that the individuals who had been assigned to the Sudanese engagement had been required to participate in a survivalist program known by the acronym THREAT–The Hostile Region Environment Awareness Training. No doubt, the firm required the staff assigned to the Somalia engagement to undergo similar training.[11]

EPILOGUE

Throughout the latter one-half of 2009 and beyond, Somalia continued to be plagued by violence that often resulted in significant casualties for the TFG militia, al Qaeda-trained and financed guerillas, and innocent civilians. Charges of government corruption also continued unabated following the retention of PwC by the TFG. In early 2010, the UN and U.S. government began quarreling over the issue of foreign aid for Somalia. According to *The New York Times*, the UN was upset because U.S. government officials were stymieing the flow of foreign aid into Somalia due to "unfounded allegations" that much of the aid was being "diverted to terrorists."[12] Two weeks later, those U.S. officials referred to a report prepared by the UN's own Security Council to support those unfounded allegations. This report indicated that as much as one-half of the foreign aid flowing into Somalia was being embezzled by various parties including corrupt TFG officials and "radical Islamist militants."[13]

Questions

1. What type of professional service engagement is PwC providing to the TFG? What professional standards apply to such engagements?

2. Do you agree that the client confidentiality rule prohibits PwC from disclosing the contractual details of the Somalia engagement? Defend your answer.

3. In addition to client confidentiality, what other ethical issues or challenges does the Somalia engagement present for PwC?

4. Identify the specific risks that the Somalia engagement poses for PwC as a firm. Do you believe that PwC has properly considered and mitigated each of these risks? Explain.

---

11. Those parties who criticized PwC for accepting the lucrative Somalia engagement failed to comment on the prominent firm's involvement in important humanitarian activities around the globe. In 2008, the firm committed millions of dollars to a program to help educate Sudanese children living in refugee camps in Chad. Among the many other humanitarian activities supported by PwC is the global initiative of the Save the Children program that provides educational and healthcare services to impoverished children around the globe.

12. J. Gettleman, "U.N. Criticizes U.S. Restrictions on Aid for Somalia," *The New York Times* (online), 18 February 2010.

13. J. Gettleman, "Somalia Food Aid Bypasses Needy, U.N. Study Finds," *The New York Times* (online), 9 March 2010.

OAO Gazprom

In February 2002, a lengthy *Business Week* article examined a major financial scandal swirling around one of the large international accounting firms. Key features of the scandal included the accounting firm allegedly "overlooking wildly improper deals" in its audits of a huge client that ranked among the "country's biggest energy firms," a company that had become a symbol "for the evils of crony capitalism."[1] The opening prologue for the article went on to note that the scandal involved "billions and billions" of dollars of losses as well as "leaked documents, infuriated shareholders, and threatened lawsuits."[2] Several major political figures had been caught up in the scandal, including the President. No, the article was not dissecting the sudden collapse of Enron Corporation in December 2001. Instead, the article focused on the international controversy sparked by the relationship between the largest energy producer in Russia, OAO Gazprom, and that company's independent audit firm, PricewaterhouseCoopers (PwC).

The commotion surrounding PwC's audits of Gazprom was ignited by the accounting firm's alleged failure to report candidly on a series of huge transactions involving that company and several smaller firms owned or controlled by Gazprom executives or their family members. Principal among these entities was Itera, a secretive company with U.S. connections. Criticism of PwC's audits of Gazprom became so intense that the prominent accounting firm was forced to purchase full-page ads in the major Moscow newspapers to defend itself.

Rogue Capitalism

Throughout the 1990s, the dominant international accounting firms pursued strategic initiatives to expand their worldwide operations. Many of these initiatives targeted Russia and the cluster of smaller countries carved out of the former Soviet Union when it suddenly disintegrated in 1991. *The New York Times* reported that the major accounting firms were among the first foreign firms to establish significant operations in Russia following the collapse of the Soviet Union.[3] In their "competitive rush" to establish an economic beachhead in Russia, these firms may have underestimated the many risks posed by that country's rapidly evolving business environment.

The massive reorganization of Russia's political, social, and economic infrastructure in the 1990s produced widespread chaos within the suddenly "new" country that had a proud history that was centuries old. Russia's political leaders wanted to quickly embrace capitalism. To accomplish this objective, Russia's new democratic government implemented a "privatization programme" intended to convert the country from communism to capitalism in a span of a few years. The first and most important phase of this enormous project gave Russian citizens the right to acquire

---

1. P. Starobin and C. Belton, "Russia's Enron?" *BusinessWeek Online*, 18 February 2002.

2. *Ibid.*

3. S. Tavernise, "U.S. Auditors Find Things Are Different in Russia," *The New York Times*, 12 March 2002, Section W, 1.

ownership interests in thousands of Russian firms at a nominal cost by using state-issued "privatization vouchers." These Russian firms were formerly state-owned companies or agencies that had established corporate governance structures equivalent to boards of directors to oversee their operations. From 1992 through 1999, more than 75 percent of Russian companies were handed over to the private sector, although the federal government retained a sizable minority ownership interest in the nation's largest and most important companies.

The privatization program succeeded in quickly converting Russia's controlled economy into a free market economy. However, the project was flawed in many respects. For example, more than one-half of the newly created companies were technically insolvent and able to survive only with subsidies and other economic support from the federal government. Complicating everyday life for these new firms and their managers was the rampant inflation in the Russian economy that exceeded 2000 percent annually.

Arguably the most pervasive weakness of the privatization program was that it allowed thousands of the individuals who had overseen the formerly state-owned businesses to acquire top management positions in the newly organized companies. The Russian press commonly referred to these individuals as "red directors," since most of them had been Communist Party "apparatchiks" or operatives. Not surprisingly, few of these corporate managers shared or even understood the capitalistic principles they were being asked to embrace. As *Business Week* noted, these individuals "cling to the view that the enterprise is an engine to generate wealth for themselves."[4] This pervasive attitude among the newly minted corporate executives spawned a rough-and-tumble version of capitalism in Russia that sparked widespread violence–including hundreds of murders and contract killings, kickbacks, bribes, and "organized robbery."[5] Critics of the privatization program often pointed to OAO Gazprom, a huge Russian company, as a prime example of this "rogue" capitalism.

Gazprom, a term that means "gas industry," was initially a privately owned company created by officials of the Soviet Union to assume control of the country's natural gas industry. The company's most important assets are the enormous natural gas reserves discovered in Siberia following World War II. Gazprom was one of the first publicly owned firms created by Russia's privatization program. Fifteen percent of Gazprom's common stock was given to employees and 28 percent to customers, while the federal government retained a 40 percent ownership interest in the company. Most of Gazprom's remaining common stock was sold to foreign investors. To ensure that domestic investors maintained control of major Russian companies, foreign investors were permitted to buy only a small fraction of a Russian company's stock.

Gazprom's initial stockholders' meeting was held in 1995. At that meeting, the stockholders endorsed the board of directors' selection of PwC as the company's audit firm. Rem Vyakhirev, Gazprom's top executive at the time, reported that the world's largest audit firm had been chosen to enhance the credibility of his company's financial statements and financial disclosures.[6]

During the 1990s, Gazprom was arguably the most important Russian company and the largest by most standards. The massive company accounted for nearly 10 percent of Russia's gross domestic product and 20 percent of its exports and tax revenues. Gazprom had an estimated 400,000 employees and provided directly or indirectly a

---

4. P. Starobin, "Russia's World-Class Accounting Games," *BusinessWeek Online*, 5 March 2002.

5. Tavernise, "U.S. Auditors Find Things Are Different."

6. P. Kranz, "Boris' Young Turks," *Business Week*, 28 April 1997, 52.

livelihood for more than 6 million Russians. The company's influence stretched far beyond Russia's borders. Gazprom supplied more than one-half of the natural gas used in Europe and controlled one-third of the world's natural gas reserves.

Gazzoviki

Victor Chernomyrdin was born ten years following the Russian Revolution of 1917. Chernomyrdin's parents were peasants who worked on a Russian collective farm. As a young man faced with limited educational opportunities, Chernomyrdin decided to become a skilled craftsman, a machinist. Following World War II, he acquired a job working in his country's rapidly developing natural gas industry that was controlled by the Ministry of the Gas Industry. The Soviet Union citizens fortunate enough to have the relatively stable and lucrative jobs in this field became known as the gazzoviki.

Chernomyrdin gradually rose through the ranks of the gazzoviki. His career success was due to his hard work, dedication to the Communist Party to which he belonged, and, most important, his ability to foster mutually beneficial relationships with key superiors and subordinates. Chernomyrdin spent much of his long career with Gazprom in frigid Siberian oil and natural gas fields. For most of that time he worked side by side with Rem Vyakhirev, his most trusted ally and protégé whose first name was an acronym for "Revolution Engels-Marx," a common name given to Russian males in the years following the Russian Revolution. In a retrospective article examining the history of Gazprom, a British reporter commented on the company's culture and the close relationship that developed between Chernomyrdin and Vyakhirev, the two individuals who had the greatest impact on the company during its formative years.

> Gazprom is a closed world obsessed by status and hierarchy, and disdainful of outsiders. It is dominated by the macho gazzoviki, lifelong gas workers, including Mr. Vyakhirev and Mr. Chernomyrdin, who speak an earthy slang. They are united by years of working and drinking together in production plants in Russia's most remote and inhospitable regions. "You can't believe how much they drank," says one company insider. "Life was simpler in Siberia. They knew what was expected of them."[7]

In 1992, Boris Yeltsin became the new Russian republic's first president. Yeltsin chose Chernomyrdin, Gazprom's chief executive, to serve as the nation's prime minister, the second-highest-ranking position in the federal government. Before leaving Gazprom, Chernomyrdin appointed Rem Vyakhirev as the company's new chief executive. Despite being the senior member of Yeltsin's administration, Chernomyrdin kept a close watch on Gazprom's financial affairs and frequently communicated with Vyakhirev regarding the company's operations. Together, Chernomyrdin and Vyakhirev guided the company through its turbulent early years as a publicly owned company when it became known officially as OAO Gazprom. (The "OAO" prefix indicates that Gazprom is an open-stock or publicly owned company.)

During Yeltsin's administration, Russian journalists took advantage of their country's new freedoms to openly and harshly criticize top governmental officials. A common target of that criticism was Chernomyrdin. Gruff and terse by nature, Chernomyrdin was frequently derided by the Russian press for his unpolished social skills, his poor mastery of the Russian language, and his refusal to provide candid answers to questions posed to him by reporters.

---

7. A. Jack, "Is Time Up for the 'Secret State'?" *Financial Times* (London) 25 May 2001, 33.

Chernomyrdin's critics charged that he used his political power to grant large tax concessions and other economic benefits to Gazprom. These critics also maintained that Chernomyrdin and Vyakhirev diverted billions of dollars of Gazprom's assets to themselves and family members. Allegedly, the two men and their colleagues established a network of private companies and then channeled Gazprom assets to those companies through an array of complex and clandestine transactions. The Russian press also claimed that Chernomyrdin routinely used Gazprom funds to finance the election campaigns of political candidates in his Our Home Is Russia political party. Likewise, although Chernomyrdin frequently insisted that he had cut all ties to his Communist background, he reportedly used Gazprom funds to finance the election campaigns of several longtime colleagues running for office under the banner of the still active and powerful Communist Party.

In responding to the persistent stream of allegations and innuendos directed at him by the Russian press, an indifferent Chernomyrdin typically resorted to a brief phrase that is the Russian equivalent of "that's nonsense."[8] Another tactic Chernomyrdin used to rebuff allegations that he and his former subordinates at Gazprom were misusing corporate funds was to point out that the company's financial affairs were being closely monitored by a prestigious CPA firm, namely, PwC.

Chernomyrdin's relationship with Boris Yeltsin deteriorated over the years. In 1998, Yeltsin forced Chernomyrdin to resign as prime minister. Later that year, Chernomyrdin failed in his bid to replace Yeltsin as Russia's president. Following Yeltsin's resignation in 2000, former KGB intelligence agent Vladimir Putin was elected the new Russian president. In the meantime, Chernomyrdin had returned to Gazprom, assuming the position of chairman of the board while his close friend Rem Vyakhirev remained the company's chief executive.

Putin had campaigned as a reform candidate, promising to clean up the fraud and bribery that pervaded Russian business. Putin realized that for the Russian economy to become viable, Russia's major companies had to raise large amounts of debt and equity capital from foreign investors. But as long as self-interested "red directors" were in charge of those companies, Putin knew that foreign investors were unlikely to make major financial commitments to the Russian economy.

Putin singled out Gazprom and its management team as prime examples of what was wrong with the Russian economic system. He was particularly offended that Gazprom's executives viewed themselves as being "above the law"[9] and not accountable to the Russian public or elected officials. In fact, while serving as Gazprom's chief executive, Vyakhirev had his company acquire Russia's only independent television network, ostensibly to silence his critics.

Vyakhirev took pleasure in bragging about the power that he exercised as Gazprom's top executive. Vyakhirev "liked to boast of dispatching flunkies in the company jet to pick special tundra grass to feed the reindeer on his private Moscow estate."[10] A British periodical claimed that such abusive practices were commonplace and carried out "under the noses" of the firm's independent auditors.

> Under . . . Rem Vyakhirev, Gazprom resembled a badly run country more than it did a publicly traded energy company: it had its own intelligence service, fleet of aircraft, hotels, media outlets and even a yacht club. Under the noses of its Western auditors,

---

8. *Global News Wire* (online), "Gazprom Denies Making Contributions to Election Campaigns," 24 January 2000.

9. *The Irish Times* (online), "Russian Gas Chieftain Pushed Out by Putin," 8 June 2001.

10. *Ibid.*

billions of dollars of cash and assets leaked to companies where ownership was at best murky, at worst startlingly close to Gazprom's chiefs.[11]

True to his word, shortly after becoming president, Putin began forcing large numbers of red directors of major Russian companies to resign. Among the first such executives to lose their lucrative positions with major Russian firms were Vyakhirev and Chernomyrdin who were allowed by Putin to voluntarily "retire" from Gazprom.[12] Unlike most Russian retirees, Chernomyrdin and Vyakhirev would not have to rely on a meager government pension for their retirement income. In 2001, *Forbes* reported that the two former Russian peasants were among the 500 richest individuals in the world. *Forbes* pegged Vyakhirev's personal wealth at $1.5 billion, while Chernomyrdin's more modest fortune was estimated at $1.1 billion.[13]

Accounting and Auditing on the Fly

Banishing corrupt corporate executives was an important first step in Vladimir Putin's campaign to entice foreign investors to provide desperately needed debt and equity capital for large Russian companies. However, Putin also realized that his country's accounting and financial reporting practices had to be revamped before foreign investors would commit significant funds to those companies. The new country's existing financial reporting framework was a holdover from the system used in the Soviet Union, a system that was poorly suited for the needs of a free market economy.

> *In the chaotic early years of new Russian capitalism, accounting standards here were poorly suited to market economics. They were built around reporting to tax authorities, not gauging a company's financial health for investors. Oversight was all but nonexistent and the legal system was undeveloped, leaving room for manipulation and theft.*[14]

Russia's move toward a Western-style accounting and financial reporting system actually began shortly after the creation of the new Russian republic in 1991, well before Putin became the nation's top elected official. In 1992, Russia's new federal government approved "Regulation on Accounting and Reporting in the Russian Federation," an administrative decree intended to provide a blueprint for radically changing the nation's accounting and financial reporting system. The primary responsibility for implementing this decree would rest with the Ministry of Finance, the government agency charged with overseeing the country's financial infrastructure. Several organizations, among them the United Nations, the European Union, and the World Bank, pledged to help the Ministry of Finance implement the decree. The international accounting community, including the major international accounting firms and professional accounting organizations in leading industrialized nations, also offered to help the Ministry of Finance in its effort.

The most important feature of the plan to overhaul Russia's accounting and financial reporting system was the adoption of the fundamental accounting concepts and procedures that had become generally accepted in major industrialized countries over the previous two centuries. Even before the break-up of the Soviet Union, Russian accountants had recognized the concept of "fair presentation." However, an

---

11. *Economist.com*, "Last Night at the Gazprom," 31 May 2001.

12. Although Chernomyrdin had to give up his position with Gazprom in 2001, a few months later Putin appointed him Russia's ambassador to Ukraine. This appointment surprised foreign journalists since the two men had been fierce political rivals over the previous several years.

13. *The Russian Business Monitor* (online), "Eight Russians Put on Billionaires List," 22 June 2001.

14. Tavernise, "U.S. Auditors Find Things Are Different."

entity's financial statements were considered to be "fairly presented" if they complied with the arcane taxation, reporting, and administrative requirements of the federal government. The new accounting framework introduced into Russia in the early 1990s required companies to adopt such revolutionary concepts as recognizing revenues when earned and realized, properly matching revenues and expenses each accounting period, and invoking the historical cost principle for most assets.

Because Russia did not have a rigorous rule-making process for the accounting domain, the major international accounting firms and other influential parties encouraged the Russian federal government to endorse the accounting standards being promulgated by international rule-making bodies. In 1999, the Ministry of Finance announced that Russian companies could apply either the loose amalgamation of Russian Accounting Standards that had developed over the previous several years or the much more comprehensive and logically consistent International Accounting Standards (IAS), which are now known as International Financial Reporting Standards (IFRS).[15]

In 2001, the Ministry of Finance, with the full support of Vladimir Putin, made another bold and progressive decision when it announced that publicly owned Russian companies would be required to adopt IFRS. The conversion to IFRS was expected to take several years, possibly as long as a decade. (Russian authorities announced in 2011 that the switch to IFRS was still in progress and should be completed over the next several years.)

In addition to higher-quality accounting and financial reporting practices, Putin and other leading reformers in Russia realized that their nation needed a rigorous independent audit function to enhance the credibility of publicly issued financial data. The large international accounting firms that established practice offices for the first time in Russia during the early 1990s found that most large Russian companies required so-called statutory audits. Statutory audits were effectively "compliance" audits intended to determine whether a given company's periodic financial reports and internal accounting functions complied with the various governmental decrees and regulations to which they were subject.

In the Soviet Union, "independent audits" intended to enhance the credibility of publicly released financial statements in the minds of investors and creditors had not been necessary since the federal government controlled practically all economic resources. Exhibit 1 presents an example of a statutory audit report issued by PwC in April 2000 for one of its large Russian clients, the Joint-Stock Commercial Savings Bank of the Russian Federation. Notice that the third section of the report indicates the various rules, regulations, and standards that PwC followed in performing the given audit.

EXHIBIT 1

EXAMPLE OF
A RUSSIAN
STATUTORY AUDIT
REPORT ISSUED BY
PRICEWATERHOUSE-
COOPERS

> To the Shareholders of Joint-Stock Commercial
> Savings Bank of the Russian Federation (an open joint-stock company):
>
> 1. We have audited the accompanying 1999 statutory accounting reports of Joint-Stock Commercial Savings Bank of the Russian Federation (open joint-stock company) (hereinafter–the Bank). These statutory accounting reports were prepared by the management of the Bank in accordance with the Chart of Accounts for credit institutions prescribed by the Bank of Russia and other regulatory documents. These statutory accounting reports differ significantly from financial statements prepared in accordance with International Accounting Standards mainly in areas of valuation of assets and capital, period of recognition of revenues and expenses, recognition of liabilities and disclosures.

---

15. The IASB adopted the phrase "International Financial Reporting Standards" in 2001.

EXHIBIT 1—
continued

EXAMPLE OF
A RUSSIAN
STATUTORY AUDIT
REPORT ISSUED BY
PRICEWATERHOUSE-
COOPERS

2. Preparation of the statutory accounting reports is the responsibility of the management of the Bank. Our responsibility as statutory auditors is to express an opinion on the trustworthiness in all material respects of these statutory accounting reports based on our audit.

3. We conducted our statutory audit in accordance with:

   The Temporary Rules of Audit Activity in the Russian Federation adopted by Decree of the President of the Russian Federation of 22 December 1993, No. 2263;

   The Regulations on Audit Activity in the Banking System of the Russian Federation No. 64 approved by the Order of the Bank of Russia of 10 September 1997, No. 02-391;

   The Regulations of the Bank of Russia "On the order of compiling and presenting to the Bank of Russia the audit report on the results of checking the credit institution's activity for the reporting year" of 23 December 1997, No. 10-P;

   The rules and standards on auditing approved by the Commission on Audit Activity under the President of the Russian Federation;

   The standards of Banking Auditing approved by Expert Committee under the Bank of Russia;

   International Auditing Standards; and

   Internal standards of the firm.

   These standards require that we plan and perform the statutory audit to obtain reasonable assurance about whether the statutory accounting reports are free of material misstatement. An audit includes examining, on a test basis, evidence supporting the amounts and disclosures in the statutory accounting reports. An audit also includes assessing the accounting principles used and significant estimates made by management, as well as evaluating the overall presentation of the statutory accounting reports in order to assess compliance with laws and current regulations of the Russian Federation. We reviewed a sample of business transactions of the Bank for compliance with the effective legislation solely to obtain sufficient assurance that statutory accounting reports are free of material misstatements. We believe that our statutory audit provides a reasonable basis for our opinion.

4. In our opinion, the audited annual statutory accounting reports are prepared in all material aspects in accordance with legislation and statutory requirements regulating the procedure of accounting and preparation of statutory accounting reports in the Russian Federation and the principles of accounting accepted in the Russian Federation. On this basis, the proper preparation of the balance sheet and of the profit and loss account is confirmed.

5. Without qualifying our opinion, we draw attention to the fact that the operations of the Bank, and those of similar credit organisations in the Russian Federation, have been affected, and may be affected for the foreseeable future by the economic instability of the company.

PricewaterhouseCoopers
28 April 2000

Source: 1999 Annual Report of the Joint-Stock Commercial Savings Bank of the Russian Federation.

International accounting firms encouraged Russian federal officials to adopt an audit model patterned after the independent audit function in Western countries. These firms generally supported a move toward the British audit model, which requires independent auditors to decide whether a given client's financial statements present a "true and fair" view of its operating results and financial condition. A Moscow-based PwC audit partner reported that his firm had encountered major resistance to this radical change.

> *Companies say, "I don't need this. I want you to check our compliance with the law and regulations and that is all." If the local law does not require something, it is difficult to persuade clients to buy it. They don't understand the process of [conforming] to a true and fair view.*[16]

In 1999, the Institute of Professional Accountants of Russia (IPAR), a leading professional organization roughly comparable to the American Institute of Certified Public Accountants (AICPA), applied for admission to the New York-based International Federation of Accountants (IFAC). The IFAC's website notes that it is "an organization of national professional accountancy organizations that represent accountants employed in public practice, business and industry, the public sector, and education." More than 150 professional accountancy organizations are IFAC members, including the AICPA.

A major thrust of the IFAC is to develop International Standards of Auditing (ISAs) that can be readily applied in developing countries without a formal rule-making body for the auditing domain. The IFAC's auditing standards tend to be broad conceptual guidelines rather than detailed rules. Nevertheless, ISAs are generally consistent with the professional auditing standards applied in the major free market economies, including Great Britain and the United States.

The IPAR became an IFAC member in 2000. In the fall of that year, the first official Russian translation of ISAs was made available to the Russian accounting profession and the foreign accounting firms with practice units in Russia. At that point, the Big Five accounting firms, each of which had a major presence in Russia, began encouraging their clients to obtain ISA-based audits and began lobbying government officials to formally endorse the ISAs. In 2008, a new federal law finally mandated that ISAs be adopted in Russia. (The transition to ISAs, which was expected to require several years to complete, was still in progress in 2011.)

A key factor that impeded the spread of Western-style auditing in Russia during the 1990s was the existence of so-called "pocket auditors." Many, if not most, new Russian companies created in the early 1990s retained accounting firms run by friends and relatives of their executives to audit their financial statements and provide related professional services. These accounting firms allegedly helped their clients "cook their books" and "evade taxes and disguise asset-stripping."[17] Executives of Russian companies feared that PwC and the other international accounting firms would not be as cooperative or compliant as pocket auditors. However, the controversy spawned by PwC's audits of Gazprom caused many critics to suggest that the prestigious accounting firm was firmly "in the pockets" of Gazprom's top executives.

---

16. PricewaterhouseCoopers, "Russia: Hammering Out Standards, Hitting a Mindset," *WorldWatch*, March 2000, 14–15.

17. Starobin, "Russia's World-Class Accounting Games."

Wildest Dream or Worst Nightmare?

In July 1997, a reporter for the London-based *Financial Times* interviewed Bruce Edwards, the PwC audit partner who had just completed supervising his firm's first annual audit of Gazprom. The reporter noted that "to most auditors, Gazprom would rank as their wildest dream–or their worst nightmare."[18] The "dream" feature of the engagement was that it provided instant credibility for PwC in the Russian audit market. Another "dream" feature of the engagement was the $12 million annual fee that the accounting firm earned for the audit. On the downside, the Gazprom audit required the 70 PwC personnel assigned to the engagement to travel the length and breadth of Russia. To accomplish their audit objectives, the PwC auditors had to inspect many of the company's more than 1,000 operating units, which included slaughterhouses, media outlets, hospitals, a yacht club, and dozens of other ventures unrelated to the company's primary line of business.

In the *Financial Times* interview, Edwards downplayed the suggestion that audits of large Russian companies were markedly different from audits of comparable U.S. firms: "There is nothing mystical about Russian accounts. There is a huge misconception that Russia is somehow different, but I do not see it being much different to anywhere else."[19] Edwards did admit that Gazprom executives and employees were initially reluctant to share information with PwC auditors. However, that reluctance was "short-lived"; Edwards assured the newspaper reporter and then went on to maintain that the quality of financial information Gazprom personnel provided to PwC auditors "was extremely high."

One feature of the Gazprom audit on which Edwards did not comment was the company's extensive related-party transactions. During the late 1990s, major Russian newspapers and other media outlets charged that Gazprom's top executives were routinely siphoning off enormous amounts of assets to related-party entities that they or their family members controlled.

According to press reports, Gazprom officials sold a huge amount of natural gas at nominal prices to Itera, a privately owned company based in the Netherlands that has major operating units in Russia and the United States. Throughout the 1990s, Itera's top executive was Igor Makarov, a former Gazprom employee and Olympic biking champion for the Soviet Union. Makarov had been taught the intricacies of the natural gas industry by his close friend and mentor, Rem Vyakhirev. In one confirmed case, Gazprom sold a large volume of natural gas to Itera for $2 per cubic meter, which Itera then resold to European customers for more than $40 per cubic meter. In another transaction, Gazprom sold its 32 percent ownership interest in a gas-producing subsidiary, Purgas, to Itera for $1,200. Industry insiders estimated that the market price of that ownership interest was approximately $400 million. Thanks to such transactions, Itera grew from a small, unknown entity to the world's seventh-largest natural gas company in a span of only seven years during the 1990s.

Although Itera appears to be the company that has profited the most from Gazprom's generosity, several other firms have been the beneficiaries of similar sweetheart deals. Among these firms is Stroitransgaz, a pipeline construction company that landed a large number of lucrative contracts with Gazprom during the 1990s. According to the Russian press, Stroitransgaz's principal owners include Viktor Chernomyrdin's two sons and Rem Vyahkirev's daughter.

---

18. J. Thornhill, "Behind the High Walls at Gazprom," *Financial Times* (London), 11 July 1997, 24.
19. *Ibid.*

In 2001, Boris Fedorov, who had previously served as the head of the Ministry of Finance, was appointed to Gazprom's board of directors. Shortly after joining the board, Federov told the *Moscow Times* that Gazprom was losing the equivalent of $2 billion to $3 billion each year due to "corruption, nepotism, and simple theft."[20] That same newspaper went on to report that its own five-week investigation had uncovered evidence that Gazprom assets "have been systematically handed over to company managers–including Vyakhirev, his deputy Vyacheslav Sheremet, and former Prime Minister Viktor Chernomyrdin–throughout Vyakhirev's tenure."[21]

The increasingly revealing and hostile reports focusing on Gazprom's business dealings with Itera and other related companies outraged the international investment community and foreign political officials whose countries had provided billions of dollars of aid to jumpstart the fledgling Russian economy. Even more outraged were foreign investors who owned Gazprom stock. Among these investors were the stockholders of Hermitage Capital, Russia's largest private equity fund, which held a large minority ownership interest in Gazprom's outstanding stock. Most of Hermitage's stockholders were U.S. citizens.

William Browder, Hermitage's chairman and a former partner with the Wall Street investment banker Salomon Brothers, had begun accumulating Gazprom stock for Hermitage in the mid-1990s. Browder, an American citizen whose father had served decades earlier as a top official of the Communist Party in the United States, recognized that the huge natural gas reserves owned by the company were not properly impounded into Gazprom's stock market price. He expected that the stock's market price would rise dramatically when Western investors realized the massive resources controlled by the company. Unfortunately for Browder and his fellow Hermitage investors, Gazprom's stock price stubbornly refused to move higher.

A frustrated Browder reported in 2001 that if Gazprom's petroleum reserves were valued by the stock market on approximately the same basis as the comparable reserves of Exxon Mobil, the company's stock price would be 132 times higher.[22] Browder attributed the lack of interest in Gazprom's common stock to the fact that the company was literally "giving away" huge chunks of its natural gas reserves each year to Itera and other privately owned companies controlled by Gazprom executives, their family members, and their close friends and associates.

The growing controversy surrounding Gazprom's bizarre deals with Itera, which was fueled by the Russian press, forced the company's board to call for a "special audit" of the Gazprom–Itera transactions in January 2001. Ironically, that announcement sparked even more controversy and negative publicity for the company. When Gazprom's board announced that PwC had been retained to perform the Itera audit, critics immediately charged that PwC would effectively be auditing "itself," since the firm had given its implicit approval to the suspicious Itera transactions during its prior audits of Gazprom. Most galling to critics was that PwC had failed to even require Gazprom to disclose Itera as a related party in the footnotes to the company's financial statements over the previous several years.

Boris Fedorov, the sole Gazprom board member who voted to retain an accounting firm other than PwC to perform the special audit, publicly criticized the board's decision. "There is no way you can believe in an assignment which asks an auditor to check their own figures. It is spitting in the face of investors."[23] PwC's appointment

20. *Moscow Times*, "Time to Say Farewell to Vyakhirev," 22 May 2001, 12.

21. *Ibid.*

22. W. Browder, "Gazprom Investors Are Sold Short," *Moscow Times*, 30 July 2001, 8.

23. A. Jack and A. Ostrovsky, "Gazprom Vote Raises Concerns," *Financial Times* (London), 24 January 2001, 32.

to perform the special audit even caused dissension among the accounting firm's partners. *Business Week* reported that several senior PwC partners in the firm's Moscow office believed "that any self-review [of the Itera transactions] would lack credibility."[24]

Shortly after Gazprom's board hired PwC to investigate the company's business deals with Itera, a group of minority stockholders led by Federov appointed Deloitte & Touche to perform a parallel investigation of those same transactions. The other members of Gazprom's board squelched that effort by refusing to provide Deloitte access to the company's accounting records. Federov responded by claiming that the board's decision "showed that it [Gazprom's management] had something to hide."[25] Federov went on to demand that PwC rigorously interrogate Gazprom's executives and family members known to have ties to Itera. Within days, Federov found himself the target of anonymous threats by hostile adversaries. Accustomed to the often treacherous business environment of his country, Federov dismissed the threats and insisted that he would continue demanding that Gazprom provide more transparent and reliable financial reports to investors, creditors, and other third parties.

No Smoking Guns

PwC completed its four-month investigation of Gazprom's business dealings with Itera in the summer of 2001 and filed a 67-page confidential report of its findings with Gazprom's board. Within days, much of PwC's report had been leaked to the press. According to the *Financial Times*, PwC did not identify any "deals in which Itera benefited at the expense of Gazprom."[26] Subsequent press reports undercut the credibility of PwC's investigation. These reports indicated that PwC's investigation had been severely hamstrung by a lack of cooperation on the part of both Itera and Gazprom officials. Itera's management had refused to provide documents requested by PwC auditors, while 19 executives and former executives of Gazprom, including Rem Vyakhirev, had refused to answer questions posed to them by the auditors.

Not surprisingly, the results of the PwC investigation failed to placate Boris Federov, William Browder, and other critics of Gazprom's management. Instead, the tepid PwC report served to focus increasingly harsh criticism on the large accounting firm. In early 2002, Gazprom's board announced a "contest" to retain an accounting firm to audit the company's financial statements for the fiscal year ending June 30, 2002. Although Gazprom invited PwC to prepare a bid for the 2002 audit, the Russian and international business press indicated that there was little chance PwC would be selected given the adverse publicity that continued to plague the firm. Diminishing even further PwC's chances to retain the Gazprom engagement was a recommendation issued in early 2002 by the Russian Securities Commission, a federal agency equivalent to the U.S. Securities and Exchange Commission. That agency strongly encouraged large Russian companies to change their auditors periodically.

A few days after Gazprom announced the auditor contest, PwC purchased full-page ads in major Russian newspapers. These ads attempted to rebut much of the criticism that had been directed at the firm over the previous two years for its Gazprom audits. The ads suggested that PwC had been singled out for criticism based on "an inaccurate understanding of the roles and responsibilities of auditors."[27]

---

24. Starobin and Belton, "Russia's Enron?"

25. "Gazprom Won't Permit Audit by Deloitte," *National Post*, 21 March 2001, C2.

26. A. Jack, "Auditors Find No Evidence of Deals That Aided Itera," *Financial Times*, 6 July 2001, 22.

27. A. Jack, "PwC Acts to Defend Itself in Russia," *Financial Times* (London), 28 February 2002, 20.

In April 2002, Hermitage Capital filed multiple civil lawsuits against PwC in Russian courts alleging, among other charges, that the accounting firm had performed "deliberately false" audits of Gazprom. At the same time, Hermitage filed a request with the Ministry of Finance to suspend PwC's license to practice in Russia. A PwC spokesperson maintained that the allegations in the lawsuits were "completely unfounded" and that the firm's audits had "met all applicable legal and professional standards."[28]

The Hermitage lawsuits were the first such lawsuits filed against a major international accounting firm in Russia. Many legal experts questioned whether there was a valid basis for the lawsuits under the emerging but scanty Russian securities laws and legal precedents. Nevertheless, the Hermitage lawsuits startled PwC and the other major accounting firms operating in Russia. The lawsuits raised in a new context a slew of "old" issues that had pestered audit firms since the inception of the independent audit function.

> Whatever the truth, the audit profession in Russia faces the same difficulties as elsewhere in arguing that it is "watchdog not bloodhound"–with a remit to verify information, but not to actively sniff out fraud, and not to assume greater responsibility than management itself for errors they have committed. But the profession is also caught in a conflict of interest. Each firm is nominally charged with reporting to all shareholders whether a company's financial statements are "true and fair." In reality, it is appointed, paid by, and reports to executive management, which may be involved in activities to the detriment of outside investors.[29]

The inherently problematic nature of the auditor–client relationship is made even more problematic within Russia by two key factors. *The New York Times* reported that "fierce competition" among the major accounting firms to acquire and retain the relatively few large and lucrative Russian audit clients had resulted in auditors feeling pressured to "sign off on questionable practices by such clients to avoid alienating them."[30] A former Ernst & Young employee who had been assigned to that firm's Moscow office was more blunt. "A big client [in Russia] is god. You do what they want and tell you to do. You can play straight-laced with minor clients, but you can't do it with the big guys. If you lose the account, no matter how justified you are, that's the end of a career."[31]

The second factor complicating the quality of independent audits in Russia has been the haphazard, if not ragtag, nature of the country's auditing rules. Critics of independent auditors in Western countries have long suggested that professional auditing standards are too "flexible," which ultimately results in less rigorous audits and lower-quality financial statements. This problem has been exacerbated in Russia by the lack of consensus on what accounting and auditing rules should be applied while the country slowly transitions to professional standards comparable to those applied in Western democracies.

The evolving nature of Russia's professional standards have allowed auditors in that country to interpret their mission too narrowly, according to one former governmental official. Auditors "check that the paperwork was done correctly, but look right past the corrupt heart of the matter."[32] One former PwC auditor provided an example of this mindset in an interview with *The New York Times*. This individual reported that a large automobile manufacturer that was a PwC audit client effectively gave away

---

28. S. Tavernise, "Shareholder in Gazprom of Russia Sues Auditor," *The New York Times*, 16 April 2002, W1.

29. A. Jack, "Testing Times for Auditors in Russia," *Financial Times* (London), 17 April 2002, 27.

30. Tavernise, "U.S. Auditors Find Things Are Different."

31. *Ibid.*

32. *Ibid.*

huge amounts of inventory by routinely shipping cars to supposed "dealers" who never paid for those shipments. The former PwC auditor recalled thinking, "What's going on? You aren't getting paid—no guarantees, no nothing. Are you stupid?' It was clear to me that it was organized robbery."[33] In its audit report, PwC commented on the fact that the client was using different methods to account for certain domestic sales and sales made to foreign customers. But, according to *The New York Times*, the firm failed to convey in its audit report "what was actually going on at the company."[34]

A PwC spokesperson refused to respond directly to the charges made by his firm's former employee but did insist that PwC "stood by its audits" of the given client. *The New York Times* reporter then asked an audit partner with Arthur Andersen about an Andersen client that routinely sold merchandise to related parties at deeply discounted prices. The nature of these sales was not disclosed in the company's financial statements or in Andersen's audit reports on those financial statements. When asked why such disclosures were not made, the Andersen audit partner replied that Russian law did not require them. This attitude on the part of major international accounting firms operating in Russia has proven to be extremely detrimental to domestic and foreign investors.

> In this environment, Western auditing firms could have and should have held their Russian clients to higher standards of behavior, investors in Russian companies are now saying. But, instead . . . the auditors chose to play by Russian rules, and in doing so sacrificed the transparency that investors were counting on them to ensure.[35]

Profit after Stealing and Subsidies

Despite earlier reports that Gazprom would likely retain a new audit firm, in May 2002 the company issued a press release indicating that PwC would remain its independent auditor. Of 29 accounting firms that had submitted bids for the Gazprom engagement, the company's board reported that PwC was the firm that best met its "requirements."[36]

Throughout the late spring and summer of 2002, PwC received more good news as one by one the Russian courts dismissed the lawsuits filed against the company by Hermitage Capital. The Russian courts ruled that under existing Russian law only the audited entity could sue its accounting firm for defective audits. Since the majority of Gazprom's board of directors and stockholders refused to side with the plaintiffs in the lawsuits, the courts' only alternative was to rule that the lawsuits were invalid. The Ministry of Finance also denied Hermitage's request that PwC's license to practice be rescinded.

William Browder reacted angrily to the dismissal of the lawsuits his firm had filed against PwC and the news that the accounting firm would remain Gazprom's auditor. Browder argued that, at a minimum, PwC and Gazprom officials should provide more detailed disclosures regarding the company's key operating results. For example, Browder suggested that in the future the company report in its income statements, "Profit after Stealing and Subsidies" and "Profit If Stealing and Subsidies Are Eliminated."[37]

---

33. *Ibid.*

34. *Ibid.*

35. *Ibid.*

36. In 2011, PwC was still Gazprom's independent audit firm.

37. M. Waller, "Fingered," *The Times* (London), 12 July 2002, 27.

Questions

1. List the challenges that a major accounting firm faces when it establishes its first practice office in a foreign country. Identify the key factors that accounting firms should consider when deciding whether to establish a practice office in a new market.

2. Suppose that a U.S. based accounting firm has a major audit client in a foreign country that routinely engages in business practices that are considered legal in that country but that would qualify as both illegal and unethical in the United States. What specific moral or ethical obligations, if any, would these circumstances impose on this accounting firm? Explain.

3. What responsibilities, if any, do you believe PwC had to Gazprom's minority investors?

4. In your opinion, should PwC have agreed to perform the "special audit" of the Itera transactions? Defend your answer. In your answer, identify the specific ethical issues or challenges that the engagement posed for PwC.

5. In the United States, what responsibility do auditors have to determine whether or not "related parties" exist for a given audit client? Explain.

6. Explain how the British "true and fair" audit approach or strategy differs from the audit philosophy applied in the United States. In your opinion, which of the two audit approaches is better or, at least, more defensible?

Societe Generale

Qui seme le vent recolte la tempete.
(he who sows the wind shall reap the whirlwind)

French proverb

Jerome Kerviel was born and raised in Pont-l'Abbe, a small coastal village in the Brittany region of northwestern France. His father was a blacksmith, while his mother worked as a hairdresser. Throughout his adolescent years, Kerviel dreamed of experiencing the excitement of nearby Paris, the City of Lights. Not surprisingly then, after completing undergraduate and graduate degrees in finance, the 23-year-old Kerviel accepted an entry-level position in Paris with Societe Generale, France's second largest bank.

Kerviel's job at Societe Generale involved working in the financial institution's "back office." For four years, Kerviel effectively served as an internal auditor ensuring that the bank's employees were complying with applicable company policies and procedures. His responsibilities included monitoring the bank's securities transactions to identify unauthorized trades, for example, trades that exceeded the monetary limits that had been established for individual securities traders.

Although polite and well-mannered, the handsome Kerviel made few friends within the bank and was thought of as "loner" by most of his co-workers. In 2004, Kerviel accomplished his goal of being promoted to a securities trader. This new position provided Kerviel an opportunity to make better use of his educational background while at the same time allowing him to escape the relative anonymity and boredom of Societe Generale's back office.

Unlike Kerviel, Societe Generale's typical securities trader was a graduate of one of France's high-profile universities and had been immediately assigned to the bank's trading staff when hired. In France's hierarchical society, one's educational background and socio-economic status tend to have a disproportionate influence on not only employment opportunities but also the ability to progress rapidly within an organization once hired. Reportedly, Kerviel wanted to prove that despite his modest credentials and lower-middle class upbringing, he could complete with his more blue-blooded colleagues when he finally landed a job in Societe Generale's trading division.

After becoming a securities trader, Kerviel worked hard to impress his superiors. Neighbors reported that he left his home in a Paris suburb early each morning and returned late every evening. Kerviel was so dedicated to his job that he refused to take advantage of the several weeks of vacation time that he was entitled to each year. By late 2007, Kerviel's annual salary was approximately 100,000 euros, an impressive sum by most standards but just a fraction of what many of his fellow traders earned.

In late January 2008, Daniel Bouton, Societe Generale's chief executive officer (CEO) and chairman of the board, startled the global financial markets by announcing that over a period of just three days his bank had suffered losses of more than six billion euros on a series of unauthorized securities trades made by a "rogue trader." According to Bouton, the trader had used his knowledge of the bank's accounting and computer systems to circumvent the labyrinth of internal control policies and procedures designed to prevent and detect unauthorized securities trades. That individual was none other than Jerome Kerviel.

Within two days of Bouton's announcement, Jerome Kerviel was arrested by France's gendarmes. For 48 hours, law enforcement and regulatory authorities grilled the young Parisian to uncover the details of the largest fraud in the history of the banking industry. According to his attorneys, Kerviel held up extremely well during the intense interrogations. At one point, the stoic Kerviel offered one of the greatest understatements in the sordid history of crime when he casually told his interrogators that "I just got a bit carried away."[1]

Fraud, French Style

Societe Generale was founded in 1864 during the reign of Napoleon III, the nephew of Napoleon Bonaparte and France's final monarch. The bank quickly became an important source of capital for the nation's rapidly growing economy during the final few decades of the nineteenth century. By the onset of World War II, Societe Generale operated 1,500 branches, including branches in the United States and dozens of other countries.

Following World War II, France's federal government nationalized Societe Generale to finance the reconstruction of the nation's economic infrastructure that had been decimated by the war. The government returned the bank to the private sector in 1987. By the turn of the century, Societe Generale had reestablished itself as one of the world's largest and most important financial institutions. By 2007, the bank operated in almost 90 countries, had total assets of 1.1 trillion euros, and had more than 130,000 employees worldwide.

In the global banking industry, Societe Generale and several other large French banks are best known for developing a wide range of exotic financial instruments commonly referred to as derivatives. "Societe Generale pioneered equity derivatives, which allows investors to bet on future movements in stocks or markets."[2] Because of their leadership role in the development of financial derivatives, French banks control nearly one-third of the global market for those securities, a market that is measured in trillions of dollars. These same banks have also become well known for the "sophistication of their computer systems"[3] that are necessary to maintain control over their financial derivatives operations.

Societe Generale's 2007 annual report revealed that nearly 3,000 employees were assigned to control and manage the risks posed by the institution's around-the-clock and around-the-globe market trading activities. The most important of these activities are housed in the bank's equity derivatives division, the large bank's most profitable operating unit. The majority of the bank's control specialists work in Societe Generale's so-called back office where Jerome Kerviel began his career.

When he left Societe Generale's back office, Kerviel joined a relatively minor department within the bank's equity derivatives division. The mission of Kerviel's new department was to mitigate the risks that Societe Generale faced due to its high volume of derivatives trading. Kerviel's job involved making "plain vanilla hedges on European stock-market indices."[4]

Beginning in 2005, Kerviel began exceeding the maximum transaction size in euros that he had been assigned for individual securities trades as well as engaging in

1. P. Allen, "'I Just Got A Bit Carried Away,' says Trader Behind EUR5BN Fraud," *The Mirror* (online), 6 February 2008.

2. J. Eyal, "Breaking the Bank, French Style," *The Straits Times* (online), 2 February 2008.

3. *Ibid.*

4. S. Kennedy, "France's SocGen Hit By $7.1 Billion Alleged Fraud," *Marketwatch.com*, 24 January 2008.

other unauthorized transactions. Because he was very familiar with the electronic and manual control procedures used in the bank's back office to monitor trading activities, he was able to use a variety of means to circumvent those controls and thereby conceal his unauthorized trades. These measures included creating phony e-mails from superiors authorizing illicit transactions, intercepting and voiding warning messages triggered by unauthorized trades that he had made, and preparing false documents to corroborate such trades.

In the weeks following the disclosure of Kerviel's fraud, the bank's board of directors established a "Special Committee" to investigate the fraud–the board retained PricewaterhouseCoopers to assist this committee. The interim report of that committee revealed that Kerviel was particularly adept at manufacturing impromptu explanations for apparent irregularities discovered in his trading activities by back office personnel. Kerviel's explanations were laced with impressive but nonsensical jargon intended to confuse those personnel and discourage them from pursuing the given issues any further. In addition, the report suggested that back office personnel were intimidated by Kerviel and his trading colleagues, which caused them to be reluctant to vigorously investigate apparent trading irregularities.

The lynchpin of Kerviel's fraud was a technique that has been used in several previous stock market frauds, namely, recording fictitious transactions that appeared to be hedges or offsetting transactions for unauthorized securities trades that he had placed. For example, if Kerviel purchased a large block of securities, he would then record an offsetting but fictitious sale of similar securities. When he "shorted" a large block of securities, the fictitious hedge transaction that he recorded would be a "long" position in those securities or similar securities. These fictitious hedge transactions made it appear as if Societe Generale faced only minimal losses, at worst, on the large securities positions being taken by Kerviel.

The ease with which he could subterfuge Societe Generale's back office controls emboldened Kerviel. By 2007, he was placing what Societe Generale executives would later refer to as enormous "bets" on future near-term moves that he anticipated in major European stock market indices. At one point, Kerviel had outstanding positions that far exceeded the bank's stockholders' equity of 33 billion euros. In late 2007, he produced more than a one billion euro gain on a series of unauthorized transactions.

During the first few weeks of January 2008, Kerviel made several huge trades predicated on his belief that European stock market indices would turn sharply higher by late January. Instead, those markets declined, resulting in an unrealized loss of one billion euros for Societe Generale. On Friday, January 18, 2008, Kerviel's open positions were discovered and reported to Daniel Bouton. Over the weekend, Bouton decided that the positions should be closed to avoid potentially catastrophic losses for the bank.

Over the three-day period January 21–23, the open positions on Kerviel's unauthorized trades were closed. Unfortunately for Societe Generale, European stock market prices fell sharply during that three-day period. Those falling stock prices caused the loss on Kerviel's January trades to sky to more than six billion euros, a figure that wiped out approximately 20 percent of the bank's equity capital.

After closing Kerviel's open positions, Societe Generale publicly reported the massive loss and the fraudulent scheme that had produced it. That disclosure unsettled stock markets worldwide, causing stock prices to fall around the globe. French president, Nicholas Sarkozy, reacted angrily to the announcement of the Kerviel fraud. "We have to put a stop to this financial system which is out of its mind and which has lost sight of its purpose."[5]

---

5. Eyal, "Breaking the Bank, French Style."

Jerome Kerviel's fraudulent scheme caused the international business press to shower Societe Generale's management team and independent auditors with a wide range of probing and embarrassing questions. Among these questions was, How could Societe Generale's supposedly sophisticated internal control system be routinely and repeatedly undermined by one "rogue trader?" Likewise, how could the bank's independent auditors fail to uncover what appeared to be pervasive deficiencies in that control system. Finally, the business press also questioned the auditors' decision to approve the highly unusual manner in which Societe Generale reported the massive fraud loss in its audited financial statements.

Internal Controls, French Style

Shortly after the turn of the century, the Enron and WorldCom fiascoes in the United States undermined the confidence of the investing public in the nation's capital markets. Congress acted swiftly to restore that confidence by passing the Sarbanes-Oxley Act in the summer of 2002. This new federal statute forced public companies to spend enormous sums to overhaul and strengthen their financial reporting functions and internal control systems.

Each of the world's major economic powers closely monitored the reaction of the U.S. Congress and regulatory authorities to the Enron and WorldCom debacles. Many of these countries passed legislation intended to mimic the reforms embedded in the Sarbanes-Oxley statute. One such country was France.

Following the passage of the Sarbanes-Oxley Act in the United States, leaders of the French business community commissioned a study to determine the measures that were necessary to strengthen financial reporting, internal controls, and corporate governance among France's large companies. Many of France's most respected business leaders were asked to serve on the committee that would carry out this study. Societe Generale's Daniel Bouton was chosen to chair the committee. In fact, the committee's lengthy report came to be referred to as simply the "Bouton Report."

According to the Bouton Report, many of the reforms included in the Sarbanes-Oxley legislation were unnecessary in France. "French companies find themselves in a very different situation from that of their U.S. counterparts. In many respects, French companies are better protected against the risks of excessive or misguided practices."[6] Despite that observation, the Bouton Report contained an impressive list of proposals. Many of these proposals were adopted by the French Parliament in 2003 when it modified the nation's federal securities laws that collectively are referred to as the French Commercial Code (*Code de Commerce*).

One of the Bouton Report recommendations incorporated into the French Commercial Code requires each public company's chairman of the board to include a report on his or her organization's internal controls in the company's annual financial report. Among other disclosures, this report should discuss a company's broad internal control objectives, key internal control procedures intended to accomplish those objectives, and factors that may limit the effectiveness of those procedures. In addition, the company's independent or "statutory" auditors must prepare an accompanying report that comments on the completeness and reliability of the chairman's internal control report. Statutory auditors are also required to disclose major control deficiencies that they discover during their annual audits to the chairman. The chairman must then include these items in his or her internal control report.

---

6. E. Didier, "Overview of Recent Corporate Governance Reforms," *globalcorporategovernance.com* (2003).

Exhibit 1 presents a brief excerpt from the seven-page internal control report included in Christian Dior's 2007 annual financial report. Christian Dior is a Paris-based company founded by the famous fashion designer of the same name. The company's many well-known brand names include Louis Vuitton, Givenchy, and, of course, Christian Dior. The excerpt in Exhibit 1 provides a concise summary of the internal control procedures employed by Christian Dior. Included in Exhibit 2 is the report issued by Christian Dior's statutory auditors on their client's 2007 internal control report.

The internal control report included in Societe Generale's 2006 annual financial report, the company's final annual report released prior to the discovery of Jerome Kerviel's fraud, included the following definition of internal control: "Those resources that enable the [bank's] management to ascertain whether the transactions carried out and the organization and procedures in place within the Company are compliant with the legal and regulatory provisions in force, professional and ethical practices, internal regulations and the policies defined by the Company's executive body." The report, which was the responsibility of Daniel Bouton, also identified the organization's three key internal control objectives:

- To detect and measure the risks borne by the Company, and ensure they are adequately controlled;
- To guarantee the reliability, integrity and availability of financial and managerial information;
- To verify the quality of the information and communication systems.

An important focus of the 2006 Societe Generale internal control report was the principal risks faced by the bank. These risks were intended to be mitigated by the large number of employees that staffed the bank's risk management functions, which included more than 1,100 internal auditors. A primary "operational" risk faced by the bank, according to the report, was the "risk of loss or fraud or of producing incorrect financial and accounting data due to inadequacies or failures in procedures and internal systems, human error or external events."

The 2006 internal control report provided no indication that the integrity of the bank's accounting data could by undermined by one employee. To the contrary, the

---

EXHIBIT 1

EXCERPT FROM INTERNAL CONTROL REPORT INCLUDED IN CHRISTIAN DIOR'S 2007 ANNUAL FINANCIAL REPORT

II.   Internal Control Procedures

The purpose of internal control procedures at Christian Dior is as follows:

- To ensure that management and operations-related measures, as well as the conduct of personnel, are consistent with the definitions contained in the guidelines applying to the Company's activities by its management bodies, applicable laws and regulations, and the Company's internal values, rules and regulations.
- To ensure that the accounting, financial, and management information communicated to the Company's management bodies reflect a fair view of the Company's activity and financial position.

One of the objectives of the internal control system is to prevent and control risks resulting from the Company's activity and the risk of error or fraud, particularly in the areas of accounting and finance. As with any control system, however, it cannot provide an absolute guarantee that these risks are completely eliminated.

Source: 2007 annual financial report of Christian Dior.

EXHIBIT 2

STATUTORY
AUDITORS' REPORT
ON CHRISTIAN
DIOR'S 2007
INTERNAL CONTROL
REPORT

To the Shareholders,

As Statutory Auditors of Christian Dior and in accordance with Article L. 225-235 of the French Commercial Code (*Code de Commerce*), we hereby report to you on the report prepared by the chairman of your Company in accordance with Article L. 225-237 of the French Commercial Code for the year ended December 31, 2007.

In his Report, the Chairman reports, in particular, on the conditions for the preparation and organization of the Board of Directors' work and the internal control procedures implemented by the Company.

It is our responsibility to report to you our observations on the information set out in the Chairman's report on the internal control procedures relating to the preparation and treatment of financial and accounting information.

We have performed our work in accordance with the professional guidelines applicable to France. These guidelines require that we plan and perform procedures to assess the fairness of the information set out in the Chairman's report on the internal control procedures relating to the preparation and treatment of the financial and accounting information. These procedures notably consisted of:

- obtaining an understanding of the objectives and general organization of internal control as well as the internal control procedures relating to the preparation and treatment of financial and accounting information, as set out in the Chairman's Report;
- obtaining an understanding of the work underlying the information set out in the report;
- assessing whether major deficiencies related to internal control procedures and treatment of financial and accounting information have been appropriately reported in the Chairman's Report, if any.

On the basis of the procedures we have performed, we have nothing to report with regard to the information concerning the internal control procedures of the Company relating to the preparation and treatment of the financial and accounting information, as included in the Report of the Chairman of the Board of Directors, prepared in accordance with the Article L. 225-237 of the French Commercial Code.

Courbevoie and Paris-La Defense, March 10, 2008.
The Statutory Auditors:
Mazars & Guerard Ernst & Young

Source: 2007 Annual Financial Report of Christian Dior.

report noted specifically that "accounting data" were compiled "independently" by the bank's accounting staff "thereby guaranteeing that information is both reliable and objective." The report went on to note that "the economic reality" of that data was subject to "daily verification" by the bank's internal control specialists. In their accompanying report, Societe Generale's statutory auditors did not challenge the accuracy of the bank's internal control report.

Following the public disclosure of Kerviel's fraud, the business press chastised Societe Generale's management team for failing to implement and maintain proper internal controls for the bank. Daniel Bouton responded to those critics by insisting that Societe Generale, in fact, had maintained strong internal controls. He then went on to suggest that Kerviel's fraud was so ingenious that even the most sophisticated internal controls would have been no match for the scheme. According to Bouton, Kerviel's fraudulent scheme had been comparable to a "mutating virus" since the nature of that scheme was constantly changing and evolving. "And when the controls detected an anomaly, he managed to convince control officers that nothing was wrong."[7]

Bouton's assertion that Societe Generale had strong internal controls was challenged by several parties. For example, the decision to allow Kerviel to transfer from the back office to the bank's trading operations was questioned. "He [Kerviel] knew what the cops were looking for. That's what I find surprising about this–to let someone who knew how a fox might act, who knew the best way for a fox to act, get into the henhouse."[8] Another critic questioned why Societe Generale had neglected one of the most fundamental control procedures, namely, requiring employees in sensitive positions to take annual vacations.

> *A low-level French employee who declines to take his vacation entitlement is already an extraordinary anomaly, enough that Kerviel's superiors should have gone on immediate and full alert. As Kerviel himself acknowledged to French police investigators, "It's one of the elementary rules of internal control. A trader who doesn't take any days off is a trader who doesn't want to leave his book to another."[9]*

Several skeptics maintained that given the size of the trades made by Kerviel, someone other than him, possibly even top management, had to have been aware of them. Kerviel gave credence to this theory during his interrogation by law enforcement authorities shortly after he was arrested. The unfazed and self-assured Kerviel told those authorities that "I accept my share of responsibility, but I will not be made a scapegoat for Societe Generale."[10] Kerviel testified that his superiors had "turned a blind eye" to his unauthorized trades "as long as he was in the black"[11] and only took exception to them when he incurred the huge loss in mid-January 2008. Kerviel went on to maintain that "his activities were part of a culture of lawlessness among other SocGen traders which had the bank's broad approval."[12]

Daniel Bouton and his fellow Societe Generale executives were not the only third parties who were held at least partially responsible for the massive loss incurred by Jerome Kerviel. Shortly after Kerviel's scheme was revealed, *The New York Times* questioned why Societe Generale's statutory auditors had not uncovered the fraud.[13] Throughout the time frame that Kerviel's fraud was ongoing, those auditors had issued unqualified opinions each year on the bank's annual financial statements.

The failure of Societe Generale's auditors to uncover the fraud was particularly perplexing to many parties since France's federal securities laws require that public companies retain not one but rather two independent accounting firms to audit their periodic financial statements. So-called joint auditing is not unique to France, but the history of the nation's independent audit function is very different from that of other major economies. To better understand the role of Societe Generale's auditors

---

7. D. Jolly and N. Clark, "Greater Details Emerge of Bank's €4.9 Billion Loss," *International Herald Tribune*, 28 January 2008, 1.

8. A. Hanes, "Suspect 'A Fragile Being;' Trader's Best Intentions Can Go Wrong, Prof Says," *National Post*, 25 January 2008, A3.

9. J. Peterson, "Societe Generale's 2007 Annual Report–Jerome Kerviel is So Last Year," *jamespeterson.com*, 17 March 2008.

10. Allen, "'I Just Got A Bit Carried Away."

11. *Ibid.*

12. J. Lichfield, "'Rogue Trader' Freed on Bail after Judges Drop Fraud Charges," *The Independent*, 29 January 2008, 18.

13. N. Clark and K. Bennhold, "French Inquiry: Bank's Inaction Grows as Issue," *The New York Times* (online), 29 January 2008.

in the Kerviel affair, it will be helpful to review the history of independent auditing in France with a particular focus on the nature of joint auditing in that nation.

Independent Audits, French Style

The accounting profession within France consists of two distinct disciplines. Statutory auditors (*commissaries aux comptes*) perform independent audits, while public accountants (*experts-comptables*) provide a wide range of accounting and related professional services. Most statutory auditors are also public accountants, but these individuals cannot provide auditing and accounting services to the same client.

Although the accounting profession has existed in France for several hundred years, the nation's independent audit function was slow to evolve. A reputable independent auditing discipline was not firmly established until the late 1960s. According to a French academic, independent auditing was effectively a laughing stock in the country until that time because of the absence of any meaningful oversight by a regulatory body or professional organization.[14]

To help modernize the French economy and integrate it into the European Economic Community, now referred to as the European Union, the French government adopted several reform measures in the late 1960s. The goal of these reforms was to create a regulatory infrastructure for the nation's financial reporting function that was comparable to that of the United States and the United Kingdom. These reforms included the creation of the *Commission des Operations de Bourse* (COB), a federal agency equivalent to the U.S. Securities and Exchange Commission. The French government also established a federal agency to oversee the nation's independent audit function. This latter agency is *La Compagnie Nationales des Commissaires aux Comptes* (Institute of Statutory Auditors), which is commonly referred to as the CNCC.[15] The CNCC was given a wide range of responsibilities. These responsibilities include establishing standards of ethical conduct for statutory auditors, sanctioning auditors who violate those standards, establishing educational requirements for statutory auditors, and issuing professional auditing standards.[16]

Since the creation of the CNCC in 1969, the French government has periodically adopted measures to further strengthen the nation's independent audit function. The 2003 reforms prompted by the Sarbanes-Oxley Act included several new rules intended to strengthen the independence of statutory auditors. The French government now prohibits statutory auditors from providing public clients any services that are "unrelated" to the annual audit and requires such clients to have audit committees. Statutory auditors are also limited to one six-year "mandate" with each public client; that is, auditor rotation is mandatory after six years. During the term of the six-year mandate, audit clients can dismiss their auditors only under very rare circumstances.[17] When an auditor–client engagement terminates, five years must elapse before statutory auditors

---

14. C. Ramirez, "Exporting Professional Models: The Expansion of the Multinational Audit Firm and the Transformation of the French Accountancy Profession Since 1970." Working paper, HEC School of Management, Paris, January 2007, 23.

15. The comparable federal agency that regulates the practice of public accounting is the Order of Chartered Accountants or *l'Ordre des Experts-Comptables* (OEC).

16. In 2000, the CNCC began effectively requiring French auditors to apply International Standards of Auditing (ISAs). In May 2006, the European Parliament, which is the legislative arm of the European Union (EU), decreed that independent audits throughout the EU must be performed in compliance with ISAs. Member countries of the EU were required to adopt this new rule by 2010.

17. Likewise, statutory auditors are effectively prohibited from resigning during the term of a six-year mandate.

can accept employment with the former client. Finally, public companies must disclose in their annual reports the total fees paid to their statutory auditors each year. In 2007, Societe Generale paid its statutory auditors approximately 26 million euros.

In 2001, two years prior to the auditor independence reforms adopted by the French government, Societe Generale's board implemented several new policies to enhance the independence of its statutory auditors. These voluntary measures included prohibiting the bank from purchasing non audit services from any member of its statutory auditors' worldwide networks.

When the French government initiated the reforms to modernize the nation's economy in the late 1960s, the U.S.-based Big Eight accounting firms targeted France as a potentially lucrative market. The aggressive client development activities of the Big Eight firms–which were reduced to the "Big Four" firms by 2002–caused France's domestic accounting firms to feel threatened. To mitigate the impact of the Big Eight's intrusion into their market, the domestic accounting firms lobbied the government to require public companies to have joint audits.[18]

The lobbying efforts of the domestic firms were successful. The requirement that French public companies be jointly audited doubled the size of France's audit market for those companies and increased the domestic firms' chances of retaining a significant number of them as audit clients. Although the Big Four firms are easily France's largest audit firms in terms of annual revenues, most public companies in France have at least one French domestic accounting firm serving as their statutory auditors. By comparison, in Italy, which does not mandate joint audits, the Big Four accounting firms audit more than 95 percent of all public companies.

Christian Dior is an example of a major French company that retains a Big Four accounting firm and a domestic accounting firm to serve as its joint auditors. Mazars & Guerard, one of Christian Dior's joint auditors and France's largest domestic accounting firm, is a French accounting firm that has benefited significantly from the joint audit requirement.

The French affiliates of two Big Four accounting firms, Ernst & Young Audit and Deloitte & Associes, served as Societe Generale's statutory auditors throughout the time period that Kerviel was making unauthorized securities trades. The rule limiting audit engagements to one six-year mandate went into effect in August 2006. Societe Generale agreed to a final six-year mandate with its auditors in 2005, meaning that Ernst & Young and Deloitte would serve as the bank's auditors through 2011.

France's joint audit requirement for public companies has been controversial. In fact, in 1984, the CNCC recommended that joint audits be voluntary rather than mandatory for public companies. The CNCC recommended the change because it believed that the joint audit rule unnecessarily increased the cost of independent audits for large French companies. That proposal was never enacted, largely because domestic accounting firms strongly objected to it.

Despite the CNCC's decision to retain the joint audit rule, critics of that rule continued to insist that it unnecessarily increased the cost of independent audits while having little impact on their overall quality. In recent years, academic researchers have addressed each of those issues. In terms of cost, one academic study demonstrated that joint audits performed in France are generally no more costly than comparable single-firm audits performed in other countries.[19]

---

18. Publicly, the domestic firms justified the proposal for joint audits as a measure to enhance the overall quality of independent audits.

19. J. Francis, C. Richard, and A. Vanstraelen, "Assessing France's Joint Audit Requirement: Are Two Heads Better than One?" Presented at the International Symposium on Audit Research, Sydney, Australia, 2006.

Another academic study found the surprising result that the quality of joint audits may actually be lower than that of single-firm audits, particularly when a company retains two Big Four firms, which was true of Societe Generale during the course of the Kerviel fraud.[20] The researcher in the latter study speculated that when both joint auditors are Big Four firms it is possible, if not likely, that neither firm will subordinate its judgment to the other firm. Such a lack of cooperation between the firms could impair the quality of an audit. An alternative explanation for the surprising result is that when Big Four firms serve as joint auditors, they may rely too heavily on each other, thus reducing audit quality.

The ongoing investigations of the Societe Generale fraud have provided few insights regarding the nature of the company's joint audits performed by Ernst & Young and Deloitte and whether the relationship between the two firms affected the quality of those audits. Despite being badgered and widely criticized by the press, neither firm has publicly commented on those audits. To date, a focal point of the criticism of Ernst & Young and Deloitte has been those firms' decision to endorse the unusual manner in which Societe Generale reported the massive loss due to Kerviel's fraud in its audited financial statements.

Creative Accounting, French Style

When Societe Generale released its 2007 financial statements in March of 2008, the global investing community was shocked to discover that the 6.4 billion euro loss incurred by Kerviel in January 2008 had been recorded by the company's accountants in fiscal 2007, which ended December 31, 2007. Even more puzzling, Societe Generale's two audit firms had acquiesced to that financial statement treatment of the loss and issued an unqualified opinion on those financial statements.

As explained in Exhibit 3, which contains an excerpt from Note 40 to Societe Generale's 2007 financial statements, Societe Generale netted the 1.5 billion euro gain that it realized from Kerviel's unauthorized trades in 2007 against the 6.4 billion euro loss that his illicit trades produced in January 2008. Recognize that the 6.4 billion euro loss incurred by Kerviel in January 2008 resulted from the sale of securities that he had purchased that same month. None of that loss related to securities purchased by Kerviel during 2007.

In justifying its decision to shift the 6.4 billion euro loss from 2008 to 2007, Societe Generale invoked the "true and fair override" included in *International Accounting Standard No. 1 (IAS 1)*, "Presentation of Financial Statements." That override clause allows reporting entities to depart from an accounting or reporting standard if compliance with the given standard would result in misleading financial statements. Societe Generale maintained that Kerviel's January 2008 trades on which he incurred the 6.4 billion euro loss were a continuation of the "unauthorized activities" that resulted in a 1.5 billion gain in 2007. As a result, the bank concluded that the net gain or loss on those activities should be recorded in the year in which the unauthorized activities had been initiated. Note 40 failed to point out that Kerviel's unauthorized activities had actually extended back to 2005 when he became a securities trader.

Exhibit 4 presents the audit report that Societe Generale's joint auditors issued on the bank's 2007 financial statements. That audit report contains the three standard

---

20. S. Marmousez, "Conservatism and Joint-Auditing: Evidence from French Listed Companies." Working paper, HEC School of Management, Paris, October 2006. However, a subsequent study suggested that the "earnings quality" of French companies was enhanced if they had at least one Big Four auditor and further enhanced if both auditors were Big Four firms. See J. Francis, C. Richard, and A. Vanstraelen, "Assessing France's Joint Audit Requirement: Are Two Heads Better than One?" *Auditing: A Journal of Practice & Theory*, November 2009, 35–63.

The application of the provisions of IAS 10 "Events after the balance sheet date" and IAS 39 "Financial instruments: Recognition and Measurement," for the accounting of transactions related to those unauthorized activities and their unwinding would have led to recognizing a pre-tax gain of EUR 1,471 million in consolidated income for the 2007 financial year and only presenting the pre-tax loss of EUR 6,382 million ultimately incurred by the Group in January 2008 in the note to the 2007 consolidated financial statements.

For the information of its shareholders and the public, the Group considered that this presentation was inconsistent with the objective of the financial statements described in the framework of IFRS standards and that for the purpose of a fair presentation of its financial situation at December 31, 2007, it was more appropriate to record all the financial consequences of the unwinding of these unauthorized activities under a separate caption in consolidated income for the 2007 financial year. To this end in accordance with provision of paragraphs 17 and 18 of IAS 1 "Presentation of Financial Statements" the Group decided to depart from the provisions of IAS 10 "Events After the Balance Sheet Date" and IAS 37 "Provisions, Contingent Liabilities and Contingent Assets", by booking in estimated consolidated income for the 2007 financial year a provision for the total cost of the unauthorized activities.

Source: 2007 Annual Financial Report of Societe Generale.

EXHIBIT 3

EXCERPT FROM NOTE 40 ACCOMPANYING SOCIETE GENERALE'S 2007 FINANCIAL STATEMENTS

To the Shareholders,

In compliance with the assignment entrusted to us by your Annual General Meeting, we have audited the accompanying financial statements of Societe Generale for the year ended December 31, 2007.

These consolidated financial statements have been approved by the Board of Directors on February 20, 2008. Our role is to express an opinion on those financial statements based on our audit.

I – OPINION ON THE CONSOLIDATED FINANCIAL STATEMENTS

We conducted our audit in accordance with the professional standards applicable in France; those standards require that we plan and perform the audit to obtain reasonable assurance about whether the consolidated financial statements are free of material misstatement. An audit includes examining, on a test basis, evidence supporting the amounts and disclosures in the financial statements. An audit also includes assessing the accounting principles used by the management, as well as evaluating the overall financial statement presentation. We believe that our audit provides a reasonable basis for our opinion.

In our opinion, the consolidated financial statements give a true and fair view of the assets, liabilities, financial position and results of the consolidated group in accordance with IFRS as adopted by the European Union.

Without qualifying the opinion expressed above, we draw your attention to:

• notes 1 and 40 to the consolidated financial statements that describe the accounting and tax treatments of the net loss on unauthorized and concealed trading activities and the reasons which led the Group to make use of the exception under IAS 1 in order to present fairly its financial position as at December 31, 2007;

EXHIBIT 4

STATUTORY AUDITORS' REPORT ON SOCIETE GENERALE'S 2007 FINANCIAL STATEMENTS

EXHIBIT 4—
continued

STATUTORY
AUDITORS' REPORT
ON SOCIETE
GENERALE'S
2007 FINANCIAL
STATEMENTS

- note 40 to the consolidated financial statements that indicates that, on the date the accompanying financial statements are authorized for issue, Corporate and Investment Banking operations are currently the subject of various internal and external investigations as a result of which new facts, unknown to date may emerge.

II – JUSTIFICATION OF ASSESSMENTS

In accordance with the requirements of Article L. 823-9 of the French Commercial Code (*Code de Commerce*) relating to the justification of our assessments, we bring your attention to the following matters:

BACKGROUND OF THE FINANCIAL STATEMENTS CLOSING PROCESS

Following the uncovering of the unauthorized and concealed activities described in note 40, we have reconsidered and extended our audit procedures to be in a position to issue an opinion on the consolidated financial statements taken as a whole, keeping in mind that the purpose of these procedures is not to issue an opinion on the effectiveness of internal control over financial reporting. Accordingly, we have:

- extended the scope and nature of the audit procedures performed on Corporate and Investment Banking trading activities;
- reconsidered the General Inspector's intermediary conclusions and work performed following its assignment as of January 24, 2008, which was primarily intended to check that all unauthorized positions and related losses have been comprehensively identified and which conclusions have been endorsed by the Special Committee after receiving the comments of its advisor;
- reviewing the documentation supporting the amount of the recorded loss.

ACCOUNTING POLICIES

Note 1 to the financial statements describes the reasons that led the Group to depart from the application of IAS 10 and IAS 37 on the basis of the exception provided under IAS 1 for purpose of providing with a fair presentation of its financial position as at December 31, 2007, by recording a provision for net loss resulting from the unwinding on January 23, 2008, of the unauthorized and concealed activities. As part of our assessment of accounting principles applied, we have assessed the basis for applying these provisions of IAS 1 as well as whether appropriate disclosure is included in the notes.

ACCOUNTING ESTIMATES

- As detailed in Note 1 to the financial statements, the Group uses internal models to measure financial instruments that are not listed on liquid markets. Our procedures consisted in reviewing the control procedures related to the designed models, to assess the data and assumptions used as well as the inclusion of the risks and results related to these instruments.
- In the specific context of the current credit crisis, the Group discusses in note 3 its direct and indirect exposure to the US residential real estate market, the procedures implemented to assess this exposure as well as the process for measuring related financial instruments. We have reviewed the control procedures implemented to identify and measure such exposure, as well as whether appropriate disclosure is included in the notes with respect thereto.
- As mentioned in note 3, the Group assessed the impact relating to changes in its own credit risk on the measurement of certain financial liabilities measured at fair value through profit and loss. We have reviewed that appropriate data have been used for that purpose.
- For purpose of preparing the financial statements, the Group records impairments to cover the credit risks inherent to its activities and performs significant accounting estimates, as described in note 1 to the financial statements, related in particular to the assessment

EXHIBIT 4—
continued

STATUTORY
AUDITORS' REPORT
ON SOCIETE
GENERALE'S
2007 FINANCIAL
STATEMENTS

of the fair value of financial instruments accounted for at amortized cost, of goodwill and pension plans and other post-employment benefits. We have reviewed these processes, the underlying assumptions and valuation parameters and assessed whether these accounting estimates rely on documented procedures consistent with the accounting policies disclosed in note 1.

These assessments were performed as part of our audit approach for purpose of expressing the audit opinion on the consolidated financial statements taken as a whole that is stated above in the first part of this report.

III – SPECIFIC VERIFICATION

In accordance with professional standards applicable in France, we have also verified the information given in the Group management report. We have no matters relating to report regarding fair presentation and conformity with the consolidated financial statements.

Paris – La Defense and Neuilly-sur-Seine,
February 29, 2008
The Statutory Auditors
Ernst & Young Audit
Deloitte & Associes

Source: 2007 Annual Financial Report of Societe Generale.

sections of a French audit report; the actual audit opinion is included in Section I of that report. The audit opinion was unqualified, although the joint auditors included an explanatory paragraph relating to the Kerviel affair. In Section II of the 2007 audit report, "Justification of Assessments," the auditors reveal that they "reconsidered and extended our audit procedures" after learning of Kerviel's unauthorized activities. In that section, the auditors also note that they "assessed" Societe Generale's reliance on *IAS 1* as the justification for the accounting treatment applied to the net loss produced by Kerviel's unauthorized activities during 2007 and 2008.

Critics of Societe Generale's decision to backdate the 6.4 billion euro loss incurred in January 2008 speculated that the bank did so to "clear the decks," that is, to put the embarrassing incident behind it as quickly as possible. If the loss had been included in the bank's 2008 financial statements, the incident would have lingered and resurfaced again when the bank released those financial statements in March or April of 2009.

In commenting on Societe Generale's use of the "true and fair override" to justify its controversial decision, the *New York Times* reported that "There is nothing true about reporting a loss in 2007 when it clearly occurred in 2008."[21] The newspaper went on to berate the bank's management team and auditors for apparently attempting to "appease" investors and other parties by backdating the January 2008 loss. A former member of the International Accounting Standards Board (IASB) and the Financial Accounting Standards Board (FASB) flatly stated that the bank's reporting of the 6.4 billion euro loss was "inappropriate" and that the prominent bank was "manipulating earnings."[22] A member of the IASB at the time added to that sentiment by noting that "This raises a question as to just how creative they are in interpreting accounting rules in other areas."[23] Finally, another critic noted that "What Societe

21. F. Norris, "Loophole Lets Bank Rewrite the Calendar," *The New York Times* (online), 7 March 2008.
22. F. Norris, "Societe Generale Invokes Special Accounting Rule to Absorb Kerviel Losses," *International Herald Tribune* (online), 6 March 2008.
23. *Ibid.*

and its auditors have perpetrated would be regarded here [the United States] as the accounting equivalent of pornography."[24]

Societe Generale's controversial decision was untimely and extremely embarrassing for the IASB, the London-based rule-making body that issues *International Financial Reporting Standards* (IFRS). Over the past two decades, the IASB had been involved in a contentious struggle with the FASB to determine whether IFRS or U.S. GAAP would emerge as the pre-eminent set of international accounting standards. Prior to the Societe Generale incident, the IASB had clearly gained the upper hand in that struggle. However, that incident made many parties question the wisdom of adopting IFRS as the worldwide standard for financial reporting.

A Canadian journalist suggested that the Societe Generale incident had exposed just one of many "tricks" that IFRS would make available to creative accountants around the globe and suggested that "there is mounting evidence that IFRS is a step backwards for financial comparability."[25] In the United States, the editor of an accounting periodical observed "Investors should be troubled by this in an IASB world"[26] and suggested that the range of accounting and financial reporting decisions permitted under IFRS encourages self-interested accounting and financial reporting decisions. The latter point was reinforced by another IASB critic who noted that "Simply put, if you give management and auditors the opportunity to obfuscate, they will take it."[27]

The *New York Times* argued that the most troubling facet of the Societe Generale incident was not the IFRS loophole that permitted the bank to backdate the large trading loss incurred by Jerome Kerviel. Instead, the newspaper maintained that the primary issue raised by the incident was the absence of a worldwide international regulatory body for the accounting and financial reporting profession: "How well can international accounting standards be policed in a world with no international regulatory body?"[28]

EPILOGUE

The Special Committee appointed by Societe Generale's board to investigate the Jerome Kerviel affair issued its final report in May 2008. That report largely contradicted Daniel Bouton's assertion that the bank had adequate internal controls but had been victimized by an ingenious fraud. The *New York Times* summarized the lengthy report by observing that "weak management and insufficient risk controls" permitted Kerviel to sustain his fraud for

several years.[29] Shortly after this report was released, Bouton resigned as Societe Generale's CEO, and Kerviel's two former supervisors were dismissed by the bank.

Numerous civil lawsuits stemming from the Societe Generale fraud have been filed in France and the United States. One of the largest of these lawsuits, a class-action lawsuit filed by Societe Generale's U.S. stockholders against the company and its management

24. *Accountingonion.typepad.com*, "IFRS Chaos in France: The Incredible Case of *Societe Generale*," 7 March 2008.

25. A. Rosen, "*SocGen* 'Rogues' Show Flaws in Accounting Rules," *National Post*, 9 April 2008, FP11.

26. F. Norris, "Loophole Lets Bank Rewrite the Calendar."

27. Rosen, "*SocGen* 'Rogues' Show Flaws in Accounting Rules."

28. Norris, "Loophole Lets Bank Rewrite the Calendar."

29. K. Bennhold, "Rogue Trader May Have Had Help, Audit Finds," *The New York Times* (online), 24 May 2008.

team, was dismissed in late 2010 by a U.S. federal judge. The judge ruled that the plaintiffs could not pursue the lawsuit in U.S. courts because they had purchased their Societe Generale stock principally on foreign stock exchanges.

In October 2010, Jerome Kerviel was found guilty of the three criminal charges that had been filed against him. Kerviel was sentenced to three years in prison. In what was characterized by the French press as a largely "symbolic" move, the presiding judge also ordered Kerviel to repay Societe Generale the more than six billion euros that the bank had lost on the unauthorized securities trades he executed in January 2008.

Questions

1. Research relevant databases to identify important recent developments within France's accounting profession, including the nation's independent audit function. Summarize these developments in a bullet format.

2. Societe Generale maintained that because Jerome Kerviel's "unauthorized activities" were initiated in 2007, the 6.4 billion euro loss that he incurred in January 2008 should be recorded in 2007. Do you agree with that reasoning? Why or why not?

3. Societe Generale was criticized for invoking the "true and fair override" in IFRS. Is there a comparable clause or rule in GAAP? If so, identify two scenarios under which a departure from GAAP would be necessary to prevent a set of financial statements from being misleading.

4. Compare the general format and content of the audit report shown in Exhibit 4 with the standard audit report issued under U.S. GAAS. What are the key differences between those two audit reports? Which report format is the most informative?

5. This case lists Societe Generale's three principal internal control objectives. Compare and contrast those objectives with the primary internal control objectives discussed in GAAS.

6. Identify countries in addition to France where joint audits are performed. What economic, political, geographic or other characteristics are common to these countries?

7. Identify audit risk factors common to a bank client. Classify these risk factors into the following categories: inherent, control, and detection. Briefly explain your classification of each risk factor that you identified.

Institute of Chartered Accountants of India

The spice trade first brought European explorers, most notably the Portuguese adventurer Vasco da Gama, to the shores of the Indian subcontinent in the late fifteenth century. In the mid-eighteenth century, Great Britain used a series of military excursions to gain control over several major Indian provinces and effectively made the country the largest colony within its far-flung empire. For almost a century, Britain's colonial rule of the country was administered through the infamous British East India Company. After Great Britain thwarted the bloody Indian Rebellion of 1857, the British East India Company was abolished and India became subject to direct rule by the British monarchy. Periodic rebellions, civil unrest, and ultimately the massive civil disobedience campaign orchestrated by Mahatma Gandhi culminated in India gaining its independence from Great Britain in August 1947.

Britain's colonial rule would leave a lasting imprint on all aspects of Indian society, including its economy, financial reporting system, and accounting profession. During the two centuries that Britain controlled India, a large number of British citizens immigrated to India seeking opportunities in banking, insurance, accounting, and other financial services industries and professions. Alexander Fletcher Ferguson arrived in India in the late 1880s. A few years later, he organized A. F. Ferguson & Co., which would become one of India's most prominent professional services organizations and its largest accounting firm.

Native Indians typically did not welcome British immigrants who, like Ferguson, often took advantage of their British "connections" to further their careers and otherwise elevate their social status. Making matters worse, the new immigrants often treated Indians as second-class citizens in their own country. Not surprisingly, after India gained its independence, an isolationist mindset prevailed in the country. Because of that mindset, India's central government established protectionist policies to prevent foreign companies, professional firms, and other organizations from dominating the new nation's economy. These policies included significant tariffs on imported goods, limits on equity investments in Indian companies by foreign nationals, and, most important, the so-called "License Raj." The License Raj was an extensive set of government rules and regulations established by India's first Prime Minister, Jawaharlal Nehru, which gave India's central government effective control over the nation's economy.[1] Under the License Raj, any major business venture proposed by a domestic or foreign entity had to be approved by a central government planning commission.

India's protectionist economic policies discouraged the major international accounting firms from establishing significant operations in India. However, when India's central government announced that it planned to relax its protectionist policies in the early 1990s, those firms quickly began pursuing practice development opportunities in the world's second-largest nation. Over the following decade, a bitter controversy erupted regarding the aggressive expansion efforts of the major

---

1. Prime Minister Nehru, an admirer of Joseph Stalin, intended to develop an economy for India patterned after the Soviet economic system.

international accounting firms within India. Before examining that controversy, it will be helpful to review the recent history of the Indian accounting profession.

Birth of a Profession

Shortly after India gained its independence from Great Britain, India's Parliament passed the Companies Act to set up a regulatory infrastructure for the new nation's capital markets. That infrastructure closely resembled the regulatory framework for Britain's capital markets that was created by the series of Companies Acts adopted by the British Parliament beginning in the mid-nineteenth century. Britain's Companies Act also served as a blueprint for the federal securities laws enacted by the U.S. Congress in the 1930s. The regulatory agency charged with overseeing India's capital markets is the Securities and Exchange Board of India (SEBI), the equivalent of the Securities and Exchange Commission in the United States. Similar to the comparable federal statutes in Great Britain and the United States, India's Companies Act mandates that publicly owned companies issue periodic financial statements audited by an independent accounting firm.

In 1949, India's Parliament passed the Chartered Accountants Act. This statute created the New Delhi–based Institute of Chartered Accountants of India (ICAI) to oversee the nation's accounting profession. In carrying out its responsibilities, the ICAI works closely with the SEBI. Unlike such professional organizations as the American Institute of Certified Public Accountants (AICPA), the ICAI is a federal agency that has a wide range of statutory authority. The ICAI's regulatory mandate includes, among other responsibilities, issuing accounting standards and ethical rules of conduct for Chartered Accountants (CAs), overseeing India's independent audit function, administering the series of examinations that must be passed to become a CA, and sanctioning CAs and public accounting firms that violate their statutory, ethical, or other professional responsibilities.

Since its inception, the ICAI has embraced Great Britain's financial reporting model that requires public companies to prepare periodic financial statements providing a "true and fair" view of their financial condition and operating results. Although not expressly defined,[2] "truth" and "fairness" in this context are generally determined in reference to the economic environment in which a company is operating, unique conditions or challenges facing the company, and accounting and financial reporting concepts relevant to the company's financial affairs. Most important, the true and fair view demands that the economic substance of transactions prevails over their legal form. The true and fair reporting model is not nearly as "prescriptive" as the "fair presentation" model that underlies the U.S. financial reporting system. That is, the British and Indian financial reporting model relies more heavily on general concepts to guide financial reporting and accounting decisions rather than a large number of detailed accounting standards, such as those issued by the Financial Accounting Standards Board in the United States.

Shortly after its creation, the ICAI began issuing *Statements on Accounting Standards* to provide guidance for accounting and financial reporting decisions by Indian companies. Collectively, the ICAI's accounting standards were referred to as "Indian Accounting Standards" or IAS. In late 2007, the ICAI announced that it would "fully converge" IAS with International Financial Reporting Standards (IFRS)

---

2. "While the term *true and fair view* originated in U.K. company law, U.K. law does not spell out what the term means" [D. Alexander and S. Archer, *Miller European Accounting Guide*, 2nd ed. (San Diego: Harcourt Brace, 1995), 24–25].

by 2011. The ICAI also has the legislative authority to establish or sanction professional auditing standards for India's accounting profession. The ICAI has endorsed the International Standards of Auditing issued by the International Federation of Accountants (IFAC), of which it is a member. Although the ICAI has its own rule-making body for the auditing domain, namely, the Auditing and Assurance Standards Board, it generally integrates the provisions of the relevant ISAs into the auditing standards that it issues.

Watchdogs vs. Bloodhounds

Despite the apparent similarities between India's independent audit function and that of the United States, independent audits performed within India are widely viewed as being less rigorous than U.S. audits. One possible explanation for the less-rigorous nature of Indian audits is the legal climate that Indian accounting firms face as compared with their counterparts in the United States.

Consider the following important legal precedent embraced by India's courts that addresses the nature of the independent auditor's role:

> An auditor is not bound to be a detective or to approach his work with suspicion or with the foregone conclusion that something is wrong. He is a watchdog but not a bloodhound. He is justified in believing tried servants of the company, and is entitled to rely upon their representation, provided he takes reasonable care.[3]

Because of this legal precedent, India's legal system seldom holds independent auditors responsible for failing to detect accounting and financial reporting frauds. No doubt, this legal precedent has influenced the audit policies and procedures of India's accounting firms. In commenting on the overall audit philosophy applied by his firm, the managing partner of one of India's largest accounting firms noted, "Operating under the constraints of time and cost, we presume full honesty from our clients. After all, an audit is not an investigation."[4]

As in the United States, independent auditors in India face criminal prosecution under various federal statutes and sanctions for unethical and otherwise unprofessional conduct by various law enforcement and regulatory authorities. The principal responsibility for punishing Indian auditors has been delegated to the ICAI. However, critics of the ICAI maintain that the federal agency historically has been reluctant to act on that responsibility. "The ICAI has been singularly lax in ensuring high standards of professionalism and conduct among auditors."[5]

In fact, the ICAI is the most common target of critics who claim that India's independent audit function has lagged far behind that of other countries in terms of professionalism, rigor, and overall effectiveness. Much of this criticism has been directed at the ICAI by representatives of the major international accounting firms. In recent years, that criticism prompted a large-scale and highly publicized counterattack against those firms by parties defending the ICAI, including the ICAI itself. These parties maintained that the major problems facing India's accounting profession were not due to ineffective regulatory oversight by the ICAI but, instead, could be traced to the major international accounting firms.

---

3. P. Ravindran, "Auditors and Fraud," *Financial Daily* (online), 11 October 2001.

4. *Flashpoint*, "Financial Chicanery," www.capitalmarket.com, 29 January 2002.

5. P. Ravindran, "Auditors and Fraud."

Barbarians at the Gate

A nationwide financial crisis in 1991 that threatened to bankrupt India prompted the so-called "liberalization movement" by the nation's central government. The principal thrust of the liberalization movement was to end the protectionist economic policies that had been the lynchpin of India's economy for the previous four decades. The opening of India's markets to the rest of the world resulted in record economic growth for the nation over the following decade. During the 1990s, hundreds of multinational companies invested heavily in a wide range of business ventures in India. The central government's abrupt change in its economic policy also resulted in billions of dollars of foreign direct investment (FDI) in India by individual and institutional investors around the world.

India's rapid economic growth during the 1990s triggered a significant increase in the demand for accounting, auditing, and other professional services offered by the major international accounting firms. The sudden increase in the demand for their services and the announced intention of India's central government to end its protectionist economic policies caused the Big Four accounting firms to begin vigorously pursuing expansion opportunities within India during the early 1990s.[6]

The enthusiasm of the Big Four accounting firms for the Indian market was soon blunted when they realized that the ICAI, unlike most other Indian regulatory agencies, had no intention of eliminating its protectionist policies. Over the previous four decades, the ICAI had erected numerous barriers to discourage foreign accounting firms from operating in India. The most problematic of these barriers was a regulation that prohibited foreign accounting firms from establishing branch offices in India. Two of the Big Eight firms—Deloitte, Haskins & Sells and Price Waterhouse—had established independent branch offices in India before this regulation went into effect. But those firms were limited to operating one practice office each with a maximum of 20 partners—a restriction imposed on domestic accounting firms as well. In addition, the two firms were not allowed to rename their Indian practice offices when each merged with another international accounting firm, which meant that those offices were required to operate under an out-of-date name for their firm.

Representatives of the Big Four firms reacted angrily to the ICAI's insistence on maintaining its protectionist policies even as most Indian markets were being opened to foreign competitors. In commenting on the regulation that prevented Big Four firms from establishing new practice offices in India, one Big Four spokesperson observed that the restriction was "part of a web of . . . protectionist restrictions that stifle foreign entrants and shield the indigenous audit profession from genuine competition."[7] An angry KPMG partner maintained that the ICAI was "outmoded" and suggested that its regulatory responsibilities should be assigned to other federal agencies.[8]

In the late 1990s and into the new century, the domestic business press in India also became critical of the ICAI, but for different reasons. An Indian business periodical maintained that the rising number of accounting frauds within the country was a direct consequence of the ICAI's lax regulatory attitude.[9] The business press also criticized the ICAI for allegedly being a "captive" of the profession that it regulated since

---

6. In fact, during the 1990s, each of the Big Five accounting firms, including Andersen & Co., pursued expansion opportunities within India. However, since Andersen effectively went out of business in 2002, "Big Four" will be used in this case when referring to the dominant international accounting firms.

7. B. Jopson and A. Yee, "Accountancy's Tangled Web," *Financial Times*, 26 July 2006, 6.

8. *Ibid.*

9. T. Ramanujam, "Checking the Explosion of Corporate Fraud," *Business Line*, 14 September 2002, 1.

the organization's governing council consisted of CAs from domestic accounting firms. One Indian journalist suggested that the ICAI should be eliminated and replaced by a regulatory agency similar to the United States' Public Company Accounting Oversight Board (PCAOB), which is controlled by a majority of nonaccountants.[10]

Mounting criticism of the ICAI greatly irritated, if not embarrassed, the members of the organization's governing council. Eventually, that criticism goaded the ICAI and its supporters to counterattack the agency's critics, principal among them the large international accounting firms. The ICAI and its supporters acknowledged that India's accounting profession was facing major challenges but contended that those problems were a direct consequence of the aggressive practice development activities of the international accounting firms within India. Despite those firms' harsh criticism of the ICAI's protectionist policies, the ICAI maintained that each of those firms, in fact, had established large-scale operations in India during the 1990s.

According to the ICAI, the so-called MAFs (multinational accounting firms) had used various subtle and, in some cases, covert methods to circumvent the laws and regulations intended to prevent those firms from wresting control of India's market for accounting, auditing, and related professional services from domestic accounting firms. As a direct result of those illicit methods, the MAFs had supposedly taken control of that market and, at the same time, undermined the credibility and integrity of India's accounting profession.

In 2002, the ICAI commissioned the Chartered Accountants' Action Committee for Level Playing Field (CAAC) to investigate the impact that the MAFs were having on India's accounting profession. Several months later, the CAAC issued its findings in a 141-page report entitled "White Paper on Multinational Accounting Firms Operating in India" ("White Paper"). The prologue to that report indicated that its principal purpose was to "inform the Indian business [community], Indian finance sector, Indian Government, Indian policy makers, Indian professionals, and also the general public about the correct facts about the Multinational Accounting Firms (MAFs) and about the state of the Indian accounting profession."[11,12] The prologue went on to note that it would demonstrate that the MAFs' presence in India was "illegitimate" and document that the MAFs had "illegally and surreptitiously taken over the attestation and audit functions of the [accounting] profession in India."[13]

The large international accounting firms have frequently found themselves the target of harsh criticism in recent years, primarily as a result of their link to such financial scandals as Enron and WorldCom in the United States, Kanebo Limited in Japan, Parmalat in Italy, Royal Ahold in the Netherlands, and HIH in Australia. Easily the harshest criticism of those firms, however, can be found in the White Paper report issued by the CAAC.

Dirty Business

Indian critics of the Big Four accounting firms maintained that the ultimate objective of those firms within India during the 1990s was to establish significant accounting and auditing practices that could then be used as a launching pad to market

---

10. S. Vikraman, "Time to Regulate the Auditing Profession?" *Business Line*, 11 March 2002, 1.

11. The multinational accounting firms specifically identified by the CAAC included Andersen & Co., Deloitte Touche Tohmatsu, Ernst & Young, KPMG, and PricewaterhouseCoopers.

12. The Group on White Paper on Multinational Accounting Firms, "White Paper on Multinational Accounting Firms Operating in India," The Chartered Accountants' Action Committee for Level Playing Field (New Delhi, 2003).

13. *Ibid.*, 3.

a wide range of consulting services to Indian businesses. Intensive marketing of such services had paid off handsomely for those accounting firms over the previous decade in the United States and Western Europe. By the early 1990s, the Big Four firms had developed large consulting divisions that provided a wide range of services, including systems design and implementation projects, cost containment studies, and internal audit outsourcing. Each of those firms' thousands of audit clients was the principal target market for such services.

The efforts of the Big Four firms to expand their consulting divisions were a direct consequence of the increasing competition within the audit market over the previous several decades that had resulted in paper-thin profit margins for audit services. Since the profit margins on consulting services were generally several times larger than those for audit services,[14] the Big Four firms easily compensated for the declining profitability of their audit practices by selling a large volume of consulting services to their audit clients and other parties.

The major roadblock that the Big Four firms faced in gaining broader access to the professional services markets in India during the 1990s was the ICAI's ban on those firms establishing their own branch offices in India. To overcome this problem, these firms began utilizing a two-pronged strategy to "invade" the Indian professional services markets. First, those firms began employing on a much larger scale a strategy that some of them had used to enter India in the first place, namely, aligning themselves with "surrogate" domestic accounting firms. Because ICAI regulations limited an accounting firm to a maximum of 20 partners and limited the number of independent audits that could be supervised by any one audit partner, the Big Four accounting firms found it necessary to establish alliances with multiple Indian accounting firms. "Each of the Big Four firms has created a messy agglomeration of Indian businesses [accounting firms] that are legally separate but in practice work together."[15]

The second tactic the Big Four firms used to establish themselves in India during the 1990s was to obtain a license to operate a business consulting firm within India. Such a license was readily available from the Reserve Bank of India (RBI), the Indian federal agency that issues those licenses. After obtaining this license, each of the Big Four firms could establish multiple practice offices within India under their global practice name–unlike the accounting profession, the consulting "profession" did not limit firms to having one practice office. These consulting practice offices then worked closely with the domestic accounting firms that were the Big Four's surrogates in the accounting and auditing services market.

Because the Big Four firms had considerably more economic resources than their surrogate firms, they reportedly dominated, if not controlled, the operations of those firms. As a result, the surrogate firms allegedly became "storefronts" through which the Big Four firms provided accounting and auditing services within India. In its White Paper report, the CAAC suggested that many Indian accounting firms aligned themselves with MAFs during the 1990s because they believed that doing so was an economic necessity if they were to survive.

> The traditional Indian [accounting] firms which had large audit and other professional presence felt too insecure about their capacity to retain their position and therefore many of them began thinking in terms of becoming [MAF] affiliates or surrogates to retain the very work they were handling and to access new work through the MAFs.[16]

---

14. N. Lakshman, "Accounting Firms: Time to Redo the Numbers," *rediff.com*, 21 September 2002.

15. Jopson and Yee, "Accountancy's Tangled Web."

16. The Group on White Paper.

A major theme of the CAAC's White Paper report was that the MAFs use of surrogate firms to "colonize" the Indian market for accounting and auditing services was, in fact, illegal since that practice allowed those firms to provide accounting, auditing, and related professional services without being subject to the ICAI's regulatory oversight. "Because the MAFs are outside the scope of the discipline of the ICAI and for that matter any discipline, no such action [regulatory oversight] is possible."[17]

One of the most important ICAI regulations that the MAFs were able to sidestep was that agency's complete ban on advertising by accounting firms. Even though the MAFs were practicing in India under their "audit" names, they were not considered accounting or auditing firms within India. So, they could advertise and use, at will, the other marketing methods that Indian accounting firms were prohibited from using. Allegedly, the MAFs used large-scale advertising and marketing campaigns not only to lure consulting clients but also to attract audit and accounting services clients for their surrogate firms. The CAAC charged that the MAFs used a wide range of unprofessional and "dishonourable" marketing methods to sell those services and that those methods had greatly diminished the integrity and credibility of India's respected accounting profession.

> *While acting and operating through their surrogates in traditional areas where Indian CAs are subject to the discipline of the ICAI . . . the MAFs began and continue to merrily advertise and brand-build their own names, and take advantage of their brand value built in defiance of the Indian CA regulations established by law. . . . This snide and devious exercise extends from holding cricket matches–to high-cost advertisements–to even higher-cost events like instituting and giving Business Leadership and Entrepreneur Awards to squeeze themselves into the high-yielding corporate and financial market for professional work.*[18]

The marketing strategies and tactics used by the MAFs were reportedly so effective that those firms quickly persuaded most large Indian corporations and even government agencies that their services were superior to those offered by domestic accounting and consulting firms. As a result, in a little more than one decade, the MAFs captured the "high-end" market for business consulting services within India and, through their surrogate firms, became the *de facto* auditors for a large number of major Indian companies. According to the CAAC, the MAFs' conquest of the accounting, auditing, and consulting services market within India "condemned" the country's domestic firms "to play a secondary role in their country, occupying just about the same position which Indian citizens occupied during the British rule in India."[19]

The CAAC maintained that the MAFs were anything but the "skilled" and "virtuous" professional services firms that they portrayed themselves to be in their elaborate marketing campaigns. Instead, the CAAC reported that over the previous few decades, the MAFs had engaged in a wide range of predatory and "dirty" business practices. Following are examples of such practices that the CAAC identified in its White Paper report, examples supported with dozens of references to specific litigation cases, news reports, and other anecdotal evidence.[20]

---

17. *Ibid.*, 35.
18. *Ibid.*, 34.
19. *Ibid.*, 37.
20. *Ibid.*, 54–56.

- "The MAFs have become skilled lobbyists and have become the tools in the hands of business to bribe the state and regulators."

- "They have become experts in money laundering."

- "The MAFs have been repeatedly caught in frauds and malpractices which have forced them to seek compromises at billions of dollars of cost."

- "Driven by their lust for money by any means, MAFs are now turning into experts in shredding evidence and in suppressing facts and evidence, to escape the consequences of their fraudulent actions."

- "The MAFs are guilty of thousands of violations of audit independence and ethical requirements."

- "The MAFs are experts in advising tax evasion and tax fraud to their clients on a global level, causing losses to governments in the billions of dollars."

The CAAC concluded its lengthy diatribe against the MAFs by declaring that the accounting profession in India was under a state of siege and that it was in the national interest that the profession be reclaimed by the nation's chartered accountants. "Finally, this is war. This cannot be won without high national spirit and without perceiving the confluence of national interest with the collective interest of the CA profession."[21] The CAAC hoped that it would be at the forefront of the effort to accomplish that goal. "This is the agenda of the CAAC. This is its goal. 'India First' is its mantra."[22]

The CAAC prepared an impressive list of action items to be considered by the ICAI and other relevant Indian regulatory authorities. Among these recommendations, two were particularly sweeping in nature. One proposal called for the ICAI to prohibit any additional multinational accounting firms from establishing practice units in India, either through an alliance with an existing Indian accounting firm or as an independent business consulting firm. For those MAFs already operating within India as consulting firms, the CAAC recommended that those firms' business licenses be revoked.

Refutation & Denial

As could be expected, the CAAC's White Paper report prompted quick responses from representatives of the Big Four accounting firms. An Ernst & Young spokesperson defended his firm's alliances with India-based accounting firms by noting that "there is no bar on establishing an alliance with a foreign firm."[23] A few months later, the managing partner of Ernst & Young's India practice unit responded curtly to a journalist when asked why his firm should not be subject to the ICAI's regulatory oversight. "We don't even fall within the jurisdiction of the ICAI, since we are just another consulting firm like Boston Consulting Group, A. T. Kearney, or McKinsey & Co. So why us?"[24] In responding to the allegation that the Big Four controlled their surrogate firms, a PwC representative noted, "The Indian firms that are members of the PwC network are home-grown organizations wholly owned in India, and have built a brand name for more than 100 years."[25] In responding to a similar assertion, a KPMG spokesperson simply observed, "KPMG has been following domestic [Indian] laws."[26]

---

21. *Ibid.*, 139.

22. *Ibid.*, 141.

23. *Business India* (online), "This Ain't GATS," August 4, 2003.

24. *Business Today*, "Four Under Peril," *indiatodaygroup.com*, 23 November 2003.

25. *Business India* (online), "This Ain't GATS."

26. *Ibid.*

The Big Four firms also insisted that they were not providing accounting and auditing services within India through their domestic affiliates. However, the CAAC's White Paper report had documented that the websites of the MAFs "proudly proclaim that they do accounting, audit, and assurance services through their Indian associates."[27] When questioned regarding the independent audits performed by one of Ernst & Young's Indian affiliates, an Ernst & Young partner reported that the affiliate was "100 percent Indian-owned and Indian-managed" and "does all the audit work" on its audit engagements.[28]

Parties other than the Big Four firms were angered and concerned by the CAAC White Paper report. In the United States, individual state boards of accountancy regulate the practice of accountancy. Collectively, those boards are represented by the National Association of State Boards of Accountancy (NASBA). The NASBA reported that if the ICAI took action against the Big Four accounting firms, it might take measures to "retaliate" against Indian accounting firms.[29] Representatives of important international accounting organizations also voiced their opinion on the CAAC report. For example, the president of IFAC encouraged the ICAI to "refrain from embracing protectionist policies in the accountancy and auditing sector."[30]

Finally, not all Indian CAs and accounting firms joined with the CAAC in condemning the Big Four accounting firms. In particular, several executive partners of Big Four–affiliated firms came to the defense of their practice partners. A partner of an Indian accounting firm aligned with PricewaterhouseCoopers (PwC) reported that the staff members of his firm benefited greatly from working alongside PwC professionals and from being allowed to participate in PwC training programs.[31]

EPILOGUE

The highly publicized release of the CAAC's White Paper report in July 2003 and the ensuing criticism of that report by a wide range of parties placed tremendous pressure on the ICAI. Both supporters and critics of the report expected the ICAI to respond quickly and decisively to the report's key findings and recommendations. But that did not happen.

At the time the White Paper report was released, the ICAI was mired in two controversies. First, the Indian business press had reported that the wife of the ICAI president was a part-owner of a large private business that provided "coaching" courses for the series of examinations that had to be successfully completed to earn the CA designation within India. The press questioned whether the CA candidates enrolled in that business's coaching courses received an unfair advantage over other candidates. To quell that controversy, the ICAI purchased newspaper advertisements insisting that the integrity of the CA examination process was not being compromised.

---

27. The Group on White Paper, 126.

28. *Business India* (online), "This Ain't GATS."

29. *Ibid.*

30. K. R. Srivats, "India Must Avoid Protectionism in Accountancy," *Business Line*, 16 March 2004, 1.

31. *Business India* (online), "This Ain't GATS."

The second controversy facing the ICAI in the summer of 2003 involved what had become known as "India's Enron." India's largest business conglomerate is the Tata Group, which consists of approximately two dozen public companies and 80 privately owned businesses. Collectively, the Tata companies account for nearly 3 percent of India's gross domestic product and employ several hundred thousand Indian citizens. India's largest accounting firm, A. F. Ferguson & Co. (AFF), audits several of the largest Tata companies.

In 2001, the Tata Group hired AFF to complete an investigation of an alleged accounting and financial reporting fraud within Tata Finance Limited, a Tata company that was not audited by AFF. In 2002, AFF released a 900-page report documenting the results of its investigation of the Tata Finance fraud. That report shocked the Tata Group, the Indian business press, and the general public by implicating several of Tata's top executives, including the chairman of the Tata Group, Ratan Tata, in the fraud. Ratan Tata purchased full-page advertisements in major Indian newspapers insisting that the report was inaccurate. AFF eventually withdrew the report and dismissed the three partners responsible for writing it. One of those partners was Y. M. Kale, who was among the most prominent members of the Indian accounting profession. Kale served on the International Accounting Standards Board, was a former president of the ICAI, and reportedly was in line to become AFF's next managing partner.

The business press, leaders of the accounting profession, and various other parties demanded that the ICAI investigate the Tata scandal and the role of AFF in that scandal. After a brief investigation, the ICAI failed to file charges against anyone involved in the matter, which renewed allegations that the ICAI was a lax and ineffective watchdog agency for India's accounting profession.

The ICAI finally responded to the CAAC White Paper report in late 2004. The ICAI identified several proposals to strengthen the competitive position of Indian accounting firms that were not affiliated with MAFs. Among these proposals was a recommendation encouraging such firms to create cooperative networks that would allow them to pool their manpower,

technological, and financial resources. The ICAI also announced that it planned to increase from 20 to 50 the maximum number of partners that accounting firms could have and that it would allow accounting firms to establish consulting divisions. Over the past decade, the so-called surrogate firms had established *de facto* consulting divisions as a result of their affiliations with MAFs. The ICAI's new policy meant that "non-affiliated" firms would have an opportunity to participate in the booming business consulting market within India.

A major problem that nonaffiliated firms had faced during the 1990s was attracting qualified professionals. India's surging economy had resulted in a large increase in the demand for accounting and accounting-related services; however, there had not been a parallel increase in the number of CAs within India. In 2004, there were only 120,000 CAs in India, meaning that on a per capita basis India had considerably fewer professional accountants than any other major country, with the exception of Japan. Making matters worse for nonaffiliated firms was a large increase in the hiring of CAs by surrogate firms during the 1990s. Because the surrogate firms offered considerably higher salaries than other Indian firms, the nonaffiliated firms found it increasingly difficult to hire sufficient CAs to staff their professional engagements. To mitigate this problem, the ICAI shortened the minimum time required to obtain a CA license from nearly five-and-a-half years to approximately four years.

Supporters of the CAAC's more radical proposals were disappointed by the ICAI's decision not to pursue the imposition of sanctions or other operating constraints on the MAFs or their surrogate firms. The ICAI did report that it would ask other Indian regulatory agencies to review MAFs' operations in India to ensure that those firms were not violating the terms of their business licenses or other relevant federal rules or regulations. In responding to the allegation that MAFs were indirectly providing audit and attestation services in India, the ICAI reported it had found no direct evidence supporting that allegation but would continue to investigate that possibility.

The most important policy initiative the ICAI pursued as a result of the CAAC White Paper report was the seeking of reciprocity agreements with regulatory agencies overseeing the accounting professions of other countries. The ICAI's president noted that "while global [accounting] firms may be keen on becoming Indian, we at the ICAI are keen on making Indian firms global."[32] Reciprocity agreements with foreign countries that are signed by the ICAI would allow Indian CAs to be recognized as qualified professional accountants in those countries. For example, a reciprocity agreement with the United States would permit Indian CAs to practice public accounting in the United States—and U.S. CPAs to practice in India.

The ICAI's pursuit of reciprocity agreements was generally met with a lukewarm response by the relevant regulatory agencies of major developed countries. For decades, India had such a reciprocity agreement with Great Britain. However, Great Britain unilaterally canceled that agreement in the early 1990s, a decision that surprised and offended the ICAI. The United States has a reciprocity agreement that allows professionally registered accountants in certain countries to practice in the United States after successfully passing the IQEX–International Uniform CPA Qualification–examination administered by the NASBA. However, presently, the NASBA only allows certain professionally registered accountants from Australia, Canada, Hong Kong, Ireland, Mexico, and New Zealand to sit for the IQEX examination.

A major reason that the ICAI decided to pursue reciprocity agreements with other nations was the large outsourcing industry for accounting services that quickly developed within India following the turn of the century. Thanks to the Internet, thousands of small Indian accounting firms found a new market for their services in other countries, in particular the United States. By 2006, an estimated 360,000 individual tax returns for U.S. citizens were being prepared by Indian accounting firms, a number that was expected to grow into the millions, if not tens of millions, in the following years.[33] Indian accounting firms were also providing a large amount of rudimentary accounting services such as "write-up" work or bookkeeping for small U.S. businesses. U.S. accounting firms were outsourcing such work to India because Indian firms could perform that work much more cheaply. To make Indian accountants "globally competitive" and, in particular, better prepared to address accounting issues faced by their U.S. "clients," the ICAI added the study of U.S. generally accepted accounting principles (GAAP) to the required curriculum for the CA licensing program in 2006.[34]

Ironically, the sudden growth in the outsourcing of accounting and taxation services to India caused the AICPA to consider taking steps to protect the U.S. market for such services from Indian accounting firms. The AICPA was also troubled by the fact that U.S.-based accounting firms could not always ensure that outsourced services were being performed in compliance with the standards of the U.S. accounting profession. Many parties within the U.S. profession insisted that, at a minimum, U.S. accounting firms had an ethical responsibility to notify their clients when they were outsourcing the services for those clients to accounting firms in foreign countries. An article in *The CPA Journal* succinctly summarized this controversy.

> *Clearly, firms that outsource the preparation of income tax returns are likely to achieve significant cost savings. But at what cost? The profession does not need more scandals, and one must wonder why many CPA firms have an unspoken rule that the client does not need to know about outsourcing. Deep down, we know taxpayers entrusting their return with a CPA are likely to respond negatively if their tax returns are prepared in India without their knowledge or consent.[35]*

32. D. Murali, "ICAI Is Not Averse to Opening Up of the Accounting Sector," *Business Line* (online), 14 September 2006.

33. *rediff.com*, "Tax Advisor Shortage: U.S. Returns Prepared in India," 24 November 2006.

34. *International Accounting Bulletin* (online), "The Price of Audit on Rise in India Again after Two Years," 12 August 2006.

35. R. Brody, M. Miller, and M. Rolleri, "Outsourcing Income Tax Returns to India: Legal, Ethical, and Professional Issues," *The CPA Journal* (online), December 2004.

Questions

1. Research online and hardcopy databases to identify important recent developments within the Indian accounting profession. Summarize these developments in a bullet format.

2. In the United States, the accounting profession is regulated at the state level, while in India the accounting profession is regulated by a federal agency. Identify and briefly discuss the comparative advantages and disadvantages of each regulatory structure.

3. In India, independent auditors are considered to be "watchdogs," not "bloodhounds." How, if at all, does that concept of the auditor's role differ from the prevailing concept of the independent auditor's role in the United States? Explain.

4. Do you believe it was appropriate for the major international accounting firms to establish networks of "surrogate" firms in India for the purpose of gaining wider access to the professional services markets in that country? Was that decision "ethical"? Defend your answers.

5. State boards of accountancy in the United States have allowed accounting firms and individual CPAs to advertise for approximately three decades. Identify the pros and cons of allowing professionals to advertise. In your opinion, should professional accountants be allowed to advertise and otherwise market their services?

6. In a bullet format, identify the parties impacted by regulatory policies designed to protect domestic professionals from foreign competitors. Briefly explain how each of these parties is affected by such policies. In your opinion, are such policies justified or appropriate? If so, under what circumstances?

7. What are the principal issues that organizations such as the ICAI and NASBA should consider in deciding whether or not to establish reciprocity agreements with other countries?

8. When CPAs outsource professional services to accountants in other countries, do they have an ethical responsibility to disclose this fact to their clients? Does your answer change depending on the type of professional service being outsourced?

Republic of the Sudan

No investor should ever have to wonder whether his or her investments or retirement savings are indirectly subsidizing a terrorist haven or genocidal state.

Christopher Cox, SEC Chairman

In 1956, Sudan obtained its independence from Great Britain. Although unified, Sudan was effectively two countries within one. Northern Sudan, home of the nation's capital, Khartoum, was controlled by Islamic fundamentalists, while southern Sudan was controlled by Christian fundamentalists. In 1989, a military coup led by General Omar Hassan al-Bashir, leader of the National Islamic Front, overthrew Sudan's central government and took control of Khartoum. Almost immediately, the new government imposed Islamic law or *Shari'a* on southern Sudan, triggering widespread violence between the Islamic-controlled Sudanese military and rebel forces organized by Christian leaders in southern Sudan. By the early years of the twenty-first century, the primary battleground in Sudan was the large western region of the country known as Darfur.

Over the past several decades, various organizations, including the United Nations and the International Criminal Court, have documented atrocities on a massive scale that have been inflicted on the citizens of Sudan, principally residents of Darfur and southern Sudan. The *Christian Science Monitor* reported in 2008 that as many as two million Sudanese have died as a result of those atrocities, while four million other Sudanese have been displaced from their homes.[1] In June 2004, UN Secretary General Kofi Annan and U.S. Secretary of State Colin Powell visited the war-torn country. During that visit, Annan referred to the ongoing civil war in Sudan as the worst humanitarian crisis facing the world, while Powell described the situation as a "humanitarian catastrophe."[2]

Government officials in numerous Western countries have insisted that the Sudanese government is responsible for the war crimes committed in Darfur and southern Sudan. Allegedly, the military dictatorship that has controlled the Sudanese government since 1989 organized large bands of armed mercenaries or *janjaweed* to attack and wipe out entire villages in those regions of the country. The Sudanese government reportedly used revenues produced by the nation's large oil industry to finance this campaign of terror against its own citizens.

In recent years, governmental authorities and private interest groups across the globe have undertaken initiatives to end the widespread suffering in Sudan. Many of these efforts have involved economic sanctions intended to limit the Sudanese government's ability to finance terrorist attacks on its own citizens. In 1998, President Bill Clinton imposed an economic embargo on Sudan that effectively prevented U.S. companies from engaging in commerce with Sudanese companies or the Sudanese government. During President Clinton's administration, Sudan was also included on the U.S. State Department's list of "state sponsors of terrorism" (SSTs), a list that

---

1. J. Adams, "Renewed Sudan Violence Raises Fears of Return to Civil War," *Christian Science Monitor* (online), 16 May 2008.

2. *CNN.com*, "U.S. Circulates U.N. Resolution on Sudan," 30 June 2004.

includes such countries as Cuba, Iran, and Syria.[3] More recently, several states have passed laws requiring state employee pension funds to divest themselves of investments linked to Sudan.

In 2004, a U.S. House of Representatives committee issued a report calling for the SEC to require companies with securities listed on U.S. stock exchanges to disclose any business operations within, or other relationships with, nations identified as SSTs. The House committee maintained that such information qualified as "material information" under the far-reaching "full and fair disclosure" regulatory mandate of the SEC and thus should be disclosed to investors.

> *A company's association with sponsors of terrorism and human rights abuses, no matter how large or small, can have a material adverse effect on a public company's operations, financial condition, earnings, and stock prices, all of which can affect the value of an investment.*[4]

The SEC responded to this directive by requiring public companies to disclose any and all ties to SST countries. To promote compliance with this new policy, the SEC established the Office of Global Security Risk (OGSR) within its Division of Corporation Finance. The OGSR monitors SEC filings to ensure that SEC registrants make all appropriate SST-related disclosures.

The most controversial measure to date to help investors identify companies with links to SSTs was an Internet search tool created by the SEC in June 2007. This search tool scanned the huge number of documents filed by SEC registrants on the agency's EDGAR (electronic data gathering and retrieval system) website and tagged companies with ties to one or more SSTs. After these companies were identified, they were included on a list that was posted to a Web page on the EDGAR website. The SEC reported that the intent of this new procedure was to provide investors and other parties with direct access to company disclosures involving "past, current or anticipated future business activities in one or more of these [SST] countries."[5] In fact, such disclosures were already available to investors and other parties who wanted to search for them by utilizing the existing search tool on the EDGAR website.

Nearly one hundred companies appeared on the initial SST "blacklist" that was generated by the SEC's Internet search tool. Because of the economic embargo imposed by the U.S. on Sudan, nearly all of these companies were foreign firms that had securities listed on U.S. stock exchanges. Among the more prominent of these companies were Alcatel, Benetton, Cadbury Schweppes, Credit Suisse, Deutsche Bank, HSBC, Nokia, Reuters, Siemens, and Unilever. The SEC reported "exceptional traffic" on the SST Web page. The agency also reported that individuals who visited that Web page typically "clicked" on individual company names to access the relevant financial statement disclosures made by those companies.[6]

Within a matter of days after the SEC initiated its new disclosure policy, the companies affected by that policy began complaining bitterly to the federal agency. Executives of many of these companies insisted that it was unfair for them to be singled out by the SEC

---

3. According to the *Encyclopedia Brittanica Online*, terrorism is the "systematic use of violence to create a general climate of fear in a population and thereby to bring about a particular political objective."

4. Steptoe & Johnson, "International Law Advisory–SEC Disclosure for Operations in Sensitive Countries," 17 May 2004 (steptoe.com/publications-3091.html).

5. Securities and Exchange Commission, *Release Nos. 33-8860 & 34-56803*, "Concept Release on Mechanisms to Access Disclosures Relating to Business Activities in or with Countries Designated as State Sponsors of Terrorism," 23 November 2007.

6. A. Rappaport, "SEC Removes Terrorism Tool Amid Backlash," *CFO.com*, 23 July 2007.

since they had only minimal operations in, or some other tenuous connection to, one or more SST countries. For example, a major pharmaceutical company in India, Dr. Reddy's Laboratories, admitted that it marketed several of its products in Sudan. However, the company's CEO maintained that those sales were not "viewed as material to our business or our overall revenue."[7] Despite that point of view, under the SEC's disclosure policy any sales to an SST nation qualified as "material." As a result, when such information was disclosed in an SEC registration statement, the federal agency's search tool ensured that the given company appeared on the Web page listing registrants with SST ties.

Another common complaint voiced by executives of companies appearing on the SEC's SST list was that many firms avoided being included on that list by not disclosing links to terrorist countries in documents filed with the federal agency. One such company was the large U.S.-based investment firm Berkshire Hathaway. In its 2006 annual report, Berkshire Hathaway failed to disclose that it had a large investment in PetroChina, a company with extensive business operations in Sudan. When contacted about this matter, Berkshire Hathaway officials insisted that the PetroChina investment was not material to their company's financial statements and thus did not have to be disclosed as an SST-linked investment in its SEC registration statements. In late 2007, Berkshire Hathaway announced that it had liquidated its PetroChina investment. Warren Buffett, the company's chief executive officer, reported that the PetroChina investment was sold for economic reasons and not because of pressure to do so by parties who had criticized his company for having a Sudan-related investment.[8]

Other critics of the SST disclosure policy suggested that it was inappropriate for the SEC to "single out" registrants involved in one type of questionable business activity while ignoring companies involved in a wide range of other such activities. An officer of the National Foreign Trade Council noted that "Providing enhanced access . . . in this particular case is selective and ignores the fact that there are a multitude of other social and political issues that do not receive similar treatment."[9] A similar point of view was expressed by an executive of the American Bankers Association—many large international banks appeared on the SEC's SST Web page. "Some investors feel strongly about activities supporting gambling enterprises, others oppose those businesses generating excessive greenhouse gases, still other investors avoid companies that are not unionized, while others avoid companies that are unionized . . . There is simply no basis for the Commission to dedicate special resources to a particular kind of taboo business activity."[10]

Finally, two top executives of the Securities Industry and Financial Markets Association maintained that the SST disclosure policy went beyond the SEC's regulatory mandate by involving the federal agency in "foreign policy and national

---

7. K. Datta and P.B. Jayakumar, "Dr. Reddy's in SEC List for Terrorist State Links," *Rediff India Abroad* (online), 30 June 2007.

8. In fact, Berkshire Hathaway's board of directors asked the company's shareholders to vote on whether the PetroChina investment should be sold. In presenting that proposal to the stockholders, the board indicated that it did not believe that "Berkshire should automatically divest shares of an investee because it disagrees with a specific activity of that investee" ("Shareholder Proposal Regarding Berkshire's Investment in PetroChina," www.berkshirehathaway.com/sudan.pdf). The stockholders voted not to require the board to sell the PetroChina shares by a margin of 97.5 percent to 2.5 percent.

9. W.A. Reinsch, Letter filed with the SEC in response to SEC *Release Nos. 33-8860 & 34-56803*, "Concept Release on Mechanisms to Access Disclosures Relating to Business Activities in or with Countries Designated as State Sponsors of Terrorism," 18 January 2008 (www.sec.gov).

10. S. Behram, Letter filed with the SEC in response to SEC *Release Nos. 33-8860 & 34-56803*, "Concept Release on Mechanisms to Access Disclosures Relating to Business Activities in or with Countries Designated as State Sponsors of Terrorism," 22 January 2008 (www.sec.gov).

security matters."[11] These individuals went on to raise the issue that became a focal point of the controversy surrounding the SEC's new disclosure policy. The issue was whether or not the SEC should be allowed to decide what information in registration statements is particularly "material" and thus should be highlighted or otherwise brought specifically to the attention of the investing public.

> We are not aware of the SEC having previously singled out companies based on disclosures that they have made, unless those disclosures were materially misleading or otherwise violated the law. With any website tool designed to draw attention to disclosures involving activities in countries designated as State Sponsors of Terrorism, however, the SEC in effect would determine what information should concern investors. Though this kind of judgment may be well-intentioned . . . it directly conflicts with the SEC's longstanding disclosure-based regulatory scheme, which is designed to elicit material information and then to let investors evaluate the disclosures for themselves.[12]

EPILOGUE

In July 2007, five weeks after the SEC instituted its new SST disclosure policy, the federal agency yielded to vocal critics of that policy by eliminating the Web page that contained the SST blacklist. At the time, the SEC reported that it would possibly re-institute the SST disclosure policy or an amended version of it in the future.[13]

Four months later, in November 2007, the SEC issued a "request for comment" release asking for public input regarding the issue of terrorism-linked financial disclosures. The key question raised by the SEC was whether such disclosures in SEC registration statements should be highlighted in some way on the EDGAR website. The large majority of the responses received by the SEC indicated that the federal agency should not bring special attention to such disclosures. To date, the SEC has taken no further action on this matter.

Sudan President al-Bashir bowed to intense pressure in 2005 and accepted a peace agreement brokered by international mediators. The arrangement called for a ceasefire of all hostilities, established a semi-autonomous government for southern Sudan, and called for a nationwide referendum on independence for that region of the country. That referendum in

January 2011 resulted in nearly 99 percent of the electorate in southern Sudan voting for secession. Later that year, the Republic of South Sudan became an independent country.

The 2005 peace agreement did not end the violence in Sudan. Even after the secession vote in 2011, southern Sudan continued to experience frequent confrontations between its military and bands of armed rebels from northern Sudan. This violence claimed hundreds of lives in early 2011 and delayed the planned return of millions of Sudanese citizens that had been uprooted by the civil warfare to their former homes.

In March 2009, the International Criminal Court in The Hague, Netherlands, issued an arrest warrant for President al-Bashir. That court, which is recognized by nearly 150 nations worldwide, indicted al-Bashir for a series of war crimes and crimes against humanity. The following year, the court indicted al-Bashir on charges of genocide and issued a second arrest warrant for him. The two arrest warrants were the first ever issued by the court for a national head of state. To date, al-Bashir has ignored the arrest warrants and insisted that the International Criminal Court has no jurisdiction over him.

---

11. D. Preston and D. Strongin, Letter filed with the SEC in response to SEC *Release Nos. 33-8860 & 34-56803,* "Concept Release on Mechanisms to Access Disclosures Relating to Business Activities in or with Countries Designated as State Sponsors of Terrorism," 22 January 2008 (www.sec.gov).

12. *Ibid.*

13. Despite closing the Web page that reported companies with links to SSTs, the SEC continues to require public companies to disclose in their SEC registration statements any relationships they have with SSTs.

Questions

1. Do you agree with the assertion that any and all associations that SEC registrants have with SSTs qualify as "material information" for financial reporting purposes and thus should be disclosed in their SEC filings? Are there other "sensitive" or questionable business activities that SEC registrants should be required to disclose? Defend your answers.

2. Should the SEC have the authority to highlight or bring special attention to certain disclosures made by SEC registrants? Why or why not?

3. How does the SEC define "materiality"? How does that definition differ, if at all, from the definitions of materiality included in accounting and auditing standards?

Shari'a

Live together like brothers and do business like strangers.

Arabic proverb

The surging demand for petroleum products in recent decades has produced a windfall of revenues for many oil-rich Islamic countries in the Middle East, including, among others, Kuwait, Saudi Arabia, and the United Arab Emirates. Because Islam limits the types of investments and business ventures in which the world's 1.6 billion Muslims can become involved, the Middle Eastern oil boom has resulted in the emergence of an Islamic economy that is largely distinct from the rest of the global economy.[1] In recognition of this new economy, which is the world's most rapidly growing economic sector, major business publications have established market indices devoted strictly to Islamic business enterprises. These indices include the Dow Jones Islamic Market World Index and the FTSE Global Islamic Index.

Banking ranks among the fastest growing and most important components of the burgeoning Islamic economy. In the early 1970s, only a few small Middle Eastern banks expressly embraced the restrictive conditions imposed on business transactions and relationships by the Islamic religion and thus qualified as "Islamic" banks. Collectively, the assets of those banks totaled less than $20 million. Four decades later, approximately 300 major banks around the globe cater exclusively or primarily to devout Muslims. Those Islamic banks boast total assets of more than one trillion dollars.

Although modern Islamic finance is still in its infancy, major Islamic banks have implemented most of the high-tech banking functions and practices used by their Western counterparts. The principal Islamic banking centers are Malaysia, the Middle East, and the United Kingdom, but financial institutions throughout the world have developed aggressive marketing campaigns to attract Muslim clients. By 2011, approximately two dozen banks in the United States offered financial services designed exclusively for the estimated five million Muslim-Americans.

Tenets of the Islamic religion dramatically influence the nature of banking practices within the Islamic economy. Easily the biggest difference between Islamic banking and Western banking is the prohibition against interest payments on capital within the Islamic world.

Islamic religious law or *Shari'a*[2] forbids the payment or receipt of *riba* (interest) in personal or business relationships. Islamic banks have been forced to develop unique and elaborate profit and risk-sharing contracts known as *mudarahah* to allow them to provide financial services without paying interest on their depositors' funds or charging interest to their "borrowers." As noted in a special report on Islamic finance published by the London-based *Financial Times*, "Islamic finance tries to replicate the conventional [banking] market, but in a structure that uses profits rather than interest."[3]

---

1. For example, Islam generally prohibits Muslims from being associated with companies whose lines of business involve alcoholic drinks, destructive weapons, gambling, illicit drugs, pornography, pork and pork products, and tobacco.

2. Western publications spell this term in several different ways. The most common spellings include *Shari'a*, *Sharia*, *Shari'ah*, and *Shariah*.

3. *Financial Times*, "Islamic Finance: An FT Special Report," *ftalphaville.ft.com*, 23 May 2007.

The literal interpretation of the term *Shari'a* in Arabic is "path to the water source." Wikipedia defines *Shari'a* as "the legal framework within which the public and private aspects of life are regulated for those living in a legal system based on Islamic principles of jurisprudence." Unlike legal codes in the United States and other Western countries, *Shari'a* is not a compendium of static laws but rather an evolving set of guiding principles and interpretations derived principally from the *Qur'an* and teachings of the Prophet Muhammad. The dynamic nature of *Shari'a* results from numerous religious opinions or *Fatwa* issued periodically by Islamic religious scholars on a wide range of contemporary issues facing Muslims.

Shari'a influences every aspect of day-to-day life in the Islamic world, including politics, family issues, personal hygiene, and business relationships. Within the Islamic economy, the term "*Shari'a*-compliant" is used to refer to business practices, economic ventures, and individual transactions that have been sanctioned by Islamic religious scholars. An audit partner of Ernst & Young Global Limited recently observed that "*Shari'a* compliance is the essence of Islamic banking and finance."[4] In fact, only those banks that offer *Shari'a*-compliant financial services and products are considered to be Islamic banks.

The development of *mudarabah* and other *Shari'a*-compliant banking practices have contributed significantly to the growth of Islamic finance in recent years. Islamic banks presently account for less than 3 percent of the worldwide financial services market, but economic experts expect that market share to grow significantly in coming decades if the Islamic banking industry can overcome several major challenges that it faces. A major European financial publication has reported that "Islamic banking's long-term ambition"[5] is to become a dominant force in international financial markets. This same publication noted that among the biggest obstacles to accomplishing that goal is the "lack of uniform and consistent accounting and auditing standards"[6] within the Islamic economy.

The Islamic View of Accounting

Since the inception of the accounting profession, cultural norms have influenced the development of accounting standards within every country, including the United States. Likewise, cultural differences across countries and regions of the world have complicated recent efforts to develop a common set of international accounting standards. Nowhere have cultural nuances had a greater impact on efforts to develop uniform accounting standards than in the Islamic world. Because of its growing size and prominence, the Islamic banking industry has been the principal focus of efforts within Islamic nations to develop domestic accounting standards that cohere with *Shari'a*, or, alternatively, to modify international accounting standards to achieve the same goal.

Similar to every other aspect of Islamic life, accounting principles are considered subordinate to the dictates of *Shari'a*. As one Islamic accounting scholar has noted, "Islam accepts the fact that accounting is a social construction and itself constructs social reality but this social reality which the accounting constructs must conform to the dictates of Islamic belief."[7]

---

4. O. Ansari, "Audit & Shari'a Compliance–Issues in Islamic Banking and Finance," www.icmap.com.pk/ppt/sem_asc_khi.pps, 20 September 2008.

5. N. Dudley, "Islamic Banks Aim for the Mainstream," *Euromoney* 349 (May 1998), 113–116.

6. *Ibid.*

7. B. Maurer, "Anthropological and Accounting Knowledge in Islamic Banking and Finance: Rethinking Critical Accounts," *Journal of Royal Anthropological Institute* 8 (2002), 660.

A more blunt point of view was expressed by another Islamic scholar who suggested that accounting principles can induce behavior inconsistent with fundamental tenets of his religion.

> *"The problem with modern corporate accounting is not a matter of just numbers but a whole philosophy. Accounting can lead to perceptions of reality . . . Ultimately, what accounting tells us [is that] what makes more money is the best thing. Over time, people will become mesmerized with this infatuation and act accordingly."*[8]

Auditing in the Islamic World

Either because of governmental regulations in their home countries or because of economic necessity brought on by their growing size and involvement in international commerce, most Islamic banks have their annual financial statements audited by an independent accounting firm. In addition to annual financial statement audits, Islamic banks must also have their business activities "audited" each year to determine whether they are in compliance with *Shari'a.* An accounting professor provides the following description of *Shari'a* auditing.

> *We can define Shari'a auditing as a systematic process of objectively obtaining and evaluating evidence regarding assertions about socio-economic, religious and environmental actions and events in order to ascertain the degree of correspondence between those assertions and Shari'a (Islamic law), and communicating the results to users.*[9]

There is a wide divergence in *Shari'a* auditing practices across the nearly 60 Asian and African countries that are predominantly Muslim. This variance results principally from diverse interpretations and applications of *Shari'a* within individual Islamic countries that not only ultimately determine what business practices are acceptable in those nations but also influence how *Shari'a* audits are performed. Similar to Christianity, there are numerous factions or schools of thought within Islam, each of which share certain fundamental beliefs while disagreeing, often significantly, on other facets of their religion. For example, in certain Islamic countries, the *Qur'an* tends to be interpreted literally, while in other Islamic countries the *Qur'an*'s teachings are subject to more expansive or liberal interpretations.

The most common *Shari'a* auditing "model" applied presently is prevalent in the Middle East. Under this audit model, the principal responsibility for determining whether an Islamic bank has complied with *Shari'a* rests with the institution's *Shari'a* Supervisory Board (SSB). An SSB is typically composed of a minimum of three Islamic religious scholars who are independent of the given bank. When an Islamic bank is considering new business ventures, banking practices, or other major operational changes, its SSB will be asked to determine whether the changes are acceptable under *Shari'a.* Under the conventional *Shari'a* audit model, an SSB also reviews the given bank's financial statements and underlying transactions, accounting records, business contracts and other relationships at the conclusion of each year to determine that the institution has complied with *Shari'a* throughout that period.

---

8. *Ibid.*

9. S. Ibrahim, "The Case for Islamic Auditing," *International Accountant* 41 (2008), 21, 23.

Esteemed Shareholders,

According to our signed contract, we have applied the required auditing for Stehwaz Holding's achieved transactions and concluded contracts to ensure their compliance to Islamic *Shari'ah* principles, as already revealed by our submitted reviews, *Shari'ah* instructions and our decisions during the period ended 31st December, 2008.

The commitment to execute these transactions and contracts in compliance with *Shari'ah* guidelines is Stehwaz's liability, whereas our responsibility is restricted to reviewing the submitted models and agreements.

We hereby certify that all Stehwaz's activities and transactions as well as Zakat calculations were practiced in compliance with the Islamic *Shari'ah* principles and provisions, and no violations have occurred to the best of our knowledge.

Sheikh Dr. Nayef Hajaj Al Ajmi, Board Member
Sheikh Dr. Essam Khalaf Al Inizi, Board Member
Sheikh Dr. Essa Zaki Shaqra, Chairman

Source: 2008 Annual Report of Stehwaz Holding Company.

Exhibit 1 presents a recent *Shari'a* audit or compliance report prepared by the SSB of Stehwaz Holding Company, a large Kuwaiti company that has significant investments in Islamic financial institutions.[10] Stehwaz's annual report in which this *Shari'a* report was included was very comparable in terms of content and appearance to an annual report of a large U.S. company. For example, Stehwaz's annual report contained a standard set of financial statements–prepared in accordance with International Financial Reporting Standards (IFRS) rather than U.S. GAAP, an accompanying set of detailed financial statement footnotes, and traditional "front matter" including a letter to the company's shareholders from Stehwaz's chairman of the board.

An unqualified audit opinion issued by a Kuwaiti chartered accounting firm preceded Stehwaz's financial statements in the company's annual report. Stehwaz's audit report was comparable to unqualified audit reports issued in the United States with one principal exception–the report indicated that the audit had been performed in accordance with International Standards of Auditing (ISAs). Stehwaz's audit report did not explicitly address the question of whether the company had complied with *Shari'a* during the year under audit. Nevertheless, *Shari'a* compliance is an important issue for independent auditors of Islamic banks and other Islamic entities to consider whether or not they address that issue explicitly in their audit reports. Because violations of *Shari'a* could have serious financial consequences for an Islamic company, independent auditors in the Islamic economy must consider that possibility in designing and carrying out audit engagements.

A second but less common *Shari'a* audit model results in a financial statement audit report that contains multiple references to *Shari'a*. Exhibit 2 presents the independent audit report issued by Ernst & Young on recent financial statements of Al Baraka Banking Group, a large international bank based in the Kingdom of Bahrain. Notice in this report that Ernst & Young's audit opinion includes an assertion that the

---

10. Notice the reference to *zakat* in Exhibit 1. *Zakat* is one of the Five Pillars of Islam, that is, the five specific duties of devout Muslims. Under *Shari'a*, individual Muslims and Muslim businesses are required to contribute a certain percentage of their wealth each year to individuals less fortunate than themselves.

bank's financial statements are in compliance with "*Shari'a* Rules and Principles" as determined by the bank's *Shari'a* Supervisory Board.

In addition to approving new business ventures, banking practices, or other major operational changes, Al Baraka Banking Group's SSB also periodically reviews or "audits" the bank's compliance with *Shari'a*. Under this *Shari'a* audit model, the *Shari'a*-related procedures performed during an entity's independent audit effectively provide a second layer of assurance that the given entity has complied with relevant Islamic religious principles during the year under audit.

The principal *Shari'a*-related procedures integrated into a financial statement audit under this second *Shari'a* audit model are performed by one or more Islamic religious scholars independent of the given audit client. These scholars are retained by the client's accounting firm. If an accounting firm does not have *Shari'a* scholars on its professional staff—which most firms do not, then the firm will retain the services of one or more such scholars on an engagement by engagement basis.

We have audited the accompanying consolidated balance sheet of Al Baraka Banking Group B.S.C. ("the Bank") and its subsidiaries ("the Group") as of 31 December 2009, and the related consolidated statements of income, cash flows, changes in equity and restricted investment accounts for the year then ended. These consolidated financial statements and the Group undertaking to operate in accordance with Islamic *Shari'a* Rules and Principles are the responsibility of the Group Board of Directors. Our responsibility is to express an opinion on these consolidated financial statements based on our audit.

Board of Directors' Responsibility for the Consolidated Financial Statements

The Board of Directors is responsible for the preparation and fair presentation of these consolidated financial statements in accordance with the Financial Accounting Standards issued by the Accounting and Auditing Organization for Islamic Financial Institutions and to operate in accordance with Islamic *Shari'a*. This responsibility includes designing, implementing, and maintaining internal controls relevant to the preparation and fair presentation of consolidated financial statements that are free from material misstatement whether due to fraud or error, selecting and applying appropriate accounting policies, and making accounting estimates that are reasonable in the circumstances.

Auditor's Responsibility

We conducted our audit in accordance with both International Standards on Auditing and Auditing Standards for Islamic Financial Institutions. Those Standards require that we plan the audit to obtain reasonable assurance about whether the consolidated financial statements are free of material misstatement. An audit includes examining, on a test basis, evidence supporting the amounts and disclosures in the consolidated financial statements. An audit also includes assessing the accounting principles used and significant estimates made by management as well as evaluating the overall consolidated financial statements presentation. We believe that our audit provides a reasonable basis for our opinion.

Opinion

In our opinion, the consolidated financial statements present fairly, in all material respects, the financial position of the Group as of 31 December 2009, the results of its operations, its cash flows, changes in equity and changes in restricted investment accounts for the year then ended in accordance with the Financial Accounting Standards issued by the Accounting and Auditing Organization for Islamic Financial Institutions and the *Shari'a* Rules and Principles as determined by the *Shari'a* Supervisory Board of the Group.

EXHIBIT 2

ERNST & YOUNG AUDIT REPORT ON RECENT FINANCIAL STATEMENTS OF AL BARAKA BANKING GROUP B.S.C.

(continued)

EXHIBIT 2—
continued

ERNST & YOUNG
AUDIT REPORT ON
RECENT FINANCIAL
STATEMENTS OF AL
BARAKA BANKING
GROUP B.S.C.

Other Regulatory Matters

We confirm that, in our opinion, proper accounting records have been kept by the Group and the consolidated financial statements, and the contents of the Report of the Board of Directors relating to these consolidated financial statements, are in agreement therewith. We further report, to the best of our knowledge and belief, that no violations of the Bahrain Commercial Companies Law, nor of the Central Bank of Bahrain and Financial Institutions Law, nor of the memorandum and articles of association of the Bank, have occurred during the year ended 31 December 2009 that might have had a material adverse effect on the business of the bank or on its consolidated financial position and that the Bank has complied with the terms of its banking license.

Ernst & Young
24 February 2010
Manama, Kingdom of Bahrain

Source: 2009 Annual Report of Al Baraka Banking Group B.S.C.

Just because an Islamic bank fails to issue a separate *Shari'a* audit report does not mean that the bank's independent auditors will necessarily refer to the issue of *Shari'a* compliance in their audit report on the bank's annual financial statements. Consider Arab National Bank, a large Islamic bank headquartered in Riyadh, Saudi Arabia. Although Arab National Bank has an internal *Shari'a* compliance function, the only reference to *Shari'a* compliance in a recent annual report released by the company was a brief narrative statement included in the letter to stockholders by the bank's chairman. That statement assured the bank's stockholders that all necessary procedures had been taken during the year in question to ensure that the institution complied with *Shari'a*. There was no indication in the bank's annual report of the degree of involvement, if any, of the entity's independent auditors in the *Shari'a* compliance audit.

Enhancing the Uniformity of *Shari'a* Auditing

The wide disparity in *Shari'a* auditing practices has become an increasingly controversial issue within the Islamic economy in recent years. KPMG, a leading supplier of professional accounting and auditing services for Islamic banks, reported in 2009 that there was a strong need for *Shari'a* compliance audits to be "standardized" since they were highly "subjective" and applied on a "case-by-case basis."[11] Many parties have suggested that the most effective way to accomplish this objective would be to establish a rule-making body that issues authoritative *Shari'a* auditing standards for all Islamic banks and other Islamic businesses. But the lack of consensus in interpreting and applying *Shari'a* across Islamic countries has so far prevented that goal from being accomplished.

To date, the most comprehensive effort to develop a body of consistent standards for *Shari'a* audits has been undertaken by the Accounting and Auditing Organization for Islamic Financial Institutions (AAOIFI). The AAOIFI was founded in 1991 in Bahrain by a cartel of large Islamic banks. By 2011, more than 200 Islamic banks in 46 countries were sponsoring members of the AAOIFI.

---

11. *KPMG.com*, "Supporting the Global Islamic Finance Industry's Aspirations," 2009.

The AAOIFI employs approximately 20 Islamic religious scholars who review new transactions, contracts, and business structures being considered by Islamic banks. Periodically, the AAOIFI issues "*Shari'a* standards" to be used by SSBs and other parties, such as independent auditors, involved in the *Shari'a* compliance function of Islamic banks. *Shari'a* standards issued by the AAOIFI address a wide range of business transactions and circumstances that are impacted by Islamic religious tenets such as insurance contracting, currency trading, and debt collection. These standards are intended to enhance the consistency of *Shari'a* compliance decisions across the Islamic banking industry. The AAOIFI also has a staff of professional accountants who monitor emerging accounting and independent auditing issues. When deemed appropriate, the AAOIFI releases best practices accounting and independent auditing standards for Islamic banks.

By 2011, the AAOIFI had issued 45 *Shari'a* standards, 26 accounting standards, and five independent auditing standards. These standards are either mandatory or used as the principal regulatory framework by Islamic banks in Bahrain, Dubai, Jordan, Lebanon, Malaysia, Qatar, Saudi Arabia, Singapore, South Africa, Sudan, and Syria. In other Islamic countries, the AAOIFI's standards are consulted on a regular basis by religious scholars, accountants, and independent auditors of Islamic banks.[12]

Many Islamic academics have suggested that *Shari'a* compliance audits and financial statement audits should be merged. This proposal would leave intact SSBs and other oversight bodies that are charged with making initial decisions on which economic ventures, contracts, transactions, and other business practices are *Shari'a*-compliant. However, the responsibility for recurring periodic audits of *Shari'a* compliance by Islamic banks and other Islamic businesses would be delegated to professionally trained *Shari'a* auditors.

An Islamic academic who supports this proposal suggests that the effectiveness of the *Shari'a* compliance function is being undercut by the lack of formal training in auditing concepts and auditing methodologies on the part of the religious scholars principally responsible for that function. "While members of the *Shari'a* Supervisory Boards are pre-eminently qualified for their role of issuing *Fatwa* on the *Shari'a* permissibility of a financial product, they are not qualified auditors because they are not trained in the collecting and evaluating of evidence."[13, 14]

This problem could be eliminated, according to the Islamic academic, by developing a "new breed" of Islamic accountants and auditors. "What is required is a new breed of Islamic accountants and auditors who would have both a Western

---

12. The AAOIFI is the most prominent standard-setting body for the accounting profession within the Islamic global economy. In 2009, officials of the IASB announced that they would be meeting with the AAOIFI to discuss how to go about converging IFRS and AAOIFI accounting standards. Presently, most Islamic countries apply IFRS that is modified to reflect the unique requirements or features of Islamic business. However, within the banking sector of the Islamic economy, financial institutions domiciled in the same country do not necessarily use the same subset or variation of IFRS. In terms of financial statement auditing, International Standards of Auditing (ISAs) are used extensively in the Islamic world. Many Islamic countries have formally adopted ISAs, while in other Islamic countries the relevant government agency has informally endorsed the use of those standards. In countries that embrace the AAOIFI's auditing standards, such as Bahrain, independent auditors jointly apply the two sets of auditing standards.

13. Ibrahim, "The Case for Islamic Auditing," 25.

14. Another complicating factor is the lack of consensus within the Islamic world on exactly who qualifies as a "religious scholar" and is thus qualified to be involved in the *Shari'a* compliance function for Islamic banks and other organizations. Individuals recognized as religious scholars in one Islamic country may not necessarily be recognized as such in other Islamic nations.

accounting qualification and possibly a degree or certification in *Shari'a*."[15] To accomplish this goal, the scholar suggests that intervention by the Organization of the Islamic Conference (OIC) may be necessary.

The OIC is an organization sponsored by 57 Islamic countries that represents Islamic interests at the United Nations and other global tribunals. Because of its important position in the Islamic world and its financial resources, the OIC may be the only Islamic organization that could eventually persuade differing factions of the Islamic faith to adhere to a common body of *Shari'a* compliance standards, such as those issued by the AAOIFI. The OIC would also likely have the authority and ability to sponsor or oversee a certification program to train accountants capable of performing joint financial statement and *Shari'a* compliance audits.

The Big Four: Gaining Access to the Islamic World

A spokesperson for KPMG recently acknowledged that auditors of Islamic banks require a unique skill set. "It has become evident that the role of the external auditor to Islamic financial institutions requires a different skill set and experience to that possessed by some accounting organizations today."[16] Because of their international credibility and extensive resources, KPMG and the other Big Four accounting firms are well suited to develop accountants who have the skills necessary to perform joint financial statement and *Shari'a* audits.

In recent years, each of the Big Four firms has established an economic beachhead in the Islamic economy. In 2008, KPMG International issued a marketing brochure entitled *Islamic Finance Credentials* that identified the wide range of professional services the firm could offer Islamic banks. According to that brochure, "KPMG was one of the first accountancy organizations to meet the needs of Islamic financial institutions across national boundaries and we continue to be one of the industry's top international advisors."[17] At approximately the same time, PricewaterhouseCoopers (PwC) made a similar bid to attract clients in the Islamic banking sector.

> *PricewaterhouseCoopers in the Middle East has played an important role in the development of the [Islamic finance] industry . . . Our clients in the Islamic financial services sector include local, regional, and international banks, insurance companies, real estate investment trusts, mutual funds, as well as some of the major regulators and regulatory bodies.*[18]

Both Ernst & Young and Deloitte also claim to be leading providers of professional accounting, auditing, and consulting services to the Islamic finance sector. In late 2007, Deloitte became the first of the Big Four firms to appoint an Islamic religious scholar to its Middle Eastern professional staff. In commenting on this appointment, a Deloitte partner observed that "We hope by this to create a gap big enough to make it difficult [for the other Big Four firms] to compete."[19]

An Ernst & Young partner downplayed the significance of Deloitte's hiring of an Islamic religious scholar. "We have good relationships with a number of scholars and a sound understanding of major *Shari'a* issues. There are variances of opinion

---

15. Ibrahim, "The Case for Islamic Auditing," 25.

16. KPMG International, *Islamic Finance Credentials* (New York: KPMG International, 2008), 2.

17. *Ibid.*, 4.

18. PricewaterhouseCoopers, "Middle East Region: Industries–Islamic Banking & Takaful," www.pwc.com, September 2008.

19. *Islamic Finance News* (online), "Deloitte 'First' with Shariah Scholar Post: Appoints Mufti Hassan Kaleem," 28 November 2007.

among the scholars and, accordingly, the selection of scholars is particular to every organization."[20] In a subsequent press release, Ernst & Young "one-upped" Deloitte by announcing that it was the first of the Big Four firms to actually begin offering *Shari'a* audit services.

> *Ernst & Young was the first professional services firm to establish a dedicated team to service clients in this [Islamic finance] industry . . . and is the only professional services firm to offer Shari'a auditing. We have an unshakeable belief in the future of Islamic Finance. As a reflection of the changing needs of the industry, we currently offer more services in more markets and more industry segments in the Islamic financial services industry than any other professional services firm.[21]*

Questions

1. Identify specific financial statement auditing concepts and procedures that could be applied in determining whether an Islamic bank has been *Shari'a*-compliant during a given financial reporting period. Would these concepts and procedures be applied differently in *Shari'a* compliance audits compared to conventional financial statement audits? Explain.

2. Do you believe that the proposal to merge *Shari'a* compliance audits with financial statement audits is feasible? Explain.

3. Do you agree with the assertion that "accounting can lead to perceptions of reality"? Explain. In deciding whether to adopt a proposed accounting standard, should accounting rule-making bodies consider whether that standard might induce socially irresponsible behavior on the part of economic decision makers? Defend your answer.

4. Identify the key challenges that the Big Four firms will likely face in their efforts to establish a major presence in the Islamic banking industry.

---

20. *Ibid.*

21. Ernst & Young, "Islamic Financial Services Group," www.ey.com/global/content.nsf/MiddleEast/ services, September 2008.

Mohamed Salem El-Hadad, Internal Auditor

The world is moved along, not only by the mighty shoves of its heroes, but also by the aggregate of the tiny pushes by each honest worker.

Helen Keller

In 1976, Mohamed El-Hadad earned an undergraduate accounting degree in his native Egypt. Before he began his accounting career, El-Hadad completed his compulsory service in the Egyptian military forces. El-Hadad accepted an entry-level position with a large hotel in Alexandria after being honorably discharged from the military in 1979. Two years later, El-Hadad immigrated to Abu Dhabi, the capital of the United Arab Emirates (UAE), after he learned that there were excellent employment opportunities for accountants in that small Middle Eastern nation.[1]

The determined young accountant soon landed a job with the UAE's Ministry of Education. For 10 years, El-Hadad worked as an auditor with that government agency. Throughout his tenure with the Ministry of Education, El-Hadad regularly received excellent performance appraisals from his superiors.

While on a vacation in the United States in 1992, El-Hadad visited the UAE's embassy in Washington, D.C. During that visit, he became acquainted with the embassy's cultural attaché and the deputy cultural attaché. The cultural attaché was impressed with El-Hadad and his employment history and encouraged him to apply for an open auditing position with the embassy. The position involved "the audit and review of all expenditures and accounting methods of the cultural attaché and the educational expenditures for UAE students in the United States, and reconciliation of all bank accounts."[2] The job would require El-Hadad to supervise eight other accountants. El-Hadad's immediate superior would be the cultural attaché.

El-Hadad was excited by the new job opportunity and the possibility of relocating to the United States. When he returned to the UAE, he informed his superiors in the Ministry of Education of his interest in the Washington, D.C., job. They encouraged him to apply for the position and gave him excellent personal references that were forwarded to the cultural attaché of the UAE's Washington, D.C., embassy. Among other complimentary remarks, the recommendations indicated that El-Hadad "was an exemplary employee who displayed seriousness and integrity."

In January 1993, El-Hadad accepted the supervisory audit position in Washington, D.C. El-Hadad enjoyed his new job and the relationships he developed with his superiors, his subordinates and the remainder of the embassy staff. He was certain that the increased scope of responsibilities he assumed in the new position would

---

1. Approximately 95 percent of UAE's workforce is made up of foreign nationals. For decades, the small, oil-rich country has actively encouraged immigration of foreign nationals to bolster its rapidly growing economy.

2. This and all subsequent quotes were taken from the following source: *Mohamed Salem El-Hadad v. The Embassy of the United Arab Emirates, et al.*, Civil Action No. 96-1943 (RWR), U.S. District Court for the District of Columbia, 2006. Much of the background information included in this case was drawn from other legal transcripts and news reports.

help him develop professionally. El-Hadad also realized that the cultural, educational, and recreational opportunities offered by the dynamic Washington, D.C., metropolitan area would be beneficial for himself and his family.

Reluctance and Regret

Unfortunately, within a matter of months, El-Hadad's American "adventure" turned bittersweet. During the performance of routine audit procedures in April 1993, El-Hadad discovered a secret bank account being used by the embassy. Upon further investigation, he determined that his new boss and friend, the embassy's cultural attaché, was maintaining the account with the assistance of the deputy cultural attaché and the embassy's chief accountant. He also determined that the three individuals were diverting UAE government funds into the secret account.

One method used by the conspirators to embezzle funds involved healthcare payments made by embassy employees. The embassy provided healthcare coverage for its employees but not for employee dependents. If an employee elected to have dependents covered by the embassy's healthcare plan, the employee was required to pay the monthly premiums directly to the embassy. The conspirators deposited these payments into the secret bank account and then used UAE government funds to pay the healthcare premiums for employees' dependents. In fact, the monthly amounts that El-Hadad paid to the embassy to provide healthcare coverage for his wife and children were included in the funds diverted into the secret bank account.

Another method used by the conspirators to misappropriate UAE government funds involved tuition refunds that the embassy received from a large number of U.S. universities. The UAE government had established an educational program that paid the college tuition of UAE citizens who chose to attend a U.S. university. The UAE embassy made these tuition payments directly to the given U.S. universities. Not unlike other college students, UAE students frequently dropped courses early in the semester for various reasons. The resulting tuition refunds remitted to the UAE embassy were funneled into the secret bank account discovered by El-Hadad.

Despite harboring feelings of reluctance and regret, El-Hadad knew that he had to "blow the whistle" and report the embezzlement scheme orchestrated by his boss and friend. Instead of informing top officials in the UAE embassy, El-Hadad chose to pass the information to a government official in the Ministry of Education, the agency for which he had worked the past 10 years. This individual in turn notified UAE's Minister of Finance. The Minister of Finance promptly contacted El-Hadad to question him about the scheme and then traveled to the United States to discuss the matter with him in person. The Minister of Finance then sent a team of auditors from his agency to carry out a comprehensive and secret investigation of the fraud. This team of auditors discovered two additional secret bank accounts used by the conspirators and determined that the three individuals had stolen at least $2 million. In early 1994, the cultural attaché, his deputy, and the embassy's chief accountant were fired. Three other embassy employees who were aware of the embezzlement scheme were also dismissed.

Prior to learning that El-Hadad had uncovered his embezzlement scheme, the embassy's cultural attaché completed his annual performance appraisal of El-Hadad for 1993. The cultural attaché indicated that El-Hadad was an "excellent employee" and gave him 99 out of a possible 100 points on the scale used for the performance appraisal. El-Hadad received a similar performance appraisal near the end of 1994 by the embassy's new cultural attaché. The new cultural attaché also recommended that he be promoted, receive a salary increase, and a merit bonus for his excellent work. During 1994, El-Hadad also received plaudits from numerous UAE government officials, most notably the Minister of Finance, for his role in uncovering the embezzlement scheme.

Retribution and Recriminations

Not surprisingly, the Minister of Finance, the new cultural attaché and several other UAE government officials were stunned in late 1995 when the UAE State Audit Division announced that Mohamed El-Hadad had been involved in the embezzlement scheme that he had reported. The State Audit Division, a government agency that provides audit services for other UAE government agencies, reported that El-Hadad had received several improper payments from the conspirators who had maintained the three secret bank accounts. These improper payments included compensation for overtime that he had not worked, expense reimbursements to which he was not entitled, and payment of healthcare premiums for his family.

The State Audit Division investigation that culminated in the charges being filed against El-Hadad had been initiated by another government agency, the Ministry of Higher Education and Scientific Research (HESR). Officials in the latter agency had been embarrassed when the embezzlement scheme at the UAE's Washington, D.C., embassy was publicly revealed in early 1994 since it involved an educational program that fell under the purview of their agency. These same officials also reportedly had an ongoing feud throughout 1994 and beyond with the embassy's new cultural attaché, who was a staunch supporter and ally of El-Hadad. Following the startling announcement that El-Hadad had been involved in the embezzlement scheme, a top official of the HESR Ministry traveled to the Washington, D.C., embassy and personally told several of El-Hadad's co-workers that he was dishonest and a poor employee.

In early 1996, the UAE cultural attaché capitulated to relentless pressure from government officials in Abu Dhabi and fired El-Hadad for his alleged role in the embezzlement scheme. El-Hadad, who had consistently and vehemently insisted that he was innocent of the charges, immediately appealed his dismissal. While his case was being reviewed, El-Hadad secured an entry-level auditing job for the UAE's military attaché in the Washington, D.C., embassy. When the HESR Minister learned of El-Hadad's new job, he notified government officials in Abu Dhabi. Within a matter of days, El-Hadad was fired once more.

In late 1996, El-Hadad's appeal of his dismissal from the supervisory audit position with the UAE embassy was denied. His appeal was denied despite several prominent individuals interceding on his behalf with the appellate tribunal. Among the individuals who wrote letters testifying to El-Hadad's work ethic and integrity was the cultural attaché who had been pressured to fire him, the UAE Minister of Finance, and the U.S. Ambassador to the UAE who was well acquainted with El-Hadad. Despite this impressive show of support for the Egyptian accountant, the appellate tribunal ruled that because El-Hadad's involvement in the fraudulent scheme had been well documented, his dismissal had been justified. The documents used to corroborate his role in the fraud had been provided by the Ministry of HESR.

Throughout the remainder of 1996 and much of 1997, El-Hadad searched for employment as an auditor or accountant in the Washington, D.C., area. Each time that he applied for a job, however, the prospective employer contacted the UAE embassy and learned that El-Hadad had been terminated because of his role in an embezzlement scheme. Economic necessity forced El-Hadad to return with his family to his native Egypt in late 1997 and seek employment there. Similar to his experience in Washington, D.C., each time that he applied for an accounting or auditing position, the prospective employer learned of his past history and refused to consider him any further.

Frustrated and disheartened, El-Hadad eventually realized that his career in auditing, a career that he had loved and a career to which he had devoted nearly two decades of his life, was over. El-Hadad then decided to pursue a new livelihood. For several years, he sold cosmetics through a small business that he organized. But in 2003 that business failed, and El-Hadad was forced to rely on family members for economic support.

Redemption

Prior to leaving the United States in 1997, El-Hadad had retained an attorney to file a lawsuit against the UAE's Washington, D.C., embassy. In this lawsuit, El-Hadad alleged that the embassy had wrongfully terminated him, that he had been defamed, and that his accounting career had been destroyed. Attorneys for the UAE attempted to have El-Hadad's lawsuit dismissed due to the concept of sovereign immunity. This concept generally prohibits criminal or civil lawsuits from being filed in U.S. courts against foreign embassies in the United States. However, the U.S. federal law that dictates the nature and scope of sovereign immunity, the Foreign Sovereign Immunities Act, includes an exception for lawsuits related to "commercial activity." Because the U.S. District Court in which El-Hadad filed his lawsuit ruled that his work as an auditor for the UAE embassy had qualified as "commercial activity," the federal court refused to dismiss the lawsuit.

During El-Hadad's civil trial in July 2001, his attorneys addressed one by one the allegations of dishonesty that had been filed against him by the UAE State Audit Division. The attorneys presented to the court the documents that had been used as the basis for those allegations and easily established that they had been forged. The attorneys also presented other documents and evidence that had been submitted to the State Audit Division during its investigation of El-Hadad, which clearly demonstrated he had not been involved in any way in the embezzlement scheme. For whatever reason, the State Audit Division had ignored that exculpatory evidence. El-Hadad's attorneys went on to prove that not only had he not been involved in the fraud, he had been known for being scrupulously honest while employed by the UAE embassy. For example, evidence presented by his attorneys demonstrated that when filing for expense reimbursements, El-Hadad had understated the amounts to which he was entitled to reimbursement.

The federal judge who presided over El-Hadad's civil trial agreed with his attorneys that he had had been victimized by false and "trumped-up" charges intended to discredit him. The federal judge also ruled that El-Hadad had been defamed by his former employer and that the defamation had ended his career as an accountant and auditor. At the conclusion of the trial, the UAE was ordered to pay El-Hadad $1.25 million for lost wages, $500,000 of damages related to the defamation he had suffered, and accrued interest on both amounts since the date of his termination in 1996.

The UAE's attorneys refused to accept the court's verdict and filed repeated appeals to have it overturned. At each level of the federal court system, the appeals filed by those attorneys regarding major issues central to the case were rejected. In 2007, the verdict was appealed to the U.S. Supreme Court. When the Supreme Court refused to review the case, Mohamed El-Hadad could finally claim victory. At last report, the UAE had yet to pay El-Hadad the more than $2 million that it owes him.

Questions

1. Identify and briefly describe the legal protections that "whistleblowers" have in the United States.

2. Should U.S. companies integrate legal protections for internal whistleblowers into their internal control systems? Defend your answer.

3. Suppose that during your career you discover a fraud similar to that uncovered by Mohamed El-Hadad. List specific measures that you could take to protect yourself from recriminations by your employer or other parties.

4. Did El-Hadad face an ethical or moral dilemma when he discovered the fraud being perpetrated by his superior and friend? Before responding, define ethical dilemma and moral dilemma.

Tae Kwang Vina

During the 1970s, the public accounting profession eliminated its bans on competitive bidding, advertising, direct solicitation, and related practices that the Federal Trade Commission maintained were restraints of trade. The decision to drop those restrictions contributed to the increasingly competitive nature of the market for independent audits over the following decades. That escalating competition was manifested by a rapid increase in the rate of auditor changes by public companies, "lowballing" on the part of certain accounting firms to obtain new clients, and stagnant or declining audit fees.

By the late 1990s, many leading accountants suggested that the independent audit "product" was diminishing in value. The American Institute of Certified Public Accountants (AICPA) concurred with that point of view in an article that appeared in its monthly newsletter. To counter the declining value of independent audits, the AICPA recommended that accounting firms begin developing and marketing other services.

> *The audit–the CPA profession's core assurance product–has been declining in value over the past few years, becoming a less marketable product. In fact, revenues from traditional accounting and auditing services have been flat for the past seven years . . . Where challenges exist, however, opportunities abound . . . [nontraditional] assurance services provide a lucrative opportunity to expand [accounting] practices. CPAs are singularly qualified as independent assurance providers to furnish businesses and their customers with the certainty they need to compete in today's marketplace.*[1]

To identify new professional services that accountants could begin providing, the AICPA created the Assurance Services Special Committee that was chaired by Robert Elliott, a senior audit partner with KPMG. Elliott's committee recommended a wide range of new services that accounting practitioners could market. Specific examples of such services included the following: ascertaining the quality of home healthcare providers and assisted living (nursing home) facilities, identifying security breaches of Internet-linked information systems, and helping companies and other organizations identify and manage the economic risks they faced. The AICPA believed that these and other nontraditional services would provide accounting firms an opportunity to significantly increase their revenues while at the same time enhancing their overall stature and reputation within the business community.

Among the boldest initiatives taken by the AICPA in the late 1990s to expand the product line of services offered by CPAs was a proposal to create a new professional designation for accountants. This new credential would be awarded to individuals who passed a rigorous examination to demonstrate that they qualified as "multidisciplinary business advisers and strategic thinkers."[2] The AICPA believed this new professional designation would help existing CPAs strengthen their credibility as

---

1. American Institute of Certified Public Accountants, "Assurance Services: Transforming the Quality of Information," *The CPA Letter* (online), May 2001.

2. American Institute of Certified Public Accountants, "Internet Portal, Broad-Based Global Credential Discussed at Regional Council Meetings," *The CPA Letter* (online), May 2000.

general business consultants and thereby allow them to gain a larger share of the rapidly expanding market for business consulting services worldwide.

Throughout the 1990s and into the new century, the major international accounting firms began offering an extended product line of nontraditional services. These firms invested heavily in advertising programs and other promotional activities to market these new services. However, as these firms attempted to develop new markets and encroach on existing markets served by other professionals, they encountered unexpected challenges and problems.

Nontraditional professional services marketed by the major accounting firms during the 1990s included "environmental and labor practices audits." These engagements were not financial statement audits but rather examinations intended to determine whether a given company, organization, or specific production facility was complying with state and federal laws, industry rules and regulations, and other predetermined criteria relevant to environmental issues and labor practices.

The accounting profession's dominant firms recognized that there was a growing demand for environmental and labor practices audits and similar engagements during the 1990s. This demand sprang from a social activism movement during the latter part of the twentieth century, which targeted high-profile companies in the United States that allegedly operated, or purchased goods from, "sweatshops" in foreign countries. Ernst & Young and PricewaterhouseCoopers (PwC) were the most prolific providers of environmental and labor practices audits within the accounting profession. In 1998 alone, PwC performed 1,500 such audits in China's Guangdong province, that nation's industrial epicenter.[3]

Wikipedia defines a sweatshop as a "working environment with very difficult or dangerous conditions, usually where the workers have few rights or ways to address the situation." These conditions may include "exposure to harmful materials, hazardous situations, extreme temperatures, or abuse from employers." Social activists claimed that many large U.S. companies were maximizing their profits by using sweatshops in third-world countries to minimize the production cost of the merchandise they sold.

In 1996, Wal-Mart was blindsided by a firestorm of unfavorable media attention ignited by a social activist organization. This organization revealed that Wal-Mart's popular line of Kathie Lee Gifford apparel was being manufactured under sweatshop conditions in the Central American nation of Honduras. Over the following several years, many other U.S. companies would face similar charges. The company targeted more than any other by the anti-sweatshop activists was Nike, Inc., the world's largest producer of athletic shoes.

Nike's critics insisted that the working conditions in the company's Far Eastern production facilities were harsh, hazardous, and in violation of the given countries' labor laws. Those production facilities were located principally in China, Indonesia, Taiwan, and Vietnam. The company was also lambasted for paying multi-million dollar endorsement fees to sports celebrities such as Michael Jordan and Tiger Woods while factory workers in its foreign production facilities received weekly wages of $10 or even less for working upwards of 60 hours.

In early 1997, threats of Congressional investigations and consumer boycotts persuaded Nike to hire Andrew Young, a former U.S. Congressman and leading civil rights advocate, to inspect production facilities in countries where the company's products were being manufactured. After visiting several of those factories, Young

---

3. *The Economist*, "Business Ethics: Sweatshop Wars," 27 February 1999, 62.

submitted a written report to Nike's board in which he indicated that the workers in those facilities were being treated well. To garner public support and quell its critics, Nike included favorable comments excerpted from Young's report in full-page ads that it purchased in several major metropolitan newspapers.

Andrew Young's report failed to placate Nike's critics. The company's detractors claimed that Young's visits had been brief and less than rigorous and that he was not qualified to assess the working conditions in the given facilities.

The next measure Nike took to silence its critics was to retain Ernst & Young to perform an environmental and labor practices audit of one of its major Far Eastern production facilities. The facility chosen for that audit was a Vietnamese factory operated by Tae Kwang Vina Industrial Company, Limited, one of Nike's largest manufacturing contractors. That factory, Nike's newest and most modern production facility in the Far East, employed 9,200 workers and produced 400,000 pairs of athletic shoes each month. During the 1990s, U.S. companies that outsourced production operations to Vietnam were responsible for much of that nation's impressive economic growth. In fact, by the late 1990s, Nike's Vietnamese factories accounted for more than 5 percent of that country's gross domestic product.

In the spring of 1997, Ernst & Young submitted a ten-page report to Nike management that summarized the principal findings of its Tae Kwang Vina audit. Only a brief excerpt from that confidential report was released to the press. That brief excerpt suggested that Ernst & Young's overall conclusion regarding the working conditions at the Tae Kwang Vina site was consistent with the conclusion reached by Andrew Young.

The excerpt from the Ernst & Young report provided to the press also indicated that the Tae Kwang Vina facility was complying with Nike's code of conduct. Among many other stipulations, that code required Nike's "business partners" to pay no less than the minimum wage mandated in a given country, to fully compensate workers for overtime hours, and to provide a safe working environment for those workers.

Ernst & Young's conclusion that the Tae Kwang Vina factory was operating in compliance with Nike's code of conduct infuriated the company's critics. In November 1997, several months after Ernst & Young submitted its final report to Nike, one of them covertly obtained a copy of the complete report and turned it over to the *New York Times*.

Ernst & Young's ten-page report painted a much different picture of the working conditions at the Tae Kwang Vina facility than the brief excerpt from that report initially provided to the press. The full Ernst & Young report documented numerous abusive labor practices and hazardous working conditions at that site. The *New York Times* summarized some of the more egregious of the deplorable working conditions that the accounting firm had found at the factory.

> *Ernst & Young wrote that workers at the factory near Ho Chi Minh City were exposed to carcinogens that exceeded local legal standards by 177 times in parts of the plant and that 77 percent of the employees suffered from respiratory problems. The report also said that employees at the site . . . were forced to work 65 hours a week, more than Vietnamese law allows, for $10 per week.*[4]

Other improper practices or incidents reported by Ernst & Young included inadequate ventilation systems, excessive noise levels and temperatures within the factory, insufficient safety equipment, inadequate training for employees required to work

---

4. S. Greenhouse, "Nike Shoe Plant in Vietnam is Called Unsafe for Workers," *The New York Times* (online), 8 November 1997.

with dangerous chemicals, failure to provide workers with sufficient water, refusal to pay wages owed to employees after they were terminated, and mistreatment of workers by supervisors.

The release of the complete Ernst & Young report to the press provoked an angry public outcry against Nike. In response, the company initially insisted that the problems identified in the report had been largely remedied over the more than six months that had elapsed since Ernst & Young completed its audit of the Tae Kwang Vina facility. That assertion was met with disbelief and ridicule by the company's critics. Several of those critics banded together and filed a lawsuit against Nike that charged the company with intentionally misrepresenting the working conditions within its foreign production facilities.

Ironically, the release of the full Ernst & Young report also resulted in heated criticism of the prominent accounting firm. Although Ernst & Young's report disclosed serious problems at the Tae Kwang Vina factory, a subsequent investigation by Dara O'Rourke, a consultant to the United Nations and a leader of the anti-sweatshop movement, revealed that the facility's working conditions were much worse than reported by Ernst & Young.

O'Rourke suggested that the Ernst & Young personnel involved in the Tae Kwang Vina engagement did not have the necessary qualifications and training to perform environmental and labor practices audits, which had resulted in the engagement being seriously flawed. Alleged deficiencies in Ernst & Young's Tae Kwang Vina engagement included, among others, relying heavily on the factory's management and other secondary sources for the information collected during the engagement, failing to properly test air quality and other working conditions in the factory, and failing to ensure that employees questioned during the engagement were free to respond candidly without any fear of reprisals from management.

Sweatshop activists also challenged Nike's claim that Ernst & Young performed the Tae Kwang Vina engagement as an "independent" third party. A governmental health and compliance officer for the state of California maintained that Nike's hiring of Ernst & Young to complete the Tae Kwang Vina "audit" was equivalent to "putting the fox's paid consultant in charge of the henhouse."[5] Corporate Watch, an international organization that monitors the social responsibility of multinational organizations, pointed out that rather than being independent of Nike, the Ernst & Young auditors had simply followed specific instructions given to them by Nike management in completing the Tae Kwang Vina engagement. To prove this point, the organization quoted the following statement directed to Nike by Ernst & Young it its ten-page report: "The procedures we have performed were those that you [Nike] specifically instructed us to perform. Accordingly, we make no comments as to the sufficiency of these procedures for your purposes."[6]

The Corporate Watch organization went on to suggest that accounting firms were not well suited to perform environmental and labor practices audits. "Indeed, Ernst & Young's incompetence as a social and environmental auditor, combined with Mr. O'Rourke's own findings inside the plant, present a strong argument against using accounting firms to conduct labor and environmental audits."[7] This latter opinion

---

5. D. Rourke, "Vietnam: Smoke from a Hired Gun," November 1997, www.corpwatch.org/article.php?id=966%20.

6. *Ibid.*

7. *Ibid.*

was seconded by the *New York Times,* which called for companies such as Nike to use "truly independent monitors" to complete such engagements.[8]

EPILOGUE

In 2003, the U.S. Supreme Court agreed to hear arguments in the lawsuit filed against Nike that charged the company with falsely denying that it used foreign sweatshops to produce the merchandise that it sold. However, the case was ultimately settled out of court when Nike agreed to pay $1.5 million to help monitor and improve factory working conditions in third-world countries. In 2005, Nike published a self-study of the working conditions in 700 factories scattered around the world that manufactured the merchandise it sold. The report documented that "widespread problems" still existed within those factories.[9] Nike executives pledged to work with social activist groups to resolve those problems.

In a nationwide vote in late 2001, the rank-and-file members of the AICPA rejected the proposal to create a new professional designation to recognize expertise in the field of general business consulting. Several months later, the U.S. Congress passed the Sarbanes-Oxley Act of 2002 in response to the massive losses imposed on investors by the Enron and WorldCom scandals. That statute included a wide range of reforms intended to strengthen independent audits. The Sarbanes-Oxley Act served not only to enhance the perceived importance of the independent audit function in the United States but also refocused the attention of the major accounting firms on the "independent audit product." Thanks largely to the Sarbanes-Oxley reforms, the audit fees charged to public companies by the major accounting firms rose dramatically over the following several years.

Questions

1. Define each of the following types of professional services: consulting services, attestation services, agreed-upon procedures engagements, and assurance services. Explain how, if at all, these services overlap.

2. Visit the websites of the major international accounting firms. Identify nontraditional services currently marketed by these firms. List several of these services and briefly describe their nature. Of the services you identified, are there any that you believe accounting firms should not provide? If so, explain.

3. On what types of engagements must CPAs be "independent"? Identify types of engagements on which CPAs are not required to be independent. What other traits should CPAs possess on professional services engagements?

---

8. *Ibid.*

9. *The Guardian* (online), "Nike Acknowledges Massive Labor Exploitation in its Overseas Markets," 14 April 2005.

INDEX

SUMMARY OF TOPICS BY CASE

The following index lists the auditing-related topics addressed directly or indirectly in each case included in **Contemporary Auditing: Real Issues and Cases, Ninth Edition**. Those topics followed by the letter "Q" are the subject of a case question.

Enron Corporation, Case 1.1 3–22

1. "Scope of services" issue facing audit firms (Q)
2. Involvement of auditors in client accounting and financial reporting decisions (Q)
3. Preparation and retention of audit workpapers (Q)
4. Recent "crisis of confidence" facing the public accounting profession (Q)
5. Recent recommendations to strengthen the independent audit function (Q)
6. Evolution of concept of "professionalism" in public accounting discipline over past several decades (Q)
7. Auditors' responsibilities regarding a client's quarterly financial statements (Q)
8. History of public accounting profession in the United States
9. Roles and responsibilities of key regulatory and rule-making bodies in the public accounting profession
10. Corporate culture as a key determinant of an audit client's control environment
11. Criminal liability faced by auditors and audit firms

Lehman Brothers Holdings Inc., Case 1.2, 23–38

1. Involvement of auditors in the development of a new accounting policy by a client (Q)
2. Responsibility of auditors to approve/review a new client accounting policy (Q)
3. Does "intent matter" in the application and/or development of accounting policies? (Q)
4. Auditors' consideration of whether specific client transactions are "accounting-motivated" (Q)
5. Allocation of responsibility for different facets of a multinational audit (Q)
6. Auditors' responsibility for client financial data external to the audited financial statements (Q)
7. Materiality assessments by auditors (Q)
8. Responsibility of auditors to investigate whistleblower allegations (Q)
9. Factors influencing auditors' legal liability in state vs. federal courts (Q)
10. Auditor consideration of whether a client's application of GAAP resulted in materially misleading financial statements
11. Responsibility of auditors to ascertain which financial statement elements are of primary concern to financial statement users
12. Auditor communications with client audit committee
13. Substance over form concept in financial reporting

Just for FEET, Inc., Case 1.3, 39–52

1. Use of analytical procedures to identify high-risk financial statement items (Q)
2. Identifying internal control risk factors (Q)
3. Impact of control risk factors on audit planning decisions (Q)
4. Identifying inherent risk factors (Q)
5. Impact of inherent risk factors on audit planning decisions (Q)
6. Identifying the most critical audit risk factors for a given audit engagement (Q)
7. Resolution of ethical dilemma faced by a corporate executive (Q)
8. Need to consider economic health of client's industry in audit planning decisions
9. Nature, purpose, and importance of accounts receivable confirmation procedures
10. Role of the SEC in policing financial reporting process and independent audit function
11. Importance of investigating unusual and/or suspicious client transactions

Health Management, Inc., Case 1.4, 53–70

1. Problems posed by relationships between client personnel and auditors (Q)
2. Audit-related implications of a job offer made by a client to one of its auditors during the course of an audit (Q)
3. Performance of inventory rollback and rollforward procedures (Q)
4. Weighing the cost of an audit procedure against the quantity and quality of audit evidence it yields (Q)
5. Documenting audit test results in audit workpapers (Q)
6. Identifying "red flag" fraud risk factors and determining their impact on each phase of an audit (Q)
7. Auditors' responsibilities for discovering and reporting illegal acts by clients (Q)

8. Historical overview of class-action lawsuits and their impact on public accounting firms
9. Impact of PSLRA of 1995 on auditors' legal exposure under the Securities Exchange Act of 1934
10. Proportionate vs. joint and several liability for auditors
11. Resolution of proposed audit adjustments
12. Nature of GAAS and the responsibilities they impose on auditors
13. Definition of "recklessness" and its implications for auditors' legal exposure under the Securities Exchange Act of 1934

The Leslie Fay Companies, Case 1.5, 71–82

1. Use of analytical procedures to identify high-risk financial statement items (Q)
2. Financial information needed for audit planning decisions (Q)
3. Non-financial information needed for audit planning decisions (Q)
4. Control environment issues pertinent to independent audits (Q)
5. Impact on auditor independence of litigation that names client and audit firm as co-defendants (Q)
6. Audit implications of important changes and developing trends in a client's industry
7. Identifying fraud risk factors and determining their impact on each phase of an audit

NextCard, Inc., Case 1.6, 83–92

1. Auditors' consideration of a client's business model (Q)
2. Identifying fraud risk factors (Q)
3. Objectives of audit workpapers (Q)
4. Identifying violations of generally accepted auditing standards (Q)
5. Responsibility of audit partners to serve as mentors for their subordinates (Q)
6. Ethical responsibilities of an auditor who is instructed to violate professional standards by his or her superior (Q)
7. Criminal liability of auditors
8. Impact of Sarbanes-Oxley on accounting profession

Lincoln Savings and Loan Association, Case 1.7, 93–106

1. Substance over form concept in accounting and its audit implications (Q)
2. Threats to auditor independence (Q)
3. Audit implications of related-party transactions (Q)
4. Assessment of a client's control environment (Q)
5. Determination of when gains resulting from the disposition of assets can be recognized (Q)
6. Identification of key management assertions (Q)
7. Audit evidence needed to support management assertions (Q)
8. Identifying appropriate audit procedures to collect desired types of audit evidence (Q)
9. Audit implications of auditor-client personnel relationships (Q)
10. Collegial responsibilities of auditors (Q)
11. Auditors' responsibility for detection of fraud (Q)
12. Societal role of independent auditor
13. SEC's oversight role for the independent audit function

Crazy Eddie, Inc., Case 1.8, 107–116

1. Use of financial ratios and other financial measures to identify high-risk financial statement items (Q)
2. Audit procedures used to detect fraudulent misstatements of inventory, accounts payable, and sales (Q)
3. Effect of important changes in a client's industry on audit planning decisions (Q)
4. Potential impact of "lowballing" on the quality of audit services (Q)
5. Objective of year-end inventory cutoff tests (Q)
6. Implications for the independent audit function of audit clients hiring former auditors (Q)
7. Impact of collusion among client executives and employees on auditors' ability to detect fraudulent misrepresentations in a client's accounting records
8. Importance of assessing the integrity of client management
9. Incentive for companies to retain large audit firms when going public

ZZZZ Best Company, Inc., Case 1.9, 117–130

1. Key differences between audits and review engagements (Q)
2. Identification of key management assertions (Q)
3. Audit evidence needed to support management assertions (Q)

4. Identifying appropriate audit procedures to collect desired types of audit evidence (Q)
5. Limitations of audit evidence (Q)
6. Predecessor-successor auditor communications (Q)
7. Auditors' responsibility for a client's earnings press release (Q)
8. Client-imposed restrictions on the scope of an audit (Q)
9. Content of an audit engagement letter
10. SEC's 8-K auditor change disclosure rules

Gemstar-TV Guide International, Inc., Case 1.10, 131–142

1. Revenue recognition issues (Q)
2. Factors or conditions commonly associated with "audit failures" (Q)
3. Quality control measures used by audit firms (Q)
4. Materiality judgments by auditors (Q)
5. Ethical vs. legal conduct (Q)
6. Need to thoroughly investigate suspicious and/or unusual client transactions
7. Limitations of client representations as audit evidence
8. Auditors' consideration of a client's business model
9. Role of SEC in financial reporting function

New Century Financial Corporation, Case 1.11, 143–160

1. Advantages and disadvantages of having a heavy concentration of audit clients in one industry (Q)
2. Quality control considerations for independent audits (Q)
3. Section 404 of the Sarbanes-Oxley Act (Q)
4. Auditors' responsibility to discover and report significant deficiencies and material weaknesses in internal controls (Q)
5. Auditing accounting estimates (Q)
6. Violations of generally accepted auditing standards (Q)
7. Mark-to-market rule for securities investments (Q)
8. Potential impairment of auditor independence
9. Impact of auditor-client conflicts on audit engagements
10. Audit implications of accounting changes
11. Auditor reviews of quarterly financial statements

Madoff Securities, Case 1.12, 161–170

1. Audit procedures applied to client investments (Q)
2. Nature and purpose of peer reviews (Q)
3. Fraud triangle (Q)
4. Common fraud risk factors (Q)
5. Regulatory reforms necessary to improve auditors' fraud detection capabilities (Q)
6. Impairment of auditor independence
7. Criminal liability faced by auditors
8. Civil liability faced by auditors
9. Societal role of independent audit function
10. SEC's regulatory mandate

Jack Greenberg, Inc., Case 2.1, 173–180

1. Audit risk factors commonly posed by family-owned businesses (Q)
2. Key audit objectives for inventory (Q)
3. Quality of audit evidence yielded by internal versus external documents (Q)
4. Nature and purpose of a walk-through audit procedure (Q)
5. Auditors' responsibility to inform client management of significant internal control weaknesses (Q)
6. Whether or not auditors have a responsibility to insist that client management correct significant internal control deficiencies (Q)
7. Segregation of duties concept and its impact on a client's internal controls
8. Need for auditors to thoroughly investigate suspicious transactions and circumstances

Golden Bear Golf, Inc., Case 2.2, 181–188

1. Identifying relevant management assertions for individual financial statement items (Q)
2. Choosing appropriate audit procedures to corroborate specific management assertions (Q)

4. Principal audit objectives for a client's discretionary expense accruals (Q)
5. Conservatism principle in context of accounting estimates (Q)
6. Auditors' responsibilities when reviewing a client's interim financial statements (Q)
7. Career planning for public accountants

Regina Company, Inc., Case 2.9, 227–234

1. Use of analytical procedures to identify high-risk financial statement items (Q)
2. Audit procedures that may uncover fraudulent misstatements of sales and related accounts (Q)
3. Audit objectives associated with year-end sales cutoff tests (Q)
4. Auditors' responsibility to follow-up on suspicious transactions (Q)
5. Extent to which auditors should trust client management (Q)
6. Methods client management may use to manipulate reported earnings
7. Audit implications of lack of management integrity

The Trolley Dodgers, Case 3.1, 237–238

1. Tests of controls and substantive tests for the payroll transaction cycle (Q)
2. Identifying internal control weaknesses in the payroll transaction cycle (Q)
3. Audit procedures useful in detecting payroll fraud (Q)
4. Control environment issues

Howard Street Jewelers, Case 3.2, 239–240

1. Importance of internal controls for small retail businesses (Q)
2. Responsibility of a small business's CPA when alerted to potential control problems facing the client (Q)
3. Meetings with prospective clients (Q)
4. Control environment issues

United Way of America, Case 3.3, 241–246

1. Cost-effective internal controls to limit organizations' exposure to theft losses (Q)
2. Social responsibilities of CPA firms (Q)
3. Client development activities for CPA firms (Q)
4. Audit risk factors commonly posed by not-for-profit organizations (Q)
5. Adoption of Sarbanes-Oxley internal control reforms by not-for-profit organizations

First Keystone Bank, Case 3.4, 247–250

1. Internal control procedures applied to banking operations (Q)
2. General conditions or factors influencing choice of auditing procedures (Q)
3. Auditing procedures applied to cash maintained on a client's premises (Q)
4. Auditing procedures that may uncover client embezzlement schemes (Q)
5. Impact of collusion on integrity of an organization's internal controls

Goodner Brothers, Inc., Case 3.5, 251–258

1. Identifying internal control objectives for a wholesale business (Q)
2. Identifying and remedying internal control weaknesses (Q)
3. Importance of an effective control environment for a business (Q)
4. Impact of management style and operating policies on an entity's internal controls
5. Role of internal auditors in an entity's internal control process
6. Need for auditors and client management to investigate suspicious transactions

Buranello's Ristorante, Case 3.6, 259–264

1. Identifying internal control weaknesses (Q)
2. Identifying remedial measures to eliminate or mitigate internal control weaknesses (Q)
3. Evaluating the cost-effectiveness of internal controls (Q)
4. Identifying internal control procedures for a restaurant (Q)
5. Assessing the ethical quality of management decisions (Q)
6. Integrating ethical considerations into internal control policies and procedures (Q)

Foamex International Inc., Case 3.7, 265–268

1. Ultimate responsibility for an organization's internal controls (Q)
2. Auditors' responsibility to identify client's internal control weaknesses (Q)

3. Auditors' communication responsibilities for internal control weaknesses (Q)
4. Differences in auditor responsibilities for public versus private clients (Q)
5. Conditions under which public companies can dismiss their auditors (Q)
6. Conditions under which auditors may resign as the auditor of a public company (Q)
7. SEC disclosure requirements for auditor changes (Q)
8. Enforcement policy of SEC (Q)
9. Section 404 assessment of a client's internal controls

Creve Couer Pizza, Inc., Case 4.1, 271–274

1. CPAs serving as the moral conscience of small business clients (Q)
2. Conflict between auditors' responsibility to the public interest and the obligations imposed on them by the client confidentiality rule (Q)
3. Resolution of ethical dilemmas by auditors (Q)
4. Privileged communications between auditors and clients (Q)

F&C International, Inc., Case 4.2, 275–278

1. Professional responsibilities of a business's financial executives and high-ranking accountants (Q)
2. Nature of the interaction between client management and independent auditors (Q)
3. Ethical responsibilities of management when they suspect subordinates are engaging in fraud (Q)
4. Need for an entity's executives and financial managers to thoroughly investigate suspicious transactions and events coming to their attention (Q)
5. Common methods used to misrepresent an entity's reported profits
6. SEC's oversight role for the accounting and financial reporting domain

Suzette Washington, Accounting Major, Case 4.3, 279–280

1. Resolution of ethical dilemma faced by an accounting student (Q)
2. Ethical responsibilities of private accountants (Q)
3. Responsibility of accountants to report unethical conduct by their colleagues (Q)
4. Internal controls for a retail business (Q)

Freescale Semiconductor, Inc., Case 4.4, 281–284

1. Exceptions to client confidentiality rule (Q)
2. Analyzing decision contexts involving the client confidentiality rule (Q)
3. Differing professional responsibilities of CPAs for consulting and audit engagements (Q)
4. Ethical challenges posed for CPAs due to their access to confidential client information (Q)
5. Negative impact on accounting profession of ethical breaches by individual professionals

Wiley Jackson, Accounting Major, Case 4.5, 285–286

1. Resolution of ethical dilemma by an accounting student (Q)
2. Disciplining of accountants who engage in unethical behavior (Q)
3. Responsibility of accountants to report unethical conduct by their colleagues (Q)

Arvel Smart, Accounting Major, Case 4.6, 287–288

1. Resolution of an ethical dilemma by an accounting student (Q)
2. Ethical issues accounting majors may face when they have multiple job offers outstanding (Q)
3. Internship opportunities available to accounting majors

David Quinn, Tax Accountant, Case 4.7, 289–292

1. Nature and purpose of the client confidentiality rule (Q)
2. Identifying violations of the client confidentiality rule (Q)
3. Resolution of disputes with fellow professionals regarding ethical issues (Q)
4. Responsibility of accountants to report unethical conduct by their colleagues (Q)

Cardillo Travel Systems, Inc., Case 5.1, 295–300

1. Ethical dilemmas that accountants and auditors must resolve (Q)
2. Parties affected by the resolution of ethical dilemmas facing accountants and auditors (Q)
3. Auditors' responsibilities when reviewing a client's interim financial statements (Q)
4. Importance of communication among members of an audit engagement team (Q)

Hamilton Wong, In-Charge Accountant, Case 6.3, 335–338

1. Ethical issues related to the underreporting of time worked by auditors (Q)
2. Effect of underreporting time worked on quality of independent audits (Q)
3. Measures needed to mitigate the underreporting of time worked (Q)
4. Potentially dysfunctional effects of competitive promotion system within accounting firms on quality of independent audits (Q)
5. Nature of in-charge accountant's work role and responsibilities

Tommy O'Connell, Audit Senior, Case 6.4, 339–342

1. Key differences between the professional roles of audit seniors and staff accountants (Q)
2. Interpersonal conflicts between members of an audit engagement team (Q)
3. Auditor's responsibility when he or she suspects that a colleague is not completing assigned audit procedures (Q)
4. Audit partner's responsibility when a subordinate reports that a member of the audit engagement team is not completing assigned audit procedures (Q)
5. Need for public accountants to achieve a proper balance between their personal and professional lives
6. Impact of a lack of client cooperation on the performance of an audit

Avis Love, Staff Accountant, Case 6.5, 343–346

1. Parties potentially affected by ethical dilemmas facing auditors (Q)
2. Auditors' ethical obligations to third-party financial statement users (Q)
3. Auditors' responsibility to document and investigate financial misstatements revealed by audit procedures (Q)
4. Potential audit impact of personal relationships between auditors and client personnel (Q)
5. Audit objectives of year-end cash receipts and sales cutoff tests (Q)
6. Assessing materiality of financial statement errors (Q)

Charles Tollison, Audit Manager, Case 6.6, 347–350

1. Requisite skills for promotion to partner in a major accounting firm (Q)
2. Partner promotion criteria in large vs. small accounting firms (Q)
3. "Up or out" promotion policy of many accounting firms (Q)
4. Need for public accountants to achieve a proper balance between their personal and professional lives
5. Need for a public accountant to actively plan and manage his or her professional career

Ligand Pharmaceuticals, Case 7.1, 353–358

1. Engagement risk vs. audit risk (Q)
2. Factors influencing engagement risk (Q)
3. Quality control issues for public accounting firms (Q)
4. Application of the revenue recognition principle (Q)
5. Subsequent discovery of material errors in audited financial statements (Q)
6. Nature and purpose of PCAOB's regulatory mandate (Q)
7. Recent criticism of PCAOB (Q)
8. Recommendations for improving effectiveness and efficiency of PCAOB (Q)
9. Impact of Sarbanes-Oxley Act on independent audit function
10. Nature of work role and responsibilities of an audit engagement partner
11. Auditing sales returns
12. Performance appraisal within accounting firms

Sarah Russell, Staff Accountant, Case 7.2, 359–362

1. Interpersonal conflict between an employee and partner of a CPA firm (Q)
2. Responsibility of public accountants to respect personal rights of colleagues (Q)
3. Office managing partner's responsibility to protect the personal rights of each office member (Q)
4. Nature of staff accountant's work role and responsibilities

Bud Carriker, Audit Senior, Case 7.3, 363–368

1. Client management effort to influence staffing of audit engagement team (Q)
2. Racial discrimination within the auditing discipline (Q)
3. Responsibility of senior members of an audit practice office and/or audit engagement team to protect the civil rights of their subordinates (Q)

4. Resolution of an ethical dilemma by an audit partner (Q)
5. Issues relevant to staffing of audit engagement teams

Hopkins v. Price Waterhouse, Case 7.4, 369–376

1. Responsibility of public accounting firms to facilitate the career success of their female employees (Q)
2. Informal employee networks within public accounting firms and related personnel and professional implications (Q)
3. Nepotism rules of public accounting firms (Q)
4. Acceptance of female and minority public accountants by clients (Q)
5. Partnership promotion process of large public accounting firms
6. Requisite skills for promotion to partner in a major public accounting firm

Fred Stern & Company, Inc. (*Ultramares*), Case 7.5, 377–384

1. Implications for the public accounting profession of the apparent move by the courts to socialize investment losses (Q)
2. Auditors' legal exposure under the Securities Act of 1933 and the Securities Exchange Act of 1934 (Q)
3. Auditors' legal exposure under the common law versus the federal securities laws (Q)
4. Evolution of the standard audit report form (Q)
5. Evolution of standard financial statement package prepared by most companies (Q)
6. Effect on audit planning decisions of the number and type of third-party financial statement users (Q)
7. Purpose of an audit engagement letter (Q)
8. Effect of audit engagement letters on auditors' legal liability (Q)
9. Joint and several liability of partners of public accounting firms for their subordinates' malfeasance

First Securities Company of Chicago (*Hochfelder*), Case 7.6, 385–390

1. Responsibility of auditors to discover and disclose serious internal control deficiencies (Q)
2. Audit implications of significant internal control deficiencies (Q)
3. Key distinctions between and among negligence, gross negligence, and fraudulent conduct in an audit context (Q)
4. Differences in auditors' legal exposure under the Securities Act of 1933, the Securities Exchange Act of 1934, and the common law (Q)
5. Objectives of the federal securities laws and the independent audit function
6. Need for auditors to be skeptical even when the integrity of client management appears to be beyond reproach

Livent, Inc., Case 8.1, 393–406

1. Identification of inherent risk factors (Q)
2. Role and responsibilities of audit partners (Q)
3. Client attitudes toward auditors (Q)
4. Reports prepared by accounting firms on the application of accounting principles by non-audit clients (Q)
5. Revenue recognition issues (Q)
6. Responsibility of accountants to investigate potential misrepresentations in their employers' accounting records (Q)
7. Potential conflict-of-interests faced by auditors who accept accounting positions with former clients (Q)
8. Accounting firms' responsibilities in due diligence investigations (Q)
9. Forensic investigations by accounting firms
10. Identifying "red flags" indicative of financial statement fraud
11. Audit firms' legal exposure under the Securities Exchange Act of 1934

Parmalat Finanziaria, S.p.A., Case 8.2, 407–420

1. Factors that complicate the audits of multinational companies (Q)
2. Audit procedures that may be effective for uncovering financial statement fraud (Q)
3. Identifying fraud risk factors (Q)
4. Allocating the responsibility for "shared audits" across the accounting firms involved in those audits (Q)
5. Legal liability issues for the global networks of multinational accounting firms (Q)
6. Impact of cultural norms and nuances on the performance of audits (Q)
7. Advantages and disadvantages of mandatory auditor rotation (Q)
8. Legal liability strategies of major accounting firms (Q)
9. Evolution of a nation's financial reporting and independent audit functions

10. Differing responsibilities of Italian statutory and independent auditors
11. Criminal liability of independent auditors
12. Conflict between client executives and auditors
13. Overview of historical development of international accounting firms

Kansayaku, Case 8.3, 421–430

1. Impact of macroeconomic variables on a nation's independent audit function (Q)
2. Impact of differing barriers to entry on the accounting professions of individual nations (Q)
3. Advantages and disadvantages of an oligopolistic market structure for independent audit services (Q)
4. Measures necessary to promote and protect auditor independence (Q)
5. Impact of cultural norms and nuances on the performance of independent audits and the overall nature of a nation's independent audit function
6. Common challenges and problems faced by independent auditors around the globe
7. Nature and structure of regulatory oversight for the accounting profession and auditing discipline across different nations
8. Criminal and civil liability of audit firms and auditors

Registered Auditors, South Africa, Case 8.4, 431–442

1. Impact of political forces on the development of a nation's independent audit function (Q)
2. Advantages and disadvantages of a separate professional credential for independent auditors (Q)
3. Nature and purpose of South Africa's "reportable irregularities" rule (Q)
4. Impact of South Africa's reportable irregularities rule on that nation's independent audit function (Q)
5. Measures necessary to persuade individuals from underrepresented groups to pursue careers in the accounting profession (Q)
6. Impact of recurring audit failures on the international reputation and credibility of a nation's capital markets
7. Nature and structure of regulatory oversight for the accounting profession and auditing discipline across different nations
8. Criminal and civil liability of accounting firms and individual auditors

Zuan Yan, Case 8.5, 443–454

1. Impact of differing cultural norms on the ability of the worldwide accounting profession to reach a consensus on important ethical principles (Q)
2. Impact of differing economic systems on the nature of financial reporting objectives (Q)
3. Relevance of fundamental accounting concepts and principles across the globe (Q)
4. Nature and purpose of independent audits across the globe (Q)
5. Challenges and problems faced by accounting firms when performing audits in countries with authoritarian central governments (Q)
6. Impact of political forces on the development and evolution of a nation's accounting profession and independent audit function
7. Unique challenges and problems faced by the accounting profession of the People's Republic of China
8. Nature and structure of regulatory oversight for the accounting profession and auditing discipline across the globe
9. Civil liability of accounting firms

Kaset Thai Sugar Company, Case 8.6, 455–458

1. Problems faced by accountants when performing independent audits and other professional services in hostile countries (Q)
2. Responsibility of accounting firms to provide for the safety of their employees (Q)
3. Impact of cultural norms and nuances on the performance of professional services engagements

Republic of Somalia, Case 8.7, 459–462

1. Differentiating between and among types of professional services engagements provided by accounting firms (Q)
2. Identifying the professional standards that apply to specific types of professional services engagements (Q)
3. Application of the client confidentiality rule (Q)
4. Ethical issues and challenges posed by high-profile and high-risk professional services engagements (Q)
5. Measures that can be taken to control or mitigate risks posed by high-profile and unusual professional services engagements (Q)
6. Problems faced by accountants when providing professional services in hostile countries
7. Responsibility of accounting firms to provide for the safety of their employees

OAO Gazprom, Case 8.8, 463–476

1. Challenges that accounting firms face when they establish practice offices in foreign countries (Q)
2. Impact of cultural differences on business practices and ethical norms (Q)
3. Responsibilities of auditors to client stockholders (Q)
4. Threats to auditor independence (Q)
5. Auditors' responsibility to identify related parties and related-party transactions (Q)
6. British "true and fair" audit philosophy vs. the U.S. philosophy of "fairly presented" (Q)
7. Philosophical differences between IASB and FASB and resulting impact on standards promulgated by those two organizations (Q)
8. Impact of social and governmental influences on the development of accounting and auditing practices
9. Legal exposure faced by accounting firms in foreign countries
10. Professional and business risks faced by accounting firms that audit high-profile clients

Societe Generale, Case 8.9, 477–492

1. Timing of loss recognition for income statement purposes (Q)
2. Departures from GAAP necessary to prevent financial statements from being misleading (Q)
3. Similarities and differences between French and U.S. audit reports (Q)
4. Similarities and differences between internal control objectives in France and United States (Q)
5. Nature and purpose of "joint audits" (Q)
6. Audit risk factors common to bank clients (Q)
7. History of the independent audit function in France
8. Internal control reporting in France
9. Big Four firms' involvement in the French audit market
10. Key differences between IFRS and U.S. GAAP

Institute of Chartered Accountants of India, Case 8.10, 493–504

1. Comparative advantages and disadvantages of a centralized vs. a decentralized regulatory infrastructure for a nation's public accounting profession (Q)
2. Philosophical differences regarding the purpose of the independent audit function that impact the nature of that function across different cultures (Q)
3. Strategic initiatives used by major international accounting firms to enter new markets (Q)
4. Ethical issues that the major international accounting firms have faced when entering new markets (Q)
5. Ethical and competitive issues posed by allowing accounting firms to advertise (Q)
6. Using economic policies to shield a nation's domestic accounting firms from foreign competition (Q)
7. Nature and purpose of reciprocity agreements between national regulatory organizations within the global accounting profession (Q)
8. Ethical, competitive, and regulatory issues posed by the outsourcing of professional accounting services (Q)
9. Impact of political and social forces on the development and evolution of a nation's accounting profession and independent audit function
10. International criticism of operating philosophy, policies, and procedures of major international accounting firms
11. Conflict between and among the accounting profession's international regulatory bodies

Republic of the Sudan, Case 8.11, 505–510

1. Regulatory mandate of the SEC (Q)
2. Definition of "material information" for financial reporting purposes (Q)
3. Materiality standard applied by the SEC (Q)
4. Differences in materiality concept in accounting context vs. auditing context (Q)
5. SEC's concept of "full and fair disclosure"

Shari'a, Case 8.12, 511–520

1. Financial statement audits vs. *Shari'a* compliance audits (Q)
2. Application of compliance audit procedures (Q)
3. Merging of financial statement and *Shari'a* compliance audits (Q)
4. Socially responsible accounting standards (Q)
5. Competitive conditions faced by Big Four firms in Islamic economy (Q)
6. Lack of uniformity in *Shari'a* audit practices
7. Promulgation of professional standards in Islamic economy
8. Financial statement audit report in Islamic economy vs. *Shari'a* compliance audit report

Mohamed Salem El-Hadad, Case 8.13, 521–526

1. Legal protections afforded whistleblowers in the United States (Q)
2. Integration of whistleblowing measures into internal control systems (Q)
3. Measures that whistleblowers can use to protect themselves from recriminations (Q)
4. Responsibility of organizational insiders to report fraud (Q)
5. Ethical dilemmas vs. moral dilemmas (Q)

Tae Kwang Vina, Case 8.14, 527–532

1. Differences between and among: consulting services, assurance services, attestation services and agreed-upon procedures engagements (Q)
2. Nontraditional accounting services offered by major accounting firms (Q)
3. Services requiring CPAs to be independent (Q)
4. Required qualifications of CPAs on various professional service engagements (Q)
5. Commercialism within public accounting profession
6. Provision of environmental and labor practices audits by major accounting firms

SUMMARY OF CASES BY TOPIC

Advertising by Accounting Firms: ICAI.

Analytical Procedures: Crazy Eddie, Just for Feet, Leslie Fay, Regina.

Assessment of Adequacy of Client Disclosures: American Fuel & Supply, Gemstar, General Motors, Geo Securities, Lehman.

Assessment of Client Management Competence: Crazy Eddie, Lincoln, North Face, ZZZZ Best.

Assessment of Client's Going Concern Status: Geo Securities.

Assurance Services: Somalia, Tae Kwang Vina.

Attorney Inquiry Letter: Geo Securities, Phillips.

Audit Engagement Letter: Stern, ZZZZ Best.

Audit Evidence—General: Cardillo, General Motors, Geo Securities, Golden Bear, Happiness Express, Health Management, Jack Greenberg, Lehman, Lipper, New Century.

Audit Evidence—Limitations: Bill DeBurger, CBI Holding, Gemstar, Geo Securities, Golden Bear, Health Management, Ligand, Lincoln, Lipper, Phillips, Regina, ZZZZ Best.

"Audit Failures:" Gemstar, Golden Bear.

Audit Implications of Control Deficiencies: Crazy Eddie, First Securities, Goodner, Health Management, Jack Greenberg, Leslie Fay, New Century, United Way.

Audit Planning Issues: Crazy Eddie, First Keystone, Just for Feet, Leslie Fay, Lipper, New Century, ZZZZ Best.

Audit Review Process: North Face, Tommy O'Connell.

Audit Risk (and/or its components): Crazy Eddie, Jack Greenberg, Just for Feet, Leslie Fay, Lincoln, Lipper, Livent, NextCard, Parmalat, Regina, Societe Generale.

Audit Sampling: Stern.

Audit Staffing Issues: New Century.

Audit Time Budgets/Audit Deadlines: Charles Tollison, Hamilton Wong, Tommy O'Connell.

Audit Workpapers: Enron, Health Management, Leslie Fay, New Century, NextCard, North Face, Phillips, Tommy O'Connell.

Auditing a Multinational Company: Gazprom, Lehman, Livent, Parmalat, Societe Generale, Zuan Yan.

Auditing Accounting Estimates: Belot, General Motors, Golden Bear, Health Management, Just for Feet, Ligand, NextCard, New Century.

Auditing Accounts Payable (and other liabilities): CBI, Crazy Eddie.

Auditing Cash: Avis Love, First Keystone.

Auditing Contingencies: Cardillo, Geo Securities.

Auditing Contracts and Commitments: Cardillo, Creve Couer, Enron, Gemstar, Geo Securities, Golden Bear, Lehman, Lincoln, ZZZZ Best.

Auditing Expense Accruals: Belot.

Auditing Investments: Lipper, Madoff.

Auditing Inventory: Crazy Eddie, F&C, Goodner, Health Management, Jack Greenberg, Just for Feet, Leslie Fay.

Auditing Payroll-Related Financial Statement Items: Trolley Dodgers.

Auditing Pension-Related Financial Statement Items: General Motors.

Auditing Receivables: Happiness Express, Health Management, Just for Feet, NextCard.

Auditing Revenues: Avis Love, Crazy Eddie, Gemstar, Golden Bear, Ligand, Lincoln, Livent, North Face, Regina, Stern.

Auditor Independence: AIG, Avis Love, Belot, Crazy Eddie, Enron, Gazprom, Health Management, ICAI, Kansayaku, Leslie Fay, Lincoln, Madoff, New Century, Parmalat, Societe Generale, South Africa, Zuan Yan.

Auditor Rotation: Parmalat.

Auditor-Client Interaction Issues: AIG, Avis Love, Belot, Bud Carriker, Cardillo, CBI, Enron, F&C, General Motors, Health Management, Howard Street, Jack Greenberg, Kansayaku, Kaset Thai, Lincoln, Livent, New Century, North Face, Parmalat, South Africa, Tommy O'Connell, Zuan Yan.

Career Development Issues: Arvel Smart, Belot, Bill DeBurger, Bud Carriker, Charles Tollison, David Quinn, Hamilton Wong, Hopkins, Leigh Ann Walker, Livent, NextCard, Sarah Russell, Tommy O'Connell, Waverly Holland, Wiley Jackson.

Client Acceptance/Retention Issues: Bud Carriker, CBI, Gazprom, Jack Greenberg, Kansayaku, Kaset Thai, Lincoln, Parmalat, Somalia, Zuan Yan.

Client Confidentiality: American Fuel & Supply, Creve Couer, David Quinn, Freescale, ICAI, Phillips, Somalia, South Africa, Waverly Holland.

Client Development Activities: Charles Tollison, Hopkins, United Way.

Client Management Integrity Issues: Belot, Bud Carriker, Cardillo, CBI, Crazy Eddie, Enron, F&C, First Securities, Foamex, Gazprom, Gemstar, General Motors, Golden Bear, Happiness Express, Health Management, Jack

Identification of Management Assertions: Geo Securities, Golden Bear, Lincoln, ZZZZ Best.

IFRS vs. U.S. GAAP: Societe Generale.

Impact of Cultural Norms and Values on Independent Audit Function: Gazprom, ICAI, Kansayaku, Parmalat, Shari'a, Societe Generale, South Africa, Zuan Yan.

Internal Auditors: First Keystone, Goodner, Mohamed Salem El-Hadad.

Internal Control Deficiencies: Buranello's, First Keystone, First Securities, Foamex, Goodner, Health Management, Howard Street, Jack Greenberg, Leslie Fay, Lipper, New Century, Trolley Dodgers, United Way.

Internal Control Objectives: Goodner, Howard Street, Mohamed Salem El-Hadad, Societe Generale, Trolley Dodgers, United Way.

Internal Control Reporting: First Securities, Foamex, Jack Greenberg, Lehman, Lipper, New Century, Societe Generale.

Internal Control, Ethical Considerations: Buranello's.

Internal Controls for Not-for-Profits: Mohamed Salem El-Hadad, United Way.

Internal Controls for Small Businesses: Buranello's, Howard Street, Suzette Washington.

Internal Controls, Cost-Effectiveness: Buranello's, Goodner, Howard Street, United Way.

Internal Controls, Remedial Measures: Buranello's, Foamex, Goodner, United Way.

International Accounting Issues: Gazprom, Shari'a, Societe Generale, South Africa, Zuan Yan.

International Audit Reports: Gazprom, Shari'a, Societe Generale.

International Auditing Practices: Parmalat, Shari'a, Societe General.

International Markets, Competitive Issues: Gazprom, ICAI, Kansayaku, Parmalat, Shari'a, Societe Generale, Tae Kwang Vina, Zuan Yan.

Issues Related to the Global Accounting Profession: Gazprom, ICAI, Kansayaku, Kaset Thai, Parmalat, Shari'a, Societe Generale, Somalia, South Africa, Sudan, Tae Kwang Vina, Zuan Yan.

Lack of Definitive Guidelines for Client Transactions: Enron, Lehman, Livent, Societe Generale.

Legal Liability—Common Law: First Securities, Stern.

Legal Liability—Criminal: Enron, Freescale, Kansayaku, Madoff, NextCard, Parmalat, Phillips.

Legal Liability—General: American Fuel & Supply, First Securities, Hopkins, Leslie Fay, Lehman, Lincoln, Lipper, Madoff, New Century, Parmalat, Somalia, Stern, Waverly Holland.

Legal Liability—International Markets: Gazprom, ICAI, Kansayaku, Parmalat, South Africa, Zuan Yan.

Legal Liability—1933 Act: First Securities, Stern.

Legal Liability—1934 Act: First Securities, Health Management, Livent, Stern.

Letter of Representations: Livent.

"Lowballing" Phenomenon: Crazy Eddie, Scott Fane, Tae Kwang Vina.

Materiality Issues: Avis Love, Belot, Gemstar, General Motors, Lehman, New Century, North Face, Sudan.

Need to Follow-up on Suspicious or Unusual Client Transactions: AIG, Avis Love, Cardillo, CBI, Enron, Gazprom, Gemstar, Golden Bear, Goodner, Happiness Express, Health Management, Jack Greenberg, Just for Feet, Lehman, Lincoln, Livent, New Century, NextCard, North Face, Parmalat, Regina, Stern, ZZZZ Best.

Negligence vs. Gross Negligence: Stern.

Negligence vs. Recklessness: Health Management.

Negligence vs. Recklessness vs. Fraud: First Securities, Happiness Express.

Nontraditional Professional Services: AIG, Freescale, Kaset, Shari'a, Somalia, Tae Kwang Vina, Zuan Yan.

Opinion Shopping: Cardillo, Foamex, Lincoln, Livent.

Outsourcing of Accounting Services: ICAI.

Peer Reviews: Madoff.

Personal Integrity of Auditors: Arvel Smart, Avis Love, Belot, Bill DeBurger, Bud Carriker, Cardillo, David Quinn, Enron, Freescale, Hamilton Wong, Health Management, Kansayaku, Kaset, Leigh Ann Walker, Madoff, New Century, NextCard, North Face, Parmalat, Phillips, Sarah Russell, South Africa, Tommy O'Connell, Wiley Jackson.

Personal Lives vs. Professional Work Roles: Avis Love, Belot, Bill DeBurger, Charles Tollison, Hamilton Wong, Health Management, Hopkins, Kansayaku, Leigh Ann Walker, Ligand, Sarah Russell, Tommy O'Connell, Wiley Jackson.

Personnel Issues within Audit Firms: Bill DeBurger, Bud Carriker, Charles Tollison, Hamilton Wong, Hopkins, Kaset Thai, Leigh Ann Walker, Ligand, New Century, NextCard, Sarah Russell, South Africa, Tommy O'Connell.

Practice Development Issues—International Markets: Gazprom, ICAI, Kansayaku, Kaset Thai, Parmalat, Shari'a, Societe Generale, Somalia, South Africa, Tae Kwang Vina, Zuan Yan.

Predecessor-Successor Auditor Communications: Lincoln, ZZZZ Best.

Premature Signoff of Audit Procedures: New Century, Tommy O'Connell.

Privileged Communications for Auditors: Creve Couer, Phillips.

Professional Roles of Auditors: Avis Love, Belot, Bill DeBurger, Bud Carriker, Charles Tollison, Enron, Hamilton Wong, Health Management, Leigh Ann Walker, Ligand, New Century, NextCard, Sarah Russell, Tommy O'Connell.

Professional Service Engagements Requiring Independence: Tae Kwang Vina.

Professional Skepticism: Belot, CBI, Enron, First Securities, Gemstar, General Motors, Golden Bear, Happiness Express, Health Management, Lehman, Ligand, Lipper, New Century, North Face, Regina.

Professional Standards, Audits vs. Consulting Engagements: Freescale.

Proposed Audit Adjustments (Auditor-Client Negotiations): Belot, Health Management, Livent, North Face.

Public Company Accounting Oversight Board (PCAOB): Ligand.

Quality Control Issues for Audit Firms: Bill DeBurger, Bud Carriker, Cardillo, CBI, Freescale, Gemstar, Hamilton Wong, Hopkins, ICAI, Leigh Ann Walker, Lehman, Ligand, Lincoln, Lipper, New Century, NextCard, North Face, Parmalat, South Africa, Tae Kwang Vina, Tommy O'Connell, Zuan Yan.

Reciprocity Agreements between International Regulatory Bodies: ICAI.

Recklessness: Happiness Express, Health Management.

Regulation of the U.S. Accounting Profession: Enron, Freescale, NextCard, North Face, Madoff.

Regulatory Issues Related to Global Accounting Profession: Gazprom, ICAI, Kansayaku, Kaset Thai, Livent, Parmalat, Shari'a, Societe Generale, South Africa, Sudan, Zuan Yan.

Related-Party Transactions: Enron, Gazprom, Lincoln, Livent, Parmalat.

Review of Client Accounting Policies/Procedures: General Motors, Lehman, New Century.

Review of Client's Tax Returns: Phillips.

Review of Interim Financial Statements: Belot, Cardillo, Enron, Lehman, New Century, North Face, ZZZZ Best.

Rule-Making Processes: Gazprom, ICAI, Kansayaku, Shari'a, South Africa, Zuan Yan.

Sarbanes-Oxley Act of 2002: Ligand, New Century, NextCard, Societe Generale, United Way.

***SAS No. 50* Reports:** AIG, Livent.

Scope of Services Issue (provision of non-audit services by auditors): AIG, Enron, ICAI.

Securities and Exchange Commission: AIG, Cardillo, Crazy Eddie, Enron, F&C, First Securities, Foamex, Freescale, Gemstar, General Motors, Geo Securities, Health Management, Just for Feet, Leslie Fay, Lincoln, Lipper, Livent, Madoff, New Century, NextCard, North Face, Sudan, ZZZZ Best.

SEC's 8-K Auditor Change Rules: Cardillo, Foamex, ZZZZ Best.

Section 404 Engagements: Foamex, New Century.

"Shared Audits": Parmalat.

Societal Role of Audit Function: Enron, First Securities, Gazprom, ICAI, Kansayaku, Lincoln, Madoff, New Century, Parmalat, South Africa, Stern, Zuan Yan.

Subsequent Discovery of Errors: American Fuel & Supply, Ligand, New Century, North Face.

Substance over Form Concept: AIG, Enron, Gazprom, Lehman, Lincoln, Societe Generale.

Supervision of Staff Accountants: Leigh Ann Walker, Tommy O'Connell.

Supplementary Information Accompanying Audited Financial Statements: General Motors, Geo Securities, Lehman.

Understanding the Client's Industry/Business Model: Crazy Eddie, Enron, Gemstar, Happiness Express, Jack Greenberg, Just for Feet, Lehman, Leslie Fay, Lincoln, Lipper, Livent, New Century, NextCard, North Face, Regina, ZZZZ Best.

Walk-through Audit Procedure: Jack Greenberg.

Whistleblowing: Enron, Freescale, Lehman, Mohamed Salem El-Hadad.

Withdrawal of an Audit Report: American Fuel & Supply, CBI, Happiness Express, Health Management, Leslie Fay, Livent, New Century, Regina.